AGATHA CHRISTIE:
A LIFE IN THEATRE

Julius Green has numerous West End plays and musicals to his credit as a theatre producer. In 2001 he produced the twelve-week Agatha Christie Theatre Festival, uniquely presenting a repertoire of Christie's complete plays as then known, and in 2006 he created the Agatha Christie Theatre Company.

He studied history at Corpus Christi College, Cambridge, and is a Fellow of the Birkbeck Centre for Contemporary Theatre, University of London. He has served on the Board of Management of the Society of London Theatre and the Board of Directors of the Edinburgh Festival Fringe and is a director of the Academy of Circus Arts.

Julius is a regular columnist for *The Stage* newspaper and was invited by HarperCollins to write the introduction to a new edition of Agatha Christie's *The Mousetrap and Other Plays* celebrating *The Mousetrap*'s 60th anniversary in 2012. In the same year Oberon published his first book, *How to Produce a West End Show*, described by *WhatsOnStage* as 'An exceptionally well-written, drily inflected and amusing book . . . full of useful words of wisdom'. He lives in Cambridge.

T0312410

Agatha Christie on the set of *Witness for the Prosecution* (1953).

Agatha Christie: A Life in Theatre

JULIUS GREEN

'Agatha has the gift of doing what all women want to do, but only men have the chance. She achieves something. Men climb Everest, race fast cars, invent atom bombs, fight wars, become famous surgeons and man lifeboats. In her heart every woman, too, would like to do these things. But all we can do is dream. It is all we can do. It's a man's world. The only consolation I get is that Agatha kills off a few of you.'

MARGARET LOCKWOOD
17 January 1954

HarperCollins*Publishers*

HarperCollins*Publishers*
1 London Bridge Street
London SE1 9GF
www.harpercollins.co.uk

Revised and expanded edition published 2018
First published by HarperCollins*Publishers* as *Curtain Up* 2015

1

Photographs courtesy of The Christie Archive Trust, The Shubert Archive,
The University of Bristol Theatre Collection/ArenaPAL, The National Portrait
Gallery, The Peter Saunders Archive, The Museum of the City of New York
Theatre Collection, The Theatre Royal Bath Archive and Getty Images.

ISBN 978-0-00-754696-1

Typeset in Linotype Centennial by Palimpsest Book Production Limited,
Falkirk, Stirlingshire

Printed and bound in Great Britain by
CPI Group (UK) Ltd, Croydon CR0 4YY

Foreword

A couple of years ago, my friend Julius Green came to see me looking unusually nervous! He said he wanted to write an important history of my grandmother Agatha Christie's plays and asked if I would give my approval. I did so immediately, because I knew of Julius' huge knowledge about her plays, and the admiration and passion he had for them. I remembered when we shuttled back and forth on a train to Westcliff-on-Sea in 2001, when Julius organised a festival of all her plays, which was not only a huge success but became a piece of history in itself. Recalling that time, and Julius's long involvement with the Agatha Christie Theatre Company, I knew I could rely on him to be the right man for the job.

But then there was something more. Although my grandmother wrote plays before the 1950s, the great explosion of interest that occurred around the time of the opening of *The Mousetrap* and her other successes coincided with the period in my childhood when I spent the most time with her, and became aware what a *star* she was (even though she hated people saying that!). Therefore nobody could appreciate more than I do how much of a contribution her dramatic output made to her unrivalled reputation, and I am delighted to have in Julius's book such a fitting tribute to the genius of Agatha Christie as a playwright to help balance her better known achievements as an author.

In addition, I was fascinated by Julius's insight into the theatrical history of the period, to learn of the forthright personalities of the major players, and to read how my grandmother coped so calmly whilst all around her were living their theatrical lives.

All in all, a real treat for everybody!

MATHEW PRICHARD
June 2015

Acknowledgements

I am enormously grateful to all those who have supported me in the research and writing of this book by offering their expert guidance and allowing me to quote from documents and publications.

Mathew Prichard has always encouraged me in my belief that there is a significant story to be told about his grandmother's work for the theatre, and generously granted me access to her papers so that I could tell it. Mathew and Lucy's boundless hospitality made every visit to their family's archive a delight, and both of them have spent time and energy assisting me in my endeavours.

William Collins first published Agatha Christie in 1926, and I was delighted to find that David Brawn at HarperCollins shared our enthusiasm for the project; it was benefited hugely from his diligent guidance throughout the process. Agatha Christie Ltd, the company that continues to mastermind the global distribution of her work in all media, has been another significant partner in the book's realisation.

Dr John Curran, the acknowledged leading authority on Agatha Christie's work, has generously made available to me unpublished material from his detailed research on her notebooks, and has been an invaluble guide when my own enquiries have entered uncharted territories. Although we approach our subject from very different angles, John is a valued colleague;

we enjoy both applauding and shooting down each other's theories as yet more new discoveries about this extraordinary writer's work come to light.

I am particularly fortunate to be the first researcher granted access to the extensive business papers of Agatha Christie's friend and colleague Sir Peter Saunders, who produced most of her theatrical successes, and I am grateful to their owner, Sir Stephen Waley-Cohen, for allowing me to access them in the midst of his busy theatrical production office, and to Jane Tichband and her colleagues for their patience and good humour in facilitating this. Sir Stephen also agreed to be interviewed about *The Mousetrap*, as did the play's longest-serving resident director, David Turner, and they both gave me valuable insights into the production's history and the care and diligence with which it continues to be nurtured. Nick Salmon, Rupert Rhymes and Diana Rawstron kindly approved my quotation of Saunders' correspondence.

Of the many archivists who have helped me to access original material relating to Agatha Christie's theatre work, Joe Keogh at the Christie Archive Trust and Gemma Poulton at Exeter University have been tireless in their assistance over the course of the book's writing, and I am also particularly grateful to Sophie Stewart at the National Co-operative Archive, Ourania Karapasia at The John Rylands Library, University of Manchester, Jill Sullivan at the University of Bristol Theatre Collection, Samantha Gilchrist at Glasgow University's Scottish Theatre Archive, and Alan Brodie and L. J. Elliott at the Noël Coward Archive Trust.

James Hallgate at Lucius Books in York generously allowed me to sit in his shop and pore over a collection of the papers of theatre director Hubert Gregg. Other antiquarian booksellers and rare manuscript dealers who have kindly assisted me include Rick Loomis of Sumner and Stillman (Yarmouth, Maine), Sanna Lorentzi Rosander of Peter Harrington Rare Books and Manuscripts (London), Richard Ford of Richard Ford Manuscripts (London), James Pickard of James M. Pickard Fine and Rare Books (Leicester), Daniel Weschler of Sanctuary Rare Books (New York),

Don Longmuir of Scene of the Crime Books (Ontario) and Claudia Strauss-Schulson of Schulson Autographs (New Jersey).

Danny Moar and Nicky Palmer at the Theatre Royal Bath provided copies of material from their archive, and Alex Brown at *The Bath Chronicle* and Ann Buchanan Smith at Bath Central Library were also most helpful; as were Carl Smith at Torquay Museum, Jessica Bowles at the Royal Central School of Speech and Drama, Rhian Latham at Companies House and Cecile Chaffard at the Société des Auteurs et Compositeurs Dramatiques. My thanks, too, to the staff of Cambridge University Library, the Victoria and Albert Museum's Theatre and Performance Collections and the British Library Manuscripts Reading Room for their unfailing courtesy and efficiency; and to Christie Scholar Tony Medawar and Christie fan extraordinaire Scott Wallace Baker for their valued comments and suggestions.

In New York, I was welcomed to the Shubert Archive by Maryann Chach, Mark E. Swartz and Sylvia Wang. Mark's prompt responses to my numerous subsequent enquiries constitute a substantial contribution to the research for this book, and I am greatly indebted to him and to all at the Shubert Organisation. I am also most grateful to Walter Zvonchenko at the Library of Congress, Washington, DC, for his expert guidance regarding Gilbert Miller's papers, and to Morgen Stevens-Garmon at the Theatre Collection of the Museum of the City of New York and Sharon Rork at the Billy Rose Theatre Division of the New York Public Library for enabling me to access a wealth of material. Hilary Wall at the archive of the *Martha's Vineyard Gazette* responded to my email on the same day, attaching a copy of a historic document that was critical in developing a particular line of enquiry, and Abbie Van Nostrand at Samuel French, Inc., New York, gave me some helpful pointers for reading material. Harold Ober Associates in New York very kindly approved my quotations from their agency's founder's correspondence, and I am particularly grateful to Craig Tenney for facilitating this.

Back in the UK, the following people have helped me by assisting with specific enquiries, opening doors or generally

lending their support: Torquay tour guide John Risdon; the
National Trust's team at Greenway House; Louise Cooper of
the Garden History Society; Eileen Cottis of the Society for
Theatre Research; Garrick Club librarians Marcus Risdell and
Dr Moira Goff; Sue Parrish at Sphinx Theatre Company; Jess
Coleman at Curtis Brown; David Corley at Noel Gay; Keeley
Spindler at HMRC; and Lord Willoughby de Broke, Robert
Maas, Charles Duff, Dr Aoife Monks, Michael Thornton, Rod
Coton, Lee Menzies, Robert Noble, Warner Brown, Pamela
Douglas, Thelma Holt, Malcolm Browning, Robert Israel, Brian
Kirk, Patrick Sandford, Michael Sommers, Gyles Brandreth,
James Hogan, Olivia Kelly, Sacha Brooks, Jo Blatchley, Martin
Burton, Dick McCaw, Chloe Bennett, Philippe Carden, Mondane
Carden, Dawn McLoughlin, Moira Goff, Rebecca Treanor and
Simon Goose.

Historian Dr Peter Martland has been particularly generous
with his time, guidance and good counsel; and Andrew
McKinnon, Programme Director of Birkbeck College's MA in
Creative Producing, has also been an invaluable source of
information. Both also provided helpful feedback on early drafts.
Professor Martin Daunton and Professor Kathy Mezei kindly
offered their guidance on particular areas of my research.

I am grateful to the Master, Fellows, students and staff of
Corpus Christi College, Cambridge for their hospitality, support
and good company during the writing of this book, in particular
to Stuart and Sibella Laing, Professor Christopher Andrew and
Jenny Andrew, Professor John Hatcher, the Revd James Buxton,
Dr Richard McMahon, Dr Patrick Zutshi, Professor Hyman
Gross, Dr David Burke, Tim Harvey-Samuel, Vanessa Addison,
Kate Williams, Michael Martin and Andrew Baughan. I was
delighted to be appointed Fellow Commoner at the College
during the first year of the book's writing, and it continues to
provide a stimulating and supportive environment in which to
conduct my research.

As a producer, I have been privileged to stage over thirty
productions of Agatha Christie's plays. These were made possible
by Ian Lenagan (the 2001 Agatha Christie Theatre Festival) and

Bill Kenwright (The Agatha Christie Theatre Company), and by the talent and commitment of the creative teams and performers involved. Of my many friends and colleagues in these ventures, actor and director Roy Marsden, designer Simon Scullion and the ACTC's long-serving artistic director, Joe Harmston, have provided me with particularly valuable insights into the staging of Christie's work.

Very special thanks to my parents, Eileen and Trevor Green, and my friends Ray Cooney, Keith Strachan, Tim Halford and Lee Waite, for joining me on this journey.

JULIUS GREEN
January 2018

To Dianne

A Note from the Author

Given the quantity of published and unpublished material that is quoted in this book, I have decided to standardise various elements of it in order to assist the reader. This includes the layout of playscripts and the style in which the titles of works are expressed: in italics if quoting from a publication and not so if quoting from correspondence. My own occasional comments in the midst of quoted material are indicated by [square brackets]. Minor spelling and typographical errors in original documents have been corrected unless I believe them to be of interest, in which case they are indicated with (sic). Documents quoted in this book which date from before the 1950s tend to refer to what we now call the director of a play as the 'producer' and what we now call the producer as the 'manager'. In such cases I have included a clarification. A number of Agatha Christie's plays underwent changes of title; where this occurred, the title used in this book is that of the particular draft, production or published edition being discussed.

Contents

Agatha Christie

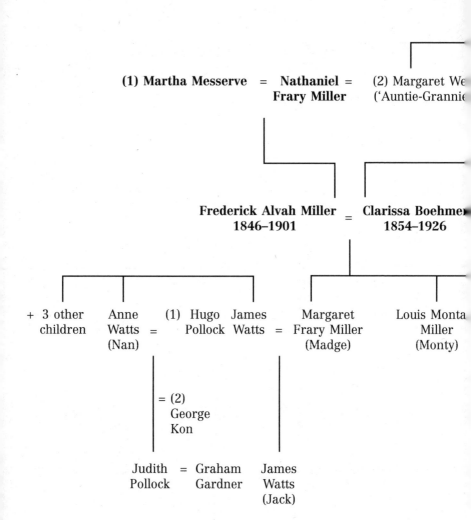

(1) Martha Messerve = **Nathaniel** = (2) Margaret We
　　　　　　　　　　 Frary Miller　('Auntie-Grannie

Frederick Alvah Miller ＿ **Clarissa Boehmer**
1846–1901　　　　　　**1854–1926**

+ 3 other　　Anne　　(1) Hugo　James　　Margaret　　Louis Monta
children　　Watts　 = 　Pollock　Watts =　Frary Miller　　Miller
　　　　　　(Nan)　　　　　　　　　　　(Madge)　　　(Monty)

　　　　　　　　= (2)
　　　　　　　　George
　　　　　　　　Kon

　　　　Judith　=　Graham　　James
　　　　Pollock　　Gardner　　Watts
　　　　　　　　　　　　　　　(Jack)

Family Tree

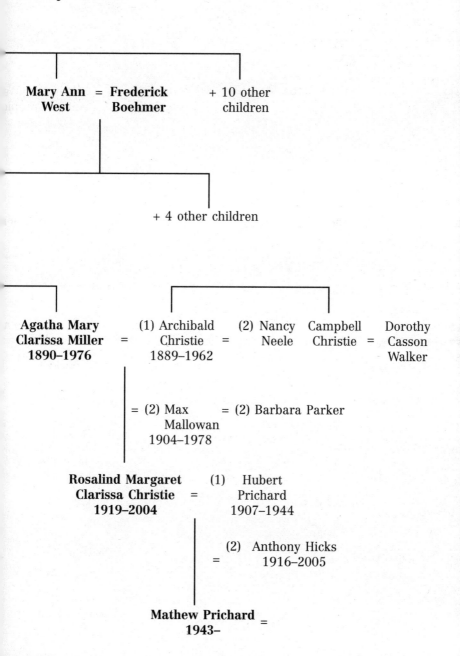

Mary Ann West = **Frederick Boehmer**   + 10 other children

+ 4 other children

Agatha Mary Clarissa Miller 1890–1976 = (1) Archibald Christie 1889–1962 = (2) Nancy Neele   Campbell Christie = Dorothy Casson Walker

= (2) Max Mallowan 1904–1978   = (2) Barbara Parker

Rosalind Margaret Clarissa Christie 1919–2004 = (1) Hubert Prichard 1907–1944

= (2) Anthony Hicks 1916–2005

Mathew Prichard 1943– =

Behind the Scenes

This is the story of the most successful female playwright of all time. She also wrote some books.

Agatha Christie (1890–1976) is universally acknowledged as the world's best-selling novelist, and yet the significance of her contribution to theatre has been largely overlooked by historians. This despite the fact that she is responsible for a repertoire of work that enjoyed enormous global success in her own lifetime and continues to do so more than forty years after her death. She not only holds the record for the world's longest-running theatrical production, but is also the only female playwright to have had three of her works running in the West End simultaneously. Her first attempts at playwriting date from around 1908 and her last completed play premiered in 1972. Nine of her plays opened in the West End in the 1940s and 1950s alone, and two of them were big hits on Broadway. For Christie, theatrical success arrived relatively late in life; it brought her much pleasure and, despite her legendary shyness, she enjoyed the company of theatrical people and relished their eccentricities.

From the point where she finally broke through as a playwright in the 1950s, it is clear that Christie continued to regard writing books as her day job, but that she found true creative fulfilment in her work for the stage. In her autobiography she notes:

Of course I knew that writing books was my steady, solid profession. I could go on inventing plots and writing my books until I went gaga . . . writing plays seemed to me entrancing simply because it wasn't my job, because I hadn't got the feeling that I *had* to think of a play – I only had to write the play that I was already thinking of. Plays are much easier to *write* than books, because you can see them in your mind's eye, you are not hampered by all the description that clogs you so terribly in a book and stops you getting on with what's happening. The circumscribed limits of the stage simplify things for you. You don't have to follow the heroine up and down the stairs, or out to the tennis lawn and back, thinking thoughts that have to be described. You only have what can be seen and heard and done to deal with. Looking and listening and feeling is what you have to deal with.[1]

In a 1951 article on Christie, *The Stage* newspaper reported that she found writing plays easier than writing books because 'With a play you can go straight to your plot and characters and you have not to deal with the problem of describing scenes and the movements and habits of people. If you are at all successful, all this appears automatically through your characters and the action in which they are involved.'[2] And, in an interview for the BBC Radio Light Programme in 1955, she once again stated that 'Of course writing plays is much more fun than writing books . . . you must write pretty fast, keep in the mood and keep the talk flowing naturally.'[3]

Some commentators have interpreted such remarks as implying that, whilst writing books was Agatha Christie's profession, writing plays was simply her hobby. My own view is that, for a writer who had a real aptitude for dialogue and who, by her own admission, felt hampered by 'description', playwriting was her true vocation. And her determined, twenty-year struggle to gain recognition as a dramatist bears witness to this. Like most playwrights, Agatha Christie has her good and her bad days but, speaking as a theatre practitioner rather than an academic, it seems to me that she is both a master of her craft and a unique and witty voice with a great deal to say about the human condition. Actors always seem to enjoy engaging with her characters and find much in them to relate to, belying the popular misconception that they are thinly drawn caricatures. Her work is laced, whether consciously or not, with echoes of the other great playwrights of the era, and some of the most celebrated actors of the day appeared in her plays.

So why has history been so unkind to Agatha Christie, playwright? At the height of her popularity in the 1950s the dominant producing force in the West End was Binkie Beaumont, but Christie's most enduring working relationship was with Peter Saunders, a rival impresario who was openly critical of the monopolistic tendencies of the Beaumont empire. So, despite her popular success, Christie was notable for working outside the established (and at times fearsomely ruthless) West End oligarchy of the day; a fact that makes her achievements all the more remarkable. As a doyenne of the 'well-made play' she remained delightfully untouched by the Royal Court revolution and consequently does not even feature in the vocabulary of those academics for whom the history of twentieth-century British playwriting started with *Look Back In Anger* in 1956. She thus occupies a unique position as a playwright, outside both the prevailing theatrical culture and its counter-culture; and her theatrical vocabulary suits the historians of neither.

Another very straightforward reason for the neglect of Christie as a playwright is continued confusion over the authorship of the plays credited to her. As well as her own work for the stage there have been a number of second-rate adaptations of her novels by third parties; and this, combined with the enduring success of third-party film and television adaptations, has led to an assumption that the plays credited to her were not from her own pen. There is an immediate and obvious qualitative difference between Christie's own work for the stage and that of her adaptors, but the staging of a number of such works in her own lifetime, and several more since, has inevitably diluted her own stock as a playwright. Christie herself was unequivocal on the subject, repeatedly expressing her displeasure at her stage adaptors' work: 'Several books of mine were dramatised by other people and they all dissatisfied me intensely,' she told the *Sunday Times* in 1961.[4] Ironically, though, whilst arguably initially hindering her own development as a playwright, the adaptors' efforts provided her with an entrée to the world of theatre and its practitioners, where she became a willing student and gained the confidence to promote her own work: 'I think what started me off was my annoyance over people adapting my books for the stage in a way I disliked.'[5] Certainly, she is the only playwright I can think of whose reputation has had to contend with the truly bizarre obstacle of a body of work for the stage penned by others but promoted to the public and the critics in her name.

And then there is the question of collaboration. Playwriting is often a shared undertaking, and writers from Shakespeare to Brecht to David Edgar have worked with others in the preparation of their scripts. There can be no doubt that one of the things that most attracted Christie to the stage was the collaborative nature of the process, enabling her as it did to exchange ideas with others in a way that her largely solitary work as a novelist did not. She was a willing and adept participant in script discussions, either as a commentator on other people's adaptations of her novels or as a playwright herself attempting to address the concerns of producers, directors and actors. Despite the patronising claims of certain directors about the level of their own input, the fourteen full-length plays and three one-act plays that were premiered on stage in Christie's lifetime, and which carry her name as sole playwright, are indisputably her own work. She only ever incorporated the suggestions of others up to a point, and always remained in control of the script development process. And when she was convinced that she was in the right she was legendarily immovable. Ironically, her own highly accomplished adaptation of one of her short stories was appropriated wholesale by an 'adaptor' without so much as an acknowledgement of her own dramatisation as source material. And, conversely, she had very little to do with the only script for which she is actually credited as co-adaptor. In such cases Christie herself acted in good faith at the behest of agents and producers, but it doesn't help when it comes to establishing the extent of her own contribution to the dramatic canon that bears her name.

There is also perhaps a misconception that Christie exploited her reputation as a novelist to promote her career in the theatre, and that her theatrical successes were in some way dependent on the success of her books. If anything, as we shall see, the opposite was the case, and the expectations raised by the popularity of her detective fiction frequently hampered her progress as a playwright and prejudiced critical opinion against her work on the stage. Whilst her producers inevitably attempted to capitalise on her existing fan base, the adaptations of some of her best-selling novels proved to be critical and box office disasters, and theatregoers repeatedly demonstrated themselves to be more than capable of judging her work for the stage on its own merits. Christie's success as a playwright was exceptionally hard-won and, far from resting on her laurels as a popular novelist, she consistently dedicated herself to honing her craft, observing and willingly learning from the numerous leading theatrical practitioners with whom she worked. In any case, Christie was writing at a time when combining careers as a novelist and a playwright was not uncommon; amongst the contemporary female playwrights who did so were Clemence Dane, Margaret Kennedy, Enid Bagnold, Dodie Smith and Daphne du Maurier. Christie was simply both a more successful novelist and, ultimately, a more successful playwright than any of them. And, for those who carp that her plays were simply adaptations of existing works, it is instructive to note how far these adaptations diverge from their source material and that, amongst her full-length plays, there are nine totally original works, six of which were premiered in her lifetime. Christie herself said, 'I prefer to write a play as a play, that is rather than to adapt a book.'[6]

Christie was passionate about theatre and was deeply involved in the processes of making it. She attended and contributed to rehearsals, and her delightful 'author's notes' at the front of some of the published editions of the plays show her engaging with everything from the mechanics of creating the effect of a lift ascending and descending in *Appointment with Death* to the problems associated with the unusually large dramatis personae of *Witness for the Prosecution* and the 'ageing' of actors and multiple locations in *Go Back for Murder*. She was very aware of the practicalities of putting on a play, favouring single sets and relatively small casts (*Appointment with Death* and *Witness for the Prosecution* are notable exceptions), and this partly accounts for her enduring popularity with cash-strapped repertory theatres and touring companies over the years, and the consequent law of diminishing returns in terms of both production values and credibility within the theatre community.

Born in 1890, for the first ten years of her life Agatha was a Victorian; Gladstone became Prime Minister for the fourth time shortly before her first birthday. As a teenager and a young woman she was an Edwardian. She waved husbands off to both world wars, and women got the vote on the same basis as men when she was thirty-eight. In 1969 she watched man land on the moon on television, and when she died in 1976, Harold Wilson was Prime Minister. Her first success as a novelist came when she was thirty; but although she started writing plays as a teenager, none of her work was staged until she was forty, and her playwriting career didn't really take off until she was in her sixties. This is an interesting inversion of the timeline of Noël Coward's career; Coward and Christie were contemporaries, but his success as a playwright came much earlier in life and reached its pinnacle in the Second World War with *Blithe Spirit* and *Present Laughter*, just as Christie was experiencing her first West End hit with *Ten Little Niggers*. (The history of this play's problematic title is examined later in this book.)

All but one of Christie's plays are firmly set in the period in which they were written, and they resist any attempt at updating in just the same way that the work of Noël Coward does. Although the moral dilemmas faced by the characters and their guilt, obsession, love and jealousy are timeless, their behaviour and interactions are very much a function of the social *mores* of the time in which each play is set; not to mention the fact that modern communications technology would severely compromise key elements of the plotting. The stakes are raised in several of the storylines by the ever-present threat of the hangman's noose; particularly in *Verdict*, where the existence of the death penalty clearly informs the protagonist's decision not to turn the murderer over to the police, and in *Towards Zero*, where it accounts for an extraordinary plot twist. The acceptability of smoking provides a continuous subtext of cigarettes, pipes and cigars both as a form of social interaction (offering someone a cigarette can be as good as a chat-up line) and to underscore key moments of tension. A nervous character will reach for a cigarette and a pipe smoker is usually to be trusted.

But it would be a mistake to assume that the society reflected in the majority of Christie's stage work is a halcyon one of pre-war vicarage tea parties. Ironically, this relatively elderly woman, whose upbringing was defined by the *mores* of the previous century and whose frame of reference is generally assumed to be that of the pre-war era, found lasting fame as a playwright in the decade when 'angry young men' were allegedly redefining the theatrical playing field at the Royal Court. Christie did not live a cocooned middle-class life. She was adventurous, widely travelled and politically aware, and encountered people of all classes and cultures. She worked in a hospital dispensary during the First World War (gaining a comprehensive knowledge of poisons in the process), was one of the first people to surf standing up on a surfboard (whilst visiting South Africa) and made use of recent changes in the law to divorce her cheating first husband, Archie Christie, in 1928. Her work spans a century of massive social and political change and this does not go unacknowledged within it, from *The Hollow* with its crumbling aristocracy facing up to the loss of empire to the overtly political challenge to the conservative orthodoxy represented by Alderman Higgs in *Appointment with*

Death, the 'not a Red, just pale pink' Miss Casewell in *The Mousetrap*, the post-war suspicion of foreigners in *Witness for the Prosecution* and the persecuted East European immigrants at the centre of *Verdict*.

Whilst the received wisdom is that Christie's novels are to a certain extent formulaic, and much scholarly time has been devoted to analysing these alleged formulae, the same most definitely cannot be said of her work as a playwright, and it almost seems that she found herself enjoying greater freedom of expression as a writer in this genre. A repertoire encompassing the edge-of-your-seat chiller *Ten Little Niggers*, the definitive courtroom drama *Witness for the Prosecution*, the Rattiganesque psychological drama *Verdict* and the 'time play' *Go Back for Murder* can hardly be described as formulaic and there is no such thing as a 'typical' Agatha Christie play. Despite the enduring perception of her work as little more than an extended game of Cluedo, Christie's plays tend to be character-led rather than plot-led, and she clearly relishes entrusting the entire momentum of the story-telling to the voices of her ever-colourful dramatis personae. Her dialogue fairly trips off the tongue and is spiced with witticisms and observational comedy frequently worthy of Wilde. In her plays the detectives and police inspectors are usually relegated to minor roles, with the solving of a crime taking second place to the human drama that is being played out. It is as if we come closer to what Christie wants to say as a writer without the dominating presence of Poirot and Marple. With the exception of Poirot's appearance in *Black Coffee*, the first play of hers to be produced (in 1930), neither character features in any of her own stage plays, and indeed she removed Poirot from the storyline when undertaking her own adaptations of four of the novels in which he appears, maintaining, doubtless correctly, that he would pull focus on stage.

Explorations of guilt, revenge and justice loom large in Christie's stage work and are timeless subjects that go back to the very dawn of playwriting, but although the concept of justice and the many forms that it can take is central to many of her plays, the image of the policeman leading away the guilty party in handcuffs is rarely part of her theatrical vocabulary. An inability to escape the past is a recurring theme, and man's infidelity is often the catalyst for its exploration, a frequently used storyline that some have attributed to the philandering of Christie's own first husband. In Christie's work for the stage, the murder itself is usually nothing more than a plot device to move forward the action and to set the scene for Christie's exploration of the human condition and the dilemmas faced by her characters. 'Who' dunit is far less important than 'Why'.

Agatha was a regular theatregoer from childhood and engaged in theatrical projects from an early age, was hugely theatrically literate and drew on a broad frame of reference from Grand Guignol to Whitehall farce, all of which can be seen in her work. But her lifelong passion was for Shakespeare, and her theatrical vocabulary was defined in particular by an enjoyment and understanding of his works, gained as an audience member and a reader rather than a scholar. In a 1973 letter to *The Times* she wrote: 'I have gone to plays from an early age and am a great believer that that is the way one should approach Shakespeare. He wrote to entertain and he wrote for playgoers.'[7] And in her autobiography she says,

> Shakespeare is ruined for most people by having been made to learn it at school; you should see Shakespeare as it was written to be seen, played on the stage. There you can appreciate it quite young, long before you take in the beauty of the words and the poetry. I took my grandson, Mathew, to *Macbeth* and *The Merry Wives of Windsor* when he was, I think, eleven or twelve. He was very appreciative of both, though his comment was unexpected. He turned to me as we came out, and said in an awestruck voice, 'You know, if I hadn't known beforehand that that was *Shakespeare*, I should *never* have believed it.' This was clearly meant to be a testimonial to Shakespeare, and I took it as such.[8]

Agatha and her grandson particularly enjoyed the knock-about comedy of *The Merry Wives of Windsor*:

> In those days it was done, as I am sure it was meant to be, as good old English slapstick – no subtlety about it. The last representation of the *Merry Wives* I saw – in 1965 – had so much arty production about it that you felt you had travelled very far from a bit of winter sun in Windsor Old Park. Even the laundry basket was no longer a laundry basket, full of dirty washing: it was a mere symbol made of raffia! One cannot really enjoy slapstick farce when it is symbolised. The good old pantomime custard trick will never fail to rouse a roar of laughter, so long as custard appears to be actually applied to a face! To take a small carton with Birds Custard Powder written on it and delicately tap a cheek – well, the symbolism may be there, but the farce is lacking.[9]

Agatha's letters to her second husband, Max, during his wartime posting to Cairo are full of enthusiastic descriptions of her visits to the major Shakespearian productions of the day, including those presented by the Old Vic Company at the New Theatre, their London base towards the end of the war. Her critiques of the productions and the performances of the leading classical actors of the day, and her insightful interpretations of the characters' motivations, display a comprehensive knowledge of the Shakespearian repertoire. She also shows a keen interest in Shakespeare's craft as a playwright. Commenting on the fact that he did not devise original plots she says, of the era in which he wrote:

> I think the playwright was rather like a composer – he had to find a libretto for his art (like a ballet nowadays). 'I should like to do a setting of Hamlet, or my version of Macbeth etc.' Inventing a story was not really thought of. 'What is the argument?' Claudius asks in Hamlet before the players begin. The argument was a set thing – you then exercised your art on it . . . I think plays tended to be loose on construction,

because they incorporated certain 'turns' – like the music halls . . . He saw a play as a series of scenes in which actors got certain opportunities. Rather like beads on a necklace – the thing to him remained always individual beads strung together.[10]

Shakespeare's portrayal of female characters particularly engaged Agatha – 'All Shakespeare's women are very definitely characterized – he was feminine enough himself to see men through their eyes'[11] – and she was intrigued by Oxford academic A.L. Rowse's disputed identification of the 'Dark Lady' of Shakespeare's sonnets. Rowse, in turn, was an admirer of Christie; 'We must not underrate her literary ambition and accomplishment, as her publishers did, simply because she was the first of detective story writers.'[12] Meanwhile, Christie trivia buffs can spend many happy hours identifying the numerous Shakespearian references in the titles and texts of her works. To get the ball rolling, I will pose the question, what were the *two* plays she wrote that took their titles from *Hamlet*?

Agatha was as enamoured with the backstage world of theatre as she was with the performance itself. 'I don't think, that there is anything that takes you so much away from real things and happenings as the acting world,' she wrote to Max in 1942.[13] 'It *is* a world of its own and actors never are thinking of anything but themselves and their lines and their business, and what they are going to wear!' And she says in her auto-biography, 'I always find it restful to stay with actors in wartime, because to them, acting and the theatrical world are the *real* world, any other world was not. The war to them was a long drawn-out nightmare that prevented them from going on with their own lives, in the proper way, so their entire talk was of theatrical people, theatrical things, what was going on in the theatrical world, who was going into E.N.S.A. – it was wonder-fully refreshing.'[14] To Agatha Christie, whose imaginary world has offered a welcome escape for so many, the world of theatre offered one to her.

Agatha shared with her theatrical friends the excitements and disappointments of live performance – 'Lights that do not go out when the whole point is that that they *should* go out, and lights that do not go on when the whole point is that they *should* go on. These are the real agonies of theatre'[15] – and in particular the agonies of first nights:

> First nights are usually misery, hardly to be borne. One has only two reasons for going to them. One is – a not ignoble motive – that the poor actors have to go through with it, and if it goes badly it is unfair that the author should not be there to share their torture . . . The other reason for going to first nights is, of course, curiosity . . . you have to know *yourself*. Nobody else's account is going to be any good. So there you are, shivering, feeling hot and cold alternately, hoping to heaven that nobody will notice you where you are hiding yourself in the higher ranks of the Circle.[16]

Christie trivia buffs can again spend happy hours identifying the numerous theatrical references, characters and scenarios in her novels; I offer for starters 1952's *They Do It with Mirrors*, in which Miss Marple is fascinated by the stage illusion involved in the creation of a production of a play that rejoices in the Christiesque title 'The Nile at Sunset'. And it is no coincidence that disguise is a recurring plot device in her plays, a number of which feature characters who are impersonating someone else. This conceit accounts for Christie's two greatest *coups de théâtre*, in *The Mousetrap* and *Witness for the Prosecution*; the latter is carried out with a high level of theatrical skill by a character who is a professional actress, in a plot twist with echoes of her 1923 short story, 'The Actress'.[17]

Agatha Christie is herself one of the most written about of writers. Much of what has been published about her, however, engages either with the highly seductive imaginary world of her novels or with endlessly re-examined elements of her personal life; even those writers who do make a serious attempt to place her work in a historical and literary context tend to overlook her contribution as a dramatist. Alison Light's persuasive study of Christie's work as an example of 'conservative modernity' in *Forever England* (1991) focuses on the inter-war period and so can be excused for overlooking her plays. But other serious assessments of her work, from Merja Makinen's *Agatha Christie: Investigating Femininity* (2006) and Susan Rowland's *From Agatha Christie to Ruth Rendell* (2001) to Gillian Gill's *Agatha Christie: The Woman and her Mysteries* (1999) and *Agatha Christie* in the Modern Critical Views series (edited by Harold Bloom; 2001), are united in their neglect of her work as a playwright. Ironically, many of the writers concerned may well have found an engagement with Christie's work for the stage to have been beneficial to their arguments.

An honourable exception is Charles Osborne's 1982 book *The Life and Crimes of Agatha Christie*. Osborne, a theatre critic and former literature director of the Arts Council, is less academic in his tone than the writers listed above, but is diligent in affording Christie's dramatic work equal prominence with her novels. Other than Osborne's book, the only significant overviews of Christie's plays in the context of appraisals of her own work are in J.C. Trewin's lively and opinionated contribution to *Agatha Christie; First Lady of Crime* (edited by H.R.F. Keating; 1977) and a chapter in Peter Haining's workmanlike *Murder in Four Acts* (1990). Two histories of crime drama, Marvin Lachman's *The Villainous Stage* (2014) and Amnon Kabatchnik's epic, five-volume *Blood on the Stage* (2009–2014), each contribute some original research to the subject, and at least acknowledge Christie's significance as a writer of stage thrillers if not as a playwright in a wider context. Several of the multifarious Christie 'companions' and 'reader's guides' dutifully list the plays and recite the often inaccurate received wisdom about their origins and first productions (an honourable mention here to Dennis Sanders and Len Lovallo's 1984 *The Agatha Christie Companion*, which is a cut above many of its competitors); but I have seen 'encyclopedias' of her characters which omit completely those which appear only in the plays.

Perhaps most saddening, though, is the fact that Christie has even been eschewed by feminist theatre academics such as those responsible for *The Cambridge Companion to Modern British Women Playwrights* (2000), meriting not so much as a footnote in the chapter covering the 1950s in a book that purports to 'address the work of women playwrights in Britain throughout the twentieth century'. Whilst not notable for chaining herself to railings, Christie challenged the male hegemony in West End theatre more successfully than any other female playwright before or since. She took on her male contemporaries on their own terms, and in many respects beat them at their own game. She created a series of strong and memorable female protagonists of all ages, and any actress complaining that there are not enough substantial stage roles for women need look no further than her plays. Most disappointing is Maggie B. Gale's *West End Women* (1996). Although Gale's book, which covers the period 1918–1962, offers a fascinating insight into a neglected area of theatre history, and acknowledges Christie's commercial success as a playwright, it largely overlooks her contribution in favour of the usual suspects: Clemence Dane, Enid Bagnold, Gertrude Jennings, Dodie Smith and others. This is a missed opportunity in an otherwise excellent book. Gale does, however, make the following interesting point: 'Research on women playwrights, let alone performers, managers, directors and designers is, in real terms, only just beginning. It is important that we look at what was there, rather than trying to fit our findings into some preconceived notion of what it is that, for example, women should have been writing.'[18]

And, examining Clemence Dane's work in *Women, Theatre and Performance* (2000), Gale observes that Dane 'falls foul of many failings in theatre historiography: the unwillingness to view women's work in the mainstream; the fear of the "conservative"; and the general lack of interest in mid-twentieth century theatre. It remains quite extraordinary that there is so little critical, biographical and historical material on a playwright so recently working in theatre, a playwright, once a household name, who has somehow been removed from fame to obscurity.'[19]

It could so easily be Agatha Christie to whom Gale is referring that I have gladly taken this as the starting point for my own book. 'Suffrage theatre' gets a great deal of attention from historians of women's writing for the stage, but theatre written by women simply in order to entertain audiences tends to be overlooked. Gender history is a fascinating subject, but the problem with it is that it tends to be written by gender historians. Lib Taylor, in *British and Irish Women Dramatists since 1958* (1993), dismisses Christie's plays solely on the basis that she believes them to exhibit an 'underlying collusion with patriarchy'. This view is based on a comprehensive misreading of a small number of the later works, and seems to be a common misapprehension amongst academics. And even if it were true, a playwright is surely free to 'collude' with whoever they like. In 1983, seven years after Christie's death, the Conference of Women Theatre Directors and Administrators undertook a major survey of women's role in British theatre.[20] Amongst the many interesting statistics arising from this important exercise was that of the twenty-eight plays written by women produced in the previous year on the main stages of regional repertory theatres, twenty-two (or 80 per cent) were penned by Agatha Christie. More recently, on the eve of her 125th anniversary year, Christie was the only woman with a play running in the West End. It is a shame that the preconceptions and prejudices of many historians of women's theatre appear to have dictated against a proper analysis of her achievements as a playwright.

Of the two 'authorised' biographies, Janet Morgan's (1984) does its best to examine the importance of theatre in Agatha's life and work, whilst Laura Thompson's (2007) marginalises it in favour of an emphasis on the widely accepted thesis that much of Agatha's work under the pen name of Mary Westmacott was semi-autobiographical. Both contain significant inaccuracies in relation to the plays, the former due mostly to the notorious difficulty of correctly dating Agatha's correspondence (which Morgan quotes extensively) and the latter due to the author's evident lack of interest in this area of Agatha's work. The book you are reading is not a biography; I have had the privilege of being able to investigate in detail a particular aspect of Agatha Christie's work, and I do not underestimate the task of attempting to chronicle the entire life of such a multi-faceted individual. So if you want to find out more about her personal life, and in particular her family history, then I recommend both of these books.

The journalist Gwen Robyns wrote an unauthorised biography, *The Mystery of Agatha Christie*, in 1978, based largely on interviews with people who knew and worked with Christie. Although somewhat unorthodox in its approach, it acknowledges the importance of theatre in her work, and is of particular interest in that Robyns appears to have spoken with some of the key players, including Peter Cotes, the original director of *The Mousetrap*, and Wallace Douglas, who as director of *Witness for the Prosecution* and *Spider's Web* was responsible for two more of Christie's biggest hits. Whilst inaccurate in a number of respects, Robyns' book gives a good flavour of the spirit of Christie's engagement with the world of theatre. As is often the case, though, her list of 'Agatha Christie plays' makes no distinction between those written by Christie herself and those which are the work of third-party adaptors.

It is autobiographies, rather than biographies, that provide the most fruitful source of published material for the Agatha Christie theatre researcher. In 1972, Agatha wrote the introduction to *The Mousetrap Man*, the autobiography of Peter Saunders, who produced all of her work in the West End between 1950 and 1962, including her biggest successes. An entertaining and opinionated romp, it gives an interesting, but nonetheless selective, insight into Agatha's work at the height of her playwriting career, as well as Saunders' own views on matters such as investors, critics and his fellow producers. In 1977, Agatha's own autobiography was published posthumously. Written between 1950 and 1965, when she was aged between fifty-nine and seventy-five, it is a compelling read and gives some fascinating insights into her personality and her love of theatre, but is notoriously selective and not always entirely accurate in points of detail and chronology. Because of its focus on her early life, and the fact that her work as a playwright met with success relatively late in her career, it ironically is not the most reliable of sources on the subject. Agatha's second husband, the archaeologist Max Mallowan, published his own autobiography, *Mallowan's Memoirs*, in the same year. His opinions on his wife's theatrical efforts are perceptive and insightful, if relatively brief.

In 1980 Hubert Gregg, who directed *The Hollow*, *The Unexpected Guest* and a couple of Christie's later, less successful plays, published *Agatha Christie and All That Mousetrap*. In this bizarrely self-satisfied and resentful book from a relatively minor player in the story of Christie on stage, Gregg complains that Christie underplayed Peter Saunders' contribution to her theatrical success in her own autobiography. What Gregg really objected to, of course, was that she had failed to mention his own modest contribution at all. I have had access to a small but very interesting privately held collection of Gregg's rehearsal scripts and correspondence with Christie, which does not entirely bear out his version of events.

Peter Cotes, the original director of *The Mousetrap*, uses his 1993 autobiography, *Thinking Aloud*, to establish (at some length) his own position in respect of his lifelong dispute with Peter Saunders, the play's producer. In doing so he quotes Gwen Robyns in support, although Robyns was presumably simply repeating information that Cotes had himself given to her. Saunders, Gregg and Cotes between them provide lively and often conflicting first-hand accounts of the production process of Christie's plays from 1950 onwards, but tend to marginalise the role of Christie herself.

No Christie scholar's bookshelf is complete without the extraordinary contribution of John Curran, whose meticulous transcriptions from and analyses of her seventy-three notebooks in his own two-volume work, *Agatha Christie's Secret Notebooks* (2009) and *Agatha Christie's Murder in the Making* (2011), provide a vital key to Christie's imaginary world. Largely undated and frequently illegible, these copious, gloriously disorganised, handwritten *aides memoires* show work in progress as Christie developed ideas for storylines for both her novels and plays. The notebooks themselves are particularly interesting for their outlines of plays that never made it as far as a draft script, and Dr Curran has been unstintingly generous as an expert guide in this respect, sharing his knowledge in a manner that enabled me quickly to locate the particular nuggets that I was seeking. For plays that reached script stage, however, the notebooks are frequently less informative as a source for examining the work's development than the often numerous versions of the draft scripts themselves, the typed and handwritten amendments made to them, and Christie's sometimes extremely detailed correspondence with directors and producers as new ideas were explored and incorporated. The draft scripts for *Three Blind Mice* (which became *The Mousetrap*) and *Witness for the Prosecution*, for instance, are full of alterations, insertions, amendments and pencil notes made as she developed the scenarios and characters. We often see quite radical changes to plotting and outcomes taking place before us on the page. The draft scripts are, in effect, the 'notebooks' for the plays.

Many of these drafts are held by the Christie Archive Trust, whose collection consists mainly of papers that were removed from Christie's cherished Devon estate Greenway when it was handed over to the National Trust in 2001, and includes a vast quantity of personal correspondence, as well as the legendary notebooks and drafts of many of the books and plays. The correspondence, mostly between Christie and her second husband Max, at times when he was either away on archaeological work or on wartime military service, gives a fascinating and deeply personal insight into Agatha's devotion to family, the wide range of her interests and her delightful sense of humour. Almost entirely absent is any reference to her work as a novelist (which, to her, would have been the equivalent of discussing her 'day job'). She does, however, frequently refer with obvious delight to progress on her numerous theatrical projects. The letters themselves, like the notebooks, are mostly undated (or not fully dated; we are usually told the day of the week) and often illegible; at one point even Max asks if she would mind typing her next epistle. Analysing the correspondence when a line about a play rehearsal could read either 'it was absolutely marvellous' or 'I was absolutely furious' is a labour-intensive but deeply rewarding operation. Dating the letters is an equally time-consuming process, although made easier by Max's completely legible and meticulously dated side of the correspondence, where available. Some of the previous mistakes that have been made in documenting Christie's theatre work have arisen from the misdating of letters, but ironically taking note of their theatrical context is often one of the most accurate ways of identifying the time of writing. When and where certain productions that she refers to were actually staged is, after all, a matter of record. Five key scripts are missing entirely from the archive: *Black Coffee*, *Ten Little Niggers*, *Appointment with Death*, *The Hollow* and *Go Back for Murder*; but it more than redeems itself by housing five unpublished and unperformed full-length scripts and a further seven one-act plays, all of them of considerable interest to the historian of her work as a playwright.

One of the many problems with assessing historic play texts is that what we currently accept as the published version may well contain significant changes to the draft that was accepted for production, and equally to the version that was eventually performed in front of the critics following amendments made during the rehearsal process. It is here that the Lord Chamberlain's Plays collection at the British Library provides an invaluable resource. From 1737 until 1968 all new plays produced in the UK were subject to approval by the Lord Chamberlain's office, thus effectively conferring a censorship role on a department of the royal household. Almost every play submitted has been retained in the collection, and scripts from the period 1824–1968 are housed at the British Library, referenced through thousands of handwritten index cards. Significantly, the script held in this collection would be exactly that performed on the first night, and thus reviewed by critics, because changes were not permitted once a licence had been issued.

Scripts had to be submitted to the Lord Chamberlain no later than a week before the first scheduled performance, and to allow for changes to be made right up to the last possible moment they were often sent at very short notice; it has to be said that the Lord Chamberlain's office seems to have been remarkably good-natured and diligent in processing scripts and responding to them in what were frequently very short time-frames. The result of this was that playwrights effectively self-censored, as nothing could be more catastrophic than to have your play postponed by a last-minute spat with the censor when the production was paid for and in rehearsal. Each play was subject to an Official Examiner's report on a single sheet of paper, which make for interesting reading and often show the censor in the role of would-be critic. There is also a file of correspondence between the Lord Chamberlain's office and the producer of each production.

The card index is by play title and the handwritten, 17-volume chronological list of plays submitted for licensing between 1900 and 1968 is similarly far from user-friendly when it comes to identifying works by a particular writer; but amongst the collection's many Christie treasures is a rare copy of the script for *Chimneys*, which was cancelled at the last minute in 1931, and some interesting correspondence that gives lie to the assumption that the censor never found cause to interfere with her work.

Another significant copy of any play that gets as far as production is the 'prompt copy' used by the stage manager to record technical cues and stage directions in rehearsal. Few of these still exist, although *The Mousetrap*'s is housed in the V&A Theatre Archive. The 'acting edition' of Christie's plays, which was usually published by Samuel French within a year of the first performance, would often incorporate stage directions from the prompt copy which Christie herself had not actually written.

Christie researchers and biographers are also fortunate to have access to the archives of Hughes Massie Ltd, her agent, relating to her work. Edmund Cork, who took over the company from the eponymous Massie, started representing Christie in 1923 and masterminded her business affairs until his death in 1988. Central to this extensive collection are the file copies of his regular updates to Christie on the progress of her work with publishers and theatre producers. What is immediately apparent from this correspondence is that under Cork's guidance 'Agatha Christie' rapidly became the first truly global, multi-media business empire based on the intellectual property of one individual. One woman with a typewriter was creating the work and one man with a typewriter (assisted by a small staff that latterly included his daughter, Pat) was responsible for selling it throughout the world; in print and on stage, as well as on film, sound recording, radio and television. Cork not only had to grapple with prototype contracts in many of the media concerned, but also with the complex and burdensome UK and international tax implications of individual worldwide royalty income on such an unprecedented scale. His unceasing labours on Christie's behalf, and his unfaltering loyalty, charm, tact, discretion and good humour, led Christie to place a complete and deserved trust in her agent, who was four years her junior. Taking on a role which these days would be described as 'personal manager', he dealt with everything from organising tickets for her regular theatre visits to dealing with troublesome tenants and the purchase of a new car. So complete was the trust between them that she would give him power of attorney when she and Max were away together on archaeological digs, to avoid their work being interrupted by business matters.

Cork had an eloquent and witty turn of phrase and his correspondence, both with Christie herself and with his New York counterpart, her American agent Harold Ober, make both for an entertaining read and a comprehensive narrative of Christie's business affairs. He may have made some mistakes, particularly when grappling with the unprecedented complexities of the network of companies and family trusts that latterly master-minded the collection and disbursement of Christie's royalty income, but on the front line of dealing with the sale and licensing of her work he was a canny businessman and a shrewd judge of character.

The Hughes Massie archive is housed at Exeter University and contains extensive correspondence between Cork and Christie, but sadly it only commences in 1938, and is sparse before 1940, so we have to look elsewhere for information regarding the business side of Christie's theatrical work prior to this date. Here her own correspondence with her husband can be used to fill in some of the gaps, as too can the archives of theatrical producer Basil Dean, with whom she discussed some of her work, although he never produced any of it.

Despite the huge success of adaptations of Christie's work on both large and small screens, she herself had absolutely no interest in film or television. She disliked the majority of the film adaptations of her work that she saw and, apart from a lengthy and diligent, but unused, film adaptation of Dickens' *Bleak House*, and a speculative, and equally unused, two-page film treatment for her play *Spider's Web*, she never wrote for the medium. She took part in a couple of radio 'serial' stories on behalf of the Detection Club (of which she was appointed president in 1957) and wrote four original radio plays which were broadcast live on the BBC but, despite misinformation to the contrary, she never wrote for television. Theatre, on the other hand, was her lifelong passion, both as a creator and a consumer.

Although Cork was initially sceptical about the commercial value of Christie's theatre projects, and was delightfully and wittily cynical about what he referred to as the 'vicissitudes of theatre' and the colourful personalities who populate its world, it is apparent that he quickly came to understand that the way to engage her attention was to prioritise her theatre work in his correspondence. And the result is that, doubtless against his own inclinations, a remarkably large amount of it relates to matters theatrical. As Christie herself commented in a 1951 press interview, 'with a book you have fewer anxieties. You write it, send it to your publisher, and, after a time, it appears. In the case of a play such things as the right cast, the most suitable sort of theatre, the best time for its production, the success or not of the first night, and a dozen other things have to be taken into consideration.'[21] It is evident from both her personal and her business correspondence that Christie greatly enjoyed engaging in these theatrical debates.

Eventually, though, even Cork had to admit that Christie's work for the stage was not simply an intellectual diversion on her part but a valuable source of core income to the business empire that he masterminded. At the time when Christie's plays were first being produced, London's West End 'theatreland' as we now know it, comprising around forty high-profile commercially oper-ated theatres, was a relatively recent phenomenon.[22] A theatre building boom, facilitated by the 1843 Theatres Act's removal of draconian licensing restrictions, had taken place between the last decades of the nineteenth century and the eve of the First World War, and playwrights now aspired to have their work presented in one of these prestigious London venues. A West End produc-tion, which would be reviewed by the national newspapers' theatre critics and would gain considerable publicity, could greatly enhance a play's value, making it attractive to repertory theatres, amateur groups, touring and international producers and even film companies. The key, therefore, did not necessarily lie in the success or otherwise of the first West End run but in the ability subsequently to exploit a title in these other markets. The licences issued to theatre producers by literary agents such as Hughes Massie consequently put a huge premium on achieving a West End production, rewarding producers who did so with partici-pation in the subsidiary income thus derived and thereby ensuring that they shared an interest with the agent in achieving the maximum exploitation of a title. New York's Broadway theatre district, which owes its current configuration to a theatrical building boom in the first three decades of the twentieth century, fulfilled a similar role to the West End in providing a valuable showcase for a playwright's work. The licences issued to theatre producers today still reflect the importance of both West End and Broadway productions for this reason.

This book focuses on the journey that each of Agatha Christie's plays took from page to stage in their original productions; there is simply not space to enumerate or evaluate the countless subsequent presentations of each title. Peter Haining sums it up well: 'the number of productions of her work plus the adaptations in this country, let alone the rest of the world, has passed into the realms of the uncountable. The performances of touring companies, repertory theatres and amateur dramatic societies are simply legion . . . Though, like all playwrights, Agatha Christie had her flops and short runs, her name outside a theatre has long exercised a tremendous attraction for the public, and spelt gold for the management.'[23]

The volume and complexity of the licensing of Christie's stage work is apparent from the enormous typewritten card index which constitutes Hughes Massie's Agatha Christie licensing records from the 1920s to the 1990s, housed in twenty-one leather-bound volumes at Agatha Christie Limited, the company which is now responsible for the global exploitation of her work. The two files labelled 'DD – apart from radio' are those of the Hughes Massie Drama Department, and detail the numerous global licensing and sub-licensing transactions relating to her dramatic work (apart from radio!). In most cases amateur rights for the English speaking world were licensed to Samuel French Ltd (who also publish the 'acting editions' of the playscripts), and in many other overseas territories deals were done with licensing sub-agents for both professional and amateur rights. These unique records confirm once again that the plays of Agatha Christie were, and remain, a vast international industry. As soon as each West End production opened, licences were being issued from Iceland to Kenya.

Of course, commercial success is a double-edged sword when it comes to critical reputation. Christie believed that critics resented the success of *The Mousetrap*, the longevity of which has become something of a theatrical running joke and which is by no means her best work as a playwright; and Hubert Gregg blamed the poor critical response to *Go Back for Murder* in 1960 on the fact that on the same day the newspapers had announced that Christie had signed a lucrative film deal with Metro-Goldwyn-Mayer. It is undeniable, though, that the enormous and enduring popularity of Christie's stage work in the repertory, secondary touring and amateur markets inevitably resulted in an association with cut-price and sub-standard productions, and a consequent law of diminishing returns as regards theatrical quality. Christie's estate have become sensitive to this in recent years and have done their best to reverse the trend, with a licensing policy that prioritises quality rather than quantity.

The story of Christie's contribution to theatre is very definitely a drama of two acts; that which predates her alliance with producer Peter Saunders in 1950 and that which follows it. Up to that date her own stage work and that of her adaptors was produced for the most part by Alec Rea and Bertie Meyer who, although great men of the theatre, failed to leave us either autobiographies or any substantial accessible business records. Until now, the Saunders archives have also been unavailable, but I am privileged to have been granted unique access to them for the purpose of researching this book. Sir Stephen Waley-Cohen, who bought Sir Peter Saunders' business, including *The Mousetrap*, when Saunders retired in 1994, thereby took ownership of two metal filing cabinets in the bottom drawer of each of which are files relating to Saunders' wide-ranging portfolio of productions and theatrical investments, including a meticulously ordered file relating to each of the nine Christie-authored plays that he produced in the West End. Here, for the first time, we see the story as it unfolded from the point of view of those responsible for the staging of Christie's work: literary licences, theatre and artiste contracts, publicity material, budgets, accounts, and lively correspondence with directors, designers and Christie herself, including handwritten missives from her about script changes and casting, often sent from archaeological digs in the Middle East. Here we also see further confirmation of Christie's box office success in the 1950s, in the form of statements to investors detailing the considerable profits that were being made from her work.

There can be no doubt that Saunders' meticulous attention to detail, exemplary financial housekeeping and understanding of publicity in all its forms was instrumental in establishing Christie's unassailable position as Queen of the West End in the 1950s. Without Saunders at the helm *The Mousetrap* may well not have run, and Christie would certainly never have penned her dramatic masterpiece *Witness for the Prosecution.* The former journalist, who was a relative newcomer to theatre when she first entrusted him with her work, became a lifelong friend and a frequent visitor to Greenway, the family home. In any event, the triumvirate of Cork, Harold Ober and Saunders proved an unstoppable force in ensuring the business success of Christie's theatrical work. But Saunders, for all his achievements, carved his own niche in theatreland based largely on a profitable, populist repertoire rather than allying himself with the theatrical oligarchy of the day and their aspirations to educate audiences as well as to entertain.

The irony is that Christie herself didn't need the money – her 'day job' took care of that – and it would have been interesting to see what history would have made of her as a playwright if she had persevered with some of her interesting early theatrical associations. The first Christie play to be produced was directed by a leading light of the Workers' Theatre Movement, and her first West End hit was directed by the first woman to direct Shakespeare at Stratford and co-produced by a female producer and a co-operative founded by a leading Labour politician. The first 'director' Saunders introduced Christie to was Hubert Gregg, a comedy actor even less experienced in the role of director than Saunders himself was at the time in that of producer. The taxman might have been less happy if Christie had never met Saunders, but the chances are that theatre historians might have taken her work more seriously. And to me that is a poor reflection on theatre historians rather than on the resourceful, diligent and hard-working Saunders.

The combination of the Cork and Saunders archives furnishes a comprehensive backstage picture of the 'Saunders years', but although the British side of the operation prior to that is sparsely documented, the American side is not. Christie's first Broadway venture as a playwright (a couple of third-party adaptations from her novels had preceded it) was an even bigger hit than it had been in London. The retitled *Ten Little Indians* was produced by the Shuberts, America's leading theatrical producers of the day, in 1944. The company, set up by three brothers from Syracuse at the end of the nineteenth century, still flourishes; and their archive, located at the Lyceum Theatre on New York's West 45th Street, in a splendid office complete with the brothers' original furnishings and photographs, provides an unparalleled insight into American theatre history. As with Saunders' archive, a wealth of original documentation has been retained, along with a well-resourced script library. It was the latter that took me to New York, on the trail of the only copies of a completely overlooked Christie script, which turned out to have been the only play of hers to receive its world premiere in America in her lifetime. Not only did I find exactly what I was looking for, but also a whole lot more . . .

The only other play of Christie's to transfer to Broadway was an even bigger hit there: *Witness for the Prosecution* in 1954. By this time Saunders was at the helm in the UK, and he was not alone in finding the Shuberts frustrating to deal with. The more affable Gilbert Miller was therefore offered the licence to co-produce on Broadway, and while I was in New York unearthing the Christie treasures in the Shubert archive I also tracked down some of Miller's papers, which resulted in a visit to the Library of Congress in Washington DC. Several other important theatrical archives in both the UK and the USA have assisted hugely in completing the picture of Agatha Christie, playwright from the 'backstage' perspective.

So, what is this book exactly? It is not a biography – if you want the story of Agatha's childhood or her two marriages, or an analysis of how her life is reflected in some of her lesser-known works, then please look elsewhere. It is not about the 'eleven missing days', or 'one missing night', as I prefer to call it, since we know exactly where she was for the rest of the time. One of the 'missing' plays, I believe, may have some bearing on this over-reported episode; but you must draw your own conclusions, and my book will no doubt avoid the best-seller list by failing to come up with yet another 'definitive' new theory on the subject. It is not a literary analysis; there is no point at all in engaging in the long-running debate between the 'highbrow' and the 'middlebrow' when it comes to popular culture. I have neither the vocabulary nor the patience for it. Neither is it a 'reader's companion'. If you want to find out about the plots and the characters then I suggest you read the plays themselves or, better still, go and watch a production of them; and if you want to play 'spot the difference' between the novels and short stories and their adaptations then read the originals as well. This is not a book about Christie's imaginary world, it is about the very real world of a playwright struggling to get her work produced, enduring huge disappointment and finally enjoying success on a scale that she could only have dreamt of. Because the playwright concerned happens to be female, it is unusual in not having been written by a feminist academic; as a theatre producer I have no agenda other than to set the record straight about Christie's contribution to theatre on a number of levels. I am hoping that by offering more detail about what she achieved, particularly as an older woman in a male-dominated industry, working at a time of enormous social, political and cultural change, the value of her work for the theatre, over and above its purely monetary one, may come to be more widely acknowledged than it currently is.

To understand the unique trajectory of Christie's playwriting career, it needs to be set within the theatrical history of the time. In Christie's case this means charting a timeline from around 1908, when she made her first attempts at writing scripts, through to the last premiere of her work in 1972. In so doing, I will introduce a whole new cast of characters to the oft-told story of this extraordinary lady; the colourful and eccentric cast that populated Agatha Christie's much-cherished world of theatre.

One thing that this book is definitely not about is detectives, and I am sorry if that disappoints some readers. But I have often felt like a detective myself as I have hunted down, assembled and analysed the evidence from a variety of different sources, and from often conflicting accounts of the same events. I hope that Hercule Poirot would have approved of my efforts and that what emerges is something approaching the truth behind the remarkable and previously untold story of Agatha Christie, playwright.

Act One

The People's Playwright

SCENE ONE

The Early Plays

Agatha Mary Clarissa Miller was fascinated by theatre from an early age. In sleepy, Victorian middle-class Torquay, 'one of the great joys in life was the local theatre. We were all lovers of the theatre in my family,' she writes in her autobiography. Older siblings Madge and Monty visited the Theatre Royal and Opera House in Abbey Road practically every week, and the young Agatha was usually allowed to accompany them. 'As I grew older it became more and more frequent. We went to the pit stalls always – the pit itself was supposed to be "rough". The pit cost a shilling and the pit stalls, which were two rows of seats in front, behind about ten rows of stalls, were where the Miller family sat, enjoying every kind of theatrical entertainment.'[1] Clara and Frederick Miller clearly did everything they could to encourage this interest in their children, and Agatha was always captivated by the colourful dramas unfolding in front of her:

> I don't know whether it was the first play I saw, but certainly among the first was *Hearts and Trumps*, a roaring melodrama of the worst type. There was a villain in it, the wicked woman called Lady Winifred, and there was a beautiful girl who had been done out of a fortune. Revolvers were fired, and I clearly remember the last scene, when a young man hanging from a rope from the Alps cut the rope

and died heroically to save either the girl he loved or the man whom the girl loved.

I remember going through this story point by point. 'I suppose,' I said, 'that the really bad ones were Spades' – father being a great whist player, I was always hearing talk of cards – 'and the ones who weren't quite so bad were Clubs. I think perhaps Lady Winifred was a Club – because she repented – and so did the man who cut the rope on the mountain. And the Diamonds' – I reflected. 'Just worldly,' I said, in my Victorian tone of disapproval.[2]

The first story Agatha ever wrote took the form of a play, a melodrama concerning 'the bloody Lady Agatha (bad) and the noble Lady Madge (good) and a plot that involved the inheritance of a castle'. Madge only agreed to take part in the production on condition the epithets were switched round. It was very short, 'since both writing and spelling were a pain to me', and amused her father greatly.[3] Agatha's parents often travelled, and when they did so she would stay in Ealing with great-aunt Margaret, who had been responsible for the upbringing of Agatha's mother and was thus referred to by her as 'Auntie-Grannie'. Even when Agatha was away from home, theatre 'never stopped being a regular part of my life', she recalls. 'When staying at Ealing, Grannie used to take me to the theatre at least once a week, sometimes twice. We went to all the musical comedies, and she used to buy me the score afterwards. Those scores – how I enjoyed playing them!'[4]

The family spent some time in France during her childhood, and seven-year-old Agatha, inspired by the local pantomime in Torquay, began staging her own work for the enjoyment of her parents, using the window alcove in their bedroom as a stage, and assisted by her long-suffering young French chaperone, Marie. 'Looking back, I am filled with gratitude for the extraordinary kindness of my father and mother. I can imagine nothing more boring than to come up every evening after dinner and sit for half an hour laughing and applauding whilst Marie and I strutted and postured in our home-improvised costumes. We went through the Sleeping Beauty, Cinderella, Beauty and the Beast and so forth.'[5] Although young Agatha studied piano, dance and singing, and at one point had aspirations to become an opera singer, she appears to have gained the greatest fulfilment from her various youthful theatrical ventures, a natural progression from the dreamy childhood role-play games that, as a home-educated child, she created to pass the time.

The Christie archive contains a delightfully witty, meticulously handwritten twenty-six-page 'acting charade in three acts' called *Antoinette's Mistake*, with a colourful hand-drawn cover that is clearly the work of a child. The play concerns the exploits of a French maid in the house of one Miss Letitia Dangerfield and her niece Rosy, and features characters called Colonel Mangoe and Major Chutnee. The closest handwriting match with that of family members is to Frederick's, and I like to think that this piece was perhaps penned by Agatha's father as a tribute to the long-suffering Marie (Antoinette?), whose performance in one of Agatha's fairy tale dramatisations 'convulsed my father with mirth'. Agatha's father was a leading light of the local amateur dramatics, and it was perhaps in recognition of the enjoyment which this brought the family that she agreed, in later life, to become president of the Sinodun Players, an amateur group based in Wallingford where she owned a house. She received numerous such requests throughout her life, but the local amateur dramatics and the Detection Club were the only societies of which she accepted the presidency.

Frederick died aged fifty-five, when Agatha was eleven and both of her siblings had already left Ashfield, the family home in Torquay; but her mother continued to nourish young Agatha's enthusiasm for theatre, whisking her off to see Irving perform in Exeter. 'He may not live much longer, and you must see him,' she insisted.[6] Agatha herself, notoriously averse to public speaking in later life, enjoyed venturing onto the stage in her youth, and an ambitious production of Gilbert and Sullivan's *The Yeomen of the Guard*, produced by a group of young friends at the Parish Rooms in Torquay, gave her the opportunity to show off her singing voice in the role of Colonel Fairfax. 'As far as I remember I felt no stage fright . . . There is no doubt that *The Yeomen of the Guard* was one of the highlights of my existence.'[7]

Finishing school in Paris at the age of sixteen was an opportunity to sample the French capital's theatrical delights. She enjoyed herself in drama class, and had a remarkable ability to appreciate a fine theatrical performance:

> We were taken to the *Comedie Francaise* and I saw the classic dramas and several modern plays as well. I saw Sarah Bernhardt in what must have been one of the last roles of her career, as the golden pheasant in Rostand's *Chantecler*. She was old, lame, feeble, and her golden voice was cracked but she was certainly a great actress – she held you with her impassioned emotion. Even more exciting than Sarah Bernhardt did I find Rejane. I saw her in a modern play, *La Course aux Flambeaux*. She had a wonderful power of making you feel, behind a hard repressed manner, the existence of a tide of feeling and emotion which she would never allow to come out in the open. I can still hear now, if I sit quiet a minute or two with my eyes closed, her voice, and see her face in the last words of the play: '*Pour sauver ma fille, j'ai tué ma mere*,' and the deep thrill this sent through one as the curtain came down.[8]

After spending a 'season' as a seventeen year old in Cairo with her mother, Agatha found herself a regular guest on the house party circuit. This served its purpose of introducing her to a number of eligible young bachelors, and she also became friends with the colourful theatrical impresario C.B. Cochran and his devoted and long-suffering wife, Evelyn. Charles Cochran was indisputably the greatest showman of his generation, in a career that included productions of Ibsen alongside the promotion of boxing, circus and rodeo as well as the management of Houdini. He was also to be instrumental in launching the career of Noël Coward. That was still ahead of him when he met the young Agatha, but for one thing he could take credit. Cochran was responsible for introducing the roller-skating craze which swept the country in the early 1900s, and a famous photograph shows Agatha and her friends enjoying some skating on Torquay's Princess Pier. The Cochrans eventually invited her to their house in London, where she was 'thrilled by hearing so much theatrical gossip'.

As a young woman, Agatha continued her own forays onto the stage. Photographs show her and her friends gloriously costumed for *The Blue Beard of Unhappiness*, which the programme (printed on blue paper of course) reveals to be 'A drama of Eastern domestic life in two acts'.[9] An open air production with a dozen in the cast, it is, we are told, set on a part of the terrace in Blue Beard's castle in 'Bagdad'. The folktale of wife-murderer Bluebeard was to provide Agatha with inspiration on more than one later occasion. In the 'Confessions Album', in which members of the Miller family regularly made light-hearted entries listing their current likes and dislikes, a 1910 entry from Agatha nominates Bluebeard as one of two characters from history whom she most dislikes.[10] The other is nineteenth-century Mormon leader Brigham Young, the founder of Salt Lake City: another extravagantly bearded polygamist, though in this case not a serial killer. 'Why did they Bag-dad?' asks *The Blue Beard of Unhappiness*'s programme, and goes on to state 'Eggs, fruit and other Missiles are to be left with the Cloak Room Attendant'. No playwright is credited and, sadly, no script survives.

Many of Agatha's earliest writings were in verse, and her first published dramatic work took this form. *A Masque from Italy*, originally written in her late teens, was later included (with the subtitle 'The Comedy of the Arts') in the 1925 self-published poetry volume *Road of Dreams*, and has thus been overlooked as a playscript. Although it is structured as a series of solo songs (which she set to music shortly before the book was published), the piece is clearly intended as a short theatrical presentation, as indicated by the word 'masque' in its title, and may have been written as a puppet show. There is a cast list, consisting of six characters from Italian *commedia dell'arte*; and a clear dramatic through-line based on the love triangle between Harlequin, Pierrot and Columbine, delivered in a prologue, seven songs and an epilogue. Punchinello serves as a master of ceremonies and is here envisaged as a marionette rather than as the 'Mr Punch' glove puppet. We know that Agatha was intrigued by a Dresden China collection of these characters owned by her family, but the piece shows a thorough understanding of their traditional dramatic functions and motivations (apart from some ambiguity over a female counterpart of Punchinello), and it is more than possible that local pantomimes were still including a traditional Harlequinade sequence featuring them when she was in the audience as a child at the turn of the century. Her lifelong interest in the Harlequin figure, later to manifest itself in the Harley Quin short stories, is here informed by his role as the dangerous and exciting stranger stealing women's hearts, which was to be a recurring theme in her early plays.

> And when the fire burns low at night, and
>   Lightning flashes high!
> Then guard your hearth, and hold your love,
>   For Harlequin goes by.[11]

The pain of lost love and the tensions between these passionate and flamboyant characters are well drawn, and with Harlequin in his 'motley array' and Punchinello inviting the audience to 'touch my hump for luck', the whole effect is deeply theatrical. Whether performed by puppets or people, it would have been fun to watch.

Encouraged by her mother, and perhaps in the hope of emulating her sister who had had some success with the publication of short stories in *Vanity Fair*, Agatha began writing stories in her late teens. 'I found myself making up stories and acting the different parts and there's nothing like boredom to make you write.'[12] Adopting the pseudonyms Mac Miller,

Nathaniel Miller and Sydney West, Agatha set about composing a number of short stories on her sister's typewriter, but they failed to impress the editors of the magazines she sent them to.

'Sydney West' had a particularly idiosyncratic style, and was responsible for a short one-act play entitled *The Conqueror* which, like the short story 'In the Market Place', also authored by West, is a parable with a mythological flavour. The Ealing address of Agatha's great-aunt is inked on the script, which does not list a dramatis personae. Subtitled 'A Fantasy', the scene is 'a great Mountain overlooking the Earth. On a throne sits a huge, grey Sphinx like figure, veiled and motionless. Around her are Messengers of Fate, and the air is full of winged Destinies who come and go ceaselessly.'[13] A blind youth ascends the mountain and exposes the Sphinx, who appears to represent Fate, as a sham. Like 'In the Market Place', the whole thing is rather baffling and appears to be some sort of morality tale. It is intriguing to imagine what future Agatha envisaged for this play, particularly given the practicalities of 'winged destinies'. Though atmospheric, and not without its interest as a stylistic experiment, it is hard to imagine that it would have proved particularly popular with the local teams responsible for putting together *Antoinette's Mistake* and *The Blue Beard of Unhappiness*. What this odd little offering does do, though, is once again confirm the broad range of Agatha's theatrical vocabulary.

When eighteen-year-old Agatha produced her first novel, *Snow Upon the Desert*, her mother suggested that she send it to local author Eden Phillpotts for his comment. Phillpotts became Agatha's valued mentor, and it was his literary agent Hughes Massie & Co. which, having rejected *Snow Upon the Desert*, would eventually take her under their wing fifteen years later, the imposing Massie himself having by then been succeeded by the more affable Edmund Cork.

A long-time neighbour of the Millers in Torquay – his daughter Adelaide attended the same ballet class as Agatha – Eden Phillpotts was forty-six when he started advising Agatha, and already a successful novelist. A sort of Thomas Hardy of Dartmoor, specialising in work written in Devon dialect and set in Devon locations, his prolific output would eventually exceed even Agatha's, and he enjoyed some success latterly with detective fiction. Well connected in literary circles – he had undertaken collaborations with Arnold Bennett and Jerome K. Jerome – Phillpotts had originally trained as an actor in London but had been forced to abandon his thespian aspirations due to a recurring illness that made him unable to control his legs. His love of the theatre never left him, though, and although he had experienced no great success as a playwright by the time he counselled Agatha, he went on to write some thirty plays, a number of which were notable and longrunning West End successes.

In 1912 Phillpotts famously refused to concede to the request of the Lord Chamberlain's office that he alter two lines in his play *The Secret Woman*, about a man who starts a relationship with his son's lover, with the result that they refused to issue it with a licence. The ensuing furore saw many of the great writers of the day sign a letter to *The Times* in his support and contribute to a fund to enable performances to take place in a 'club' theatre where a licence was not required. Amongst the signatories was Bernard Shaw, whose work 'in its massive and glittering magnificence' Phillpotts admired greatly, in particular 'the thousand challenges he offers to humanity on burning and still living questions'.[14] Phillpotts and Shaw would later meet at Birmingham Repertory Theatre which, under its legendary founder Barry Jackson, regularly produced the work of both men. There can be no doubt that Phillpotts shared his enthusiasm for Shaw with the young Agatha and that this informed some of her early, unpublished playwriting ventures, which deal with such Shavian preoccupations as variations on the marriage contract, grounds for divorce and eugenics. The lengthy and witty preface to Shaw's 1908 *Getting Married* has particular resonances in some of Christie's early work.

In any event, contact with Phillpotts would have broadened

young Agatha's mind when it came to the issue of human relations, as is evidenced by his recommended reading for her. In
a letter to her he suggests that she try 'a few of the Frenchmen',
including Flaubert's *Madame Bovary*. 'But this last is very
strong meat and perhaps you had better wait till you have
taken some lighter dose first of the more modern men. When
you come to it, remember that *Madame Bovary* is one of the
greatest works in the world.'[15] Although one may concur with
his literary appraisal, *Madame Bovary* seems a particularly
daring recommendation for an eighteen-year-old Edwardian
girl, given its subject matter and the lifestyle of its author, who
stood trial in France for obscenity in 1857 after it was published
in a magazine.

Sadly, Phillpotts' advocacy of unconventional human relations
extended beyond literature and into his family life. His daughter
Adelaide, who collaborated with him on a number of books
and plays, including the 1926 Theatre Royal Haymarket success
Yellow Sands – and whose literary career was to cross paths
with Agatha's in the future – was the long-term victim of his
incestuous attentions, as is apparent from his correspondence
with her and, indeed, her own autobiography.[16] This bizarre
obsession was confined to the one relationship, and there is
no indication of any impropriety as far as the young Agatha
was concerned. There can be no doubt that Phillpotts' advice
and input, and his role as a sounding board for her early work,
was critical to Agatha's blossoming as a writer, enabling her
to gain confidence in her writing and widen her horizons.
Indeed, her 1932 novel *Peril at End House* was dedicated to
Phillpotts 'for his friendship and the encouragement he gave
me many years ago'. He doubtless, too, encouraged her interest
in theatre, and they maintained a sporadic correspondence
until the 1950s. In 1928 Phillpotts' wife died and the following
year he married a young cousin. We will hear more of Adelaide
later.

Nobody would publish Agatha's novel *Snow Upon the Desert*,
but she carried on producing short stories and one-act plays.
Amongst these, *Teddy Bear* is an endearing and performable

comedy for two male and two female actors, written under the pseudonym of George Miller. A well-constructed but lightweight romp, it centres around young Virginia's attempts to attract the attention of Ambrose Seaton, a fellow who is involved in an impressive array of charitable ventures:

> VIRGINIA: He's so good looking and – and so splendid. Look at all his philanthropic schemes, the Dustmen's Christian Knowledge, and the Converted Convicts Club, and the Society for the Amelioration of Juvenile Criminals.[17]

Virginia eventually adopts a strategy of attracting Ambrose's attention by herself becoming a 'juvenile criminal'. Needless to say, things do not go according to plan, and after the farcical unravelling of her scheme she abandons her attempts to ensnare the virtuous but elusive (and possibly gay) Ambrose and settles instead for her long-suffering admirer, Edward:

> EDWARD: You heard me say I wasn't going to propose again?
> VIRGINIA: (smiling) Yes.
> EDWARD: (with dignity) Well, I'm not going to.
> VIRGINIA: (laughing) Don't.
> EDWARD: Not in that sense. I was going to suggest a business arrangement.
> VIRGINIA: Business?
> EDWARD: You see, you've got a lot of money, and I'm badly in need of some. The simplest way for me to get it would be to marry you. See?
> VIRGINIA: (still laughing) Quite.
> EDWARD: No sentiment about it.
> VIRGINIA: Not a scrap.
> EDWARD: Well – what do you say?
> VIRGINIA: (very softly) I say – yes.
> EDWARD: Virginia! (tries to take her in his arms)
> VIRGINIA: (springing up) Remember you're only marrying me for the money . . .

This is nicely constructed comic banter, although there is already an undercurrent of more serious debates about the nature of the marriage contract. In this case, it all ends happily, although it is clear who the dominant force in the relationship is going to be:

> VIRGINIA: (tragically) . . . a confession of weakness. I've fallen from the high pinnacle of my own self esteem. I fancied that I was strong enough to stand apart from the vulgar throng, that I was not as other women (sits upright) but I am beaten, I am but one of the crowd after all, (slowly) I have –
> EDWARD: (breathlessly) Fallen in love?
> VIRGINIA: (dramatically) No. Bought a Teddy Bear!

Eugenia and Eugenics, another of Agatha's unpublished and unperformed early one-act plays housed at the Christie Archive, is a more ambitiously constructed comedy which explores a popular theme of the day. We are told that it is set in 1914, which may be either the present or the future, given that it deals with the repercussions of a fictitious piece of legislation. In 1905 Shaw's *Man and Superman* had received its London premiere, with a plot that underlined his belief that women are the driving force in human procreation, and that the development of the species is dictated by their success in finding biologically (rather than socially or financially) suitable partners: a quest which essentially constitutes the 'Life Force'. There can be no doubt that Agatha's work was also informed by this philosophy, although by what route it reached her is unclear. 'What are men anyway?' asks Kait in the 1944 novel *Death Comes as the End*. 'They are necessary to breed children, that is all. But the strength of the race is in the women.'[18] This novel is set in ancient Egypt, but time and again we see in Christie's plays examples of the weak male either dominated or rejected by the superior female.

Shaw's take on the topic, which challenged received Darwinian theory, was just one aspect of a much wider debate about the subject of eugenics that was current at the time, leading to the first International Eugenics Conference, held in London in 1912. Although there were ethical issues from the outset with a philosophy that advocated the genetic improvement of humanity, this was well before the concept of breeding a 'master race' took on a much more sinister aspect. Whilst Christie seems at home with Shaw's approach to the matter, her comedy both makes merciless fun of the wider philosophy's advocates and touches on some other burning issues of the day. Faced with an upcoming new law that will enforce eugenic philosophy by allowing only the physically and mentally perfect to marry, Eugenia has taken herself to what she believes to be a eugenics clinic advertising perfect partners. Her maid, Stevens, accompanies her:

EUGENIA: Talking of divorce, Eugenics will revolutionise the divorce laws.
STEVENS: Indeed Ma'am. Well I've heard as in Norway and Sweden and such countries you can get rid of your 'usband as easy as asking, with no more reason than just losing your taste for him. Very unfair I calls it. All men is trying at times, but don't turn them helpless creatures adrift, call 'em your cross and put up with 'em.[19]

In the preface to his 1908 play *Getting Married*, under the heading 'What does the word marriage mean?' George Bernard Shaw had written: 'In Sweden, one of the most highly civilized countries in the world, a marriage is dissolved if both parties wish it, without any question of conduct. That is what marriage means in Sweden. In Clapham that is what they call by the senseless name of free love.'[20] The divorce laws were the subject of much debate in the early twentieth century, and it was not until 1923's Matrimonial Causes Act that women were able to file for divorce on the same basis as men. Prior to that, men had simply to prove infidelity on the part of their spouse, whilst women had to establish further exacerbating circumstances such as rape or incest.

Christie's play goes on:

EUGENIA: It's an equal law for men and for women. Men can obtain a divorce with equal ease.

STEVENS: Ah! Ma'am, but a wife's an 'abit to a man, and we all know how attached a man is to his 'abits, drinking and smoking and such like.

EUGENIA: So you class a wife with drinking and smoking, Stevens!

STEVENS: Well, Ma'am it's true she comes more expensive sometimes.

EUGENIA: Stevens, you are lamentably behind the spirit of the age . . .

STEVENS: (thoughtfully) It seems to me M'am, what with the gentlemen being as difficult and scarce to get hold of as they are, that it's a pity to ask too much of 'em . . .

EUGENIA: . . . next week, the Marriage Supervision Bill will become Law. It ensures that only the physically and mentally sound shall marry . . . I'm sure I don't know what society is coming to. A few years ago money was everything – like birth used to be, and now nothing counts but notoriety. To be anybody one must have a new religion, or a new pet. My baby kangaroo, in spite of the fuss with the police, kept me in the forefront of society last season. But this year, Hyde Park is a walking menagerie, and an elephant would hardly attract attention. Eugenics, I feel assured, will be the next society craze. Let me then, be the first to take it up . . . This advertisement caught my eye this morning (reads) 'Eugenic Institute. Men and Women of England. Protect the Race. Choose mates of physical and mental perfection. Come here and find your mate (Guaranteed with Medical Certificate). Remember the Race and Come. And here we are. What do you think of it, Stevens. Shan't I be the most talked of woman in society?

STEVENS: It's my experience, M'am, as anything that mentions racing, is shady.

Even the suffrage movement does not escape Stevens' wisdom: 'I holds as votes is very much the same as husbands, they're a lot of trouble to get, and not much use once you've got 'em.'

Women over the age of thirty were finally enfranchised in Britain in 1918, but this play's 1914 setting places it at the height of the suffrage campaign; the previous year, the Women's Social and Political Union had mobilised thousands of supporters to march through the streets of London behind the coffin of suffragette Emily Davison, who had thrown herself in front of the king's horse at Epsom. The characters in a play, of course, all speak with their own voices and without the benefit of authorial comment. Agatha's writing, as ever, is well considered and fully engaged with the issues of the day, but it is up to the audience whether they believe Stevens to be speaking from a position of ignorance or whether they think her homespun philosophy may contain some pearls of wisdom.

Meanwhile, the 'Eugenic Institute' in the play turns out not to be all that Eugenia had hoped. The farcical construction of the piece is not as well handled as the comic dialogue, but suffice to say that Eugenia's schemes to find the physically perfect partner are frustrated, and she resigns herself to marrying the devoted but self-professedly imperfect Goldberg who, from his name, we may assume to be Jewish. Agatha's play thus wittily subverts eugenic philosophy and underlines the importance of putting the heart first. They decide to tie the knot immediately, before the new 'Marriage Supervision Bill' takes effect:

> GOLDBERG: It seems to me, the only solution is for us to get married before next Wednesday.
>
> EUGENIA: (reflectively) After all, if everyone is forced into Eugenics it will be far more chic to have an uneugenic husband . . .
>
> GOLDBERG: Well, you know man hunting's quite ousting foxhunting as a sport amongst the fair sex. You can hunt a man all the year round, you see, and English women are so deuced sporting.

Agatha's own hunt for a husband, which had started in the social whirlwind of colonial Cairo and moved on to the more genteel setting of English house parties, was about to result in her marriage, at the age of twenty-five. Abandoning her fiancé, family friend Reggie Lucy, she opted instead for love from a stranger, and the promise of adventure offered by dashing young airman Archie Christie.

'Archie and I were poles apart in our reaction to things. I think that from the start that fascinated us. It is the old excitement of "the stranger".'[21] Married on Christmas Eve 1914, their early years together were disrupted by war, with Archie gaining distinction for his contribution to the ground-based operations of the Royal Flying Corps, mostly on overseas postings, while Agatha remained in Torquay as a member of the Voluntary Aid Detachment at the Red Cross hospital in Torquay, completing the examination of the Society of Apothecaries and becoming a dispenser.

At the end of the war Archie, by now a colonel, was stationed at the Air Ministry in London, and after the war ended he found himself a job in the City. The couple divided their time between a flat in St John's Wood and Ashfield, Agatha's mother's house in Torquay, where their daughter Rosalind was born on 5 August 1919.

The following year Agatha enjoyed a successful publishing debut with her novel *The Mysterious Affair at Styles*. Written on a break from her hospital work during the war, it was finally accepted for publication by Devon-born John Lane of the idiosyncratic and often controversial publishing house The Bodley Head, which specialised in books of poetry, and whose authors included Eden Phillpotts' friend Arnold Bennett. The Bodley Head had been responsible at the end of the previous century for the notoriously decadent literary quarterly *The Yellow Book*. The five-book deal she signed with the firm was to establish her profile as an author, but it was to be another ten years until a play of hers was produced.

In 1922, Archie was engaged to take part in a world tour to promote the forthcoming British Empire exhibition, and Agatha took the opportunity to join her husband on this eye-opening voyage, which took in South Africa, Australia, New Zealand, Hawaii and Canada, with a stop for Agatha in New York in November on the way back, while Archie continued his work in Canada. In New York, Agatha stayed with her elderly American godmother Cassie Sullivan, and it is her name and address, along with the date 9 November 1922, that tantalisingly appears in handwriting on the front of the typed one-act playscript *The Last Séance*. In her autobiography, Agatha remembers this as one of her very first short stories, later rewritten for publication (which occurred in the American magazine *Ghost Stories* in 1926). The scenario works much better as a short play, however, and I believe that it was in this format that she first envisaged and wrote it, as an exercise in the then popular theatrical genre of Grand Guignol. In a letter to her mother from Melbourne in May 1922, Agatha writes, 'I've been rather idle – but have written a Grand Guignol sketch and a short story.'[22] Notes for *The Last Séance* (titled 'The Mother') appear in Notebook 34, along with those for the novel *The Man in the Brown Suit* (1924). 'Passed Tenerife last night' she observes at one point.[23]

At the time of Agatha's stay in Paris as a teenager, the original Parisian Théâtre du Grand-Guignol was under the direction of Max Maurey, and at its height as a 'horror theatre' venue, with André de Lorde its celebrated and prolific principal writer. An ever-changing programme of evening entertainments consisting of a collection of graphically bloodthirsty and macabre one-act plays, occasionally interspersed with comedies by way of light relief, were the talk of the town. It was widely advertised that audience members frequently passed out from fear, but the public proved themselves more than happy to rise to the challenge, and flocked to the small theatre in the Quartier Pigalle. It seems unlikely that those responsible for the education of a group of teenage girls would have allowed their charges to sample the delights of the Grand Guignol, but in 1908 the French company made headlines when it toured to London, including in its repertoire a play called *L'Angoisse* (*The Medium*).

In the early 1920s the Little Theatre on the Strand hosted London's own Grand Guignol season, with a poster so horrifying that it was banned from the London Underground. A total of forty-three plays were produced in its rolling repertoire and the Lord Chamberlain's office added to the publicity by refusing a licence to several more. Rarely out of the newspapers, the regular casts included such stalwarts of the English stage as Sybil Thorndike and her husband Lewis Casson, and a repertoire of work that included translations of some of the original French pieces (including *The Medium*) along with pieces by several English writers of the day. Noël Coward even contributed a short play, although he opted for a comic interlude rather than a horror piece. *The Better Half*, which was another play highlighting the inadequacies of the divorce laws, culminates in this heartfelt plea from its heroine:

> ALICE: I tried to make him strike me, so that I could divorce him for cruelty – but No. He wouldn't! He did just twist my arm a teeny bit but not enough even to bruise it . . . As somebody so very truly remarked the other day, the existing Divorce laws put a premium on perjury and adultery! Therefore I am going to find a lover and live in flaming sin – possibly at Claridges.[24]

As regards the horror element of the programme, the following review from *The Times* sums up the sort of evening that audiences could enjoy:

> The other new feature of the evening is probably familiar to most visitors to the Paris Grand Guignol, and it has already been seen in both French and English in this country. It is *The Medium*, the gruesome little play about a sculptor who is filled with strange imaginings on moving into a new studio. His model is a medium and goes off into a trance . . . during which she reveals the grizzly secrets which the studio holds . . . Those who like two series of shudder in one evening

will probably appreciate *The Medium*, particularly as it gives
Miss Sybil Thorndike another opportunity for a hair-raising
performance . . . but we confess that for us *The Hand Of
Death* is quite enough for one evening.[25]

There is no record of Agatha having attended a Grand Guignol
performance at the Little Theatre, but she was living in London
at the time and would have read the numerous press articles
and reviews that the season generated. The genre's preoccupations would certainly have resonated with her interest in the
occult and with some of her own literary experimentations,
including a few published stories and a number of unpublished
ones such as 'The Green Gate', 'The Woman and the Kenite',
'Stronger than Death', 'Witch Hazel' and 'The War Bride'.[26]

The Last Séance itself is a short, atmospheric and effective
shocker in the true Grand Guignol tradition. Written for two
male and two female actors, and set of course in Paris, it
concerns a medium, Simone Letellier, who is persuaded to
communicate with the spirit of a dead child. The outcome is
marvellously gory, as a curtain is pulled back to reveal that
'Simone is lying on the marble floor in a pool of blood which
is dripping down the steps.'[27] This would be a gripping *coup
de théâtre*, but it does not make for a satisfactory short story.
The dialogue, which in the story simply appears to have had
speech marks put around it, works well when spoken but not
when read, and the highly theatrical denouement, when briefly
described on the page, goes for nothing. We don't know whether
the play was submitted for performance, but in these early
days Agatha found it a lot easier to get her work published
than produced, so this is likely to have accounted for the change
of format.[28]

Agatha also continued to write one-act plays on themes that
seem likely to have been suggested by the writings of George
Bernard Shaw, but which latterly sound as if they may also
have been informed by her own experiences as a wife and
mother. *Ten Years* concerns a couple who have lived together
as man and wife on the basis that they will review their

relationship after a ten-year trial period. Elliot, the husband, is an author who has begun to enjoy some success, here talking to his lawyer, Rogers:

ROGERS: I fancy your – early views – were rather unpopular.
ELLIOT: Oh! They gained me a sort of notoriety. But unorthodoxy is for the young, Rogers – the young who imagine they're going to remake the world on their own improved pattern. As we go on in life we find that the old pattern is not so bad after all! . . .

. . . I admit that my one aim then was to free the world from many of its existing conventions which I considered hampering and degrading. You may have heard that I met my – that I met Desiree when she was studying art in Paris. She too held unorthodox views. We both agreed in condemning the convention of marriage, which seemed to us then an ignoble bondage. Instead we favoured what is known as the ten years marriage system.[29]

When the time comes, however, Desiree decides that, despite having been entirely faithful for ten years, she wants to leave Elliot and set up home with another male friend.

DESIREE: I've been a good wife and mother – but – I'm still young. Young enough to feel the divine fire, and long for it. I'm only thirty-three, remember. And something cries out in me – for more life! I want romance – passion – fire – the things we had once and can never have again. I want to feel the first exquisite thrill of mingled fear and joy. I want the beginning of love – not its end. I don't want peace and security, and calm affection. I want to *live* – to live *my* life – not yours.

This comes as a shock to Elliot, who believes that the ten-year experiment has been a success. He and Desiree argue over custody of their child and, in a sentimental ending, resolve to stay together for the child's sake.

Marmalade Moon is another four-hander one-act play, this time a comedy reminiscent of Noël Coward. As usual with most of these early, unpublished works, the typescript is undated, the author's name is not given, and the researcher has to turn detective, scouring the script for contemporary references, or comparing stylistic traits or even paper quality, typefaces and layouts with other works the dates of which are known. In this case, it seems likely that the play predates Coward's *Private Lives* by several years, although the scenario is not dissimilar to his 1930 comedy about a divorced couple reuniting during their honeymoons with their new spouses.

There are two versions of the script in the Christie archive, *Marmalade Moon* being a slightly amended version of the earlier *New Moon*. The location is a continental hotel, the second draft rationalising the first's two settings into a more user-friendly single one. Here we meet two couples, one celebrating their honeymoon and the other the first anniversary of their divorce. In this extract, the divorced man offers some words of wisdom to the female honeymooner:

BRANDON: As a matter of fact, I'm here to commemorate my wife's divorce.

SYLVIA: Who from?

BRANDON: Regrettably, but inevitably, myself. She didn't start threatening soon enough. She just went (flicking his fingers) – like that. That's why I advised you to start threatening now. Then you may not have to leave later.

SYLVIA: Since you seem so frank about it, perhaps you wouldn't mind telling me why your wife left you?

BRANDON: (lightly) – You mean why I left my wife. Certainly. We couldn't agree on how to pronounce 'Wagner'. She would call him 'Oo-agner'. She was an American. They said it was incompatibility of temperament. Anyway, I never loved her.

SYLVIA: Oh dear!

BRANDON: Yes, it distressed me greatly, in fact, almost as much as her quite indecent mispronunciation of Wagner!

(slight pause, then seriously) But perhaps the real trouble
was that neither of us would give in to the other. In married
life you have to have a master – or a mistress.[30]

Again, there are echoes of Shaw's preface to *Getting Married*,
in which he asserts, 'the sole and sufficient reason why people
should be granted a divorce is that they want one', and indeed
to the play *Getting Married* itself, which involves a couple who
are hesitant to marry and another who are divorced. In Agatha's
play, as in Shaw's, the happy outcome follows a traditional
dramatic convention. The newlyweds split up and then reunite,
and the divorced couple are eventually reconciled. In the first
version, *New Moon*, Brandon concludes, 'This is just the beginning of a new era of our married life – a new moon.' In the
wittily retitled *Marmalade Moon* he states, 'This is just the beginning of a new era of our married life – our second honeymoon!
Our Marmalade Moon. That's it – a little less sweet, perhaps, but
a lot less sticky, and a thousand times more satisfying!'

It is not clear for what purpose the four playlets *Teddy Bear*,
Marmalade Moon, *Eugenia and Eugenics* and *Ten Years* were
intended; it may be that they were designed to be Guignol
comic interludes. They appear to have been written over a
number of years, but in terms of their subject matter they
share a frame of reference informed by Shavian explorations
of the theme of marriage. If performed together the effect would
not have been dissimilar to Noël Coward's popular 1936 short
play compilations *Tonight at 8.30*.

Agatha's early playwriting experiments demonstrate a natural
aptitude in a variety of styles, but she had yet to see any of
her work reach the stage. Then, in 1924, her sister Madge (or,
perhaps, a clever agent working on her behalf) suddenly raised
the stakes by somehow persuading impresario Basil Dean to
produce her own full-length play, *The Claimant*, in the West
End. Madge's penning of short stories for magazines had ceased
when she married the wealthy and quietly charming businessman James Watts and moved into his impressive Victorian

mansion Abney Hall, near Manchester. Meanwhile, Agatha's career as a writer had been successfully launched with three novels in three years for The Bodley Head. But now, suddenly, it was Madge's name that was in lights, albeit the non-gender specific name 'M.F. Watts' under which she now wrote. 'Awfully exciting about her play!' Agatha wrote to her mother from the Grand Tour in May 1922. 'And I shall be furious if she arrives "on film" before I do! It seems as though there was such a thing as an agent who is some good.'[31]

Basil Dean, who at this time was in his mid-thirties, had abandoned a career on the Stock Exchange in favour of training as an actor in repertory at Manchester, before becoming the first director of the Liverpool Repertory Theatre (later Liverpool Playhouse). During the First World War, in which he became a captain in the Cheshire Regiment, he had been director of the Entertainment Branch of the Navy and Army Canteen Board, supervising fifteen theatres and ten touring companies. Such experience served him well when he set up a theatrical production company in partnership with businessman Alec Rea, one of the principal sponsors of the Liverpool Rep project. As the Theatre Royal Windsor's *Curtain Up* magazine commented: 'One of the great men of the theatre of our time, Basil Dean began his remarkable career as a West End producer and manager in 1919 in partnership with Alec Rea. For the twenty years between 1919 and 1939, which at the beginning saw Galsworthy at his height and later Priestley at his prime, Basil Dean held a position in the West End theatre quite as powerful and influential as any of the big London managements of our post-war days. Under his sure guidance, plays by nearly all the leading dramatists of that period saw the light of day.'[32]

A passionate commentator on theatre, and an early advocate of a National Theatre, Dean wrote a highly readable two-part autobiography, in which he remembers Alec Rea's offer to him to go into business:

> had I dreamed for a hundred years I could not have imagined
> an opportunity more suited to my circumstances . . . I needed

a business manager whom I could trust. My choice fell on E.P. Clift, who was doing an excellent job as manager of the latest garrison theatre at Catterick Camp. He jumped at the chance, and thereafter wove himself in and out of my story with persistent self-interest . . . Meanwhile Alec [Rea] busied himself with the legal formalities of registering our company, to which he gave the name ReandeaN, always printed with capital letters at either end. People scoffed to see this name at the head of our playbills . . . Eventually the public came to accept it as the hallmark of an efficient presentation . . . I felt an urge to replace the ramshackle productions of the wartime theatre by the standards of acting and homogeneity of production in which I had been trained . . . Inspiring the new company with these ideals would not be easy. Actors trooping back from the battlefields and munitions factories were discomfited, more anxious about future employment than present perfection.[33]

Rea paid Dean a salary of £20 per week, and set about looking for a theatre to use as a base for their operations. He settled on the St Martin's, a small and elegant playhouse and London's newest theatre, built by theatrical manager Bertie Meyer for Lord Willoughby de Broke and opened in 1916. C.B. Cochran had taken a lease on the building but failed to make a success of it and was keen to dispose of it. Rea eventually paid £20,000 for the remaining nineteen and a half years of the lease – as Dean put it, his 'enthusiasm overcame his business caution' – and ReandeaN took over the theatre on 11 February 1920.

The new company's first major success was to be a play by a new female playwright. 'Still walking the tight-rope between success and failure,' writes Dean, 'I decided that my only course was to go forward boldly . . . so I chose *A Bill of Divorcement*, a first play by Clemence Dane, a young writer who had already attracted the attention of the literary critics with two early novels. This moving play would have stood no chance of acceptance by a commercial management because the subject of

madness was taboo on the London stage.'[34] Clemence Dane
was the pen name of Winifred Ashton, whose work merits
many a chapter in the established histories of female playwriting. The production, directed by Dean himself, was by all
accounts an extraordinary one, not least due to the performance
of ReandeaN's ill-fated young starlet Meggie Albanesi, and it
ran at the St Martin's for over four hundred performances. It
was also to launch Dane's career as one of the best known
and most prolific women dramatists of the inter-war years. A
friend of Noël Coward, who based *Blithe Spirit*'s Madame Arcati
on her, she continued writing plays until her death in 1965.

As with Agatha's early plays, the issues of the divorce laws
and eugenics were primary themes of Dane's West End debut.
Following the First World War the divorce rate in England
had quadrupled, fuelled by hurried courtships, enforced separ-
ations, wartime adultery (both at home and abroad) and a
new-found independence enjoyed by women, not least in the
realm of employment. The resulting public and political
debate lent renewed urgency to the recommendations of a
1912 Royal Commission, which had suggested a liberalisation
of the divorce laws, and Clemence Dane's 1921 play, set in
1933, controversially considered a future in which some of
the proposed reforms had been introduced. As a dramatic
exercise, this was not dissimilar to Agatha's examination of
the potential consequences of the fictional 'Marriage
Supervision Bill' in *Eugenia and Eugenics*. When, in 1923,
the Matrimonial Causes Act removed the additional exacerbating circumstances that women needed to prove in order
to obtain a divorce, the immediate result was that the number
of cases brought by women rose from 41 per cent to 62 per
cent of the total. However, the only grounds for divorce on
either side remained proven adultery until the 1937
Matrimonial Causes Act, which additionally allowed for
cruelty, desertion or incurable insanity to be cited as reasons.
The latter reason, of course, was kept firmly on the agenda
by the eugenics movement.[35]

Dane's play concerns war veteran Hilary Fairfield, who

suddenly returns to his wife and daughter one Christmas Day, having been hospitalised for over seventeen years with mental problems, thought to be shellshock. Citing the 'incurable insanity' clause in the fictional new divorce law, his wife Margaret has divorced him and is on the verge of remarriage. His daughter Sydney, meanwhile, is about to marry the son of the local rector. Although he claims to be cured, it comes to light that the mental illness from which Fairfield is suffering is in fact hereditary, and the play's debate, whilst sympathetic to his predicament, involves a wide-ranging consideration of the issues of women's rights in the matter of divorce and the ethical implications of knowingly passing on hereditary illness to the next generation. Eventually Sydney, fearful of passing on the illness to her own children, gives up her own aspirations of marriage in order to care for her father, thus liberating her mother to find happiness with a new husband.

Critics and audiences welcomed the play's bravery and, as Dean's obituary in *The Times* summed it up, 'Basil Dean excelled himself as a director, and his young contract players, Meggie Albanesi and Malcolm Keen, excelled themselves in the roles of the daughter and the father.'[36] In Dean's words, the response to Albanesi's sensational performance as Sydney was 'The only instance within my memory of a young actress achieving an international reputation by virtue of her performance in a single play.'[37] Three years later the object of Dean's heartfelt admiration was dead, at the age of twenty-four, most probably as the result of a botched abortion.

Quite what attracted Basil Dean to produce and direct Madge Watts' *The Claimant* is unclear. He perhaps hoped to repeat his success promoting the work of a female writer and *The Claimant*, like *A Bill of Divorcement*, concerns a man re-entering the family circle after a long absence. But there the similarities end. The play was cleared by the censor on 9 August 1924 for 'performance at St Martin's in a few weeks',[38] but actually opened on 9 September at the Queen's Theatre. It ran for forty-four performances and was not a success, although Madge's letters from rehearsals to her husband and son are full of theatrical gossip and details of her involvement – clearly encouraged by Dean – in the process of creating the production.[39] She stayed in London during rehearsals and frequently visited Agatha and Archie, entertaining them with news of the latest dramas from the rehearsal rooms. Agatha herself attended rehearsals on at least one occasion, and doubtless enjoyed her first experience of the making of professional theatre. She also may well have noted the immaculate work of Marshall's typing agency in the preparation of her sister's playscript, and certainly entrusted them with much of her work thereafter.

As for the play itself, it has been said that it is inspired by the notorious case of the 'Tichborne Claimant', Roger Tichborne, who having been assumed dead in an 1854 shipwreck, turned up almost twenty years later to claim his inheritance. This resulted in a celebrated 1874 court case, following which the claim was rejected and the 'claimant' subsequently imprisoned for perjury. Madge's play is a relatively light-hearted domestic drama, in which the protagonist abandons his claim and admits his true identity when it is discovered that the man he is impersonating was married, and that if he keeps up the pretence he will thus be unable to marry the young lady with whom he has fallen in love. There is an almost incomprehensible back-story and the central family's relationships are so labyrinthine that a family tree is included in the script by way of explanation. This relatively trivial affair is a long way from the courtroom drama that gripped the nation in the 1870s. As G.S. Street at the Lord Chamberlain's office put it, 'I see no harm in the play. The Tichborne case has inspired many stories; in this case (except for calling the hero Roger) the resemblance is quite remote.'[40]

The Times, which the week before opening had announced a new play by 'Mr M.F. Watts',[41] corrected itself with its review headline 'Woman Dramatist's new play' and went on to say

The history of the Tunstall family is a little complicated, even with the aid of a genealogical table kindly issued by the management with the programme . . . The author, Mrs M.F.

Watts is, we take it, new to the stage, and inexperienced dramatists are apt to be over-lavish with their plots. There was, for instance, a first act exhibiting various members of the Tunstall family who were never seen again. You identified them carefully by the aid of the genealogical table, but it was labour wasted; the play got on very well without them . . . But there is plenty of competent acting from an exceptionally choice cast . . . And, for an 'extra', there was Mrs Lottie Venne, in a yeomanry helmet and Union Jack as Britannia ruling the waves and evidently wondering, as well she might wonder, why she was there.[42]

The latter is a reference to a fancy dress party scene, which may have inspired a scene in Agatha's 1930 short story, 'The Dead Harlequin', later adapted by her for the stage as *Someone at the Window*. In *The Claimant*, a footman comments on seeing the cream of society in fancy dress: 'To see all these 'Arliquings and Pantomimes and Columbias, and then to think 'oo they are . . . well, reelly!'

The Claimant, which appears to have been the only play by Madge to reach the stage, sank without trace and has never been revived, although forty-five years later the seventy-nine-year-old Agatha would request a copy of it from the Lord Chamberlain's office; to what purpose we will probably never know.[43] The irrepressible Madge, undaunted by the reception of her play, expressed her intentions to write a piece about Warren Hastings, but the only other script of hers that remains is another three-act drama, *Oranges and Lemons*, in which the widow Octavia has to choose between Junius, the young radical MP, and Rockhaven, the Conservative Prime Minister, both of whom are up against the machinations of a Labour leader of the opposition. The saying 'Life's a comedy to those who think, a tragedy to those who feel', usually attributed to seventeenth-century French playwright Jean Racine, appears on the title page. Yet again, there are shades of eugenics in the play's debates, as in this conversation between young Junius and the older Octavia:

JUNIUS: We're not intended to be saints. We've got *bodies*.
We're born into a cruel animal world whose only design
is – creation . . .
   . . . if you deny . . . frustrate my love, I've nothing. *Nothing*
left. It's all of me.
OCTAVIA: It isn't natural. You must turn to Spring, not autumn.
JUNIUS: I want no April to freeze me. I want the gold of
October. Can't you see, can't you understand?[44]

The central political argument, however, is a debate about land
value tax, a policy advocated by the American political econo-
mist Henry George in the late nineteenth century which found
favour with Asquith and Lloyd George, and subsequently the
Labour Party, in the early twentieth:

JUNIUS: All that results from unimproved land should be sacred.
ROCKHAVEN: Humph! You differ from the socialists there.
JUNIUS: Land is different from everything else. It's not for
some men, or a few men, but for all men. Man *must* pay
that one tax to mankind, then, for God's sake leave him
alone to work or starve! He's had his opportunity.
ROCKHAVEN: How are you going to value your land?
JUNIUS: The value of land alters from day to day. But there's
already a rent paid for every plot and field in England.
Deduct the value of buildings and improvements and
there's your ground rent.
ROCKHAVEN: You wouldn't collect enough from this one
source to run the country.
JUNIUS: The rent roll of England is roughly four millions. It
ought to be enough if the government only stuck to essen-
tials.
ROCKHAVEN: Essentials?
JUNIUS: The Army, the Navy and the Administration of
Justice. Now we pay for a grandmother not a government!
ROCKHAVEN: The incapables would loathe to lose their
grandmother.

. . .

ROCKHAVEN: I suppose you believe that all men are born
   equal?

JUNIUS: No. But there is a chance they might be bred equal
   if they had an equal chance.

ROCKHAVEN: You'll never eliminate human nature.

JUNIUS: I want to eliminate poverty. Now we're taxing wealth.
   What harm does wealth do a country? If there *is* a man
   capable of making money, for Heaven's sake encourage
   him to make more!

This is hardly the stuff of gripping drama, but neither is it
what immediately springs to mind as the likely subject of
breakfast conversation in the Miller/Watts/Christie house-
holds. *Oranges and Lemons* does not appear to have been
performed. Agatha says in her autobiography that after *The
Claimant* Madge 'wrote one or two other plays, but they did
not receive London productions',[45] which does not rule out
the possibility that they were performed at regional repertory theatres in productions listed in the Lord Chamberlain's
plays card index (which *Oranges and Lemons* isn't), or indeed
by amateurs. We are told by Agatha that Madge was 'quite
a good amateur actress herself, and acted with the Manchester
Amateur Dramatic' so, after her brief spell as a West End
playwright, we must assume that this is where she focused
her theatrical energies.

Amongst Agatha's own unpublished and unperformed early
works are two very different full-length plays, *The Clutching
Hand* and *The Lie*. The first of these, 'A Play in Four Acts by
A. Christie', states on the title page that it is 'Adapted from
the novel *The Exploits of Elaine* by Arthur B. Reeve'.
Significantly, this is undoubtedly her first dramatic adaptation
of a novel, albeit not one of her own.[46]

Arthur B. Reeve was a journalist who became America's
most popular writer of detective fiction in the second decade
of the twentieth century. His recurring character, 'scientific
detective' Craig Kennedy, was billed as 'The American Sherlock

Holmes', and Kennedy's investigations are characterised by the use of pioneering forensic techniques and bizarre gadgets created by him in his lab. In fact he would probably have had more success than me in dating some of Agatha's manuscripts and correspondence. Of course this particular detective's investigative techniques may well have appealed to Agatha the chemist, although it is notable that her own sleuths tend to treat forensic evidence as secondary to an analysis of character and an understanding of motive.

The Exploits of Elaine itself is an odd hybrid. Conceived by Pathé in 1914 as a fourteen-part film serial, it was primarily a vehicle for their star Pearl White, who had been a huge success in the *Perils of Pauline* series. Arthur B. Reeve was employed to create the storyline, and included the character of Craig Kennedy. This meant that the syndicated newspaper instalments of the story, when compiled into a book the following year, effectively became both the next Craig Kennedy novel and the 'book of the film' of *The Exploits of Elaine*. It has to be said that the result is far from being a literary masterpiece; Reeve is no Raymond Chandler, and the disjointed 'novel', the chapter titles of which exactly reflect the titles of the film serial's episodes, very much betrays its origins.

Quite how this ended up on Agatha's bookshelf, and why she felt drawn to adapt it for the stage, is something of a mystery; it may have been done in response to her sister's challenge to write a piece of detective fiction, which more famously resulted in her first published novel, *The Mysterious Affair at Styles*. We know that she had read Gaston Leroux's *The Mystery of the Yellow Room*, Edgar Allan Poe's short story 'The Murders in the Rue Morgue', Maurice Leblanc's Arsène Lupin stories and, of course, Arthur Conan Doyle and Wilkie Collins; but we can now add Arthur B. Reeve's brand of pulp fiction to the august roll-call of those who inspired Agatha's early experiments in crime fiction.

The book and play concern the efforts of the plucky young Elaine Dodge to track down her father's murderer, a master criminal known as The Clutching Hand, who leaves 'a warning letter signed with a mysterious clutching fist' next to the body of each of his victims. In order to do this, she enlists the help of Craig Kennedy, scientific detective, and his 'Doctor Watson', the journalist Walter Jameson. Other characters include the lawyer Perry Bennett and three gangsters named Limpy Red, Dan the Dude and Spike. For good measure, the book also includes Chinese devil worshippers and even a medium performing a séance, none of whom, perhaps thankfully, make it into Christie's dramatisation.

Whilst the play is an interesting early exercise in the efficient adaptation of a novel for the stage, it would be fair to say that Agatha is no Damon Runyon when it comes to a grasp of New York vernacular. Her leading characters tend to speak in cut-glass English accents and her gangsters endearingly lapse into cockney while referring to 'drug stores' and 'janitors'. Agatha's father was a New Yorker, but although she was proud of her American ancestry she herself did not travel to America until she was thirty-one, and it seems either that Frederick Miller's American accent cannot have been a strong one, or that by the time Agatha wrote *The Clutching Hand* her memory of it was distant.

Although *The Clutching Hand* never made it as far as the stage, the influence of *The Exploits of Elaine* can be seen in Christie's early adventure fiction; in particuar, the pursit of an elusive master criminal was a theme that she would return to on a number of occasions. As she says in her autobiography, "Thriller plays are usually much alike in plot – all that alters is the Enemy. There is an international gang *à la* Moriarty – provided first by the Germans, the "Huns" of the first war; then the Communists who in turn were succeeded by the Fascists. We have the Russians, we have the Chinese, we go back to the international gang again and again, and the Master Criminal wanting world supremacy is always with us.'[47]

Arthur B. Reeve's adventurous young heroine undoubtedly held a particular appeal for Agatha. Tuppence Beresford (*The Secret Adversary*, 1922), Anne Beddingfeld (*The Man in the Brown Suit*, 1924) and Virginia Revel (*The Secret of Chimneys*,

1925) would all appear to owe something to Reeve's Elaine
Dodge. Here, to cherish, is his description of her: 'Elaine Dodge
was both the ingénue and the athlete – the thoroughly modern
type of girl – equally at home with tennis and tango, table talk
and tea. Vivacious eyes that hinted at a stunning amber brown
sparkled beneath masses of the most wonderful auburn hair.
Her pearly teeth, when she smiled, were marvellous. And she
smiled often, for her life seemed to be a continuous film of
enjoyment.'[48]

When, in 1922, Christie was writing notes for *The Man in
the Brown Suit* while on the Grand Tour, they appear under
the heading 'Adventurous Anne Episode 1'.[49] Reeve's heroine
and 'episodic' format were therefore very much on her mind
– although she later claimed that 'Anne the Adventuress', the
title under which the novel was serialised in the *Evening News*
the following year, was 'as silly a title as I had ever heard'.[50]
All of this, though, seems to indicate that the script for *The
Clutching Hand* pre-dates 1922, and Agatha's own first visit to
America.

And now on to more serious matters, in the shape of an
unpublished and unperformed three-act 'domestic drama'
called simply *The Lie*. In her autobiography Agatha mysteriously states, 'I wrote a gloomy play, mainly about incest. It
was refused firmly by every manager I sent it to. "An
unpleasant subject". The curious thing is that, nowadays, it
is the kind of play which might quite likely appeal to a
manager.'[51] I believe *The Lie* to be that play and, although
the chronology in her autobiography is notoriously inaccurate,
Agatha clearly places it in the mid-1920s after her and Archie's
return from the Grand Tour. The action of the play, of which
there are two drafts, takes place in a suburban house, located
in Wimbledon (amended to Putney) in version one or
Hampstead in version two. The house belongs to John, who
is married to Nan. Nan's mother and grandmother live with
them, and her younger sister Nell, who is fighting off the
attentions of an ineffectual young suitor, shares a flat with a
female friend elsewhere.

Nan is disillusioned with the boredom of her marriage to John, whom she married when she was seventeen, and the fact that he lavishes more of his attention on her golf- and tennis-playing younger sister than on her. In an attempt to get some excitement back into her life, she spends a night with an older admirer, Sir Peter (whom we never meet), claiming that she is staying with family friends. But when she returns home the next day she discovers that a friend of John's has told him that he has seen her dining with Sir Peter, and it is not long before he establishes that she has not in fact been staying with the family friends. As Nan explains to her mother, Hannah:

I suppose he's a good husband. He's kind and polite, and feeds and clothes me well, and doesn't beat me. Oh! A model husband! But I'm outside his life – right outside it. He goes to his business in the morning, and when he comes back in the afternoon, if it's summertime, he plays golf or tennis with Nell. In the evening there's music – with Nell. He'd sooner talk to her than to me. He never cares to be with me – he never wants me – I don't interest him. Although I'm his wife I never dare laugh and joke with him as Nell does. And so it's gone on from day to day – until I felt I couldn't bear it any longer! (a pause) And then, Sir Peter came. *He* wanted to talk to me, *he* liked to be with me – I was *the* person to him! What happened? John told me to drop him! Altogether! Told me quite coldly and calmly, not because he cared – not because he was jealous – but because I was his wife, and he disliked having his property talked about![52]

As Hannah explains to her own mother, 'A love not expressed is no love at all to Nan. And a man like John, upright, honourable, and straight as a die, lacks one thing – imagination.' We are told that Hannah herself followed her dream: 'I loved him! He was fascinating. His bad qualities were all beneath the surface. I promised to marry him. My people did their best to stop it, they knew him better than I did, but I was young and headstrong, I wouldn't listen! I went my own way, and shut my eyes to the truth.' As a result of this experience, she now advises, 'Love isn't everything. Marry a man you can respect and admire. Love will come.'

In order to preserve Nan's marriage, and indeed in order to prevent three generations of her family becoming homeless, Hannah enlists the assistance of Nell, who is asked to lie for her sister and claim that Nan in fact stayed overnight with her after dining with Sir Peter. This is 'the Lie' of the title. It is believed that this plan will work, because of John's apparent affinity with Nell. Hannah persuades Nell with the forceful argument, 'I believe with all my heart and soul, that in every life there comes a moment, one supreme and all powerful moment, when we hold our fate in our hands, to decide our entire life for good or evil! Nell! Don't let this moment pass by!'

The whole drama is played out in the course of one evening – 'one never knows what a day might bring forth' is a repeated line in the play – and the tension that Agatha builds as the various revelations unfold in a suburban front room over a matter of hours is skilfully sustained. The final scene is brilliantly dramatic as, with the disgraced Nan upstairs in her room, Nell faces her brother-in-law to tell him 'the Lie'. His astonishing response, having seen through and dismissed Nell's fiction for the attempt to protect her sister that it is, is to declare his secret love for Nell – which is clearly reciprocated as they embrace and 'he kisses her long and passionately'.

Rather than John divorcing Nan for her infidelity, Nell and John vow to elope and allow Nan to divorce him, so that the shame of her own indiscretion is thereby not revealed. 'Let the disgrace be ours,' says Nell, 'We're doing a far worse thing than she has done.' At this moment Nan walks in and, oblivious to developments between her husband and her sister (of which she continues to remain blissfully ignorant), falls to her knees, confesses her infidelity and begs John to forgive her. In a final twist, Nell fights her sister's corner and begs John to return to the realities of married life rather than pursuing the fantasy of what might have been, echoing her mother's words: 'A moment comes to everyone – a moment when they hold their life in their hands . . . Sometimes – it's not only *one* life – there might be *three* – three lives and we hold them all! It's our moment!'

John is persuaded to forgive his wife and is reconciled with her, forgoing the possibility of a relationship with the younger Nell, and unwittingly echoing his mother-in-law, 'We'll both start again, Nan – together . . . Someday – who knows? – happiness may come . . .' In the final moments of the play Nell is left alone on the stage, repeating John's words:

> Someday – who knows? – happiness may come . . .
> Someday . . . (she stands over the lamp, preparing to blow
> it out. In a final tone of doubt and wonder.) Someday? (she
> blows out the lamp. The stage is in darkness. Curtain.)

This play is about many things: infidelity and divorce, sisterly and motherly love, and the familiar Christie theme of choosing between the excitement of dangerous, passionate love and the perceived tedium of steady commitment. One thing it may at first not appear to be about is incest.

However, as with all things Christie it is important to set the subject matter in context. In 1907, the Deceased Wife's Sister's Marriage Act had ended decades of controversy by allowing widowers to marry the sister of their deceased spouse. This form of marital union had been made illegal in 1835, and remained a topic of lively debate, both inside and outside Parliament, throughout the Victorian period. The controversy centred around the effects of sexual desire on the purity of the English family, not to mention the ability of government to legislate on issues of morality, control individual behaviour and regulate the family. During the second half of the nineteenth century, the relationship between sisters was used to make the domestic sphere part of the public, political world. The sisterly bond was used by politicians as the catalyst for discussions about marriage, the sanctity of family life and even threats to the authority of the Church of England. The issue even merits a mention in Gilbert and Sullivan's *Iolanthe* (1882); when Strephon is sent by the Queen of the Fairies to stir up Parliament, one of his tasks is to 'prick that annual blister, Marriage with deceased wife's sister'. In the end, the change in law was to an extent an acknowledgement of the status quo. It was common in the nineteenth century for single women to move in with a sister's family and assist with the raising of the children; and it was a small logical step, at least in nineteenth-century terms, for that role to be formalised in the event of the married sister's death.[53]

The Deceased Wife's Sister's Marriage Act, however, permitted only what was referred to in its somewhat convoluted title. It was not until the 1960 Marriage (Enabling) Act that a man could marry his former wife's sister whether that wife was 'living or not'. So, when Christie started writing her autobiography in 1950, she might well still have regarded the relationship between John and Nell as 'incestuous' (although there are wider theological issues here that we need not concern ourselves with). Readers who have been paying close attention to the intricate legislative subplot of this chapter will note that, prior to 1923, the 'incestuous' nature of John's relationship with Nell may well have assisted Nan in obtaining a divorce from him. Meanwhile, John and Nell discuss fleeing the country, perhaps not only in order to escape the scandal but possibly also so that they can marry, once his divorce comes through, without the requirement for Nan to be 'deceased'.

Christie underlines this theme in the play when John declares to Nell, 'I love you – and you love me – Oh! Why did I marry Nan? *Nan* – when you were there, growing up day by day, from childhood to womanhood . . . You! My Nell!' He goes on to refer to her as his 'little sister', asserting 'I look upon you as my sister' and 'Haven't I always been a brother to you?' Further emphasis is given to the relationship between John and his sister-in-law by a change in title in the second draft from *The Lie* to *The Sister-In-Law*.[54] I prefer the original. All of this, I am sure, was done in ignorance of the darker side of life in the Phillpotts household.

The fact that 'The scene represents a typical suburban drawing room' and not some distant, imagined country house, only serves to add to our discomfort, and gives the astonishing subject matter of this relentlessly unfolding drama even more impact. This could happen to any of us, Christie seems to be saying. John sums up the frustrations of the daily grind that have led both his wife and himself to seek illicit adventure elsewhere: 'Oh! I know! I was keen on my work – that dull, plodding work, the same day after day! It seems incredible now to think of it! I meant to wear the collar steadily year after year. I never dreamed of any other life. The 8.16 train up to town every morning, the 5.10 back, the annual holiday to the sea side – I thought all that was life! How narrow and paltry it all seems now! Why did I do it? Because everyone does. There's a reason for you!'

But, however enticing the forbidden fruit, as Nell reminds us, 'It's the dull brown earth that endures, not the gay flowers that grow there.' Feminist writers would no doubt consider the play's resolution as somehow involving 'an underlying collusion with patriarchy', but I believe there is a far more complex appraisal of human emotions going on here than there is in Clemence Dane's *A Bill of Divorcement*.

The circumstances of Christie's own 1928 divorce were, as it happens, every bit as dramatic as something on the West End stage. Following their return from the Grand Tour at the end of 1922, and reunited with Rosalind (who had been left in the care of her grandmother and aunt), Agatha and Archie settled in Sunningdale in Berkshire, eventually moving into a house they bought together, which they named Styles. Agatha bought a two-seater Morris Cowley coupé and took on a secretary, Charlotte Fisher ('Carlo'), who made a substantial contribution to her employer's wellbeing in the following years, and whose arrival, amongst other things, coincided with a vast improvement in the typing of Agatha's draft playscripts.

Agatha's six-book deal with The Bodley Head ended with *The Secret of Chimneys* in 1925, and her new agent, Edmund Cork of Hughes Massie, negotiated much-improved terms for her with her new publisher, Collins. The following year Collins published *The Murder of Roger Ackroyd*, which proved to be her biggest success to date. Archie, meanwhile, resumed work in the City. Perhaps the excitement of their round-the-world adventure underlined the relative dullness of the return to normality, or perhaps their wartime separation and lengthy travels in the company of others meant that they had never really got to know each other properly, but in any event Archie the City commuter was no longer Archie the dashing young airman and adventurer. In 1926, following the death of her beloved mother, Agatha spent time at Ashfield in Torquay, where she found the process of clearing out her mother's belongings enormously stressful. This was exacerbated when Archie arrived and announced that he was in love with Nancy Neele, a younger woman with whom she shared an interest in golf, and wanted Agatha to divorce him. Agatha's autobiography describes this distressing period of her life with moving sincerity and economy. Clearly to the frustration of many, she offers no detail at all about what happened next. I will keep it brief.

We will never know what exactly motivated Agatha's sudden decision to abandon her cherished car, take a train to Harrogate and there book into a hotel, in a name similar to that of her husband's mistress, between 4 and 14 December 1926. Whether it was the result of some sort of stress-induced anxiety attack, or the botched playing-out of a scenario intended to win back her husband, or – as seems most likely – a combination of the two, the only winners at the time were the press, who succeeded in boosting their circulations by drumming up one of the first celebrity media frenzies; an outcome which appears to have surprised and distressed the very private Agatha in equal measure. One of the many who has subsequently perpetuated this intrusive reportage by claiming to 'provide the answers to the mystery' is Jared Cade who, in his book *Agatha Christie and the Eleven Missing Days* (1998), bases his claims on information received from Judith Gardner, the daughter of Agatha's close friend Nan Kon. Cade incorrectly describes Nan as Agatha's 'sister-in-law', when she was not in fact a relation, but simply Agatha's sister's husband's sister. Cade informs us that Nan told her daughter, amongst other things, that Agatha stayed with her on 3 December, the one night on which her whereabouts is unaccounted for. Biographer Laura Thompson painstakingly employs antique train timetables to disprove this theory and goes on to berate Cade for describing scenes that 'he cannot possibly know about', having herself given a detailed and lengthy fictionalised account of events. Surely the biggest flaw in Cade's theory is that we are asked to assume that the 'sister-in-law', Nan, if she did indeed claim that Agatha stayed with her on the night in question, was actually telling the truth.

Following a recuperative sojourn in the Canary Islands with Rosalind and Carlo, Agatha attended a court hearing in April 1928, at which, in order to avoid embarrassment to Nancy Neele, falsified evidence of Archie's adultery with an unknown party was offered. Agatha was granted the divorce that Archie wanted in October of that year. Unlike in *Ten Years*, the fact that the couple had a young child proved insufficient to keep them together; Agatha was granted custody of Rosalind. And Archie was never to speak John's line from *The Lie*, 'We'll both start again – together . . . Someday – who knows? – happiness may come . . .' Archie stuck to his own script, and life on this occasion failed to imitate art.

Christie's early, unpublished playwriting, much of it very accomplished, takes an often witty and always idiosyncratic look at many of the burning social issues of the day, particularly as they affected women. As Christie herself implies, in the mid-1920s *The Lie* was undoubtedly ahead of its time, not only in terms of its themes but also of its setting and characters. If a producer had been brave enough to accept it, then the Lord Chamberlain's office may well have raised objections. The script is perhaps too short, and is by no means perfect in its construction, but with the benefit of a little dramaturgy from an experienced director it could have made for a highly impactful evening of theatre. Had it been performed when it was written, and been presented to the public as Christie's first play, then the history of Agatha Christie, playwright might have been very different.

As it turned out, though, all her early playwriting efforts were to be upstaged by a moustachioed French detective, who inevitably stole the show as soon as he set foot in front of an audience. Yes, French.

SCENE TWO

Poirot Takes the Stage

By early 1928, at the age of thirty-seven, Agatha had become a best-selling novelist, a media celebrity, a mother and a soon-to-be divorcee. As a playwright she had experimented with a wide variety of genres, including *commedia dell'arte*, Grand Guignol, American pulp fiction, comedy and passionate domestic drama. Much of her work had touched on socio-political issues such as divorce and eugenics, and some of it had embraced controversial subject matter that would have raised eyebrows in the Lord Chamberlain's office.

It must have been particularly frustrating for her, then, not only that her sister achieved her West End debut before she did, but also that the first time her own name appeared on a theatre marquee was in relation to another playwright's less than satisfactory adaptation of one of her detective novels.

In April 1927, touring actor-manager Lionel Bute paid £200 to Hughes Massie for the right to produce an adaptation of Christie's hugely popular 1926 novel *The Murder of Roger Ackroyd*.[1] The script was not yet written at this point, but the chosen adaptor was Michael Morton, a prolific playwright who between 1897 and his death in 1931 would be responsible for numerous dramas and comedies, as well as a number of successful stage thrillers including *The Yellow Passport* (1914), *In the Night Watch* (1921) and *The Guilty One* (1923). Since the archives of Hughes Massie in relation to the agency's dealings with Christie do not commence until 1940, it is difficult to establish why Morton was chosen as the adaptor, and indeed whether it was Bute or Hughes Massie who commissioned the play. Given Christie's penchant for playwriting, it seems odd that the job wasn't given to her, particularly as it is highly likely that she had herself by this time delivered an original play featuring Poirot and called *After Dinner*; although the engagement of an adaptor may well have been due to the reluctance of Hughes Massie's Edmund Cork to see his novelists spending their time writing plays. The £200 Bute paid was by way of an advance against royalties, which were to be paid at between 5 and 15 per cent on different levels of box office income. Morton was to share this royalty income 50/50 with Christie, a ratio that would become standard with respect to third-party stage adaptations of her work.

In 1921 Bute had created Lionel Bute Ltd, 'to send out on tour London successes played by first rate artists'. As an actor-manager he saw himself as having his performers' 'artistic as well as their material welfare at heart, and he would be deeply hurt if anyone regarded the firm as merely commercial'.[2] He was a popular character whose troupe affectionately adopted the motto 'Bute-iful plays Bute-ifully acted'. A sort of touring repertory company, Lionel Bute's players enjoyed great success throughout the 1920s, with up to five units on the road simultaneously.

Hughes Massie had given Bute until 1 November 1928 to produce the play or lose his £200, but for some reason in February 1928 he assigned his licence to the West End impresario Bertie Meyer. Bute presumably felt that his chances on tour would be enhanced by a West End production (the remit of his company was, after all, to tour 'London successes') but that he needed a heavyweight partner in order to achieve this. Once Morton had delivered the script, he therefore seems to have gone about finding a business partner with the resources to create a West End production, but in a deal that would still give him the ability subsequently to tour the title. There are no records of the detail of this arrangement, but the West End programme, whilst stating that it is presented by 'B.A. Meyer', notes in the small print that it is 'produced by arrangement with Lionel Bute'.[3] It also notes that the actor Norman V. Norman (playing Roger Ackroyd) appears 'by permission of Basil Dean', Dean having allowed him an early release from Margaret Kennedy's *Come With Me*.

Bertie Meyer, the man who built the St Martin's Theatre, had originally been a tea planter in Ceylon. Whilst on a visit to London in 1902, he became engaged to Dorothy Grimston, daughter of celebrated actress Mrs Kendal, and having married into a theatrical dynasty, decided to apply his business acumen to theatrical matters. As a French speaker, he was engaged in a management role by the company presenting Réjane's 1903 London season at the Garrick Theatre, where the actress who was later to so impress the young Agatha in Paris scored a great hit. Continuing with the French theme, he himself presented the legendary Coquelin in his defining role as Cyrano at the Shaftesbury Theatre in 1905. His marriage to Dorothy didn't last, but his love affair with theatre did and, following these early successes, he went on to become one of the most respected London producers and theatre managers of the day. In 1927 he enjoyed a big hit with Edgar Wallace's *The Terror* at the Lyceum Theatre, a drama which, like much of the hugely popular crime novelist's work for the stage, owed a substantial debt to Grand Guignol.

Meyer's two big coups in the production of the stage version of *The Murder of Roger Ackroyd*, which – after the issue of its licence but before the script's submission to the Lord Chamberlain's office – had been retitled *Alibi* by its adaptor, were the engagement of Gerald du Maurier to direct and Charles Laughton to play Poirot. Du Maurier, one of the most respected actors and directors of the day, was the son of the novelist George du Maurier (of *Trilby* fame) and the father of novelist Daphne du Maurier, who was herself to enjoy three West End hits as a playwright in the 1940s. Gerald du Maurier, who had been knighted in 1922, is credited with having masterminded Edgar Wallace's first big West End success, *The Ringer*, a melodramatic adaptation of his 1925 novel *The Gaunt Stranger*. Engaged as director of *The Ringer*, du Maurier was generous with his dramaturgical assistance in the preparation of the script, which generosity Wallace reciprocated by sharing his royalty income with him. Wallace even revised the original novel and reissued it as *The Ringer*, taking on board the lessons learned from du Maurier. We should note in passing that, during the play's successful 1926 run at Wyndham's Theatre, Wallace had jumped on the bandwagon of press speculation about Christie's disappearance by contributing a piece on the subject to the *Daily Mail* at the height of the furore.

With Meyer as producer and du Maurier as director, the credentials of the team responsible for the production of *Alibi* were promising. All that remained was to cast the role of Poirot, who had already appeared in four novels and a book of short stories, for what was to be the character's stage debut. In February 1928 Meyer had produced *A Man With Red Hair* at the Little Theatre; in this gruesome shocker, adapted from a Hugh Walpole novel by Benn Levy, the leading role of the grotesque sadist Crispin was played to great acclaim by a twenty-eight-year-old RADA graduate, Charles Laughton, 'a very gargoyle of obscene desires' according to the *Observer* critic.[4] The production ran for only seventy-nine performances, but served as the springboard to Laughton's distinguished acting career. Although borrowing from the Little Theatre's Grand Guignol repertoire of horrors, this play lacked the essential larkiness of the genre, and Meyer decided to replace it with a successful revival of 'London's Grand Guignol' itself, taking a large advertisement for the season in the programme for *Alibi*.

Despite his recent critical success in *A Man With Red Hair*, Laughton was by no means the obvious choice for the role of Poirot. Too young, and physically too portly, there was also the problem that he was now associated in people's minds with the unsavoury Crispin. Christie herself was more concerned with changes to the storyline and characterisation made by Michael Morton. As she states in her autobiography:

Alibi, the first play to be produced from one of my books – *the Murder Of Roger Ackroyd* – was adapted by Michael Morton. He was a practised hand at adapting plays. I much disliked his first suggestion, which was to take about twenty years off Poirot's age, call him Beau Poirot and have lots of girls in love with him . . . I strongly objected to having his personality completely changed. In the end, with Gerald Du Maurier backing me up, we settled on removing that excellent character Caroline, the doctor's sister, and replacing her with a young and attractive girl . . . I resented the removal of Caroline a good deal.[5]

In a 1961 *Sunday Times* interview Christie comments, 'I disliked Poirot being made into a young man, and having a sort of sentimental love affair. Charles Laughton played Poirot extremely well, but it was made into rather a sentimental part.'[6] And in her introduction to Peter Saunders' *The Mousetrap Man*, she remarks that Laughton was 'entirely unlike Hercule Poirot but a wonderful actor'.[7] Christie herself believed that Miss Marple, who was to make her first print appearance in 1930's *The Murder at the Vicarage*, may have been inspired by the discarded character of Caroline, 'an acidulated spinster, full of curiosity, knowing everything, hearing everything; the complete detective service in the home'.[8]

The frustrations of the rehearsal process were many for the would-be playwright: 'I had no idea when it was first suggested what terrible suffering you go through with plays, owing to the alterations made in them.'[9] In the end, 'Beau Poirot' remained in the version of the script licensed for performance by the Lord Chamberlain, but perhaps the biggest surprise is that Christie appears not to have made any objection to her famous Belgian creation being referred to as French.[10]

In the event the cast, which also included 'Lady Tree' (Helen Maud Holt – Sir Herbert Beerbohm Tree's widow) as Mrs Ackroyd, acquitted themselves well and the play, though attracting only mediocre reviews, enjoyed a successful run of 250 performances. It opened at the Prince of Wales Theatre on 15 May 1928, a few weeks after the initial court hearing relating to Agatha's divorce, and transferred to the Haymarket on 20 August, where it ran until the end of the year. On 6 August Lionel Bute opened a touring production at the Grand Theatre, Swansea, with the ensemble temporarily renamed 'Lionel Bute and B.A. Meyer's Company'.[11]

The play itself suffered from the fact that the impact of the book's denouement relies on a device that is simply not transferable from page to stage. And the script's obvious shortcomings appear only to have been emphasised by Laughton's consciously stellar performance. As playwright St. John Ervine put it, reviewing for the *Observer*:

This is an actor. Let me not be afraid to use superlatives. Mr Laughton is about to become a *great actor*. I hereby announce to the world that this young man, whose age is less than thirty, is likely to be as fine a character actor as Coquelin. He has the most malleable body and pliable face of any actor I know. He acts with his mind and with his body. He knows that he has a face and he acts with it. He acts with his hands and with his legs and feet, and I should not be at all astonished to find that if his boots were removed, each one of his toes would be acting hard. He seizes the stage and firmly controls the audience. He fills me with a sense of his power, and makes me intensely aware of him from the moment he comes on to the stage until the moment he leaves it . . . The play begins badly but steadily improves; the first two scenes, which are dull and slow, might be telescoped . . . Mr Laughton, however, added so much to the part of Poirot that the play seemed far bigger than it is. I am about to repeat myself. Mr Laughton, I say, is an actor. The whole of the cast is excellent. They must pardon me if I do no more than note their names . . . It was Mr Laughton's night. An actor, ladies and gentlemen.[12]

Laughton was the first of numerous actors to appropriate the role of Poirot as a vehicle for their own talents, and Christie herself was disconcerted by the manner in which the character pulled focus on stage. The function of a detective, after all, is to observe; and in a detective novel the reader is invited to join the detective in this process. On film, camera angles and editing can focus the audience's attention on specific characters and events. But on stage the audience is liable to be distracted from the observational process by the detective's constant presence in their line of vision. Ironically, rather than observing what the detective is observing (as in a book or a film), they end up observing the detective; especially if a particularly flamboyant actor has commandeered the role.

For all its frustrations, the process was hugely enjoyable for Agatha, as it had been for her sister. Agatha, of course, had no one at home at this time other than her nine-year-old daughter to share her excitement with, but the following interview in *The Star* gives an insight into the enjoyment she derived from her involvement in the production of *Alibi* (it is interesting to note that, even at this early stage, a play not actually written by Agatha Christie is referred to as an 'Agatha Christie play'):

'It's all great fun!' Such was the enthusiastic comment with which Agatha Christie today greeted a 'Star' woman who went along to the flower-like Kensington home of the novelist-playwright to see how she felt about last night's production of her play, 'Alibi'.

This new piece at the Prince Of Wales theatre, in which Charles Laughton has made so great a hit as the famous fictional detective Hercule Poirot, is the first Agatha Christie play to be staged. It has been dramatised by Michael Morton from the Christie novel called *The Murder Of Roger Ackroyd*. Mrs Christie confessed today that this was not her idea of a title at all, 'I wanted to call the book "The man who grew vegetable marrows" but nobody would let me!' she said sadly.[13]

Christie goes on to reiterate her own interest in playwriting. 'Certainly I hope to write more plays – now! . . . I have not actually got one begun, and I am not sure whether my next work will be a novel or a play.' Her beloved dog Peter was at rehearsals with her. 'He is such a sensible dog, and knows everybody connected with the play, and sometimes at rehearsals he has taken orders from Sir Gerald Du Maurier.'

Impressively, on 5 July 1928, less than two months after this interview, Christie's own dramatisation of her 1925 novel *The Secret of Chimneys* came back from the Marshall's typing bureau.[14] Her response as a playwright to seeing Poirot on stage was thus to adapt a book in which he did not feature. One of her notebooks (that now numbered 67) contains some thoughts on the adaptation, which she called simply *Chimneys*, and there is nothing in these notes or the chronology of the surrounding material to indicate that the play itself could not have been written between May and July 1928. I suspect that nothing would have pleased her more than to see this Buchanesque romp, with its echoes of Arthur B. Reeve, presented as her own first work for the stage. But ironically it would be Poirot who was to facilitate her own playwriting debut.

Christie's own world and the post-war world around her were changing, and the certainties of her Victorian and Edwardian upbringing were being challenged on all fronts. In 1922 Stalin became General Secretary of the Central Committee of the Communist Party of the Soviet Union. 1924 had seen the short-lived first Labour government under Ramsay MacDonald, while 1926 had brought the disruption of a general strike. On 2 July 1928 the Representation of the People (Equal Franchise) Act finally enabled women to vote on the same basis as men and, as a result of the election in May the following year (dubbed 'the flapper election' in recognition of the newly enfranchised young female voters), MacDonald again became Prime Minister.

Throughout the 'Roaring Twenties' London's entertainment scene thrived as never before, and amongst the numerous women playwrights who found a voice alongside Clemence

Dane in the West End were Gertrude Jennings, Adelaide Phillpotts (in collaboration with her father) and Basil Dean's latest discovery, Margaret Kennedy. Meanwhile the public's appetite for thrillers remained unabated, and at the end of the decade audiences flocked to the West End premieres of Patrick Hamilton's *Rope*, *Murder on the Second Floor* (a hit for writer/ director/actor Frank Vosper), Emlyn Williams' *A Murder Has Been Arranged*, and Edgar Wallace's *On the Spot* (starring Charles Laughton). No one in theatreland yet fully appreciated the significance of the British premiere, at the Piccadilly Theatre on 27 September 1928, of *The Jazz Singer* – the first 'talkie'; and the long-term economic impact of the 1929 Wall Street Crash had yet to be felt.

In October 1928 the Christies' divorce was finalised and Archie married Nancy Neele, although it was agreed that Agatha would continue to use 'Christie' as her *nom de plume*. That autumn, she travelled on the Orient Express and visited Baghdad and the archaeological dig at Ur, staying as a guest of the renowned archaeologist Leonard Woolley and his wife Katharine. Edmund Cork had been working hard on her behalf, and the year also saw her sign lucrative new contracts with publishers Collins (in the UK) and Dodd, Mead & Co. (in America). Agatha's wayward older brother Monty died in 1929, and at the end of the year she was invited back to Ur where she was introduced to the archaeologist Max Mallowan. Although Max was fourteen years her junior, the pair fell in love. There was an undoubted intellectual meeting of minds that had been notably absent with Archie, but it is clear from their letters to each other that Agatha and Max's mutual devotion went far deeper than that, and on 11 September 1930 they married in Edinburgh. Max was obliged to return to Ur without Agatha that winter, but in subsequent years she was to accompany her husband on his expeditions. As his reputation as an archaeologist grew she became a valued contributor to his work, cataloguing and photographing artefacts as they were unearthed. A few years after their marriage Max and Agatha bought a house in London, 58 Sheffield Terrace on

Campden Hill, with another, Winterbrook House in Wallingford, as a weekend retreat. But Agatha was to spend the first winter of her second marriage alone with her daughter.

It was at this moment that, suddenly and unexpectedly, Agatha made her debut as a playwright. Although she herself clearly had hopes for her 1928 adaptation of *The Secret of Chimneys*, the success of *Alibi* had inevitably popularised the idea of Poirot on stage, and *After Dinner*, a play she had written some years previously featuring the Belgian sleuth, was consequently now in demand. It is not clear exactly when *After Dinner* dates from. Her autobiography is vague and inaccurate about this play on a number of levels (including its original title, the theatre that premiered it and the length of its run), while her introduction to *The Mousetrap Man* dates it as 1927. However, John Curran in an entertaining article for *Crime and Detective Stories* magazine makes a persuasive argument for it having actually been written in 1922, based partly on a meticulous chronology of Captain Hastings' love life.[15] The history of the play's production does nothing to contradict this theory, and the script lodged with the Lord Chamberlain is quite clearly an early work, very different from the heavily revised version that was eventually published by Alfred Ashley and Son in 1934. The script is not typed by the Marshall's agency, which she used for *Chimneys* in 1928, does not carry a Hughes Massie label and, intriguingly, includes the note 'Left and Right are seen from the point of view of the audience'; a very basic error corrected in *The Clutching Hand* and *The Lie*, in both of which Christie makes a point of stating, unnecessarily, that stage directions are given from the point of view of the actors. This would not only appear to suggest that *After Dinner* is Christie's first full-length stage play, but, given that *The Clutching Hand* may well pre-date 1922, could indicate that its origins are even earlier than Dr Curran has deduced.

According to Christie's autobiography, at the time of *Alibi* 'I had already written a detective play of my own, I can't remember exactly when. It was not approved of by Hughes Massie; in fact they suggested it would be better to forget it entirely, so I didn't press on with it . . . It was a conventional spy thriller, and although full of clichés it was not, I think, at all bad. Then, in due course, it came into its own. A friend of mine from Sunningdale days, Mr Burman, who was connected with the Royalty Theatre, suggested to me that it might perhaps be produced.'[16]

It seems likely that Christie presented the play to her new agency when she joined them in 1923 and they discouraged their valuable new signing from getting involved with dramatic distractions. Believing that the project had been abandoned, she rescued the character of Tredwell the butler from Sir Claud Amory's house Abbotts Cleve in *After Dinner*, and relocated him to Lord Caterham's house Chimneys, where he made his debut two years later in *The Secret of Chimneys*. By 1930 he had also appeared at Chimneys in the novel *The Seven Dials Mystery* (1929); but audiences for Agatha's debut play now found the familiar character in his originally intended location.

The 650-seat Royalty Theatre in Dean Street, which had hosted the West End transfer from the Hampstead Everyman of Noël Coward's *The Vortex* in 1924, would indeed have been a suitable home for *After Dinner*, and a Mr L.E. Berman was staging work there at that time. But in the end the producer who took the play on was Alec Rea, who in partnership with Basil Dean had produced Madge's play *The Claimant*. The Hughes Massie paperwork relating to Rea's licence is headed 'not our sale. For reference only' and lists the deal as having been done 'by L.E. Berman', whose Shaftesbury Avenue address appears on a recently discovered typescript of the play.[17] It seems that Christie's friend Berman had approached Rea directly with a copy of the play which he must have had in his possession since the early 1920s, thus accounting for the fact that it had not been updated or retyped. *Alibi* had suddenly put a premium on a Poirot play written by Christie herself and, in a wonderful piece of opportunism, Berman appears to have taken the initiative and presented the script to one of London's leading producers. One can only imagine

that, at the time, Edmund Cork was less than delighted by
this development.

The ReandeaN company, which had become one of the West
End's leading producing managements, had experienced a high-
profile rollercoaster of success and failure in equal measure.
In 1925 Alec Rea had terminated his contract with Basil Dean,
appointing the company's business manager, E.P. Clift, in his
place and continuing to trade under the banner of Reandco.
Dean's hectic personal life (a close friendship with the tragic
Meggie Albanesi, a divorce and a remarriage), an ill-advised
and short-lived attempt by him to juggle the joint managing
directorship of the Theatre Royal Drury Lane with his ReandeaN
responsibilities, and his not always successful attempts to
balance the demands of the company's ever-growing production
portfolio with the need to provide a programme of work for
the St Martin's Theatre, had tested the patience of his mild-
mannered business partner to breaking point.

The ending of ReandeaN was not a good thing for either
partner, says Basil Dean in his autobiography:

> Alec Rea, its financial head, loved the theatre, not because
> he was a playwright *manqué*, not because of some profes-
> sional diva whose interests he sought to advance, but for its
> own sake. Yet he never really understood it, and his judge-
> ment of plays was poor, as the subsequent record shows. He
> was suspicious of plays breaking fresh ground, especially if
> they revealed leftist tendencies, a surprising trait in a member
> of a distinguished Liberal family. His rejection of Shaw's
> *Heartbreak House* was a case in point. Generally speaking,
> the plays he produced during the remainder of his tenancy
> of the St Martin's Theatre with Paul Clift as his manager,
> lacked distinction and brought only limited commercial
> success. Yet he deserves high place in the annals of the
> English Theatre, for as Patrick Hastings [an MP and barrister
> who wrote plays produced by ReandeaN] pointed out in his
> autobiography: 'ReandeaN was virtually the last organised
> management under a private patron.'

The parting was largely my fault. I should have restrained my impatience to conquer on so many fields at once . . . When all's said I owe Alec Rea an incalculable debt, for without his warm friendship and loyal support during my early struggles I might not have achieved anything very much.[18]

After the end of ReandeaN, Alec Rea and Basil Dean continued to be linked by a number of joint business ventures, but the partnership was effectively over. Rea's new company, Reandco, continued its involvement with the St Martin's and then, in September 1930, announced that it had also taken over the lease of the Embassy Theatre in Swiss Cottage and was establishing a repertory company there, a move that was widely welcomed in the theatrical community. Sydney W. Carroll, who two years later was himself to found the Regents Park Open Air Theatre, wrote in the *Daily Telegraph*, under the heading 'Latest Repertory Idea',

Keep both eyes on the Embassy Theatre, Swiss Cottage, Hampstead. It is a beacon flaming on the heights that overlook London. It can only be seen, at the moment, gallantly flickering through the fog. But when the mists break and the sky grows clear the blaze will be apparent to all theatre lovers, brilliant and leaping to the sky . . . It is a Repertory venture, and out of repertory and repertory alone will come salvation for modern theatre. The Embassy has recently been taken over by Alec L. Rea, a manager who has been creditably associated with the repertory movement for years, first chairman of the Liverpool Repertory Company, a position he held for six years, and who, in conjunction with Basil Dean, has been identified with some of the most notable and distinguished productions in the West-end theatre of recent years.

Mr Rea believes, as I do, that actors must be properly and thoroughly trained. They must get constant exercise in their craft. And repertory, with its quick succession of different experiences in play by play, offers the young actor and actress the ideal and only public opportunity for a thorough practical grounding in the actor's art. Nothing is more deadening to the mind, the soul, and the sensibilities of a player than to be compelled to enact the same role night after night for months . . .

Mr Rea is ambitious of finding, with the aid of the Embassy, new players, new dramatists with original ideas. He hopes after the fashion of Miss Horniman at Manchester to found a school of young playwrights. He has catholic tastes and aspirations. His arms embrace equally both classic and commercial. He will do his best to encourage both highbrow and box-office alternately in the hope of making a unison ultimately between them . . .[19]

The Embassy Theatre had opened in 1928 in a building that had originally housed the Hampstead Conservatoire of Music. It initially operated as a 'try-out house', much like the 'Q' Theatre at Kew Bridge, giving often challenging plays a run of a fortnight in the hope that they might prove attractive to West End managements; but prior to Rea's takeover its programming had become increasingly *ad hoc*. The short-lived Everyman Theatre in nearby Hampstead had served much the same purpose from 1920 to 1926, and had enjoyed a number of West End transfers before a succession of box office failures forced its closure; and it is the Everyman that Christie erroneously credits in her autobiography as the theatre which premiered her own play. Such theatres always found it difficult to maintain a permanent company of actors on the salaries they could offer, and it was Rea's commitment to establishing a full-time team of players at the Embassy in a proper two-weekly repertory system that endeared him to the theatrical establishment.

The permanent ensemble of performers, who Sydney W. Carroll described as 'remarkably talented', included Joyce Bland, Judy Menteath, Francis L. Sullivan, John Boxer and Donald Wolfit, all of whom were to appear in Christie's play, and Andre van Gyseghem, who directed it. Robert Donat also appeared regularly, though not in this particular production, and further performers were engaged on a show-by-show basis as required. 'These facts,' concludes Carroll, 'are of sufficient importance and interest to justify circulation all over Greater London. Already, I understand, people are coming from considerable distances to see the art of these players, and my own experience of their work leads me cordially to recommend them to the public patronage.'

Rea's creative partner in the venture was A.R. Whatmore, who had been running the Hull Repertory Theatre Company to great acclaim for the previous six years. And, of course, if any of the productions did merit a West End transfer, then Rea still owned the lease on the St Martin's, so such a thing would be easy enough to facilitate.

Agatha's excitement at being included in the opening season of this widely publicised venture was justified. In an early November 1930 letter to Max, who had returned to the excavations at Ur, she wrote: 'Very exciting – I heard this morning an aged play of mine is going to be done at the Embassy Theatre for a fortnight with the chance of being given West End production by the Reandco – of course nothing may come of it – but it's exciting anyway – shall have to go to town for a rehearsal or two end of November, I suspect – I wish you were here to share the fun (and the agony when things go wrong and everyone forgets their part!!) But it's awfully fun all the same.'[20]

After Dinner was licensed to Reandco on 18 November 1930, for a two-week try-out at the Embassy Theatre within three months, with a West End option to be taken up within six weeks of the Embassy production on payment of £100. The Lord Chamberlain's office issued a licence on 4 December to the play – which was now called *Black Coffee*, the title having been changed by hand on the script they received[21] – and the production opened on 8 December. To today's theatre producers these lead-times would seem unfeasible, but with a permanent company on retainer, and rehearsing the next show whilst playing the current one, the repertory

system allowed for the confirmation of future programming
to be left until the very last minute. The extraordinary logistics
of scheduling in the London and regional repertory theatres
and London 'try-out' theatres at this time, and the manner
in which they constantly fed new productions into the West
End system alongside a seemingly inexhaustible supply of
new plays generated by the West End's own managements,
all of it without the benefit of a penny of public subsidy,
makes the operation of today's theatre industry look positively leisurely.

On 26 November Agatha wrote to Max from Ashfield: '"After
Dinner" or (according to my *Sunday Times* which seems to
know more than I do!) "Black Coffee" – comes on on Dec 8th
– so I will have to go up to town for rehearsals next week . . .
Six *eminent* detective story writers have been asked to broadcast again – we're all getting together on December 5th to plan
the thing out a bit – Me, Dorothy Sayers, Clemence Dane,
Anthony Berkeley EC Bentley and Freeman Wills Croft . . . all
rather fun.'[22]

Here she is referring to a project which was to be broadcast on the radio in early 1931, in which members of the
Detection Club created a sort of literary game of consequences, each writing and broadcasting an episode of a crime
story which was to be aired over a number of weeks. The
Detection Club, comprising the elite of British crime writers,
had undertaken a similar project with great success in 1930,
and the authors contributed their income from the BBC to
the club's coffers.

In 1928 Clemence Dane had co-authored with Helen Simpson
the first of two crime novels she was to pen, *Enter Sir John*,
about an actress wrongly convicted of murder. Filmed as *Murder!*
by Alfred Hitchcock in 1930, it earned Dane a place in the
Detection Club. I do hope that Agatha and Clemence Dane did
actually meet on 5 December. The successful forty-two-year-old
playwright who had just published her first detective novel and
the successful forty-year-old detective novelist, who was about
to have her own first play performed, would have got on well,

I think. Clemence Dane's name appears on a reading list of Agatha's in one of her notebooks.

The opening night of *Black Coffee* at the Embassy was a success. Although Max was absent, Agatha's sister Madge was in the audience, just as Agatha had been for *The Claimant* six years previously, and with Madge was her husband, James, along with his sister Nan and her husband George Kon. Agatha wrote to Max two days after the opening:

> Oh it has all been fun – Black Coffee. I mean it was fun going to rehearsals and everything went splendidly on the night itself except that when the girl said (in great agitation!): 'This door won't open!' it immediately did! Something like that always happens on a first night. They had a larger audience . . . than they've ever had before, and the Repertory Company were so pleased . . . The girl was *awfully* good – couldn't have had anyone better – well, let us hope 'something will come of it' as they say – preferably in May. The Reandco have an option for six months. I do hope they take it up. This week has been simply *hectic*.[23]

The actress she so admired playing the role of Lucia Amory was Joyce Bland, who had just completed a busy and successful season at Stratford. Agatha was wrong about the length of the West End option; Reandco actually had six weeks in which to take it up, and they did, although a log-jam of productions at the St Martin's meant that, following the two-week run at the Embassy in December 1930, the play would not appear in the West End until the following April.

Although there is a sub-plot relating to spies, and a remarkably prescient storyline relating to weapons of mass destruction created by 'disintegration of the atom', *Black Coffee* is, to all intents and purposes, an efficient and well-crafted, if relatively simple, country house murder mystery. It engages both some of the plot devices and some of the characters – not only Poirot but also Captain Hastings and Inspector Japp – who, at the most likely time of the play's writing, had just been introduced to the public in Christie's first novel, *The Mysterious Affair at Styles*. *Black Coffee* thus ticks all the boxes for a 'typical Agatha Christie play' and, ironically, was both the first and last that she wrote in this idiom.

As with *Alibi*, Christie's own principal concern was with the portrayal of Poirot. Although she ultimately preferred Francis L. Sullivan's interpretation to Charles Laughton's, she laments in her autobiography, 'It always seems strange to me that whoever plays Poirot is always an outsize man. Charles Laughton had plenty of avoirdupois, and Francis Sullivan was broad, thick and about 6'2" tall.'[24]

Sullivan, like Laughton, saw Poirot as an ideal vehicle for his talents, and had actually first performed the role in the post-West End tour of *Alibi*. In fact he made something of a career of being the poor man's Charles Laughton, not only taking over his role in *Alibi* but also starring in a 1942 revival of *A Man With Red Hair*. Sullivan would receive his final 'review' in 1956 in the form of his *Times* obituary, which opined, 'Corpulence, sharp eyes embedded in florid features, and a deep, plummy voice suited him admirably for the part of the suave but foxy lawyer. He was generally too much of a carica-ture to be unrelievedly sinister, and though he was sometimes cast as a comic, his talents were wasted if there was no streak of evil in the part. His acting had a wider range than his exag-gerated physique might suggest. He was an obvious choice for Bottom, and perhaps for Mr Bumble, but not for Hercule Poirot . . .'[25]

Although Christie had objected to the amorous antics of a French 'Beau Poirot' in *Alibi*, she was not above introducing an element of romantic frisson when it came to her own portrayal of her Belgian sleuth. Here are the final moments of *Alibi*, as performed by Charles Laughton:

CARYL (softly) I don't care what anyone says, you will always
    be "Beau Poirot" to me! (holds out her hand) Good-night!
POIROT: (Taking both her hands, kisses first one, then the
    other) Good-bye. (Still holding her hands) Believe me, Mees

> Caryl, I do everything possible to be of service to you!
> (drops her hands)
> (CARYL goes out)
> Good-bye!
> POIROT stands at the open window looking out after her as the Curtain slowly falls.[26]

And here are the not dissimilar final moments of *Black Coffee*, written several years before *Alibi*, in the original script approved by the Lord Chamberlain and performed by Francis L. Sullivan at the Embassy:

> LUCIA: M Poirot – (she holds out both hands to him)
> Do not think that I shall ever forget . . .
> (Lucia raises her face. Poirot kisses her.)
> (She goes back to Richard [her husband]. Lucia and Richard go out together . . . Poirot mechanically straightens things on the centre table but with his eyes fixed on the door through which Lucia has passed.)
> POIROT: Neither – shall I – forget.[27]

Reviews from the Embassy, as with *Alibi*, inevitably focused largely on the interpretation of Poirot. 'Mr Sullivan is obviously very happy in the part, and his contribution to the evening's entertainment is a considerable one,' said *The Times*.[28] Amongst the other characters are Dr Carelli – played at the Embassy by Donald Wolfit – the archetypal Christie 'unexpected guest' who has echoes in *The Mousetrap*'s Mr Paravicini; and, more interestingly, a wittily executed portrayal of a young 'flapper' girl, the murder victim's niece. The flapper phenomenon was at its height in 1922, as a generation of young women threw off the restrictions of the Victorian and Edwardian era and defined their own agenda in terms of fashion, entertainment and social interaction with men. The sexual revolution of the 1920s, in its subversion of what went before it, was arguably far more radical than anything that happened in the 1960s, and although Agatha herself would have been a decade too old to qualify as a flapper or to embrace their style and philosophy, there is a distinct affection in her writing for what they stood for, albeit informed by her trademark observational humour. In *Black Coffee*, Barbara Amory is described as 'an extremely modern young woman of twenty-one'. She dances to records on the gramophone and flirts mercilessly with Hastings, describing him as 'pre-war' ('Victorian' in the original script) and exhorting him to 'come and be vamped'. When criticised by her aunt for the brightness of her lipstick, she responds, 'take it from me, a girl simply can't have too much red on her lips. She never knows how much she is going to lose in the taxi coming home.'

When the play did finally open in the West End, at the St Martin's Theatre, it was in a much-changed production. Christie had undertaken rewrites, as she had felt that her 'aged' play seemed out of date when she saw it at the Embassy. 'Have been working very hard on Black Coffee. Some scenes were a little old fashioned, I thought,'[29] she wrote to Max. Tricks she uses in order to achieve a more 'contemporary' feel include a joke about the brand-name vitamins Bemax, which were advertised widely in 1930. The script published by Arthur Ashley in 1934 included these changes, along with the following more straight-laced version of the final scene:

> LUCIA: (Down to Poirot, takes his hand, she also has Richard's hand) M.Poirot, do not think I shall forget – ever.
> POIROT: Neither shall I forget (kisses her hand.)
> (Lucia and Richard go out together through window. [Poirot] follows them to window, and calls out after them.)
> POIROT: Bless you, mes enfants! Ah-h!
> (Moves to the fireplace, clicks his tongue and straightens the spill vases.)[30]

At the Embassy, *Black Coffee* had been directed by Andre van Gyseghem, a radical young director who, as a RADA-trained actor, had worked for the theatre's creative head A.R. Whatmore in his previous post at the Hull Repertory Theatre. A leading light of the Workers' Theatre Movement, van Gyseghem was to become a member of the Communist Party and a frequent visitor to the Soviet Union, and later penned a surprisingly readable book entitled *Theatre in Soviet Russia* (1943). The West End production of *Black Coffee* was redirected by Oxford-educated Douglas Clarke-Smith, an actor-director who appears to have had no association with the Embassy, but who had cut his teeth at Birmingham Rep after distinguished service in the First World War, and who went on to direct over twenty productions for pioneering touring group the Lena Ashwell Players, the peacetime incarnation of the company that had provided entertainment for the troops throughout the conflict.

As well as a new director, all but one of the supporting cast to Sullivan's Poirot were also new to the piece. Joyce Bland was amongst those who were replaced, along with van Gyseghem himself, who had doubled his directing duties with the small but significant role of Edward Raynor. Given that the delay in transferring had allowed for the luxury of a new rehearsal period, the Embassy had clearly decided not to commit too many of their core ensemble to a potentially lengthy West End run. On 9 April 1931, the day Alec Rea presented the West End premiere of *Black Coffee*, *The Times* was listing attractions at thirty-one West End theatres, including revivals of Shaw's *Man and Superman* at the Court, Ibsen's *Hedda Gabler* at the Fortune and Somerset Maugham's *The Circle* at the Vaudeville. At the Queen's Theatre, Rudolf Besier's *The Barretts of Wimpole Street*, directed by Barry Jackson, was advertising itself as 'London's Longest Run' (which, of the productions then running in London, it was; it went on to complete 530 performances).

In the end, *Black Coffee* itself was to enjoy only a very short West End run. Reviews of the new production were not unfavourable, and the *Observer*'s influential Ivor Brown noted, 'Mr Francis Sullivan prudently refraining from a Charles Laughton pastiche does not tie the "character" labels all over the part, but plays it quietly and firmly, trusting that the story will do its own work of entertainment.' But he concluded, 'Black Coffee is supposed to be a strong stimulant and powerful enemy of sleep. I found the title optimistic.'[31]

Reandco soon found that they needed the St Martin's in order to gain a West End foothold for another production; as *The Times* reported: 'In order that Messrs. Reandco may present Mr Ronald Jeans's new play *Lean Harvest* at the St Martin's Theatre on Thursday next, Mrs Agatha Christie's play *Black Coffee* will be transferred on Monday to the Wimbledon Theatre, and on the following Monday, May 11, it will resume its interrupted run at the Little Theatre.'[32] Although Reandco owned the lease on the St Martin's, Bertie Meyer remained the building's licensee on behalf of its freeholders, the Willoughby de Broke family. Having enjoyed a successful association with the Little Theatre as a producer, he was doubtless instrumental in facilitating *Black Coffee*'s transfer there, although he was not directly involved with the production. *Black Coffee* was sent away from the West End to Wimbledon in order to fill an unsatisfactory week's gap between its scheduling at the St Martin's and the Little. But the production never really recovered from this disruption, and closed on 13 June.

Between the St Martin's and the Little Theatre, *Black Coffee* had completed a total of sixty-seven West End performances over two months, which was, at least, slightly longer than *The Claimant*'s run. It was to be more than twenty years until the premiere of the next Christie play that was not based on one of her novels.

Agatha herself had missed her West End debut as a playwright in order to join her new husband at the archaeological dig in Ur. In the autumn of 1931 Max Mallowan relocated his archaeological work in Iraq to Nineveh, and at Christmas Agatha hurried home in the hope of catching the premiere of *Chimneys*, which Reandco had now scheduled for a December opening at the Embassy, clearly in the hope of enabling a West End transfer as they had done the previous year with *Black Coffee*.

The fate of *Chimneys* has taken on an almost mythical status amongst Christie scholars as a 'play that never was'. Having been advertised as opening at the Embassy, gone into rehearsal and been licensed by the Lord Chamberlain, it suddenly disappeared from their schedule, apparently without explanation. It was not heard of again until it was unearthed by Canadian director John Paul Fishbach in 2001 and given its world premiere in Calgary in 2003, almost twenty-eight years after Christie's death. As is often the case with matters theatrical, however, the reality of the '*Chimneys* mystery' was far more prosaic than may at first appear, and those previously attempting to establish the facts of the matter may have enjoyed more success if Agatha had dated her letters with the year as well as the day and month. Once her letters are placed in the correct sequence, the order of events surrounding the cancelled production becomes apparent.

There are in fact no fewer than four copies of the script amongst Christie's papers, all of them very similar. Three of these are duplicates, two clearly dated 5 July 1928 by the Marshall's typing agency stamp and carrying Agatha's address in Ashfield, Torquay. The unstamped duplicate carries the Hughes Massie label and has been annotated in pencil by the actress playing the role of Bundle. The fourth copy includes some slight variations in the typescript and handwritten notes by Agatha, and has the Hughes Massie address handwritten on it. The first point to establish, therefore, is that the script itself never actually 'disappeared', even if the scheduled premiere production appears to have done; assuming that Fishbach's copy is now amongst those at the archive, we know of at least four other 'originals', including the one lodged with the Lord Chamberlain's office. Hughes Massie's records show that Reandco acquired the rights in the play as early as 22 April 1931, shortly after the opening of their West End run of *Black Coffee*, for production at the Embassy Theatre within six months of signature and with a West End option to be taken up within six weeks of the Embassy production.[33] This time the sale had been co-ordinated by Hughes Massie themselves. As was standard practice, the royalties payable by the Embassy, as a small repertory theatre, were at the reduced rate of 5 per cent of box office income. Although the scheduling of the production would be subject to the vagaries of the repertory system and its short lead times, Reandco clearly wanted to ensure that the next Christie play would appear as part of their own repertoire rather than someone else's.

The Times of Thursday 19 November 1931 duly announced that 'The next production at the Embassy Theatre will be *Chimneys*, by Agatha Christie, which Mr A.R. Whatmore will produce [i.e. direct] on Thursday 1 December.' This was slightly outside their six-month option period, but that would not have been an issue for a management of good standing who had given Christie her West End premiere, and an informal extension of the option had doubtless been negotiated. Based on the previous year's experience, Rea and Whatmore clearly felt that a pre-Christmas Christie at the Embassy was a good formula for box-office success.

On the same day as *The Times*'s announcement, *Chimneys* arrived at the Lord Chamberlain's office. Act One of the script submitted to the Lord Chamberlain is clearly from a different copy of the play to the rest of it, and includes rehearsal notes written in pencil apparently by the actor playing Lord Caterham.[34] Interestingly, the list of characters at the front shows evidence of what appears to have been an earlier attempt to cast the production, with 'Wolfit' pencilled in as one of two suggestions for George Lomax and 'Sullivan' for Superintendent Battle. Neither of these were still under contract to the Embassy repertory company by the time the play went into production – Donald Wolfit was by then touring Canada with Barry Jackson's company. 'Boxer' (John Boxer) is pencilled in as Bill Eversleigh and Agatha's favourite, 'Joyce' (Joyce Bland), as feisty heroine Virginia Revel, and it is fairly safe to assume that these two were cast in these roles when *Chimneys* finally went into rehearsal, particularly as they were both appearing in the Embassy's previous production, *Britannia of Billingsgate* – Bland in a small role no doubt in order to allow her to prepare for her leading role in *Chimneys*. A note next to the role of

Anthony Cade says 'Oliver' or perhaps 'Clive'. I don't know who this is, but I'm sorry to disappoint those who believe that 'Olivier' may have been been considered for the production.

Writing to Max from a bug-infested train on her journey back from Nineveh in early December, Agatha, having just seen the 19 November copy of *The Times*, probably in a hotel lobby, laments:

> Darling – I am horribly disappointed, Just seen in the Times that Chimneys began December 1st, so I shall *just* miss it. I did want to hear how this child of mine sounded on the stage. I *could* have gone on the Saturday convoy because my passport came back in time and then I'd have got home on the Friday and could have seen the last night Saturday. What I ought to have done was wired to Carlo . . . 8th or 1st? I've been getting out of my good telegraphy habits lately – with bad results! If *she* had had any sense she would have wired the date to *me*![35]

Agatha had commenced her journey too late to return by Saturday 12 December, which would have been the last night of a run commencing on 1 December. In reality, under a two-weekly repertory system, with *Britannia of Billingsgate* having opened on 10 November and announcing in its programme, 'Change of programme every fortnight' and 'production in preparation: Chimneys, a new play by Agatha Christie',[36] the scheduled opening date for *Chimneys* would originally have been Tuesday 24 November (the date for which it was licensed by the Lord Chamberlain's office). But in the event the unexpected success of *Britannia*, a new comedy by Jope Slade and Sewell Stokes about a charwoman at a film studio who 'walks on' in a film and is such a hit that she later becomes a famous character actress, meant that it had been extended for a week at the Embassy and was thought worth transferring to the St Martin's thereafter. *Chimneys* was therefore pushed to 1 December by the extended run at the Embassy, rather than being brought forward as Agatha seemed to believe it had been. It could only ever have opened on 8 December if there was another production scheduled between *Britannia* and it, which clearly there wasn't.

Agatha arrived in Istanbul in mid-December, writing to Max, 'Am now at Tokatlian [hotel] . . . looked at Times of Dec 7th and "Mary Broome" is on at the Embassy!! So perhaps I shall see Chimneys after all? Or did it go off after a week? All book-shops etc are closed of course – so can't get any other papers.'[37]

Mary Broome, featuring Robert Donat and Joyce Bland, had indeed followed *Britannia of Billingsgate* into the Embassy on 1 December instead of *Chimneys*. With the transfer of *Britannia* to the St Martin's went, presumably, the majority of the cast who would have been in rehearsal for *Chimneys*. The 'exten-sion' of *Britannia* at the Embassy for a week would have helped to buy some time in respect of organising a new cast for *Chimneys* and was announced on the same day as the news that *Chimneys* was to follow it into the Embassy, so the original intention still seems to have been to make *Chimneys* work. But at some point it must have been decided that the logistics of re-casting *Chimneys* to open by 1 December were simply too daunting. Christie's play is a relatively complex piece of theatre and not without its challenges; *Mary Broome*, on the other hand, was a twenty-year-old comedy by Allan Monkhouse which had become a firm favourite with repertory companies. Only two cast members of *Britannia of Billingsgate* did not transfer with the production, one of them being Joyce Bland, whose small role allowed her to be replaced and to take up the lead in *Mary Broome* rather than *Chimneys*. John Boxer was amongst those who departed with *Britannia*. Had Robert Donat, who was not in the cast of *Britannia*, perhaps been in rehearsal for *Chimneys* when the switch was made? The programme for *Mary Broome* states: 'Production in preparation: to be announced later (see Daily Press)',[38] indicating the disarray into which the Embassy's scheduling had been thrown by the sudden departure to the West End of a number of the resident ensemble. With the transfer of *Black Coffee*, this had of course been avoided by taking a break in which to recast the production.

This piece of opportunism on the part of Reandco paid off for them, and *Britannia of Billingsgate* enjoyed a successful West End run, moving on from its launching pad of the St Martin's to the Duke of York's in much the same way that *Black Coffee* had moved on to the Little. The fact that they had produced *Britannia* in the West End would doubtless also have secured Reandco a share of the proceeds when it was filmed two years later, just as their brief West End presentation of *Black Coffee* had cut them in on 50 per cent of Christie's income from the 1931 film of her play. The reason for the rescheduling given to Agatha on her return was rather different, however. On 23 December 1931 she wrote to Max, 'Chimneys is coming on here but nobody will say when – I fancy they want something in Act One altered and didn't wish to do it themselves' She also mentions that 'Alibi *may* come on in New York with Charles Laughton.'[39]

Chimneys was eventually rescheduled to commence at the Embassy on either 23 February or 1 March 1932. On 31 December 1931 Agatha wrote to Max from the Torquay Medical Baths, 'I'm going to have a sea water bath (HOT!) to buck me up after Christmas . . . If Chimneys is put on on Tuesday 23rd I shall stay for first night. If it's a week later well I shan't wait for it. I don't want to miss Nineveh and shall have seen rehearsals, I suppose. By the way, Alibi *is* being put on in New York after being rewritten and "Americanised" by someone. Charles Laughton to be Poirot.'[40]

What Agatha didn't realise was that Reandco were about to relinquish their lease on the Embassy. Business had not lived up to expectations and the commitment to repertory, with fortnightly productions and a permanent ensemble, whilst highly regarded in theatrical circles, was putting the company under financial pressure. Ticket prices had been lowered in the hope of attracting more customers, but the struggle proved an unequal one and Rea, ever the pragmatist, decided to cut his losses, terminating his arrangement with the venue at the end of February 1931, just prior to the rescheduled dates for *Chimneys*. There can be no doubt that for Rea, balancing the demands of a full-time repertory company with those of a West End theatre (the St Martin's) and a portfolio of commercial productions was proving unfeasible.

Ivor Brown, writing in the *Observer*, commented, 'The suitable play is scarce and one fortnight of poor houses will swiftly obliterate the small profit derivable from two or three of reasonably crowded attendance. The policy of the house seems to have been to give everything a turn and balance a few high-aspiring swings with the more ordinary jollity of the roundabouts. I suspect that the management attracts the critics rather than the public when it goes for the swings and has to pay for its receipts of complimentary writing by some bestowal of complimentary seats.'[41]

The Times also lamented the Embassy's loss: 'Valuable work in London has been done by the Embassy Company at Swiss Cottage, where under the skilful direction of A.R. Whatmore many plays . . . were performed in London for the first time. In its comparatively short life the company has created for itself a public which will learn with regret that the lease at the Embassy is not to be renewed and that the theatre is to become a cinema.'[42]

The rumours of the Embassy's change of use proved unfounded, however, and it soon reopened under Ronald Adam, who had been its business manager under Reandco. He turned it into a club theatre, thereby avoiding the need for the Lord Chamberlain's approval and facilitating a sometimes more radical programme of work. Andre van Gyseghem replaced A.R. Whatmore as the venue's artistic figurehead, directing a number of notable productions including two plays starring Paul Robeson. Adam ran the Embassy until 1939, and his business model appears to have been more robust than Rea's, with numerous plays going on to enjoy West End success.

Chimneys, therefore, was to an extent a victim of the organised chaos of the repertory system, the very system that had given Christie her West End debut with *Black Coffee*. There was actually no mystery about its sudden disappearance from the schedule; she was clearly advised that it had been postponed, purportedly to enable rewrites, and the management that had optioned it then ceased their involvement with the theatre that was to have presented it shortly before the rescheduled dates. The truth is, however, that had Rea been particularly enamoured with the play he could easily have renewed his licence and facilitated its production elsewhere. Similarly Ronald Adam and Andre van Gyseghem, both of whom had been involved with it at the Embassy, could easily have acquired a new licence on the Embassy's behalf. In December 1931 it had clearly been felt that *Britannia of Billingsgate* was a safer bet than *Chimneys*. The critics had been lukewarm towards *Britannia*, but it proved popular with audiences and was perhaps a more obvious candidate for a pre-Christmas West End run than Christie's new work, particularly if they did feel that it needed rewrites.

In any event, Alec Rea presumably felt that it was ultimately worth sacrificing *Chimneys* to ensure a future for *Britannia*. In reality, too, he must have known some time in advance that he was going to give up the lease on the Embassy, and one cannot help surmising that it was more than coincidence that the new dates for the production given to Agatha turned out to be just after the theatre's enforced temporary closure. By the time that the Embassy and Reandco parted company Agatha was already back at the archaeological dig at Nineveh with her new husband, and the problems with *Chimneys* were no doubt soon forgotten. Whatever the truth of the matter, the situation had been finessed in a manner that carefully avoided putting the firm of Reandco out of favour with Agatha Christie, playwright, and they were to work together again in the future.

It is not difficult to see why the ensemble of a small repertory theatre might have lost their initial enthusiasm for Christie's rambling, light-hearted melodrama once they started rehearsing it. As a piece of theatre, it offers many more unwelcome challenges to the director, designer and actors than *Black Coffee*. *The Secret of Chimneys* does not immediately lend itself to stage adaptation, and limiting the action of the novel to two rooms in a country house necessitates the cutting of various multi-locational escapades in its early chapters, which are set in Bulawayo and London. As a result the stage version is burdened with a great deal of back-story and this, combined with a convoluted plot involving diamonds, oil concessions, exiled royalty from a fictional principality, international diplomacy, secret societies, an elusive master criminal, suspicious foreigners, wily assassins, blackmail, deception, multiple impersonations, unexpected guests and an unexpected corpse can make the whole thing a bit impenetrable. The Lord Chamberlain's reader's report, dated 20 November 1931, describes the play as 'harmless' and 'melodramatic', noting that it is 'excessively complicated to read but I dare say will be less complicated when acted; it is naturally written'.[43]

Virginia Revel, the heroine of *Chimneys*, is very much a British 'Elaine', 'about twenty-six and bursting with vitality, a radiant gallant creature'. As she becomes embroiled in various potentially dangerous exploits she exclaims, 'You don't know how I'm enjoying myself. After years of Ascot and Goodwood and Cowes and shooting parties and the Riviera and then Ascot all over again – suddenly to be plunged into the middle of this! (Closes her eyes in ecstasy).'[44]

The Foreign Office's Honourable George Lomax, however, represents a more traditional view. 'I disapprove utterly of women being mixed up in these matters. It is always dangerous. Women have no sense of the importance of public affairs. They display a deplorable levity at the most serious moments. The House of Commons is ruined – absolutely ruined nowadays – all the old traditions – (He breaks off) I am wandering from the point.' At time of the play's writing 1929's 'flapper election' was yet to come, and Lomax is referring to the tiny number of women MPs who had been returned to Parliament since 1918, when women over thirty were given the right to vote (subject to minimum property qualifications) and women over twenty-one were given the right to stand for Parliament.

The feisty Virginia finds a natural ally in adventurer Anthony Cade, who remarks, 'Perhaps I was born colour blind. When I see the red light – I can't help forging ahead. And in the end, you know, that spells disaster. Bound to. (a pause) Quite right, really. That sort of thing is bad for traffic generally.'

When the two eventually but inevitably tie the knot he confesses:

> ANTHONY: Darling! I have let you believe such a lot of lies about me. And I have married you under false pretences. What are you going to do about it?
> VIRGINIA: Do? Why we will go to Herzoslovakia and play at being kings and queens.
> ANTHONY: The average life of a king or queen out there is under four years. They always get assassinated.
> VIRGINIA: How marvellous! We'll have a lot of fun – teaching the brigands not to be brigands, and the assassins not to assassinate and generally improving the moral tone of the country.

Christie's dialogue is seen to best advantage when presented in dramatic form, and it is notable that, in the plays which are adaptations of novels, it is often an improvement on the equivalent passage in a book from which it is taken; this delightful banter being a case in point. Indeed, her stated frustrations with the need to break up the flow of dialogue in a novel with descriptive passages are never more apparent than in the novel of *The Secret of Chimneys* itself where, instead of a description of the house, she gives us this: 'The car passed in through the park gates of Chimneys. Descriptions of that historic place can be found in any guidebook. It is also No 3 in Historic Homes of England, price 21s. On Thursday, coaches come over from Middlingham and view those portions of it which are open to the public. In view of all these facilities, to describe Chimneys would be superfluous.'[45]

Intriguingly, sections of *The Secret of Chimneys* are written as though they were themselves part of a playscript. Here is the start of Chapter 10: 'Inspector Badgeworthy in his office. Time, 8.30am. A tall, portly man, Inspector Badgeworthy, with a heavy regulation tread. Inclined to breathe hard in moments of professional strain . . .' And most of the final chapter is written in the present tense, again in the idiom of a playscript:

> Scene – Chimneys, 11am Thursday morning.
>   Johnson, the police constable, with his coat off, digging.
>   Something in the nature of a funeral feeling seems to be in the air. The friends and relations stand round the grave that Johnson is digging . . .

The play, like the book, features a character named Herman Isaacstein, who represents the interests of a British oil syndicate. Although his position as a high-powered man of finance is clearly respected by the other characters, they occasionally make reference to him, usually humorously, in a manner typical of the casual anti-semitism of the pre-war upper middle classes. Like that of Hergé, the Belgian creator of boy detective Tintin, Christie's work was published between the 1920s and the 1970s, spanning and reflecting for popular consumption a century of extraordinary social and political upheaval; and it is important to consider the context in which it was written before passing judgement. Because Christie was still writing in the 1970s it is easy to forget that she was raised an Edwardian and, like Hergé's, some of her early work contains elements of racial stereotyping that typify her class and the era in which she was writing. Suffice to say that, when *Chimneys* finally received its stage premiere in Calgary in 2006, certain lines relating to Isaacstein were subtly adjusted to take account of the sensibilities of modern audiences.

For all her efforts to provide audiences with alternative fare, however, Poirot was to continue to weigh heavily on Christie's theatrical ambitions and, on Broadway as in the West End, the character was to make his debut before his creator. Key to successfully dating Agatha's correspondence relating to *Chimneys* (previous misdating has exacerbated the perceived problem of the 'disappearing play') are the references to the forthcoming Broadway production of *Alibi*, starring Charles Laughton, which received its premiere at the Booth Theatre

on 8 February 1932. Laughton had already made his own
Broadway debut, enjoying a modest success in *Payment
Deferred*, an adaptation of a 1926 C.S. Forester crime novel
presented at the Lyceum Theatre at the end of 1931. *Payment
Deferred* was produced by Gilbert Miller, a defiantly independent producer who was a friend of Basil Dean's and who
was later to play a key role in Agatha's own Broadway success.
Broadway was a calling-card for Hollywood for British actors
in the 1930s, and Laughton felt that *Alibi* would provide a
notable showcase for him, as it had in London. The play had
been successfully revived in repertory, notably at London's
Regent Theatre in 1931, and in the same year the clean-shaven
young Austin Trevor, a former ReandeaN player, had improb-
ably played Poirot in British film versions of both *Alibi* and
Black Coffee.

For the Broadway production of *Alibi*, Laughton teamed up
with the notoriously acerbic and bullying Jed Harris, a prolific
thirty-two-year-old producer/director whose various Broadway
producing successes to date had included journalistic comedy
The Front Page at the Times Square Theatre in 1929. Harris,
who had changed his name from Jacob Horowitz, purchased
a licence for $500 from Hughes Massie at the end of 1931 and
engaged John Anderson, a critic on the *New York Evening
Journal*, to revise the script for the American market; a process
which Agatha was not involved in but which, from her letters
to Max, she was evidently aware of. Authors' royalties were
split three ways, between Christie, Michael Morton and John
Anderson, unusually giving Christie herself a minority share
in the work.[46] The title was also changed, to *The Fatal Alibi*,
and the production was credited as 'staged by Mr Laughton'
although Harris was closely involved in the rehearsal process.

The cast also notably included Broadway veteran Effie
Shannon, but it was Laughton who once again stole the show.
The Booth Theatre's playbill (i.e. programme) shows a moustachioed Laughton in a gaudy pin-striped suit and carnation
gurning and waving his hands in the air. 'Look at me,' it clearly
states.[47]

The three-act, five-scene acting masterclass that *The Murder of Roger Ackroyd* had become was not welcomed by the American critics. The *New York Times* commented, 'Since Mr Laughton enjoys playing the part, a guileless theatregoer may enjoy watching him. But colourful acting, slightly detached from the flow of narrative, can also temper a drama's illusion. In the opinion of this department, Mr Laughton's lithographic performance has that subtle effect. It diverts attention from the play.'[48]

Legendary Hollywood gossip columnist Sidney Skolsky in his syndicated 'Tintypes' column led off an affectionate character sketch with:

Charles Laughton is the latest English actor to invade Broadway and capture the critics and the public – a neat trick. Although movie companies have already tried to entice him to go to Hollywood, little is known about him here. And even less is known about him in London . . . Is sensitive about his weight. Wants to forget about it and not step on the scales. The wife has a scale in the house and tries to coax him to step on it by placing a piece of cake on the machine . . . Normally retires between one-thirty and two in the morning. When with Jed Harris between six and seven in the morning . . .

His nicknames are Fatty, Henry VIII and Pudge and Billy. The wife's pet name for him can't be printed.[49]

The Fatal Alibi ran for only twenty-four performances on Broadway, but it was enough for Laughton to make his mark, and it served its purpose as a springboard for a successful Broadway and Hollywood career. 'The wife', of course, was the actress Elsa Lanchester, whose film career was to take off alongside Laughton's; according to Skolsky, Laughton designed 'most of her clothes'.

And so Agatha Christie made her Broadway debut; in her own absence, her work processed by not one but two adaptors, and with her 'French' detective once again stealing the limelight. Later in 1932 he would appear in Paris in yet another re-adaptation of *Alibi*, this time by French dramatist Jacques Deval. With *Black Coffee* Christie had, however, finally seen her own work reach the West End stage, albeit for a very brief run. It was to be over a decade before another of her own plays was to be produced, a decade in which adaptors misleadingly continued to keep her name on theatrical marquees on both sides of the Atlantic, and in which she herself wrote four further full-length scripts, none of which were to achieve West End productions in her lifetime.

SCENE THREE

Stranger and Stranger

Charles Laughton made his Broadway exit as Poirot on 1 March 1932, and six weeks later Hughes Massie issued Francis L. Sullivan with a licence for a new Poirot stage script written by Christie herself.[1] This was a one act play (or 'Sketch' as it was titled) based on the short story 'The Wasp's Nest', which had been published in the *Daily Mail* in November 1928. The licence allowed Sullivan to perform the piece at a 'royal charity matinee' in June 1932, which appears to have been the purpose for which it was written, and to present it at London's Arts Theatre. It also gave him the right to perform it as a 'music hall' act, in return for 10 per cent of his income therefrom; the concept of a Poirot play featuring on a variety bill is indicative of the theatrical curiosity that the character had rapidly become.

On Tuesday 7 June 1932 the King and Queen attended a gala matinee in aid of the British Hospital in Paris at the Theatre Royal Drury Lane.[2] The production consisted of a variety of numbers and sketches, in one of which Gerald du Maurier caused much hilarity by playing the role of a non-speaking butler. This may well have been the event for which *The Wasp's Nest* was originally written, although it did not in fact form part of the programme. Neither did it turn up at the Arts Theatre or on the music hall stage, although in 1937 it was broadcast live by BBC television, with Sullivan as Poirot. Also in the cast were Douglas Clarke-Smith, who had directed the West End transfer of *Black Coffee*, and Wallace Douglas, who would go on to direct the London premiere of *Witness for the Prosecution*. The broadcast took place on 18 June at 3.35 p.m., with the *Radio Times* announcing that

> Viewers will be the first to see this Agatha Christie play, which has never previously been performed anywhere. Francis L. Sullivan, who will bring to the television screen the famous detective character, Hercule Poirot, originally made a great hit in another Poirot play, *Alibi*, which he toured for almost a year, and subsequently in the same characterisation in *Black Coffee*. In addition to being familiar to theatre audiences in New York, London and Stratford upon Avon, he has appeared in a number of films, amongst them *Jew Suss*, *Great Expectations*, *Chu Chin Chow* and *The Mystery of Edwin Drood*. The character of Poirot is one of his favourite parts, and with the exception of a notable portrayal by Charles Laughton, the character has been almost permanently associated with him for the past six years.[3]

A myth has grown up that the play was actually written by Christie for television and, as such, is her only work for the medium. The contractual trail, however, makes it clear that she originally wrote it for theatrical presentation, and that it was subsequently sold to the BBC for the princely sum of £4, and simply broadcast as written. The BBC Television Service had been established at Alexandra Palace the previous year, and the broadcasting of drama was in its infancy, so the straightforward live transmission of a short stage script would have been entirely in keeping with the methodologies of the day.

Significantly, the script itself does not immediately lend itself to presentation as part of a variety bill, either in the context of a gala event or a music hall presentation. It is a gentle fourhander concerning a love triangle and the redeployment to murderous purpose of the cyanide being used to destroy a wasp's nest. Poirot is at his most contemplative and unshowy. There is nothing at all 'Guignol' about the piece, and the murder is prevented before it can actually take place. It is almost as if Christie had deliberately undermined the brief that she had been given in order to avoid Poirot being reduced to a music hall turn. Yet, although Christie herself had no interest in television – far from being a pioneering dramatist in the medium, she positively disliked it – all of these qualities in the script make the piece perfectly suited to presentation as a television studio drama. It seems likely that it was Sullivan himself who identified and promoted this opportunity, thereby securing himself a place in history as television's first Poirot.

A 1949 letter from Edmund Cork to Christie's American agent, Harold Ober, provides an interesting postscript to the *Wasp's Nest* affair. 'The Mallowans have just gone off to Baghdad for five months, and Agatha has left me with her power of Attorney and instructions not to trouble her about any business matter!' says Cork, before going on to discuss the issue of an American offer for Poirot television rights. He advises Ober against accepting the deal due to problems that Christie was experiencing with the American tax authorities, and also because 'television is so much in its infancy that there is the danger that rights may be disposed of now for trifling royalties that would otherwise be extremely valuable in the future – I believe many mistakes were made in the early days of movies.'[4]

This remarkably prescient advice undoubtedly paved the way for more lucrative deals in the future and is an insight into the dilemmas faced by those responsible at the time for licensing intellectual property rights in the 'new media' of radio, film and television; not dissimilar to the challenges currently faced by those licensing work for use on the similarly unknown quantity of the internet. There had also been an enquiry about Sullivan reprising *The Wasp's Nest* on television in the USA. Cork continues:

I think, however, I ought to explain the personal background. Francis Sullivan is a close friend of the author of many years standing, and The Wasp's Nest, which was originally a short story written in 1928, was dramatised for Sullivan to appear in at a charity matinee in 1932. He has always regarded the play as more or less his, although in point of fact he has no rights in it, and the author received the fee when it was televised by the BBC in 1937. Sullivan, like many successful actors, is a most temperamental person, and makes the most of his personal standing with Agatha whenever we have had to refuse him his own way. He is certainly making a lot of excitement over this proposed production . . . and while I do not want to influence you in any way, it might make life momentarily simpler if Larry Sullivan got his way!

I shall leave it to television historians to establish whether the production actually took place, as we return to the world of theatre, but I do rather like Cork's frank appraisal of Francis L. Sullivan, who was widely known as 'Larry' (though the 'L' in his name actually stood for 'Loftus').

The next full-length play based on Christie's work to receive a West End production was *Love From a Stranger*, which opened at the New Theatre on 31 March 1936 for a relatively successful run of 149 performances, and was purportedly adapted by Frank Vosper from her short story 'Philomel Cottage'.

The story itself was first published in the *Grand Magazine* in November 1924, and was included in the collection *The Listerdale Mystery* ten years later. It is the gripping and dramatic tale of a woman who unexpectedly inherits a sizeable sum of money, effectively liberating her to reject her uninspiring and prevaricating suitor in favour of an alliance with a man who she has just met and about whose background she knows nothing. They settle in the country, in apparently blissful surroundings, but her new husband turns out to be a notorious wife murderer and she, it appears, is intended to be his next victim. In an astonishingly tense final scene she manages to outwit him and turn the tables by herself pretending to be a killer. The short story picks up the narrative at the point where they have moved into Philomel Cottage and are apparently living in wedded bliss. The two-hander denouement and country cottage location are echoed in one of Christie's four scripts for radio, 1948's *Butter In a Lordly Dish*; and the mythical serial wife murderer Bluebeard, who featured in one of Agatha's youthful dramatic enterprises, would again be the inspiration for a villain in her 1954 radio script *Personal Call*. As for the story's premise, the excitement of striking up a relationship with a stranger is a sensation that was not unfamiliar to Christie herself; in her autobiography she observes, 'Archie and I were poles apart in our reactions to things. I think that from the start that fascinated us. It is the old excitement of "the stranger".'[5] As Christie herself well knew, however, there can be a price to pay for such adventuring. In 1924, when the story was published, she was still living with Archie at Sunningdale and, I believe, about to write the play *The Lie*.

'Philomel Cottage' is an intense and engaging psychological thriller, a battle of wills between two people which examines the extremes to which the power of suggestion can be pushed. There is (technically) no murder and there is no detective to pull focus. The setting is straightforward, there are two central characters and a minimal supporting dramatis personae, and there are echoes of Grand Guignol in its construction. It is, in short, ideal for dramatic adaptation. Which is why Agatha Christie chose to adapt it herself, as her fifth full-length stage play.

The Agatha Christie archive contains two copies of a script called 'The Stranger', a three-act play 'by Agatha Christie' which carries a typist's stamp dated 10 March 1932, two years before the short story was to appear in the collection *The Listerdale Mystery* and three years before Frank Vosper was licensed by Hughes Massie to create his own adaptation. Not that he did.

Vosper, who was nine years younger than Christie, was already an established and popular stage and screen actor and playwright by the time he became involved with the project. He had started his career immediately after the First World War, doing tours of military camps for Basil Dean, and in 1926 scored a hit in the role of Joe Varwell in Eden and Adelaide Phillpotts' *Yellow Sands* at the Theatre Royal, Haymarket. As a playwright he was known for writing pieces in which he could cast himself in the lead, notably *Murder on the Second Floor* and *People Like Us* (both 1929) and *Marry at Leisure* (1931). *Murder on the Second Floor* had been a particular success, playing for over 300 performances in London, with Vosper taking the central role of playwright Hugh Bromilow, although when the production transferred to New York with an English cast, Laurence Olivier took over the role. Vosper was an amateur criminologist (he listed his interests in *Who's Who in the Theatre* as 'criminology and blackberrying'), so it was hardly surprising that he found Christie's psychological study of a serial killer intriguing. Here was a perfect subject for him as a playwright, and one in which he could assay the leading role of a charismatic and attractive villain.

What has been overlooked is that Vosper's source material for the play that he eventually called *Love From a Stranger* was not in fact Christie's short story, but her own unpublished, unperformed full-length play based upon it. Although the script of *Love From a Stranger*, like the advertising for it at the time, credited the piece as being 'by Frank Vosper, based on a story by Agatha Christie', there has always been some disagreement amongst commentators as to whether Christie herself contributed to Vosper's adaptation. The version submitted to the Lord Chamberlain's office, although it carries Vosper's address, clearly states 'by Agatha Christie and Frank Vosper', and Vosper's *Times* obituary categorises the play as a 'collaboration' with Christie.[6] Gwen Taylor, intriguingly, writes that Christie was 'helped by Frank Vosper' to adapt the story into a play.[7] But Charles Osborne, who is usually a reliable source on the plays, states categorically, and entirely wrongly, that 'Other writers on Agatha Christie have described the play as having been adapted jointly by Christie and Vosper. This is incorrect: it was the work of Frank Vosper alone, and the credit for its shape and dialogue must be entirely his.'[8]

Nothing could, in fact, be further from the truth. Hughes Massie's summary of the adaptation licence issued to Vosper on 1 February 1935 clearly shows that his play is to be based on both 'The Stranger' and 'Philomel Cottage', with Christie's own dramatisation listed first.[9] The entire dramatic structure of Vosper's piece, which interpolates additional scenes prior to the starting point of the short story before leading to the same terrifying denouement, is in fact the uncredited work of Agatha Christie, playwright.

In fact, Christie's is arguably the better play. Her adaptation is fast-moving, witty and suspenseful, a neat six-hander with three acts of one scene each. Vosper increases the dramatis personae to eight, and divides each act into two scenes. It becomes a long-winded affair in which the leading male role has clearly been built up as a star vehicle for himself, to the detriment of that of the female protagonist, with whose predicament we engage more fully in Christie's own version. Most significantly, the conceit of two independent young women giving up their London flat following a sweepstake win, and the eponymous 'stranger' turning up to look round it as a prospective tenant, as well as the entire 'love from a stranger' motif, are all absent from the short story and are intrinsic to Christie's play. In the short story's own back-story, our heroine simply inherits her windfall and meets the stranger at a friend's party.

It doesn't help in establishing the facts that Christie's own memory on the subject was unreliable. In 1968 she wrote thus to a Californian student who had requested information about her plays for his thesis: 'Love from a Stranger was originally a short story written by me called Philomel Cottage. I re-wrote this as a one act play, Love from a Stranger, and agreed to Frank Vosper extending it into a three act play. The two first acts being his, and the third act being principally the one act play as I had written it.'[10] Although this is incorrect in its detail, it clearly establishes that she was the first to adapt the story as a play and that Vosper used her own playscript as his source material. Whilst the early sections of Vosper's play clearly owe their structure to Christie's adaptation, it is indeed in the final act where the textual similarities are most striking. Here is an extract from Christie's *The Stranger*:

GERALD: All the trouble women get, they usually deserve. They've no sense – absolutely no sense.

ENID: I expect that's true sometimes.

GERALD: Born fools, the little angels! (Kisses the tips of his fingers) Woman's weakness is man's opportunity. Did Shakespeare say that or did I think of it myself? I believe I thought of it. If so, it's good, it's damned good!

ENID: Have some more port? . . .

GERALD: I'm a remarkable man. I'm – well – different to other men.

ENID: Yes, I think you are.

GERALD: I've a lot of power over women for instance. I've always had it. I discovered quite young that I could twist women round my little finger. It's like a useful gift. Boyish – that's the note they like. Makes them feel maternal. The eternal boy – it fetches every time.[11]

And the corresponding section in Vosper's *Love From a Stranger*:

BRUCE: You're a sensible girl, aren't you?

CECILY: How do you mean?

BRUCE: You don't 'go on' at a man. Very few women can say 'Oh, all right,' and leave it at that . . . But, then, most women are fools. (He smiles to himself)

CECILY: (trying to be conversational) Do you think so?

BRUCE: I don't think, I know – born fools! . . .

CECILY: Perhaps you're right.

BRUCE: And women's weakness is man's opportunity. Did someone write that, or did I think of it myself? – If I did it's good, damn good! 'Women's weakness is man's opportunity.'

CECILY: You have extraordinary insight into things. Have some more coffee.

BRUCE: Please . . . Yes, you're right, I have great insight. I've a lot of power over women. I discovered quite early in life that I could twist women round my little finger. It's a useful gift.

CECILY: It must be.

BRUCE: Boyish – that's the note they like – makes them feel sort of maternal . . . It gets them every time . . .[12]

The characters, as it happens, get through three names each, from their first appearance in the story to Vosper's script via Christie's. The original story's female protagonist, Alix Martin, becomes Enid Bradshaw in Christie's play and Cecily Harrington in Vosper's. The abandoned suitor, who, in another echo of Christie's own experience, becomes an abandoned fiancé in both her dramatisation and Vosper's, similarly morphs from Dick Windyford to Dick Lane to Nigel Lawrence, and the story's murderous husband, Gerald Martin, becomes Gerald Strange and eventually Bruce Lovell. Enid's female friend Doris West, a character introduced in Christie's play, becomes Cecily's friend Mavis Wilson in Vosper's. Christie's script keeps the cast to an absolute minimum: Enid Bradshaw, Doris, the two men in Enid's life and a pessimistic but highly entertaining housekeeper in each of her London and country properties. The two house-keepers, Mrs Huggins and Mrs Birch, each outdo the other in their condemnation of the male sex, and are particularly sorely missed in Vosper's script, which clumsily introduces a gardener from the original story, and adds a maid, a doctor and an unnecessary comic aunt to the cast list.

Mrs Huggins is clearly cast from the same mould as Stevens in *Eugenia and Eugenics*:

MAVIS: According to you Mrs Huggins, married life is a continuous battle.

MRS HUGGINS: And so it is, Miss. With one party always defeated. And what I say is this – take care as you're the winning party from the start!

She goes on to sing to herself, 'tunelessly' and prophetically, 'It brings you but trouble and danger to listen to Love from a stranger', thereby giving Vosper the title of his version of the play. When Enid arrives at Philomel Cottage, the idyll is somewhat undermined by the presence of Mrs Birch, who 'has none of Mrs Huggins' cheerful pessimism' and who has discovered that her own husband is a bigamist.

Since the Hughes Massie correspondence archives relating to Christie's work do not commence until 1940, quite how or why Christie handed over her script and the credit for it to Vosper, not to mention 50 per cent of the theatrical royalty and film rights income, is unclear. One can imagine, though, that he may have been approached about playing the role of Strange and made his own authorship a condition of his involvement. Like Laughton and Sullivan before him, Vosper evidently saw Christie's work as a vehicle for advancing his own career, and in engaging with it as such inadvertently conspired to delay and compromise the arrival of an interesting new female playwriting voice.

Vosper's option gave him a year to write the piece and get it produced in the West End but, as he neared completion of the script, an unexpected problem arose. Thirty-six-year-old actor/writer Vosper was a friend of thirty-year-old actor/writer Emlyn Williams, who tells the extraordinary story in his autobiography of being invited to dinner at Vosper's house late in 1935:

One night we were at Frank Vosper's house in St John's Wood. I liked him more and more, for his generous character and for the sensitive talent under the buffoonery. He mentioned that he was in the middle of writing a new play. I mentioned that I was too and he asked me how mine was getting on . . .

'What's yours about, or aren't you telling?

'Oh, it's another murder play . . .'

He looked at me. 'Really? So's mine.'

'Oh, really?'

'Based on an Agatha Christie short story.' That sounded safe.

'A detective play like *Alibi*?'

'Oh no, not a mystery. I've turned it round so I could base it on the Patrick Mahon case.'

I stared at him. He went on. 'D'you remember it? He cut the woman up and no-one would believe it, he was such a charmer.'

I had to say something. 'Mine's about a charmer too, who cuts up a woman.'

It was his turn to stare. 'Is there a girl who falls for him?'

'Yes.'

'What are you calling yours?'

I told him.

'Good title. Mine's *Love From a Stranger*.'

That was a good title too. They were interchangeable. Then he said, 'Are you by any chance writing a part for yourself?'

'Yes.'

'So am I. Who d'you have in mind for the girl's part?'

'A star if possible,' I said, 'emotional but with restraint. Edna Best, for instance.'

'I've just written asking her if she'll read my play when it's finished.'

Another silence. Then he beamed and added, 'Just as well we like each other. We need a drink.'[13]

And so started the astonishing parallel histories of Emlyn Williams' breakthrough play, *Night Must Fall*, and Vosper's Christie adaptation. Perhaps as a result of this conversation, Vosper appears not to have pursued the Patrick Mahon angle. Mahon was a killer notorious for having dismembered his victim in a gruesome 1924 murder case, and although this aspect of the murder in question adds a dramatic *frisson* to *Night Must Fall*, it would have been an unnecessary embellishment to Christie's work. Nonetheless, from their beginnings in Scotland to their eventual Broadway presentations, the two plays continued to dog each other's progress.

That both writers should have been in pursuit of Edna Best to play the female lead in their plays was not surprising. Best had been the talk of the town ten years previously when she appeared alongside Noël Coward (replaced soon after

Agatha the actress, as Sister Anne in *The Blue Beard of Unhappiness*.

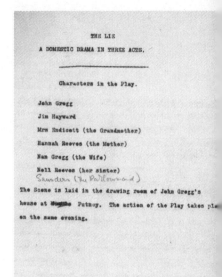

THE LIE

A DOMESTIC DRAMA IN THREE ACTS.

Characters in the Play.

John Gregg

Jim Hayward

Mrs Endicott (the Grandmother)

Hannah Reeves (the Mother)

Nan Gregg (the Wife)

Nell Reeves (her sister)

Saunders (the Parlourmaid)

The Scene is laid in the drawing room of John Gregg's house at Putney. The action of the Play takes place on the same evening.

Top left: Agatha and Archie.

Top right: Script page from *The Lie*.

Bottom left: Bertie Meyer.

Bottom right: Agatha's sister, Madge.

Top: ReandeaN: Alec Rea (left) and Basil Dean (right).

Bottom: Poirot on stage. Charles Laughton (left) in *Alibi* (1928) and Francis L. Sullivan (right) in *Peril at End House* (1940).

Top left: Advertisement for *Chimneys* in the Embassy Theatre programme for *Britannia of Billingsgate* (1931).

Top right: Francis L Sullivan with Christie stage directors Douglas A. Clarke-Smith and Wallace Douglas in the 1937 television performance of *The Wasp's Nest*.

Bottom left: Writer and actor Frank Vosper.

Bottom right: Script page from Agatha Christie's *The Stranger*.

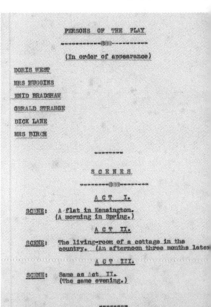

opening by John Gielgud) in Margaret Kennedy's *The Constant Nymph*, produced, directed and co-adapted from Kennedy's novel of adolescent sexuality by Basil Dean. She had previously been part of the regular ReandeaN ensemble, playing Meggie Albanesi's twin sister in *Lilies of the Field* in 1923. 'Two of the most popular young actresses of the day', according to Dean, although Best, he observed, was 'always true to the limitation of her own talent'.[14] The fact that in 1935 she chose Vosper's play rather than Williams' may have had something to do with the fact that they had worked together the previous year in Alfred Hitchcock's *The Man Who Knew Too Much*. But although Vosper had secured his leading lady of choice, he himself was not in the cast when the production's pre-West End tour opened in the spring of 1935. On 17 March the *Observer* had announced that 'Miss Edna Best and Mr Frank Vosper are to appear together in *Love From a Stranger* by Mr Vosper and Miss Agatha Christie', but on 7 April it carried the news that 'Mr Frank Vosper has given up the leading man's part in his play, written in collaboration with Miss Agatha Christie, *Love From a Stranger*. The two chief parts will be played by Mr Basil Sydney and Miss Edna Best.' The way that Christie's contribution to the script is acknowledged in these reports is notable; she is credited as joint author of the play rather than simply the writer of a story from which it is adapted. It is unclear what led to this very late change of plan on Vosper's part; it may be that his instincts told him that the script needed more work and that he felt he could better fulfil his role as writer from a position in the stalls. Basil Sydney, his substitute, was a British film and stage actor who had spent much of his career on Broadway.

The licensing records for *Love From a Stranger* in the Hughes Massie ledgers are incomplete, but in April 1935 *The Stage* announced that 'Hugh Beaumont, of the firm of Moss Empires and Howard & Wyndham Tours Ltd, is busily engaged upon three new productions. One is "Love From A Stranger" by Frank Vosper and Agatha Christie.'[15] There is also reference in the files to correspondence with 'H M Tennent';[16] Harry Tennent, along with Beaumont, had set up Moss Empires and Howard & Wyndham Tours Ltd in 1933 to provide touring productions for the theatre-owning chains that were later to form a cornerstone of the notorious cartel that became known as 'the Group'. And so it was that Hugh 'Binkie' Beaumont, of whom we will hear a great deal more, became one of the first producers of plays from the work of Agatha Christie, although one suspects that twenty-six-year-old Beaumont may have been more attracted by Vosper's charms than by Christie's talent.

According to Williams, 'the Stage announced that "Emlyn Williams' new thriller *Night Must Fall* will open on 29 April at the King's Theatre, Edinburgh. On the same evening, Frank Vosper's new thriller *Love From a Stranger* will open at the King's Glasgow." For one bemused moment I thought the two plays were opening not only on the same night, but in the same theatre.'[17] *Love from a Stranger* actually premiered at the Theatre Royal Birmingham the previous week, but both plays were well received in Scotland, and Vosper's cast, and Scottish director Campbell Gullan, were praised by critics. Although Vosper himself did not appear, his sister Margery played the role of the feisty maid Edith and, intriguingly, the dramatis personae included a ninth character, a female role listed simply as 'A Stranger', who appears in no versions of the script other than that for this first tour.[18]

'Whichever play got to London first would kill the other, and nothing to be done about it,' concluded Williams. It seemed to him for a moment that both productions might be competing for a potential West End slot at the Duchess Theatre but, following a short tour, Vosper and Beaumont decided that Vosper should spend some time on rewrites and should re-rehearse the production with himself in the leading role, as had originally been intended. J.B. Priestley was running the Duchess independently of the big theatre-owning cartels at the time, and *Night Must Fall* opened there on 31 May 1935, running for 436 performances before transferring to London's Cambridge Theatre where it ran for a further 205. The production was Williams' first big success as a playwright.

On Sunday 2 February 1936, the revamped version of *Love From a Stranger* was presented for one performance at Wyndham's Theatre, with Vosper taking the role of Bruce Lovell and his sister Margery demoted to assistant stage manager. The new production was directed by Murray MacDonald and, in the absence of Edna Best, who was presumably no longer available, the role of Cecily was played by Marie Ney, who had appeared alongside Best in *The Constant Nymph*. At this time it was common practice to present one-off performances of new plays on Sundays in West End theatres in the hope of securing them a future life. In *The Stage*'s review of this presentation by one of the 'Sunday societies', the 1930 Players, it commented, 'in the desirable event of the play being put into an evening bill it should be played by the same cast . . . the play, effectively produced [i.e. directed] by Murray Macdonald, was enthusiastically received by an audience which included many well-known theatrical folk.'[19] This showcase performance had the desired effect: nine days later, Moss Empires and Howard & Wyndham Tours Ltd took up the West End option, opening it at one of their parent company's own theatres, the New in St Martin's Lane, on 31 March 1936.

The production was very well reviewed. Ivor Brown in the *Observer* remarked that 'this play soon sails away into those profusions of homicidal mania and sadistic frenzy which are the cordials and sweetmeats of this curious age.' He felt that Vosper's performance maybe gave the game away too soon: 'it is unwise to make us so early certain that Lovell is fully qualified for the chairmanship of the United Society of Operative Homicides and Dirty Workers. Or else he should declare himself straight away, as the author-actor of "Night Must Fall" has done.' But he was full of praise for the 'authentic and tremendous suspense about the struggle between Bruce and his captive wife', admiring Vosper's 'very clever performance, a first rate study of disintegration', and Marie Ney's 'charming and persuasive picture of the fluttering and rather foolish young woman . . . with a very powerful grip on the second half of her part, when the amorous lady becomes the Amazon and fiercely fights for her life with wit and grit, since tooth and claw are of no avail.'[20]

The Times reserved its praise primarily for the final scene, the acting of which 'could scarcely be bettered', although it observed that the 'whole play is an elaborate approach' to this moment.[21] Muriel Aked made the most of the gratuitous comedy role of Auntie Loo-Loo and the *Daily Herald*, *Daily Telegraph* and *Daily Mail* were prominent in the general chorus of approval. The production moved to the Queen's Theatre (the owners of which later became major share-holders in H.M. Tennent Ltd) and played for a total of 149 performances; a respectable run, but significantly less successful than *Alibi*. A month after it opened in the West End, members of the cast could be heard performing live extracts from *Love From a Stranger* on BBC Radio's Regional Programme.

Sadly Vosper, like Laughton before him, could not resist the lure of Broadway. On 21 September 1936, he led an American cast, including Jessie Royce Landis (later a Hitchcock regular) as Cecily, in a new production at the Erlanger Theatre, Philadelphia, produced by former press agent Alex Yokel, who had recently enjoyed a huge hit as a producer with *Three Men On a Horse*. The Broadway production of *Love From a Stranger* was directed by British former actress Auriol Lee, who had been successful as the director of a number of West End productions, recently and most notably a three-year run of Merton Hodge's *The Wind and the Rain*, co-produced by Alec Rea and Moss Empires and Howard & Wyndham Tours Ltd. On 29 September, *Love From a Stranger* starring Frank Vosper opened at Broadway's Fulton Theatre. The previous night, *Night Must Fall* starring Emlyn Williams had opened at the Ethel Barrymore Theatre.

Critics were, understandably, bemused by this sudden influx

of British psychopaths. The *Daily News* commented:

> I don't know how you feel about murder plays, but if you are interested in collecting this season's crop then you may have both of these for all of me. I shall not be using either of them again . . .
>
> Frank Vosper is both author and star of *Love From A Stranger*, which he took from a story by Agatha Christie. Like young Mr Williams of *Night Must Fall* he rather fancies himself, I gather, in roles of violent contrast and psychological significance . . .
>
> It might be wiser in the future to import only the last acts of English murder-melodramas; in fact to import the last acts of three such murder-melodramas simultaneously and then, after rewriting them enough to provide a slight continuity, produce them all on one evening as parts of the same thriller.[22]

Vosper had chosen Christie's work as the vehicle for his Broadway acting debut and, like Laughton and Sullivan, was relentless in his self-promotion. The title page of the playbill is clear that this is 'A new play by Frank Vosper from a story by Agatha Christie', with his own name in significantly larger type than hers; and the playbill's text notes:

> Frank Vosper adapted *Love From a Stranger* from an Agatha Christie story as a result of his interest in criminology, a hobby that has long occupied his off-stage moments. He created his present role in the successful production of the drama in London, where he is one of the ranking stage and screen favourites. The account of Mr Vosper's writing and acting activities takes up two and a half columns in *Who's Who in the Theatre*. A remarkable feat, considering he is still in his thirties. He has played in Shaw, Shakespeare, Pirandello at the Haymarket and Old Vic, and countless British movies.[23]

The *New York Times*, however, felt that 'Mr Vosper has taken this tale from one of Agatha Christie's stories, and has spun it out to dangerous length . . . as the leading player Mr Vosper gives the part the works. His interpretation of Bluebeard is a head-holding, shoulder-straightening, partly ranting person instead of a cool and calm characterization that would have seemed more dangerous.'[24]

The *New York Evening Journal* concurred: 'Mr Actor Vosper is in fact almost as disastrous as Mr Author Vosper . . . until he gets to the aforementioned last act. Until that horror-ridden business he and his fellow players work pretty hard over a play that is so flagrantly inert that I half expected the actors to resort to sticking pins in it. Or, anyway, into the audience.'[25]

The aforementioned inertia is entirely the result of Vosper's own unnecessary embellishments of Christie's original script. Christie's piece is anything but overblown. It is economical in the extreme, and wastes no time in getting to its deadly point. This is perhaps why she herself remembered it as a one-act play, although she had in fact provided two neatly and wittily executed opening acts. She in any case claimed the denouement as being largely her own work, and it was this element of the play that won critical approval and, in the Grand Guignol tradition, allegedly saw audience members fainting on both sides of the Atlantic.

Love From a Stranger closed at the Fulton after only twenty-nine performances, and Christie's name had now been associated with two Broadway flops, neither of her own making. It can have been little consolation to Vosper that *Night Must Fall* only ran for sixty-four; his Broadway acting debut had been an ignominious failure.

Four months later, under the headline 'Actor Missing from Liner', *The Times* ran the story that

Mr Frank Vosper, the stage and film actor and author, was missing from the French liner *Paris* when she arrived at Plymouth on Saturday from New York. It is believed that Mr

Vosper, who was 37, was lost overboard. He was one of several present at an 'end of voyage party' in the cabin of Miss Muriel Oxford, aged 22, who won the title 'Miss Europe' in 1935, in a beauty contest, and had been undergoing film tests in Hollywood . . . there is no question of a love affair between herself and Mr Vosper.'[26]

There certainly was 'no question' of such an affair. Vosper's lover, the twenty-three-year-old actor Peter Willes, later to be a TV producer and friend of Joe Orton and Kenneth Halliwell, was also at the party.

Vosper was short-sighted and may have been drinking, but the location of the porthole he appears to have fallen through in relation to the cabin balcony on which he had apparently been standing alone, seemed to rule out an accident, leading to speculation that he had taken his own life. It seems unlikely that any interaction at the party between Willes and Oxford would have triggered this, but one wonders how the slightly inebriated star, having just made a humiliating exit from Broadway, might have responded to the news of Hollywood's apparent interest in the ebullient young beauty queen. The press went to town on the story, skirting around the issue of Vosper and Willes' relationship (homosexuality was not decriminalised in England until 1967), but, after the body was washed up near Eastbourne with one leg and a quantity of cash missing, the coroner returned an open verdict. And so shall we.

Unusually, Collins themselves published *Love From a Stranger* in both hardback and paperback in 1936, while Samuel French issued their standard 'acting' edition for amateurs and repertory companies – with both of which it enjoyed enormous popularity – the following year. In 1937 Basil Rathbone played Gerald Lovell in the first film version of *Love From a Stranger* and in 1938 Edna Best reprised the role of Cecily on television, playing opposite Bernard Lee.

Christie's original version of the play appears never to have been performed although, intriguingly, a script called *L'Inconnu*, with her credited as sole writer, was registered with the French

Society of Dramatic Authors in 1935, two months before the UK premiere of Vosper's version. It was translated by popular French actor Pierre Palau for presentation at the *Théâtre Des Deux Masques* in Paris, but it is unclear whether the production actually took place.[27] In a strange postscript, playwright Louise Page wrote yet another stage adaptation of the story in 2010, which was performed at the Mill at Sonning Theatre under the title of Vosper's version. Perhaps the people who licensed it were unaware of the two copies of 'The Stranger by Agatha Christie' held in the Agatha Christie archive. As her first exercise in expanding a short story for the stage rather than, as had been the case with *Chimneys*, compressing a novel, it is arguably the best constructed of the five full-length plays that she had written by 1932. Under the circumstances, a third adaptation seems somewhat surplus to requirements.

Christie followed the same model of expanding a short story for what I believe to have been her next full-length script, although like so many of her writings it is, frustratingly, undated. *The Mysterious Mr Quin* is a collection of short stories published in 1930, having originally appeared in magazines throughout the previous decade, which centre on the enigmatic Harley Quin. Quin's brief and almost spiritual interventions enable his more corporeal friend, Mr Satterthwaite, to resolve a number of problems and mysteries. Although the setting of the stories is contemporary, the elusive protagonist is inspired by the mythical Harlequin figure which featured in Agatha's family's china cabinet and in her script *A Masque from Italy*. Amongst the stories is 'The Dead Harlequin', first published in the American magazine *Detective Fiction Weekly* in 1929, although neither Quin nor Satterthwaite is technically a detective. The play *Someone at the Window* expands at length upon the plot of 'The Dead Harlequin' but abandons the characters of both Mr Quin and Satterthwaite.

This is the first of many instances where Christie's dramatisations of her previously published work exclude what appears to be the pivotal character. Following *Black Coffee*, she never wrote another full-length play featuring Poirot, and her four stage adaptations of novels in which he appears exclude him completely. Similarly, following Superintendent Battle's appearance in *Chimneys*, she cut the role when next adapting a work in which he featured, and although it seems that Christie was not averse to the idea of Miss Marple on stage, she herself never wrote a Marple play. In the case of Harley Quin, the very act of physicalising the character would have undermined his spiritual essence. In 1928 there had been a poorly executed film based on one of the stories, and one can well imagine that her worst nightmare would have been the image of Francis L. Sullivan lumbering around a stage in a Harlequin costume.

The Agatha Christie archive holds two loose-leaf draft copies of the script of *Someone at the Window*; one, which is a duplicate of the other, contains a small number of handwritten amendments. There is also a bound final version which appears to be professionally typed, although there is no agency date stamp in evidence. The address of Lawn Road Flats in Belsize Park, where Christie lived in the early 1940s, has been handwritten on the cover, and another name and address has been heavily crossed out. On close examination, it is that of L.E. Berman, who sold the licence for *Black Coffee* to the Embassy Theatre, and seems effectively to have been Christie's play agent at this time.

The play is a 175-page epic, and is Christie's first theatrical experiment with the themes of time and memory, later to be explored more fully in 1960's *Go Back for Murder*. An intriguing two-hander prologue is set in a first class railway carriage in January 1934, following which there is a two-act flashback to 'the big hall at Carnforth Castle' in 1919 (very deliberately post-war), and a third-act return to June 1934 in London. In this context, it is a not unreasonable assumption that 1934 is the year of writing, although we should not rule out that it takes place in the past or indeed, being Agatha Christie, in an imaginative leap to the future.

In the opening scene, the two characters who meet in the railway carriage disagree about the potential healing qualities of time:

FRANK: . . . Time gives you a new angle of vision – the true angle.

SYLVIA: I see what you mean.

FRANK: Doesn't it help you?

SYLVIA: No, in my case facts were facts.

FRANK: You're looking at it as it appeared then. I want you to look at it now.

SYLVIA: Nothing can help me but forgetfulness.

FRANK: You can't forget to order. You can thrust a thing down out of sight – but it's there still – growing in the dark.[28]

On a lighter note the artist Frank, who is endearingly described as 'a big simple looking likeable young man – rather like a friendly dog that hopes it is welcome but is not quite sure about it', regrets the passing of the Victorian age: 'I'd love to have lived in the days of good old Victorian melodrama with the heroine turned out into the snow, and a thorough-paced villain with a black moustache. It must have been fun. They did have fun – the Victorians. They had something we haven't got nowadays – gusto – enjoyment of life.'

The play is brimming with witty banter and social commentary about inter-war Britain, courtesy largely of a pair of society *grandes dames* who we meet when we go back in time to Carnforth Castle. Mrs Quantock, who is married to a colonel, and her friend Lady Emily, delight in making candid observations about relations between the sexes:

MRS QUANTOCK: My experience of life has taught me that you can trust nothing and no one. Always expect the worst and you'll be surprised how often you're right . . . Take Arthur now – in the regiment he was considered a perfect martinet – but if any woman were to come to him with a hard luck story – why he'd be as soft as butter. He's much too soft-hearted.

LADY EMILY: It is a good thing he has you to look after him.

MRS QUANTOCK: It takes a woman to see through women.

Men say 'Poor little woman, all the others are so down on her.'

The bitter governess, here in conversation with the seventeen-year-old lady of the house, is similarly cynical on the subject:

MISS GREY: You've been living in a fairy tale all your life. (She speaks with real bitterness) You've been sheltered and protected. You've gone about believing fine things about men and women. Now your eyes are opened and you can see what life is really like. Ugly – ugly. It's everyone for himself and the devil take the hindermost. Love a man and believe in him – he'll let you down every time. You've got to use the whip. Treat him like dirt, trample on him, don't ever let him think he's got you. Life's a dirty business – a sordid ugly business. You can't afford to play fair if you want to win. It's cheat or go under – down into darkness . . .

SYLVIA: Don't – don't . . . I feel as though you were thrusting me into a prison – away from the sun and the air.

MISS GREY: Not at all. I'm introducing you to real life.

The final, two-scene act brings us back to 1934 and is set in an art gallery and at the house of an art collector, the locations of the short story. Art is a major theme of the piece, and Christie's observations on the art world are perceptive and informed. It was the impresario C.B. Cochran who nurtured her own interest in art in her late teens, after a childhood being dragged reluctantly around galleries: 'Charles Cochran had a great love of painting. When I first saw his Degas picture of ballet girls it stirred something in me that I had not known existed.'[29] In the following extract, Mrs Quantock and Lady Emily gossip about life as they inspect an exhibition of modern paintings. I include it for no other reason than that it is a wonderfully well-written and witty piece of theatrical dialogue and, as nobody has ever seen it performed on a stage, it seems a shame not to share it . . .

MRS QUANTOCK: I hope Arthur won't keep us waiting. I'm surprised he's not here. There's one thing to be said for military men – they do know the meaning of punctuality. These young people are past anything . . . No manners . . . No consideration for others. They come down to breakfast at all times of the morning.

LADY EMILY: And the girls' nails! Too terrible! Just like blood!

MRS QUANTOCK: (inspecting a picture severely through a lorgnette) 'The Cafe Beauvier'. All these modern pictures are exactly alike.

LADY EMILY: What I say is, there is so much that is depressing in the world. Why paint it? These very peculiar looking men and women sitting at curious angles – where is there any *beauty*? That's what I want to know.

MRS QUANTOCK: You heard about the Logans' butler?

LADY EMILY: Yes, most distressing. Why, they trusted the man completely. (Consults catalogue) 'Meadow in Dorset'. What a very *odd* looking cow. They came back unexpectedly, I suppose?

MRS QUANTOCK: Yes, and found his wife and six children occupying the best bedroom, and the wife wearing one of Mary Logan's tea gowns.

LADY EMILY: No!

MRS QUANTOCK: A fact I assure you. 'Spring in Provence'. Nonsense – not in the least like it. I've been to Provence.

LADY EMILY: What people *suffer* through their servants.

MRS QUANTOCK: Did I tell you about the housemaid that came to see me? Quite a nice respectable looking young woman. She asked me how many there were in family and if there were any young gentlemen. I said there was the general and myself and our two young nephews. And do you know what she had the impertinence to say?

LADY EMILY: No, dear.

MRS QUANTOCK: She said. Very well, I'll come on Tuesday. But seeing there are young gentlemen, I'll have a bolt on my bedroom door, please. I said, you'll have no such thing for you won't have a bedroom in *my* house. The impudence of the girl.

LADY EMILY: 'La Nuit Blanche'. Dear, dear the bed looks very comfortable. Mrs. Lewis has had to get rid of her nurse. The woman simply wouldn't allow her to come into her own nursery. Said she had entire charge and wouldn't brook interference. Interference from the child's own mother!

MRS QUANTOCK: Amy Lewis is a fool – always was. Look how she's mismanaged that husband of hers.

LADY EMILY: He behaved very badly.

MRS QUANTOCK: I've no patience with women whose husbands behave badly. It's a woman's job to see that a man behaves properly. Do you think I would have stood any nonsense from Arthur?

LADY EMILY: But, we can't all be like you, Maud. You've such a force of character.

MRS QUANTOCK: Men have got to be looked after. Left to himself a man always behaves badly. It's only natural.

LADY EMILY: Everything seems very odd nowadays. Midge tells me that young people – people of different sexes – can go away and stay at hotels and positively *nothing happens*.

MRS QUANTOCK: I can well believe it. This generation has no virility.

LADY EMILY: It seems so unnatural.

MRS QUANTOCK: Of course it's unnatural. Why, when I was a girl, if I had gone away for a week-end with a young man – Not that my parents would have permitted it for a minute – I repeat *if* I had gone away with a young man – everything would have happened.

(Examines wall)

This young man can't paint a horse. I expect he lives in a nasty unhealthy studio and never goes into the country.

LADY EMILY: I expect you're right, dear. That cow over there was most peculiar. I couldn't even be sure if it was a cow or a bull.

MRS QUANTOCK: People shouldn't try and paint nature when they know nothing about it. 'The Dead Harlequin'. Very confusing – all these squares and diamonds. Nobody studies composition nowadays. There should be proper grouping in a picture – light and shade.

LADY EMILY: How right you are, Maud. I was very artistic as a girl. I used to do flower painting when I was at school in Paris.

MRS QUANTOCK: You sang, too, Emily.

LADY EMILY: Oh, I only had a very small voice.

MRS QUANTOCK: Nobody sings nowadays. They turn on that atrocious wireless. Even expect you to play Bridge with some annoying American voice wailing about Bloo-oos, or else a dreadful lecture on pond life – or some nonsense about Geneva.

LADY EMILY: What do you think about the League of Nations?

MRS QUANTOCK: What every sensible person thinks. (looks at catalogue) 'Three Women'. H'm. I suppose you *could* call them women at a pinch.

LADY EMILY: Their faces seem to have been squeezed sideways and they've got no tops to their heads. Even an artist can't think women look like that.

(Enter MIDGE . . . a charming young woman with great assurance of manner.)

MIDGE: Hullo, darlings. Fancy finding you here. (looks at picture) Oo-er, scrumptious. That's amusing. I say, the man can paint, can't he?

LADY EMILY: They're all so ugly.

MIDGE: Ugly? Oh, no, they're not. They're marvellous. Do you think that rather attractive-looking man is the artist?

MRS QUANTOCK: Very likely. He looks very odd.

MIDGE: I thought he looked rather nice. So alive. Like his pictures.

LADY EMILY: Do you call these women alive?

MIDGE: I know. One looks at these pictures and one says no

women were ever like that and then one goes out into the
street and one suddenly sees people that remind one of
the pictures.

MRS QUANTOCK: I don't.

Thank you for indulging me with that lengthy quotation; I hope
that you found it as entertaining as I do.

Someone at the Window is a theatrically ambitious piece
with a colourful sixteen-person dramatis personae, and as
such would not have been immediately attractive to repertory
theatres of the time. It is, sadly, let down slightly by the
clumsy staging of the murder at a fancy dress ball and a
rather contrived and rushed ending. The murderers plot and
carry out their plan in front of the audience; this is not a
whodunit, but a 'will-they-get-away with it'. Plodding police
investigations undertaken in the middle of the play by
Inspector Rice and Sergeant Dwyer only serve to slow down
the action. They conclude, as the murderers intended, that
the victim committed suicide as a result of shellshock
sustained in the First World War, but the murderers' plan to
inherit a fortune goes unexpectedly askew when the victim's
young wife gives birth to an heir after his death.

There is no reference to *Someone at the Window* in Christie's
autobiography, in her correspondence or in the licensing
records of Hughes Massie, although her notebooks do contain
some work in progress. The final script appears to be 'performance ready', but was never submitted to the Lord
Chamberlain's office, and neither does there appear to be any
record of it having been tried out by one of the club theatres,
where the audience had to sign up as members and which
therefore did not require a licence. Unlike other unperformed
work of hers, she appears not to have returned to it, reworked
it or lobbied for its production. She perhaps appreciated that
its dramatic construction rendered it unattractively cumbersome as a production proposition. With its loss, sadly, we have
in my opinion been deprived of some of her best dialogue for
the stage.

One work which Christie did return to was the similarly lengthy *Akhnaton*, her remarkable historical drama about the idealistic pharaoh, father of Tutankhamun. Akhnaton, who dreams of 'a kingdom where people dwell in peace and brotherhood' and spends much of his time composing poetry, attempts to promote a pacifist philosophy and to unite the polytheist Egyptians under one god; policies which inevitably do not go down well with either the army or the priesthood. The action of the play takes place over seventeen years, moving from Thebes to Akhnaton's purpose-built Utopia, the City of the Horizon, and involves a cast of twenty-two named roles, including an Ethiopian dwarf, not to mention scribes, soldiers and other extras, as well as a spectacular parade featuring 'wild animals in cages' and 'beautiful nearly nude girls'.

Christie commentators tend to be united in their praise for the piece; including even biographer Laura Thompson, who is generally dismissive of her work for the theatre. In the absence of a response from critics, Charles Osborne sums it up well: '*Akhnaton* is, in fact, a fascinating play. It deals in a complex way with a number of issues: with the difference between superstition and reverence; the danger of rash iconoclasm, the value of the arts, the nature of love, the conflicts set up by the concept of loyalty, and the tragedy apparently inherent in the inevitability of change. Yet *Akhnaton* is no didactic tract, but a drama of ruthless logic and theatrical power, its characters sharply delineated, its arguments humanized and convincingly set forth.'[30]

The play, eventually published in 1973 and not performed in Agatha's lifetime, is usually dated as having been written in 1937. The earliest surviving copy is clearly stamped by the Marshall's typing agency as having been completed on 12 August of that year, and the ancient Egyptian subject matter certainly makes sense in the context of her involvement with the archaeological community since her marriage to Max Mallowan. In introductory material written for its publication, Christie refers to the date of its writing as 1937,[31] although thirty-six years later she may well simply have been using the date on the typescript's cover as an *aide memoire*.

Mallowan himself touches briefly but perceptively on a small number of Agatha's plays in a chapter towards the end of his autobiographical *Mallowan's Memoirs*, published in 1977, a year after her death. *Akhnaton*, he says, is

> Agatha's most beautiful and profound play . . . brilliant in its delineation of character, tense with drama . . . The play moves around the person of the idealist king, a religious fanatic, obsessed with the love of truth and beauty, hopelessly impractical, doomed to suffering and martyrdom, but intense in faith and never disillusioned in spite of the shattering of all his dreams . . . In no other play by Agatha has there been, in my opinion, so sharp a delineation of the characters; every one of whom is portrayed in depth and set off as a foil, one against the other . . . the characters themselves are here submitted to exceptionally penetrating analytical treatment, because they are not merely subservient to the denouement of a murder plot, but each one is a prime agent in the development of a real historical drama.[32]

Mallowan appreciates the play's classical dramatic construction – 'the play moves to its finale like an Aeschylean drama' – and, like other commentators on the piece, notes its contemporary relevance: 'Egypt between 1375 and 1358 BC is but a reflection of the world today, a recurrent and eternal tragedy'. He does, however, appreciate why theatrical producers might hesitate. 'Good judges of the theatre have deemed it beautiful, but would-be promoters are daunted by the frightening thought of an expensive setting and a large cast.'

Max introduced Agatha to Howard Carter at Luxor in 1931, describing the man who discovered Tutankhamun's tomb in 1922 as 'a sardonic and entertaining character with whom we used to play bridge at the Winter Palace hotel', and also to his friend Stephen Glanville, another leading Egyptologist who later became Provost of King's College Cambridge and who Max claims offered Agatha guidance relating to source material for her historical drama. However, although Agatha's new-found archaeological connections were understandably instrumental in the realisation of the script for *Akhnaton* that we now know, there are some ambiguities about the play's inception that indicate that it may have had an earlier existence. In her autobiography, Agatha credits Glanville at some length for his assistance with the 1944 novel *Death Comes as the End*, which is set in ancient Egypt, but not with having helped her with *Akhnaton*. This may, of course, simply be because the play had not been published when she finished writing her autobiography, and she did not want to confuse readers with detail about its creation. She refers to it only twice, on the first occasion noting that 'I also wrote a historical play about Akhnaton. I liked it enormously. John Gielgud was later kind enough to write to me. He said it had interesting points, but was far too expensive to produce and had not enough humour. I had not connected humour with Akhnaton, but I saw that I was wrong. Egypt was just as full of humour as anywhere else – so was life at any time or place – and tragedy had its humour too.'[33]

Despite the notoriously inaccurate chronology of Agatha's autobiography, not least when it comes to her plays, one thing it tends to be very clear on is which part of her life she spent with Archie and which with Max. Her first mention of *Akhnaton* occurs very much in the former section of the book, in a sequence where she is recounting her activities after returning from the Grand Tour in 1922 and before her divorce. Immediately before this she mentions 'the play about incest' (i.e. *The Lie*) and there is no link with her second husband or his archaeological interests. To me, this indicates that she is placing the origins of *Akhnaton* in the pre-Max era of the mid-1920s. Agatha was of course no stranger to Egypt prior to meeting Max and his friends, having spent some time in Cairo with her mother as a seventeen-year-old, although one suspects that she was more interested in potential suitors than mummified Pharoahs during this particular visit. She notes that Gielgud wrote to her 'later', and this handwritten letter, dated simply 'Friday evening', was doubtless in response to the version of the script that was typed up in 1937 and which may well by then have benefited from Stephen Glanville's input; Gielgud writes from an address in St John's Wood which he occupied between 1935 and 1938. Gielgud felt that *Akhnaton* requires 'a terrific production in a big theatre with a great deal of pageantry. Personally I think it would have a great deal better chance of success if it was simplified and so made possible to do in a smaller way.'[34]

Agatha was a great admirer of Gielgud, but although he appeared in various screen adaptations of her work (and the novel *Sleeping Murder* even involves a visit to one of his stage performances), they never met and he never appeared in one of her plays. Gielgud later became both personally and professionally linked with the H.M. Tennent theatrical empire, and would have been unlikely to put his name to a production by Peter Saunders, Christie's producer at the height of her playwriting career. Max invited him to speak at Agatha's memorial service, but he was unable to do so.

As well as its dating, there is a further mystery surrounding the script that Gielgud was responding to. In 1926 Thornton Butterworth published a verse play called *Akhnaton* by Adelaide Phillpotts, the daughter of Agatha's mentor Eden Phillpotts. There are striking similarities between Adelaide Phillpotts' play and Christie's, over and above the fact that they clearly share source material.

The story of Adelaide Phillpotts is a fascinating one, and would easily fill a book in its own right. An accomplished writer, and the author of forty-two novels, plays and books of poetry, her autobiography, *Reverie*, was published in 1981 when she was eighty-five, under her married name Adelaide Ross. It tells of her childhood in Torquay, where attending the local theatre was a highlight, her early naïve attempts at playwriting, finishing school in Paris, her adventures in London as a young woman where she became an admirer of Lilian Baylis' Shakepeare productions at the Old Vic, and her various playwriting collaborations with her father, particularly the 1926 success *Yellow Sands*. It also makes reference, without recrimination, to the incestuous attentions that her father paid her from an early age, and to the oppressive closeness of both their personal and professional lives, until she finally married, despite his protestations, at the age of fifty-five. After which he never spoke to her again. 'As to Father,' concludes Adelaide simply, 'he should be judged, as he wished, and it must be favourably, by his works.'[35]

Writing of her life in London in 1925, Adelaide says, 'I spent several hours in the British Museum Reading-room, where I procured books, recommended by Arthur Weigall, concerning the life and times of Pharaoh Akhnaton, about whom Father had urged me to write a blank verse play – a splendid theme which I had promised to attempt.'[36] Weigall was an Egyptologist and theatre set designer who in 1910 had authored the book *The Life and Times of Akhnaton, Pharoah of Egypt*. Publisher Thornton Butterworth's *Times* advertisement for a 'new and revised edition' in 1922 trumpeted, '"the world's first idealist" . . . "the most remarkable figure in the history of the world" . . . such are some of the praises given to the young Pharaoh of over 3,000 years ago whose strange and pathetic story is here told by the distinguished Egyptologist, Mr Weigall'.[37] The author was part of a team that he believed had discovered the mummified remains of Akhnaton, although from my necessarily brief dip into Egyptology it appears that correctly identifying and dating ancient Egyptian remains is a challenge equal only to that of establishing a chronology for the work of Agatha Christie. I suspect that Weigall's archaic and occasionally melodramatic prose style may have influenced that adopted by Agatha in writing her own play.

Like Agatha's play, Adelaide's was never performed, but it was well reviewed in the February 1927 edition of *The Bookman*:

Some thirty-three hundred years separate the periods of *Akhnaton* and *Yellow Sands*. Yet two characters are common to each play – the Pharoah of the one and the socialist of the other. During the war they would have been described – and derided – as Pacifists; in these less disruptive days they may be accepted as idealists . . . This has not been written to gratify historical or archaeological curiosity, but to display the character and difficulties of a ruler who dared to place himself in opposition to the powerful priestly and military castes of his period. Akhnaton is seen in conflict with all types, from the father he succeeded to the scullions of his kitchen, and in every varied circumstance his character is depicted with unfailing consistency and ever-growing charm. But it is not merely on her interpretation of Akhnaton that Miss Phillpotts is to be congratulated; her sketches of the general Horemheb, of the aggressive sculptor Bek, and of the subtle and wavering High Priest are also drawn with a firm hand. And many of her episodes have a high dramatic quality, which culminates in a scene of great tensity in the tomb of Akhnaton fifteen years after his death. What theatrical producer will enrich the intellectual and moral life of the nation by an adequate performance of this remarkable play?

Eden Phillpotts was delighted by his daughter's play. He wrote to her from Torquay, 'My darling dear, I love to have the dedication of the Akhnaton and am very proud to think that you dedicated it to me. It will be my most cherished possession after your dear self and I shall value it beyond measure,'[38] and, 'I gave Mrs Shaw Akhnaton and she was very pleased with the gift and I hope will tell me what she thought of it.'[39]

Adelaide's and Agatha's plays, of course, share much the same cast list of historical characters and both use as their ultimate source material translations of the Armana letters, a remarkable collection of around three hundred ancient Egyptian diplomatic letters, carved on tablets and discovered by locals in the late 1880s. Whilst Adelaide meticulously credits her sources, however, Agatha does not; so it is difficult to tell where they end and her own invention begins. Adelaide's play is written in accomplished blank verse and Agatha's in a sort of poetic prose that makes it completely different in style from any of her other writing. Whilst Adelaide's is arguably the more accomplished literary work, Agatha's is definitely the more satisfactory as a piece of drama, with more developed intrigue and conflict amongst the courtiers, the dramatic licence of the introduction of the then newsworthy character of Tutankhamun (played as a young adult rather than the child that he would then have been) and, for good measure, a climactic poisoning and suicide (although there is no mystery as to how or why).

Amongst the striking parallels between the plays are the use of Akhnaton's coffin inscription as his death speech. In Adelaide's version,

> I breathe the sweet breath of thy mouth,
> And I behold thy beauty every day . . .
> Oh call my name unto eternity
> And it shall never fail (Akhnaton falls back dying)[40]

And in Agatha's,

> I breathe the sweet breath which comes from thy mouth . . .
> Call upon my name to all eternity and it shall never fail (he dies)[41]

Immediately after this, both plays feature an epilogue set in Akhnaton's tomb, in which people are erasing Akhnaton's name and someone gives a speech. In Adelaide's version,

> . . . A ghost with Amon's dread wrath upon thy head –
> eternally forgotten by God and man.
>
> (Priests, raising their torches) Amen! Amen! Amen!

And in Agatha's,

. . . So let this criminal be forgotten and let him disappear
from the memory of men . . . (a murmur of assent goes up
from the People)

There is a scene in Adelaide's version where a sequence of
messengers read out letters bringing news of military calamity
from the far reaches of the empire. In Agatha's version of what
is effectively the same scene, there are no messengers but
Akhnaton's general Horemheb reads out the letters himself. In
both cases, the readings are interrupted by a comment from
Horemheb. In Adelaide's version,

> My lord, troops disembarked at Simyra
> And Byblos, could be quickly marched to Tunip

In Agatha's,

> My lord, it is not too late, Byblos and Simyra are still loyal.
> We can disembark troops at these ports, march inland to
> Tunip.

Again, the source material (credited by Adelaide but not by
Agatha) is clearly the same, so the similarities in the phraseology are less remarkable than the dramatic construction of
an intervention by Horemheb with these words. But perhaps
even more notable are some similarities in stage directions.
Adelaide: 'The high priest . . . with shaven head, wearing a
linen gown . . .'; Agatha: 'The high priest . . . his head is
closely shaven and he wears a linen robe . . .'
So, what to make of all this? On one level it may appear
that in writing *Akhnaton* Christie simply 'did a Vosper' on the
work of her mentor's daughter. But when Christie's own play
finally saw the light of day in 1973, Adelaide was still very
much alive (she died, aged ninety-seven, in 1993); and Christie
is unlikely to have allowed its publication in the knowledge
that she had consciously borrowed from another living writer's
work. It has to be said, too, that each writer puts her own very

distinctive touches into the story. Adelaide includes the characters of Akhnaton's and Queen Nefertiti's two daughters, who some historians believe he took as additional wives, with the following exchange between father and daughter as one of them is married off to a young prince:

> AKHNATON . . . I think thou art still a child?
> MERYTATON: A woman, my lord.
> AKHNATON: Then art thou willing to be wed?
> MERYTATON: No sire,
>   If husband gained mean father lost. But, yes,
>   If I may keep them both

Christie, on the other hand, explores in some detail the relationship between the artistic, poetry-reciting Akhnaton and his muscular general, Horemheb. One wonders what the Lord Chamberlain's office would have made of this exchange between the two men:

> AKHNATON: (after looking at him a minute) I like you, Horemheb . . . (Pause) I love you. You have a true simple heart without evil in it. You believe what you have been brought up to believe. You are like a tree. (Touches his arm) How strong your arm is. (Looks affectionately at Horemheb) How firm you stand. Yes, like a tree. And I – I am blown upon by every wind of Heaven. (wildly) Who am I? What am I? (sees Horemheb staring) I see, good Horemheb, that you think I am mad!
> HOREMHEB: (embarrassed) No, indeed, Highness. I realize that you have great thoughts – too difficult for me to understand.

As it happens, Adelaide's was not the first verse play on the subject by a female writer. In 1920 *The Wisdom of Akhnaton* by A.E. Grantham (Alexandra Ethelreda von Herder) had been published by The Bodley Head, the company that in the same year gave Christie her publishing debut. Grantham's introduction cites the Amura tablets as her source and advocates the relevance of Akhnaton's philosophy:

> There was no room for greed or hate and war in this conception of man's destiny; no occasion for those ugly and gratuitous rivalries which make human history such a never-ending tragedy . . . never has mankind stood in direr need of a real faith in the indestructability and the supreme beauty of this great Pharaoh's ideals of light and loveliness in life . . . the episode chosen for dramatisation is the conflict between the claims of peace and war and Akhnaton's successful struggle to make his people acquiesce in his policy of peace.[42]

The Bodley Head's *Times* advertisement for Grantham's *The Wisdom of Akhnaton* read, 'A remarkable play about Akhnaton, the father of Tutankhamen, and the Pharoah who tried to establish the pure monotheistic religion of Aton and a religion of Love and Peace thirteen hundred years before Christ . . . this is one of the few works of fiction ever written about the Egypt of those days, which are now being made to live again so vividly by Lord Carnarvon's discoveries.'[43]

Despite covering approximately the same period of history and including several of the same characters, however, there are no echoes of Grantham's work in either Adelaide's or Agatha's, a fact which only serves to highlight further the similarities between those of Eden Phillpotts' two protégées. Whilst Grantham chooses to halt the story at the point where Akhnaton has been 'successful in his struggle to make his people acquiesce in a policy of peace', both Adelaide and Agatha go on to show Akhnaton's ultimately tragic failure. In doing so they are not, in my view, opposed to the value of striving for Akhnaton's aspirations, even against all the odds and in the face of human nature.

During the First World War, Adelaide had worked for Charles Ogden's *Cambridge Magazine*, which controversially gave a balanced view of events by publishing throughout the conflict translated versions of foreign press articles, as well as pieces by writers such as Shaw and Arnold Bennett. By the early 1920s, newspapers were full of reports of the latest archaeological finds in Egypt, and Egyptologists were front page celebrities as they continued to unveil the 'secrets of the tombs'. Western writers and intellectuals were intrigued by the lessons that could be learned from this ancient culture, particularly in a world still reeling from the devastation of war, and it is little wonder that the Phillpotts circle found the pacifist philosophy of Akhnaton in particular worth exploring, and that at least two female playwrights, A.E. Grantham and Adelaide Phillpotts, thought him a worthy subject for a verse play.

It thus seems plausible that Agatha's autobiography could well be correct in appearing to date the origins of her own Akhnaton play to the mid-1920s, and that it may have been, at least initially, the product of this post-war zeitgeist and her association with Eden Phillpotts rather than her more specific interest in archaeology in the 1930s. It may even be that it was Phillpotts himself who suggested the idea to Agatha, just as he had to his daughter. Even if one dismisses the similarities between Agatha's Akhnaton play and Adelaide's as pure coincidence, there seems to me to be a Phillpotts stamp on the project that is hard to ignore.

In a further twist to the tale, in 1934 Adelaide Phillpotts and her friend and writing partner Jan Stewart wrote a three-act murder mystery play, which was performed in repertory at Northampton. It was called *The Wasps' Nest*.[44] Like Christie's at that time unperformed 1932 one-act play of the same title, it revolves around the destruction of a wasp's nest in a country house and the murderous application of the cyanide used to achieve this. Although the outcome is entirely different, it contains some remarkably similar plot devices to Christie's story, and shares a storyline about a woman returning to her previous lover having abandoned him in favour of another man.

Did Agatha read Adelaide's 1926 Akhnaton play? Did

Adelaide read Agatha's 1928 'Wasp's Nest' short story in the *Daily Mail*? We do know that Agatha and Adelaide exchanged some affectionate correspondence in the late 1960s, in which the two old ladies charmingly reminisced about their Torquay childhoods and shared news of family and friends.[45] There is no mention at all of matters Egyptian. Or of wasps.

Another long-term playwriting project of Christie's was the compelling domestic drama, *A Daughter's a Daughter*, which she wrote in the 1930s but which was not to receive its premiere until 1956. Taking its title from the saying, 'Your son's a son till he gets a wife, but a daughter's a daughter all your life', it concerns the friction between a widow, Anne Prentice, and her adult daughter, Sarah, as each in turn contrives to destroy the other's opportunities to find fulfilment in love. As with *The Lie* and *The Stranger*, we see a young woman torn between a dull but reliable suitor and the excitement of a potentially more dangerous liaison.

In the third week of March 1939, a letter from Bernard Merivale, Edmund Cork's business partner at Hughes Massie, landed on the desk of Basil Dean.

Dear Basil Dean,

I would be very glad if you would read the enclosed play by Agatha Christie.

The play has nothing whatever to do with Poirot or crime solution. It impresses me as being another manifestation of this author's undoubted genius.

I would be very interested to know your reaction.[46]

Dean appears to have responded positively although, sadly, his side of the correspondence is in the missing early years of Hughes Massie's Christie archive. Merivale acknowledged his 'interesting letter' about the play, and on 5 April Agatha sent Dean a handwritten note from Sheffield Terrace:

Dear Mr Dean,

I should be so pleased if you could lunch here on Wednesday 12th 1.15. I should be most interested to hear your ideas about A Daughter's a Daughter.

Yours sincerely,

Agatha Christie[47]

There is no record of what took place at this lunch, although it seems that Dean suggested various alterations to the script. The sudden death of Merivale interrupted the correspondence, and put the matter into the hands of Cork, who wrote to Dean in late May:

We really ought to have written to you regarding the Agatha Christie play . . . I am afraid the insistent demand for her literary work has prevented Mrs Christie from doing any work on A Daughter's A Daughter, and there doesn't seem any prospect of her being able to get down to possible alterations in the immediate future, but perhaps I may come and see you about it on your return from America.[48]

It is interesting that Hughes Massie should have approached Basil Dean about this project rather than his former business partner, Alec Rea, who had produced *Black Coffee*. But as well as being a producer, Dean had a track record of successfully directing work by women playwrights, including Clemence Dane and Margaret Kennedy, both of whose playwriting careers he had effectively launched. And although Rea had co-produced *The Claimant* with Dean, it was Dean, as director, with whom Agatha's sister had had the working relationship. Madge had invited Dean to lunch as recently as 1937,[49] although there is no indication as to how he responded to this suggestion, or as to what Madge's agenda was in making it. She had possibly hoped to interest him in an updated version of *Oranges and Lemons*, for which there are some handwritten notes on the script; Junius adds the air force to the army and navy in summarising the list of 'essential' government expenditures, and 'Bolshevists' are now described as 'Communists'.[50]

The move to Dean, then, was a logical one for Agatha, and was vindicated when, undeterred by her own lassitude, he appeared to be on the brink of pulling an extraordinary piece of potential casting out of the bag. In June 1939 Cork wrote to Dean, 'The pressure of her literary work made it difficult for Agatha Christie to get down to the alterations in A Daughter's a Daughter, but your exciting news about Miss Lawrence's interest enabled us to persuade her to do so, and I have great pleasure in sending you the revised script herewith. I shall look forward keenly to developments.'[51]

Gertrude Lawrence had become the talk of the town for her 1936 partnership with Noël Coward in his *Tonight at 8.30* playlets, and her interest in the role of Ann Prentice certainly had the desired effect. The revised script cleverly specified Ann's age as thirty-nine, as against Lawrence's forty-one, and in her covering letter to Dean Christie wrote,

> I return the play. I have completely rewritten the third act, following the scene order you suggested and I really do think it is a great improvement . . . I still feel that Sarah's rudeness ought to arise spontaneously – like a jealous and undisciplined child, and that any deliberate 'trick' on her part does make her an 'unpleasant character' which she should not be. However, it may seem different when played.
>
> I think I'm by now quite incapable of doing any more to it – so if you feel it needs further alterations, I suggest you do them and tell me what you have done!'[52]

This last suggestion is not as extraordinary as it seems. Dean's input on Margaret Kennedy's stage version of her novel *The Constant Nymph* had, after all, been sufficiently substantial to earn him a co-writing credit.

Although Christie had used the pen name Mary Westmacott for her non-crime novels *Giant's Bread* (1930) and the semi-autobiographical *Unfinished Portrait* (1934), there was at this stage, as we can see from the wide frame of reference of her dramatic work, no indication that the name Agatha Christie, as a playwright, was necessarily going to be associated exclusively with the crime genre. Indeed, the Christie archive's copies of the 1930s version of *A Daughter's a Daughter* state clearly that it is 'by Agatha Christie'. And so it was that, in mid-August 1939, Agatha Christie seemed poised to have her passionate, witty and cleverly constructed drama about the conflict between mother and daughter presented in the West End. Undoubtedly her finest work for the stage, and compared by surprised critics to the work of Rattigan at its eventual West End premiere thirty-three years after her death, it was to have been produced and directed by the man who launched the playwriting careers of Clemence Dane and Margaret Kennedy and seems likely to have starred one of the most popular actresses of the day. Within three weeks, though, Britain had declared war on Germany, and the story of Agatha Christie, playwright, was to take a very different turn.

The next we hear about *A Daughter's a Daughter* is in a letter from Cork to Christie in January 1942: 'I was on to Basil Dean the other day about A Daughter's a Daughter and he asks me to tell you that he still hopes to be able to do the play, but that all his plans have been disorganised by E.N.S.A. What he asks now is that we give him another month in which to make a definite proposal.'[53]

Dean's passionate commitment to his work as the co-founder of the Entertainments National Service Association, which provided entertainment of all varieties to British troops during the war, is well documented, not least by himself in his very readable 1956 book *The Theatre at War*. Although Cork, in correspondence with Agatha, still appeared to be holding out some hope of achieving a production of *A Daughter's a Daughter* as late as 1943, it was not to be, and the play would not be heard of again until the 1950s.

A Daughter's a Daughter was not the only Christie theatrical project to be interrupted by the war. In July 1938 Agatha had entered into an agreement with Arnold Ridley, another Hughes Massie client, allowing him to adapt her 1932 Poirot novel *Peril at End House* for the stage.[54] Hughes Massie's records refer to the licence granted to Ridley as a 'collaboration agreement',[55] a description which might more correctly have been applied to that granted to Frank Vosper; it is clear though that in this instance Christie was the 'author' and Ridley the 'adaptor'. At this stage it was agreed that royalty income was to be split 50/50, although Hughes Massie would later take half of Ridley's share, possibly as a result of some sort of 'buy-out'. A month later, Francis L. Sullivan's company, Eleven Twenty Three Ltd, paid an advance against royalties of £100 to commission a script from Ridley for delivery by the end of September.[56] Given the promptness of Sullivan's arrival on the scene, it seems likely that he had been involved in the deal from the outset. In any event, whoever's idea it was, a Ridley adaptation of a Christie novel with Sullivan as Poirot certainly had commercial potential.

Ridley was, on the face of it, an ideal adaptor for Christie. He had begun his career as an actor, joining Birmingham Rep after the First World War, in which he was wounded at the Somme. He continued to act in plays and films, and occasionally to direct for the stage, once his playwriting career took off with the enormously successful 1925 melodrama, *The Ghost Train*. The original production of *The Ghost Train* played 655 performances and, having opened at the St Martin's, transferred to three further West End theatres. It is perhaps ironic that this enormously busy and successful playwright and actor, who fought in both world wars and was awarded an OBE for service to theatre, is best remembered for his role as Private Godfrey in the television comedy series *Dad's Army*.

The script for *Peril at End House* was duly delivered, and on 23 November Sullivan paid a further £100 advance against royalties (of between 5 and 10 per cent on different levels of box office income) for an option to produce the play which, if exercised, would also have given him the American rights and a one-third share in any film sale.

The credited producer, however, when the play was eventually staged in 1940, was Ellen Terry's nephew, the film director Herbert Mason.[57] Although he had worked as a stage manager, Mason had no track record of presenting West End productions and I suspect that he may have been something of a front man in order for Sullivan to avoid appearing to be self-producing his return to the stage in the role of Poirot. There may also, of course, have been some hope of a film deal arising from the production; as was standard practice, the film rights in the book and play were 'indissolubly merged'. Mason may well have been a director of Eleven Twenty Three Ltd but, in common with many other theatrical production companies of this era, its company records no longer exist. In any event, the engagement of Charles Landstone as general manager for the production indicates that the nominal producer may not himself have been actively at the helm. Landstone was more than a safe pair of hands, and in 1942 was to become Assistant Drama Director of the Council for the Encouragement of Music and the Arts (CEMA), the wartime precursor to the Arts Council. His book *Off-Stage: A Personal Record of the First Twelve Years of State Sponsored Drama in Great Britain*, offers an interesting counterpoint to Basil Dean's book about the work of ENSA.

In January 1940, Cork wrote to Agatha, 'We will pay your membership dues to the Dramatists Guild. Their organisation has a "closed shop" in America and managers cannot make a contract with any dramatist who is not a member. I have no doubt we shall ultimately have a production of *Peril at End House*. I understand Francis Sullivan's present plan is to take it out in the country about the end of March and to bring it into town towards the end of his option period, which expires in May.'[58]

Cork was not wrong. On 7 March he wrote:

I was talking to Francis Sullivan this morning. I find he has completed all his arrangements for the Richmond production of *Peril at End House* on April 1st. It is a little unusual that he shouldn't have consulted anybody about them, but he seems to be within his legal rights. I don't know very much

about any of the people that he has got, but he seems to be
satisfied that they will give a very good show, and of course
if he should happen to be wrong about any of them then
they can be changed before the play comes to the West End.
AR Whatmore is to produce [i.e. direct] – I don't think he is
at all bad, although once again he is not very well known.

Everyone was delighted that you will be able to attend
some of the rehearsals. The play is to be read over next
Wednesday and obviously rehearsals start on the following
Monday, but Sullivan is getting in touch with you himself
about the arrangements.[59]

As artistic head of the Embassy during Alec Rea's tenure, A.R.
Whatmore had been instrumental in the West End transfer of
Black Coffee nine years previously. Sullivan's wife, Danae
Gaylen, was one of a number of female stage designers coming
to prominence at this time, and she was put in charge of the
production's design.

Peril at End House opened at Richmond and, following a
short tour, on 1 May in the West End, at the independently
owned Vaudeville Theatre. Despite the play's somewhat cumbersome three-act, seven-scene construction, reviews were encouraging, both at Richmond and in the West End, and it was
generally felt that the suspense was sustained, although Sullivan
inevitably stole the limelight once again. The *Daily Telegraph*'s
review, headed 'FRANCIS SULLIVAN AS POIROT', remarked
that 'The Belgian sleuth has been highly theatricalised and, as
impersonated by Francis Sullivan, physically he will be a slight
shock to Mrs Christie's admirers. But it is a good performance,
in which his charming conceit is admirably justified . . . The
play has been effectively produced by A.R. Whatmore.'[60]

Critics also particularly enjoyed the performances of character actor Ian Fleming (no, not *that* Ian Fleming!) as Captain
Hastings and young South African actress Olga Edwardes (later
to be known as artist Olga Davenport) in her first West End
leading role as 'Nick' Buckley.

Despite the favourable critical reception, the West End run

only lasted for twenty-three performances, and in this case there can be no mystery as to why. Ten days after it opened, German forces began the invasion by air and land of Belgium, France, the Netherlands and Luxembourg, and Prime Minister Neville Chamberlain resigned, enabling Winston Churchill to form a coalition government. Chamberlain, like Akhnaton, had paid the price of advocating a policy of appeasement. As Charles Landstone notes, 'Any further theatrical activities were interrupted by the end of the "phoney war". At the time of the German invasion of the Netherlands, I was at the Vaudeville with aspiring actor-manager, Francis Sullivan, with a new Agatha Christie play. The audience melted away, and practically the whole of London theatre closed down for the second time.'[61] Landstone clearly considered himself to be working for Sullivan rather than Herbert Mason.

A touring production of the play was licensed the following year, but Samuel French Ltd did not enter into their usual agreement for amateur and publishing rights until 1944, and publication was held back until the end of the war. Of the income generated for the writers by the deal with French's (including the usual 50 per cent of amateur licensing income), Ridley's share was payable to 'Mrs Ridley' and Hughes Massie's to 'Mrs Cork',[62] a manoeuvre that one suspects probably had less to do with husbandly devotion than with avoiding the attentions of the taxman. Unsurprisingly, the American production that Cork had anticipated did not occur.

Shortly after Ridley completed his adaptation of *Peril at End House*, Frank Vosper's sister, Margery, wrote a very straightforward, one-act, four-hander play called *Tea For Three*, based on Christie's short story 'Accident'. The story had first been published, under a different title, in the *Sunday Despatch* in 1929 and was subsequently included in Christie's collection *The Listerdale Mystery* in 1934. Following her job as assistant stage manager in the West End run of *Love From a Stranger*, Margery had gone on to work as a literary agent in the Dorothy Allen agency, which she eventually inherited, changing its name to hers at its former owner's insistence. Amongst

Margery's clients was Dorothy L. Sayers, who in 1936 had enjoyed an extraordinary West End hit with *Busman's Honeymoon*, the only stage appearance of 'gentleman detective' Lord Peter Wimsey, a play co-written with her friend Muriel St Clare Byrne and novelised the following year as the last in the Wimsey series. And with playwriting clients also including Emlyn Williams and John Osborne, the Margery Vosper agency was to become a major force in the West End. As her *Times* obituary remarked, 'Next to her family the theatre was Margery's life; a dedication largely attributable to her devotion to her famous actor brother, Frank, twelve years her senior, whose tragic death at sea in 1937, when Margery was 25, ended prematurely a brilliant career on stage and screen.'[63] Quite how or why *Tea for Three* came to be written is unclear, but it was published in 1939 in Book Two of Nelson's *Theatrecraft Plays*, a book of one-act plays by various writers, and appears to have been aimed entirely at performance in the amateur market.

The London theatrical calendar in the 1930s had been even busier than in the previous decade. Noël Coward and Gertrude Lawrence were the hot ticket in *Tonight at 8.30*, audiences were fascinated by J.B. Priestley's 'time plays', T.S. Eliot left his dramatic calling card with *Murder in the Cathedral* and, almost a decade after his successful 1929 thriller *Rope*, Patrick Hamilton followed it with *Gas Light*. Compared to now, women playwrights were relatively well represented in the West End. Clemence Dane continued to have work performed, and in 1937 A.P. Herbert's Matrimonial Causes Act finally introduced the divorce legislation anticipated by *A Bill of Divorcement* in 1921. Amongst a number of other women who saw their plays premiered in the West End at this time was Gertrude Jennings, whose 1934 success *Family Affairs* was directed by Auriol Lee, director of the Broadway production of *Love From a Stranger*. But the decade belonged to Dodie Smith, who enjoyed a succession of hits from *Autumn Crocus* in 1931 through to *Dear Octopus* in 1938. The latter, produced by the fledgling production company H.M. Tennent Ltd and starring John Gielgud, won her particular acclaim and ran for 376 performances at the Queen's Theatre. And just as Christie the novelist was to blossom as a playwright in later life, so Smith the playwright was later also to achieve success as a novelist.

Despite her own disappointments in pursuing her vocation as a playwright, the 1930s had proved a remarkably productive decade for Christie in her day job as a thriller writer. Successfully combining her writing career with accompanying her husband on his archaeological digs, she had published no fewer than seventeen mystery novels, including such classics of the genre as *The Murder at the Vicarage* (1930), *Peril at End House* (1932), *Lord Edgware Dies* (1933), *Murder on the Orient Express* (1934), *The ABC Murders* (1936), *Death on the Nile* (1937) and 1939's *Ten Little Niggers*, which under various titles was to become one of the best-selling novels of all time. It is little wonder that Cork had to explain to Basil Dean that she was rather busy. Agatha's happy marriage to Max, marred only by a miscarriage in 1932, was fulfilling and intellectually stimulating, and in October 1938, they bought Greenway, a classic Georgian house built in 1771 and set in thirty acres of woodland on the banks of the River Dart. Agatha dubbed it, with good reason, 'The most beautiful place in the world', and it was to become the Mallowans' regular summer retreat.

To some commentators, the decade that began with the Depression, saw the death of the monarch and the abdication crisis, and ended in war, was for Agatha, professionally and personally, her most fulfilling. But for Agatha Christie, playwright, it had been full of frustration and disappointment. In 1940 Christie turned fifty and, despite having penned seven full-length plays encompassing a variety of styles and subjects, had so far seen only one of them performed, and that for an interrupted West End run of just two months. Her name had, admittedly, frequently been seen by the public on theatre marquees, but most often in the context of its appropriation by egotistical showmen like Charles Laughton, Francis L. Sullivan and Frank Vosper.

The outbreak of war, which had put paid to Arnold Ridley's *Peril at End House* and to Christie's own *A Daughter's a Daughter*, was however destined to change everything. Within four years, Agatha Christie would have established herself as a celebrated West End and Broadway playwright in her own right.

SCENE FOUR

Broadway Bound

The war, inevitably, brought disruption to Agatha's life. Max secured a job at the Directorate of Allied and Foreign Liaison (part of the Intelligence branch of the RAF), working alongside his old friend, Egyptologist Stephen Glanville. The Mallowans lived at a number of London addresses in the early part of the war, including their house at Sheffield Terrace once it had been vacated by tenants, but in March 1941 Glanville introduced them to the stylishly modernist Lawn Road Flats ('the Isokon Building') in Belsize Park. Here they took up residence alongside a colourful group of emigres, artists and Soviet spies whose acquaintance doubtless broadened Christie's creative, social and political frame of reference and helped to inform her characterisations and plots in what was to be another remarkably productive period of book writing.[1] In 1942 Max volunteered to head the Cairo branch of the Directorate, where he could make use of his knowledge of Arabic, and he and Agatha were separated for the first time in ten years. In the autumn of 1943 Greenway was requisitioned by the Admiralty for use by the American navy, but Agatha was happily ensconced in Lawn Road Flats, where she dined regularly in the Isobar restaurant in the company of her intellectually stimulating new neighbours. By way of light relief, occasional weekends were spent in Haslemere at the home of Francis L. Sullivan and Danae Gaylen.

In November 1939, two months after the declaration of war,

Collins published Christie's masterful mystery *Ten Little Niggers*, which had been serialised in the *Daily Express* that summer. The deeply chilling conceit of the novel is that eight strangers are lured to the only house on an island, only to discover that their unknown and mysteriously absent host is methodically committed to executing each of his guests, as well as the two domestic staff hired for the occasion, in a manner inspired by a popular children's nursery rhyme of the time. Each of the intended victims is exposed as having escaped retribution for previous misdemeanours, so that their deaths appear to represent some sort of vengeful justice. In a delicious detail, a framed copy of the rhyme hangs on the wall, and ten figurines representing the protagonists are also on display. As one by one they meet their fate by an unseen hand, a corresponding figurine is also mysteriously dispensed with. There is no means of escape from the island, and the terrifying conundrum throughout these events is that the killer must be one of the group; as the number of survivors diminishes so too, apparently, does the number of potential suspects.

Several of Christie's books draw their titles from nursery rhymes, and I will not spoil the fun for Christie trivia buffs by providing a list. In this case the rhyme, which was at the time the subject of a garishly illustrated large-format children's book, was drawn from Frank Green's 1869 music hall song of the same title, which in its turn was based on an American song, 'Ten Little Indians', written by Septimus Winner the previous year.[2] The word 'nigger', as generally used in the UK at this time, had yet to develop the deeply pejorative overtones with which it is now associated, and to most Britons would simply have described, albeit with the inherently patronising overtones of imperialism, the apparently exotic inhabitants of some far-flung corner of the Empire.

Christie's masterpiece of suspense received excellent reviews and its highly theatrical premise made it an obvious candidate for dramatisation. Inevitably it wasn't long before Edmund Cork started to receive requests from would-be adaptors, and in January 1940 he wrote to Agatha, 'I think I told you last autumn that Reginald Simpson wanted to make a play of *Ten Little Niggers* and at that time I wasn't quite sure he was the right dramatist to do it. I would rather like to know what your general feeling about dramatising this book is, as I am sure we will have to deal with the question before long as we have both an English and an American manager interested in the idea.'[3] Simpson was a film actor and scriptwriter who had enjoyed some West End success in 1934 with a play co-written with Frank Gregory called *Living Dangerously*. Christie responded immediately, 'As regards Ten Little Niggers – if anyone is going to dramatise it, I'll have a shot at it myself first!'[4]

This was clearly the reply that Cork had been hoping for: 'I am delighted to hear that you are thinking of dramatising Ten Little Niggers yourself – generally speaking, I am all against such valuable professional time as yours being spent on anything so speculative as the drama, but Ten Little Niggers is different.'[5]

Notwithstanding Hughes Massie's support of *A Daughter's a Daughter*, Cork's reservations may go some way towards explaining Christie's lack of progress as a playwright since signing up with the agency seventeen years previously. Christie and Cork met for lunch to discuss the matter further, and Cork wrote to her afterwards, 'I would like to say thank you for one of the most heartening of lunches. I feel tremendously enthusiastic about the dramatisation of Ten Little Niggers . . .'[6]

There are no surviving scripts for *Ten Little Niggers* in the Agatha Christie archive, which is a shame, as Christie undertook substantial rewrites between the first and final drafts and it would be intriguing to be able to see how the material developed. Her wartime separation from her husband, however, means that there are letters from her to him which include details of the mounting of the production itself; and Hughes Massie's Christie archive finally connects with our story in 1940, meaning that this is the first Christie dramatic venture for which we can see a full exchange of correspondence between the playwright and her agent. At this stage in the game, though, there are still no producers' archives in evidence, so the picture we get of the creation of this important production remains frustratingly incomplete.

For Christie, with a drawer full of her own original plays, to stand aside while others adapted *The Murder of Roger Ackroyd*, *The Stranger* and *Peril at End House* (although the latter had not yet been performed) must have been deeply frustrating. As she notes in her autobiography, 'It suddenly occurred to me that if I didn't like the way other people had adapted my books, I should have a shot at adapting them *myself*. It seemed to me that the adaptations of my books to the stage failed because they stuck far too closely to the original book. A detective story is particularly unlike a play, and is so far more difficult to adapt than an ordinary book. It has such an intricate plot, and usually so many characters and false clues, that the thing is bound to become confusing and overladen. What was wanted was *simplification*.'[7] Significantly, the second of her own novels that she chose to adapt for the stage was not, strictly speaking, a detective story, and her dramatic instincts in this regard were to prove entirely correct.

The first producer to be approached was her old friend C.B. Cochran, now sixty-eight. As Christie says of the adaptation in her introduction to Peter Saunders' *The Mousetrap Man*, 'Charles Cochran who was a great friend of mine liked it and wanted to put it on, but his backers were against it. "Impossible," they said, "to have ten people dying on stage – it would just make audiences roar with laughter."'[8]

In mid-April Christie wrote to Cork, 'Maddening about Cochran. Why will they go round and listen to people? All full of enthusiasm one minute, and just as easily put off the next! I got quite a nice letter from him, but he'd obviously got doubts about it all. Oh well, build no hopes on the theatre! Am looking forward to Peril at End House if the Vaudeville isn't bombed from Norway first.'[9] A few days later, Cork replied, 'Most certainly Ten Little Niggers haven't gone down the drain. Mr Cochran still says that he is going to do it, and in any other business this, from a man in his position, would be good enough to count on. It is only because it is a theatrical deal that one feels unsure about it.'[10]

In the autumn of 1940 both the Hughes Massie offices and Agatha's London house in Sheffield Terrace experienced narrow escapes from German bombs. On 10 September Cork wrote to Agatha, 'The raid last night shook us up a bit. Contract books thrown all over the office by the explosion but everyone seems to be carrying on much as usual.'[11] And on 22 October she wrote to Cork, 'Sheffield Terrace was hit a few days after we left! . . . houses next door and opposite completely flattened – so we would have had a rude awakening had we been there!'[12] Five months later, the Mallowans would move to the relative safety of the Lawn Road Flats.

Towards the end of 1942, Bertie Meyer, who had produced *Alibi* fourteen years previously, began to express an interest in Agatha's dramatisation of *Ten Little Niggers*, but felt that changes would be necessary in order for it to go forward to production. In September Christie wrote to Cork, evidently responding to Meyer's suggestions for script changes, 'As to Ten Little Niggers I don't think I like these cheap comedy effects and silly to build up a love interest unless (quite possible) you end play by Vera and Lombard turning tables on Judge – L having been shamming dead to catch him and being really a hero who risked his life to save natives – this could be managed and would make for a good end – but *I* know how to do it . . . I do not think I want anyone messing about with my play . . . they can back it or leave it!'[13] Cork replied immediately, 'My first thought was that it would be sacrilege to alter Ten Little Niggers as you suggest, but I am coming round to thinking that you could do it – and of course if you did it would make much easier theatre. I have put the idea to Bertie Meyer, and I will let you know what transpires.'[14] Christie's willingness to make changes had the desired effect. A week later, Cork wrote to her:

> I have just had another talk with Mr Bertie Meyer regarding your play Ten Little Niggers. He and his associates are willing to enter into a contract to acquire the British stage rights . . . this is subject to certain alterations being carried out in the script, but it is agreed that you should do these yourself. One

of Mr Meyer's associates would like to discuss these alterations with you, and I had thought that this matter might be
done over lunch . . . Would you let me know if you want this
matter to go forward, and when you would care to have a
talk about the alterations?[15]

Because of the very short timeframe between Christie's original undertaking to write the script at the end of January 1940
and Cochran's rejection of it in mid-April, my original thought
was that Cochran had simply shied away from the idea of
commissioning a script from Christie. But the language in which
the involvement of both Cochran and Meyer is discussed by
Cork and Christie raises the intriguing prospect that there was
an existing script, completed by Christie in less than two months
at the beginning of 1940, in which all ten of the visitors to the
island end up dead, as they do in the novel. This speed of
delivery would not have been atypical of Christie, who is on
record as saying that three months is the ideal time in which
to write a book, but that a play should take less.[16] It seems
that Cochran and his investors turned down the script on the
basis that its original premise was dramatically unfeasible, but
that the revised ending, which was clearly Christie's own idea
and evolved out of other amendments she had been asked to
make, succeeded in bringing Meyer to the table.

The 'associate' of Bertie Meyer's who Cork is referring to
was thirty-four-year-old Barbara Toy, one of the most interesting
of the extraordinary cast of characters who Christie came into
contact with through her theatre work. Brought up in Sydney,
Australia, where her father was the editor of the *Sydney
Bulletin*, she worked in a bookshop as a teenager and later
travelled extensively with her husband, a member of the Royal
Geographical Society, before drifting apart from him and moving
to London in 1935. In an unpublished letter she later said that
'the biggest influence in my life was my father, whom I adored.
We went off on holiday together. There was a great affinity
and looking back I realise I had a real father-complex which
probably didn't help my relations with other men!'[17]

On arrival in London she made some undistinguished appearances as an actress, the first of these being at the Q Theatre in *The Good Old Days* by Eden and Adelaide Phillpotts, before becoming a stage manager at Richmond Theatre and later working at a film studio in Welwyn Garden City where she met the director Norman Lee. A popular English writer of American-style thrillers, Lee had been a script writer on Hitchcock's 1927 film of Eden Phillpotts' hugely successful play *The Farmer's Wife*. He had gone on to write a number of documentaries, mainly about London life, before turning to writing and directing comedy films. Toy and Lee collaborated, under the pen name Norman Armstrong, on a three-act 'play of the Merchant Navy', *Lifeline*, which had a run of eighty-five performances at the Duchess Theatre in 1942, produced by the independent management Linnit and Dunfee. *Lifeline* had just closed when Meyer requested that Agatha meet Toy.

At the end of the war Barbara Toy travelled to Germany and Holland to compile a report for ENSA on the state of theatre in the occupied territories. She went on to pen three further plays, all in collaboration with her friend Moie Charles, including a modestly successful adaptation of James Hilton's *Random Harvest*; but in 1950 she would suddenly embark on an extraordinary career change and reinvent herself as a globetrotting solo adventurer, travelling alone to remote corners the world in a Land Rover she named Pollyanna and writing up her exploits in a series of eight entertaining and highly readable books.

Quite what brought this extraordinary woman to the offices of Bertie Meyer in the autumn of 1942 is unclear. Her signature appears next to Meyer's in a copy of the nursery rhyme book *Ten Little Niggers* which all those involved in the production signed for Agatha, presumably as a first night gift,[18] indicating that she enjoyed considerable status within the management of the project. She appears to have had some association with a company called Farndale, which would eventually co-produce the play with Meyer and which took first position producer billing (i.e. before Meyer) in the West End programme. Farndale Pictures had been set up in 1936 with a

board of directors consisting mainly of solicitors and accountants; its name implies that it was conceived as a film production
company, but it registered as a 'Theatrical Employer' the
following year. Barbara Toy and Moie Charles replaced two
female literary agents as directors of the company for almost
a year from July 1944 (immediately after the West End run of
Ten Little Niggers), at which time they were also both directors
of Overture Theatres Ltd, which managed the repertory company
at the Connaught Theatre, Worthing. Toy and Charles were not
shareholders of Farndale, and it is not clear from the paperwork
whether their association with the company pre-dates the *Ten
Little Niggers* project or whether it came about because of it.

In any event, between signing the rights and opening Christie's
play, Farndale produced its first West End venture, Enid Bagnold's
first play, *Lottie Dundas*. If Toy was indeed a senior figure within
Farndale prior to becoming a director of the company, it is odd
that the company appears to have had no involvement in the
1942 production of her own play, *Lifeline*. At this point, though,
irrespective of her status within the production companies associated with the project, Toy's only literary qualification for giving
Christie notes on her work was the fact that she had anonymously
co-authored one modestly successful play.

Unsurprisingly, Christie appears not to have responded to
the idea of meeting Barbara Toy. A month later, Cork gave her
a nudge: 'Mr Bertie Meyer has just been talking to me again
about Ten Little Niggers. Apparently several producers [i.e.
directors] feel that the play cannot be put on as it stands, but
says that his people are convinced that it can be put right if
you will only listen to them. The present suggestion is that you
might meet Barbara Toye [sic] and Derrick de Marney some
time next week to hear their ideas. Shall I arrange such a
meeting? I think perhaps it should be held here for reasons I
will explain to you before it takes place.'[19]

Thirty-six-year-old Derrick de Marney and his brother, thirty-
three-year-old Terence, were a busy pair of actor-directors.
Terence had just appeared in Barbara Toy's play *Lifeline* and
was to play the role of Lombard in *Ten Little Niggers*, but Derrick

spent much of the war involved in documentary film projects. There is a frustrating lack of extant paperwork relating to Meyer's Christie productions, but I am assuming from the role that Derrick de Marney played in later projects that his involvement here was as an investor or even an uncredited co-producer.

Cork's suggestion that the meeting be held at the Hughes Massie office was no doubt simply a tactical ploy to establish that Christie herself was in the driving seat. It took place on 4 November 1942 and went well. The next day Agatha wrote to Max:

> Another crisis arising with Ten Little Niggers – usual talk of immediate production. I met yesterday 'under the auspices' of Cork with an eloquent girl with a Cockney accent [had Agatha perhaps mistaken an Australian accent for a Cockney one?] and an intense young man with masses of black hair to discuss the usual alterations. Their suggestions were for once sensible and in fact an improvement – the alternative 'happy ending' 'He got married and then there were none', I have always contemplated as a possibility if I can do it my own way which is agreed – well I shall believe nothing until the contract is signed![20]

Christie here refers to two different endings that were used for the nursery rhyme. The one in which the final boy 'went and hanged himself, and then there were none' leads to the novel's truly mystifying outcome, where all ten of the visitors to the island are found dead. The alternative, where the final boy 'got married, and then there were none', offers up the possibility of a 'happy' ending, and was in fact the version used in the children's book of that time. This was the ending that she now adopted for the playscript, but it necessitated a further twist in that the survivor required someone to marry; so in the event not one, but two, of the play's protagonists escape the killer's clutches. This entails one of the characters, who has apparently been shot dead, standing up and declaring the immortal line, 'Thank God women can't shoot straight.'

When the play is performed these days, and in the absence

of the first version of Christie's script, the last two pages are usually subtly edited to reinstate the far more sinister ending that Christie herself originally intended. Although she appears to have been quite happy with the revised ending, and even takes full credit for it in her autobiography, it clearly came about as the result of pressure from producers and, to a modern playgoer, undermines the carefully crafted tension that has been built up throughout the piece. For wartime Britain, though, it has to be said that the instincts of all concerned (including Christie's in readily agreeing to the alteration) were probably correct, and that the counterpoint of the upbeat and humorous ending to the horrors that preceded it was doubtless appreciated by audiences as they stepped out into war-torn London.

Agatha got down to work immediately on the script amendments, and on 20 November Cork wrote to her, 'I have just been talking to Barbara Toy on the telephone. She is delighted that you have carried out the alterations so quickly, and she is so anxious to see what you have done that she can't wait for the script to be typed. I have therefore sent it along to them as it is – they can do what retyping is necessary!'[21] A week later, Bertie Meyer invited Christie to lunch at the Savoy restaurant, and it seems that at this lunch he confirmed his intention to produce the play.

On Christmas Eve Cork wrote to Christie, 'Here is the contract for Ten Little Niggers. Would you sign and return it so that we can complete early next week? It has been tentatively fixed for Monday . . . this deal seems to be "all set" . . .'[22] On 30 December 1942, the following Wednesday, a stage licence for *Ten Little Niggers* in the territories of Great Britain, Ireland, South Africa, Australia and New Zealand was issued jointly to Bertie Alexander Meyer and Farndale Pictures Limited. A £100 advance was paid against royalties on the usual sliding scale of between 5 and 10 per cent on banded levels of box office income, with the licence to run for seven years from the date of the first performance. The producers were granted an option on the American territory and a share of amateur income, but the film rights to the book had already gone elsewhere.[23]

The play had secured its producers, and they in turn quickly moved to secure a director. On 18 February 1943 Agatha wrote to Max, 'latest news of Ten Little Nigs good. Irene Hentschel likes it and is willing to produce [i.e. direct] it – hesitated because she likes a rest in between productions – but at this critical moment her husband Ivor Brown got a boil – and anything which she produces when he has a boil is always lucky!!! Can you beat it?! Aren't theatrical people extraordinary? Tentative date April 19th – I said quickly April was my lucky month and 19 my lucky number, and that made a great impression.'[24] Agatha's affection for the quirkiness of theatrical people, and her quick-thinking bluff, paid off. The woman entrusted with the first of Christie's adaptations from one of her novels to reach the stage was one of the most successful and sought-after directors of the day. Notably, she was a regular director for H.M. Tennent Ltd, a new venture established by Harry Tennent and Hugh 'Binkie' Beaumont and now run solely by Beaumont following Tennent's death in 1941. Hentschel's recent work for the company had included highly regarded productions of Frederick Lonsdale's *On Approval* at the Aldwych Theatre and Shaw's *The Doctor's Dilemma*, starring Vivien Leigh, at the Theatre Royal, Haymarket.

A year younger than Christie, Hentschel had trained as an actress at RADA and first worked as a director at Hampstead's Everyman Theatre in 1926. According to her 1979 *Times* obituary (which, unsurprisingly, fails to mention her successful foray into the work of Agatha Christie),

for a quarter of a century she was among the most skilful and respected members of a highly specialized branch of the theatre that, when she entered it, was dominated by men . . . the 1930s was an exceedingly fruitful decade with seventeen or eighteen successes and very few failures. Priestley's *Eden End* (1934) was the first piece in which people remarked upon Irene Hentschel's loving instance on realism; nothing, in performance or décor, must be out of place. Companies liked acting for her; she was positive, friendly, and a thorough-going professional.[25]

Perhaps Hentschel's greatest claim to fame was as the first woman to direct Shakespeare at the Shakespeare Memorial Theatre in Stratford upon Avon where, in 1939, she staged a controversial production of *Twelfth Night*. Designed by the women's design team Motley, who went on to work regularly at Stratford, it featured Joyce Bland as Viola. Bland was the young actress who had caught Agatha's eye in the role of Lucia Amory in *Black Coffee* at the Embassy, and Agatha's unerring theatrical judgement also told her that Hentschel was a formidable talent.

Writing her autobiography some thirty years later, Agatha recalled:

> Irene Henschell [sic] produced [i.e. directed] the play, and did so remarkably well, I thought. I was interested to see her methods of production because they were so different from Gerald Du Maurier's. To begin with she appeared to my inexperienced eye to be fumbling, as though unsure of herself, but as I saw her technique develop I realised how sound it was. At first she, as it were, *felt* her way about the stage, *seeing* the thing, not hearing it; seeing the movements and the lighting, how the whole thing would *look*. Then, almost as an afterthought, she concentrated on the actual script. It was effective, and very impressive. The tension built up well, and her lighting, with three baby spots, of one scene where they are all sitting with candles burning as the lights have failed, worked wonderfully well.[26]

Of course, a first-rate director was able to attract a first-rate cast. Christie appreciated this, too: 'With the play also well acted, you could feel the tension growing up, the fear and the distrust that rises between one person and another; and the deaths were so contrived that never, when I have seen it, has there been any suggestion of laughter or of the whole thing being too ridiculously thrillerish.'

Although the pair only worked together once, the praise Christie heaps on Hentschel's work as a director is unparalleled. Christie recognised theatrical quality when she saw it, and her failure to mention in her autobiography some of the male directors who were later to work with her more frequently, to the considerable chagrin of at least one of them, is, I believe, calculated.

Hentschel's husband Ivor Brown, whose boil was to change the course of Christie's theatrical fortunes, was as theatre critic (and later editor) of the *Observer* one of the most influential (and, indeed, most readable) critics of the day. Professor of Drama at the Royal Society of Literature and CEMA's Director of Drama for the first two years of its existence, Oxford graduate Brown was a distinguished and provocative theatrical commentator, whose reviews of Christie's work, including that directed by his wife, are witty and insightful. Amongst his many writings was a one-act play called *Beauty Spot*, contained in the same 1939 collection as Margery Vosper's Christie adaptation *Tea For Three*. The man with the boil wrote a play called *Beauty Spot*.

As it happens 'lucky' 19 April was not to be, and Christie's scepticism about the 'immediate' production proved justified. Hentschel spent April directing J.B. Priestley's *They Came To a City*, produced by Tennent Plays Ltd (a sister company to H.M. Tennent Ltd) at the Globe, the theatre which housed the blossoming empire's offices. She then went on to direct Enid Bagnold's first play, the Farndale-produced *Lottie Dundas*, which opened at the Vaudeville Theatre on 21 July 1943. It must have been a bad year for boils for Ivor Brown.

On 23 June an excited Agatha wrote to Max, '10 Little Niggers *really* coming on – I believe Sept 6th. I wish it was later now.'[27] The rescheduled production dates had brought the opening perilously close to the anticipated birth date of Agatha's first (and, as it happened, only) grandchild, and Agatha would clearly have preferred to know that all was well with her growing family before throwing herself into her new theatrical venture. In the end, the dates were indeed pushed back, but the outcome was not to Agatha's advantage: the opening of the production's pre-West End tour at Wimbledon Theatre eventually came so close to the date the child was due that Agatha was unable to attend the performance.

Her daughter Rosalind had married Welsh Fusilier Hubert Prichard in 1941, and the absence at war of each of their husbands contributed to the anxiety of both Agatha and Rosalind. Perhaps as a result, Agatha may not have been in the best of moods when she attended the dress rehearsal of *Ten Little Niggers* on 19 September (theatrical folk don't seem to have minded working on a Sunday in those days). The next day she wrote hurriedly to Max in handwriting even less legible than usual; it is difficult to make out many of the words, but it is clear that she is less than happy. 'Dress rehearsal of 10 Little Niggers yesterday and I really was *furious*! – between Friday's rehearsal and Sunday they had altered the whole of the . . . and made it . . . idiotic . . . all down to this girl Barbara Toy – and without a word to me . . . and no shot at the right moment . . . I'm delighted not to be going to the first night tonight – shall come back end of week if all is well and see it then.'[28]

Ten Little Niggers opened at Wimbledon on 20 September 1943 and Mathew Prichard, Agatha's grandson, was born the next day. Both productions were a triumph and received excellent reviews.

On 1 October Agatha wrote to Max, 'You will have got my wire and also my letter telling of the safe arrival of Master Mathew Prichard . . . Yes, R's baby is a great relief. And Ten Little Niggers has been such a success at Wimbledon. Full houses and likely come to London in about 6 weeks – so I am pleased and happy – only nothing can take away that ache inside that is wanting you.'[29] For once, the schedule didn't change, and at the end of the month Agatha confirmed, 'It is coming on at the St James Theatre on the 17th – I went up to Oxford with the producer [i.e. director] Irene Hentschel and her husband Ivor Brown (whom you would like – very silent and devoted to Oxford . . .) and Barbara Toy – and we really had great fun.'[30] Agatha's faith in Barbara Toy seems to have been restored following the disastrous dress rehearsal; the superstitious Hentschel herself doubtless subscribed to the old theatrical adage that a bad dress rehearsal usually results in a good opening night. The Oxford day trip group of Agatha Christie, Irene Hentschel, Ivor Brown and

Barbara Toy was an interesting one indeed, and one wonders whether Agatha was fully aware of what distinguished theatrical company she was keeping in Hentschel and Brown.

It seems likely moreover that it was Hentschel who created a link between Bertie Meyer, Farndale and the third major party responsible for co-producing the project. J.B. Priestley's *They Came To a City*, directed by Hentschel in April 1943, had been co-produced with Tennents by the newly formed People's Entertainment Society (PES). This extraordinary organisation was the brainchild of East End MP Alfred John Barnes, a leading light of the co-operative movement and a founder of the Co-operative Labour Party. He was to become Minister of Transport in the post-war Attlee government, masterminding the nationalisation of the country's transport infrastructure.

The People's Entertainment Society, founded by Barnes and others in 1942, was conceived as nothing less than the theatrical production wing of the co-operative movement, and by rights should take its place in theatrical history alongside the well-documented work of CEMA and ENSA. Like most such enterprises, the PES was a stickler for constitutions, rules and regulations. The 'Rules of the People's Entertainment Society', printed by the Manchester Co-operative Press, state that the organisation's remit was to produce and co-produce plays and films and to run theatre and cinema buildings; all of which, if their annual reports and accounts are anything to go by, they went on to do with a remarkable degree of success. Their proud aspiration was that 'The business of the Society shall be conducted . . . to foster and further the art of the drama in accordance with the principle that true art, by effectively presenting and truthfully interpreting life as experienced by the majority of the people, can move the people to work for the betterment of society.'[31]

The society's Annual Report and Balance Sheet for the year ended 4 December 1943 states, 'We are associated with Farndale Pictures Ltd and B.A. Meyer in the production of Agatha Christie's play *Ten Little Niggers*. After a short successful provincial tour, this play is now running at the St James's Theatre. We have every reason to believe that it will prove to be a financial success.'[32] Sadly there are no detailed records as to the size of their investment in the production or the returns that they achieved, but the society's overall accounts appear to be buoyant, and it seems safe to assume that their investment in Agatha Christie's play got them off to a good start. The first year's trading having been conducted without a loss, and in anticipation of a successful outcome on *Ten Little Niggers*, the organisers campaigned to recruit further investors, wisely warning: 'We desire to emphasise that there is a considerable element of risk in creating an entertainment organisation governed by democratic principles and practice; consequently we would prefer numerous small investments rather than a few large ones . . . we have reasonable grounds to believe that, with widespread public support, we shall eventually make the PES a steady and profitable investment.' It was, in effect, an early experiment in theatrical 'crowdfunding'.

According to the literature accompanying a 1944 share application form, the society had a 'capital interest' in J.B. Priestley's *How Are They At Home?* at London's Apollo Theatre, and in the tours of *Ten Little Niggers* and Terence Rattigan's *Flare Path*. It had also 'been associated with' successful West End runs of *They Came to a City* and *Ten Little Niggers*, a Wigmore Hall recital by Australian soprano Austra Bourne and a provincial tour of the London Philharmonic Orchestra. The PES had also 'provided artistes, and given advice to many Co-operative Societies', purchased the Theatre Royal in Huddersfield and set up a film unit.[33] The following year it was to add to its West End repertoire *Duet for Two Hands* by Mary Hayley Bell, starring her husband John Mills and co-produced with Jack Buchanan at the Lyric Theatre. After the war it would create a 'National Theatre Club' based at the Royalty Theatre in Dean Street (Agatha's friend L.E. Berman's old stomping ground).

In the 1944 leaflet, ninety-one co-operative societies from around the country are shown as being shareholders, as well as various other affiliated groups such as the Crompton Boot Manufacturers and the Co-operative Press. The society's publicity material described its supporters as 'Individual members, democratic organisations, and those engaged in providing entertainment, being bound together for the purpose of securing the best performances under good conditions for the common people.'

The *Co-Operative News* of 2 February 1946, reporting on the Society's AGM the previous week, ran the headline 'HOPES AND CONFIDENCE IN PES HAVE BEEN JUSTIFIED' and announced that an annual honorarium of £100 to Alfred Barnes, MP, had been unanimously approved in recognition of his 'invaluable' services to the society since its foundation. Barnes had resigned from the society in 1945 upon his appointment as Minister of War Transport.

The Co-operative Society's December 1946 edition of its *London Citizen* magazine announced on its front page, 'SWITCH FROM WAR TO PEACE GOES SMOOTHLY – ERA OF SOCIAL SECURITY STARTED', and included inside a double-page article headlined 'Ringing up the Curtain. Democracy makes a hit on the stage.' The text ran:

In its mission of providing millions of people with the essentials of life, democracy has never lacked courage. The vast Co-operative movement, with its millions of capital invested in countless factories and shops, is an impregnable example of the organised strength of the little man.

It is true to say, however, that although for many years some of our first-class brains had realised that food for the mind can be as important as food for the body, no real attempt had been made to gain a footing in Shakespeare's own profession.

That was until 1942, when there was formed a body under the title the People's Entertainment Society, now familiarly and affectionately referred to as the PES.

The PES financed itself in a simple and direct way. Co-operative societies, Trade Unions and other democratic organisations were invited to take up shares in the society up to £200. These shares not only carry the usual right of democratic control, but entitle the holders to beneficial block-bookings in the Society's theatrical ventures in London and the provinces. Individuals may also take up £1 membership shares and may hold shares up to £200 and participate in any surpluses.

This was the cash side of one of the most successful efforts to break into what had hitherto been a mysterious capitalist 'closed shop' . . . Despite scepticism about the Co-op's lack of experience in this field, they went to JB Priestley, who agreed to work with them.

'Oh!' said the critics, 'Intellectual highbrow stuff, eh! That will soon cure 'em when they back a flop. JB can't turn out plays to order. He's not the type.'

So to show the complete Catholicity of their tastes and to live up to the creed plainly set out in their charter, 'To provide for the People the best entertainment *in all its most infinite variety*,' the PES associated itself with the famous detective thriller writer Agatha Christie in the presentation of Ten Little Niggers.

With her endorsement by the PES as the populist antidote to the 'highbrow' Priestley, Agatha Christie had, in a very real sense, been adopted as the people's playwright, and in *Ten Little Niggers* was to give the PES its first big commercial success, with a substantial West End run followed by an extensive national tour. By the time of its West End opening, the production had collected another co-producer, the classical music promoter Jay Pomeroy. So it was under the auspices of Farndale, Meyer, the PES and Pomeroy that it finally opened at Prince Littler's St James's Theatre on 17 November 1943. When Agatha arrived home that night she wrote to Max, 'Just back from first night of Niggers – I felt *awful* of course – It *is* an agony – but Stephen came again and was very kind and soothing and he and Rosalind pulled me through. I *do* wish you had been there.'[34]

Stephen Glanville who appears also to have seen a previous performance, had clearly enjoyed himself and wrote the next day:

Agatha darling –

Last night was really something to remember – in Vera's words, 'until I die'. The whole thing was FUN – it was lovely to watch the play without half an eye on a wilting child and be able to revel in its mounting horror without misgiving, and it was exciting to pose as a dramatic critic and compare the two performances; it was delightful to make a party with so many altogether enjoyable people, with the spice of meeting some of them for the first time. But best of all was the diverse experience of Agatha: Agatha really nervous (as she must be till the show is over) – not just shy – even in the midst of close friends; Agatha in the moment of triumph, quite radiant, but still asking only for her friends, and incredibly un-egotistical; and last, and perhaps most precious, Agatha still quietly excited, but beautifully poised and content, balanced between the success of the immediate achievement and the purpose to achieve more, and blessing the moment with the intimacy of friendship.

Bless you and thank you, my dear, for a never-to-be-forgotten night.[35]

I like this letter from her infatuated friend because it beautifully captures Agatha's excitement at her achievement; the publication of a book would never occasion such intense emotions in relation to her work. This is why Agatha loved theatre.

The critics were unanimously supportive. *The Times* remarked that 'This is not a play. It is a kind of theatrical game, with Miss Irene Hentschel pitting her wits as a producer against our natural tendency to weary of flagrant absurdity prolonging itself through three acts. She has some admirable actors at her disposal; the stage action she invents for them is unfailingly ingenious; and she wins her game very comfortably . . . the company as a whole is splendidly responsive to the producer's adroit ideas.'[36]

Ivor Brown, inevitably, felt it best to avoid such direct praise of the director in his *Observer* review, but clearly enjoyed the play a great deal more than he had *Black Coffee*:

Miss Agatha Christie does not stint on things. Like Hotspur, who could kill six dozen Scots at breakfast, complain of his quiet life, and then ask for work, she is not one to be concerned about a mere singleton corpse. But she can add quality to quantity in her domestic morgue. In *Ten Little Niggers* she shows an intense ingenuity in adapting that very lethal rhyme (so oddly deemed a nursery matter) to modern conditions . . . they are guilty parties lured to an island off Devon where it seems that some President of the High Court of Summary Justice is to have his sport with them; this he intricately does, thus giving abundant sport to the audience.[37]

Amongst a distinguished cast, those singled out for critical praise included veteran stage and screen actor Allan Jeayes as Sir Lawrence Wargrave, and Linden Travers (Bill Travers' sister) as typically feisty Christie heroine Vera Claythorne, the character mentioned by Glanville in the first line of his letter. Christie's own verdict was that 'I don't say it is the play or book of mine I like best, or even that I think is my best, but I do think in some ways that it is a better piece of craftsmanship than anything else I have written.'[38] It is hard to disagree. Putting aside the issue of the ending, the play is a masterpiece of dramatic construction, set in one room on the only house on the island and taking place over two consecutive nights. The potentially laboured conceit is handled with great skill and unfailing theatricality, and the ever-diminishing row of figurines provides a compelling dramatic focus.

The published version of the play (Samuel French, 1994) differs in a number of respects from that submitted to the Lord Chamberlain. For reasons unknown, a number of sections of dialogue were trimmed down or removed completely prior to publication and, gripping storyline aside, the resulting text can as a result appear somewhat underwritten and even slightly disjointed. There are no clues as to when or why these changes were made, although it seems most likely that they were instigated during the pre-West End tour and, as they are all cuts rather than additions, it would not have been necessary to inform the Lord Chamberlain. In the absence of any typescripts of the play at the Agatha Christie Archive, the only known copy of Christie's own final draft of her adaptation of *Ten Little Niggers* is thus that held in the Lord Chamberlain's Plays Collection at the British Library. It is, in a number of interesting respects, a richer text than the one we now know.

Amidst the carefully-constructed thrills of the piece, Christie takes time to explore various issues of morality and justice, and to make known her own views on them. Most notable is the following exchange between Vera and the embittered spinster Emily Brent, which has survived intact from Christie's final draft:

EMILY: Now that we are alone, I have no objection to telling you the facts of the case – indeed, I should like you to hear them. It was not a fit subject to discuss before gentlemen – so naturally I refused to say anything last night. That girl, Beatrice Taylor, was in my service. I was very much deceived in her. She had nice manners and was clean and willing. I was very pleased with her. Of course, all that was sheerest hypocrisy. She was a loose girl with no morals. Disgusting! It was some time before I found out that she was what they call 'in trouble'. It was a great shock to me. Her parents were decent folk, too, who had brought her up strictly. I'm glad to say they didn't condone her behaviour.

VERA: What happened?

EMILY: (self-righteously) Naturally, I refused to keep her an hour under my roof. No one shall ever say I condoned immorality.

VERA: Did she drown herself?

EMILY: Yes.

VERA: How old was she?

EMILY: Seventeen.

VERA: Only seventeen.

EMILY: (with horrible fanaticism) Quite old enough to know how to behave. I told her what a low depraved thing she was. I told her that she was beyond the pale and that no decent person would take her into their house. I told her that her child would be the child of sin and would be branded all its life – and that the man would naturally not dream of marrying her. I told her that I felt soiled by ever having had her under my roof –

VERA: (shuddering) You told a girl of seventeen all that?

EMILY: Yes, I am glad to say I broke her down utterly.

VERA: Poor little devil.[39]

The West End remained remarkably buoyant throughout the war. On the day *Ten Little Niggers* premiered, thirty-one West End theatres were open, and amongst the productions with which it was competing for audiences were Ivor Novello's *The Dancing Years* at the Adelphi, produced by Tom Arnold (who had hosted *Ten Little Niggers'* opening at his Wimbledon Theatre); Terence Rattigan's RAF play *Flare Path*, produced by H.M. Tennent Ltd at the Apollo; the PES's Priestley play *They Came to a City*, co-produced with Tennent Plays Ltd at the Globe; John Gielgud in Congreve's *Love For Love*, produced by Tennent Plays Ltd at the Haymarket; and the final week of Enid Bagnold's *Lottie Dundas*, produced by Farndale Pictures Ltd and starring Sybil Thorndike at the Cambridge Theatre.

In many histories of British theatre, chapters on the war years focus almost entirely on the roles of ENSA and CEMA. ENSA, under the irrepressible Basil Dean, took responsibility for providing entertainment for the troops (who dubbed it Every Night Something Awful) whilst the work of CEMA, the precursor of the Arts Council, was directed at audiences on the home front. Under the chairmanship of John Maynard Keynes, and with Ivor Brown as its first Drama Director, CEMA undertook a wide-ranging programme including tours to factories and garrisons by the Sadler's Wells Ballet and Ballet Rambert and the dispatch of the Old Vic Company (temporarily based at Burnley) to perform Shakespeare plays starring Sybil Thorndike in Welsh mining villages.[40]

It is clear that the government, through its promotion of both these organisations, subscribed to the belief that the provision of live entertainment in all its forms was a crucial wartime morale booster. But to focus exclusively on their work is to overlook not only the contribution of the PES but also the fact that the foundations of two of the century's biggest commercial theatre empires were laid during the war; the theatre-owning 'Group' consolidated its position, and the recently formed production company H.M. Tennent began to flourish. As we have seen, the pre-war West End puts the current one to shame with regard to its promotion of work by female playwrights, as well as that of directors such as Irene Hentschel, Auriol Lee, Leontine Sagan and Margaret Webster; and in the early 1940s the absence at war of a generation of men, as with so many other industries, helped further to consolidate women's position in the theatre. Amongst the many women who saw their plays produced in the West End at this time were Esther McCracken, Enid Bagnold, Daphne du Maurier, Rose Franken, Margaret Mayo and Lillian Hellman.

It must be remembered too that wartime conditions prevailed throughout the first West End run of *Ten Little Niggers*. This was reflected in particular in the performance times, with daily matinees at 2.30 p.m. and only two evening shows per week, on Wednesdays and Saturdays at 6 p.m. The programme carried the following announcements:

Important notice
During 'Alerts' no trains from Piccadilly Circus to Charing Cross, Waterloo or Elephant; but there are special buses from Haymarket and Jermyn Street.

The Booking Hall, Piccadilly Circus station, is NOT an air-raid Shelter. If you wish to take shelter, see list in Vestibule.

Warning of an AIR RAID will be given by a RED electrical sign above the orchestra pit. ALL CLEAR will similarly be shown in GREEN. Patrons are advised to remain in the Theatre, but those wishing to leave will be directed to the nearest official air-raid shelter, after which the performance will be continued for so long as is practicable.

Should any news of particular interest be received during

a performance it will be announced from the stage at the end of the succeeding scene or act of the play.[41]

And, on a lighter note,

> Ladies are earnestly requested to remove their Hats or any kind of Head-dress. The rule is framed for the benefit of the audience and the Management trusts that it will appeal to everybody, and that Ladies will kindly assist in having it carried out.

Fortunately, a performance was not in progress when the St James's Theatre suffered bomb damage at the end of February 1944. The production was forced to relocate to the Cambridge Theatre for several weeks before returning to its original home, where it continued until July, clocking up a very respectable total of 261 performances.

It may seem surprising that Christie's first really successful venture as a playwright was staged in these adverse circumstances. One reason for good ticket sales may well have been the co-operative movement's support for the venture, not simply in terms of its direct financial input but also through its constant publicity for the production amongst its members, including the promotion of group bookings. But there was clearly also an intrinsic quality to the piece which struck a chord with wartime theatregoers. On one level, the play explores the familiar Christie themes of guilt and the nature of justice, and employs her oft-used device of bringing together a diverse group of people in an isolated location. All of these ideas, however, are here developed to an extreme, enhanced by the claustrophobia of the setting and the characters' growing anxiety in the face of the inexorable progress of an all-knowing unseen adversary who clearly intends that all present will be his or her victims. Paranoia sets in as the norms of social interaction begin to disintegrate, and the characters expose their own vulnerability as they each begin to suspect the others.

Christie's play, like William Golding's *Lord of the Flies* a decade later, examines the disintegration of social order amongst

a group marooned on a small island. In one of the lines unaccountably cut from the published script, Vera makes the point
that, after the horrors of the night, the remaining protagonists
have effectively become a 'zoo'. It does not take a huge leap of
the imagination to see how this scenario might have resonated
with the vulnerable inhabitants of an island state at war with
a powerful enemy and where, as the programme's notes on
evacuation procedures make clear, everyone is a potential victim.
During the war many of the established niceties of the theatregoing experience itself were abandoned; travel to and from
theatres was a challenge (as it is to and from the island in the
play) and, with most performances being matinees, evening
dress and post-show dining in swanky restaurants were things
of the past. At the outset of the play, in the host's absence,
dressing for dinner is 'optional', and the image of characters
running short of food and serving up tinned meat would have
had a particular resonance.

The original novel had been written on the very eve of war,
but the final script of the play was not completed until the autumn
of 1942, by which time the country had experienced the Blitz.
Without consciously creating a wartime or a military piece Christie
had exactly tapped into the contemporary zeitgeist, and her agreement to the new upbeat ending undoubtedly sealed its success
in this context. In the play the two surviving characters are shown
to be innocent of the 'crimes' of which they are accused, and
their ultimate vindication, defeat of their persecutor and escape
from the island thus inadvertently turned the play into a morale
booster as well as a thriller. It was not the last time that Christie
the playwright would find success by connecting with audiences
on a subliminal level in this way; her natural empathy with her
public was indicative of an instinctive appreciation of their
concerns rather than the exercise of a particular agenda. 'The
People' had adopted Agatha Christie as their playwright, and they
could not have chosen anyone better qualified for the role.

Not everyone was happy, however. Although publication of the
original novel had apparently not provoked any debate regarding
the use of the word 'nigger' in its title, the publicising of the play's

arrival at St James's Theatre had, of necessity, resulted in posters proclaiming it being displayed all over London. The play had already received a licence from the Lord Chamberlain at the commencement of its tour, but the Lord Chamberlain's correspondence files held at the British Library reveal a fascinating series of seemingly panicked internal memos in the days immediately prior to its West end opening. The first of these notes that the Colonial Office has 'received a very strong complaint by a newly formed society of Coloured People, who have appealed to have the title of the play changed, as they greatly object to the word 'nigger' being used in the advertisements of a play. The Colonial Office realise that this is the title of a nursery rhyme, but they are very anxious to meet the wishes of the Coloured Society, and have asked the Lord Chamberlain's office if the title can be changed. Unfortunately, the play is already being advertised under the title Ten Little Niggers and is to be produced at the St James's Theatre on Wednesday.'[42]

Remarkably, given that this was 1943, it was immediately ruled that in view of the Colonial Office's representations the title of the play must be changed. Bertie Meyer was contacted, but argued that to do so at such a late stage in the game would simply be impractical. The Under-Secretary for the Colonies was consulted, and it was eventually concluded that changing the title of a play just before it was due to open 'would bring the question too much in the limelight.' It is noted that 'The Lord Chamberlain was accordingly informed and agreed to withdraw his ban.' The views of the Coloured Society on this outcome are not recorded.

It is not clear exactly who was behind the 'newly formed society of Coloured People', but it seems likely that it was the same 'Coloured Committee' that was invited to a meeting at the BBC a month later, and whose declared aim it was to combat cases of colour discrimination in the press, the theatre and broadcasting. Also in attendance was the same Colonial Office representative who had represented their views to the Lord Chamberlain's Office. According to the minutes of the meeting the BBC representative, whilst confirming the corporation's commitment to opposing racism, was of the opinion that the

Committee should not be concerned by traditional music hall terms such as 'Black Sambo', 'Ten Little Nigger Boys' and 'Nigger Minstrels' as in his view they did not provoke 'anti-colour feeling' in British audiences.[43] Both the Lord Chamberlain's files and the BBC minutes relating to this matter give a fascinating insight into contemporary British views on what was known at the time as the 'colour question'.

It seems that Christie herself remained blissfully unaware of this controversy, even though it had involved the Lord Chamberlain himself, not to mention a junior government minister. What is for certain, though, is that had the Lord Chamberlain's office elected to pursue the matter then her career as a playwright might well have taken a very different course.

As soon as *Ten Little Niggers* opened in London, English producer/director Albert de Courville started negotiations for an 'exclusive US and Canadian Licence' with permission to 'assign to Select Operating Corp (A Shubert subsidiary)'.[44] An advance of $2,500 was paid against an author's royalty of 10 per cent, of which Christie was to receive two-thirds. Meyer and Farndale were to receive one-ninth and two-ninths respectively; Farndale was by now operating from the same address as Meyer, and clearly from this had been responsible for the majority of the project's finance. The People's Entertainment Society's involvement ended with the 1944 post-West End UK tour of the production, and of West End co-producer Jay Pomeroy we hear nothing more. A note on the Hughes Massie summary memo relating to the American licence states, 'A Christie's two thirds temporarily held up in US against the General Tax Settlement'; this refers to an epic and, for Christie, demoralising battle with the American tax authorities that she was engaged in throughout the 1940s relating to income from all of her work.

Fifty-seven-year-old Albert de Courville seems an unlikely choice for the valuable American rights to the piece. Although he had obtained the rights with a view to the American production being a vehicle for himself as a director, his credentials in this regard could not have been more different from Irene Hentschel's. He had made a career in London and the UK provinces as a director and promoter of light entertainment revues rejoicing in such titles such as *Fun and Beauty* and *Flirts in Skirts* before moving into film as a director of comedies and musicals. When he moved to New York in 1940, his theatrical work continued in much the same vein. The key to the deal was the intention that his rights were to be assigned to the Shuberts, and one suspects that it was probably in this role as an intermediary with Broadway's most powerful producers that he was perceived by Cork as bringing value to the project.

Brothers Sam, Lee and Jacob J. Shubert had set up in business at the turn of the century, buying up theatre leases in their native Syracuse, New York, and setting out to challenge the then nationwide theatre-owning and production monopoly of the Klaw and Erlanger empire; they had achieved this feat by the 1920s, by which time they had interests in hundreds of theatres nationwide and controlled half of Broadway. The eldest brother, Sam, had died in a train crash in 1905, five years after they leased their first Broadway venue, the Herald Square Theatre, but Lee and 'JJ' had continued to provide a seemingly unstoppable momentum to the company, so that by the time Agatha Christie was working with them they had become indisputably America's most important theatrical powerbrokers.

As Gerald Schoenfeld, who ran the Shubert Organization from 1972 to 2008, noted in the introduction to its official history, 'these brothers were not ordinary men. For while they possessed courage, ruthlessness, and an innate intelligence, they had no regard for what others thought of them or their actions. Devoid of guilt and lacking the desire to be liked, admired, or respected, they conducted their business and personal lives as they saw fit.'[45] Lee Shubert's 1953 *Times* obituary remarked that the brothers 'produced more than 500 plays and every successful performer since 1920 had at one time or another contributed to their profits. It is more difficult to say that they in return contributed much that was creative to theatre.'[46] Basil Dean regarded the Shuberts as extraordinarily penny-pinching and difficult to deal with when negotiating the Broadway transfer of one of his projects, and found Lee Shubert

to be particularly irksome, 'a quiet little man with hard unre-
lenting eyes that belied his gentle voice . . . I grew tired of
waiting about in one or other of his corridors of power, listening
to angry arguments over the telephone by members of his staff,
who all seemed to be living in a mild state of frenzy lest "Mr
Lee's" displeasure should put their livelihoods at risk.'[47]

The Shuberts were indeed legendarily tough cookies, but as
Schoenfeld comments, 'through their undying devotion these
two brothers undoubtedly saved the institution of commercial
theatre from the threats posed by the advent of motion pictures,
the Depression, bankruptcy, and the coming of television. In
retrospect they were to the theatre what Ford was to the motor
car and the Wright brothers to aviation.' They were, undoubtedly, the biggest players to date to express an interest in the
work of Agatha Christie, playwright.

The immaculately maintained Shubert archives, which document over one hundred years of Broadway theatre history,
demonstrate the company's dispassionate and meticulous attention to business detail under 'Mr Lee's' regime, with younger
brother 'J.J.' a constant presence in the background. An
exchange of correspondence between Lee Shubert and his
lawyers in the months before the New York opening of Christie's
play shows the organisation level-headedly dealing with a
complicated chain of paperwork and negotiating for improved
terms right down to the wire. It is evident that, although the
licence with the English producers is in the name of de Courville,
negotiations are taking place directly between Hughes Massie
(represented here by Christie's New York agent, Harold Ober)
and the Shubert office. Amongst other complications were the
paperwork between de Courville and the Shuberts assigning
his rights to them, which he did in return for 25 per cent of
profits over and above his director's fee of $750 and expenses
of $1,250, and the necessity for a standard Broadway Dramatists
Guild Dramatic Production Contract. Although Christie herself
had become an associate member of the Guild in anticipation
of an American production of *Peril at End House*, the Guild
contract, like the contract that de Courville was assigning, was

actually with Farndale and Meyer, meaning that they in turn had to become Guild associate members.

A confidential memo to Lee Shubert from Adolph Kaufman (who worked for the Shuberts' fearsome lawyer, William Klein) clarifies that 'Miss Christie is involved in some tax litigation and wants to be kept out of it.'[48] The Shuberts nonetheless required Christie to sign a warranty that she had assigned her interest, at least on paper, to Farndale and Meyer. Although the Shuberts were entitled to 50 per cent of income from 'stock' (i.e. repertory) licensing, Kaufman, who was clearly as sharp as a knife, was particularly concerned that 'reserved rights' (i.e. those in which they did not participate) could 'very seriously interfere with the stage performance rights' if exercised by Christie. These included the amateur, broadcasting, television, operatic, musical comedy, play publishing and film rights. Undertakings had to be obtained that they would not in any event be exercised until after the Broadway run.[49]

With the film rights, Kaufman went one better. Critical to the Shuberts' involvement was a separate deal that they negotiated with RKO[50] – who had bought the film rights to the novel in 1941 – whereby, following the Broadway opening, they had the option to purchase RKO's rights for $50,000. As it happens, the Shubert/RKO deal proved to be just the start of a complex and bitter series of wranglings concerning control of the film rights, about which no doubt another book will one day be written. In the meantime, de Courville himself was clearly playing both ends against the middle and ensuring that, whatever the outcome of the stage rights negotiations, it was a good one for himself. The fact that much of the key paperwork relating to the rights in the production does not appear to have been signed until the day before the first Broadway performance, several weeks after the production's 5 June 'out of town' opening in Washington, is evidence of the Shuberts' own confidence in the strength of their position; but the trouble they were clearly prepared to go to in order to safeguard their investment, and their apparent confidence in a lucrative outcome, is indicative of the value that they placed on Christie's play.

The Shuberts had in fact been keeping an eye on Christie's work for some time. An internal memo from their publicist gloats at the poor reviews received by upstart independent producer Jed Harris for Morton and Anderson's *The Fatal Alibi* in 1932,[51] but their archive nonetheless includes file copies of the 1931 West End script of *Black Coffee* and of Frank Vosper's version of *Love From a Stranger*. The Shuberts were no doubt right in not considering *Black Coffee* to be Broadway material (it had, after all, only run in London for two months) and Christie's name, through no fault of her own, had so far been associated on Broadway only with two flops. So it is a tribute to the potency of the London success of *Ten Little Niggers* that the Shuberts elected to make the play Agatha Christie's own Broadway debut.

Christie's story had originally been serialised in the US by *The Saturday Evening Post* in May 1939 (pre-dating its UK publication) as *And Then There Were None*, the title which was then used for its 1940 US release as a novel by Dodd, Mead & Co. I suspect, however, that history may have been kind to both publishers in attributing a post-civil rights motivation to them for the title change. The pre-war *Saturday Evening Post* was not noted for its liberal views, and Dodd, Mead & Co. was the publisher who, some forty years earlier, had changed the title of Joseph Conrad's *The Nigger of the Narcissus* because, according to Conrad, they believed that 'America would not buy a book about niggers.'[52]

When Christie's play opened in 1944, America was a country where racial segregation was the norm in the Southern states and in the army that was fighting in Europe, and yet the musical *Carmen Jones* was enjoying huge success on Broadway ('A performance by Negroes – yes – and they do a highly creditable job!' applauded the *New York Times*[53]). What is certain is that the play's original title would have had very different connotations in America than in the pre-*Empire Windrush* UK. The Shuberts, however, did not elect to adopt the book's American title, but instead came up with their own; *Ten Little Indians* (an alternative, *The Unknown Host*, had also been considered)[54]. As with the American edition of the novel, the protagonists of the poem at the centre of events were duly changed to the 'Injuns' of Septimus Winner's original American song of the same name, although their actual fates continued to follow Frank Green's version. No correspondence exists to substantiate how, why or at whose instigation the play's British title was rejected, but the resolution of the play's plot was certainly more attractive to Hollywood than that of the novel, and it was effectively now identified as a separate intellectual property; a fact that was to strengthen the Shuberts' negotiations with film makers. In any event, there appears to have been no shame in handing out audition scripts for Broadway carrying the original title, which also appears on the director's rehearsal script and the stage manager's prompt copy; and the first typescript of the Shuberts' rebranded version clearly states 'Ten Little Niggers (Indians)'.

In its direct reference to the play's ten potential murder victims, the Shuberts' title is certainly closer to Christie's original intention than that used for the novel in America, and it was perhaps felt that the reference to native Americans, whose ten befeathered silhouettes adorned the posters, added a touch of exotic mystery to proceedings for 1940s New York theatre-goers. In any event, the new title clearly resonated with the American public in a way that the British one would not have done, and doubtless sold a great many more tickets than 'The Unknown Host' would have.

Given the amount of negotiation and the extensive paperwork involved in preparing the production, Lee Shubert, who was by then seventy-three and still firing on all cylinders, must have been delighted with the financial outcome. The play opened at the Broadhurst Theatre on 27 June 1944 and transferred to the Plymouth Theatre on 9 January 1945 where it ran until 30 June, clocking up a total of 426 Broadway performances. This is the first Christie-related stage work for which any accounts are available. An interim statement of operating profit from December 1944 shows that, with more than six months left to run, the Broadway production had repaid its set-up costs of $17,157.38 and generated a profit after running costs and royalties of $46,977.17.[55] Of this, Hollywood talent agent Frank Orsatti received 10 per cent, presumably on behalf of a client or clients appearing in the production, and the Shuberts then split the balance 75/25 with de Courville, whose perspicacity seems to have paid off. A touring production which had been launched in October was already adding to the project's profitability. Never ones to miss a trick, the Shuberts negotiated a reduced author's royalty for the tour, which then ran well into 1946, latterly under licence to another producer. According to Christie biographer Laura Thompson, 'The play of the book also ran on Broadway where it caught the attention of the theatrical impresario Lee Shubert.'[56] I would say it probably did, given that he made a great deal of money out of it.

Probably of less concern to Shubert would have been the reviews, which were generally not as supportive as those for the London production had been. It does seem, though, that despite their reputation for penny-pinching, the Shuberts pushed the boat out with the production values. The production design by Howard Bray, which was based on that of the London production by Clifford Pember, came in for particular praise. The *New York Times*'s verdict was that 'The Messrs. Shubert and Albert De Courville have given the play a good American production. Like the number of corpses and potential corpses, all the ingredients were there. But as it turned out *Ten Little Indians* does not climb far above the potential stage.'[57] Howard Barnes in the *Herald Tribune* felt that the play was 'A high class melodrama . . . mannerly, literate and occasionally terrifying . . . a superior bit of nonsense . . . Miss Christie writes well for the theatre . . . the ending is definitely anti-climactic. With the excellent acting and the taut staging by Albert de Courville, it still manages to be a pleasantly chilling hot-weather entertainment.'[58] The *New York Post* remarked that 'The change in ending, which will be pounced upon at once by all avid Christie readers, is in the interests of romance. It removes some of Mrs Christie's original ruthlessness, but it does not violently distort the plot, nobody is going to care very much, especially since she herself is credited with the dramatization.'[59] The *New York Journal-American* lamented that the production 'left me the way it found me, damp, dejected and disinterested'[60] but the *New York Word-Telegram* countered that it was 'Top-notch escapist stuff, sheer unmitigated, fantastic, enjoyable nonsense. Last night's audience were wildly enthusiastic about it.'[61]

It seems, however, that American audiences were watching a rather different play from that seen in Britain. Christie herself did not attend, but one suspects that she would have been dismayed to see her work advertised variously as a 'hilarious chiller thriller', a 'hilarious mystery thriller' and a 'superlative comedy mystery'.[62] Significantly, when Cork requested a copy of the performance script for his records, Kaufman advised Lee Shubert to send him 'the manuscript of the original play Ten Little Niggers as it was written by Miss Christie, and not the playing version which is being produced'.[63]

In the absence of a resonance with the inhabitants of a beleaguered island state, de Courville had clearly decided to play to his own strengths and direct the piece as straightforward comedy melodrama. In this context it still appears to have struck a chord as wartime entertainment, albeit in a far less sophisticated way than Hentschel's production. Again, the wartime context is evident in the playbill text, which includes the following notice from the Mayor of New York: 'The way that the Theatre has responded to our defense effort is a matter of pride to every citizen, for the work of the Theatre in keeping up the morale of the members of our armed forces is something which in its way is as vital to our war effort as the production of additional military equipment.'[64]

The playbill also carries a note that 'Because of governmental restrictions, The Playbill, in common with all publications, will have to curtail its consumption of paper. During this emergency it will not be possible to furnish a copy of The Playbill to every person. With your co-operation this regulation can be met without hardship if you will share your copy of The Playbill with your companion.' Paper was by no means the only thing in short supply. In the Shubert production office's day files, we find a certificate dated 7 December 1944 from the Office of Price Administration, Shoe Division, allowing the company to issue four of the actors with pairs of rationed shoes, and carrying the warning: 'For you or anyone else to transfer these stamps or shoe ration check for any purpose other than that for which they are issued is a violation of the regulation and subjects violators to certain penalties.'

The day files give a fascinating insight into the running of a Broadway show in the 1940s, with the production team having to deal with a number of issues as they arise. Just as rehearsals were about to start it was discovered 'by purest coincidence' that Pat O'Malley, playing the role of Blore, was British, and the Shuberts had to appeal to the actors' union, Equity, for permission to allow him to continue in the role: 'The part of Blore is characterised as a provincial detective and written in the vernacular of that County (Devonshire, England). It requires a player thoroughly versed in the peculiar accent and dialect of that particular locality, and moreover, an artist with a sense of comedy.' Mr O'Malley, claimed the Shubert office, 'will be a featured member of the cast, commanding one of the highest salaries in the play', and it was simply too late to replace him. 'In view of the extraordinary circumstances and the impossibility of replacing Mr O'Malley at such short notice with an actor capable of playing this unique part . . . we trust that you will give this application your favourable consideration.'[65] O'Malley was indeed amongst the production's highest earners. Veteran stage and film actor Halliwell Hobbes, playing Wargrave, and debonair Hollywood leading man Michael Whalen, playing Lombard, were earning $400 per week in performance, while O'Malley was next in line on $350. However, whilst the character of Blore claims to operate a detective agency in Plymouth, the Shuberts are somewhat over-stating the case about the necessity for a Devonshire accent (a good South African accent would actually be more useful for the role), and it seems that O'Malley's expertise in any case lay elsewhere when it came to accents; his playbill biography reveals that he 'is a well-known radio personality, creator of such ether-famed favourites as Sam Small and 'Erbert Pinwinkle; his Lancashire dialect songs and stories have won him a wide following on the coast-to-coast networks, Hollywood and radio. This is his second US stage appearance.'[66]

Even if they knew they were being bluffed, Equity decided not to take on the Shuberts over this matter, and replied the next day that, following a meeting, they had 'granted your request permitting Equity members to work with Mr O'Malley, subject to all the rules and regulations of Equity's Alien Actor Policy, particularly the payment of the alien actor dues.'[67] Less happy was the outcome for Claudia Morgan, playing Vera Claythorne, sacked by the Shuberts when a Sunday evening radio commitment of hers was rescheduled to Fridays, causing a scheduling clash with the play.

Most importantly, as the production playbill remarked, this was Agatha Christie's 'first play of her own writing to be presented in this country'. For one glorious week there were productions running simultaneously in the West End and on Broadway. Legendary *New York Times* cartoonist Al Hirschfeld drew caricatures of the play's ten protagonists, which ran across the top of two pages. Agatha Christie, playwright, had not only arrived, but was suddenly big business. The London run had been a great success, but following its Broadway premiere it was immediately clear that her classic suspense drama was desitined to become a truly global phenomenon.

Options for professional productions had already been sold for a number of overseas territories during the war, including some that were under Nazi occupation at the time. On 13 November 1944 a licence was issued to the Czech-born film actor Herbert Lom, who had moved to the UK in 1939, to produce the play 'in Czechoslovakia for five years from the liberation of Czechoslovakia or from the cessation of hostilities in Europe whichever is the earlier'.[68] On 1 December 1944 five year options on the Finnish and Swedish rights – along with those for Norway and Denmark from the date of 'liberation or the cessation of hostilities in Europe, whichever is earlier'[69] – were sold to the Finnish director Arvid Englind. Interestingly, Hughes Massie had allowed for the eventuality that hostilities might cease without the territories concerned actually having been liberated. In support of the continued effort to make them so, ENSA was licensed on 23 June 1944 to undertake a six-week tour, and *Ten Little Niggers* followed *Love From a Stranger* into the fray. The play had already become a forces favourite, with a special performance in London attended by Montgomery; and a group of Dutch prisoners of war even staged their own dramatisation at Buchenwald concentration camp.

In September 1945 Hughes Massie took an advertisement in *The Stage* newspaper:

TEN LITTLE NIGGERS
As played at the St James's Theatre, London; Broadhurst Theatre, New York; Theatre Maringy, Paris; Stockholm, Brussels and Buenos Aires
NOW AVAILABLE FOR REPERTORY
Apply: Hughes Massie[70]

Amongst a number of high-profile repertory productions of *Ten Little Niggers* in the 1940s were those staged at the Embassy Theatre (1948) and the Theatre Royal Stratford East (1949). The Embassy, which in the 1930s had staged controversial plays addressing the 'colour question', evidently had no issue with the play's title.

This was just the beginning of what was to prove an extremely lucrative international and repertory market for Christie's work, and it was her world-wide appeal, as evidenced by Hughes Massie's voluminous licensing records, that within two decades was to confirm her position as without question the most performed female playwright in history. Although many of her contemporaries, including Clemence Dane, Dodie Smith and Enid Bagnold saw their work premiere both in the West End and on Broadway, none of them come close to achieving Christie's lasting domestic and international success at all levels of production. Even the plays of hers that were to fare less well in the West End and on Broadway went on to carve a lucrative niche in secondary touring and repertory markets, trading on the reputation of their more successful counterparts.

And all of this was masterminded by Edmund Cork, as it slowly dawned on him that the licensing of subsidiary rights of Christie's work for the stage, if properly managed, could be a substantial revenue source for both his client and his agency.

When Hughes Massie placed their advertisement, six weeks after the surrender of Japan finally ended the Second World War, Agatha Christie had just celebrated her fifty-fifth birthday. She rightly saw *Ten Little Niggers* as the turning point in her playwriting career, and later wrote to Rosalind:

> I remember when I had hopes of Ten Little Niggers being put on – Charles Cochran was mad about it – naturally I was very excited however his backers refused point blank to put up the cash – they were united in their opinion that it would be a terrible flop – laughed off the stage – one after another of the characters being killed off – the silliest plot they'd ever heard of – Cochran was very angry but he couldn't win them over – when Bertie Meyer put it on quite unexpectedly a couple of years later, he was furious. Nobody laughed at everyone getting killed. Irene Hentschel produced it beautifully. It played at the St James Theatre till that was bombed in the war and then shifted to the Cambridge. All theatrical things are a pure gamble.[71]

For Christie, though, the theatrical gamble wasn't over, and there were to be some bitter disappointments before her position as the most successful female playwright of all time became unassailable.

SCENE FIVE

Towards Zero

The triumphant progress of *Ten Little Niggers* was marred for Christie by the failure of three further full-length plays that she wrote, and that were premiered, during the war: her own adaptations of her novels *Death on the Nile*, *Appointment with Death* and *Towards Zero*.

Christie remained enormously productive as a novelist during this period; between 1939's *Ten Little Niggers* and 1945's *Sparkling Cyanide*, she penned a further nine books, including such classics as *Evil Under the Sun*, *The Body in the Library* and *Five Little Pigs*. The year of 1944 alone saw the publication of *Towards Zero*, *Death Comes as the End* (the Egyptian historical mystery which benefited from the advice of Stephen Glanville) and a new Mary Westmacott novel, *Absent in the Spring*. Yet, while she rarely mentions her work as a novelist in her correspondence, her wartime letters to Max are brimming with news of her latest theatrical ventures, and of her close involvement in the process of nurturing them from page to stage. She also reports on her own frequent visits to the theatre in London where she enjoyed many of the great Shakespearian productions of the day, including those given by the Old Vic Company when it returned from its Blitz-imposed exile in Burnley to play at the New Theatre. Her commentaries on these productions are insightful and demonstrate a playwright's appreciation of the craft.

Given the volume of her own theatre work at this time, the frequent illegibility of her writing and her failure to date the majority of her correspondence, it is hardly surprising that disentangling her wartime theatrical activity has not been a priority for biographers who, in any case, tend to marginalise her work for the stage. The resulting picture, inevitably, has tended to be somewhat inaccurate. Her letters contained so much news of casting, rehearsals, rewrites and opening nights on tour and in the West End that even Max became confused. 'Now pay attention,' she chided him in October 1943, 'Ten Little Niggers is not the Sullivan play! Allan Jeayes is playing the judge.'[1]

Ten Little Niggers was, of course, Christie's main theatre project throughout this period. As we have seen, the first draft was written in early 1940 and it eventually played in the West End between November 1943 and July 1944. A simultaneous touring production, commencing in April 1944 and for which Agatha attended rehearsals, was again directed by Irene Hentschel and presented by Meyer, Farndale and the PES. It starred Arthur Wontner as Wargrave, well known to the public for his 1930s film portrayals of Sherlock Holmes, in a performance that Agatha felt was even better than that of Allan Jeayes. The Shuberts' Broadway production ran from June 1944 to January 1945 at the Broadhurst Theatre, continuing at the Plymouth Theatre until June 1945, and their US tour was on the road for two years from the autumn of 1944. The three further novel dramatisations that ran parallel with all this may well have been an exciting prospect for Christie at the time, but they ultimately did her reputation as a dramatist no favours with producers, actors or critics. Given her intense book writing schedule during this period, she may perhaps have been spreading her playwriting skills rather thin.

The dramatisation of *Death on the Nile*, which turned out to be a massively time-consuming and frustrating project, had originally been conceived as another vehicle for Francis L. Sullivan, following the ill-fated *Peril at End House*. The first title to be discussed with Sullivan for this purpose was *Triangle at Rhodes*, a Poirot novella originally published in the *Strand Magazine* in 1936, and in the four-novella collection *Murder in the Mews* the following year. It was a sort of prototype for the 1941 novel *Evil Under the Sun*, but Edmund Cork clearly had reservations about its suitability for stage adaptation. In September 1942 he wrote to Agatha at Lawn Road, 'I read Triangle At Rhodes last night. It certainly is a perfectly marvellous dramatic situation and would probably make just as good a play as any of them, but it is not the later, highly characterised Poirot, is it?'[2] Agatha wrote back, 'I feel rather "anti" Poirot play.'[3] As she later explained with reference to *Black Coffee*, in a letter to a researcher, 'After seeing that and the previous plays dramatised from my books I decided, quite definitely that Hercule Poirot was utterly unsuited to appear in any detective play, because a detective must be necessarily the onlooker and observer, and can only succeed if he abandons detection for positive action. That is, he should not be in a detective play but in a thriller.'[4]

Unsurprisingly, the less 'characterised' Poirot did not suit Sullivan himself, and in October Cork wrote:

Francis Sullivan came in to see me yesterday. I gather that he is not so keen on the Triangle at Rhodes idea, but he is very keen to make an arrangement for a play based on Death On The Nile, if the difficulties can be overcome. The complication that we particularly wanted to avoid was not to involve another Poirot subject while the present negotiations regarding a blanket Poirot film contract are in hand, but I find that Sullivan was more favourably inclined towards your idea of having the Poirot part played by say, a rather fleshy canon, as he would then enter into the action more, and even come under suspicion.[5]

Agatha described to Max the moment when she persuaded her friend Sullivan to abandon Poirot, 'leading him gently to the idea of Death On The Nile without Poirot – suggested instead a retired Barrister – a solicitor – a diplomat – a clergyman – canon or bishop. And suddenly he bit! His eyes half closed – "oh yes – purple silk front and a large cross" He saw it, you see. Not the speaking part – the *appearance*! I bet you whoever played Hamlet argued a good deal as to whether to play it in a hat or not!'[6] Sullivan, as it happens, was at the time once again following in the footsteps of Charles Laughton by appearing in a short-lived revival of Laughton's 1928 *succès d'estime*, *A Man With Red Hair*, produced by himself at the Ambassadors Theatre, directed by *Black Coffee*'s Andre van Gyseghem and designed by Danae Gaylen. The *Times* reviewer felt that Sullivan's performance was no match for Laughton's.

The 1937 Poirot novel *Death on the Nile* confusingly shares a title with a 1934 short story featuring portly investigator Mr Parker Pyne, whose declared aim in life is to resolve unhappiness. Elements of this story are to be found in both the *Death on the Nile* novel and the 1938 Poirot novel *Appointment with Death*, and all of this material finds its ultimate source in a Nile cruise undertaken by Agatha and Max in 1933. Christie is likely to have been mightily relieved that Sullivan was not insistent on reprising his theatrical party piece as Poirot, and the character of the 'fleshy canon' who replaced him in the play (variously named in different versions of the script, but originally known as Canon Pennefather) perhaps owes more to Parker Pyne than to Poirot. Christie's notes indicate that she had in fact experimented with adapting the original Parker Pyne short story for the stage, a venture from which Parker Pyne himself appears to have been similarly absent. The major significance of the switch from Poirot to Pennefather is that, as a character unknown to the audience, he can, as Sullivan himself noted, be portrayed as morally ambiguous and thus himself fall under suspicion in a way that Poirot couldn't.

By the end of 1942 the script, entitled *Moon on the Nile*, had been written; it is clearly an adaptation of the novel *Death on the Nile*, although without Poirot and with a much reduced, conflated and renamed dramatis personae. Amongst

the absentees from the stage version are novelist Salome
Otterbourne, who Christie had originally put down in her
notes as 'Mrs Pooper – cheap novelist', a joke at her own
expense (Max and Agatha referred to each other for reasons
unknown as 'Mr and Mrs Puper'). The dramatisation benefits
instead from the introduction of the formidable Miss ffoliot-
ffoulkes, one of a number of Bracknellesque *grande dame*
characters which Christie drew particularly well for the stage.
Agatha wrote to Max, 'I have finished the Death From [sic]
the Nile play. Larry very keen for it – I think I've written him
quite a good part as Canon Pennefather – a kind of budding
Archbishop of Canterbury and Sir W. Beveridge rolled into
one!'[7] The Beveridge Report, the foundation of the post-war
Welfare State, had been published the previous week, and
Canon Pennefather is raising funds for what his niece
describes as 'some wonderful scheme for rebuilding a new
England – self-supporting communities and industries – a
kind of Christianised Soviet it seems to me'.[8] Agatha's letter
continues, 'Sidney Smith [a distinguished archaeologist friend
of the Mallowans] has lent me some books with good illustra-
tions of Abu Simbel for Danae to enjoy herself with for the
scenery.'

On Christmas Eve Cork wrote to Christie, 'I had a long
session with the solicitor representing Mr Sullivan and the
people who are going in with him on Moon on the Nile, and
I am glad to say that we reached a consensus without giving
up anything that mattered to us.'[9] Three weeks later, Sullivan's
company Eleven Twenty Three Ltd paid £100 for a licence for
the UK and its colonies, to be exercised within one year.[10] A
Broadway option could be taken up within two months of a
London opening and, again provided the play was produced
in London, Sullivan would benefit to the extent of one-third of
the proceeds of any film sale of the original novel. Significantly,
Sullivan did not pay a commissioning fee, as he had done to
Arnold Ridley for *Peril at End House*, although the play had
clearly been written at his behest. It was not, as has been
implied elsewhere, a script that Christie took 'off the shelf' for

him, and neither, as has also been suggested, did it pre-date the novel.

In February 1943 Agatha wrote to Max, 'Larry's play will, I feel, go on – as I believe either he or Danae put up some of the money – Do hope it will be a success as I have convinced him that *I* characterise my books much better than Ridley.'[11] But then, a week later, 'Dead silence from Larry Sullivan but then Danae is getting on with the scenery – am now thinking of . . . a play about a WAAF (. . . spy drama!)'[12] It seems that *Moon on the Nile* was being developed during Agatha's regular weekend visits to the Sullivans' house in Haslemere, which was to inspire the country house setting of her 1946 novel *The Hollow*.

In the event, it was to be a year before the play, now retitled *Hidden Horizon*, opened for a short 'try-out' production at Dundee Repertory Theatre. Christie's choice of titles, both the original and the replacement, is indicative of how she wished to avoid the characterisation of her stage work as thrillers. On one of the Christie archive's copies of the script, carrying Sullivan's address and presumably dating from some time in 1942, the title *Moon on the Nile* has been crossed out and 'Hidden Horizon' written in by hand. The phrase has echoes of Akhnaton's 'City of the Horizon' and is mentioned in Act One of the play in this exchange between Canon Pennefather and the tormented Jackie as the Nile steamship cruiser *Lotus*, on which they are both passengers, is about to set sail:

CANON PENNEFATHER: We shall be starting in a minute or two. Ahead of us is what the old Egyptians called the hidden horizon.
JACKIE: (thoughtfully) Hidden Horizon.[13]

Hidden Horizon, like the novel *Towards Zero* which was published six months after the play's premiere, concerns a love triangle involving one man and two women, with all three protagonists present. The shipboard setting provides a claustrophobic, self-contained scenario that allows for the dramatis personae to intermingle in similarly isolated, if far less ominous, surroundings to those in *Ten Little Niggers*. Several of the characters are motivated by their financial circumstances: as well as Pennefather, for whom fundraising is a priority, those on board include a man who has spent years unsuccessfully seeking employment, a young woman who has been removed from the school and friends she loved as a result of her father losing his money, a doctor who has escaped his country after watching his hopes of an egalitarian society being destroyed by foreign investors, a maid who fears for her livelihood and a young communist who is concealing his aristocratic background. Christie considers these matters as someone whose own upbringing was affected by the financial instability caused by her father's death and who, at time of writing, was unable to draw on any of her American earnings due to a debilitating dispute with the tax authorities there.

Similarly to *Ten Little Niggers*, the ending of the stage adaptation was to prove particularly contentious. The original *Moon on the Nile* script sees the character of Jacqueline de Severac exit with a knife, clearly to take her own life as she does in the novel, and apparently with the endorsement of Canon Pennefather:

Police are heard off . . .

JACKIE: I feel so alone – so bewildered . . . I don't know . . . Ah! (snatches up dagger) (Springs back triumphantly, watching him. He does not move. She stares at him in a bewildered way) Did you know I was going to do that?

CANON: Yes, I knew.

JACKIE: And you didn't try to stop me?

CANON: No.

JACKIE: Then I *can* take my own way out?

CANON: If you want to . . .

JACKIE: (Slowly) I see – it's to be *my* choice?

(she goes slowly L carrying dagger and to doorway. CANON sits watching her go. His face very sad. Jackie looks at him, smiles, goes out)

CURTAIN[14]

Suicide, an idea which is also explored by Christie at around this time in *Towards Zero* and the stage version of *Appointment with Death*, was, however, clearly deemed to provide too downbeat an ending, and this scene was replaced in the copy of *Hidden Horizon* that was approved by the Lord Chamberlain's office at the end of 1943 with

JACKIE: Then I *can* take my own way out?
CANON: *If* you want to . . .
JACKIE: (Slowly) I see – it's to be *my* choice?

(She stands irresolute, dagger in hand. Voices come nearer – excited jabber.)

JACKIE: All right, you win!

(She tosses dagger out of window, flings up her chin defiantly. Canon rises. They stand hand in hand as Egyptian Police official enters.)

CURTAIN[15]

Although the weapon at some point changed from a knife to a gun, this is pretty well the ending in the French's acting edition of 1948 and is the one that was used in the West End and on Broadway. It is radically different, and remarkably less dramatic, than Christie's original intention. Even more fascinating, though, is an 'alternative ending' provided on a page following this one in later drafts of the script. To understand the significance of this, we should first take a look at the end of Act One, where the Canon urges Jackie to disembark the

Lotus and avoid a confrontation with her former fiancé Simon and his new wife, Kay.

> CANON: We are casting off. For the last time I beg of you – not because of Kay's peace of mind but for your own lasting peace, and your future happiness – get off this boat. Give up this journey.
>
> JACKIE: I wish – I almost wish I could (she speaks with deep weariness)
>
> CANON: But you can. There is always a moment when one can turn back – before it is too late. This is your moment. I beg of you, my very dear child . . .
>
> JACKIE: I wish you hadn't been on board.
>
> CANON: (urgently) Go *now*.
>
> (she takes a step)
>
> SIMON: (off) No, Kay, we've got to go through with it.
>
> JACKIE: (her face changing) We've got to go through with it!

And here is the quite astonishing 'alternative ending':

> JACKIE: Then I *can* take my own way out?
>
> CANON: *If* you want to . . .
>
> JACKIE: (Slowly) I see – it's to be *my* choice?
>
> (There is a black out, the jabber of voices change to that at the end of Act 1. Sounds of paddles, bells ring.
>
> Lights on again. It is sunset at Shellal, as at the end of Act 1.
>
> Jackie standing swaying, her eyes shut.)
>
> CANON: I beg of you my very dear child. Go now, before it is too late . . .
>
> JACKIE: What – did – you – say?
>
> CANON: You're ill.
>
> JACKIE: No. I've been seeing things – imagining them . . . as they might be . . . (shivers) *Hidden Horizon*.
>
> SIMON: (off) We've got to go through with it now, Kay.
>
> JACKIE: No, no – stop. I'm getting off . . .
>
> (Runs off. Simon enters)

SIMON: What's happened?
(Paddles stop)
CANON: Jacqueline has left the boat.

CURTAIN[16]

In other words, the whole of Acts Two and Three have been
a sort of vision of the events that will unfold if Jackie stays
on the boat. She has seen the 'Hidden Horizon' and the tragic
consequences of her plan, and has decided not to proceed
with it.

Although much of *Someone at the Window* takes place in
flashback, and she was later to experiment with time in *Go
Back for Murder*, this is without doubt the most radical piece
of dramatic construction undertaken by Christie and quite
possibly was inspired by a similar device in J.B. Priestley's
1932 play *Dangerous Corner*. It creates the requisite happy
ending, but in a manner that is far more dramatically challenging than the one we have been left with. It reinforces the
concept of the life-changing moment, which we first heard
about in *The Lie*; and the significance of a young woman being
given the ability to turn back the clock on a course of action
that she will later deeply regret will not be lost on Christie
aficionados. Also included at the end of the script are the
complete lyrics for the traditional American song 'Frankie and
Johnny', with which the aggrieved and inebriated Jackie repeatedly taunts the honeymooning Simon; 'He was my man but he
done me wrong, so wrong.'

The script submitted to the Lord Chamberlain's office a few
weeks before the Dundee opening still contains both the current
and the 'alternative' endings, indicating that the alternative
was under consideration until the very last minute. Indeed,
there is even the possibility that it was used for the Dundee
premiere, as critics of course would have been honour-bound
not to reveal such a radical twist.

In January 1944 Agatha wrote to Max, 'I go to Dundee
Monday for rehearsals of Hidden Horizon . . . if well received

it may be put on in London as owing to the success of Ten Little Niggers "backers" are not now so hard to find. It's mainly taken from Death on the Nile – but no Poirot. Larry is a Canon of the Church instead. Stephen [Glanville] has been supplying Arabic . . . for bead sellers and is really longing to come to Dundee himself but his life is rather complicated at present as he has his father with bronchitis . . .'[17] A week later she wrote again, from the Royal British Hotel in Dundee:

> I am enjoying myself *immensely*. Really great fun. Feel I am practically producing [i.e. directing] the play myself . . . of course nobody knows their part and they get worse and worse and it seems as if we can't possibly open on Monday! . . . Larry and Danae are great fun to be with. Danae is like a kind of general store. She has an immense trunk with her out of which come evening dresses for actresses, coffee and household milk, smelling salts for temperamental artistes – dictionary to look up words – soap, throat pastilles . . . It all takes place on the Lotus Nile steamer in the front observation saloon. First act just before leaving Shellal – 2nd and 3rd acts Abu Simbel. Larry is a canon and is toying with the idea of being a Bishop in the London production (if there is a London production!! "Backers" are coming to see it here!) Two Arab bead sellers . . . provide comic relief – Oh I do hope it will be a success – The end of course is chancy.[18]

The reference to the ending being 'chancy' is an intriguing indication that the original Dundee production may have used the 'alternative' ending.

In January 1944 the press in Dundee was full of the local rep's 'scoop' in securing the new Agatha Christie play, and particularly the casting of 'guest artist' Francis L. Sullivan, the 'well-known British film star' who was to lead their regular company of actors. The choice of the five-year-old Dundee Repertory Theatre for the try-out production was no coincidence; its director was none other than A.R. Whatmore, who had been artistic head of the Embassy Theatre for Alec Rea when Andre van Gyseghem directed *Black Coffee* there in 1930. The *Dundee Evening Telegraph* ran the headline 'Rep Producer [i.e. director] Gave Actor First Big Chance – Why New Play Opens at Dundee' and went on to explain:

> Mrs Agatha Christie, whose new play *Hidden Horizon* has its premiere at the Repertory Theatre on Monday night, wrote the play at the suggestion of Mr Francis L. Sullivan, who plays the lead. Mr Sullivan, who has appeared in several of Mrs Christie's plays, notably in *Black Coffee*, was anxious for her to dramatise an Egyptian scene which had captured his imagination in one of her books. Mrs Christie described the play to the *Telegraph and Post* as 'not a thriller – just a murder story'. She has known Mr Whatmore, of Dundee Repertory Company, for some time, and he has produced one of her plays in London [i.e. he had directed Arnold Ridley's *Peril at End House*]. Mr Sullivan explained that he had brought the play to Dundee. He has the option on it. Mr Whatmore had given him what he described as his 'first big chance' at the Embassy Theatre, in London in 1930, when he played in a number of plays including *Black Coffee*. He had intended for some time to play for Mr Whatmore in Dundee, and thought it would be a good chance to bring a new play when he had this particular interest in *Hidden Horizon*. Dundee Repertory Theatre is the only one doing fortnightly runs just now, and this afforded an excellent opportunity for rehearsing a new play. Mr Sullivan is playing the part of a High Anglican canon who becomes involved in a mystery while sailing on the Nile, and becomes amateur detective. His wife Danae Gaylen, the stage designer, has designed the sets.[19]

Gaylen, of course, had also designed Whatmore's production of *Peril at End House*.

The paper's reviewer concluded that 'The play is definitely

one which should "go",' but intriguingly also that 'It would be helped by the elimination of a certain staginess from its last moments.' This comment again raises the fascinating possibility that the production was played in Dundee with the 'alternative ending', as the image of Jackie awaiting arrest could hardly be described as 'stagey'. According to the local critic, 'Francis L. Sullivan gave a smooth, capable performance as the central figure, although there was no great call on his acting powers . . . Mrs Christie was present, but followed her usual custom of making no curtain appearance.' A.R. Whatmore made a curtain speech about his association with Christie and Sullivan, having also played the small role of the Ship's Manager (known at that point as Tibbotts). Cabaret singer Mischa de la Motte, one of the actors playing the beadsellers for whom Stephen Glanville had provided lines in Arabic, is credited with 'oriental singing throughout the play'.[20]

Following its Dundee premiere, though, there was no news of *Hidden Horizon* for over a year. Agatha occasionally referred to the lack of progress in letters to Max but, after her initial optimism that it would be easy to finance, seems to have given up on the idea and turned her attention instead to a stage adaptation of another of her novels.

In May 1944, with his production of *Ten Little Niggers* still running in the West End, Bertie Meyer acquired the option to produce Christie's own stage adaptation of her 1938 novel *Appointment with Death*.[21] Neither Farndale nor the PES were involved on this occasion; instead, in November 1944, Meyer entered into a co-production agreement with Derrick de Marney, who put up £750, 25 per cent of the production's £3,000 capital. The cost of staging the production itself accounted for £2,000, with the remainder held as a reserve against running costs.[22]

Christie had written *Appointment with Death* immediately after the Dundee premiere of *Hidden Horizon*, and it similarly involves a group of English holidaymakers in a Middle Eastern setting that she had visited with Max. This was undoubtedly an attempt on Meyer's part to repeat the success he had enjoyed with *Ten Little Niggers*, but unfortunately the script, although not without merit, would not have met the expectations of audiences who had been gripped by Christie's first big West End hit. The Christie archive contains no drafts or scripts for this play.

As a piece, *Appointment with Death* is a somewhat cumbersome, eighteen-hander, three-act drama, which sets the designer the challenge of moving the action from the King Solomon Hotel in Jerusalem to the Travellers' Camp at the Petra archaeological site. Again, Poirot is removed from the story, and there is a significant change in the outcome of the plot which aficionados of the detective genre may justifiably find frustrating but which, once again, demonstrates Christie's eagerness to experiment when adapting her work for the stage. The characterisation of the dramatis personae, and in particular of the Boynton family and its tyrannous matriarch, are of more interest to Christie the playwright than the trail of clues and, as so often in her stage work, 'whydunit' takes precedence over 'whodunit'. Though no match for it in terms of dramatic structure, the dialogue, in many cases, is sharper than that of *Ten Little Niggers*; and some relatively light-hearted political debate is provided through the introduction of Alderman Higgs as a down-to-earth nemesis for Lady Westholme, characterised in the play as a former Conservative MP, who is described by one of the other characters as 'a political big bug. In her own eyes at any rate. She's always heckling the government about housing or equal pay for women. She was an under-secretary or something – but she lost her seat at the last election.' Christie seems to have cast Lady Westholme in the same mould as *Hidden Horizon*'s Miss ffoliot-ffoulkes and, as in her previous play, the audience is invited to judge the character of the English abroad by the manner in which each of them addresses locals, particularly the staff who are looking after them. Here is Lady Westholme introducing the local guide to another member of the party:

LADY WESTHOLME: This is our dragoman – Mohammed.

DRAGOMAN: My name not Mohammed, lady. My name Aissa.

LADY WESTHOLME: I always call dragomen Mohammed.

DRAGOMAN: I Christian dragoman. Name Aissa, all same Jesus.

LADY WESTHOLME: Most unsuitable. I shall call you Mohammed, so please don't argue.[23]

The character of Lady Westholme would give rise to a particularly intriguing example of theatre censorship. Two days after Christmas 1944, H.C. Game of the Lord Chamberlain's office, in recommending the play for licence, suggested that 'we might point out to the management that the line which I have marked on III,9, when read in conjunction with the speech on I,6, suggests that the character, a minor one, is based on Lady Astor. It would be just as well if an alteration were made.'[24] The speech referred to was the one quoted above about Lady Westholme being a 'political big bug', and the line of hers in Act III which he had underlined read, 'Alcoholic indulgence is the great evil of the present age, and I shall never rest until I have introduced prohibition into England.' Lady Astor, wife of *Observer* proprietor Viscount Astor, had been the first woman to take a seat in Parliament in 1919 and at the time was still an MP. A notorious right-winger, she was a tireless anti-alcohol campaigner and in 1923 had introduced the Intoxicating Liquor bill, which raised the legal age for the consumption of alcohol in a public house from fourteen to eighteen. The line was duly cut, and it says a lot about the priorities of the Lord Chamberlain's office that a statement about the evils of alcohol was sacrificed in order to avoid causing offence to Lady Astor by associating her with a comic character.

Before *Appointment with Death* even reached the stage, Christie found herself working on her fourth full-length script in five years; again it was her own adaptation of one of her novels. Six weeks after the Broadway opening of *Ten Little Indians* – and, like Meyer, clearly hoping to repeat its success – the Shuberts commissioned Christie to write a stage version of her hugely popular new novel, *Towards Zero*. Christie duly delivered this script to the Shuberts in December the same year. Because Christie later lent her name to Gerald Verner's 1956 adaptation of the same book, the occasional reference in 1940s correspondence to the title as a stage adaptation has always been assumed to be some sort of work in progress for that. Nothing could be further from the truth.

On 1 August 1944, Lee Shubert and his legal eagle Adolph Kaufman met Ivan von Auw, a representative of Christie's New York agent, Harold Ober, for lunch. A week later, and two months after the novel's highly successful American launch, the Shuberts issued a commissioning agreement to Agatha Christie for a stage adaptation of *Towards Zero*; the document also refers to it by the title *Come and Be Hanged!*,[25] under which it had originally been serialised. On paper, the latest play from the writer of *Ten Little Indians*, adapted from her latest book, was a hot property. This was reflected in the size of the fee: $5,000, half of which was payable on signature and half on delivery. The script was to be received by the Shuberts by 1 February and they then had six months in which to produce it. Provided it was presented on Broadway, the Shuberts would receive 40 per cent of any film sale of the title (the film rights to the book could thus not be sold separately, as they had been with *Ten Little Niggers*) and financial participation in all residual licensing, excluding production in the UK. An author's royalty of between 5 and 10 per cent was payable on different bands of box office income. These arrangements are confirmed on an index cards in a forgotten corner of the Hughes Massie licensing records, which also seems to indicate their own 10 per cent commission as being split with Ober.[26]

On 3 March 1945 the *New York Times* announced, 'Agatha Christie has dramatised another of her mysteries, *Towards Zero*, and the completed script is expected in the Shubert offices momentarily.' But in reality the script had already arrived, on 14 December, and the Shubert office was trying to work out what to do with it. It was clearly not what they had been expecting.

In the meantime, Bertie Meyer's production of *Appointment*

with Death had opened. Unlike the Shuberts, he had had the opportunity to read the script before he bought it but, despite its obvious shortcomings, he appears to have engaged in none of the diligence that had resulted in lengthy rewrites and consequent delays in the production of *Ten Little Niggers*. The strategy in this case was simply to ensure that the production was staged as soon as possible in order to cash in on the popularity of *Ten Little Niggers*, opening its pre-West End tour shortly after the end of the latter's post-West End tour. The production was directed by Derrick de Marney's brother, Terence, who had played Lombard in *Ten Little Niggers*, and featured Joan Hickson (later to play Miss Marple on television with great success) in the role of Miss Pryce.

The production process for *Appointment with Death* proved considerably less enjoyable for Agatha than that for *Hidden Horizon*, partly one suspects due to the absence of her friends, the Sullivans. She wrote to Edmund Cork complaining of frustrating cast absences from rehearsal and noting that Sullivan meanwhile appeared to have booked a tour for *Hidden Horizon* without engaging a director or cast. Her reports of rehearsals to Max were not encouraging:

> Back in the hubbub of theatrical life . . . I'm rather glad all this is happening before you come back – would hate to miss any of your company because of having to attend rehearsals, and if one doesn't go to them frightful things happen and actors write in lines for themselves which make complete nonsense of the play! This in case you are confused, is Appointment with Death, and it opens in Glasgow on the 29th (a long cold journey! Do you remember our trip to Scotland – wasn't it fun!) we have been busy seeing people for parts. Bertie Meyer fell for a red head 'Lots of sex appeal!' . . . but once she had given a reading . . . his business instincts reassembled themselves.[27]

The production 'ought to be in London when you come home', she concludes.

The play opened at the King's Theatre, Glasgow, on 29 January 1945. Two days later Agatha wrote to Max, 'Here I am up to the head in the dramatic world. It has all been rather like a nightmare.'[28] Terrible weather had caused transport delays and 'Really it seemed impossible we could ever open on Monday night but we did – notices haven't been very good – but so contradictory that it is difficult to get pointers from them. One says for two acts "nothing happens"; only in Act 3 does the play "come to life". Other says interest drops *after* first two acts. I really think that the "whodunits" like [the] 3rd act and non-detective fans like first two. I also think it is unfortunate coming after Ten Little Niggers when there were 8 murders!!' She is complimentary about the scenery, saying that it reminds her of her visit to Petra with Max, and gives a detailed analysis of the performances, criticising some over-acting before concluding, 'Of course a lot of it is very funny. I do wish you were here to laugh about it with me . . . If it's not a success I don't care – Max is coming home – that's the great thing and *nothing* else matters *at all* . . . But I think this will be all right. Now that awful snow and ice has gone the bookings are good and the audience appreciative. Well – I must go and do my stuff – Christian names and lots of "Darlings!" Your exhausted Mrs Puper.'

Immediately after its Glasgow premiere, *Appointment with Death* embarked on a short national tour, evidently with a view to securing a West End theatre as soon as possible: 'BA Meyer presents, First time on any stage prior to London Production, Full West End Company in Appointment with Death' boasted the programme.[29] Reviews were mixed, however, and on 17 February Edmund Cork decided to go and see for himself. Three days later he wrote to Agatha, 'I hear such varied reports from people who went up to see Appointment with Death last week I thought I ought to see it myself. I went up on Saturday, and I was thrilled by the reception the play got. I have seldom seen a more enthusiastic audience.'[30] He gave her some perceptive notes on the text, staging and performances before finishing, 'Doubtless, however, these sort of points will be ironed out during its triumphant progress through the North, and we shall have a marvellous show before it comes to town.'

Despite Cork's optimism, however, Meyer was not finding it easy to secure a West End theatre, and on 22 February he wrote to Christie about the matter. During the production process for *Ten Little Niggers*, he had corresponded with Christie entirely via Edmund Cork and in this, one of the very few surviving letters from him to her, it is interesting to note the informal and affectionate tone of address that had grown up between them since then:

My dear Agatha,

On Saturday last, Associated London Theatres sent a representative to see our play at Northampton, and whilst he was quite pleased with some of it, he has requested me to make certain alterations before the Company is prepared to offer me one of their theatres for a London production. I am therefore passing on the gist of their report to you. He feels that the Curtains [i.e. ends of scenes] are not quite as good as they might be, and also that some of the dialogue in the Carbury cross-examination could be improved. They have asked for one or two changes in the cast, notably 'Nadine' with which I quite agree. They are [also] of the opinion that while Carla Lehmann is very charming and looks lovely, that she does not suggest the young woman doctor, and in view of the fact that she is under contract to play the part in London, I suggest that a few lines be added intimating that she has just completed her studies and is 'blowing' say a small inheritance before actively taking up her profession. I have ordered the new stage cloth for the last Act, and I propose to redress 'Sarah', 'Nadine', 'Lady Westholme' and 'Ginerva' for London. Would you kindly let me know whether it would be possible for you to meet me in Manchester for the first night on March 5th. The Northampton week was quite satisfactory. We had our worst opening, so far, in Hull

(£90), but this does not worry me as Hull is quite one of the worst dates.

Always yours sincerely,

Bertie A. Meyer[31]

In the end, all of the principal performers in the touring company stayed with the production for the West End, if only for no other reason than that, like Carla Lehmann, they were presumably under contract to do so. If Lehmann's lines were indeed changed to take account of the fact that the Canadian actress had clearly been miscast in the role of Doctor Sarah King, then there is no evidence of this.

Associated London Theatres (as Meyer refers to Associated Theatre Properties Ltd) was at the centre of the ever-growing theatre-owning cartel that became known in the industry as 'the Group', in which their investor Howard & Wyndham Ltd was a key player. In the end ATP didn't offer one of their own theatres, but one of the Group's associates, Tom Arnold, who had hosted the pre-West End opening of *Ten Little Niggers* at his Wimbledon Theatre, found room for the production at the Piccadilly Theatre. The Piccadilly had had mixed fortunes in recent years, partly as a vaudeville venue, and *Appointment with Death* was to reopen the theatre after a period of closure following bomb damage. One wonders whether Meyer's contractual inability to recast certain players compromised the production's ability to secure a more auspicious home.

A month later, Cork was writing to Christie about arrange-ments for the West End opening night, scheduled for 31 March. He noted that *Appointment with Death* had done well at the box office in Manchester and that 'it used to be said that what Manchester likes today, London likes tomorrow.'[32] The buoyant box office on the tour and in the early weeks in the West End were, though, to a large extent based on audience expectation following *Ten Little Niggers*. The luke-warm critical response in the West End was soon to put paid to that, although popular character actress Mary Clare scored a hit as Mrs Boynton.

It is also evident from the reviews that no expense had been spared by Meyer when it came to the two settings of the hotel and Petra. The scenery, including the extra cloth especially ordered for the final scene, was 'designed and executed' by leading scenic studio The Harkers, and the critics applauded their recreation of Petra. *The Times*, however, felt that

It is not until the end of the second act that Mrs Boynton's appointment, that has always seemed imminent, is actually kept, and so what began as though it would set off the old problem of who did it turns into a prolonged query about who is going to do it. There is ingenuity here, but all the polish of the acting and the production cannot disguise the artificiality of the characters and their behaviour; and what is acceptable as a kind of crossword in crime within the pages of a book becomes tedious on the stage . . . Mrs Boynton, gloating, as someone remarks, like some obscene idol over the sufferings of her hapless family, is a murderee if ever there was one. She is a monster, an artist in mental cruelty, and since she is also Miss Clare at the top of her form, it is a good thing for the audience that death delays so long in coming to her . . . Miss Joan Hickson makes the perfect spinster tourist.[33]

The *Observer* critic, on this occasion not Ivor Brown, whilst noting that 'Mrs Agatha Christie shuns library or lounge-hall', remarked that 'Unhappily her people, with one exception, are less surprising than their surroundings.'[34] Instead, the revival of Eden and Adelaide Phillpotts' *Yellow Sands*, presented by Robert Donat, Alec Rea and E.P. Clift at the Westminster Theatre, was their critic's recommendation for the week. For *The Stage*'s critic, *Appointment with Death* was

quite a good example of sophisticated melodrama, with an unusual setting and an unusual if insufficiently explained central theme . . . It was good to welcome back Mary Clare to the West End stage. All regular playgoers have vivid memories of her performances in earlier thrillers and here she dominates the play as effectively as Mrs Boynton dominates her step-children. The effectiveness of the performance . . . is the more remarkable because for long periods Miss Clare has only to sit silent and motionless while creating an impression of fear and terror. Terence De Marney has put plenty of vitality into his production and the Harkers' scenery well meets the needs of the situation.[35]

Thirty-four West End theatres were offering alternative attractions on the night *Appointment with Death* opened. Noël Coward was enjoying success with both a revival of *Private Lives* at the Apollo and the long-running *Blithe Spirit* at the Duchess; Terence Rattigan, similarly, had both *While the Sun Shines* at the Globe and *Love in Idleness* at the Lyric; the Old Vic Company, headed by Laurence Olivier, Ralph Richardson and Sybil Thorndike, were presenting *Richard III* at the New Theatre; and Lesley Storm and Esther McCracken were amongst the female playwrights whose work could be seen in the West End. At the Ambassadors the second instalment of the popular revue show *Sweet and Low* was in full swing.

Christie's first wartime offering in the West End had found favour with the contemporary zeitgeist, but her second seemed oddly out of kilter with it, and closed after forty-two performances on 5 May 1945, five days after Hitler's suicide and three days before the end of the war in Europe. It is understandable that the public were glued to their radios during these momentous events, rather than enjoying a night at the theatre puzzling over whodunit with a group of eccentric Brits at Petra. The lack of involvement from the People's Entertainment Society also meant that, unlike *Ten Little Niggers*, the production had not benefited from the co-operative movement's considerable nationwide publicity machine. It seems unlikely that they turned the play down, after their previous success with a Christie title, and they were to work with Meyer on another Christie project in the future; it may simply have been that on this occasion Meyer did not wish to dilute the distribution of the anticipated profits beyond himself and de Marney. Although Samuel French entered into their usual deal for amateur and publication rights in 1947, they did not publish the play until 1956. With its extravagantly large dramatis personae, it has had no significant revival and is notable for its absence from Hughes Massie's regular advertisements promoting Christie's work to the repertory market throughout the late 1940s and 1950s.

Shortly after the opening of *Appointment with Death* at the Piccadilly, the long-awaited pre-West End tour of *Hidden Horizon* finally began, over a year after the play's try-out production in Dundee. In the intervening period, Sullivan had sold his company's rights in the project to Alec Rea[36] whose company Reandco had transferred Sullivan from the Embassy to the West End in *Black Coffee* in 1931. Along with his business partner E.P. Clift, Rea now become the producer of the project, and Sullivan himself remained in the role that had been written for him. On this occasion, Reandco co-produced in association with seasoned tour booker and promoter Barry O'Brien, who had produced a post-West End tour of *Peril at End House* starring Sullivan, and who was presumably responsible for booking the theatres for *Hidden Horizon*. In mid-February Agatha wrote to Max, 'Hidden Horizon is going into rehearsal March 12th and has first production at Wimbledon on April 9th. Then Birmingham and then Cardiff 23rd. By which time you might be home and we would have a visit to Ros combined with seeing Larry Sullivan in his dog collar as Canon Pennefather!'[37]

The response at Wimbledon, where *Ten Little Niggers* had also opened, was encouraging. Under the headline 'Wimbledon premiere', *The Stage* announced, 'On Monday last at Wimbledon, Alec Rea and E.P. Clift presented a new play by Agatha Christie entitled *Hidden Horizon*. Any play by Agatha Christie is bound to attract attention and *Hidden Horizon* is no exception.'[38] The fact that the play had actually premiered in Dundee the previous

year is conveniently overlooked. The review went on, 'There
are numerous "situations", plots, clues, with plenty of excitement and thrills. It is a cleverly worked-out play . . . The cast
is a strong one. Francis L. Sullivan as Canon Pennefather . . .
gives a fine rendering of the character of a middle-aged
clergyman.'

By June, though, Cork was writing to Agatha with disappointing news:

I'm afraid I have not any good news for you about Hidden
Horizon. Business was not very good either in Hammersmith
or in Glasgow, and although at the latter place there was
a very strong counter-attraction and [director Claud] Gurney
says Appointment With Death left a prejudice against
Christie plays, I do find it rather disappointing. But the
disturbing thing is that the short tour ends this week . . .
and Clift tells me that he is quite unable to get a suitable
London theatre. His suggestion was that you should be
asked whether you would be prepared to grant a further
extension of the option under which Clift has to put it on
in London by July 12th . . . I think I know the answer to
this without asking you. He then asked how we would view
the possibility of putting it on at the Westminster Theatre
– he has not the offer of it but he thinks he might be able
to arrange it. My view is that the Westminster is quite
unsuitable for this play, and I would be prepared to argue
that the Westminster is not a 'first class West End Theatre'
as required by the contract. Do you think it is? . . . Probably
from a hard business point of view it might be better for
you for the present contract to run out, which would mean
that the projected American production would come on first
under a contract granted from you as provided by the last
lot of papers that you signed. If it were successful in America,
we would be in a very strong position to deal with an English
manager. But – and I am afraid this letter seems to be all
buts and dashes – I am afraid your friend Sullivan may feel
rather badly about it.[39]

The end of the war in Europe had caused a momentary hiatus in the West End that contributed to the demise of *Appointment with Death*, but ultimately created an unprecedented boom in theatre attendance, as a celebratory mood prevailed and the long process of demobbing commenced, swelling the number of potential attendees. In August Cork wrote to Agatha again:

I have not written to you about Hidden Horizon because, despite everyone's protestations, there have not been any developments. I have just spoken to Clift again, and he tells me that though he is doing his damdest there is no progress to report. Such business as is being done today has never been known among London theatres, and there is not a single show that need come off . . .

I realise how unsatisfactory you must find all this, but I doubt if any other management could have done better – certainly the Tennents seem to have a lot of shows on, but they have many more plays that they have bought and cannot find theatres for. I suggest that we do not grant an extension to Sullivan and Clift in case another opportunity presents itself, but allow them to carry on with their efforts (which they will do as they have the production and every confidence in it) on the understanding that their position will be regularised if they can produce an acceptable proposition within a reasonable time.[40]

The possible American production of *Hidden Horizon* that Cork refers to in his earlier letter was being planned by the Shuberts under an option that they eventually obtained from Reandco at the beginning of August 1945.[41] The UK producer would not normally have been entitled to sell the US rights in advance of opening in the West End, but Hughes Massie had given them a special dispensation to do so in order to facilitate the sale without the Shuberts having to wait for Reandco to present the play in London. Presumably sensing that there were problems with their commissioned *Towards Zero* script, and eager to have a follow-up ready for *Ten Little Indians* (which had finally closed on Broadway the previous month), the Shuberts seem to have taken on *Hidden Horizon* as a fall-back position. *Ten Little Indians'* Albert de Courville was lined up to direct and again named as a co-licensee and entitled to 25 per cent of profits, indicating that he was regarded once more as a key player in securing the title for them from Hughes Massie (via Ober in New York). Significantly, the Shuberts at no point showed any interest in *Appointment with Death*, even though its American option was in the gift of Bertie Meyer, with whom they had struck the deal for *Ten Little Indians*.

Towards Zero, though, would have had greater currency as a title in America at the time than a retitled *Death on the Nile*, and the Shuberts did their best to safeguard their investment and make it work. On the day that they had issued their commissioning contract to Christie for *Towards Zero*, their lawyer Adolph Kaufman had spoken with Ivan von Auw of the Ober office about adding a clause that would enable them to make changes for the script in the event that it was 'not fit for American theatre'. But, he reported to Lee Shubert at the time, 'Mr Van Auw stated that from his past experience with Miss Christie, she has always been very co-operative with publishers in the matter of changes and he sees no reason why she would not co-operate in this case. He thinks this question should be left to the future because, very likely, you will not need many changes in any event.'[42]

Changes were duly requested, and in January 1945, Cork wrote to Christie, 'I hear from Harold Ober that Lee Shubert is enthusiastic about your play Towards Zero, but he is suggesting certain slight alterations in the last act, which have been posted to us by airmail. I should think these are just "producer's alterations" which I believe you antici-pated.'[43]

It seems though that, in the event, Christie was too busy to undertake any changes and, following exchanges with Hughes Massie in March, an American writer, Robert Harris, had even-tually been engaged to carry out some script doctoring. On

5 June 1945 the Shuberts signed an agreement to pay Harris $1,000 'to edit and re-write for us any or all parts of the play now known as Towards Zero as shall be designated by the undersigned'.[44] Harris was to waive all his rights and would not receive a credit on the play. According to a memo from Kaufman to Lee Shubert on 30 June, 'The work performed by Harris becomes the property of Select [one of the Shuberts' companies] and he has no claim of ownership or title to the work.' It added that he 'has already delivered the rewritten work and been paid in full'.[45]

I was first set on the trail of the *Towards Zero* script by a letter from Lee Shubert to Christie (care of Hughes Massie) dated 18 October 1945. It reads,

Dear Miss Christie,

We 'tried out' the above play this summer and regret to say unsuccessfully. The trouble, as Mr de Courville pointed out, lies in the last act, and, even though we went to considerable expense in an effort to correct the act, we found the climax came too suddenly and the final situation was not plausible to the audience.

We therefore decided to postpone the New York production of the play until you yourself had an opportunity to put things right. It would, in our opinion, be unwise to produce a successor to the very popular Ten Little Indians unless we felt we had an opportunity of topping, or at least equalling the success of your other play. It would not only be bad for us, but also for the name of Agatha Christie, which we wish to keep very high on Broadway . . .

Would you be good enough to undertake the work on the play yourself for, after all, we know of no one else competent enough to do it. You know, of course, the difference in the returns between a mediocre play and a good one and we hope you will agree to make the necessary alterations and give us the necessary time for producing same.

With kind regards I am sincerely yours,

Lee Shubert[46]

For Shubert himself to write to Christie in this way is indicative of the perceived value of her work to his company, but the most significant point here is that he is clearly discussing a work that, by October 1945, *has already been performed* in America in a 'try-out' production, albeit not in New York. Within hours of phoning the Shubert archive I was advised that they held copies of not only of the original commissioning agreement, but also of the script. Having cast myself in the role of detective in this particular story, I felt that it was essential that I see the evidence first hand as I had with the scripts for *The Lie*, *The Stranger* and others. This was much more than a missing Christie play; it was a missing play that had actually been performed, the only play that she wrote as a result of a commission, and the only work of hers to receive its world premiere in America in her lifetime. The Shubert archive, as it happens, held three copies of this unique and previously unknown script, one of which has now kindly been donated by the Shubert Organisation to the Agatha Christie archive.

Like the novel, Christie's play is set at Lady Tressilian's house on the coast. It follows the same plot concerning a man who flaunts his new wife in front of his previous one; and a murder, the perpetrator of which comes close to successfully framing another suspect, and has constructed the whole scenario in the hope of disposing of the wrongly accused individual via the hangman's noose (hence the original magazine serialisation title, *Come and Be Hanged!*). It is a neat plot with a surprise outcome, but it is no *Ten Little Niggers* in terms of construction and consequent dramatic potential. Instead, as is often the case with Christie's stage work, she takes the opportunity to focus on characterisation and motivation, which is of particular interest to her in a story the premise of which is to explore how, through people's interactions, the 'zero hour' of murder is actually arrived at.

Superintendent Battle, for whom this was his last appearance in a novel, is absent from the play's dramatis personae (although he had appeared in Christie's adaptation of *The Secret of Chimneys*), and local CID man Inspector Leach is left to do the honours. A cast of thirteen take part in the three-act, five-scene drama, which takes place over a period of eight days. Intriguingly, the piece is set in the open air, on the terrace and in the garden of the house and on the adjacent cliff path. We see a garden wall, a large rock at the top of the cliff and a sea view across to the hotel on the other side of the bay. Audrey, the play's female protagonist, regularly encounters the failed suicide Angus McWhirter on the cliff path, where they engage in discussions about issues of mortality:

> ANGUS: . . . If life holds nothing worth living for – the only sensible thing is to get out.
>
> AUDREY: Oh no – oh no! I don't want to believe that . . . one's life might be valuable.
>
> ANGUS: A man's the best judge of that himself.
>
> AUDREY: I meant valuable to someone else.
>
> ANGUS: If a man's all that valuable to someone else, I doubt that he'd want to commit suicide at all. His natural vanity would prevent it.
>
> AUDREY: One's life might be valuable to someone one had never seen.
>
> ANGUS: I'd be interested to hear how you make that out?
>
> AUDREY: I'm being stupid, perhaps, but it seems to me that life is a little like a play – everyone has a part.
>
> ANGUS: (quoting rather sententiously) 'All the world's a stage and every man a player'. Is that your meaning?
>
> AUDREY: (Smiling) Oh, I know that Shakespeare put it a good deal better. What I'm trying to say is – (breaks off) How difficult it is to put one's ideas into words.
>
> ANGUS: Go on. I'd be interested to hear just what you have in mind.
>
> AUDREY: (slowly and with difficulty) The actors in a play depend on each other – and so does the action of the play. If a man decides to make a final exit, shall we say, in the

first act – what's to happen in the third act when he has perhaps a small, but very important part – only a few lines, perhaps, but without them the play goes to pieces – the action is meaningless – all because a small part actor who didn't think his part sufficiently important, has walked out on the Company.[47]

Following this, of course, McWhirter goes on to play a significant role in the story's resolution. Anyone familiar with Gerald Verner's 1956 drawing-room set adaptation of the novel will immediately recognise that this is an entirely different play. Verner's eleven characters, only six of which are shared with Christie's version, include Battle but not McWhirter. Christie's work is a far more dramatically ambitious piece on all levels, but one can see why the Shuberts were perplexed by it.

A check in the *New York Times* archive for 1945 quickly revealed where and when the try-out production of their new Christie script, as doctored by Robert Harris, had taken place: 'Towards Zero, another murder mystery by Agatha Christie, will be tested for the Shuberts by Arthur J. Beckhard on Martha's Vineyard on September 11. Clarence Derwent is directing the cast, which includes Elfrida Derwent, Althea Murphy, Shirley Collier, Rand Elliot, Ned Payne, Esther Mitchell and J.P. Wilson.'[48] Arthur J. Beckhard was a prolific producer-director and Martha's Vineyard resident, who regularly promoted seasons and Broadway try-outs at the Playhouse there. London-born Clarence Derwent was a respected actor and director who carved a successful early career in the UK before moving to America where, from 1946 to 1952, he was President of American Actors' Equity. The union still gives out an annual award which he set up to recognise the work of 'non-featured' (latterly redesignated 'most promising') actors on Broadway, whilst its UK counterpart presents an award in his name for 'supporting' actors in the West End. Earlier in 1945 Derwent had directed Diana Barrymore in the short-lived Broadway premiere of Daphne Du Maurier's *Rebecca*; and now his sister, Elfrida Derwent, was to play Lady Tressilian for him in *Towards Zero*.

The *New York Times* appears to have got the date of the production wrong by a week; it seems that the world premiere of Agatha Christie's *Towards Zero* actually took place at Martha's Vineyard Playhouse on Tuesday 4 September 1945; two days after the formal surrender of Japan following the unleashing on Hiroshima and Nagasaki of weapons of mass destruction not dissimilar to those described by Christie in *Black Coffee* over two decades previously. The *Martha's Vineyard Gazette* of 7 September provides, as far as I know, the only critical appraisal of this unique theatrical event. Under the headline 'A New Mystery Play: Characteristic Touches of popular writer Make an Engrossing Play' it ran the following review:

> A new Agatha Christie mystery play, *Towards Zero*, is this week's production at Martha's Vineyard Playhouse, on East Chop . . . The action takes place on the walled terrace of Lady Tressilian's house, Gull's Nest, on the high coastal rocks of a place called Salt Creek, the atmosphere of which is excellently realized by the stage setting of Pamella Judson-Styles . . .
>
> As so often in Agatha Christie stories, the apparent facts do not coincide with the real facts, which is the sort of mystification the reader or the audience can follow with suspense and see resolved with a sense of surprise and satisfaction . . . The title of the play derives from exchanges of philosophy between Audrey and a roving Scot named McWhirter, who appears from time to time on the coastal path . . . Events move, it is pointed out, towards a zero hour of murder, with people gathered from different places as if by appointment . . . The play has been well staged by Clarence Derwent, and the cast is good.[49]

Given that this was presumably the doctored version, of which there appears to be no surviving copy, it seems not to have differed significantly from the script delivered by Christie in December the previous year. It is notable the care with which the complex exterior setting appears to have been executed for what was evidently intended in the first instance as a one-week run, and the detailed description of this set in Christie's script provides the answer to another little mystery. The Agatha Christie archive contains a small, beautifully executed water-colour which recreates in every detail the play's setting as specified by Christie. On the back of it is written 'Sketch of Scene – Towards Zero', but until the discovery of this script there was no explanation for it. The picture bears no relation to Gerald Verner's 1956 script and, whilst it is not a technical design drawing for a set, it is completely uninhabited and is an artist's impression specifically of the relevant buildings and landscape rather than of a moment from the novel. Now that we know what it portrays, my belief is that Christie commissioned the painting so that she could visualise the unusual layout of the stage while she was writing and plan the characters' positions on it and their entrances and exits. It is signed 'H. Francis Clarke' (or possibly Clark with a smudge), offering the intriguing prospect that it may have been the work of the distinguished landscape architect Frank Clark, who was resident in Hampstead (not far from Christie's Lawn Road address) at this time.

It was to the Martha's Vineyard production that Shubert is referring in his letter to Christie of the following month, expressing his hope that she herself will now undertake the necessary changes. Ober was tasked with establishing exactly what was needed, and at the end of November wrote to Cork to say that Shubert and, interestingly, de Courville both thought that 'the denoument is abrupt and does not play well. They feel that Mrs Mallowan could with very little rewriting handle this scene more adroitly.'[50] A week later he followed this up with

I had a discussion a couple of days ago with Shubert and de Courville regarding the Towards Zero contract . . . De

Courville, as a matter of fact, urged that we try to get Mrs Mallowan to come over here and work on revisions of the play and I am glad to see that this is in the realm of possibility. I think the difficulty could also be solved by having the play tried out in England first. You will have had by now my letter saying that neither de Courville nor Shubert want any drastic alterations and they do not want to change the character of the play. It has been difficult, however, to get them to be very specific about what they feel is the matter with it. They gave the play a stock try-out [another reference to the Martha's Vineyard production] and they simply feel that the denouement is abrupt and does not play well. If this is so it would be apparent in an English try-out and Mrs Mallowan could fix the script over there.[51]

He goes on to suggest that, English rights being reserved to Christie, Bertie Meyer could perhaps offer the Shuberts a co-production in London. Changes, however, were not forthcoming from Agatha, and she did not take up the Shuberts' apparently generous offer of a trip to New York to carry out the work.

After the frenzied activity of the war, Agatha was now reunited with Max and with Greenway; the former unscathed by his contribution to the air force's work in North Africa, the latter with the colourful addition of a mural depicting the American navy's war effort, painted by one of its wartime residents. Clement Attlee's Labour Party, with its full-blooded commitment to the introduction of a Welfare State, had swept Churchill from power after the end of hostilities in Europe. It was a time of austerity and of change and Agatha, like many of her contemporaries, seems to have been afflicted with post-war doldrums. Despite the safe return of Max, the war had taken its toll on her family, with the loss in October 1944 of her son-in-law Hubert Prichard, just at the moment when she had been rushing to complete the script of *Towards Zero*. Now was a time for taking stock and looking to the future rather than tidying up loose ends from wartime projects.

J.J. and Lee Shubert.

Top left: Barbara Toy in her Land Rover 'Pollyanna'.

Top right: Irene Hentschel.

Bottom: Agatha's agents Edmund Cork (left) and Harold Ober (right).

Top: Linden Travers and Terence de Marney in *Ten Little Niggers* (1943).

Bottom: The Broadway cast of *Ten Little Indians* (1944).

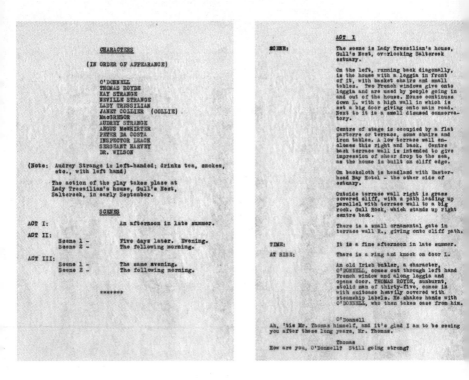

CHARACTERS

(IN ORDER OF APPEARANCE)

O'DONNELL
THOMAS ROYDE
KAY STRANGE
NEVILLE STRANGE
LADY TRESSILIAN
JANET COLLIER (COLLIE)
MacGREGOR
AUDREY STRANGE
ANGUS McWHIRTER
PETER DA COSTA
INSPECTOR LEACH
SERGEANT HARVEY
MR. WILSON

(Note: Audrey Strange is left-handed; drinks tea, smokes, etc., with left hand)

The action of the play takes place at Lady Tressilian's house, Gull's Nest, Saltcreek, in early September.

SCENES

ACT I: An afternoon in late summer.

ACT II:
    Scene 1 –   Five days later. Evening.
    Scene 2 –   The following morning.

ACT III:
    Scene 1 –   The same evening.
    Scene 2 –   The following morning.

****

ACT I

SCENE: The scene is Lady Tressilian's house, Gull's Nest, overlooking Saltcreek estuary.

On the left, running back diagonally, is the house with a loggia in front of it, with basket chairs and small tables. Two French windows give onto loggia and are used by people going in and out of the house. House continues down L. with a high wall in which is set a big door giving onto main road. Next to it is a small disused conservatory.

Centre of stage is occupied by a flat parterre or terrace, some chairs and iron tables. A low terrace wall encloses this right and back. Centre back terrace wall is intended to give impression of sheer drop to the sea, as the house is built on cliff edge.

On backcloth is headland with Easterhead Bay Hotel – the other side of estuary.

Outside terrace wall right is grass covered cliff, with a path leading up parallel with terrace wall to a big rock, Gull Rock, which stands up right centre back.

There is a small ornamental gate in terrace wall R., giving onto cliff path.

TIME: It is a fine afternoon in late summer.

AT RISE: There is a ring and knock on door L.

An old Irish butler, a character, O'DONNELL, comes out through left hand French window and along loggia and opens door. THOMAS ROYDE, sunburnt, stolid man of thirty-five, comes in with suitcases heavily covered with steamship labels. He shakes hands with O'DONNELL, who then takes case from him.

                    O'Donnell
Ah, 'tis Mr. Thomas himself, and it's glad I am to be seeing you after these long years, Mr. Thomas.

                    Thomas
How are you, O'Donnell? Still going strong?

Script for Agatha Christie's *Towards Zero* (left), description of set (right) and set illustration (below).

The Shuberts' licence was extended to enable them to open on Broadway by 1 October 1946, but it was not to be, and Agatha Christie's play of *Towards Zero* was never seen or heard of again.

One of the conditions of the contract extension on *Towards Zero* negotiated by Ober was that the Shuberts were obliged to put *Hidden Horizon*, now incorporating some changes that they had requested in Act Three, into production in the meantime. The eventual fate of *Hidden Horizon* thus appears to have been dictated more by contractual considerations than by any genuine enthusiasm for the piece on the part of either its British or American producers. In order to understand the motivations of those concerned it is necessary to appreciate the huge premium that the licensing system placed on achieving a West End (and, in America, a Broadway) production. The originating producer in the UK would secure the rights to a new play by paying an advance against the writer's royalty income (typically £100 against 10 per cent of box office sales). This would give the producer a specified period (usually one year) in which to secure a West End opening (often following a pre-West End tour or provincial 'try-out'). The option period could usually be extended in return for a further advance payment, provided that no other managements were competing for the licence. Having opened in the West End, the licensee would have the right themselves to produce the work in Great Britain, Ireland and various dominions, colonies and dependencies for a period of seven years in return for the agreed royalty payments. They would also have the right to sub-license in these territories and would have first option to acquire for sub-licence the American rights, retaining a share of the author's income from any such deals.

In the case of *Hidden Horizon*, for instance, if Reandco had produced in the West End, exercised the American option and then sub-licensed to a Broadway producer, they would have received 40 per cent of Christie's royalties. The West End production would also have entitled them to a third of her income from the play in other overseas territories. In this instance, a commission was deductible from Reandco's share and payable to Sullivan's company Eleven Twenty Three Ltd who had, with Hughes Massie's co-operation, assigned their original licence to Reandco.

Having opened in the West End, the producer would also benefit from the sale of film rights if this took place within the seven-year period, in this case receiving a third of income from the sale of either the play or the original novel, *Death on the Nile*. During the seven-year period, the producer would also receive a share (in this case 40 per cent) of the author's income from amateur, repertory, broadcasting and television rights in Britain and associated territories. A sub-licence issued by the originating West End producer to an American producer would similarly give them a timeframe in which to produce on Broadway, following which the American producer would be entitled to a share of the British producer's income from a film sale and from American sub-licensing, in particular to stock (i.e. repertory) theatres. These financial incentives offered to the originating West End producer and their Broadway counterpart were deemed to be fair recompense for the publicity that these particularly high-profile productions would bring to the work, thereby enhancing its attraction to film studios (for which a Broadway run was particularly important), repertory, touring, stock and amateur companies. They also gave the producers concerned a vested interest in assisting the writer's agent with maximising the various potential income streams from it during the seven-year duration of the original licence. Arrangements not dissimilar to these remain custom and practice in the licensing of stage works to this day. Edmund Cork was no fool, and he understood the nuances of the game very well.

Following their failure to find a West End home for the play, Reandco's West End option for *Hidden Horizon* had duly been allowed to lapse on 16 October 1945, but two weeks later a new licence was issued to them on rather different terms. Alec Rea had by now become a substantial producing force in his own right, and Cork saw no advantage in falling out of favour with him, given his continued interest in Christie's work. Reandco's prevarication had forfeited them their share of income from a film sale and various other secondary licences, although they retained post-West End touring rights, and in the new deal Christie was, unusually, entitled to 20 per cent of profits to the producer arising out of the licence.[52] All this was the price of Cork's continued patience.

Most significantly, as a special condition of the arrangement whereby they had been allowed to sell an American option to the Shuberts without themselves having presented the play in the West End, any income generated thereby for Reandco would be held in an escrow account by Hughes Massie until they themselves had staged a West End production. Reandco's new licence contained the usual provision for an American option to be taken up after the West End opening. So, with the most powerful theatre organisation on earth already holding a licence for a Broadway production, Reandco had the biggest possible incentive to achieve a West End run for the play, exercise their American option and cash in their share of the income from a likely Broadway run. Cork's strategy in reinstating Reandco's entitlement to 40 per cent of Christie's Broadway income may at first seem questionable but, as internal Shubert correspondence shows, they were, unsurprisingly, reluctant to exercise their option on an English play if that play had not been deemed worthy of a West End run. And in any case the boost to secondary markets for the play that a West End run would bring was evidently deemed worth the sacrifice by Cork. The renegotiated licence issued to Reandco in October 1945 is the first time that we see the play referred to as 'Murder on the Nile'[53] – the play's third title, for what was to be its third production. For this incarnation Reandco continued to share producing credits with Barry O'Brien.

In the circumstances, it is perhaps not surprising that the eventual West End production of *Murder on the Nile* appears to have been something of a half-hearted affair, doubtless motivated principally by Reandco's desire to secure a share of the American income and the sale of a sub-licence for the post-West End touring rights in the piece; 'direct from the West End' carried a certain cachet then, as it does now. The production opened at the Ambassadors Theatre on 19 March 1946, more than two years after it had premiered in Dundee. It ran for six weeks. This was not, as has previously been assumed, because it failed at the box office, but because it had been specifically booked in for a limited season while, according to *The Stage*, the cast of the long-running popular revue *Sweeter and Lower* took a holiday and rehearsed for the opening of its sequel *Sweetest and Lowest*.

The cast of *Murder on the Nile* was largely that which had appeared in the previous year's tour, and the director was once again Oxford-educated Claud Gurney – a safe pair of hands but no Irene Hentschel. Contrary to some accounts, the role of Miss ffoliott-ffoulkes was played not by Helen Hayes, who later portrayed Miss Marple on American TV, but by the more elderly British actress Helen Haye. Having provided 'Oriental singing' in both Dundee and on tour, Mischa de la Motte was no longer with the company, and the highly regarded Vivienne Bennett (who had appeared in the 1937 television broadcast of Emlyn Williams' *Night Must Fall*) had taken over the role of Jacqueline de Severac. But the most significant change was that the man for whom the play had been written was himself no longer in it. Francis L. Sullivan was either not available or simply didn't fancy a six-week run, and Father Borrowdale (as he was now named) was played by character actor David Horne. The next we hear of Sullivan is from Cork at the end of the following year, with regard to the possibility of him appearing in an American tour of *Alibi*. Mrs Sullivan's scenery was retained for *Murder on the Nile* and continued to receive good reviews, although for the most part the play and the actors didn't.

The Times led off the critical drubbing: 'Once more the "Who did it?" piece, and this time in its crudest form. Motives are distributed amongst passengers in the Observation Saloon of the Nile Steamer as lightly as though they were raffle tickets, and none of those who receive one has the personality to make us wish that he or she will or will not be the winner or loser . . . we cannot help hoping that it will turn out to be the parson who, whether as a platitudinous Father Confessor or a highly ratiocinative amateur detective, is no end of a bore.'[54] To save you looking it up, as I had to, ratiocination is the process of logical reasoning.

The *Daily Mail* put it even more bluntly: 'If even my gullible old eyes can spot successively the future assassin, the accomplice, and even the method of murder in *Murder on the Nile*, something is wrong. Indeed, it is a hard job to find much right with Agatha Christie's new thriller . . . the company in general seems to suffer from a lack of spirit, natural enough in the circumstances, yet something which I found myself catching.'[55]

The *Observer*'s Ivor Brown, whose wartime household income had been swelled by royalties from the West End and touring productions of *Ten Little Niggers*, was less condemnatory:

As far as plot (intricate of course) is concerned, the new Agatha Christie play might as well have tipped its corpses into the Nile. But Egypt offers the scene painter a better chance (nicely taken by Danae Gaylen) . . . The piece has the proper excitements of its hard-worked kind; a weakness lies in the blending of the usual mystery-mechanism with unusual human emotion. We have come to take our murders lightly in this kind of theatre; consequently a serious ending, with the guilty party nobly declining an obvious suicide at sacerdotal urgence, the better to find salvation via the scaffold, is too momentous a finale for so light a morsel of playmaking . . . Mr David Horne, as a detectively-minded Anglican priest, persuasively mixes clues and canonicals . . .[56]

The Stage noticed that 'Father Borrowdale has a good deal

in common with his Chestertonian counterpart Father Brown. David Horne, playing a part that has been taken on tour by Francis Sullivan, very skilfully suggests, both in appearance and manner, this subtly contrived pillar of the High Church.'[57] The *Daily Telegraph* noted that whilst 'not a vintage Christie' the production was 'likely to fill the Ambassadors Theatre for some time to come';[58] in fact it didn't, simply because of the limited engagement at the theatre. For some reason Rea does not appear to have advertised the fact that this was a limited season, but on 27 April, as scheduled, the production moved aside to enable *Sweetest and Lowest* to open. Two days previously, *The Stage* had announced that touring producer D. Rewse-White had secured the UK touring rights from Reandco and that a tour would commence in July; the deal had doubtless been brokered by co-producer Barry O'Brien, who booked touring dates for Rewse-White. The previous week Reandco had taken up their American option and thereby secured their share of any income from a Broadway production. The intentionally brief West End run of *Murder on the Nile* at least appears to have served its purpose in certain respects.

Murder on the Nile opened two weeks after the closure – having clocked up a record-breaking 1,998 performances – of Noël Coward's *Blithe Spirit*. Coward's *Private Lives* was in its second year at the Apollo, and the Old Vic Company, led by Olivier and Richardson, were playing *Henry IV Part One* at the New Theatre. Competing for the attention of Shakespeare audiences, the irrepressible Donald Wolfit could be seen in a repertoire of the Bard's work at the Winter Garden Theatre. On a lighter note, Lupino Lane was appearing in *Me and My Girl* at the Victoria Palace, and it was the last chance to see Bud Flanagan in *Cinderella* at the Adelphi. Esther McCracken's *No Medals* was in its second year at the Vaudeville and Mary Hayley Bell's *Duet for Two Hands* was enjoying success at the Lyric, co-produced by Jack Buchanan and the People's Entertainment Society.

Six weeks after *Murder on the Nile* closed, Reandco, in

co-production with the increasingly ubiquitous H.M. Tennent Ltd, opened another Christie play which ran for 289 performances at the West End's Apollo Theatre. On this occasion, the Christies concerned were Dorothy and Campbell Christie; Campbell, the younger brother of Agatha's former husband, enjoyed a successful playwriting partnership with his wife. They had already seen two of their plays performed in the West End, including 1935's 'comedy thriller' *Someone at the Door*, which appears to have been written at exactly the time when Agatha herself was penning the similarly titled *Someone at the Window*. Now, in 1946, *Grand National Night* was to be Dorothy and Campbell Christie's first big success, and would be followed by a number of other plays including *Carrington VC* and *The Touch of Fear*. Agatha had remained on friendly terms with Campbell, a well-known wit with a distinguished record of military service, following her divorce from Archie; but it must nonetheless have rankled somewhat to see her own producer score such an apparently effortless hit for a part-time writer. When in 1963 Campbell was found dead in his gas-filled kitchen at the age of sixty-nine, a hugely respectful *Times* obituary quoted his view on state subsidy for the arts as being 'Why pay people to put plays on that audiences don't want to see?'[59]

Given *Murder on the Nile*'s undistinguished West End premiere, it seems extraordinary that the Shuberts decided to proceed with a Broadway production at all. In early July 1946 J.J. Shubert wrote to brother Lee, in one of the terse internal memos that characterised the organisation: 'I notice you have Hidden Horizon which must be produced by September 30, 1946; also Towards Zero by October 1, 1946. Are you going to do anything about producing these plays?'[60] Their company had so far invested $10,000 in acquiring options on them, so the question was a legitimate one.

The Shuberts' paper trail on *Hidden Horizon* makes that for *Ten Little Indians* look relatively straightforward; this is largely due to their having been licensed by Reandco, who at the time were themselves about to lose their licence for failing to produce in the West End. The Shuberts' ever-diligent lawyers had spotted that Reandco would have no film or American stock rights to pass on if they themselves had failed to produce in the West End, and a side agreement with Christie to secure their position in this regard was therefore required, reassuring the Shuberts that in the event that Reandco's own licence lapsed, they would still receive 25 per cent of income from a film sale and 50 per cent of income from stock licences if they produced the play on Broadway. That, along with tortuous dealings with the Dramatists Guild and de Courville, numerous assignments and warranties that were required from the various parties (going back as far as Sullivan's Eleven Twenty Three Ltd) and a number of requests to extend the date on the Broadway licence, kept the Shuberts' lawyers and the Ober office busy for almost six months.

Eventually, on 27 July 1945, an exasperated Ober wrote to Lee Shubert himself ('Shubert, as you know, is a difficult man,' he had commented to Cork two weeks earlier[61]): 'With pains-taking care we have gotten all the supplementary documents which your legal department thought necessary . . . Now I am constantly getting enquiries from our London office, wanting to know what the status of the contract is. I am afraid, there-fore, that unless the contracts are returned to us fully executed by Friday, August 3rd, we will have to withdraw the play and make other arrangements for its production.'[62] Shubert signed the contract on 1 August.

The final extension on the *Hidden Horizon* licence granted to the Shuberts, to 30 September 1946, was allegedly in order to ensure de Courville's own availability to direct.[63] Throughout all this, there was clearly still some hope on the Shuberts' part that Christie might come up with the desired script amendments on *Towards Zero*, and it has to be said that Lee Shubert remained remarkably sanguine in the face of her continued refusal to do so. Finally, with licences for both plays about to run out and no further extensions on offer, the Shuberts must have decided that, of the two scripts as they stood, *Hidden Horizon* was the better bet. This was their last opportunity to present a work from the writer of the hit *Ten Little Indians* while that production was still relatively fresh in people's minds and, despite the poor critical response in London, they booked the play into the Plymouth Theatre from 19 September.

Interestingly, the Shuberts either decided against, or were not given the option to use, the title under which the play had finally premiered in the West End and, as with the West End production, it was only booked to run for a very short limited season. Over the summer, the American press had been monitoring the lack of New York theatre availability with interest; and on 30 August the *New York Times* had noted that both *Hidden Horizon* and a production of *Cyrano de Bergerac* were seeking theatres, adding that if they had to become 'stop gap shows' (i.e. occupying a theatre temporarily between other bookings) there would be no trouble finding transfer houses for them if they were hits: 'There is a tradition in the theatre forbidding any hit to go homeless.'[64]

On 14 September, the Shuberts' press agent Claude Greneker issued a press release: 'Agatha Christie, famed mystery writer who was last represented on Broadway by *Ten Little Indians*, will have another of her spine-tinglers on the boards when *Hidden Horizon* is presented here on Thursday, September 19th, at the Plymouth Theatre. It is being produced by Messrs. Shubert in association with Albert de Courville with the latter also in charge of the direction, this being precisely the same set up responsible for *Ten Little Indians*.'[65] On opening night, though, the *New York Times* announced, 'Fabricating popular mystery yarns is quite a hobby with Agatha Christie, who likes to dramatise them too. Her first attempt along these lines was *Ten Little Indians* produced by the Shuberts and Albert de Courville for a run of 424 performances here. Devoted admirers of Miss Christie, this same combination will launch unveil her latest effort *Hidden Horizon* at the Plymouth tonight. Theatres are so scarce these days that it can remain there only until *Present Laughter* is ready to open October 28 . . .'[66] For Reandco finding a West End theatre had been a genuine problem. But it is hard to believe that the Shuberts, who owned much of Broadway, could not have properly accommodated the play had they really wanted to. The fact is that they didn't.

Halliwell Hobbes, who had played Wargrave to great acclaim in *Ten Little Indians*, was cast in the role of Archdeacon Pennyfeather, and Diana Barrymore as Jacqueline de Severac. Daughter of John Barrymore, she had played the lead in the short-lived Broadway production of Daphne du Maurier's *Rebecca*, which Clarence Derwent (director of the Martha's Vineyard *Towards Zero*) had directed the previous year. Her playbill biography reads, 'Carrying the banner of the Theatre's Royal Family beginning with Louisa Drew, Diana Barrymore is well on her way to etching her own insignia on that famous escutcheon.'[67] Other playbill biographies show that, for a number of the male participants in the production, this was their first engagement since wartime military service. One only wishes that the outcome could have been happier for all concerned.

As it turns out, the production did not last even for the five and a half weeks for which it had been scheduled. *Hidden Horizon* is not, on any level, intended to be a 'spine tingler', and leading audiences and critics to believe that it was had raised false expectations. The *New York Post* described the production as a 'tragic fiasco'.[68] The *Herald Tribune* felt that 'There are more unwitting laughs than calculated thrills in *Hidden Horizon* . . . Admirers of Mrs Christie will find little of the suspense and none of the staccato action which endowed *Ten Little Indians* with a modicum of excitement.'[69] 'The most unnecessary article of the season,' said the *New York Times*' Brooks Atkinson, 'dull in theme, dull in story, dull in acting.'[70] The *New Yorker*, however, found one redeeming feature: 'The only thing, in fact, that pleased me even mildly was that somehow, in transplanting her work to the stage, Mrs Christie was persuaded to leave out her Belgian detective called Hercule Poirot, probably the most irritating little collection of mannerisms in the literature of gore.'[71] In retrospect, it is perhaps hardly surprising that Broadway audiences were bemused by the sight of American actors portraying the carefully observed idiosyncrasies of Brits abroad, and I can well imagine that, in the absence of *Ten Little Indians*' suspense and 'staccato action', the script into which Christie had put so much thought simply didn't translate. It was, almost literally, laughed off the stage.

Hidden Horizon closed on Broadway after twelve performances, having run for a week and a half, and must have been a fiasco indeed for the Shuberts thereby to sacrifice the residual rights in which they would have participated had it run for two weeks more. The remaining four weeks until the opening of *Present Laughter* were filled by Basil Rathbone in a two-hander play. There are no accounts for *Hidden Horizon* on file in the Shubert archive, but the papers of the great American stage actress and producer Katharine Cornell, held at the New York Public Library for the Performing Arts, contain a complete set. Although not credited as a co-producer, it may well have been that the 'first lady of theater', who had played Sydney Fairfield in the 1921 Broadway production of Clemence Dane's *A Bill of Divorcement* and had subsequently found fame for her Broadway role in *The Barretts of Wimpole Street*, was an investor in the project. We see from these documents that the production cost $26,111.89 to mount and incurred a further $10,359.96 of losses during its short run, resulting in a total loss of $36,471.85.[72]

Christie's critical reputation as a playwright was in tatters on both sides of the Atlantic but, thanks to the convoluted machinations of agents and producers, a lucrative long-term secondary market had been secured for *Murder on the Nile*. With its cast of thirteen and its easily achievable setting in the ship's lounge (unlike the scenically ambitious outdoor locations of *Towards Zero* and *Appointment with Death*, it was effectively a drawing room drama despite its exotic location), the play was to become an enduringly popular mainstay of the touring, repertory and amateur circuits. Without her astonishing 'alternative' ending, and rebranded from her more imaginative original title to be recognisably derived from the similarly named novel, the piece was fundamentally an undemanding whodunit that made it attractive to those of limited talent and resources. It was, in short, a prime example of what came to be regarded as a 'typical' Agatha Christie play, although in fact it was no such thing, and it thrived in markets (and productions) which inevitably undermined her aspirations of acceptance as a serious dramatist by the critical and theatrical communities.

In April 1947 Samuel French Ltd entered into their usual agreement to publish the script and deal with amateur licensing (in return for 50 per cent of licensing income) and in October Cork wrote to Ober: 'Although this play [*Murder on the Nile*] had no great run in the West End of London, it is now proving extremely popular in repertory and stock in this country, and it might also be a good road and stock proposition in the US. There will be no objection to change of title and reasonable rewriting.'[73] Six months later, Hughes Massie announced in *The Stage*:

NOW RELEASED FOR REP
MURDER ON THE NILE By Agatha Christie

Undiminished in popularity TEN LITTLE NIGGERS
By Agatha Christie
LOVE FROM A STRANGER
By Agatha Christie and Frank Vosper
PERIL AT END HOUSE By Agatha Christie and Arnold Ridley
Repertory rights from Hughes Massie & Co[74]

Whilst, as we have seen, the claim to joint authorship for the dramatisation of *Love From a Stranger* was justified (although that for *Peril at End House* was not), the motivation here was clearly not to set the record straight but simply to improve the saleability of the plays by putting Christie's name first in each case. This deliberate, and continuous, blurring of the lines by her own agent, and indeed by producers, regarding the authorship of the plays only served further to damage

Christie's reputation in the theatrical community. A number of the third-party adaptations that carry her name are markedly inferior to her own work, and where her own writing for the stage was concerned there would always be the assumption, or at least the suspicion, that other parties were involved. It is critically important to an appreciation of Christie as a playwright that a proper distinction is made between her own plays and those written by others who borrowed her name.

As it happens, the next 'Agatha Christie' play to open in the West End was to be yet another third-party adaptation, in this case of her 1930 novel *The Murder at the Vicarage*, the first to feature Miss Marple. Throughout the 1940s Christie had toyed with a number of ideas for plays of her own. As well as the possible play about the WAAF that she had referred to in a letter to Max, her notebooks from this period show that she was considering a number of other ideas for the stage. There are musings on the subject of a potential adaptation of the Poirot novel *Three Act Tragedy* (1934), as well as of *Triangle at Rhodes*, both considered as potential Sullivan vehicles before *Death on the Nile* was settled on; and, more interestingly, a play on the Harlequin theme (possibly even a ballet). 'R Helpmann?' she suggests, next to this, being a great admirer of the popular and ceaselessly energetic British-based Australian actor-dancer Robert Helpmann. She was absolutely right; there could not have been better casting for the role of Harlequin.[75]

Another idea was for an original play on 'moral issues involving husband and wife' with a plot revolving around a woman who is proved innocent of a crime (unspecified) but who turns out to be guilty, a device later used to great effect with respect to a husband in *Witness for the Prosecution*. There are also notes for an adaptation of the 1933 Parker Pyne short story 'The House at Shiraz', with a vastly enhanced back-story and potentially a new title. Like her sketch for a dramatisation of the Parker Pyne version of *Death on the Nile*, it seemingly

dispenses with the character of Parker Pyne himself. Under
consideration as well were two original plays, one about a love
triangle involving a squadron leader (Max's official rank in
Cairo) and the other, *Command Performance*, about an actor
(Francis L. Sullivan?) holidaying in either Rhodes, Egypt or
Petra, who entraps a villain by becoming a decoy.[76] Christie's
enthusiasm for playwriting must have been buoyed up by the
success of *Ten Little Niggers*, and this veritable smorgasbord
of ideas demonstrates a vivid dramatic imagination, all of it
seemingly unencumbered (after the initial work on Sullivan's
behalf) by the restrictions of the detective story format.

However, it is testament to the degree to which her playwriting aspirations must have been set back by the accumulated
frustrations of *Towards Zero*, *Appointment with Death* and
Murder on the Nile that she appears to have put up no resistance to the idea of Barbara Toy and her friend Moie Charles
adapting *The Murder at the Vicarage*. A licence for them to
do so was duly issued at the end of 1948, with the usual 50/50
royalty split between the adaptors and Christie (Toy and Charles
in turn dividing their share equally), and a six-month deadline
for them to complete the work.[77]

This apparent willingness to see the book dramatised by
others was all the more surprising given that, almost ten years
earlier, Christie had seriously considered adapting the novel for
the stage herself. In the summer of 1939, right in the middle of
her agents' attempts to interest Basil Dean in *A Daughter's a
Daughter*, she had written directly to Dean in an attempt to
interest him in the idea: 'Dear Basil Dean, I am sending you
Murder at the Vicarage to see what you think of a village murder
play – with elderly spinster detective.'[78] She goes on to explain
how the dramatis personae could be reduced and altered for
the stage before concluding, 'am hoping to tackle Mother and
Daughter play soon.' We don't know how Dean responded, but
the idea was clearly still current when, on Christmas Eve 1942,
at the conclusion of a letter to Christie about *Ten Little Niggers*,
Cork wrote, 'No news yet about either the Vicarage or a
Daughter's a Daughter, but I think something should come of

both these matters so that 1943 may be a really dramatic year.'[79]

Although Christie cut Poirot, Battle, Parker Pyne and even Harley Quin from dramatisations, or notes for dramatisations, of the stories, she seems to have been keen at this point to experiment with the idea of Miss Marple on stage. Perhaps she felt that the character of the elderly spinster was less likely to pull focus than the others, an instinct in which she was quite possibly right. She may also have been reassured by the fact that the role would have been exempt from the interpretations of Laughton, Sullivan and the other flamboyant male actors who had appropriated her work as vehicles for their talents (at least, one hopes it would!).

The six-month deadline proved academic. Moie Charles and Barbara Toy appear to have delivered the script within a month, indicating that there may have been some preliminary discussions and work before the adaptation licence was issued. In any event, by late January 1949 Christie was sending Cork her notes on the script: 'On the whole I think a very good job has been made of it. It still has the rather too cosy novelish atmosphere of "Let's sit down and wonder whodunit" – but I never could see how that could be avoided in this particular book . . . I do feel it would add greatly to the interest if Lawrence and Anna could have a moment or two of passionate love making in the first scene of all . . . I do *not* like Miss Marple fainting at the end. It is, it really is, *corny*. Just done for the curtain – and absolutely untypical of her. No, that really cannot be.'[80] Having spent a decade dealing with requests for script changes from Basil Dean, Francis L. Sullivan, Bertie Meyer and Lee Shubert, it must have given Agatha a moment of satisfaction to have been giving notes to a playwright; not least the one from whom she herself had taken notes regarding *Ten Little Niggers*.

On 2 March Cork wrote to explain that, despite the end of hostilities, Christie's theatrical projects were once again the victim of unfortunate scheduling with respect to matters military: 'The arrangements for Murder at the Vicarage have been delayed somewhat as Bertie Meyer is now in Germany where he is touring the production of Ten Little Niggers for the Army of Occupation.'[81] The involvement of Barbara Toy inevitably made Meyer the producer of choice and, in fairness, he had nurtured *Ten Little Niggers* from page to stage with great diligence, and had at least acted promptly and efficiently to ensure a West End run for *Appointment with Death* (unlike his counterparts entrusted with *Murder on the Nile*). In September 1949 he duly entered into a licence to present *Murder at the Vicarage* (now without its '*The*') on fairly standard terms. Meyer surrounded himself with co-producers on this occasion, amongst them Ted Kavanagh, creator of the BBC Radio comedy *ITMA*, who had set up his own production company in 1944, and the People's Entertainment Society. This trio of producers had toured Moie Charles and Barbara Toy's stage adaptation of James Hilton's novel *Random Harvest* the previous year, although they had been unable to find a West End home for it.

Notable by its absence from both these projects, given its association with Charles and Toy, was Farndale, the co-producer of *Ten Little Niggers*. Farndale had produced a tour of a previous Moie Charles play, *To-morrow's Eden*, in 1944 – the year in which both she and Barbara Toy sat on the board of the company. *To-morrow's Eden* was directed by Irene Hentschel, who had directed Enid Bagnold's *Lottie Dundas* for the company in 1943 immediately prior to *Ten Little Niggers*. According to Christie biographer Janet Morgan, Hentschel also directed *Murder at the Vicarage*, which would have made perfect sense given all this; but it was in fact directed by Reginald Tate, who also played the role of Lawrence Redding. And in any case, I rather doubt whether the play itself would have been Hentschel's cup of tea. In the meantime, Farndale's last contribution to West End theatre appears to have been the enormously successful R.F. Delderfield comedy *Worm's Eye View*, which opened at the Whitehall Theatre in 1945 and closed at the Comedy Theatre in 1951, having given a total of 2,245 performances.

The production of *Murder at the Vicarage* cost £2,500 to

mount (there is no record of its running costs) and the powerful theatre chain Howard & Wyndham Ltd took an investment of almost a fifth of this,[82] its interest in the project doubtless securing valuable touring dates. Contrary to some accounts, other than giving her notes on it Christie had no involvement with the script, a fact confirmed by Christie herself in a letter to a researcher: 'I had no connection with the dramatisation of Alibi, Murder at the Vicarage and Peril at End House . . . I did not consider that any of the dramatisations were in any sense my plays.'[83] The style of the piece, in any case, is clearly not hers. A reasonably efficient, two-act, thirteen-hander adaption of the novel, with a colourful array of characters, it is set entirely in the (unusually busy) study of the Reverend Leonard Clement, and simplifies the novel's plot whilst updating its action to the 1940s. Although it alters the book's ending, the identity of the murderer remains the same. It is the kind of linear 'whodunit' detective narrative that Christie herself preferred to avoid on stage, and its dialogue lacks her trademark sparkiness.

As for Moie Charles, she appears to be one of theatre history's 'missing persons'. What we do know is that she was born Marion Gwynedd Beevor in 1911, three years after Barbara Toy. Like Toy, she was a company director of Overture Theatres Ltd and, briefly, of Farndale. She wrote a number of screenplays (including *The Gentle Sex*, produced by Derrick de Marney in 1943) and, like Toy, she wrote other plays and had other collaborators, although *Murder at the Vicarage* was the only work of hers to reach the West End. Her unusual pen name, to which she officially changed her name by deed poll in 1945, has led to an assumption by some commentators that the co-author of the Christie adaptation was male.[84] She died in her Chelsea flat in 1957 aged forty-six, apparently as the result of a gas leak, at which time she was in a relationship with the celebrated bisexual actress and chanteuse Frances Day.[85]

According to Hughes Massie's accounts records, Moie Charles left her share of the royalties from *Murder at the Vicarage* to Barbara Toy, who had by then reinvented herself as a Land

Rover-driving adventurer and travel writer whose work gives us few clues about her theatrical past. The following extract from a *Times* article published in June 1959 under the headline 'Day and Night on a Haunted Peak' is how the public eventually came to know Toy:

> Miss Barbara Toy, the traveller and writer, has just spent a day and a night alone on the summit of the 19,000 ft Wehni Peak, in Northern Ethiopia, from which she landed by a helicopter . . . with a sleeping bag, a camera and some food . . . She found a dilapidated church, wells filled with leaves and stones, and a crumbling fort with its heavy wooden doors ajar. She also found many passages leading to tiny cells and rooms. At the end of her stay she was taken off by the same helicopter. The lowland natives were surprised to see her return alive.[86]

All of this seems a million miles away from the vicarage at St Mary Mead. My instincts tell me that there is probably a good story to be told about Barbara Toy, who abandoned an apparently promising career in the theatre to travel the world, her lesbian friend and collaborator Moie Charles who died young, and a theatrical production company called Farndale.

Charles and Toy's adaptation of Christie's *Murder at the Vicarage* opened on 17 October 1949 at the New Theatre, Northampton, where *The Stage* reported that it was very well performed, particularly by Barbara Mullen as Miss Marple ('It would be hard to find a part that suited Barbara Mullen better'[87]) but let down by a long drawn-out final act. The publicity leaflet at Liverpool's Royal Court Theatre, the last venue on the eight-week pre-West End tour, once again fails to distinguish between Christie's own work for the stage and that of her various adaptors:

> This thriller-masterpiece, adapted for the stage from her 'best-seller' of the same name, is perfect theatre and comes with its forceful dramatic impact and full-blooded appeal at a time when playgoers, surfeited with a procession of namby-

pamby milk and water histrionics, are crying out for virile and dynamic pyrotechnics in their plays.

Crime, brilliantly handled as it was in Agatha Christie's earlier smash-hit successes such as *Alibi, Ten Little Niggers, Love From a Stranger* and *Appointment with Death* has proved to be the most completely satisfactory of dramatic fare, which is not surprising since it is also the most effective escapism for playgoers who yearn to be carried magically away from the monotonous humdrum of everyday life.[88]

The copy-writer was no less restrained in praising the production's two key players. Of American-born Barbara Mullen, who had forged a notable career as a West End leading lady after training in London at the Webber-Douglas School, they proclaimed, 'she is able to bring to life with quite startling brilliance the personality of the alert-brained old lady whose penetrating perception elucidates seemingly unfathomable mysteries. Barbara Mullen, in fact, adds another gem to her collection of widely contrasting roles . . . Roles varying from 18 to 75 have been taken with equal success by Miss Mullen since she arrived in England, so the mature Miss Marple presents no difficulties.' The last line, presumably, was by way of reassurance to those who might have feared that, at thirty-five, Mullen was unsuitably young for the role. Of popular West End leading man Reginald Tate we are told that he is 'Equally distinguished as actor and producer [i.e. director]' and that he 'fills both these roles in *Murder at the Vicarage*. His staging of the play is carried through to achieve the dramatic results essential to a murder mystery and to retain the excitement and suspense without which a "thriller" would lose its hold and appeal. In his leading role as the easy-going artist, Lawrence Redding, he gives a performance of unusual strength and great charm.'

Meyer appears to have secured a West End theatre well in advance on this occasion and, following the week in Liverpool, the production opened at the Playhouse Theatre on 14 December 1949. The *Times* reviewer commented that 'Everyone has a motive for killing. Nobody, unhappily, has a reason for living.

It is not until the final scene . . . that we become aware that
there was, after all, an effective one act play in Miss Christie's
novel . . . Miss Barbara Mullen is Miss Marple, and once she
is allowed to take a firm practical hold on the story she manip-
ulates it with all possible skill.'[89] Ivor Brown in the *Observer*
was complimentary of his wife's associates' input – 'Neatly knit
together and tidied up for the stage by Moe Charles and Barbara
Toy' – and joined the general chorus of approval for the leading
lady, whilst harbouring doubts about the production: 'Barbara
Mullen is excellent as that sharp eyed Prodnose Miss Marple,
and her performance along with that of Reginald Tate and of
Jack Lambert as the nice, dull, dutiful vicar, gives West End
quality to a production otherwise on a less exalted level . . .
the second act was very much more persuasive than the first.'[90]

The production played for 126 performances and closed on 1
April 1950. Both Cork and the PES blamed the 1950 General
Election for its demise; the PES' annual report for the year stated
that 'The returns of the production *Murder at the Vicarage*, at
the Playhouse, London, were adversely affected, in common with
other shows, by the General Election, and it had to be withdrawn.'[91] There was indeed a great deal of interest in the election,
which was effectively the public verdict on the Labour Party's
post-war programme of nationalisation and welfare reforms, and
it turned out to be a cliff-hanger, resulting in a very slim majority
for Labour. But it took place on 23 February, over five weeks
before the production's eventual demise, and it seems somewhat
disingenuous to link the two events. Cork wrote to Christie in
Baghdad to reassure her that the production had run for long
enough to become a valuable property for amateur and repertory
companies.[92] And the People's Entertainment Society, the co-operative movement's unusual and initially highly successful venture
into show business, continued until 1955 when, following a
decline in its fortunes, it went into voluntary liquidation.

In the summer of 1944, with Irene Hentschel's masterful
production of *Ten Little Niggers* still running in the West End
and on tour, and the Shuberts about to open their hugely

successful production on Broadway, Agatha Christie, play-wright, had the theatrical world at her feet. By the end of 1946 that dream had been shattered. Her highly imaginative script for *Towards Zero* had been rejected, the exotically located *Appointment with Death* had sunk without trace, and *Hidden Horizon* (without its 'alternative' ending) was a laughing stock on Broadway. Perhaps more damagingly yet, her producers, and even her own agent, had started to characterise her dramatic work as something that could yield huge dividends in secondary markets and subsidiary rights if given even the most perfunctory of 'first-class' presentations, and they had no hesitation in deliberately confusing the issue of who had actually penned a particular script if that assisted sales of tickets or licences. Here, of course, Christie's popularity as a writer of detective novels was, to an extent, undermining her legitimacy as a playwright. Christie herself was, as a playwright, more than happy to work in a number of different genres and to tackle all sorts of scenarios and issues; but whilst egotistical actors leapt at the chance to play Poirot on stage, her domestic drama *A Daughter's a Daughter*, arguably her finest dramatic work to date, remained on the shelf in the office of Basil Dean, the producer who had given Clemence Dane her West End playwriting debut. And whilst Dane's agent, Spencer Curtis Brown, would no doubt have wept to see the global income generated by the dramatisations of both *Ten Little Niggers* and *Murder on the Nile*, not to mention some of the third-party adaptations, it was to be his client who would secure page after page in the history of female playwriting.

It is my belief that a proper understanding of when, where, how, why and by whom a play was first presented is critical to an appreciation of the subsequent fortunes and reputation of both the play and its writer. Biographer Laura Thompson's succinct summary of events may arguably be easier to digest ('The play *Hidden Horizon* flourished after its initial difficulties and it, too, went to New York'),[93] but this is to overlook the complexities of the production process and the extraordinary array of personalities involved in it; the very elements of theatre which Christie herself found endlessly fascinating, if at times perplexing.

'I should always write my one book a year,' Christie wrote in her autobiography, 'I was sure of that. Dramatic writing would be my adventure – that would always be, and always must be hit and miss. You can have play after play a success, and then for no reason, a series of flops. Why? Nobody really knows. I've seen it happen with many playwrights. I have seen a play which to my mind was just as good or better than one of their successes fail – because it did not catch the fancy of the public; or because it was written at the wrong time; or because the cast made such a difference to it. Yes, play-writing is not a thing I could be sure of. It was a glorious gamble every time, and I liked it that way.'[94]

Despite her apparent acceptance of the vagaries of theatre, we should not underestimate the damage to Christie's confidence as a playwright caused by the setbacks of the 1940s; the fact that she allowed Moie Charles and Barbara Toy to adapt a book that she herself had previously earmarked for dramatisation (although many other such requests, from both established writers and amateurs, were turned down) is indicative of the insecurity that she must now have felt about her own playwriting abilities. Perhaps even more telling is the following passage from her autobiography: 'I suppose it was *Ten Little Niggers* that set me on the path of being a playwright as well as a writer of books. It was then that I decided that no-one was going to adapt my books except myself: I would choose what books would be adapted, and only those books that were suitable for adapting. The next one I tried my hand on, though several years later, was *The Hollow* . . .'[95]

This is to ignore completely her own *Towards Zero*, *Appointment with Death* and *Murder on The Nile*, as well as Charles and Toy's *Murder at the Vicarage*. Such rewriting of history specifically in order to exclude mention of a period of heartache is in a league with the phrase 'so ended my first married life' at the point in her autobiography where one might expect some explanation of her expedition to Harrogate. As far as she is concerned, the events simply didn't happen.

At the end of 1950, as she turned sixty, it must have seemed to Christie that her playwriting ambitions were to come to nothing. And then, suddenly and extraordinarily, all that was to change. Within four years she would become the undisputed Queen of the West End.

Act Two

Saunders Saves the Day

SCENE ONE

The Binkie Effect

British post-war theatre was characterised by the dominance of the H.M. Tennent production empire, known as 'the Firm', and the theatre building-owning cartel known as 'the Group'. Whilst the two were not unconnected through various directorships and shareholdings, it is notable that in the UK the dominant theatrical production company and the major building-owning interests were at least nominally controlled by different people (the means of production and distribution, if you like, were technically separate entities), whereas in the USA at the time they were both directly controlled by the Shuberts.

'The Group' was an interconnected collection of theatre-owning and producing entities which had started to establish links in the early 1940s. It involved such potent 'bricks and mortar' managements as Prince Littler, Stoll Theatres, Associated Theatre Properties, Moss Empires and Howard & Wyndham, and included theatre buildings throughout the country as well as in London's West End. While no single company or individual within the Group could be accused of operating a monopoly, the labyrinthine network of long and short building leases, directorships and shareholdings that bound it together effectively created one. In 1952 the Federation of Theatre Unions (comprising Equity, the Musicians' Union and the National Association of Theatrical and Kine Employees) published a 280-page book called *Theatre Ownership in Britain*, which lists and analyses the directorships and holdings of all the major building owners and production companies. It is not exactly a thrilling read, but it is astonishing in its analysis and exposure of what was clearly a highly organised cartel, with a number of independently owned theatre buildings struggling to exist in its shadow.

H.M. Tennent Ltd was formed in 1936 by Harry Tennent and his assistant Hugh 'Binkie' Beaumont, who had been working together as bookers for the Group's Moss Empires and Howard & Wyndham Theatres, and who had identified a gap in the market for a new production company. Following Tennent's death five years later, the enigmatic Binkie Beaumont had found himself managing director of the fledgling enterprise, and about to launch the most successful business strategy ever conceived by a commercial theatre producer in the UK. The company was linked to the Group through substantial share-holdings by two of its major theatre-owning players, but H.M. Tennent itself had no building-owning interests and Binkie was clearly identified as its boss.

Entertainment tax, a levy on ticket sales, had been introduced in 1916 as a wartime measure. In 1942, at which time the tax typically accounted for over a third of theatre box office income, a scheme was set up offering exemption to non-profit distributing theatre companies whose productions were partly educational. The judgement as to whether a play was educational (or, indeed, 'partly' educational) was put in the hands of three CEMA-appointed 'experts', who rapidly became known as the 'three blind mice'. The 1946 Finance Act revised these terms so that the aims of the company itself, rather than necessarily all of its productions, were required to be partly educational, rendering the mice redundant. Crucially, there was nothing to prevent the company itself from trading at a profit, provided such profits were not distributed to investors. In 1942, Beaumont had established Tennent Plays Ltd, a non-profit distributing and therefore tax-exempt company, to run alongside his commercial company H.M. Tennent Ltd. Following a spat with the tax authorities in 1947, this was reconstituted as Tennent Productions Ltd. The two companies shared an office, staff and board members, many of whom were accountants and solicitors. In a move to lend the company credibility with the newly formed Arts Council – whose endorsement ('in association with the Arts Council'), though not essential to qualifying for tax exemption, clearly gave its operation kudos and legitimacy – Ralph Richardson and John Gielgud were added to the board of Tennent Productions Ltd.

The tax-exempt non-profit distributing company paid the commercial company £40 per week for managing each of its productions and, unlike its competitors, retained the full ticket price, thereby quickly accumulating cash reserves that could, by definition, only be spent on further productions. At the same time, the commercial company continued to present its own productions. As a motor for the creation of a theatrical monopoly based on volume of work this was an extraordinarily productive model, and the two companies between them soon established complete dominance over the industry, with what appeared to be exclusive access to the best theatres, writers and performers based on their ability to guarantee an unprecedented volume of high quality work. Along with this, of course, went (unproven) accusations of using their cash reserves to pay over the odds for theatre rents, actors' fees and authors' royalties, as well as a widely held perception that the companies operated blacklists and that you either worked for Tennents or you didn't work at all.

The 'educational' aims of Tennent Productions, as reflected in its repertoire, and the legality of its tax-exempt status were frequently challenged by rival managements, with matters coming to a head over their 1948 production of Daphne du Maurier's *September Tide*, directed by Irene Hentschel and starring Gertude Lawrence, and the following year's *A Streetcar Named Desire*, directed by Laurence Olivier and starring Vivien Leigh. By 1950 they had survived the scrutiny of both an Inland Revenue Board of Enquiry and a Parliamentary Select Committee and, although the Arts Council's increasingly controversial 'association' had eventually been dropped, the twin companies' dominance of the West End appeared to be unshakeable.

Kitty Black, Tennents' loyal and long-serving office manager and production assistant, in her understandably uncritical book *Upper Circle*, maintains that 'To all the critics of Binkie's methods and the acrimonious condemnation of the stranglehold he exercised over the London theatres, there is always only one reply. If he could do it, why couldn't anyone else?'[1] This is somewhat disingenuous. The fact is that by the time other managements fully understood Binkie's business model, his position was unassailable. It was simply too late to mount an effective challenge, even through the application of Binkie's own strategy. The monopoly system works very effectively in theatre, as the Shuberts had demonstrated in New York, largely due to the finite number of buildings available in which it is possible to operate. And once a particular operator is in place, it is very difficult to shake them.

At the centre of all this sat Binkie himself, in his offices at the Globe (now Gielgud) Theatre: the archetypal smooth operator, whose personal charms wooed both the Arts Council and the leading players of the day, and whose management style was characterised as an 'iron fist in a velvet glove'.[2] In the darker corners of the West End there were mutterings that the industry had fallen under the control of a gay mafia, but from the audience's point of view there had never been a better time to go to the theatre, with an array of immaculately presented, impressively cast productions filling London's best theatres every night. In Kitty Black's words:

While Harry [Tennent] concentrated on the bricks and mortar managements, Binkie used his charm and incredible energy on the stars, male and female, who guaranteed the success of the productions, wooed authors, directors and agents who provided the raw material . . . his diary was crammed with lunch dates and supper engagements . . . I have also heard that he was a dedicated poker player, keeping it up sometimes all through the night. I could well imagine those blue eyes giving nothing away while he treated the card game much as he did the wheeling and dealing he was carrying out in the cut-throat business of the theatre world.[3]

Beaumont's *Times* obituary quotes Tyrone Guthrie's comment that he was the person who, 'more than any other single individual, could make or break the career of almost any worker in the British professional theatre', and concludes that 'He did not want publicity for himself. He did not want money for its own sake. He wanted power.'[4]

Although the entertainment tax rate was reduced to around 20 per cent of box office revenue after the war, this was not a good time to be setting up in business as an independent theatre producer. But that didn't deter former journalist and publicist Peter Saunders who, in 1947 at the age of thirty-five, booked the St James's Theatre in the West End to present his first venture as an impresario, *Fly Away Peter*. The play was penned by A. P. Dearsley, an army colleague with whom he had been posted to Europe in the Intelligence Corps towards the end of the war, and it clocked up a respectable 183 performances. Working with repertory producer Geoffrey Hastings – who was to remain a close associate – and making the most of the entertainment tax-exempt status of Hastings' company, Saunders went on to produce a successful tour of the comedy *The Ex Mrs Y*, followed by an extremely unsuccessful one of *The Poison Belt*, an Arthur Conan Doyle adaptation.

Saunders' autobiography gives an entertaining and relatively frank account of the fledgling producer's early struggles, as well as treating us to his views on critics, investors and his fellow producers. He does not mince his words on the subject of Tennents, and in a chapter called 'The Power Game' explains:

> theatre was in the astonishing and seemingly immovable grip of H.M. Tennent Ltd, run by Hugh Beaumont and John Perry . . . There was some minor competition from Bill Linnit, of the Linnit and Dumfree firm, but whereas Binkie frequently had ten or twelve shows in the West End, Bill Linnit never aspired to more than four . . . What was worse, from the point of view of independent producers, was the fact that Tennents had virtually first refusal on all the stars, authors and the best West End theatres. And this state of affairs

came about through an altruistic-minded government trying to help the Arts. Binkie Beaumont brilliantly and quite legally exploited this for his own benefit and built himself up into such a power in the theatre that it looked as if nothing could ever topple him . . . when I wanted a certain star to appear in *Spider's Web* she turned down a salary of £300 per week because she said 'Binkie looks after me.' She then went down to work for Binkie at the Lyric Theatre, Hammersmith, for £40 per week . . . Seldom did other productions get the much sought after Shaftesbury Avenue theatres in the forties and the first half of the fifties . . . Drury Lane, the Haymarket, and His Majesty's Theatres were also his for the asking. Binkie's activities were strangulation to other producers.'[5]

A Tennent company also operated the Lyric Theatre Hammersmith, where it kept star actors busy while finding the next West End vehicle for them. Touring was no easier: 'if one tried to get a date from Howard and Wyndham, or Moss Empires, the two major circuits at the time, they were usually filled with Tennent shows.' Even once contracted, touring dates were liable to mysteriously 'disappear' without warning.

Urgently seeking a touring title that would replenish his coffers after the disastrous production of *The Poison Belt*, Saunders cast his eye over the West End. 'Barry O'Brien was king of the tours and had first refusal on all Tennent shows; even if Barry didn't tour them no-one else could,' he recalls, 'We had to find a play that (a) wasn't a complete flop, (b) wasn't such a success that the producing management wanted to tour it themselves, and (c) it had to be a play that was shortly coming off.'[6] It was February 1950, and *Murder at the Vicarage* was still on at the Playhouse, although clearly not shaping up to be a long runner. Saunders applied to Bertie Meyer for, and obtained, a 'Number Two' touring licence, sealing the deal by offering to hire the set from him. Saunders was minor league, a new arrival on the scene, and this is reflected in the terms of his licence.[7] Thirteen major towns were specifically excluded, including Aberdeen, Birmingham, Manchester and Bristol, enabling Meyer to tour there himself in the future if he so wished. And so it was that Moie Charles and Barbara Toy's adaptation of *Murder at the Vicarage* finally connected Agatha Christie with the man who was to ensure her enduring theatrical success.

Meyer's own deal with Hughes Massie ensured that he would receive a third of the author's royalty for the tour, with Christie herself receiving a third and the two adaptors a sixth each. There was no attempt to cast the production with stars, and Saunders makes much of the fact that he advertised it as 'Agatha Christie's *Murder at the Vicarage*', in effect making her the 'star'. (In fact, this was the way the play had been advertised in *The Times* by Bertie Meyer throughout its West End run.) As ever, the actual authorship of the work was deemed less important than the box office outcome. And in this case the outcome was a good one. Business was double what Saunders had expected and the debts from *The Poison Belt* were more than paid off. 'I suddenly thought of the possibilities of this star writer,' says Saunders, who immediately wrote to Cork boasting of his 'substantial resources' and expressing his interest in any new work that Christie might have available; provided of course her long-standing producer Meyer, now in his seventies, had no use for it. 'I assumed, rightly, that I should not have to produce evidence of my substantial resources, which was just as well,' he adds.[8]

As it happens, Meyer was at that moment toying with Christie's latest dramatic offering, her own adaptation of her 1946 novel *The Hollow*. Like much of Christie's writing for the stage, it is a detailed and thoughtful work that, although ostensibly ticking the boxes for a 'whodunit', clearly has a lot more to say.

Agatha describes its origins thus in her autobiography:

> It came to me suddenly one day that *The Hollow* would make a good play. I said so to Rosalind, who has had the valuable role in life of eternally trying to discourage me without success.

'Making a play of *The Hollow*, Mother!' said Rosalind in horror. 'It's a good book, and I like it, but you can't *possibly* make it into a play.'

'Yes, I can,' I said, stimulated by the opposition.

'Oh, I wish you wouldn't,' said Rosalind, sighing.[9]

It may well be, of course, that Rosalind's real motivation was to spare her mother the disappointment of another *Murder on the Nile* or *Appointment with Death*; nevertheless, more than twenty years later, Agatha reminded her daughter of the exchange in a letter: 'I have had to bear Alibi – I hated Murder at the Vicarage and a Miss Marple of twenty odd – and several other of the "adapted" plays from my books . . . It was because I hated them so much that I determined to adapt The Hollow myself – I did that at Pwllywrach [Rosalind's home] and you did your utmost then to persuade me not to!'[10]

The novel of *The Hollow* had been dedicated to the Sullivans, whose hospitality Agatha had so enjoyed in the war, and whose swimming pool is a feature of the story. But neither their swimming pool nor her host's favourite role were to appear in Christie's dramatisation. Christie notes, 'Anyway, I enjoyed myself scribbling down ideas for The Hollow. It was, of course, in some ways rather more of a novel than a detective story. The Hollow was a book I always thought I had ruined by the introduction of Poirot . . . so when I went to sketch out the play, out went Poirot.'[11] This was the third of her dramatisations to cut the character completely.

The Hollow is another of Christie's plays about which we hear the views of Max, whose comments on the subject of his wife's theatrical endeavours and on the theatre industry in general in his book *Mallowan's Memoirs* tend to be very perceptive: 'The Hollow was brilliantly adapted from the book by Agatha herself in a manner that shows her flair for the theatre,' says Max, 'and it is interesting to compare the book published in 1946 with the play . . . Here Agatha exploited the dramatic potential of the novel to the full, with the utmost economy in assembling the plot . . . The book itself is in my opinion not one of her best, for it is disjointed and tends to ramble, but exceptionally it features a number of romances, and the portrayal of the women is penetrating, the result of a perceptive feminine outlook.'[12]

The plot centres around the fate of self-centred Harley Street Lothario Dr John Cristow, who finds himself at a house party with his dull but devoted wife, his mistress (a sculptress) and his former lover (a Hollywood film star). His mistress, Henrietta, seems to have the measure of him:

HENRIETTA: It's dangerous to be as oblivious as you are.

JOHN: Oblivious?

HENRIETTA: You never see or know anything that people are feeling about.

JOHN: I should have said the opposite.

HENRIETTA: You see what you are looking at – yes. You're like a searchlight. A powerful beam turned to the one spot where your interest is, but behind it, and on each side of it, darkness.

JOHN: Henrietta, darling, what's all this?

HENRIETTA: I tell you, it's dangerous. You assume everybody likes you – Lucy and Gerda, Henry, Midge and Edward. Do you know what they all feel about you?

JOHN: And Henrietta? What does she feel? At least – (He catches her hand and draws her to him) I'm sure of you.

HENRIETTA: You can be sure of no one in this world, John.[13]

On one level, this neatly sets up a list of 'whodunit' (or who may be about to do it) for the audience. But there is clearly something else being said here. This is a man who describes his wife, Gerda, thus: 'I didn't want a raving beauty as a wife. I didn't want a damned egoist out to grab everything she could get. I wanted safety and peace and devotion, and all the quiet enduring things of life. I wanted someone who'd take her ideas from *me*.'

As with so much of Christie's stage work there can be no doubt that, in *The Hollow*, it is the women who are in the driving seat. Henrietta Angkatell the talented sculptress, Veronica Craye the gloriously self-centred actress and even Gerda Cristow the apparently compliant wife, run circles around a group of inept and ineffectual men. And Lady Angkatell is Christie's finest theatrical *grande dame*, though a far more amiable take on the role than her snooty predecessors Miss ffoliott-ffoulkes and Lady Westholme. Former Indian provincial governor Sir Henry comments admiringly of his wife, 'She's always got away with things. I don't suppose any other woman in the world could have flouted the traditions of Government House as she did. Most Governors' wives have to toe the line of convention. But not Lucy! Oh, dear me, no! She played merry hell with precedence at dinner parties – and that, my dear Henrietta, is the blackest of crimes. She put deadly enemies next to each other. She ran riot over the colour question. And instead of setting everyone at loggerheads, I'm damned if she didn't get away with it.' According to her autobiography, Christie herself had suffered the embarrassment of unintentionally flouting the accepted seating plan at an official dinner engagement on the Grand Tour, and it must have delighted her to create a character who made a virtue of revelling in such subversion.

The Hollow may be set at a country house party, which is, in fact, by no means typical of a Christie play, but it revels in questioning the precepts of that setting and, importantly, places the inhabitants of the house concerned very precisely in a post-war context. The play's portrayal of a crumbling aristocracy in a time of rapid social change could easily take its cue from Chekhov, and amongst the many challenges to the established order of things faced by the play's central family is one from within, as young Midge (a name we last heard in *Someone at the Window*) opts to go and work in a shop:

EDWARD: You can't really like working in a shop, Midge.
MIDGE: Who said I liked it?
EDWARD: Then why do it?
MIDGE: What do you suggest I should live on? Beautiful thoughts?

EDWARD: But my dear girl. If I'd had any idea you were hard up . . .

SIR HENRY: Save your breath, Edward. She's obstinate. Refused an allowance and won't come and live with us, though we've begged her to. I can't think of anything nicer than having young Midge in the house.

EDWARD: Why don't you, Midge?

MIDGE: I have ideas. Poor, proud and prejudiced – that's me.

(Lady Angkatell enters)

They're badgering me, Lucy.

LADY ANGKATELL: Are they, darling?

EDWARD: I don't like the idea of her working in that dress shop.

MIDGE: Well find me a better job.

EDWARD: There surely must be something . . .

MIDGE: I've no particular qualifications, remember. Just a pleasant manner and the ability to keep my temper when I'm shouted at.

EDWARD: Do you mean to say that customers are rude to you?

MIDGE: Abominably rude, sometimes. It's their privilege.

EDWARD: But my dear girl, that's all wrong. If only I'd known . . .

MIDGE: How should you know? Your world and mine are far apart. I'm only half an Angkatell. The other half's just plain business girl, with unemployment always lurking round the corner in spite of the politicians' brave words.

When Midge is later berated over the telephone by her unpleasant employer (characterised as Jewish in the novel, but not in the play), and Edward suggests that she quits, Midge responds, 'To show an independent spirit one needs an independent income . . . What do you know about jobs? Getting them and keeping them? This job, as it happens, is fairly well paid, with reasonable hours . . . Yes, money. That's what I use to live on. I've got a job that *keeps* me, you understand.'

Even the butler, Gudgeon, has had to review his recruitment policy for new staff. Here we find him training a young maid who clears glasses, empties ashtrays and folds newspapers during the following exchange:

GUDGEON: Sir Henry was the Governor of one of the principal provinces in India. He would have been the next Viceroy most probably if it hadn't been for that terrible Labour government doing away with the Empire.

DORIS: My *dad's* Labour. (there is a pause as Gudgeon looks pityingly at Doris. She takes a step back, apologetically) Oh, I'm sorry, Mr Gudgeon.

GUDGEON: (Tolerantly) You can't help your parents, Doris.

DORIS: (Humbly) I know they're not class.

GUDGEON: (Patronizingly) You are coming along quite nicely – although it's not what I've been used to. Gamekeeper's daughter or Head Groom's daughter, a young girl who knows her manners and has been brought up right. That's what I like to train.

DORIS: Sorry, Mr Gudgeon . . .

GUDGEON: Ah well, it seems those days are gone for ever.

DORIS: Miss Simmonds is always down on me too.

GUDGEON: She's doing it for your own good, Doris, she's training you.

DORIS: Shan't get more money, shall I, when I'm trained?

GUDGEON: Not much, I'm afraid.

DORIS: Doesn't seem worth being trained, then, does it?

GUDGEON: I'm afraid you may be right, my girl.

Seventy-three-year-old Bertie Meyer eventually passed up the opportunity to produce *The Hollow*, believing that it would be too difficult to cast; a fear that he shared with Peter Saunders when giving the young producer his blessing to take it on. And so it was that in September 1950 Saunders obtained a licence to be the originating producer of *The Hollow*. That month, he moved into new offices in Trafalgar Square, from where he was to work for the next twenty-one years.

Although he had at one point worked at a film studio,

Saunders was a relative newcomer to the theatrical game and not particularly well connected, so his first challenge was to find a director who would pass muster with Christie and Cork. Hughes Massie, perhaps misguidedly, persuaded him to investigate directors with an association with the work of Edgar Wallace, but Saunders' preferred candidate for directing *The Hollow* was Hubert Gregg, whose qualifications for the job at that time, as Gregg himself admits, were hardly impressive. The thirty-five-year-old show-business jack of all trades had worked as an actor, notably in comedies but also as Henry V at Regent's Park Open Air Theatre, and as an announcer for the BBC. He had directed some plays for the Sunday societies (which 'tried out' new productions in one-off performances at West End theatres), but his main claim to fame at that time was as the writer of the song 'Maybe It's Because I'm a Londoner', popularised by Bud Flanagan in 1947. Gregg eventually achieved a further modicum of celebrity as the host of BBC Radio 2's long-running 'oldies' music programme *Thanks for the Memory*.

Gregg's book, *Agatha Christie and All that Mousetrap* (1980), provides a parallel account to Saunders' of the creation of much of Christie's stage work, but has numerous flaws. In it he accuses Christie of having overlooked Saunders' contribution to her theatrical success in her autobiography when, in fact, she goes to great lengths to give credit to his role. She does not, however, mention Gregg, who directed four of her plays (as well as babysitting *the Mousetrap* for a number of years), despite devoting a paragraph to the skills of Irene Hentschel. It seems that hell hath no fury like a director scorned: as well as giving away the endings of several plays (including *The Mousetrap*), Gregg takes credit for having extensively rewritten *The Hollow*, and for coming up with the title of *The Mousetrap* and the ending of *Witness for the Prosecution*. He goes to great lengths to examine Christie's 1926 'disappearance', implying that it was a publicity stunt, accuses her of being inhospitable and, to add insult to injury, includes a remarkably unflattering photograph of 'Agatha as I remember her', doubtless in the full knowledge of how sensitive she was about photographs of herself. His *Daily Telegraph* obituary states, 'He had little affection for the author, whom he later described as a "mean old bitch".'[14] Gregg's family have subsequently edited and marketed an 'autobiography' which touches on his work with Christie and repeats some of the assertions made in his 1980 book.[15]

It was also presumably his family who put up for sale his annotated director's scripts for some of the Christie plays he directed, along with a small amount of correspondence from the playwright. I was very kindly given access to these items by an antiquarian bookshop which had purchased them at auction for resale, and will refer to them as they become relevant in our story. The antiquarian book market has not always been a friend to those protecting the Christie legacy, particularly as a quantity of original manuscripts bearing the Hughes Massie label have unaccountably come into circulation in recent years, but in this instance it came up trumps and provided a unique insight into the realities of Gregg's involvement. Although two of the Christie plays that Gregg directed were successes, and doubtless owed much of that success to the care that he invested in their production, it is all too apparent that he had no real regard for either the plays or the playwright. Christie was no fool, and doubtless detected this trait in him, so whilst she commends his work in private correspondence with others, I cannot imagine that his omission from her autobiography is entirely accidental. It is not my own intention to underplay Gregg's role in the story of Agatha Christie, playwright, but it is a sadness that the discourtesy of his book will forever taint the memory of his contribution.

Saunders arranged to introduce Gregg to Christie over lunch at the Carlton Grill, at what was also to be his own first meeting with her. The venue was Saunders' suggestion and Agatha was accompanied by Max, along with Rosalind – who had remarried the previous year – and her new husband Anthony Hicks. Trained in Oriental Studies and as a barrister, although he never practised, Hicks was to provide a calm, reassuring and trusted voice in the conduct of the family's business affairs, and became a valued advisor to Cork in the management of the ever-growing Christie brand.

'Everything depended on the impression I made, and no First Night has ever made me feel so terrified,' confesses Saunders.[16] To an extent he had already proved himself with his commitment to the tour of *Murder at the Vicarage*, but the real hurdle was Gregg's lack of credibility as a director, not to mention the fact that Saunders had persuaded him to take on the role of Cristow as well, offering him prominent 'star' billing on the production's publicity.

Both Saunders and Gregg recall the fateful meeting in great detail. I will opt for Saunders' account:

> Her husband, Professor Max Mallowan, said very little, but this wonderfully kind man must have known the strain I was under. Anthony Hicks, her son-in-law, tried to ease things by talking on every subject under the sun, from the political situation to the difficulty of telling the difference between claret and burgundy. Agatha's daughter, Rosalind, frankly frightened me. I was to learn what enormous fun she is. But she would be the first to agree that she looks very forbidding in certain circumstances, and I felt at the time she was keeping a careful watch on me in case I slipped my hand into Agatha's handbag and knocked off her purse . . . Agatha of course was her usual shy self.[17]

The meeting apparently went well despite a faux pas from Gregg, when he claimed to have preferred the 'book' of *Black Coffee* to the play. This would have been doubly embarrassing for Saunders, who had optioned the touring rights to *Black Coffee* two weeks before he signed the West End contract for *The Hollow*. Evidently designed as a follow-up to the successful tour of *Murder at the Vicarage*, his new production of *Black Coffee* went on the road in 1951 starring Kenneth Kent as Poirot, and doubtless provided a useful source of regular income for Saunders to balance the initially unpredictable fortunes of *The Hollow*. RADA-trained Kent had been a pre-war stalwart of the Old Vic Company, and appears to have been the 'go to' performer when casting the role of Napoleon on stage, resulting in his appearance in the role in no fewer than four productions. Casting a Napoleon as Poirot arguably has some logic to it, and he had also played Professor Challenger in Saunders' ill-fated Conan Doyle adaptation.

Once plans were under way for *The Hollow*, Saunders also took a West End option on *Black Coffee*, possibly by way of an insurance policy.[18] In the end, the option was never exercised, as matters had begun to develop rapidly in new directions; but Christie took the opportunity to update the twenty-year-old script for the tour, and this forms the basis of the current 'acting edition'. Saunders makes no mention of the *Black Coffee* tour. Gregg does, which makes sense as it was running when he was working on *The Hollow*; but Gregg in turn makes no mention of the fact that Saunders' first 'Christie' was *Murder at the Vicarage*.

As Bertie Meyer had predicted, casting *The Hollow* was to be no easy task. Whilst the characters themselves are well drawn, none of them has sufficient stage time to be a really attractive vehicle for a star actor. Gregg, of course, saw this as a sign of Christie's lack of experience as a playwright. I think it more likely to have been a sign of her extensive experience of dealing with star actors, and of her dislike of the manner in which they had been inclined to hijack her work when given the opportunity to do so. According to Saunders, his friend the actors' agent Dorothy Mather, of the company Film Rights, said, 'I have read the script and I beg you, dear Peter, not to put this play on. It is awful.'[19] As it happens, she greatly enjoyed the production when she saw it on tour and provided two actors when some of the cast were replaced prior to the West End.

At this point, though, financing *The Hollow* proved no easier than casting it. In the absence of 'substantial resources' of his own, Saunders initially approached 'the Group', in the form of Howard & Wyndham, hoping that their involvement might also help to secure crucial pre-West End touring dates. But, although they had been happy enough to back Meyer's production of *Murder at the Vicarage*, for a production with Saunders at the helm they declined.

Undeterred, Saunders next approached the Arts Council. *The Hollow* was to be produced in 1951, the year of the Festival of Britain. Running from May to September, to mark the centenary of 1851's Great Exhibition, the Festival was intended to celebrate Britain's contribution to the arts, science and technology, with the opening of the newly built Royal Festival Hall as its centrepiece. The Arts Council of Great Britain, the postwar successor to CEMA, was a sponsor of several key events, and had encouraged theatre producers to apply for funding or guarantees against loss. Saunders claims that the council of the Society of West End Theatre Managers delayed relaying this invitation to the society's full membership, which resulted in his application being submitted too late. In reality, although Saunders made a good case for the inclusion of *The Hollow* as a funded Festival event, his application was roundly rejected. The Arts Council's secretary general, Mary Glasgow, wrote advising him that the Arts Council felt that 'a single play on that scale is one that should be able to pay its way as an ordinary commercial proposition without any subsidy, and that it has not, in their opinion, any strong Festival appeal.'[20] This was the same Arts Council that had unblushingly endorsed Binkie Beaumont's hardly uncommercial endeavours; but Binkie had ensured his future by bedazzling John Maynard Keynes, one of its founding fathers, with his particular brand of theatrical stardust way back in the CEMA days.

Like many books with such titles, Methuen Drama's *Modern British Playwriting: the 1950s* makes no mention of Christie's contribution as a playwright. But it does contain an interesting interview with Anthony Field, finance director of the Arts Council from 1957 to 1985. The interviewer asks, 'When you first started, what were the criteria on which you were assessing [theatre]?' Field responds, 'Well a number of us evolved this over my early years, and if an organisation applied to us for a grant and say it was for a drama company presenting Agatha Christie plays on the end of the pier in Blackpool, it would go to the drama department, and the drama department would say, you know, "We're not interested: Agatha Christie plays, end of the pier, you know, that should pay for itself", so it would never come to our finance department at all . . .'[21]

I have no axe to grind with Field, who in his lifetime did enormous good as a promoter and advocate of both commercial and subsidised theatre, and in any case is here discussing the assessment methods of the Arts Council drama department rather than necessarily his own. What is instructive, though, is the equation of Agatha Christie with 'end of the pier' and the assumption that her work is automatically disqualified for funding. Field, as it happens, was responsible for persuading the Arts Council to help fund the young Cameron Mackintosh's 1978 production of *My Fair Lady*, originally staged in collaboration with the Haymarket Theatre in Leicester.[22] One can only assume that Mackintosh would have had less luck with the Arts Council ten years earlier when, aged twenty-two, he was producing tours of *Black Coffee*, *Murder at the Vicarage*, *Love From a Stranger* and *Witness for the Prosecution*, and giving interviews declaring his intention to tour Christie plays every year.[231] The fact is that Saunders' spirited attempt to garner Arts Council funding never stood a chance, not because it was an inherently commercial endeavour (which it wasn't), but because of the name of the playwright. The Arts Council's ethic, as it turned out, was very different from that of the People's Entertainment Society.

With his options running out, Saunders decided to swallow his pride and approach the one man who could 'command' a star to appear in the play. 'I wrote to Binkie Beaumont and asked if I could come and see him on business.'[24] At the ensuing meeting, Beaumont was courtesy itself. 'He made me feel I was the only person in the world who mattered at that moment,' says Saunders, and he promised to co-produce and find a star if he liked the play. But, of course, he didn't. This was probably the first time that a play with Agatha Christie's name on it had been across Binkie's desk since he and H.M. Tennent had programmed the *Love From a Stranger* tour into Howard & Wyndham theatres.

The official line on Beaumont's rejection of *The Hollow* is given in Richard Huggett's biography of the 'Eminence Grise of the West End'. Huggett's obsequious prose is symptomatic of the reverence in which Beaumont's name is held to this day in certain theatrical circles:

> He was, at all times, rather less concerned with making money than in doing plays which interested and excited him, plays which offered splendid opportunities to his favourite actors and stars, plays which would add lustre to the Firm's image. In short, it had to be a Tennent play, a category which it would be difficult to define, but was always easy to recognise. Anything which he felt did not qualify would be turned down instantly no matter how much money it was likely to make. Many of these were produced by rival managements with great success but Binkie was unresentful for he had little professional jealousy. He turned down an offer to do Agatha Christie's first play [sic], *The Hollow*, and thus lost the chance of making history with *The Mousetrap*, a fact which Peter Saunders has related with some relish, and considerable detail, in his book, *The Mousetrap Man*. Binkie didn't mind. It wasn't a Tennent play and thus he would have no interest in it.[25]

I suspect, however, that equally important was the fact that the brusque and businesslike Saunders was not a 'Binkie' producer; Beaumont had been happy enough to work with Frank Vosper on *Love From a Stranger*.

Whilst it might have improved Christie's credibility within the industry to be included in Tennents' rosta of women playwrights, which included Daphne du Maurier, Lillian Hellman and Dodie Smith, Beaumont's rejection of *The Hollow* proved to be a lucky escape for Saunders, who was thereby saved from being the junior partner in all future Christie projects. Without help from Tennents, the Group or the Arts Council, Saunders was forced to produce and raise the finance for the project himself, which ultimately proved to be the best thing that could have happened to him. His company's repertoire of thrillers and comedies had in the end proved impossible to pass off as even partly 'educational', and entertainment tax exemption had thus been forfeited. This meant, though, that he was permitted to distribute profits to investors. And with this business model in mind, he now set about raising funds from a small group of his friends, family members and business associates. All of whom were about to make a great deal of money.

Meanwhile, an inspired piece of novelty casting had solved the problem of finding a star to lead the piece. Born in the British colony of Basutoland (now Lesotho), the Paris-trained actress and comedienne Jeanne de Casalis had started her stage career in New York and France before moving to London in 1921. Her lasting claim to fame was the creation, in 1931, of the hair-brained radio character Mrs Feather, reviewed thus in her *Times* obituary:

Mrs Feather, whose adventures continued throughout the 1930s, provided a flawless reflection of the surface of life as lived by a particular type of woman at a particular social level; while Jeanne de Casalis's invention did not attempt to probe the deeper mysteries of the feminine character, it gaily and truthfully surveyed social activities and attitudes. Some of Mrs Feather's charm can be found in *Mrs Feather's Diary*, which Jeanne de Casalis published in 1936, but the printed page does not convey the intonations, the polish and the precision of timing and technique which she brought to her radio monologues.[26]

Casting a performer known to the public principally for a comic radio role was a high-risk strategy, and Max Mallowan for one, was not enamoured with the production's leading lady, describing her as 'that celebrated comedienne Jeanne de Casalis, who acted throughout as the Queen Bee, to the detriment of the hive'.[27] He was, as it happens, no more taken with Cicely Courtneidge's interpretation in a later revival, remarking that her performance 'reminded me how often a production is a battle between the playwright and the actor, and how difficult it is for the producer [i.e. director] to reconcile the two. When he succeeds, he deserves an artistic triumph.' But de Casalis proved a box office draw and, once she had settled into the role, turned out to be an accomplished performer who served the project well.

In January 1951, Christie, responding to a newspaper announcement of the forthcoming production, complained to Edmund Cork, 'Don't like the "thriller" and "whodunnit" publicity – I understood Peter Saunders was *not* approaching it that way. If he does this *play* will be a disappointment to people – Definitely *not* a thriller.'[28] Cork duly relayed this to Saunders, who responded,

> Thank you for your friendly tip. Mrs Christie had already telephoned me and I explained that the 'Whodunnit' part of 'the Star' write-up was their idea, not mine.
>
> All the printing is going out without any description of the play. It is merely billed as 'the new play by Agatha Christie' . . . I bow to her wishes, but if the play is not a thriller and if it is not a 'whodunnit', I am darned if I know what it is.[29]

The play opened its pre-West End tour at the Cambridge Arts Theatre on 5 February 1951. Agatha had attended rehearsals before setting off to Iraq with her husband, settling back into the pre-war routine where several months a year were spent accompanying him on his archaeological digs, but she arranged for the cast to receive flowers as a first night gift from her, requesting; 'something rather exotic for Jeanne de Casalis'.[30] Edmund Cork relayed the news to her of the play's successful opening, corresponding care of the British School of Archaeology in Baghdad: 'You will have received Peter Saunders' cable saying the Hollow is a great success', he wrote a few days later. 'There is no doubt at all that it is by far the best yet, and we shall have to be very unlucky not to have a really long run in town, with all the attendant subsidiaries.'[31] It is interesting to note Cork's eye for potential subsidiary exploitation, even at this early stage in the game, and the fact that he leads off with it before going on to discuss artistic matters, which would undoubtedly have been of more interest to his client. He would later write to her that 'Repertory bookings for The Hollow are coming in marvellously – this is the real justification for the vicissitudes of theatrical production.'[32]

For now, though, the issue was de Casalis' performance. 'Lady Angkatell is the perfect part for a natural droll,' wrote Cork, 'and I am sure even you would have been surprised at what Jeanne de Casalis made of it. In fact, the only thing that bothered me on Monday night was whether the drama might not be sunk by the comedy. However there was a six hour conference after the show, with the result that there were no unexpected laughs on Tuesday, and the show seemed to have already got a nice balance. By the time we get to town in April it should be absolutely right.'[33] Cork explained that the ever-loyal Stephen Glanville had already been to see the play in Cambridge and that Rosalind, who lived in Wales, was expected to attend in Cardiff the following week.

Agatha responded a week later:

I am delighted about the play and even more delighted that Peter Saunders and Hubert Gregg don't want to play the thing only for laughs. That's where they are more intelligent than Bertie. If they can get Jeanne more or less kept under so that she doesn't run away with things, I think all should be well. Cambridge, of course, was bound to be appreciative, but Cardiff is pretty wet so it will make a useful contrast. Shall get a good blast of destructive criticism from Rosalind, I expect. If she says 'not at all bad, mother' I shall go up in the air. How maddening that *I* can't see it. It's just got to be running in London in May.[34]

As it happens, Agatha's most fearsome critic appears to have very much enjoyed the performance, writing to Saunders somewhat belatedly,

Dear Mr Saunders,

I must write and tell you how much we enjoyed The Hollow. Our seats were very good, thank you, but I am sorry that you didn't come down to Cardiff.

I thought most of the cast were very good – Henrietta was a particularly pleasant surprise! She was just right. Gerda was good particularly at the end but I think she was inclined to overdo being clumsy and stupid to begin with. Jeanne de Casalis was very good and very funny I thought – not quite Lady Angkatell but that doesn't matter – Sir Henry was good but we didn't like Edward much. He looked all right but he wasn't very sympathetic. He has a loud assertive voice and sticks his chin out and would certainly never shoot himself. That scene is easily the worst part of the play in my opinion. It looks quite ridiculous when he attempts to shoot himself and made me feel quite uncomfortable. Otherwise I think Hubert Gregg directed it excellently. It goes quickly and never drags at all. He is not as unlike John Cristow as I had imagined he might be. We both thought when he is just about to be shot that he said 'Gerda' first – I know of course that he doesn't but it *sounded* like he did. The Inspector was very good, but a little indistinct at times – he slurs his words together – the maid had a very funny face! Veronica was quite good and Midge I think was good. She is very attractive and I think could be even more like Midge than she is. Her clothes aren't quite right in my opinion.

Anyway we thoroughly enjoyed it and I hope it really does well.

Yours sincerely,

Rosalind Hicks

I'm sorry I forgot to post this last week![35]

Clearly relieved, Saunders responded,

Dear Mrs Hicks,

Thank you so much for your letter. As I didn't hear from you I was wondering whether you were quite appalled at the production, and had written to your mother telling her to cable Bertie Meyer forthwith!

When you saw Gerda she had already been toned down in the first two acts, and since then Hubert has gone even further in making her a little less sub-human.

Jeanne de Casalis is not and never will be Lady Angkatell. But I do feel that the one thing lacking in this play is a personality such as Poirot or Miss Marple, and I am hoping that Jeanne will be a substitute.[36]

He went on to suggest that the scene she did not like would benefit from a rewrite, and reassured Rosalind that Midge would in any event be re-costumed for the London opening: 'Apart from the star one does not provide clothes for the women until the West End, in case there are changes of cast.'

There is no copy of Rosalind's letter to her mother in Baghdad, but she evidently had expressed many the same opinions that she had to Saunders, eliciting the response:

Very pleased to get your letter about the play – if on the whole *you* wouldn't have any one changed, it must be more or less all right. Glad you thought Henrietta good – Stephen didn't – but Beryl was madly nervous and constantly in tears and probably didn't do herself justice in Cambridge. At rehearsal I thought she and Joan Newell were very good in end scene – and you say so too – and *that's* very important. I think Hubert is on the watch to keep Joan Newell from going too far – He is a good producer [i.e. director] – streets ahead of Reginald Tate [director of *Murder in the Vicarage*].[37]

But despite the tour's success Saunders was having difficulty in securing a West End theatre for the production. A few weeks later Cork wrote to Christie:

It has been very difficult indeed to get a suitable West End theatre for it, however, the people who control several of the smaller theatres do not seem to think it is the sort of show that should be put on at an 'intimate' house, while we are quite sure on this point after seeing the effect of the vast Wimbledon stage – it was a good show there, but not the superlative attraction that it should be. The result of the negotiations is that Peter Saunders has definitely got a line on the Fortune – against no less than thirty-eight competing shows – and he plans to open during the first week in June. The Fortune would not have been my first choice, as there is very little casual business there, but it is a nice little theatre and can play to £1,600 a week – which would suit us very nicely – and what is by no means unimportant, it will come on after your return.[38]

In his autobiography, Saunders writes:

It was impossible to get a theatre at the time, and I find that in writing to Agatha Christie I told her that there were thirty-eight plays waiting to come into London. I suspect this was a gross exaggeration. So after eight weeks on tour I called it off and re-cast three parts. The Fortune theatre, which no-one wanted, was going to be available from June until the end of September, which in those days was the worst time of the year . . . Agatha had written from Baghdad hoping that I would not open the play in the summer, but again this remarkable lady accepted the fact that there was nothing else I could do.[39]

Saunders notes that the manager of the Westminster Theatre liked the play and was keen to provide a home for it, but that the theatre's owners insisted they would rather close and go dark than take the production. The lease on the Westminster had recently been taken over by Reandco, and the first play hosted by them there had been their own production of Lesley Storm's hugely successful *Black Chiffon*, starring Flora Robson.

The man who objected so strongly to *The Hollow* was none other than E.P. Clift, Alec Rea's business partner. Reandco's last Christie production having been the less than satisfactory *Murder on the Nile*, it may simply have been that they had lost faith in her as a playwright. Or perhaps Reandco, who had produced work in partnership with Tennents, had no desire to ally themselves with Saunders.

The production reopened in Nottingham on 14 May 1951 and completed a three-week tour prior to opening at the Fortune on 7 June. The opportunity was taken to recast the actors playing Midge and Sir Henry, and Hubert Gregg also left the company, in order to take on the role of Prince John in Disney's film of *Robin Hood*. He remained director and, once again, his peculiar brand of meticulous pedantry appears to have served the work well. Cork had reassured Christie that 'Hubert Gregg has been caught up by some film commitment, and had to give up the part of Cristow, but he will be available to do his producer's stuff, and in fact you really have got your own way in having him able to devote himself wholly to that side, without an actor's little vanities creeping in.'[40] He believed that the new actors were an improvement and lamented that the actress previously playing Midge just went 'down and down. She never reproduced that emotional quality that we admired at the first reading . . .'

Far from fighting off thirty-eight other productions, Saunders had actually been offered the Fortune for *The Hollow*, sight unseen, the previous year; he even mentions it in his application to the Arts Council. Despite technically being part of the Group (Prince Littler himself was listed as managing director) it was one of the least in-demand of the West End theatres, being used by amateurs for several months of the year.

On the night *The Hollow* opened in the West End, the thirty-five plays and musicals competing for audiences included Tom Arnold's production of Ivor Novello's *Gay's the Word*, starring Cicely Courtneidge, at the Saville and Farndale's production of *Worm's Eye View*, which had moved to the Comedy Theatre and was in its sixth year. Celia Johnson and Renee Asherson were appearing in *Three Sisters* at the Aldwych, Donald Wolfit could be seen in *His Excellency* by Dorothy and Campbell Christie at the Piccadilly, Terence Rattigan's *Who Is Sylvia?* was playing at the Criterion and Peter Ustinov was starring in *The Love of Four Colonels* at Wyndhams.

On opening night *The Stage* carried a report about a talk given by Christie on the forthcoming production. There is no record of where this talk was given, or to whom, but Christie appears to show none of her legendary shyness when it comes to discussing her forthcoming play. As ever, it is the issue of Poirot on stage that is her principal concern. Under the heading 'New Style Detective', the article announces:

When Agatha Christie's new play, *The Hollow*, opens at the Fortune to-night, Thursday, she will introduce a new kind of stage detective. So far as the theatre is concerned, Miss Christie's celebrated Poirot has been 'killed', chiefly because of the difficulty of casting him. 'Poirot will still appear in my books,' Miss Christie said in a talk, 'but I have a new detective for theatre purposes. I found that the difficulty of casting such an individualised character sometimes spoiled his effect in the theatre. Although the artists concerned gave excellent performances, some of those who had known him in my books had different views as to how he should look! The detective in *The Hollow* is, I think, a more usual sort of person, at least so far as appearance and personality are concerned. As he will be new to audiences, whether they have read my books or not, it should be possible for him to establish himself without undue difficulty.' Miss Christie's new play attempts to combine real-life characterisation and atmosphere with its thriller elements. 'It is more of a murder-drama set in ordinary social surroundings than a Who-done-it?' she explained. 'I believe that the more firmly you place your plot in everyday surroundings, and have characters with a life of their own, the more effective your drama will be. It is a limitation to have to rely entirely on your thrills or surprises. I have tried to make my detective as natural as possible, both in himself and in his methods. After all the 'private investigator' isn't much known in real life, apart from divorce matters.'[41]

Poirot's replacement, the diligent, methodical and rather colourless Inspector Colquhoun, certainly runs no risk of upstaging the characters who Christie is really interested in.

Despite Gregg's claims to have won the day as a result of his application of directorial thriller gimmickry, Christie must have been gratified to see the West End reviews recognising a quality of realism in the writing. 'Full marks to Miss Christie,' said the *Evening Standard*, '*The Hollow* is in fact that rarity; a thriller about reasonable and interesting people, intelligently and credibly acted.'[42] The *Evening News* concurred: '"Keep the secret locked in your hearts" said Jeanne de Casalis at the curtain-call of *The Hollow* by Agatha Christie . . . but I think, even knowing "whodunit" I might nerve myself to sit out this play again because of the highly entertaining dialogue and the penetrative character-acting with which it is adorned.'[43] J.C. Trewin, writing in the *Illustrated London News*, commented, like *The Times*, that the opening scene dragged a bit, but noted that

> to the end her listeners stay rapt . . . The main interest of the play, as a piece of writing, is in the mystery; but Mrs Christie writes quick, speakable dialogue and, gleefully, her cast keeps us guessing until the dying minutes of the third act . . . And, for once, Mrs Christie does not ask us to solve the mystery of a detective, to fathom why so strange a fellow should be down from Scotland Yard. Martin Wyldeck's detective is an Englishman. He is a professional. He has no catchwords, no foibles, no oddities of dress or manner. He merely does his job. It is all very curious and unexpected.[44]

Ivor Brown, in the *Observer*, also approved of Christie's specially created new stage detective: 'Martin Wyldeck is an admirable Detective Inspector, neither smart nor smart Alec, but just humanly and taciturnly natural.'[45] It seems that Christie had finally expunged the curse of Poirot from her stage work.

Other preconceptions about her plays were less easily dispensed with than the inclusion of Poirot, however. The *News of the World* wrote:

> Agatha Christie, sitting well back in a box at the Fortune theatre, listened to the rounds of applause and knew that the old, old formula had worked once more. For her new play, *The Hollow*, faithfully follows the pattern of her countless other 'whodunit' stories which have made the 60-year-old authoress Britain's most popular thrill provider. Of course, there may be some who will cavil at this; who will demand new angles on the proven formula. But as one who rarely guesses right in the game of 'find the murderer' I personally hope that the Christie technique will continue unchanged. There is of course, a country house week-end party. There is, inevitably, a shooting on the stage by a murderer or murderess unseen. And it follows automatically that the man who is shot is loved by various women (three in this case) all of whom may have a motive for murder. Jeanne de Casalis has a perfect 'Mrs Feather' part, and supplies the laughs that according to custom must lighten the tension. It's ideal entertainment for those who can't sleep without a thriller at the bedside.[46]

This was, in fact, only Christie's fifth play to be presented in the West End, and of the previous four only two had been set in a country house, and neither of those had featured the shooting of a philandering man by an unseen murderer.

The *Sunday Chronicle* introduced an even more cynical note:

> It is reasonably safe to prophesy that eventually almost everyone in this enchanted island will see *The Hollow*, Agatha Christie's latest whodunit, which opened at the Fortune Theatre on Thursday. Only a small proportion can see it at the Fortune, even if it runs there for years, for this is one

of London's smallest theatres – with 493 seats. But this we are sure is only the launching site for a long and lucrative voyage. *The Hollow* will be filmed, televised, broadcast and for the next decade or so will head the 'surefire' list compiled for repertory companies and amateur societies. Considered purely as a play it would be a negligible contribution to the drama, but as a whodunit (and they have been woefully scarce in recent years) it is a fascinating and intriguing exhibition of sleight-of-hand on the part of the author.[47]

Although most of the reviews insisted on describing the play as a 'thriller' or a 'whodunit', Saunders remained true to his promise to Christie and removed the words from the publicist's vocabulary. Whether the alternative was an improvement is, perhaps, doubtful: 'This gripping but not gruesome comedy-mystery is the latest play from the most famous of all detective story writers', proclaimed the leaflet advertising the production, continuing, 'Jeanne de Casalis, George Thorpe and Ernest Clark co-star in this brilliant play. Glamour is provided by Beryl Baxter, star of the film "Idol of Paris" and Dianne Foster, lovely actress of the Canadian stage.'[48]

Although Hubert Gregg evidently made a good job of directing *The Hollow*, and made a good living from his association with Christie over the years, it seems a shame that someone with so little regard for her both as a writer and a person should have been so close to the centre of operations. In his book, Gregg is at great pains to emphasise what he believes to be the critical importance of his own contributions to the script, acknowledged, as he sees it, by Saunders' reference to him (on a copy of it he signed in 1952) as 'the architect of victory'.[49] 'One day, I was given the script of *The Hollow* to read,' he explains. 'It was hair-raising . . . I mean I thought it was abysmal. The dialogue was unspeakable . . . the characters were caricatures. The denouement was good. "Jesus," I said to myself quietly. "I need the job."'[50] Similarly, when offered the role of John Cristow, 'Any actor who would accept Cristow if he didn't need the money would be out of his histrionic mind.' A few months previously Christie had been awarded a Fellowship by the Royal Society of Literature. Her critic's greatest claim to fame as a writer were the lyrics to 'Maybe it's Because I'm a Londoner'.

Gregg makes great play of the fact that Christie does not allow enough time for a kettle to boil or for actors to change into evening dress, and that her set requires two French windows, a door, a fireplace and a 'breakfast nook' (all of which were, as it turned out, well within the capabilities of designer Joan Jefferson Farjeon). He claims to have cut the first act 'to ribbons', and that he had to persuade Christie to introduce a thunderstorm at the climax of the piece. In these days before lighting designers, when directors tended to light their own plays, we hear much from him of his particular skills in this department (there is a lighting plan inserted in the front of his copy of the script). No wonder it rankled when Christie not only failed to mention him in her autobiography, but heaped particular praise on Irene Hentschel's lighting for *Ten Little Niggers*. Perhaps most astonishingly, Gregg compares his dramaturgical role in nurturing *The Hollow* from page to stage with that of Gerald du Maurier's legendary (and well paid) contribution to Edgar Wallace's dramatisation of *The Ringer*, and argues that he should have received comparable acknowledgement and financial recompense for his work. He includes in his book a page of Christie's own notes as if to demonstrate the vast superiority of his own insights.

The Christie archive includes no script of any sort for *The Hollow*, but Gregg's own copy is amongst the Gregg/Christie memorabilia recently put up for sale. It has to be said that the typescript appears to have been extensively cut and annotated in (blue) ink, but whether this constitutes anything more significant than the usual adjustments made to a new play at rehearsals with the writer present is difficult to say. If the script had been definitively reworked prior to rehearsals, as Gregg suggests, then it would surely have been retyped and issued to the actors on day one. It is also worth questioning

whether Gregg's textual cuts improved the quality of the work.
Here are three separate examples of the cuts he made:

> DORIS: My dad says I ought to call myself a domestic help.
> GUDGEON: That's about all you are.
> [*Cut*: DORIS: What d'you mean?
> *Cut:* GUDGEON: In my young days when a girl wasn't bright
>   enough to be a good parlour maid or a proper housemaid,
>   or even an efficient kitchen maid, she had to call herself
>   a 'household help' and was paid accordingly. She had no
>   proper status.]

> CRISTOW [on his role as a doctor]: I don't cure them. Just
>   hand out faith, hope and probably a laxative. [*Cut*: In a
>   bottle flavoured with peppermint for the poor and wrapped
>   in cellophane and costing a guinea for the rich.]

> [*Cut:* HENRIETTA: And of course Gudgeon is the last of the
>   butlers. Any bit of human flotsam who is entrapped in
>   this house as an under-servant has to live up to Gudgeon's
>   standards or go.][51]

Gregg holds the following line up for particular ridicule as an
example of Christie's 'unspeakable' dialogue:

> HENRIETTA: Hurry up, Henry, it's nearly dinner time.
> HENRY: I'll be like greased lightning.[52]

Personally, I can't see a problem with it; and can well imagine
such a response from old Sir Henry. Some of Gregg's work on
scene structure clearly resolves issues of timing, which is, after
all, the director's job. I cannot really see, though, any marked
improvements as a result of his editing of Christie's generally
well-crafted dialogue. Gregg was horrified when, a few years
later, he was turned down for another job because of his work
on what someone had described to his potential employer as
'those awful Christie plays'. He apparently saw no irony in the

fact that his own lack of regard for her writing doubtless had
a role to play in propagating the views that condemned Christie
to the end of the Arts Council's pier.

Christie was never resistant to the dramaturgical input of
others, and was always a willing participant in the sometimes
tortuous process of script editing and development. But we can
be sure that, with the possible exception of sections of *Akhnaton*
where she draws on a range of source material, the writing
itself is always her own. She was strongly resistant to the work
of third parties being included in her scripts, and generally
insistent that she alone should be responsible for carrying out
any changes that were required. She had at one point told
Basil Dean that he could make any further changes that he
wanted to *A Daughter's a Daughter* (which he didn't); but after
Dean's successful co-adaptation with its author of Margaret
Kennedy's *The Constant Nymph*, it may well have been that
Christie felt this was a good way to maintain his interest. And
she was to allow some expert interpolations regarding legal
procedures in *Witness for the Prosecution*. But Christie's own
stage dialogue is instantly recognisable as such, and *The Hollow*
is rich with it; and although the absence of early drafts limits
our ability to understand just how this particular script developed, I do not detect any significant sections of writing in it
that are not Christie's own.

Whatever the truth of Gregg's input into the script, the
production of *The Hollow* was a great success, and at the end
of August *The Stage* ran an interview with its star:

> Jeanne de Casalis, familiar to audiences in modern drama
> and comedy parts, has established herself firmly in another
> sort of play by her performance in Agatha Christie's thriller
> *The Hollow* at the Fortune. Altogether, this play, in the first
> few weeks of what looks like being a long run, has been the
> cause of several remarkable happenings. Firstly, it is the first
> thriller to capture a London audience for several years.
> Secondly, it opened in high-summer when hopes for success
> are never very optimistic. Thirdly, it has brought back into

the crowded life of the West End the little Fortune. It has
had the patronage of Queen Mary; it is attracting full houses;
curtain speeches are in demand; and the faith of Peter
Saunders, who presents it, has been justified. 'Although *The
Hollow* is such an expertly written play' Miss de Casalis said,
'part of its success rests on Hubert Gregg's excellent production and the good acting of the entire company, as a team . . .
Acting in a thriller demands special effort in several ways.
Although the author, as in this case, makes the characters
as natural as possible, inevitably they are subject to plot-
development. There is always a sense of unreality mixed in
with the "natural". The player has to convince the audience
it is seeing real, everyday people, and yet bring out the highly
charged, artificial atmosphere of a thriller. This must be done
without disturbing the balance or conviction on either level.
So you see it is not an easy job! But I find the work particularly exciting. In my case there is another problem which
I have to resolve afresh every night. The public have come
to regard me in the last few years as a comedienne. As soon
as I come on to the stage at the Fortune they expect to laugh,
want to laugh, or do laugh. Well there is plenty of comedy
in my role of Lady Angkatell, but I have to be very careful
not to let this overflow into serious dramatic moments. This
makes acting the part very tricky, yet it is the sort of thing
almost any player revels in. It demands your best work all
the time . . . I think it is quite true to say that there is always
a place in the theatre for a good thriller, but it must have
some sense of ordinary reality blended with its excitement
and suspense, and it must be well presented.'[53]

The deal at the Fortune had been for a four-month limited
season over the summer. Although, as Saunders points out,
this is usually regarded as the worst time of the year in the
West End theatre, there is some indication that the theatre's
unenviable Covent Garden side-street location was on this
occasion beneficial, placing it on the route taken by many to
and from Festival of Britain events on the South Bank. As noted

in *The Stage*, amongst the play's many customers was avid theatregoer and Agatha Christie fan Queen Mary, the king's 84-year-old mother. By the time the engagement at the Fortune came to an end in October, the production had gained sufficient momentum to secure a transfer to the independently owned Ambassadors Theatre, where it eventually completed its run the following May, totalling 376 performances. According to Saunders, the Ambassadors' manager, Herbert Malden, didn't like the play and had turned it down when a London home was originally being sought for it. Now his view was, 'It doesn't matter what I think. What I do like is the business you're doing.'[54]

The Stage, reviewing the play in its new home, noted that 'The production by Hubert Gregg of this engrossing murder play drew a full house on its opening night at the Ambassadors, and as the tension does not snap until a second before the final curtain, it should continue to have a strong appeal. Jeanne de Casalis, Joan Newell, Jessica Spencer, Beryl Baxter, George Thorpe, Ernest Clark [who had replaced Gregg as Cristow] and Colin Douglas repeat their ingenious performances, their unselfish team-work serving the author to the best possible advantage.'[55] Christie's failure to write star turns had seemingly paid off.

When the play transferred to the Ambassadors, the programme featured a full-page advertisement for all of Tennents' current productions.[56] The commercial wing of the organisation, H.M. Tennent Ltd, was presenting four plays in the West End including John Mills in *Figure of Fun* at the Aldwych, Robert Morley in *The Little Hut* at the Lyric and Gladys Cooper in Noël Coward's *Relative Values* at the Savoy. Meanwhile, the non-profit distributing Tennent Productions Ltd was offering a further four productions, including Emlyn Williams as Charles Dickens at the Criterion, Edith Evans and Sybil Thorndike in N.C. Hunter's *Waters of the Moon* at the Haymarket and John Gielgud in *The Winter's Tale* at the Phoenix, as well as the latest attractions at the Lyric, Hammersmith. No doubt the advertisement, which appeared on the page opposite the cast list, had the desired effect of reminding Peter Saunders who was boss.

Crucial to the operation of Saunders' enterprise was his long-serving general manager, Verity Hudson. Born in 1923 in Lahore, she had started her theatrical career as an assistant stage manager at the Theatre Royal, Windsor in 1946, joining Saunders as a stage manager two years later. She appears in Saunders' programmes under various titles including 'stage director' (senior stage manager) and 'business manager', and in 1969 she was to become an executive director of the Saunders companies. In 1975 she was the first woman to join the Executive Council of the Society of West End Theatre, going on to become its first woman president in 1986 and dying, aged sixty-four, during her second year in office.

Peter Saunders' business papers give us a delightful insight into the daily operation of the production. Beryl Baxter, playing Henrietta Angkatell, complains to Hudson about her dressing room on tour, eliciting the response from Saunders, 'Can't you see, you silly girl, that billing which the whole world (I hope) will see, is vastly more important than dressing rooms, that is known only to the cast.'[57] Baxter writes back to him immediately to apologise, with an endearing 'PS: Thank you for being so sweet.' During the London run, a clearly frustrated dressmaker refunds £28 paid for making Jeanne de Casalis a new dress and asks for the dress to be returned, declaring, 'I really am at a loss to know what to do but I do feel that after making a second one, without success, it is quite evident that we cannot please her . . . suggest that you try someone else, who I only hope will prove more successful with her.'[58] On 6 February 1952, King George VI died, necessitating the closure of all theatres for one night as a mark of respect. In settling the accounts for that week, the management of the Ambassadors Theatre offer to cover the costs of their own staff for the cancelled performance rather than recharging them to Saunders as they normally would. Saunders thanks them for their 'most kindly gesture' which he accepts 'in the very nice spirit in which it is offered'.[59]

Saunders' archive contains a full set of production accounts for *The Hollow*, as well as records of his dealings with his investors. He misleadingly maintains in his book that he 'discarded the idea' of taking 'outside backers' for his productions, but it is certainly true that he did not take many. Those he did raise finance from were a close circle of family members and business associates, and he himself would usually retain a substantial financial stake in his productions. In the case of *The Hollow*, £4,000 was raised to cover the production's set-up costs and provide a float to underwrite its weekly running expenses. There are records of four investors having subscribed £500 each and one contributing £1,000, meaning that Saunders himself retained a 25 per cent investor stake in the production. Saunders advised investors that he estimated that 'about £900 will have been spent when the curtain goes up'.[60] In the event, the first pre-London tour cost £979 to mount, and the eventual move into London (including all those ladies' dresses) a further £767. Weekly income would have been applied in the first instance to covering the running costs. The show cost £1,158 to run (including £239 theatre rent and £352 in artists' salaries) in a sample week at the Ambassadors (week ending 24 November 1951), and on the week in question made a healthy £1,360 at the box office (after the deduction of entertainment tax) to cover those costs and generate an operating profit for the week of just over £200.[61]

From the artists' contracts and weekly payroll we see that Jeanne de Casalis was significantly better paid than her colleagues, earning £75 per week plus 5 per cent of box office income over £1,250. George Thorpe, playing Henry Angkatell, took home £30 per week, Colin Douglas (Edward Angkatell) earned £25 and Beryl Baxter £20. The lowest paid cast member, Patricia Jones (Doris), earned £8 per week.[62] In our 'sample' week Agatha Christie earned £77 in royalties (although 10 per cent of that would have gone to Hughes Massie). Peter Saunders received a 'management fee' of £25 (as compared with the £40 per week charged by Tennents to their productions).

At the end of October 1951 Saunders wrote to his investors

repaying their initial stake and announcing that 'I can safely promise you a very substantial profit by the time we have finished the production.'[63] Final accounts show that the two pre-London tours and the West End run between them generated a profit of £4,737.[64] The thirty-second West End performance triggered Saunders' financial participation in a menu of subsidiary rights, and over the licence period of seven years following the final West End performance these generated a further £2,211 for him in royalties from sub-let UK tours and licences issued in the USA, South Africa, Australia and East Africa. A substantial £2,567 from Saunders' share of UK repertory rights brought the total profits for his production to an impressive £9,515. An investor of £500 was entitled to 8 per cent of all profits (including subsidiary income), so as well as receiving back their initial stake would have received a further £761 by the end of the seven-year licence period. On this basis Saunders himself would have walked away with £3,425 of profits, plus a further £1,522 resulting from his own financial stake in the project. That would make his own share of profits over £100,000 in today's money. He must have been one very happy producer.

Rather than attempting to compete with 'Binkie' Beaumont on his own territory, Saunders was to build an empire of his own by deliberately cultivating a style of work that Tennents rejected. Saunders also took on the leases of a number of West End theatre buildings shunned by the Group, and at various times would find himself running the Duchess, the Vaudeville, the Duke of York's, the Ambassadors and the St Martin's. By deliberately promoting and eloquently advocating populist and 'unfashionable' theatre, he was to build himself a position of respect within the industry (he was twice President of the Society of West End Theatre) and a not inconsiderable personal fortune. His perspicacity, business acumen and integrity enabled him to carve out something more than a niche, based on a variety of work including that of Christie and William Douglas-Home. And Cork was to find an enthusiastic fellow-traveller in Saunders when it came to his methodical exploitation of sub-sidiary rights. Christie's partnership with Saunders would ensure the systematic promotion of her work for the stage over the following decade, creating a highly lucrative global market for her work, and ensuring her position as the most successful female playwright of all time. The only sadness was that Madge Watts, the first of the Miller sisters to have a play produced in the West End, died in 1950 and was not there to enjoy Agatha's theatrical breakthrough with her.

In Saunders, Christie had at last found a producer on whom she could rely, who appreciated her value and who treated her with respect. In her introduction to his autobiography, Christie writes:

> How I came into Sir Peter Saunders' life and he into mine is a matter of vague recollection. Dates and places and times are all such indefinite things – but he certainly came to stay. He is one of my most appreciated friends; he has influenced me in many ways. I have enjoyed his friendship and his good company – his ready humour, the knowledge of the stage he has imparted to me, and I have a deep respect for the things he has made me do that I said I couldn't and didn't want to do . . . I have always been a shy person – but with Peter I never felt shy. He has a natural friendliness and kindness.[65]

Unlike Edmund Cork, whose name appears only infrequently in the Greenway visitors book, Saunders was to become a regular guest at Agatha's country residence, where he played cricket with her cherished grandson and devised theatrical projects with the delighted playwright. Commentators tend to remark on the fact that after the war Christie's output as a novelist slowed down; the official website even goes so far as to head this section of her life 'autumn'. But this is to ignore the fact that she was finally coming into her own as a playwright. She was happily dividing her time between archaeological digs and theatre, and dutifully producing a book a year to keep her publisher and her fans happy. For Agatha Christie, playwright, the 1950s were high summer.

But, as her success grew, so would the dilemma at the centre

of her work. Agatha Christie was the writer of such remarkable dramas as *The Lie, The Stranger* and *A Daughter's a
Daughter* but theatrical success, which had arrived late in life,
was seductive to her. Should she continue to write 'plays' or
should she bow to popular demand and fulfil the expectations
of her audiences (and her producer) by writing whodunits?
The creative but often chaotic days of Bertie Meyer, Francis
L. Sullivan, Basil Dean, Alec Rea, Irene Hentschel, Andre van
Gyseghem, Barbara Toy and the People's Entertainment Society
were behind her and 'Christie on stage' was destined to become
part of a well-oiled and carefully branded production machine
that existed outside both the mainstream theatre of the day
and its well-documented counter-culture in the new Arts
Council-funded subsidised sector. It was, in effect, the alliance
with fellow maverick Peter Saunders that would ultimately
result in Christie, like him, being written out of the theatrical
history books.

The establishment that Saunders fought, in the form of H.M.
Tennent Ltd and their associated companies, was effectively
able to operate a monopoly through the complex inter-linking
of a number of nominally independent concerns, but the
Shuberts' control of the American theatre industry was more
immediately obvious. Consequently, in 1950, the US government
filed a suit charging the Shuberts and their United Booking
Office with creating a monopoly in violation of the 1890
Sherman Anti-Trust Act and, following a case that rumbled on
for six years, the company was eventually ordered to divest
itself of a quantity of its holdings, including a number of the
buildings under its control.

In the meantime, Lee Shubert, now aged eighty, had not
given up on the idea of finding a successor to *Ten Little Indians*,
despite the Broadway failure of *Hidden Horizon* and his belief
that Christie's version of *Towards Zero* was not ready for
production. In June 1951 the Shuberts therefore paid a substantial £1,000 (the deal was done in sterling) for a one-year option
on the American and Canadian rights to *The Hollow*,[66] with a

further payment subsequently extending the production date to the end of October 1952. They were no longer working in conjunction with Albert de Courville, although they entered a co-production deal for the project with film producer Sherman S. Krellberg,[67] who was backing a successful comedy at one of the Shuberts' theatres at the time. As the producer of the play in the West End, Saunders had exercised his own American option and was thus a party to the agreement with the Shuberts.

To the horror of Harold Ober, the deal with Lee Shubert was done directly by Edmund Cork, apparently during a visit to London by Shubert, without involving Ober and his lawyer Howard Reinheimer. On 2 August Ober wrote to Cork listing a number of serious shortcomings in the agreement, not least that Shubert had evidently persuaded Cork not to use the Dramatists Guild standard 'Minimum Basic Agreement':

> I don't know whether you remember the trouble we had with Lee Shubert over Ten Little Indians. I imagine that he persuaded you to close the deal for The Hollow in London so that he could escape us and our lawyers! I assume from your letter that the contract has been signed and that there is nothing we can do about it unless the Dramatists Guild can force him or shame him into conforming with the Minimum Basic Agreement. I am enclosing a memorandum . . . and a copy of a letter from Howard Reinheimer. Probably the only use these will be to you will be to warn you so that you will know what to do if some other American producer tries the same tactics sometime in the future.[68]

As Reinheimer pointed out in the accompanying correspondence, the Minimum Basic Agreement was still universally adopted for Broadway productions, although it had recently been the subject of a 'restraint of trade' court case as a result of which it was now styled a 'recommended' rather than an obligatory form of author's contract. 'This business about the Shuberts telling Mr Cork that the MBA is "out" and that Lee Shubert would be a monkey for signing it is just ridiculous,' declares Reinheimer. 'The MBA *is* the standard form and *is being signed by everybody on Broadway today*.'[69] In fairness to Ober, he seemed unconcerned by the loss of his own commission on the deal, and genuinely worried about the contract that Cork had supplied. Unfortunately he was to be proved right.

Initially there was talk of *The Hollow*'s English cast going to New York in the autumn of 1951, but the production's transfer to the Ambassadors, where it ran until May the following year, meant that this idea lost impetus. Saunders reminded Shubert of this idea when he eventually announced the end of the West End run,[70] and Cork later did so as well,[71] with the extension of the Shuberts' option to October 1952 (after a bit of haggling) theoretically making it possible.[72] But in the end the idea was not pursued. Whether there would have been a happier outcome had the English cast played the piece in America we will never know.

One actor wasn't taking 'no' for an answer, though. Joan Newell, who had played Gerda in the London production, sent a telegram to Lee Shubert, 'WOULD LIKE TO PLAY HOLLOW ON BROADWAY AND REPEAT LONDON SUCCESS AS GERDA CRISTOW'. Her agent followed this up a week later with 'WOULD LIKE AGAIN SUGGEST JOAN NEWELL', eliciting the classic Shubert response 'CABLE LOWEST SALARY NEWELL'.[73] A deal was done and Newell was flown out to America, where she was contracted for $300 per week, having earned £18 per week in London. Her dream of playing Gerda on Broadway was not to materialise, though.

Rehearsals started on 15 September 1952, and the following day Shubert cabled Cork, 'IS IT AGREEABLE CHANGE TITLE HOLLOW TO SUSPECTS. PLEASE CABLE'. Having received no answer, he wrote to Cork a week later, 'I must impress upon you the importance of an immediate reply . . . we have discussed this change with a number of people and they feel that SUSPECTS is a very strong title in relation to the play . . . we will, as you suggest in your letter make suitable reference to the fact that the play refers to the London stage success The Hollow.' Cork, who had previously been asked if the title could be changed to *The*

House Guest, responded, 'PROPRIETORS LIKE SUSPECTS EVEN LESS THAN HOUSEGUEST BUT LEAVE DECISION TO YOU PROVIDED PUBLICITY CONNECTS WITH HOLLOW'.[74]

The programme's title page does indeed state 'THE SUSPECTS (From the London success "The Hollow") by Agatha Christie',[75] although one might legitimately question the use of the word 'from' in this context, implying that it was based on the original rather than simply being a retitled version. As it turns out, though, the title was not the only change made to the play by the Shuberts. As Harold Ober had pointed out in his condemnation of the deal with the Shuberts, there was nothing to stop them from making alterations to the play, and according to press reports it was indeed being 'rewritten' (although, it seems, on an uncredited basis) by 'former Dramatists Guild member' Russell Medcraft,[76] a screenwriter with a couple of Broadway shows to his credit.

Although there is a copy of the original play in the Shubert archive there is no copy of *The Suspects*, so we will probably never know what exactly American audiences were watching in the belief that it was written by Agatha Christie. Amongst the alterations we can discern were its emendation from a three-act to a two-act structure, which Christie had agreed to, although in the process of achieving this the timeframe of the action appears to have been radically condensed. *The Hollow* is a three-act, five-scene play spanning a period from Friday to Monday. According to the programme for *The Suspects*, Act One takes place on Saturday (two scenes) and Act Two on Sunday (two scenes), with the interval occurring in the middle of Act Two. Amongst other things, this presumably means that a number of the characters cannot go off to attend an inquest as they do in the final scene of *The Hollow*. The character of Doris the maid also appears to have been cut, which would have involved the removal of Christie's carefully placed subtext about the changing status of servants in contemporary England. Granted, an American audience would probably have had no idea what Gudgeon and Doris were talking about, but this again begs the question as to the advisability of staging the play in America in the first place, and particularly to an audience who had been led to believe that it was a follow-up to *Ten Little Indians*. The playwright herself, of course, had insisted from the start that it was not a 'thriller'.

The progress of *The Suspects* out of town was monitored closely by American showbiz columnists. On 10 October the *New York Times* reported that the show was to open that night in Princeton, playing two nights only, and was due to tour before its Broadway opening on 10 November. 'Just where it will open has not yet been decided. The contract is said to call for the Booth but Beatrice Lillie is playing to capacity business at that house and Lee Shubert is not exactly eager to move her. As it does so often at this time of the year, the Broadway booking will probably depend upon how well the play looks out of town.' Since the *New York Times* had previously announced *The Suspects* as being due to open at the Booth, this was presumably by way of a clarification at the Shuberts' request, so as not to affect Lillie's box office. She had just opened in *An Evening with Beatrice Lillie* and would, as it turns out, continue to play at the Booth until the end of May the following year. On Sunday 12 October, prior to the *The Suspects'* opening in Philadelphia the following week, *The New York Times* ran a photograph of cast members Anna Karen (Veronica Craye) and Jeff Morrow (John Cristow) 'in the Agatha Christie mystery play which is scheduled to arrive on Broadway the week of Nov 10'. No theatre is mentioned.

The *Boston Herald* trailed the 27 October opening of the tour in the city, announcing, 'Ever since *Ten Little Indians* terrified and excited audiences, Broadway producers have been looking around for another play which would produce the same effect. The Messrs Shubert and Krellberg believe they have found it in *The Suspects*, which was written by the same brilliant writer of thrillers, who wrote the first-mentioned play, Agatha Christie.'[77] We are even told to expect 'the most sinister police inspector ever to find his way to any stage'. With this kind of misguided publicity, the Shuberts were inevitably setting the play up for a fall, and the *Boston Post*'s review is typical of its reception:

> Since there are not many of them available any more, it is necessary to have a little patience with such mystery melo-dramas as we get to see . . . Nine little Indians out of a possible ten littered the stage in her 'Ten Little Indians' with clues all over the place . . . Here, in *The Suspects*, there is nothing but talk for the entire first act, and some of it dreary talk. And there is one lone victim of a mysterious shot . . . although there are one or two stout parts most of the actors aren't helping *The Suspects* very much so far. This play needs restaging and I am afraid, some recasting, also a good deal of speeding up. Else it will run into trouble in New York.'[78]

A week later the *New York Times* duly reported, '*The Suspects* Agatha Christie's murder melodrama will be withdrawn for repairs after tomorrow night's performance in Boston. Lee Shubert and S.S. Krellberg, the producers, feel that more rewriting and some recasting are in order before they bring the play to Broadway. Accordingly the premiere at the Lyceum [notably no longer the Booth] has been postponed until Late November or December.'[79]

One wonders what Agatha would have made of her play being described as a 'murder melodrama'. One also wonders what the actors thought of their producers sharing this infor-mation with the press in quite so much detail while they still had a performance to give – and, indeed, to what extent the success of Beatrice Lillie dictated the failure of *The Suspects* to arrive on Broadway on schedule. It does indeed look as if the Shuberts could have engineered an end-of-year opening at the Lyceum had they wanted to (the short-lived show running there eventually closed on Christmas Day), but it was not to be; and this may well have had something to do with the fact that Frederick Knott's *Dial M for Murder* started its long and hugely successful Broadway run on 30 October – at the

Shuberts' Plymouth Theatre, which had briefly been the home of *Hidden Horizon*.

A short time afterwards, Ober sent Cork a *New York Times* article dated 7 November:

> Edward Chodorov is the new director of *The Suspects*. Withdrawn in Boston last week for major repairs, the Agatha Christie mystery play is slated to resume practicing at the end of the month in anticipation of a late December arrival here. Who will appear in what may be a completely revised line-up is not definite. The management is thinking of such performers as Victor Jory, Lueen McGrath, Francis Sullivan and Jo Van Fleet. Despite the wholesale revamping, confidence in the script hasn't diminished, especially in the eyes of Marcella Swanson, whose judgment is highly respected by Lee Shubert, one of the sponsors.

Playwright and screenwriter Edward Chodorov had been a protégé of Broadway producer Jed Harris, for whom he made revisions in the script of *The Fatal Alibi*. The following year he would fall foul of the House Committee on Un-American Activities after being identified as a member of the Communist Party by choreographer Jerome Robbins.[80] Former showgirl Marcella Swanson had the distinction of being Mrs Lee Shubert (twice).

'All of these people are good and this sounds encouraging,' said Ober in his covering note.[81] But it seems unlikely that the project could have been successfully revived at this point, having been so publicly branded a failure.

There was an unfortunate postscript to the curtailment of the American version of *The Hollow*. The small print of the contract that Cork had signed with Shubert did not actually require the Shuberts to present the play in New York in order to secure the American rights on an ongoing basis.[82] The production had opened on 10 October 1952, within the extended 31 October deadline, and had played twenty-seven performances in Princeton, Philadelphia and Boston, closing on 1

November. During any three-year period after the end of the 'season' in which the first run took place, the contract allowed the Shuberts to present two hundred performances in order to retain the rights, enabling them, in effect, to do so in perpetuity. It was not specified how long the first run that triggered this arrangement needed to be. The end of 1952–3 'season' (in which the twenty-seven performances were presented) was 31 May 1953, so the Shuberts could retain the stage rights until 31 May 1959 by presenting at least two hundred further performances before 31 May 1956.

Furthermore, the contract with the Shuberts stated that their subsidiary rights participation (30 per cent of film and 50 per cent of stock) would be triggered as a result of three weeks in New York or fifty consecutive performances in any other first-class city in the USA. It wasn't clear whether this applied to the initial run only, or whether they could now qualify for subsidiaries simply by presenting a second tour of at least fifty performances within three years. In normal circumstances, only a three-week run on Broadway would have triggered their ability to participate in subsidiary rights, and then only if they took up the option to do so within a very specific and limited timeframe. But the wording in this case was ambiguous.

All of this was deeply frustrating for Saunders, who in any case only benefited to the extent of a fifth of the author's 10 per cent royalty income from the American stage production itself (instead of the usual one-third). His original 25 per cent share of the sale of film rights would have been increased to 50 per cent in the event that the Shuberts exercised their own option to participate in the film sale, enabling him to pass on the 30 per cent required by them and leaving him with 20 per cent.[83] If they didn't exercise their option, he would receive his original 25 per cent. Saunders was keen to pursue the idea of a film, but now he had no idea whether or not the Shuberts would at some point become entitled to be a party to the negotiations for the sale of film rights.

The deal had been badly botched, and became the subject of endless correspondence between Cork, Ober, Reinheimer, the

Shuberts, Saunders and Saunders' lawyers. In fairness, internal correspondence seems to indicate that Lee Shubert himself found the contract as confusing as its English signatories did, and although the situation as it stood at the end of 1952 appeared to play into the Shuberts' hands, it does not seem to have done so as the result of any premeditated strategy on their part. They could, after all, have secured their subsidiary participation simply by ensuring that the original tour had lasted for fifty performances, rather than the twenty-seven that it did.

Eventually, in January 1953, Cork wrote to Shubert telling him that his licence on the play 'has, of course, expired'[84] and asking whether he wished to renew it as there was other American interest. If the intention of this was to provoke a response then that is what he got. Shubert wrote straight back, 'I cannot agree with you that my "option on the play has expired" . . . My present intentions are to produce the play again and I am still very much interested in the property. Under these circumstances it would neither be fair or proper for you to negotiate the contract with any other producer.'[85]

Lee Shubert died at the end of 1953, aged eighty-two. The following year, in response to a continuing barrage of correspondence from parties representing Saunders and Christie, the company's new vice-president, J.J.'s son John, displaying his father's penchant for brevity, sent the following note to Ober: 'Regarding "The Hollow" this office will not make another production of this show, nor have we any enquiries from any amateur or stock companies.'[86]

Perhaps not surprisingly, Saunders did not take this as the confirmation that he needed that he was free to trade in the film rights, and his lawyers advised him that he should obtain a more definite undertaking from the Shuberts that they had no intention of engineering an option for themselves to participate in the film deal. Ober's lawyers, however, felt that this would simply antagonise the Shuberts, and that John Shubert's note would stand up in court as an undertaking that in any event they would not be presenting performances that might be regarded as triggering their participation in film rights. The resulting correspondence is quite colourful, with Ober's team pulling no punches as regards their views on the firm engaged by Saunders.

Ironically, an internal memo shows that the Shubert's lawyers felt that they would not in any case have been able to argue that any performances given after the initial twenty-seven-performance run could be counted as qualifying them for subsidiary participation.[87] In reality, therefore, Saunders had nothing to fear, but it was typical of the Shuberts' vastly superior gamesmanship that they persistently failed to give the inexperienced English producer the one piece of information that would have put him out of his misery.

Saunders had the last laugh, though. In 1956, John Shubert's assurances having proved correct, the Shuberts finally lost their stage rights to *The Hollow*. All ambiguity was thus removed, but by this time Saunders was engaged in a far more exciting Christie Broadway-to-film proposition. And the Shuberts, having driven him to distraction, had not been invited to the party.

The Shubert Organisation is still a major Broadway player and in 2000 celebrated its centenary, one hundred years after the three brothers from Syracuse purchased the lease of the Herald Square Theatre in New York. Lee Shubert's contribution to the Agatha Christie story has often been dismissed as obstructive, partly due to surviving correspondence from UK producers and agents who were embarrassed by their own relative ineptitude when it came to dispassionate business management. Shubert had one big Christie success with *Ten Little Indians*, but let it not be forgotten that he also made great efforts to present more of her work in America. Not only did he present *Hidden Horizon* for its ill-fated Broadway run, but he gave Christie her only commission as a dramatist, displaying considerable patience and courtesy in his efforts to get her to provide rewrites following its world premiere at Martha's Vineyard. And, contrary to received wisdom, *The Hollow* was also presented by the Shuberts in America following its London production, if under a different title.

SCENE TWO

The Disappearing Director

With *The Hollow* safely up and running at the Fortune, and an enthusiastic new producer delivering the goods, Agatha considered the options for her next dramatic project. Fascinatingly, the first play that her thoughts turned to was *Chimneys*, which had been cancelled at the last moment by Alec Rea's Embassy Theatre twenty years previously.

In August 1951, Christie wrote to Edmund Cork, 'Have you got an old play of mine called Chimneys, was once going to be done at the Embassy – all about oil concessions. I might bring it up to date.'[1] Cork responded, 'I am sending you a copy of Chimneys which Reandco were going to do twenty years ago. Sir St Vincent Troubridge tried it out about three years ago without any success, but as you say recent developments in the oil business do give it a new topical slant.'[2] Four months earlier, Iran's new Prime Minister, Mohammed Mossadegh, had precipitated a diplomatic crisis by moving to nationalise his country's oil reserves, largely at the expense of the British-controlled Anglo-Iranian Oil Company. Although part of the convoluted plot of *Chimneys* does indeed involve oil concessions, it is doubtful whether audiences would have shared Christie's view that her Buchanesque romp was 'all about' the subject. Interesting, though, that she felt it could potentially be worked up into something with a contemporary political resonance.

Sir Thomas St Vincent Troubridge's contribution to the promotion of Christie's work as a playwright merits more than an endnote. A colourful character who headed the Hughes Massie Drama Department after the war, he was a playwriting collaborator of their client Arnold Ridley, a popular member of the Garrick Club and an entertaining and opinionated correspondent with the press on theatrical matters. Passionate about all things dramatic, he was in 1948 a founder member of the Society for Theatre Research, where honorary secretary Jack Reading paid tribute to him in an affectionate poem whose first line runs, 'Loudly, loudly in the corner Sir St Vincent snores away . . .'[3] In 1952 Troubridge was appointed an Assistant Examiner of Plays at the Lord Chamberlain's Office, where he appeared to relish the role of the poacher turned gamekeeper, and he later penned a well-researched book (published posthumously) about the 'benefit system'; a tradition that operated until the late nineteenth century whereby the box office income from certain performances was gifted to one of the actors. The Hughes Massie Agatha Christie archive bears witness to the extent to which Edmund Cork personally managed his agency's relationship with its star client, and this mention of Troubridge gives us a rare glimpse of the endeavours of other Hughes Massie staff working behind the scenes on her behalf.

My attention was grabbed by Cork's reference to the fact that Troubridge had 'tried it out', which, in the context of the Shubert correspondence referring to a 'try-out' production of *Towards Zero*, would seem to indicate that *Chimneys* had perhaps been premiered in a small 'club' theatre somewhere, or even in a repertory theatre, given that the script had already been licensed by the Lord Chamberlain's office. But it seems here that Cork simply means that Troubridge had been trying to interest producers in the play. The piece is very much of its era, and Christie presumably sensed this when she re-read it, as we hear nothing more about the idea. Instead she wrote *The Mousetrap*.

In her autobiography Christie writes, 'I knew after I had written *The Hollow* that before long I should want to write another play, and if possible, I thought to myself, I was going to write a play that was not adapted from a book. I was going to write a play as a play.'[4] In the end, she opted to adapt one of her short stories, 'Three Blind Mice', which had itself been adapted from a short radio play of hers of the same title. The latter was part of an evening of programmes celebrating the eightieth birthday of Queen Mary, a new play by Christie having been specifically requested by her when the BBC asked the Palace what they should schedule for the evening. Christie accepted the commission and donated her fee to charity. The original radio broadcast was on the Light Programme on 30 May 1947, four days after Queen Mary's birthday, and on 21 October that year a live television transmission took place of what appears to have been the same script.

The following year Christie adapted the radio play into a short story (a very long one, perhaps more correctly described as a novella) which was first published in the US in *Cosmopolitan* magazine and subsequently serialised in the UK in *Woman's Own* magazine. In 1950 it was published by Dodd, Mead & Co. in America in the collection *Three Blind Mice and Other Stories*. At Christie's insistence the story has never been published in book form in the UK, in order to preserve the secrets of the stage adaptation, although the playscript has been in publication in the UK since 1954.

The process of adapting a short story, rather than a novel, for the stage seems to have suited Christie well. 'There can be no doubt that I think one of the advantages of *The Mousetrap*, as the stage version of Three Blind Mice was called, has had over other plays is the fact that it was really written from a précis, so that it had to be the bare bones of the skeleton coated with flesh. It was all there in proportion from the first. That made for good construction.'[5] It can be no coincidence that her two most successful plays, *The Mousetrap* and *Witness for the Prosecution*, were both adaptations from short stories.

The Mousetrap once again demonstrates Christie's uncanny knack for subtly capturing the spirit of the age. Mollie Ralston (Mollie had been listed by Agatha as a 'favourite name' of hers in the Miller family's 'Album of Confessions' thirty years previously[6]) is another feisty young Christie leading lady and, like *Ten Little Niggers*' Vera Claythorne, is not herself untainted by the events of the past. She has inherited Monkswell Manor, a country house which, with her husband of a year, Giles, she has decided to run as a guest house. They keep chickens and have no 'indoor staff', and Mollie herself prepares the meals (corned beef) and does the cleaning (crossing the stage with a vacuum cleaner at one point, much to the disgruntlement of one of the guests). Giles, meantime, does the sign writing and stokes the boiler, the fuel for which is running low. What we are witnessing is not some country house idyll, but a young couple struggling to set up a business in the post-war age of ration book austerity. 'There are one or two rather incongruous bits of Victorian furniture,' say Christie's stage directions, 'and the house looks not so much a period piece, but a house which has been lived in by generations of the same family with dwindling resources.'[7] It has to be said that, judging from photographs, Roger Furse's original set design fulfilled this brief more successfully than subsequent reworkings.

The play's subject matter is as hard-hitting as its setting is contemporary, exploring as it does the long-term consequences of child abuse, and inspired by the case of the two O'Neill brothers who were placed under the care of Reginald and Esther Gough of Bank Farm by Newport Borough Council in 1944. A doctor was called to the farm in January of the following year, having been advised that twelve-year-old Dennis O'Neill was having a fit; but when he arrived, he found Dennis dead, clearly malnourished and the victim of repeated physical assaults. The case was extensively reported and resulted in an overhaul of the fostering system. To London audiences in the early 1950s, this scenario would have stirred recent memories of their wartime evacuee children being placed in the care of strangers, and of the inevitable anxieties caused thereby.

As Harold Hobson, former *Sunday Times* drama critic, commented in an article included in the play's fortieth anniversary brochure, 'I am convinced that *The Mousetrap* would never have achieved the longest run in the history of theatre had it not been, as well as a very exciting story, a parable of the social outlook of our times.'[8] To my mind, Christie's particular skill as a playwright lies in her ability deftly to deliver this in a manner acceptable to the censor, palatable to West End family audiences of the early 1950s and within the considerable constraints of the 'whodunit' format. Straightforward 'realism', by contrast, is relatively easy to achieve on stage.

The five guests on Monkswell Manor's opening day are an odd assortment of misfits, including an effeminate young man with an 'artistic tie' and a young woman 'of a manly type'; clearly gay and lesbian characters, but sufficiently encoded to meet with the approval of the censor, who in his report describes the guests as a 'queer lot'.[9] The house gets colder and becomes snowbound, and we discover that a murderer is on the loose. As in *Ten Little Niggers*, Christie has created a scenario where an isolated group of strangers is at the mercy of a self-appointed agent of justice. Paranoia mounts and mutual suspicion sets in, even between devoted husband and wife, as this angel of vengeance starts to go about their mission of meting out punishment to those whose past negligence has contributed to the suffering of others. A young detective sergeant perhaps owes something to the role played by the eponymous inspector in J.B. Priestley's seminal 1945 play *An Inspector Calls*; and the unexpected guest whose car has run into a snowdrift, the enigmatic Mr Paravicini, ably fulfils his role of diverting attention from the two characters who really are impersonating someone else.

The single-set, eight-hander play that we now know originally involved two locations and four extra characters. Early drafts of *Three Blind Mice* held at the Agatha Christie archive include an eleven-page opening scene set in a London street on a foggy day, where we see the immediate aftermath of a murder which is reported on the radio by way of back-story at the start of the play as we now know it. The stage directions read:

> Two workmen, Alf and Bill, are sitting by a charcoal brazier – possibly in a little shelter. During their talk people pass along. This can include all the members of the cast. It is very dark and they are seen hardly at all except as moving figures. The men are wrapped up in mufflers, turned up collars, etc. Women, Mollie and Mrs Boyle have head scarves on. The

exception to this is Mr Paravacini, who is conspicuous in his fur lined overcoat and goes along uttering 'Brrrr' to himself. Bill is a typical pessimistic labourer – Alf is younger and has ideas with which he is pleased.[10]

All the men wear 'dark overcoats, light mufflers and similar hats', the significance of which will become apparent later. Much of the opening scene is taken up by Alf and Bill's views on life, the universe and everything:

ALF: Expect there'll be lots of accidents in this fog.
BILL: There's been too many accidents lately. Train accidents, air accidents, road accidents. I don't know what things are coming to.
ALF: Nature, that's what it is. The world's over-populated, and accidents is Nature's way of putting it straight, see?
BILL: There ain't nothing natural about aeroplanes. 'Ighly complex they are. You wouldn't believe. I got a nephew who's ground staff.
ALF: Got a fag?

Bill gives Alf a cigarette, just as a character walks on wearing a muffler; collar up, hat down. Alf's lighter isn't working and he scrounges a match from the passer-by, standing so that the audience's view is obstructed. The passer-by speaks in a whisper and exits whistling 'Three Blind Mice'. The workmen discuss why the passer-by may have been whistling:

ALF: What makes blokes do what they do. Unconscious motivation.
BILL: (suspiciously) You been listening to the Third Programme?
ALF: I'm a bloke what thinks about things. A chap whistles because he's pleased about somethink. Maybe that young fellow was going to be married.
BILL: If so he don't know what's what! If he did he wouldn't whistle.

ALF: Or maybe he's got himself a good job.

BILL: Wish I'd got a job inside somewhere. Straight – I'd rather be down a ruddy coal mine than here.

Alf then mimics the tune that the passer-by was whistling.

ALF: I know that tune. Now whatever is it?

BILL: God Save the King?

ALF: Nah!

BILL: Internationale?

ALF: Nah. It's a kid's tune. Nursery rhyme.

BILL: Little Jack 'Orner?

ALF: Not quite. I'll tell you another thing as I've been thinking about sitting 'ere – *Feet*.

BILL: Feet?

ALF: 'Eard it on the wireless. Charles Dickens. 'Tale of Two Cities'. London and Paris they are. All about the French Revolution. And it starts with *feet*. Trampling along. Feet what's coming into your life. And I been thinking this morning. All these feet along here. Where are they going to and where 'ave they come from?

BILL: You're barmy.

They find a notebook which the passer-by has dropped, and then Mrs Casey runs on, screaming that her lodger has been murdered . . . by a person who whistled 'Three Blind Mice' as they left the house. A police constable comes to her assistance.

Here is a unique attempt by Agatha Christie to portray working-class characters who are not domestic staff of some sort in their working environment. They talk about working down a coal mine and the French Revolution, and are familiar with the Internationale. Whilst she has an experienced ear for the banter of domestic staff, though, Christie is as endearingly out of her depth here as she was with the Cockney-accented New York gangsters of *The Clutching Hand*. This sort of material would not have won her any friends at the Royal Court, where the English Stage Company were to lead the new wave of realist 'kitchen sink' drama only four years later, and Bill's 'pessimism' would hardly have given Jimmy Porter a run for his money; but it does show that she was not unaware of the directions in which theatre was heading and not unwilling to dip her toe in the water. We are eleven pages into an Agatha Christie play, and so far all we have seen is a road works, while the only characters who have been identified are two workmen, a boarding-house land-lady and a police constable.

The idea of all the suspects that we will meet later being seen in the street outside the murder scene is a fascinating theatrical device, but the necessity for an extra set and four extra characters made the whole scene a non-starter from a practical point of view. The copy of the script submitted to the Lord Chamberlain, which was presented to Christie in a gold binding on the play's tenth birthday, includes a version of the Bill and Alf scene, as does the prompt copy of the play held at the V&A, although in the latter it has been torn out and stuck unceremoniously into the back of the script as scrap paper. The V&A's prompt copy is also notable for extensive and witty doodles and observations by a very artistic and clearly rather bored stage manager, unaware that their sketch of 'Marilyn Monroe hiding in a pile of grapefruit' (think about it!) would one day form part of a priceless museum piece. Meanwhile, the reader's report was thoughtfully removed from the Lord Chamberlain's script before it was presented to Agatha; the report describes the piece as a 'poor thriller'.[11]

The Christie archive also contains a draft script with the play's new title on the cover and 'Suggested alterations for first scene' written on the first page, followed by a badly typed three-page insert. Bill and Alf are gone, and instead we have a short scene in the snowy London street which simply involves Mrs Casey enlisting the assistance of the police constable. Intriguingly, though, three of the characters who we will see later, including the murderer, still cross the stage, muffled against the cold, in a reduced version of the full-cast dumb show that was included in the previous draft.

The original 1947 radio script for which, of course, location was not an issue, includes the first murder victim Mrs Lyon and her landlady, as well as a brief appearance by two unnamed workmen, but omits one of the characters who we will later meet in the stage play. The short story, or novella, as published in America, is even closer to the play, but the final character is still to be introduced.

The play's prologue, inevitably, was found to be surplus to requirements, and was abandoned before rehearsals started. It was replaced with a brief, atmospheric (and certainly more economical) soundscape portraying Mrs Lyons' murder, played in darkness before the curtain rises. The resulting two-act, eight-character play is lean and efficient, qualities which enhance its dramatic effectiveness and which have doubtless contributed to its longevity. The brevity of the dramatis personae serves to emphasise the writer's skill in concealing the murderer amongst them, and the fact that the action takes place over a timeframe of only two days serves to heighten the tension. *The Mousetrap*'s missing prologue, though, shows a willingness to experiment with form and content for which Christie rarely receives credit.

During the 1950s much of Edmund Cork's work focused on arrangements to enable Agatha to circumvent both punitive income tax and potentially punitive death duties, a strategy encompassing wholesale copyright assignments to a labyrinthine network of trusts and companies. One of the first beneficiaries of these arrangements was her grandson, Mathew, and in August 1951 Cork wrote to Christie confirming arrangements for a trust to which the copyrights of the novel *They Do It with Mirrors* and the play *Three Blind Mice* were assigned until Mathew's twenty-first birthday, at which point they would become his. Cork added that 'Peter Saunders is prepared to make a contract with the Trustees for Three Blind Mice [himself and Rosalind] on terms pretty similar to those we obtained for The Hollow. He does not think, however, that he should be called upon to pay the unusually heavy advance we extracted for The Hollow – you will remember I made him pay through the nose as an earnest of his seriousness and sincerity, of which I think we now have ample proof.'[12] Saunders had indeed paid an advance against royalties of £500 to option *The Hollow*, and had also just paid a considerable sum to the Ambassadors to keep the theatre dark for five weeks and enable the play's transfer from the Fortune at the end of its run there. Cork was right that his seriousness and sincerity could not be questioned.

On 3 September 1951, nineteen days before Mathew's eighth birthday, Agatha transferred the rights to *Three Blind Mice* to the trust, and a month later, Saunders acquired the UK play licence from it.[13] When he says in his autobiography that Christie gave him the finished script over lunch just after Christmas 1951, he must have known that it was on the way; what is not clear is whether he had seen an earlier draft or whether the play was actually written between November and December 1951, after he had acquired the licence. On 17 September the following year Cork wrote to Christie, 'I hear from Peter that rehearsals for The Mousetrap are going very well indeed. Mathew is a very lucky boy!'[14] Mathew was told about his ownership of the rights the following week, on his ninth birthday, but by all accounts was more interested in his new train set. 'Mathew, of course, was always the most lucky member of the family,' Agatha remarked, 'and it would be Mathew's gift that turned out the big money winner.'[15]

Legend tells of different estimates given by those involved for the length of West End run that the play would enjoy, although it should not be forgotten that, even if it had not broken all West End records, on the showing of Christie's other plays Mathew's income from residuals would have been considerable. What was to transform the fortunes of the project, though, and give it a head start over all Christie's plays to date, was the involvement from an early stage of two substantial stars: Richard Attenborough and Sheila Sim. The RADA-trained husband and wife team had enjoyed huge popular success and critical acclaim in a series of stage and screen roles, both individually and as a couple. In 1947 Attenborough had appeared in the role of the vicious young gangster Pinkie Brown in the Boulting brothers' film of Graham Greene's *Brighton Rock*, establishing his status as one of the country's most sought-after young actors. Although Sheila Sim, who played the role of the young guest-house owner Mollie Ralston to great acclaim, was to leave the company at the end of her eight-month West End contract in order to fulfil a film commitment, Attenborough was to extend his engagement as Sergeant Trotter in the production to almost two years. During the time they were both in the production they also starred as Tommy and Tuppence in a thirteen-part radio adaptation of Christie's *Partners in Crime*, providing the play with invaluable additional publicity.

Max Mallowan writes, 'The play was fortunate too in having two theatrical stars of the highest magnitude to send it off – Richard Attenborough and his beautiful wife Sheila Sim – both of them lovable and great artists with a faultless sense of timing.'[16] Attenborough's integrity, says Saunders, 'was beyond belief. No one dared not give their best when he was there, and they adored him. It was Dickie who started the *Mousetrap* snowball . . . and I have never ceased to be grateful to him.'[17] It was not only Attenborough's agreement to take part, but his obvious and unselfish dedication to the work, that helped to ensure its success. The long-term commitment to, and obvious affection for, the production shown by this giant of stage and screen is arguably the most ringing endorsement of her skills as a playwright that Agatha Christie could have hoped for, and this was not lost on Christie herself. 'Richard Attenborough and his enchanting wife Sheila Sim played the two leads in the first production,' she recalls. 'What a beautiful performance they gave. They loved the play, and believed in it and Richard Attenborough gave a great deal of thought to playing his part. I enjoyed the rehearsals – I enjoyed *all* of it.'[18]

The appointment of a director, however, was an altogether less happy process. The man who got the job, Peter Cotes, was one of the most controversial stage directors of the day. The older brother of twin film-makers John and Roy Boulting, he had changed his name to avoid being eclipsed by their success. His parents had both been performers, and he started his career playing the music halls in revue and cabaret. Amongst his own early acting ventures was a small role in the 1943 film *The Gentle Sex*, co-scripted by *Murder at the Vicarage* co-writer Moie Charles and directed by Derrick de Marney. This won him a role in the 1944 tour of Charles' *Tomorrow's Eden*, for which he also worked as assistant to director Irene Hentschel. His controversial 1946 production of *Pick-Up Girl*, a hard-hitting American play by Elsa Shelley about child abuse and venereal disease, opened at his New Lindsey club theatre in Notting Hill, a licence having been declined by the Lord Chamberlain's office because Cotes refused to cut certain lines, including a reference to abortion. Since club theatres were exempt from censorship, they had become notorious for offering a showcase for work rejected by the censor. Astonishingly, seventy-nine-year-old Queen Mary decided to attend the production in the tiny, upstairs theatre space and, following this royal endorsement, the Lord Chamberlain's office had no option but to allow the production to transfer to the West End.

As a result, the following year Binkie Beaumont offered Cotes the direction of the London premiere of *Deep Are the Roots*, a Broadway drama about racial prejudice. He argued with the actors over his interpretation of the piece and was promptly fired; if there was indeed a Tennent blacklist then Cotes was undoubtedly on it. Not surprisingly, in his 1949 book *No Star Nonsense*, an eloquent advocacy of ensemble theatre, he made a point of attacking everything that the West End stood for. A one-man theatrical awkward squad, and no stranger to litigation, Cotes was nonetheless in a different league to Hubert Gregg as a director. Adam Benedick's obituary of Cotes in the *Independent* newspaper describes him as 'a kind of pathfinder in what are considered by people who did not live through them to have been the darkest days of British theatre, the 1940s and 1950s . . . as long as he ran his own company under his own management he was happy and successful.'[19]

With Peter Saunders, Hubert Gregg and Peter Cotes all offering markedly conflicting first-hand accounts in their books (published in 1972, 1980 and 1993 respectively), it is difficult to establish a definitive sequence of events as regards the appointment of a director for *Three Blind Mice*. It is clear, though, that something was afoot from the outset. According to the chronology offered by Cotes in his book *Thinking Aloud*, he was approached by both Attenborough and Saunders at the end of February 1952. Attenborough and Sim were under contract to film with Cotes' brothers at the time, and according to Cotes this offer followed a lunch between Attenborough and John Boulting, which I believe to be a lunch at the Ivy that Saunders refers to having been present at with these two. It seems logical that Cotes would have been Richard Attenborough's first choice as director; not only was he related to the Attenboroughs' employers, who were releasing them both from their contract so that they could perform in *The Mousetrap*, but Sheila Sim had been directed by Cotes in *Come Back Little Sheba*, which her husband had seen. Having made a name for himself with *Pick-Up Girl* and, more recently, *The Biggest Thief in Town*, Cotes was in all respects a credible director who, having assisted Irene Hentschel earlier in his career, would doubtless take the same serious approach to Christie's work that Hentschel had.

Cotes claims to have read the script and lunched with Saunders at the Carlton, after which casting then proceeded, the majority of those selected being actors who had worked with him before. He makes cryptic mention of the fact that his agent was then 'called into negotiations' and that there has been 'no really comprehensive account of how it all started, when heads rolled, directors were chosen, titles changed'.[20]

According to both Hubert Gregg and Peter Saunders, however, Gregg was Saunders' first choice for director. Undeniably it was Gregg who forged the introduction with the Attenboroughs. He was at the time working at the Garrick Theatre as assistant director on *To Dorothy, a Son*, a hugely successful comedy they were starring in. Gregg introduced the couple to Saunders in their dressing room, Attenborough agreed to read the script, and shortly afterwards Saunders lunched with John Boulting and Attenborough at the Ivy. A letter from Saunders to Boulting and Attenborough dated 11 January 1952 offers them the opportunity to invest £1,000 in the production and makes reference to receipt of Attenborough's contract to appear in it,[21] so

Saunders' account of being introduced to Attenborough back-stage in February is clearly inaccurate. Attenborough's film schedule meant that a deal had to be done a long time in advance, and a rehearsal date of 15 September was set.

According to Gregg, he not only introduced the play's stars to Saunders but also came up with its eventual title – although Agatha credited her son-in-law Anthony Hicks with the idea in her autobiography, much to Gregg's inevitable chagrin. A title change was necessitated when, Saunders having announced the forthcoming production, powerful impresario Emile Littler (Prince's younger brother) advised him that he had produced a play called *Three Blind Mice* before the war and requested that Christie change the title of hers. There is no copyright in titles, and in fact no fewer than seven plays of this name had been licensed by the Lord Chamberlain's office in the previous fifty years, but you didn't argue with a Littler.

'The Mousetrap' is the title flippantly given by Shakespeare's Hamlet to a play performed by a group of strolling players for his uncle, Claudius. The play's actual title is *The Murder of Gonzago*, and Hamlet hopes that its subject matter, which parallels the murder of his father, will provoke an incriminating response from Claudius, who he believes to be the murderer. The new title resonated with Christie's play on a number of levels. Not only did it fit neatly with the theme of 'Three Blind Mice' (as the killer refers to their potential victims), but Christie's policeman has the suspects re-enact the murder at Monkswell Manor in much the same way that the players performance in effect reconstructs the murder of Hamlet's father. The re-enactment in Christie's play, however, results in the trapping of the next intended victim rather than the murderer. '*Hamlet* could certainly qualify as a detective drama,' she would later write to a fan.[22]

Gregg had played Hamlet twice and had a good knowledge of Christie's script, so in this case I'm inclined to give him the benefit of the doubt. It may be that Saunders relayed Gregg's suggestion to Cork, who then passed it on to Rosalind and Anthony, who were closely involved with the project as Mathew's trust was technically the licensor. It thus could well have been Anthony who relayed the suggested new title to Agatha on her return from that year's dig. It seems unlikely that he would have deliberately taken the credit for someone else's idea, and more probable that we are simply dealing here with a case of Chinese whispers recalled inaccurately by Agatha in all innocence some years later. Or it may be that both Hicks and Gregg really did come up with the same remarkably catchy new title for *Three Blind Mice*.

Some time after the contracting of Attenborough, Saunders obtained a licence to mount a post-West End tour of *To Dorothy, a Son*. According to Saunders, Gregg then asked if he could give up directing *The Mousetrap* in order to direct and star in this new production of Roger MacDougall's comedy ('an extraordinary decision and I think one that he later regretted'[23]). According to Gregg, he didn't ask; Saunders offered it to him.[24] I suspect that what actually happened is that Saunders, having been told by Attenborough and Boulting that they wanted Cotes to direct, took a licence for *To Dorothy, a Son* in the knowledge that Gregg would jump at the opportunity to both direct and star in it. This would get Gregg out of the way and leave the coast clear for Saunders to secure his star by engaging Peter Cotes. In any event, it seems unlikely that Attenborough would have approved as a director a man he knew as the hired-in assistant responsible for rehearsing new cast members into the West End production of *To Dorothy, a Son*. It seems that discussions must have been taking place with Cotes at a time when Gregg was nominally still at the helm of *The Mousetrap*, although it may be, of course, that Gregg was complicit in all this and happy to take the other project in the knowledge that he was clearing the way for Cotes. We are unlikely ever to discover the truth of the matter, as all of those involved put their own distinct spin on events.

Gregg's replacement, however, turned out not to be Peter Cotes, but John Fernald, whose production of *Dial M for Murder* had opened at the Westminster Theatre on 9 June. It seems that negotiations to secure Cotes' services had been lengthy, and it is perhaps not surprising that Saunders took the opportunity (and presumably persuaded Attenborough) to go with the director of the biggest hit thriller in town. In the end, Fernald withdrew from the project just as rehearsals were about to start, having disagreed with Saunders, Christie and Attenborough over the casting of the role of Miss Casewell.[25] Cotes claims to have been unaware that Fernald was the 'first director to be offered the job' and had 'turned it down'.[26] The actress who Saunders and the others wanted to play the role was Jessica Spencer, who had taken over the role of Midge when *The Hollow* moved into the West End. In 1947 she had made her TV debut as 'Molly Davis' in *Three Blind Mice*, and the following year she had won Equity's Clarence Derwent award for Best Supporting Performance for her portrayal of Barbara Martin in *Royal Circle*, directed by Ralph Richardson at Wyndham's Theatre; moreover, she had also notably played the 'Pick-Up Girl' for Peter Cotes. Fernald, according to Saunders, apparently had a more 'feminine and fluffy' actress in mind. He left the production, but there were no hard feelings, and thirty years later he became the sixteenth director to oversee its run.

If we are to believe Saunders rather than Cotes, it was at this point that Richard Attenborough suggested Cotes as Fernald's replacement. On 30 August, with the production scheduled to open in Nottingham on 6 October, Saunders wrote to Cotes saying, 'As I told you this morning, the producer [i.e. director] of this play has withdrawn and I am most happy that you agree to direct it on the terms originally agreed.'[27] It is apparent from this that there had been previous negotiations with Cotes and that a deal had at some point been agreed in principle but not signed off. Cotes evidently knew the script and the project already, if he was prepared to agree to do it on the basis of one conversation. One thing that had attracted him to it in the first place, he claims in his book, was the fact that the story had originally been written for Queen Mary, whose patronage of his production of *Pick-Up Girl* had enabled it to circumvent the censors and enjoy a West End run. This remarkable woman, an indomitable supporter of theatre in all its forms, died in March 1953 aged eighty-five, without having seen the stage production that her original request for a radio play from Christie had inspired.

In his book, Cotes goes out of his way to describe the success of his working relationship with Christie and his respect for her, no doubt in deliberate counterpoint to Gregg's portrayal of her as distant and inhospitable:

There are those connected with the theatre who have criticised Christie as a negative character when she was away from the theatre or her other work. I am bound to say that in my experience she was the soul of equanimity; throughout our association in study, dining-room, theatre and rehearsal room, not one hard word was ever heard between us. She was protective of her 'brain child' as all good mothers should be, but only up to a point. Her shrewd side was uppermost in her mind when constructive discussions had to be made about removing or adding a line or even a speech here and there. She would grasp an idea to strengthen the play or even alter characterizations wholeheartedly . . . This sort of person is sparing with her words too, with a dislike of non-essentials, and Agatha in her detailed letters to me, some of many pages, as well as her scores of postcards, showed a similar dislike. She wished at all times to relieve herself of spare talk and theatrical chitter-chatter. She refused to obscure the main issue by the side-tracking discussion that all too often passes in the world of theatre for constructive discussion. What she did possess was professionalism; a willingness to co-operate once she had made her mind up, as well as a degree of receptivity not always to be found in highly successful writers when their 'brain child' is being transferred from the page to the stage.'[28]

Cotes claims that the prologue was cut at his request, although Saunders suggests that it was he who asked Christie to remove the scene, for reasons of economic necessity. In any event, the fact that the copy submitted to the Lord Chamberlain's office included a version of it is consistent with its abandonment very late on in the process. Of the brief pre-show soundscape that was used instead, Cotes observes, 'The replacement, conceived between author and director, was played in semi-darkness with various sound effects such as police whistles, footsteps and shouts. This appeared to me to create the correct atmosphere for the play that followed.' It would be difficult to disagree. Most importantly, whilst Cotes is full of praise for Christie's openness to editing and improving on the dialogue, he is, unlike Gregg, very clear that any such changes were the work of the playwright herself rather than the director.

Cotes watched the first night of the seven-week pre-London tour in Nottingham, gave his notes and rehearsed with the company the following day, but then absented himself to work on another play, *The Man*, in which his wife Joan Newell was appearing, and which subsequently opened in the West End a month after *The Mousetrap*. Cotes made occasional appearances during the *Mousetrap* tour, and was happy to entrust Christie, Saunders and Attenborough with any changes that they felt needed making in his absence; but Saunders felt that this was negligent on Cotes' part, and was aggrieved that he had apparently not been advised by Cotes of his other commitment. The main issue that needed resolving with the play, as had been the case with *The Hollow*, was whether the comedy element was too dominant, although in this case it was down to the writing rather than the performance of the leading lady. Whether this perceived imbalance was resolved by Cotes or Saunders we will never know; they each took credit for coaxing the necessary changes out of Christie. But resolved it was.

On this occasion, with the success of *The Hollow* to his credit and his stellar leading couple contracted well in advance, Saunders experienced no difficulty in securing the £5,000 up-front finance required to stage the production; but there were still problems securing a suitable West End home for it, particularly as he was hoping to open in London at the best time of year, just in time for the pre-Christmas rush. Saunders found the Group's doors closed to him, although he did have offers from two independently owned theatres: the tiny Ambassadors, where Herbert Malden was keen to repeat the box office success of *The Hollow*, and the vast Winter Garden.

Persuaded by Attenborough, Saunders wisely opted for the smaller of the two, and *The Mousetrap* duly opened at the Ambassadors Theatre on 25 November 1952. True to form, Tennents took out an advertisement in the programme promoting no fewer than ten of their own productions.

Forty-four London theatres were advertising their wares in *The Times* that day; they included a number that were not strictly 'West End', such as the Tennent-controlled Lyric Hammersmith, not to mention *Sleeping Beauty on Ice* at the Empire Pool, Wembley. There was particularly strong competition in the thriller genre; Janet Green's *Murder Mistaken*, starring Derek Farr, had moved from the Ambassadors to the Vaudeville in order to make way for *The Mousetrap*, and Frederick Knott's *Dial M for Murder* was packing them in at the Westminster. Meanwhile, Bertie Meyer was producing *Meet Mr Callaghan* at the Garrick, Terence Rattigan's *The Deep Blue Sea* was playing at the Duchess, Peter Ustinov was still appearing in *The Love of Four Colonels* at Wyndhams and, at the Phoenix, Alfred Lunt and Lynn Fontanne were appearing in Noël Coward's *Quadrille*. The complete television listings in *The Times* on 25 November 1952 were contained in three and a half lines.

The critical response was, with the notable exception of the *Sunday Dispatch*, very supportive. Ivor Brown in the *Observer*, of course, was one of the few to pick up on the allusion to *Hamlet*. He went on to say:

Agatha Christie has a taste for Nursery Rhymes and why not? They tinkle their horrors to the tots and they will make murder wherever they go. To one who so neatly disposed of 'Ten Little Nigger Boys' three blind mice are quite a small order . . . if so many of our soubrettes now sing on skates [no doubt a reference by Brown to *Sleeping Beauty on Ice*], why not a cop gliding on skis to the scene of the crime? . . . It is all gloriously improbable and a trifle untidy, but it goes with a scream and the actors have some characters to work on. Richard Attenborough leads a capable team through the humours as well as the horrors of this hotel with death on the menu; small wonder that it could not collect any staff.[29]

The Sketch magazine concurred: 'I would say that, while this is by no means in the *Ten Little Niggers* class, it is well up to *The Hollow*, and that, if Mrs Christie can continue to reel off these theatrical puzzles, she fills again a gap in the West End list about which addicts had begun to complain.'[30]

Punch noted that '*The Mousetrap* is a delicately poised machine, and I cannot say very much about Mrs Agatha Christie's play of that name without unforgivably springing it . . . Suspicion switches cleverly, and in one tense moment after another we seem to be on the edge of the author's secret . . . Peter Cotes' direction is as discreet as a solicitor's letter, and a sound cast plays a complicated game with fairness . . . This is one of Mrs Christie's neatest puzzles and it takes the stage very naturally. Only the final moments are a trifle untidy – but then Mrs Christie was left with a great deal to clear up in a short time.'[31] *The Times* joined the general chorus of approval, noting that 'the piece admirably fulfils the special requirements of the theatre. There are only two acts, the first of exposition and preparation, the second of action and conjecture.' The characters, it says, 'provide the colour, the mystification, the suspects and the screams . . . there remain the alarming silences, which are perhaps the true test of such a piece on stage. That we feel them to be alarming can only be thanks to the producer, Mr Peter Cotes.'[32] Cotes, incidentally, provides in his book an appendix which helpfully quotes no fewer than sixteen reviews singling out his personal contribution for particular praise.

In America, where Christie's only stage hit remained *Ten Little Indians*, and where *The Suspects* had sunk without trace the previous month, the London correspondent of theatre and film magazine *Variety* reported:

Final thriller of the year is this ingenious whodunit by Agatha Christie, whose *The Hollow* last year swung the trend back to worthwhile crime plays. There is suspense and considerable speculation as to the why and the wherefore in this one, which holds attention all through. If it were less absorbing it would still command box office attention on the reputation of the authoress and popularity of the leading players, Richard Attenborough and Sheila Sim. It might stand a good chance on Broadway, although its worth would probably be minimized coming after the current successes *Dial M for Murder* and *Murder Mistaken*.[33]

In the same issue of *Variety* a news item headlined 'Christie's Mousetrap latest London Smash' goes on to say that 'It was enthusiastically received at the prem[iere], giving every indication of providing a good holiday attraction and having a protracted run.'

When *The Mousetrap* opened in London, Cotes attended on the opening night and the second day; but, according to Saunders' files, he subsequently visited the production only once, seeing only the second act. To make matters worse, *The Man* took up residence at the St Martin's Theatre next door, where it played through February and March 1953, before Cotes headed off to New York to direct his wife (and Roger Moore) in a production of the controversial anti-death penalty play *A Pin to See the Peepshow*, which, like *Pick-Up Girl*, Cotes had originally produced and directed in a London club theatre in order to avoid a ban from the censor. The production, mounted in September 1953 by an economically challenged New York producer, had the distinction of both opening and closing on Broadway on the same night.

In July 1953, hearing that his director had departed for America, again apparently without having advised him, Saunders wrote to Cotes requesting him not to return to the production, but assuring him that he would still be paid.[34] Hubert Gregg was brought in to oversee recasts of the production, and one can only speculate as to whether Saunders felt obliged to his friend to involve him in some way, having manoeuvred him out of the director's job in the first place. Although his seven-year association with the production inevitably enabled Gregg to trumpet his own contribution to its success, even he was remarkably equitable in his acknowledgement of the debt that it owed to Cotes, remarking that he had done a 'bloody good job of it' and expressing his regret that Cotes was not invited to the production's anniversary parties.[35]

In 1954 Saunders offered to pay Cotes £2,000 in exchange for relinquishing his 1.5 per cent royalty and, according to Cotes, Richard Attenborough suggested that he should accept the offer, as he was about to leave the production and it seemed unlikely that the run would continue much longer in his absence.[36] Cotes, however, insisted on sticking to his original royalty deal. His decision was to prove the correct one.

As it happens, the takings did decline sharply when Attenborough left the cast, and the next two years were bumpy ones. 'It was my faith and money that kept the play on and turned it into a success,' said Saunders in a letter that he drafted to Cotes' lawyers. 'Had the play come off as it ought to have done in 1955 Mr Cotes' £2,000 would have given him a substantial profit . . . Had he accepted this sum I also undertook to keep his name on the posters and programmes for the run.'[37] Although Saunders technically had no right to remove Cotes from the billing, he did so. By 1985 Cotes had earned £156,000 in royalties. There can be no doubt, however, that Saunders is not exaggerating his own input, and that his careful stewardship and publicist's instincts were central to establishing the production's longevity. Successive anniversaries and milestones were celebrated with publicity stunts, star-studded parties and royal visits, as the records tumbled and eventually *The Mousetrap* became the longest running theatrical production of any sort in the history of the world, eclipsing the twenty-six-year run (1933 to 1959) of *The Drunkard* in Los Angeles and outlasting the forty-two-year run (1960 to 2002) of *The Fantasticks* in New York. Christie herself was a regular attender at milestone events, posing for photographs, cutting cakes and occasionally making her legendarily brief speeches. 'I was brought in,' she recalls, 'subjected to cutting tapes (*sic*), kissing actresses, grinning from ear to ear, simpering, and having to suffer the insult to my vanity that occurs when I press my cheek against that of a young and good-looking actress and know that we shall appear in the news the next day – she looking beautiful and confident in her role, and I looking frankly *awful*. Ah well, good for one's vanity, I suppose!'[38]

Although Christie was to enjoy the first twenty-three years of *The Mousetrap*, the one sadness for her was that this longed-for theatrical success came so late in life, and that it is as an increasingly frail old lady that she will be remembered by those who attended these events and in the media records of them. The tall, spirited, strikingly beautiful girl who light-heartedly penned *Teddy Bear* and *Eugenia and Eugenics* was no doubt there in spirit to soak up the plaudits of the theatrical community that Agatha Christie so cherished being a part of.

Whatever Peter Saunders may have maintained about the way in which he made Christie the star, he was certainly not shy about announcing the participation of star actors on the occasions when he got them. Advertising for the play gave prominence to the names of Richard Attenborough and Sheila Sim, and their photographs were widely used on printed material. Amongst the items featuring their picture was a leaflet carrying the following intriguing message on the reverse:

ANSWERING YOUR QUESTIONS . . .
Whenever a new Agatha Christie play is produced, the producing management is always asked the same questions. This is some indication of the interest taken in these thrillers, and the customary questions are, therefore, answered here.
Is Hercule Poirot in the play?
The answer is 'no', and if this may disappoint Poirot fans, it should be remembered that it is very difficult to find the ideal stage Poirot and that it would be unsatisfactory to miscast such a fascinating and individual character.
Is there any comedy in it?
Answer: Emphatically YES.
Is it gruesome?

Answer: No. It is thrilling, gripping, but contains nothing that will send anyone home to have nightmares.

Was it adapted from a book?

Answer: No. It is an original play although many years ago there was a broadcast called 'Three Blind Mice' on which the play is based.

Is it a new play or a revival?

Answer: It is a new play, written by Agatha Christie during the run of her play, *The Hollow*, at this theatre.

A curious question.

Many people ask whether there are any revolver shots in the play, and the answer is no. Not one.[39]

One of the earliest records to be set by *The Mousetrap* was as the longest running play in the history of British theatre, which the production achieved on its 1,998th performance on 13 September 1957. The record had previously been held by the 1941 production of Noël Coward's *Blithe Spirit*, and Coward had the good grace to send his fellow playwright a telegram of congratulation from Bermuda: 'DEAR AGATHA CHRISTIE, MUCH AS IT PAINS ME I REALLY MUST CONGRATULATE YOU ON THE MOUSE-TRAP BREAKING THE LONG RUN RECORD. ALL MY GOOD WISHES, NOEL COWARD.'[40] Christie was delighted by this gesture and immediately replied to Coward, telling him that 'I've always been one of your most fervent admirers'[41] This particular *Mousetrap* milestone was reached during Hubert Gregg's tenure as resident director, and he proudly quotes from Coward's telegram in his own book.[42]

In addition to Saunders' tireless efforts, other factors were undoubtedly a major contributing factor to *The Mousetrap*'s success. According to Saunders, the production needed to play to 80 per cent of capacity at the then-419 seat Ambassadors simply to cover its running costs, although he eventually added a further thirty-four seats. The small theatre, as well as the play's star casting and favourable reviews, however, resulted in the display of 'sold out' signs for the first three months; someone even made a living renting chairs to the queue at the box office. As Dickens observed in *Nicholas Nickleby*, 'It is a hopeless endeavour to attract people to a theatre unless they can first be brought to believe they can never get in.'

This was not lost on Max Mallowan: 'Many things combined to contribute to its phenomenal success over and above the natural genius of the author, which is all too easy to forget in the analysis. First there was the comparatively exiguous size of the theatre . . .'[43] And Christie herself was not unaware of the advantageous nature of the project's underlying economics. In a 1961 interview with the *Sunday Times* she observed, 'I've thought a lot about it. Of course it is a small play in a small theatre, which helps. It hasn't got terrific running costs or overheads. But I think it really is probably because it is the sort of play you can take anyone to. It is not really frightening, it is not really horrible, it is not really a farce, but it has got a little bit of all those things, and perhaps that satisfies a lot of different people.'[44] And in her autobiography Christie remarks:

People always ask me to what I attribute the success of *The Mousetrap*. Apart from replying with the obvious answer, Luck! – because it is luck, ninety per cent luck, at least, I should say – the only reason I can give is that there is a bit of something in it for almost everybody: people of different age groups and tastes can enjoy seeing it . . . But I think, considering it and trying to be neither conceited nor over-modest that, of its kind – which is to say a light play with both humour and thriller appeal – it is well constructed. The thing unfolds so that you want to know what happens next, and you can't quite see where the next few minutes will lead you. I think, too, though there is a tendency for all plays that have run a long time to be acted, sooner or later, as if the people in them were caricatures, the people in *The Mousetrap* could all be real people . . . a young woman, bitter against life, determined to live only for the future; the young man who refuses to face life and yearns to be mothered; and the boy who childishly wants to get his own back . . . all these seem to me real, natural, when one watches them.[45]

As ever for Christie the playwright, her chief concern is the creation of believable characters. Those commentators who regard her primarily as a constructor of plots, and dismiss her characters as stereotypes, would do well to study her plays in more detail.

The London Council for the Promotion of Public Morality did not agree that *The Mousetrap* was the sort of play you could take anyone to. Founded in 1899 to combat vice and indecency in London, the Council was comprised of religious leaders from across the faiths as well as representatives of charitable associations and the medical profession. When *The Mousetrap* opened it ruled that the play was suitable for adults only, and it was not until 1963 that Saunders persuaded its general secretary, George Tomlinson, to get the Council to reassess the production and acknowledge that it was suitable for children. Not that it mattered; numerous children had seen and enjoyed the production in the interim. The Council was disbanded in 1969. The production sailed on.

The Mousetrap's longevity has become something of a double-edged sword, an easy target for satirists and for those who criticise the West End's inherent conservatism. Christie herself believed that its astonishing and seemingly unaccountable success turned critics and commentators against her; and for advocates of the 'new wave' in British theatre in the late 1950s, including John Osborne himself, it came to symbolise everything that they were striving to subvert. Max Mallowan observes that the production became 'so successful that it has inevitably attracted the attention of the green-eyed monster – jealousy. To jaundiced critics it has been an unpardonable offence that any one play should monopolize a theatre for so long. I have little fancy for such bitter lemons.'[46]

For a while, successive caretaker directors altered any references in the text, such as prices, that risked dating the play; but these days it is delivered resolutely as a period piece and, as such, has achieved the status of a cherished national treasure. At some point the production achieved sufficient momentum to carry on running simply because of the novelty of the fact that it does. Statistics are kept about how many miles of shirts have been ironed and how many tons of ice cream sold, and members of the company have entered the *Guinness Book of Records* for long service (although these days the full cast is changed annually). Amongst the historical curios still featured in the production are the original mantelpiece clock and the hand-operated wind machine. And the voice of Deryck Guyler can still be heard as the radio announcer, just as it was on the first night, although the stage manager no longer needs to place a needle on a record in order to create the effect. For all this, though, it shouldn't be forgotten that when *The Mousetrap* premiered it was very emphatically set in 'the present'.

In 1999 The National Theatre included *The Mousetrap* in its '100 Plays of the Century', and the resulting 'platform' performance in the Cottesloe Theatre on 30 March that year remains to this day the only occasion on which the words of Agatha Christie, playwright, have been spoken on stage at the National, although her most enduring play's title does get the occasional mention, much to the amusement of audiences for *Hamlet*.[47]

The exploitation of subsidiary rights in *The Mousetrap* has inevitably followed an unusual pattern, given the continuing West End run. Amateur and repertory rights have never been released in the UK, although there have been numerous productions throughout the world, including a successful run in Paris, a twenty-six-year run in Toronto and regular presentations in Shanghai and other Chinese cities. John Mills led the cast in a production presented by Saunders for British troops in Germany in 1954, and a major UK tour was launched in the play's sixtieth year, as were celebratory productions in sixty cities across the globe. The film rights to *The Mousetrap* were sold in 1956, but with the proviso that no film can actually be shown until after the end of the West End run. Quite how successful a film of *The Mousetrap* would be is open to question; the premise of the play is essentially theatrical, and it does not have the cinematic potential of much of Christie's other stage work. The concern, then, is presumably less that

a film would give away the play's ending (the audience's coop-
eration in this regard is enlisted in a nightly curtain speech)
and more that it would risk damaging the reputation of a
successful theatrical brand.

The same fears also led to a very considered strategy for the
play's American production. After the debacles of *Towards Zero*,
Hidden Horizon and *The Suspects*, a conscious decision was
taken by Cork and Saunders not to expose the piece to Broadway
audiences and critics. Max Mallowan identifies its very
Englishness as one of the characteristics that has led to the
play becoming a tourist attraction in London, and there can be
no doubt that this quality in Christie's work was a contributing
factor to the failure of three successive American productions.
As many transatlantic theatrical producers have discovered to
their cost, England and America can all too often be two countries divided by a common language, and in the case of *The
Mousetrap* this caution was probably justified. *Ten Little Indians*
had demonstrated that some of Christie's plays could enjoy even
greater success in New York than in London. But not all of
them. Her biggest Broadway triumph, as it happens, was still
ahead of her, and the fact that *The Mousetrap* had not been
sprung on Broadway in the interim was doubtless a contributing
factor to her ultimate theatrical success there.

Given his careful nurturing of *The Mousetrap*, Saunders came
to believe, not unreasonably, that full ownership of the project
should, as far as possible, be vested in himself. After two and a
half years at the Ambassadors he had renegotiated the rental
terms and entered into a long-term occupancy deal with its
owners. As *The Stage* reported, Saunders 'expects The Mousetrap
to run for another year. When it finishes he will present a new
Christie play.'[48] In 1958, with the play showing no signs of
finishing, he acquired the long lease on the theatre. As well as
becoming his own landlord, Saunders made outright purchases
of a number of the play's subsidiary rights and bought out several
of its investors including Richard Attenborough, who had eventually taken a 10 per cent stake in the production for £500, and
who used the money from its sale to help finance his film *Gandhi*.

In 1969 Saunders even bought out Mathew Prichard, paying a substantial sum for the ongoing rights in the play; although a quirk of UK copyright law requires that any literary rights assigned prior to 1956 must revert to the writer's 'residuary legatee' twenty-five years after the writer's death, so that in 2001 Rosalind became the legal beneficiary of the royalties for *The Mousetrap* despite the fact that her mother had assigned them to Mathew in 1951. At this point, Rosalind could technically have closed the show, but a new deal was done with Sir Stephen Waley-Cohen, who had bought the production from Saunders on his retirement in 1994, and since then the author's royalties have been assigned to a trust which distributes the income to arts charities. Cotes was thus not the only one to receive an offer to relinquish his ongoing interest, and whilst he might arguably have negotiated (and, no doubt, received) a better price than he was offered, he perhaps should not have taken it quite as personally as he did.

Cotes was a legendarily spiky customer, but it has to be said that on paper he was an inspired choice for the direction of *The Mousetrap*. Like Saunders, he was a maverick who flew in the face of 'the Firm' and 'the Group', and it is a shame that the two of them fell out. An apparent truce between the two men came to an abrupt end when Saunders published his autobiography *The Mousetrap Man* in 1972. In this he strongly implies that Cotes was negligent in his duties towards the production and that, having effectively been left holding the baby by the absentee director during the production's pre-London tour, he was himself responsible for its artistic as well as its financial success. Cotes put this down to 'the frustrated-director complex in Saunders's make-up'[49] and took the opportunity to set the record straight, as he saw it, when interviewed by Gwen Robyns for her 1978 Christie biography. He goes on to justify his position at some length in his own book, and includes a number of bizarrely scrappy appendices giving evidence in support of his own version of events. During this period Saunders' and Cotes' solicitors were in regular correspondence, and in 1985 Saunders wrote to the theatre critic, Jack Tinker, 'I am enjoying myself running up Mr Cotes' legal bills.'[50]

This forty-five-year dispute between director and producer was the only cloud to sully the production's otherwise triumphant progress. It was Saunders who was to have the last laugh. In 1992, as part of a strategy to ensure that there were no loose ends for his successors, he wrote to Cotes' agent to say that, according to their original 1952 contract, Cotes was allowed to direct any post-London tour or to 'be compensated, at my option, with £50'. He added, 'I am enclosing a cheque for £50 as a release from my obligation.'[51] Cotes does not mention this in his book. In the end, the tour that started in the production's sixtieth anniversary year was to run concurrently with the London production, not after it. It was, in my view, incorrectly advertised as the production's 'first national tour'. It was actually the second. The first was in 1952 and was directed by Peter Cotes.

So what really lay at the root of all this bitterness? Cotes' contract states that after the opening in Nottingham he would 'from time to time arrange to see the show and call rehearsals at times to be mutually agreed upon whenever this may be deemed necessary and advisable'.[52] Although he appears to have done the absolute bare minimum to fulfil this obligation, he could not actually have been accused of breach of contract, and Saunders knew this. It would have been, and in some quarters still is, standard practice for a director with other commitments to leave the rehearsals of a production after opening in the hands of an assistant, who in this case would have been the 'stage director', or senior member of the stage management team, Tony Huntly-Gordon. According to Saunders, Cotes tried to have Huntly-Gordon fired on the first day of rehearsals,[53] although he ended up staying with the production for twenty-one years.

We must remember that Cotes only got the job at the very last minute, when John Fernald pulled out, even though there had evidently been previous negotiations with him. This is reflected in the fact that Cotes' contract allows him to work evenings only during the first week of rehearsals, as he had evidently been unable to reschedule an existing commitment.

This lack of availability in the first week may well have been the reason why initial negotiations with Cotes broke down, but with two weeks to go until rehearsals were due to start, Saunders had no option but to agree to this unusual arrangement. Attenborough was available from 15 September and the production was due to open in Nottingham on 6 October. Saunders may well have felt, with some justification, that having accommodated Cotes' schedule in this way he should have gone the extra mile to attend the production during the early weeks of its tour. As a man of absolute integrity, though, Saunders never used the fact that Cotes had not been present for much of the first week of rehearsals against him. That was an agreed point of contract, and as such not a legitimate part of the argument.

More significant, though, in my view, is part of the letter of engagement which Saunders sent to Cotes on 30 August 1952, the day on which he had agreed to take over from Fernald. 'As, however, you have not used the peculiar circumstances to increase your terms,' he wrote, 'the terms I suggest are rather better than arranged. I hope you will treat this as a friendly gesture of appreciation.'[54] Saunders' appreciation of the fact that Cotes did not take the opportunity of this last-minute offer to hold him to ransom took the form of an offer to increase his royalty on box office receipts from 1 per cent to 1.5 per cent once the production was in profit. Interestingly, Saunders sent the letter, including full details of the deal, to Cotes himself rather than to his agent, Eric Glass.

Two days later, Cotes responded in a handwritten message on BBC notepaper,

My dear Peter,

Thanks for your letter the contents of which I deeply appreciate; not because of the value of the additional small percentage, but because of the thought, made doubly touching by the fact that it was spontaneous. So often in the theatre one gets one's behind kicked as reciprocation for doing one's best and not throwing one's weight about or refusing to exploit a situation; it is because of that fact that your little thought becomes both gracious and unique.[55]

This amiable initial exchange between the two notorious long-term adversaries goes, I believe, a long way towards explaining subsequent events. Saunders had not only agreed to Cotes' part-time attendance in the first week of rehearsals but had, completely voluntarily, offered an increment on his royalty as a spontaneous gesture of good will. As it is still a going concern, I have not seen the accounts for *The Mousetrap*, but received wisdom is that it was already in profit by the end of its pre-West End tour, and my assumption would be that Cotes' bonus would have been payable out of Saunders' own share of profits, so as not to raise any eyebrows amongst investors. Again, this was not something that could legitimately be used against Cotes in the ensuing flow of correspondence or in print, as it was an agreed point of contract. Saunders may well also have felt that it exposed a softness on his part which did not sit comfortably with his carefully cultivated image as the no-nonsense producer. So although Cotes' paltry attendance record may not technically have put him in breach of contract, and Saunders' removal of his name from the advertising certainly did, it is easy to empathise with Saunders' extreme disappointment that his gesture of good will did not result in an enhanced commitment to the project from its director. Cotes, on the other hand, may well have resented the fact that he was a last-minute choice, after previous negotiations with him appear to have broken down; something that he in turn would not have wanted to be made public.

On the sixth anniversary of the production, Christie herself displayed typical magnanimity by sending both Peter Cotes and Hubert Gregg specially bound copies of the script, with inscriptions thanking each them for their work. Of Saunders she wrote, 'He certainly is "the Mousetrap Man". *I* wrote it – but he put it on . . . and believed in it . . . We've all three been lucky – the Authoress – the schoolboy – and THE MOUSETRAP MAN.'[56]

SCENE THREE

Saunders' Folly

Witness for the Prosecution is Agatha Christie's undisputed theatrical masterpiece. This accomplished three-act courtroom drama with its classic 'quadruple twist' ending sets the benchmark for the genre and is a bold departure from her previous plays. In plotting terms it is another variation on the theme of female revenge on the philandering male, and once again it is a woman who is at the centre of events. It is also Christie's most detailed examination of the concept of justice in all its forms. Like *The Mousetrap, Witness for the Prosecution* is expanded from a short story, although a much shorter one than 'Three Blind Mice'. First published as 'Traitor Hands' in January 1925 in *Flynn's Weekly* in the USA, it was subsequently retitled and included in the short story collections *The Hound of Death* (published in the UK in 1933) and *The Witness for the Prosecution* (published in the USA in 1948).

It was Peter Saunders who came up with the idea of turning the story into a play, and of centring the piece on the courtroom, which is only briefly referred to in the story. He first suggested it to Christie in the summer of 1951 on one of his regular visits to Greenway, where he 'felt completely at home, and was now one of the family', but she was not immediately taken with the idea. Once *The Mousetrap* had opened Saunders reminded her of it again, and she responded that if he wanted a play of *Witness for the Prosecution* then he should write it himself.

And that is exactly what he did. 'Every night,' he recalls, 'I would go to bed and set the alarm clock for three in the morning because it was at this time I felt freshest. And, on a portable typewriter in bed, I wrote the play based on her short story.'[1]

Saunders eventually presented Christie with the fruits of his labours, and his perseverance had the desired effect. Six weeks later (as Saunders remembers it) or three weeks later (as Christie remembers it) she presented him with her own version. Sadly, there appears to be no copy of Saunders' script either in the Agatha Christie archive or amongst Saunders' own papers; that would indeed be a historic document to unearth. Whether there are any traces of Saunders' work in the play as we now know it we can only speculate. I believe not, as there is a great deal of correspondence between Saunders and Christie as she develops her own script from its first draft, and no reference at all is made to Saunders' version.

In 1978, two years after Christie's death, a courtroom drama called *Scales of Justice*, which takes its inspiration from a court case in which a naturalised German sued a popular MP for allegedly instigating his internment during the First World War, would open at Perth repertory theatre.[2] It was directed by Joan Knight, who had been a notable resident director on *The Mousetrap*. And it was written by Peter Saunders. The play is a workmanlike affair that deals with an intriguing subject, and is stylistically so dissimilar to Christie's work that it comprehensively allays any suspicion that Saunders' own hand may be evident in the finished script of *Witness for the Prosecution*. Bizarrely, though, a short story version of *Witness for the Prosecution*, written by and credited to Saunders, was serialised in the *Daily Express* in February 1956, a year after the London production closed, under the heading 'the thriller by Agatha Christie'.[3]

The play itself concerns a charming young man, Leonard Vole, who is arrested for the murder of an elderly spinster who has left him her fortune in her will. His solicitor, Mayhew, enlists the help of flamboyant barrister Sir Wilfred Robarts, and they meet with both Vole and his enigmatic East Berliner wife, Romaine, who hesitatingly confirms his alibi. The action then moves from

Robarts' chambers to Vole's trial at the Old Bailey, where most of the rest of the play is set. In tense, tightly written and authentic courtroom scenes a series of witnesses give evidence, culminating in the star witness for the prosecution who, shockingly, turns out to be none other than Romaine. She gives evidence against Vole which appears to incriminate him and to destroy the case for the defence; but, the same evening, a mysterious woman visits Robarts and Mayhew and sells them letters that will enable them to demonstrate that Romaine is lying. In a thrilling court-room denouement, Romaine is discredited and Vole acquitted. And then, in the last two pages, there are no fewer than four truly astonishing twists to the tale, an extraordinary and auda-cious piece of playwriting that trumps even the revelations at the end of *The Mousetrap*. Although the short story's premise and basic plot are the same as the play's, the original does not actu-ally take place in a courtroom, and as such does not feature the character of Robarts. Romaine is Viennese in the pre-war short story, and her reinvention as an East German in 1950s Britain cleverly tips the scales against her. And, most importantly, the short story does not feature the play's final killer twist.

The Agatha Christie archive has more work in progress for *Witness for the Prosecution* than for any of Christie's other plays, and amongst the Saunders papers there is a lengthy correspondence between Christie and her producer; she writes care of the British School of Archaeology in Baghdad (it being that time of year when she joined her husband at the Nimrud excavations), and for once uses a typewriter for most of her letters, so there is not the usual battle to decipher her hand-writing. The script material in the archive appears to reflect the issues being discussed in the correspondence quite closely, so it is a safe assumption that these were Christie's working papers on the play while she was away with Max on the annual dig.

What appears to be some sort of master working copy bears the short story's revised title, 'The Witness for the Prosecution', but with the word 'The' crossed out. The title typed in the text is actually 'Hostile Witness' although this, too, has been crossed out. In 1964 Saunders was to be involved in the creation of another courtroom drama, a play by Old Bailey official and television writer Jack Roffey, which was originally conceived as a vehicle for Margaret Lockwood (although she never appeared in it). It was given the title *Hostile Witness*.

Across the front of the draft script Agatha has scribbled the words 'legal fun to be added!' Saunders had only managed to convince her to write the play by assuring her that he would enlist the services of an expert consultant to ensure the authenticity of the legal aspects of the story. The first person Saunders approached about this was Leo Genn, the film and stage star who, after a pre-war stint in the Old Vic Company, had come to prominence in a small role in Olivier's 1944 film of *Henry V* and the following year had taken Broadway by storm in Lillian Hellman's *Another Part of the Forest*. In 1951 he had been nominated for a Best Supporting Actor Oscar for *Quo Vadis*; but for now it was his Cambridge law degree that was of particular interest. Prior to the war, Genn had combined his show-business career with work as a barrister, and after it had served as an assistant prosecutor at the Belsen trial.[4] But now he was concentrating on his acting career and, in the end, felt that a practising barrister would be better placed to assist Saunders and Christie. In his place he recommended Humphrey Tilling.

Tilling and his wife Sue were both leading lights of Canterbury's 'Old Stagers', founded in 1842 and reputedly the world's oldest amateur dramatics society. Sue's obituary in the *Daily Telegraph* notes that her husband 'was one of the best amateur actors of his day and could easily have pursued a professional career. For financial reasons he entered the bar instead, but remained the linchpin of the Old Stagers until his death in 1991.'[5] Tilling's role in bringing legal authenticity to the piece was clearly greatly appreciated by Agatha; she refers to a barrister attending rehearsals, although much of this work was actually done in advance and communicated to her in Iraq by Peter Saunders. It has to be said that Tilling's suggested interpolations on occasion appear to have strayed somewhat beyond his advisory remit, but that when this occurred Christie rejected his tamperings. A note of thanks to Saunders from Genn appears to indicate that he received payment of some kind, but there is no correspondence with Tilling on file and he is not credited for his contribution to the piece, although one assumes that he was remunerated for it.

Christie herself made no attempt to conceal that she received some expert advice for this element of the play, and neither should she have. She also refers to having read 'quantities of the *Famous Trials* series' before she started writing, by which she must mean the *Notable British Trials* books published by William Hodge & Co.; a regular editor of which was fellow playwright Fryn Tennyson Jesse, whose *A Pin To See the Peepshow* was to take Peter Cotes on his ill-fated expedition to New York. As well as ensuring that Christie herself was properly briefed, Saunders was also keen to educate himself and the rest of the creative team about both legal procedures and the play's location in the Central Criminal Court (the Old Bailey) and, to this end, his files contain correspondence with the court's officers and a judge. He himself attended some of the trial of notorious serial killer John Christie, and he made arrangements for director Wallace Douglas and designer Michael Weight to make reconnaissance visits to the Old Bailey as well.

In Christie's first draft, the play opens with a couple of legal clerks tidying up Mayhew's office, and bantering about the outcomes of trials in a manner not dissimilar to that adopted by two female characters in Christie's 1948 radio play *Butter in a Lordly Dish*. The clerks' somewhat irreverent exchanges right at the start of the piece have the same sort of effect as when we first meet Bill and Alf in *The Mousetrap*. Sadly, like their counterparts in *The Mousetrap*, the two clerks were ultimately destined for the wastepaper basket, in this case to be replaced by a Chief Clerk and a female typist. Here, the two original clerks offer odds on the outcome for Vole:

2ND CLERK: Well, reading between the lines and all the rest of it, it seems a clear case. I don't see who else could have done the old girl in.

1ST CLERK: No, shouldn't think he's got a hope. What's the starting price?

2ND CLERK: 5 to 1 against acquittal, 3 to 1 against Broadmoor.

1ST CLERK: Not taking those odds. 50 to 1 is more like it.

2ND CLERK: Ah, you wait until old Wilfred Windbag gets up and starts addressing the jury bringing in all the psychologists to say he was dropped on his head as a child, or sang too long in the choir, and was much too fond of his mother!

1ST CLERK: Live like fighting cocks at Broadmoor, so I've heard.

2ND CLERK: Well, what'll you bet?

1ST CLERK: He isn't arrested yet so he doesn't come under starter's orders. No arrest, no bet.[6]

One of the biggest problems with Christie's original draft was that the opening scene was set in the office of the solicitor, Mayhew. Mayhew meets Vole on his own, telephones the barrister Sir Wilfred (here called Sir Giles) Robarts QC, and is then visited by Romaine. He is well into his conversation with Vole's wife when he is joined by Robarts. In this scenario Robarts does not appear until page 23, and in one version he is on his way to play golf at Christie's old haunt, Sunningdale, and is dressed for it; 'I can give you ten minutes,' he declares. The issue here, as pointed out by both of the production's legal consultants, was that a QC would never visit a solicitor. The resulting relocation of the first scene to Robarts' chambers means that Robarts of necessity was on stage right from the start of the play, hosting the initial interviews with both Vole (who Mayhew brings to see him) and Romaine. We thus have this quirk of legal etiquette to thank for the fact that the role of Robarts became so dominant in the play.

In the original script we also see that DI Hearne started life as DI Warren, and the now familiar shock ending is on a three-page insert. On the dramatis personae, which lists only fifteen of the eventual thirty characters, Christie larkily suggests 'Anna Lias' as the name of the actress to be credited with playing a role which is actually another character in disguise. On a page of handwritten notes, she adds:

> Suggestions on Act I
> If it is wanted to be longer – work up scene between Romaine and Sir Wilfred. Depends rather on who is cast as Sir W – what type he is.
> Tentative Mayhew is small, dry humour, rather old fashioned –
> Wilfred – big – bombastic – dramatic changes of voice and mood – a bit of a windbag?
> They must be a contrast to each other.

Hubert Gregg, as always, places himself at the centre of events:

> In 1953, Peter Saunders gave me the script of the next Christie and offered me the direction of it. It was, I think, her best . . . I made a few suggestions after reading the play. Principally I felt that, in the climate of the day, it would be wrong if crime should be left paying a dividend. (Subsequently, to my astonishment, Agatha claimed that she insisted – above everything – upon retaining her own ending.) I outlined what I thought should happen and Christie incorporated the idea . . . *Witness for the Prosecution* is the one Christie play I am sorry I didn't direct. I had other plans and they turned out not so well. I suggested Wallace Douglas to Peter. He was an old theatre friend . . . Wally was grateful to me and said so. His success with *Witness* led to his being invited to tackle other whodunits – and, who knows, perhaps to his long association with the comedies at the Whitehall.[7]

Douglas did indeed go on the following year to direct John Chapman's long-running Whitehall Farce *Dry Rot*; he was also engaged by Saunders to direct William Douglas Home's *The Manor at Northstead*, in a production which was to mark the start of Saunders' fruitful association with the playwright. Having been an actor before the war (collectors of Christie trivia may like to observe that he had appeared as an actor opposite Francis L. Sullivan's Poirot in the 1937 television broadcast of *The Wasp's Nest*) and a prisoner of war for most of it, Douglas had turned to directing in 1945. Of his appointment, however, Saunders says simply, 'Wallace Douglas had read the play at my invitation and visualised it so much as I did that I asked him to direct it. It was a very wise choice.'[8] He makes no mention of having offered Gregg the job or of Gregg having suggested Douglas, who was in any case represented by Film Rights, a company with which Saunders did a great deal of business.

Wallace Douglas was contracted at the end of July, three months after the script was finalised and two months before the first performance, although he appears to have been working with Saunders on casting prior to then. This time there was no messing around, and the director's royalty was a flat 1½ per cent from the start.[9] Douglas is the quiet man amongst Christie directors; he delivered two of her biggest hits but, unlike some of the others, seems to have had remarkably little to say on the subject. Gwen Robyns interviewed him for her Christie biography, in which he expresses his admiration for her ability to memorise and willingness to act upon his notes – apart from his suggestion that she change the play's ending.

It may well be that Hubert Gregg introduced his friend Douglas, just as he had been the go-between with the Attenboroughs. And it may perhaps be the case that he came up with the title of *The Mousetrap*. But his suggestion that he also came up with the ending of *Witness for the Prosecution* is bizarre in the extreme. There is no record of Gregg having been involved in any way with the development of the script, and the legendary final twist was added by Christie in long-distance correspondence with Saunders. Perhaps, of course, Gregg had suggested it to Saunders, who in turn had somehow subliminally suggested it to Christie in a way that made it feel her own; Saunders was very good at this, and Christie referred to herself as 'hypnotised and always amenable to the power of suggestion' where he was concerned.[10] There is some correspondence that might appear to bear this out; but it seems unlikely as Saunders, although supportive to Christie of her ending for the play, was clearly not entirely convinced that it would work. The issue at stake was that in the original story a murderer walks away unpunished. In the play's unexpected and dramatic ending the murderer is seen to face gory retribution from an unexpected source. My own belief is that Christie's advisors encouraged her to make the murderer face justice in the stage version; there was even some feeling that the play would not get past the Lord Chamberlain's office if crime was seen to pay. But I have no doubt that Christie herself came up with the means for achieving this, and the production files show that an order for stage blood was duly placed.

Saunders claims that he and Douglas made a list of thirty-six actors for the role of Robarts, which had become a good star vehicle in its expanded form, but that they all turned it down. 'They just didn't believe this play could work, and the ending which Agatha had put in (it wasn't in the short story) was so spectacularly daring that I never knew until the first night on tour whether or not it would come off.'[11] Whether thirty-six offers were actually declined we will never know, but there is correspondence on file to indicate that casting the part proved a problem. This includes a polite letter from Robert Morley, a Film Rights client, turning down the role, and some correspondence with forty-seven-year-old film star Roger Livesey (best known for 1943's *The Life and Death of Colonel Blimp*) in which he objects to the script's two biggest *coups de théâtre* (the impersonation and the ending). The latter elicited the response from Saunders, 'I freely concede that something may have to be done about the ending of "Witness",' although he leapt to Christie's defence as regards the impersonation: 'This, to me, is a basic part of the play, and if you don't like that part then inevitably during production you would find yourself wanting to remove other oddities in the script. While one might end up with a play, I do not believe it would be a Christie play. Christie plays, whatever people may think of them, can I believe only succeed if they are written in black and white and not in grey.'[12]

At one stage Saunders even suggests changing the role to a female barrister and offering it to Flora Robson, which results in one of my favourite no-nonsense Christie responses: 'I know there are women barristers but one always feels that they are rather a joke.' I gift this to the feminist writers who make so much of Christie's alleged 'collusion with patriarchy'. But in the context of 1953 Christie is right, of course. The first female barristers had been called to the bar in the 1920s, but in Christie's story Romaine makes unashamed use of her sexuality to bamboozle the self-satisfied and easily led male lawyers, and the focus of the play would have changed beyond recognition if the barrister had been a woman. It would have become a play about a female barrister. Which it isn't.

Eventually the role went to David Horne who, as Saunders says, was 'a first class character actor but in no sense of the word a box-office draw. David looked the part and, as it was quite clear no star was going to do the play, I dived in at the deep end. From then onwards we were committed to a no-name cast.'[13] What he fails to mention is that Horne had appeared as Father Borrowdale in the brief West End run of *Murder on the Nile*. In 1964 Saunders was to cast Flora Robson in the role of a female QC in a courtroom drama called *Justice is a Woman* (although Robson withdrew from the production due to illness). The play was written by Jack Roffey, whose *Hostile Witness* he had produced two years earlier.

The part of Romaine proved no easier to cast, but eventually went to Patricia Jessel, who had played a small role for Saunders in one of his first projects, *The Ex Mrs Y*. Known principally as a Shakespearian actress, both with Donald Wolfit's company and Stratford's Shakespeare Memorial Theatre, she had impressed Saunders when he saw her playing opposite Peter Ustinov in *The Love of Four Colonels*. She was not a star, but the role of Romaine was to make her one. Her performance in the London production of *Witness for the Prosecution* would win her Equity's Clarence Derwent Award, and Saunders described it as 'one of the finest pieces of acting I have ever seen in my life'.

In a lively three-month correspondence between Saunders

(in London) and Christie (in Iraq) at the beginning of 1953, we see the producer skilfully cajoling the absent playwright into completing her script. They also discuss other aspects of the production, including advice from the legal consultants and casting. I reproduce this in full in the following pages, and have kept my own commentary to a minimum so as not to interrupt the delightful exchanges between the two as this definitive courtroom drama is created.[14]

Christie to Saunders: 24 January 1953

Dear Peter,

A friend of ours at the Embassy is flying home tomorrow so I have given him the rewritten script of the end of the play as I thought it would probably get to you quicker. I've got a carbon copy, of course, so let me know in due course if nothing turns up. I think I've got it just as you want it now – with the double punch – or indeed treble punch . . . and thank goodness no need for any explanations to hold up the Curtain.

I'm more than ever convinced that you must have your head over the casting of Romaine. The point is she must be a personality – and if not the kind of personality I had in mind – one slightly adapts the lines. After all Lady Angkatell was not at all my Lady Angkatell – but she most decidedly was a Lady Angkatell – so all went well, jelly babies and all! Yes, Ann Todd is a good actress. I don't think blondness matters. Two others I've thought of were Irene Worth and Constance Cummings. But anyone you fancy.

I'll see if I can think of anything to improve the 'letters' scene in court – if one could lead up to their production a bit? The difficulty is that it must be the actual production of the letters that (supposedly) breaks her down, because they are (supposedly) completely unexpected.

If anything strikes you about the play write out to me on the various points. I rather want not to look at it or think of it for a few weeks and then come back to it fresh. The scene between the solicitor and Counsel can be worked up when one has a better idea of who might be cast for the parts. They should be a contrast to each other. I visualise at the moment Counsel as big and blustering and Mayhew as neat and precise – but it doesn't matter really.

We arrived two days ago rather weary from our wanderings having had flu on the way and spent two days in Rome in an expensive Hotel, taking our temperatures and ordering trays of weak tea.

Glorious sunshine here and already quite warm.

Tell me the news from time to time

Love to the Dicky Birds [I wonder if this is a reference to 'Dickie' Attenborough and Sheila Sim?]

Yours

Agatha

Saunders to Christie: 28 January 1953

Dear Agatha,

I cabled you today having just read the WFTP ending. It is quite wonderful. Everything I saw in the finale is now there, and I can't wait to get on with it.

The Mousetrap obstinately continues to play to full houses, so it may be some time before I do it, but I feel I should start my plans now and will either do it next September or about Christmas.

Leo Genn, who is a distinguished actor, and was also a barrister connected with murder cases, is reading the script and says that, providing there is not a lot of work to be done (and, of course, there isn't), he will be very happy to give any help he can.

I enclose two photographs as suggested for Leonard and Romaine. Will you please let me know whether I am working on the right lines?

Patricia Jessel plays one of the wives in The Love of Four

Colonels, but if you happen to have seen The Platinum Set she plays the mistress. She is a brilliant actress, and is a rather younger version of Sonia Dresdel. Outside star names I cannot think of anybody I would prefer. Her actual age is 32.

Jack Watling played Flight Lieut. Graham in Flare Path, but you will almost certainly remember him as the son (not the young boy of course) in The Winslow Boy . . . [Watling is being suggested here for the role of Leonard Vole, which was eventually played by Derek Blomfield]

I am having your new ending incorporated into your draft, and I will get Leo Genn to do us a little bit of 'legal fun', and I will then send you a copy of the script for your observations.

Have you any strong feelings about including the jury on stage? Does it worry you if the judge and counsel address the audience, who would be the jury? . . .

No more news, except that Aubrey Dexter [playing Major Metcalf in *The Mousetrap*] has been ill for a week, and Tony Huntly-Gordon [the production's senior stage manager] has been playing for him . . .

My kind regards to Max,

[Peter Saunders]

Christie to Saunders: 1 February 1953

Dear Impressario Pete [sic] Saunders . . .

Very glad the revised end meets approval. I will admit that I think it is better myself!

Patricia Jessel looks all right and as I have said, I leave it in your hands. I thought you had to have a 'name'? I saw Four Colonels but can't remember anything about the wives except for Diana Graves who once acted in a play of mine [she played Jacqueline de Severac in the pre-London tour of *Murder on the Nile*] and who appeared to me to be singularly miscast as the French wife, and who had dyed her black hair golden to make it even more unconvincing!

I have been thinking about the opening of the play and it seems to me the 2 clerks are stagey and rather a waste and if you've got to pay two people, how would it be to have an elderly clerk, rather a type (years with the firm etc) and a pert young woman – material for a laugh or two vaguely resembling the Gudgeon Doris gambit? Also I think Mayhew could be worked up – very precise and pedantic and dry as dust and some exchanges between him and elderly clerk – and also a few laughs between him and Leonard – Leonard as the naïve young man not realising he can be really going to be arrested for murder and rather endearing himself to the old lawyer by his naïve observations.

I'd like to hear what you think of working up Act I on these lines? Does Act I want to be longer?

And now for the Gypsy's warning. Are you really sure you want to do a play like this? I can see it's a big undertaking. The Mousetrap formula seems to be a fairly safe one. Intimate murder, not taken too seriously, with plenty of rather obvious domestic humour. Even if it's not liked, I don't suppose you go down much on it. But I do feel W.F.T.P. runs a risk of being Saunders' Folly – so I don't want to urge you into it. End of Gypsy's warning.

I enclose a letter which I think you will enjoy. It is from the Leading Twin of my friends the Richmond Twins aged thirteen, impossible to tell apart and great friends of mine. I arranged with Cork to get them seats [for *The Mousetrap*], but it seems to have gone wrong and their mother rang up the box office and was put on to someone 'with a very nice voice' – sounds more like your secretary than one of Edmund's minions – anyway all ended well, and this is certainly an exact account of the effect produced by the play on Miss Emma Richmond. Keep it for me, if you don't mind, as it's one I'd like to keep [he must have returned the child's letter to Agatha, as it is missing].

Baghdad sunshine is lovely and not conducive to work.

But I really deserve a rest, after being bullied over the play by you and goaded to a book by Edmund.

Yours,

Agatha Mallowan

Saunders to Christie: 10 February 1953

Dear Agatha,

Very many thanks for your letter of February 1st, which I was delighted to receive.

I like your opening idea of a rather loveable elderly clerk and a pert young woman. It won't save any characters as far as I can see, but – as you say – it will give us some laughs to start off with.

I know that you are always satisfied that producers [i.e. directors] will always find laughs in your script, but it may be that because there may not have been enough in 'The Mousetrap' to start with, that we rather looked for them and caused some unwanted ones.

Aubrey Dexter is still off, and the more I see of Huntly-Gordon the more I prefer his interpretation.

So do please try out your idea of the new opening, and I am also very much hoping that you can work up a verbal duel before Romaine is trapped. Each time I read it I feel that she gives in far too easily.

I am most appreciative of your gipsy's warning. The old formula, as you say, is a fairly safe gamble because of the reps and tours, and you have proved with your books that the public don't get tired of your formula.

On the other hand, it does seem that this is an exciting play to tackle, and my only fear is that if the press turn round and criticise you for departing from your normal type of play, I should feel very bad about it.

I am so delighted with the script to date that I should hate to drop the thing. In fact I don't think I could. So let's jump into the deep end and see how cold the water is!

Patricia Jessel and Jack Watling are not, of course, names, but I would like to cast this play with the people you had in mind. I shall try Ann Todd, but I don't think that Romaine is a big enough part to attract her.

I mentioned this play to Dickie, and he is dying to read it. I suppose he couldn't play Leonard, and Sheila couldn't dye her hair black and play Romaine? No, I thought not!

I have not had the script back from Leo Genn, but as soon as I do I will let you know of his observations.

I have arranged with the Common Serjeant to spend the whole of the next murder trial at the Old Bailey in one of the V.I.P. seats, as I would like to get a bit of atmosphere.

I still don't know when I shall do the play. Two things would affect the date. If 'The Mousetrap' happened to flop suddenly (and I still think it will do the fourteen months I forecast at Nottingham) I should forge right ahead.

The only other danger is that there is an enormous amount of talk in theatrical circles that 'it's about time someone put on a play with a court scene in it'. To follow one with ours would make it appear as if we were copying, and if I heard any news that one was to be done I would get in first. That is another reason why I would like the script settled as far as possible.

Can you tell me why you are [seeing the] defending Q.C. as a pompous windbag? It seems that it would be more effective theatrically if the audience liked him. If they didn't like him they would more probably anticipate his eventual deflation . . .

I haven't approached any producer [i.e. director] for W.F.T.P. as yet, but I have in mind Glen Byam Shaw, who directed 'The Winslow Boy', or Charles Hickman, who has a string of successes to his name – such as 'Black Chiffon' which I seem to remember you liked. I also have a leaning towards Frith Banbury, who directed 'The Deep Blue Sea'. What do you think? [Both Hubert Gregg and Wallace Douglas are, significantly, absent from this list. It would have been interesting to see what Frith Banbury, who the previous year

had directed the premiere of Rattigan's play, starring Peggy Ashcroft, would have made of *Witness for the Prosecution*]
Kind regards and best wishes to you both,
Yours Sincerely,
[Peter Saunders]

Continued:
I have just spent two hours with Leo Genn, who says that there is rather too much work for him to tackle, but he is putting me on to another theatrical barrister [Humphrey Tilling].

He [Genn] says that there are quite a number of minor points which will present no difficulty, and he does observe that evidence is given in half an act which normally takes a couple of days.

I pointed out that the audience would get rather tired of sitting in the theatre for two days at a time.

He does, however, make one serious objection – and I do not suggest you do more than think about it until I have seen his barrister friend. He says that it is quite unthinkable that a Q.C. should visit a solicitor. This could not, he says, possibly happen because of the laws of the Temple.

He says it is just all right for the solicitor and the Q.C. to be in the solicitor's office in the Lily Moggson scene, although he should start off by being an observer.

The first scene in Mayherne's [original name of the solicitor, Mayhew] office seems to be the problem, but by no means insoluble, so don't bother about it until you hear from me again – which may not be for a week or two.

Christie to Saunders: 19 February 1953

Dear Peter
Herewith various startling improvements (?)! I think I've done what you wanted with the scene of Romaine's break down and got it more dramatic.

I've also revised the first act, and I think it now covers Sir Wilfrid being in Mayhew's office since he comes there in a friendly fashion, off duty so to speak [on his way to play golf]. Also I think it is better this way, since it builds him up better. I didn't really mean he was a windbag. Yes, he must be sympathetic. But I meant more the histrionic type of Counsel – the Marshall Hall type [Hall was a celebrated Edwardian defence lawyer] rather than the cold keen shrewd type. Really, I rather like the play now. And am getting all excited.

Let me know what you think about the revisions and don't be too much bullied by the legal pundits. 'Several days' is such a silly remark. Time on stage isn't real time, it's illusion. Only the more flagrant errors need doing. Anything exactly like a criminal court would be dull . . .

There must be a Personality for Romaine. She has all through to suggest so much that she isn't saying.

Well, here's luck. Hope this typing isn't too much of a mess but I think it's quite clear where it joins on and fits in. Court Scene can dim off anywhere we choose, but I think the sooner the better after Romaine. Anyway, I am really quite fogged now about length. Is it too short or too long? The former, I hope. So much easier to add.

Yours

Agatha

Saunders to Christie: 24 February 1953

Dear Agatha,

Many thanks for your letter of February 19th and re-writes.

I like the opening very much indeed, and I think we might get a bit of fun out of it. Also it gives us the chance to have an attractive girl in the part of Greta, which I think is a good thing in a play where there isn't much feminine appeal.

The new scene of Romaine in the box I like very much indeed, but it has disappointed my barrister friend [Tilling] who has just written his own suggestion for it. I haven't seen

it yet, but for what it is worth I will send it on to you at the
end of the week when I get it.

Regarding the arrival of Sir Wilfrid at Mayhew's office, I
am not quite sure what to say. It is still, even as re-written,
completely contrary to all the ethics of the Temple. If you
feel that it is better theatre that way, and the inaccuracy
doesn't matter, then of course I withdraw all objections.

This barrister, however, has got an idea which would not
involve great alterations but might make it 'right', so I will
send on his observations on this as well.

As you say, we must of course bear in mind that this is
the stage not a court, and I have the greatest faith in your
theatrical 'feel'.

What I am afraid of is sending you repeated screeds of
requests and notes to such an extent that you will come to
the conclusion that you shouldn't have written the play at
all.

I will send to Mosul, I hope on Friday, the barrister's
observations, but if when you get them you feel that I could
be of more use on the spot, for the purpose of discussing
how far we should go as regards accuracy, I could easily fly
out for a couple of days. Planes leave twice a week, and it
is only two and a half hours by train from Baghdad.

However, I suggest you leave everything till you hear from
me again, which would be in three or four days' time.

Kind Regards,

Yours Sincerely,

[Peter Saunders]

Saunders to Christie: 27 February 1953

Saunders' Folly

Dear Agatha,

I enclose a loose leaf edition of the play, with the barrister's observations. I have not returned your revisions (hoping

you have a copy) as I would like them by me to refer to. If you need them, a letter or a cable will bring them by return.

You will find that he has written in on the script minor changes, and anything major he has done on green paper so that you can easily pick it out.

I hope, and believe, that you will think he has done some useful work. Most of it (particularly legal arguments) I like very much, and I don't think it makes it too long winded, because his legal interpolations are usually backed up by sarcasm, irony or dramatic conflict.

The major problem is the Q.C. visiting the solicitor. As you will see, he has switched the entire thing (both scenes) to the Q.C.'s office, and if this satisfies you it certainly does me. On the other hand, if you think that the unethicality of having the Q.C. visiting the solicitor doesn't matter for the stage, then I accept this just as happily. But I am slightly inclined towards the accuracy, providing we don't lose 'theatre' by it.

But there is another snag. If you have it in the Q.C.'s office then I am afraid it might have to wash out your new beginning, as a Q.C. wouldn't deal with messages and things like that. This wouldn't worry me, as your original beginning was very acceptable.

He says, incidentally, that before Romaine arrives in the first instance the Q.C. should have been put in the picture, which of course you have done on your revised script.

Regarding his final scene, where Romaine breaks down, I don't like it. She is trapped far too easily, and I think yours is infinitely better – although he may be right in saying that for Romaine to be forced to read the letter herself might be more effective. [This suggestion wasn't taken up]

I feel I am giving you an enormous amount of work. I have a copy of all his notes and, if you agree that it is better to keep the Q.C.'s office, would it save you the trouble if I had a completely new script typed out, with all his interpolations (except the Romaine witness-box scene) and incorporating some of your revisions which you sent me?

I don't suggest that this would be the final script, but I feel it would save you a lot of time to alter a fairly up to date script, rather than to have to type most of the thing again.

If you would like me to do this, would you be good enough to cable 'Send new script' and I will know what it means.

Again, my apologies for all this extra work, but I am very excited about it, and do sincerely believe that it is going to be worth it.

Kind regards to you both,
Yours Sincerely
[Peter Saunders]

Christie to Saunders: 7 March 1953

Dear Peter,

Have just sent you a wire approving the new script which I think is excellent in every way *bar* the Romaine break-down –

(a) There should be no mention of 'fabricated evidence' – the last thing you want to do is put *that* idea into the audience's head.

(b) I think my 'trap' is better. She must appear absolutely flabbergasted by the production of letters . . .

Other points . . .

(1) The 'left handed' idea is good. I should think one small suggestion (*not* from Counsel) that Janet [the murder victim's housekeeper] is or may be left handed – perhaps when she is sworn? Take book in left hand, etc. As I see it Defence tries to indicate young intruder 'cosh murderer' what is *audience* going to be clever about? They spot – the sharper ones – that one indication of left handed Janet and say 'Ha ha!' – *I* know – the house keeper really did it.

(2) What is the point of not having any specimen of
Romaine's handwriting?

I'm enormously cheered up now by the legal embellishments
– I've got copies of my last revision so don't bother about
those – keep them . . .

Delighted to see you if you . . . fly out – but as we seem
to be in agreement I don't think there is any real need –
Mosul is not 2½ hours from Baghdad but a whole night's
journey!! And the line has just been cut for nearly a week . . .
we only got here today! . . .

Agatha

Saunders to Christie: 11 March 1953

Dear Agatha,

Just a brief note to thank you for your letter of March 7th.
I am having a script typed, and will send it to you in a few
days for your final approval.

I think the idea of no specimen of Romaine's handwriting
is that if they did have a specimen then it would be easy to
prove the letters were hers, instead of trapping her into
admitting it.

I think I shall refrain from flying over to see you, and I
do agree that the legal embellishments are extremely good.

[Peter Saunders]

Saunders to Christie: 18 March 1953

Saunders' Folly

Dear Agatha,

My secretary is away wintersporting, so please ignore
errors and omissions!

I enclose an up-to-date typed copy. Will you be good enough

to tell me whether it is now sufficiently complete to have it roneoed and sent out to various people. While it is easy to leave alterations until rehearsals, I do like to give the people concerned as far as possible the 'right' script.

The enclosed script is loose-leaved, so either send me your notes with the relevant page numbers, or send me actual pages with your alterations.

I have sent the script round to the barrister and his new notes are very few, as you will see.

There are a few minor touchings-up which I think you can trust me with. For instance, Leonard is accused of murder on Thursday, October 14th, 1952 – which happens to be a Tuesday.

The only rather more substantial change I wanted to ask about is this. Can we omit Lily Mogson's name completely. When she arrived, can she decline to give her name? Then, on the programme, she can be described as 'The Other Woman'. On the programme, 'The Other Woman' will be the girl at the end. But the audience will assume it is Lily M. If you agree, I can easily do this with a few pencil strokes.

I am delighted that you like the barrister's alterations. I did think they were so good myself, but hesitated to say so in case you hated them.

I am anxious to know if you like the idea of J.H. Roberts for Mayherne. Roberts wouldn't play the judge as the part isn't big enough. [Milton Rosmer eventually played Mayhew]

I only hope the play isn't too long. But I am sure it is good.

The Mousetrap isn't quite so healthy as before, but it is still doing excellent business and I think we shall do that 14 months.

Sorry to keep on worrying you with this play, but I think it is right now. I hope you think so too!

[Peter Saunders]

Christie to Saunders: 25 March 1953

Saunders' Folly

Dear Peter,

I think your idea of 'The Other Woman' is a brain wave, nothing less. Nothing could be more misleading and yet strictly fair. Haha!

Play, I think, is now quite all right to go ahead with, except for the first act. And that's definitely wrong. It may pass legally, but it outrages common sense. Would any level headed solicitor, if a young man rushed into his office, said he was in trouble over a murder, hare off with him to counsel without even hearing his story first? I don't want the play to seem bogus at the beginning.

We can get round this in two ways.

A. (the easiest) Leonard has already told his story to Mayherne, but M is anxious for Sir Wilfrid to hear L's story in his own words, to see if latter finds L. as convincing as he has done. This involves bringing Sir W. in almost as soon as they arrive and removes the weakness of Sir W. appearing to know all about the case without having ever been told about it!

Only disadvantage, it reduces Mayherne's part and increases Sir W's. This may suit you. I adore J.H. Roberts. He's a wonderful actor. Perfect for Mayherne. But he could play Sir W. I think. His keen brain countering Romaine's equally keen brain. Anyway, that I leave you. I enclose an outline of A.

And I might as well say now that I find myself instinctively disliking the opening between the clerks. Honestly, did I ever write it? I can't feel I did. Have a suspicion it's carried over (by me, perhaps) from the radio play done by someone else. For one thing, Leonard's picture would not have been in the paper as wanted by the police. The one thing the police know is his name which will have been given to them by Janet though it's feasible that she doesn't know his address and so it takes a little time to find him. If you definitely want two clerks talking the reference must be to an item in paper such as, 'It is believed that the last person to see the murdered woman alive was a Mr Leonard Vole who visited her that evening. The police are anxious to interview Mr Vole etc'. Something like that. But I think it's a mistake to pinpoint the thing in the first few lines. Also I don't see why we shouldn't cut out the one clerk (surely that would suit you?) All this I have incorporated in A. But if you like it, have the clerks as before.

B. Leonard follows Mayherne to Sir W's chambers. I've also done a rough outline of this. It's for you to choose. But I'm not satisfied with the opening as it is.

No more now, as I want to get this off to you as soon as possible. Vile Weather.

Yours,

Agatha

[a page of notes and rewrites is attached]

Saunders to Christie: 31 March 1953

Saunders' Folly

Dear Agatha,

Many thanks for your letter of March 25th. I am using for Act I alteration A, and have amended the rest of it as you suggest.

I am having scripts duplicated, and will send one out to you in about two weeks' time.

Giving most of Mayhew's first act dialogue to Sir Wilfrid does, as you say, make Sir Wilfrid a star part. I don't think he's ever off the stage!

It helps me from the point of view that I can now offer it to a 'name'. I think the first choice must be Ralph Richardson, but if necessary I should be very happy to finish up with J.H. Roberts.

I should like to do this play in the autumn, but – as I believe you know – Bertie is threatening at long last to do 'Towards Zero', and if he really is going to do it this time I must obviously wait for him. [Bertie Meyer had optioned a new adaptation of *Towards Zero* by Gerald Verner, which threatened to undermine Saunders' ability to schedule Christie's work successfully. More of this later.]

Edmund is away at the moment, but on his return he is going to try and find out definitely what Bertie wants to do.

I don't know if you can get England on your wireless, but we are on Henry Hall's Guest Night programme on Easter Sunday, which is transmitted at 2.15 our time.

Looking forward to seeing you,

Kind regards, and many thanks for all your trouble.

[Peter Saunders]

Saunders to Christie: 7 April 1953

Dear Agatha,

I hope to send you the script within the next few days, and as soon as I get them I want to start sending them out to various people.

I append a list of possible Sir Wilfrids, and should be grateful if you would let me know as soon as possible the order in which you would like them to be approached.

We shall probably end up with somebody like J.H. Roberts, but would like to try the stars first.

Roger Livesey: Robert Donat: John Mills: Ralph Richardson: Clive Brook: Felix Aylmer: Charles Laughton: Claude Rains (I can dream, cant I?) Cecil Parker: Eric Portman: Basil Sydney.

If Flora Robson would do it, would it be worth changing it to a woman Q.C.?

Kind Regards

Yours Sincerely,

[Peter Saunders]

Saunders to Christie: 10 April 1953

Dear Agatha,

I enclose a copy of the script, and hope that it is roughly our production to be.

I find, to my dismay, that Dorothy and Campbell Christie have written a play [*Carrington VC*] all about a court martial. I don't know if there is any similarity, but I am getting a script over the weekend, and if there is it might be necessary to go into rehearsal at the beginning of May for an immediate production.

This would mean that there would be no time to get your approval for the cast, other than the major parts, and I wonder if this would worry you.

I hope very much that it will not be necessary to rush this play on, as I really aim for a late autumn production.

I am eagerly awaiting your reaction to my Sir Wilfrid suggestions.

Kind Regards,
Yours Sincerely,
Peter Saunders

Christie to Saunders: 14 April 1953

Dear Peter,

A very handsome list of Sir Wilfrids! Not a woman Q.C. definitely. It would remove reality. I know there are women barristers but one always feels that they are rather a joke. Besides a bit of man woman sex antagonism between R. and Sir W. would be good. I'll give you my list of priority – but would prefer you to follow your own. Some of my likes and dislikes are prejudices – and I've no real objection to any of them.

1) Richardson – Because he would be a draw and is a
    good actor. I can't imagine him as it, because I've

always thought him best at unassuming everyday men, but his queer face might look rather arresting under a wig.

2) Laughton – Has great attack and temperament, and is rather 'lucky for me' I think. Haven't seen him for years, however. Don't know how popular he is or what he's like now. [Laughton would later play the role in the 1957 film of *Witness for the Prosecution*. Richardson would play it in the 1982 television film.]

3) Roger Livesey – I like him very much as an actor. Any plays he's been in I always remember the character he played. A lot of people don't like him, though. That funny voice of his might be effective.

4) Felix Aylmer – Best as a Bishop, but wonderful in his irony. A different kind of Sir Wilfrid – but effective. But isn't he much too old?

5) Claude Rains/Robert Donat – Never seen either of them on stage. Know nothing and can't judge. Obviously a great many peoples' dream?!

6) Portman – Probably good. Does he overact a bit? Probably wouldn't matter for Sir W. On reflection might be very good.

7) John Mills – Can't imagine him in a part. Always visualise him as gentle and romantic character.

8) Cecil Parker – I've never liked him in anything I've seen him in – but lots of people think he's very good.

9) Clive Brook – Nice but deadly dull. I think you want somebody who can be a personality – even an odd one.

10) Basil Sydney – Not seen him for years. Always thought him bad.

I don't suppose any of these remarks will be at all helpful to you. You just go ahead and have whoever you fancy. You're very quiet about Romaine? What are you up to?

Yours in haste,

Agatha

Just got script – but I'm sending this off.

If you want to [go] into rehearsal beginning of May, go ahead. You're very sound on casting and I do feel this is Saunders' Fun.

We shall be here until about May 3rd, I should think. Then a few days in Kurdistan, perhaps, and to Baghdad by the 7th or 8th. Flying home May 12th.

A.M. [Agatha Mallowan]

What about Jean Cadell as the housekeeper? Or is she dead? [The Scottish actress was by no means dead, though at sixty-nine would arguably have been too old for the role.] No hope of Irene Worth for Romaine I suppose?

As well as casting, the issue of its scale was at the forefront of concerns about *Witness for the Prosecution*'s potential right from the start. On the one hand, its widely advertised Old Bailey setting was one of its biggest selling points, but on the other it made the piece expensive and difficult to create and run. Christie's original dramatis personae of fifteen had expanded to thirty by the time the production opened, in order to include court officials, additional barristers and some members of the jury; although the play was widely promoted as having an actual cast of thirty it was, in fact, twenty-eight, including two doubles. Aware of the importance of her work to the repertory market, Christie herself offers some introductory notes in the acting edition, explaining how less well-resourced companies might approach the piece. There are a large number of non-speaking roles which exist largely for the purposes of courtroom authenticity, and her preferred option is to use amateur supernumeraries for some of these or, indeed, to bring members of the audience onto the stage: 'I believe this would be greatly to the benefit of the play rather than lose a lot of people in the court scene.' Failing that, she suggests how the piece could be performed by ten men and five women through the doubling and cutting of roles. Sensitive to the fact that disguise is a central feature of the story, she specifies two small female roles that should not be doubled 'as the audience will think it is "plot" – which, of course, it isn't'.[15]

And it wasn't just the cast that was unusually big. Michael Weight's set, although not an entirely accurate recreation of the Old Bailey, was an impressive representation of it. The problem lay in the fact that there are two locations in the play, and this necessitated large trucking units to effect the scene changes from Robarts' chambers into the courtroom. Built by Jack Brunskill and painted by Harkers, leaders in their respective fields, these were impressive items. Saunders' loyal lieutenant Verity Hudson, credited in the programme in bold type as 'Stage Director and Business Manager', was proud that her team were able to achieve the first scene change, which reveals the Old Bailey, in twenty-eight seconds.[16]

The question of how the jury should be portrayed is particularly interesting in terms of both cast numbers and the physicality of the set. Integral to the conceit of any courtroom drama is the fact that the audience is, in effect, the jury. Instead of struggling to second-guess a maverick detective as they unravel a mystery through a combination of homespun forensic techniques, psychological analysis and eccentric intuition, much of which would be inadmissible in court, the audience is asked to make an assessment based on the evidence as it is presented, supported by sometimes complex and often impassioned legal argument. The system itself, of course, is not infallible, so the audience must keep their wits about them; and with the character accused of murder facing the gallows if convicted, the stakes in 1953 were that much higher. Saunders and Christie exchanged notes on whether the jury should be physically represented on stage or whether the defence and the prosecution should simply address the audience. The problem with the jury being featured on stage, as well as the obvious issue of increasing the payroll by twelve people, was the practical one of where to seat them, without pulling focus from the important characters and while remaining relatively faithful to the Old Bailey's layout. Having actors playing the jury also to an extent disenfranchises the audience, who want to inhabit their own role as jurors. In the end, the set was designed so that only three jurors were visible, effectively minimising their on-stage impact and giving the audience the opportunity to make up the numbers.

Saunders' problems were not limited to the production's large, non-star cast and its outsize set. Despite the success of *The Hollow* and *The Mousetrap* (or maybe because of it), 'the Group' was still not opening its doors to him and, once again, he found himself struggling to secure a West End theatre. The only one available was the independently owned Winter Garden, which Saunders had wisely turned down for *The Mousetrap* and which, according to him, was 'the worst of all the white elephant theatres and an enormous sixteen hundred and forty seater . . . By this time all my capital had gone. I found I had underestimated the enormous cost of this production and I would be responsible for any excess. I was so scared of the Winter Garden that I would only agree to go there provided I could give one week's notice at any time within the first five days of the run.'[17] His contract with the Winter Garden confirms this unusual arrangement, and the fact that the theatre was prepared to offer such terms is indicative of how desperate they were to secure a production.[18]

In order to help take the curse off the Winter Garden, Saunders engaged a ten-piece 'entr'acte orchestra' to play before the performance and during the interval, having first obtained an agreement with the Musicians' Union that the musicians would be retained only so long as business permitted,[19] after which they would be replaced with the more usual Hammond organ. The leaflet advertising the production also boasts, 'This theatre has now been entirely re-seated, with more leg room and wider and more comfortable seats for patrons. Clean towels and soap are provided in all cloakrooms – without charge of course.'[20]

Even booking theatres for the short pre-West End tour proved problematic, particularly when Howard & Wyndham suddenly and inexplicably cancelled an engagement at one of their theatres. Following what Saunders believes to have been the personal intervention of Howard & Wyndham boss Prince Littler,[21] the booking was replaced with one at the Empire Theatre, Edinburgh, a variety theatre controlled by Moss Empires. Hardly ideal, but better than nothing; Saunders was grateful to Littler for getting involved, and where the Group was concerned there was nothing to be gained by arguing.

The tour opened on 28 September in Nottingham, where *The Hollow* and *The Mousetrap* had both started out, before moving on to Glasgow, Edinburgh and Sheffield. Notices were 'mixed', even in Nottingham, while business, particularly at Sheffield, was not sufficient to sustain the size of the production. Saunders was clearly becoming nervous that he should have heeded Christie's 'gipsy warning' and that the whole enterprise was indeed about to prove to be 'Saunders' Folly'.

He needn't have worried. When Witness for the Prosecution opened at the Winter Garden on 28 October, its first night was, by all accounts, an unqualified triumph, magnified by the sheer size of the audience. Saunders writes:

> If I had to choose my supreme moment in my theatre life this was it, and I shall never forget it as long as I live . . . Everything went perfectly. After innumerable curtain calls . . . the cast turned to the upper box where Agatha was sitting, and the entire company bowed. There was pandemonium in the theatre. Not only clapping and shouting, but people standing and waving. I have never in my life been at any theatre and heard such a reception. Dickie Attenborough had rushed round from *The Mousetrap* to be there at the end. John Mills was there, too, standing at the back of our box, clapping and cheering, and shouting as loudly as anyone. And Agatha Christie, completely stunned by the reception, was beaming and waving at the audience . . . as she left, she whispered to me the understatement of all time, 'it's rather fun, isn't it?[22]

Max Mallowan recalls, 'This is the only occasion on which I have known Agatha enjoy the agony of a first night: from the opening it was clear that this was a winner, and at the end the cast bowed in unison to the authoress. Peter Saunders, who produced a wonderful scenario and who has never stinted any production said that he had never seen the like of this *finale* in which one and all displayed their sincere admiration.'[23]

Malcolm MacDougall, a business contact of Saunders, had persuaded his client, a Mrs Duke, to invest £500 in the production, and wrote to Saunders to congratulate him and thank him for the first night tickets for his wife and himself. Saunders replied, 'You mention my courage in taking this big theatre for this very big show, but I in turn would like to congratulate you on your courage in advising a client to put money into a show with a person that you know only slightly. I am certain that it will show a substantial profit.' Rather alarmingly, he continues, 'I am terribly sorry about Gwenda's dress. I saw it from my box, and was about to come down and see if I could do anything when I saw the flames had been extinguished. I really think Mrs Duke should buy her a new dress.'[24] The mind boggles.

In a week in which the Old Vic Company were presenting *King John*, the *Sunday Express* ran the headline 'AGATHA TOPPLES THE BARD OFF HIS PEDESTAL' above a review that declared, 'This is a rattling good play, Agatha Christie has the stuff of playwriting in her. Her paradox is that her characters are unreal, and yet she makes them live. *Witness For the Prosecution*, as a matter of fact, is a much better play than *King John*, which is also by a British author. Yes, the Old Vic is right to give us Shakespeare's failures as well as his successes . . . At any rate, it was Agatha Christie's week in the theatre, and not even Shakespeare can deprive her of that honour.'[25]

The *Daily Telegraph* remarked:

Of late there have been unhappy signs that the Winter Garden might be lost before long in the trackless hinterland of unexplored London, as happens to theatres when they go out of fashion.

But the production there last night of Agatha Christie's exciting murder trial *Witness for the Prosecution* puts it fairly back on the map again; this play might run for a century. Once more the Christie conjuring trick has come off. Once more in the plain sight of the audience the pea has been insinuated under the wrong thimble. Once more we have been led down the garden path – or at least I have . . . Apart from being a clever puzzle, this is an extremely actable play. Trial scenes are proverbially effective, and this one is jam for a number of players. Patricia Jessel in particular, as the German woman, gets a big chance and takes it in a big way. She gives a beautifully judged and controlled performance, and has a great share in the play's success.[26]

And the *Daily Express* reported the rapturous reception of the audience: 'They cheered, they stamped, they shouted "Author!" All thirty of the cast bowed solemnly to a stage-box. But Agatha Christie, 62, sat alone in the dark, looking like Queen Victoria, smiling . . . "If you dare shine a light on me," she had told her backer, Peter Saunders, "you'll never have another play of mine." He kept faith . . . I salute Patricia Jessel for a brilliant impersonation as the wife. D.A. Clarke-Smith is an iron prosecuting attorney. And Mrs Christie is the most infuriating darling of them all.'[27]

The *Daily Mail* reported, 'This is not only Agatha Christie's biggest play (it has a cast of thirty) but her best; an ingenious and absorbing murder thriller with more than the usual share of comedy . . . We have had court scenes often enough before, and impoverished young men accused of killing rich elderly women are no novelty but Miss Christie stirs these familiar ingredients into an evening of crisp excitement.'[28] And the *Daily Mirror* joined it in applauding the playwright's successful experiment with the courtroom drama genre: 'Agatha Christie must be happy this morning. While one thriller, *The Mousetrap*, is packing them in at the Ambassadors Theatre, another play of hers called *Witness for the Prosecution* opened with great success last night at the Winter Garden Theatre. The Old Bailey murder trial is a good theatrical bet, but the way Miss Christie treats this one makes it outstanding . . .'[29]

One fascinating press analysis of the Christie theatrical phenomenon came the following August in an article in the *New York Herald Tribune* headlined 'Second-Rate London Plays Have Rewarding Virtues'. In it, Walter F. Kerr compared the Broadway and West End theatregoing experiences, from the American perspective:

One of the nicest things about the London theatre is that you can go to a second-rate play on purpose.

You wouldn't do that in New York. You may, indeed, find yourself staring at second-rate stuff on Broadway with alarming frequency – but never because you meant to. If you wind up at a routine domestic comedy hereabouts it is only because someone has told you that it is really much more than a routine domestic comedy – that it is, in fact, first rate.

Or you may conceivably settle for an inferior entertainment out of sheer desperation, because you've got out of town friends on your hands and you can't get into anything you know to be better. The tacit understanding in the American theater is that every theater-going adventure is going to be – and had darn well better be – of the highest quality. An understandable bitterness is often the result.

The British theater is a great deal more candid and a great deal more relaxed about the matter. It offers, with no apologies at all, at least two flatly and imperturbably opposed levels of playgoing. During the current summer in London it is possible to satisfy one's presumably better higher tastes by traipsing off to the Haymarket, where John Gielgud, Ralph Richardson and Irene Worth are giving superb performances in a quasi-Chekhovian cameo called 'A Day by the Sea' . . .

But it is also possible – in London – to turn squarely about and march off to an Agatha Christie thriller that doesn't pretend to be anything more than an Agatha Christie thriller.

Going to one of these straight-faced, but unmistakenly

genial, entertainments is, in fact, an experience exactly comparable to settling down for the evening with any detective novel you happen to fancy. As theater it is depressurized – casual, undemanding, irresponsible, amiable.

You drop in, let's say, on Miss Christie's 'Witness for the Prosecution.' You notice at once that the hushed and slightly frigid atmosphere that pursues the 'best' in theater is missing. The audience certainly hasn't dressed – what's good enough at noon around the house is good enough here. Nor has the tempo of the day undergone any solemn change for the worse: the playgoers are flushed, busy, noisy, pleasantly knockabout.

Even the ushers are at their chattiest and most companionable, the starch all gone from their uniform and manners. The actors are by no means embarrassed by the relatively primitive work they are called upon to do; they love it, are loved in return and are never above glancing directly at the audience for approval after a particularly good riposte.

When the evening is over, no one is in a hurry to go home. And no one hates himself for having come. He knew exactly what he was getting into . . .

The London theater is lucky I think. By refusing to be on its very best behaviour all the time, it has left room for the idler, the family outing and the lowbrow. (We have more or less effectively discouraged the lowbrow from bothering with Broadway.)

And the virtue of this amiable conspiracy isn't just that it keeps so many actors and writers at work. It has the good grace to invite a much larger segment of the public into the playhouse. It helps form a habit.[30]

In response, Saunders wrote to Kerr, not to object to the 'lowbrow' label but to applaud his perspicacity in celebrating it. This was typical of former journalist Saunders' direct level of engagement with critics, and the letter provides a fine example of his committed and articulate advocacy of populist theatre:

My Dear Kerr,

I was most interested in your article, date lined London, August 14th, headed 'Second rate London plays have rewarding virtues', as I produce plays – including 'Witness For The Prosecution'.

At least I see in your article a clue as to why so many British plays fail on Broadway.

From what you say, the American theatregoers live on a diet of caviar and grilled nightingales' tongues on toast. There is no room for the hunk of bread and cheese.

London critics can be as devastating and hypercritical as those in New York. But in the past twenty years they have gradually come round to the view that they must judge plays not on the grounds of 'Is it good?', but 'Is it good of its kind?'

London critics have frequently panned plays, at the same time qualifying their disapproval with 'The public liked it' and 'The audience laughed hugely'. Those plays have frequently become box office successes, and yet the critics' integrity has been retained.

Now I think that these critics have done a vast service to the London theatre. The theatregoing public is no longer confined to London's West End, but is 90% comprised of the outlying districts and provincial towns. The critics, by not strangling at birth plays which are good in their own sphere, have encouraged a brand new theatregoing public. This same theatregoing public might have to be dragged into the theatre by Agatha Christie or broad farce, but they may end up by taking a look in at Chekhov.

I regret deeply that you say that lowbrows have been discouraged from bothering with Broadway. You cannot surely expect to have all the New York theatre full of what you call first-rate plays? Or if they are first-rate in type, some of them must be inevitably fifth rate in quality.

Is it not better to see a good play by Agatha Christie than a bad one by Chekhov? The wine connoisseur may disdain the common beer, but beer will always have a larger public than wine.

I am sorry I did not happen to meet you when you were in London, as I should have liked to have discussed the subject with you at length.

Kind regards

Yours sincerely,

Peter Saunders[31]

Needless to say, Kerr responded positively to Saunders' missive, and the two struck up a dialogue.

For all its populist appeal, or perhaps because of it, Christie's work was also an enduring favourite with the royal family. Both Princess Margaret and the Duchess of Kent attended *Witness for the Prosecution*, the latter on two occasions, and on 1 December 1953 the Duke and Duchess of Windsor made their first appearance at a London theatre since their intended marriage led to the 1936 abdication crisis. The audience stood and applauded when they took their seats. The ultimate royal command performance, though, took place after the end of the West End run, when a production was specially mounted for two weeks in May 1955 by the Theatre Royal Windsor to coincide with a visit to their local theatre by the Queen and the Duke of Edinburgh. John Counsell, the theatre's director, believed that the visit was intended by the royals to be a gesture of support for the repertory movement, and as such it was no doubt a welcome one. He and the Queen's private secretary had both suggested *Witness for the Prosecution* as the play to mark the occasion, as the newly crowned monarch had been sorry to miss it in the West End. When the Duke of Edinburgh enquired of a member of the theatre's staff whether the news of the royal visit had made any difference to business, the response was, 'Well, sir, to a play by Agatha Christie on a Saturday night, the honest answer must be "No"!'[32]

If ever a playwright could boast of being 'by Royal Appointment' then it was Agatha Christie; but royal endorsement, of course, wins you no friends amongst the chroniclers of post-war theatre history. And, ironically, neither does successfully appealing to the widest possible market. Theatre histories tell us that in 1953 Joan Littlewood's pioneering Theatre Workshop took over the Theatre Royal Stratford East, but not that a play by Agatha Christie was filling the Winter Garden.

Amongst the many publicity schemes devised by Saunders to promote *Witness for the Prosecution*, arrangements were made to cancel a performance early in the run so that a five-minute extract could be performed live on *Face the Music*, a television programme then fronted by popular bandleader Henry Hall. Although it is not entirely clear from the surviving paperwork whether this scheme reached fruition, pay rates for the actors were agreed with the BBC and Saunders himself prepared a five-minute script featuring a narrator that he had written in for the occasion. 'I am no script-writer,' he modestly declared to his BBC contact.[33]

A combination of critical approval and astute marketing ensured that *Witness for the Prosecution* was another financial success for Saunders, despite the perceived disadvantages of its West End home. In a letter to a prospective investor, he had warned, 'Before definitely deciding to participate, I do feel I should stress the fact that this particular play is a complete speculation, and unlike The Mousetrap has a negligible value as to its subsidiary rights.'[34] He presumably meant by this that the play's large scale was likely to deter repertory productions. Ironically, it was *The Mousetrap* that would fail to realise the full potential of its subsidiary income, owing to the withholding of repertory and amateur rights during the West End run. The investors in *Witness for the Prosecution*, on the other hand, were destined to make an astonishing return on subsidiary rights; when the final accounts were drawn up in 1962, seven years after the end of its West End run, the profit distributed to investors, including income from repertory, touring and international sales, as well as a substantial film deal, stood at £98,812.[35] Not bad for a play that cost £4,200 to put on.

Six investors had between them contributed £2,000 to a

£5,000 capitalisation, including reserve funds, leaving Peter Saunders responsible for £3,000. As Saunders states, the costs of the production were higher than anticipated, meaning that the reserve fund (£800) was unusually low as a proportion of the capital raised, and he is therefore likely to have had to underwrite the project himself in its early performance weeks. It is perhaps indicative of his nervousness that the production was technically mounted by Aurora Productions Ltd, another company he owned, rather than by his main company, Peter Saunders Ltd. This also effectively protected *The Mousetrap* from any potential financial fallout from *Witness for the Prosecution*. In the event, the gamble paid off handsomely. As well as its 37.5 per cent producer's share of the profit, its own investment meant that Aurora Productions benefited from 60 per cent of the investors' 62.5 per cent share; this amounted to 75 per cent of the overall profit, well over a million pounds in today's money. With her £500 investment, Mrs Duke would have received her money back plus £6,176 (around £92,000 today). She would certainly have been able to afford to buy Mrs MacDougall a new dress.

The play's investors were not entitled to a share of amateur licensing income, although, perhaps precisely because of its large number of small roles, it was to prove hugely popular in this market too. Samuel French entered into their usual deal for English language publishing and amateur rights as soon as the play had opened in the West End, and Saunders benefited from half of Christie's 80 per cent of amateur fees for the duration of his own licence.

Forgive me if I pause to quote almost two pages about *Witness for the Prosecution* from Agatha Christie's autobiography. To me, this passage sums up perfectly the huge thrill she got from her involvement with every element of the process of creating a piece of theatre and her deep understanding of and engagement with that process. Nowhere does she share with us the experience of writing a novel with the passion and detail that she does here:

It was one of my plays that I liked best myself. I was as nearly satisfied with that play as I have been with any. I didn't want to write it; I was terrified of writing it. I was forced into it by Peter Saunders, who has wonderful powers of persuasion. Gentle bullying, subtle cajoling.

'Of course you can do it.'

'I don't know a thing about legal procedure. I should make a fool of myself.'

'That's quite easy. You can read it up and we'll have a barrister on hand to clear up anomalies and make it go right.'

'I couldn't write a court scene.'

'Yes, you could – you've seen court scenes played. You can read up trials.'

'Oh, I don't know . . . I don't think I *could*.'

Peter Saunders continued to say that of course I could, and that I must begin because he wanted the play quickly. So, hypnotised and always amenable to the power of suggestion, I read quantities of the *Famous Trials* series. I asked questions of solicitors as well as barristers; and finally I got interested and suddenly I felt I was enjoying myself – that wonderful moment in writing which does not usually last long but which carries one on with a terrific verve as a large wave carries you to shore. 'This is lovely – I am doing it – it's working – now, where shall we go next?' There is that priceless moment of seeing the thing – not on the stage but in your mind's eye. There it all is, the real thing, in a real court – not the Old Bailey because I hadn't been there yet – but a real court sketchily etched in the background of my mind. I saw the nervous, desperate young man in the dock, and the enigmatic woman who came into the witness box to give evidence not for her lover but for the Crown. It is one of the quickest pieces of writing that I have done – I think it only took me two or three weeks after my preparatory reading.

Naturally it had to have some changes in the procedure, and I also had to fight desperately for my chosen end to the play. Nobody liked it, nobody wanted it, everyone said it would spoil the whole thing. Everyone said: 'You can't get away with that,' and wanted a different end – preferably one used in the original short story I had written years ago. But a short story is not a play. The short story had no court scene in it, no trial for murder. It was a mere sketch of an accused person and an enigmatic witness. I stuck out over the end. I don't often stick out for things, I don't always have sufficient conviction, but I had here. I wanted that end. I wanted it so much that I wouldn't agree to have the play put on without it.

I got my end, and it was successful. Some people said it was a double cross, or dragged in, but I knew it wasn't; it was logical. It was what could have happened, what might have happened, and in my view what probably would have happened – possibly with a little less violence, but the psychology would have been right, and the one little fact that lay beneath it had been implicit all through the play . . .

Of all the stage pieces I have had produced this came closest in casting to my own mental picture: Derek Bloomfield [sic] as the young accused; the legal characters whom I had never really visualised clearly, since I knew little of the law, but who suddenly came alive; and Patricia Jessel, who had the hardest part of all, and on whom the success of the play most certainly depended. I could not have found a more perfect actress. The part was a difficult one, especially in the first act, where the lines cannot help. They are hesitant, reserved, and the whole force of the acting has to be in the eyes, the reticence, the feeling of something malign held back. She suggested this perfectly – a taut, enigmatic personality. I still think her acting of the part of Romaine Helder [sic] was one of the best performances I have seen on a stage.[36]

There speaks a true playwright, fully engaged with her art on all levels. And, if nothing else, this passage gives the lie to Hubert Gregg's accusation that Christie never credited Saunders sufficiently for her theatrical successes. In her introduction to

Saunders' *The Mousetrap Man*, written after this but published before it, she reiterates, 'His principal victory was making me write my play, *Witness for the Prosecution* . . . I still think it is the best play I have written and both Peter Saunders and others agree – but without him it would never have been written.'[37]

Her husband also agreed with Agatha that it was her best play:

> Some of Agatha's plays have earned as much fame and popularity as her books, and I think that most critics would name *Witness for the Prosecution* as the tops: The Old Bailey as the theatrical *mise en scene* held a magnetic attention for the audience, which felt itself in the dock; no-one who has seen the play will be able to forget it – the highest tribute one can pay to a work of art. Patricia Jessel gave a brilliant performance, and the play was destined for a good run, but the size of the cast, the amplitude and inconvenience of the theatre, prevented it from enjoying the long run that it deserved.[38]

Max, interestingly, is the name of the female protagonist's alleged lover in the play, taken from the short story which pre-dates Agatha's relationship with Mallowan. There are some jottings which indicate that she toyed with changing the name to Ivan from that of her own husband for the play, but in the end she stuck with the reference to 'my beloved Max'.

In January 1954 Agatha booked a big group of friends to see *Witness for the Prosecution* and in February, buoyed by her theatrical success, she hosted a party at the Savoy for one hundred friends and relations. The guest list included Dorothy L. Sayers and Campbell and Dorothy Christie, whose successful court-martial drama *Carrington VC* had opened at the Westminster Theatre three months ahead of *Witness for the Prosecution*. Although a success, it had not proved to be the threat to Agatha's play that Saunders had feared.

In May 1954, declining box office income justified replacing the orchestra with an organist and Saunders negotiated a rent reduction with his landlords. These belt-tightening measures enabled *Witness for the Prosecution* to continue to run success- fully at the Winter Garden until the end of January 1955, where it eventually completed 458 performances. Edmund Cork was a happy man. When the production had been running for just over a month, he wrote to Harold Ober in New York, 'This play is the biggest success we have had for years. It was put on at the worst time of year in the worst theatre in the West End, and it is just packing out. We are selling rights for it all over Europe on terms which we had only heard about before!'[39] And it wasn't just Europe that was interested. Broadway was also beckoning again, and this time all were agreed that Christie's play was sufficiently 'first rate' to pass muster on the Great White Way.

As soon as the London production of *Witness for the Prosecution* opened, American producers started to bid for the Broadway rights. In New York Christie was still celebrated for the outstanding success of *Ten Little Indians* a decade earlier. The brief pre-war appearances of Morton's *The Fatal Alibi* and Vosper's *Love From a Stranger* were long forgotten, *Hidden Horizon* had sunk without trace after twelve performances in 1946, *Towards Zero* and *The Suspects* had never made it to Broadway and *The Mousetrap* had deliberately been withheld. The scene was well and truly set for a second Broadway triumph for Christie.

Saunders and Cork's growing impatience with the Shuberts over their handling of *The Hollow* effectively ruled them out as Broadway partners for *Witness for the Prosecution*, and Lee Shubert's death in December 1953 in any case drew a conven- ient line under their dealings with his company. In his autobi- ography, Basil Dean recounts how he had found some respite from his own wearisome dealings with the Shuberts in the good company of independent New York producer Gilbert Miller, a Sullivan-sized personality who took Dean under his hospitable wing: 'I should have had a thin time of it during those first days in New York but for Gilbert Miller's friendliness.'[40] Now, over thirty years later, it was to this characterful figure that Saunders also turned.

Sixty-nine-year-old New Yorker Miller was well known on the London theatre scene, where he was involved in the St James's Theatre, and had enjoyed success as a producer on both sides of the Atlantic. Indeed, it was as a West End producer that Miller had first made his mark, clocking up sixteen West End productions, including the 1916 hit *Daddy Long Legs*, before his first Broadway venture in 1922. His London years had been notable for a successful business relationship with Gerald du Maurier, and although since the 1930s he had focused more on his work in New York, he continued to produce regularly in London as well. No one could have been better positioned to deal with the issues surrounding the presentation of Christie's sometimes very 'English' work on Broadway, and Miller personified a showbiz pizzazz that Saunders and Cork had doubtless found lacking in their seemingly interminable dealings with the Shuberts' lawyers.

Ably supported by his Hungarian general manager, George Banyai, Miller was very much the man of the moment in New York; in 1951 he had presented the Oliviers in a transfer of their London success alternating Shaw's *Caesar and Cleopatra* with Shakespeare's *Antony and Cleopatra* and, by way of contrast, had introduced Broadway to twenty-two-year-old Audrey Hepburn in *Gigi*. His *Times* obituary would note that 'Miller's association with a play was a guarantee that, whether it was by Harold Pinter or Terence Rattigan, by Anouilh or Agatha Christie, it would be presented with theatrical glitter, excitement and a conscientious regard for its style and purpose.'[41] Better still, Miller operated Henry Miller's Theatre (now the Stephen Sondheim), founded by his father in 1918, a truly independent concern that had escaped the clutches of the Shuberts. And it was here that *Witness for the Prosecution* was destined to find its Broadway home.

'A lot of American producers wanted to buy *Witness for the Prosecution*,' writes Saunders, 'and I decided to co-produce it with Gilbert Miller, chiefly because he seemed quite happy for me to take a much more active part in the production than the others wanted me to do.'[42] It was perhaps because Miller was such a well-known figure on the London scene that Cork and Saunders felt confident to draw up the American paperwork themselves and, despite the tortuous *debâcle* with the Shuberts over *The Hollow*, that they once again did so without consulting Harold Ober and his lawyers. They did, however, take on board Ober's previous warning that it was essential to use the Dramatists Guild Minimum Basic Agreement, ensuring that this labyrinthine document formed the basis of the contract. Additional paperwork[43] specified that principal roles should be played as far as possible by Englishmen (leaving the large number of non-speaking roles to American Equity members) and emphasised that no changes to the script could be made without the author's permission. It was also explicitly stated that a share in the income from the sale of film rights would only be triggered by a minimum run of six weeks on Broadway.

Saunders had exercised his own American option,[44] so the agreement was technically between him and Miller. It stipulated that he would receive 10 per cent of the Broadway box office (of which two-thirds was passed on to Christie) as well as 25 per cent of profits. The production was to be billed as co-produced by Peter Saunders, and he was to receive 'first class transportation' to New York and 'reasonable hotel and travel expenses' during rehearsals. The production's playbill,[45] as well as its glossy souvenir brochure,[46] does indeed clearly announce that it was presented by 'Gilbert Miller and Peter Saunders', although one suspects that the playwright herself might have taken issue with the tagline describing the play as a 'Murder Mystery'. I's were dotted and T's were crossed on matters relating to the division of income from stock rights (which were to prove a substantial source of earnings) and the date by which a production had to be achieved in order for Miller's licence to be activated; the latter was specified as 31 October 1954, subsequently extended to 30 November, failing which his £1,500 advance payment would be strictly non-refundable. All bases had been covered. Or so it seemed . . .

Miller signed his deal with Saunders on 27 November 1953,[47] a month after the West End opening. Two months later he heard from Francis L. Sullivan, who had been notable by his absence from Christie's theatrical projects since relinquishing his role in *Murder on the Nile* to David Horne. With Horne now playing Robarts in London and Miller under pressure from Saunders to cast English actors, this was clearly an opportune moment for Christie's portly thespian friend, who had worked for Miller in London, to throw his hat into the ring: 'A few months ago Mrs Mallowan, who is an old friend of mine, sent me the play *Witness for the Prosecution* as she thought the part of the QC for the defence would be an ideal part for me. Unfortunately I was engaged on a movie at the time and unable to do anything about it. Recently I heard from her again that you have now acquired the play for Broadway and so I am writing to you to ask you to consider me when you are casting the play. I am particularly anxious to do a play again as I have not done one for about five years, and think this part would suit me admirably. I hope you agree!'[48]

Like Saunders, Miller had found that performers and investors to whom he sent the script did not like the ending; indeed, correspondence indicates that, as well as half an hour of material being cut from the original, an alternative ending had been prepared in case audiences did not respond well to it on the pre-Broadway tour. There is no reference in the extensive Saunders–Christie casting correspondence to Sullivan ever having been offered the role in the West End production, but his letter to Miller was timely, and Miller wrote back immediately to say that he thought it would be an excellent idea for him to play Robarts. Saunders assisted the casting process by releasing Patricia Jessel from her West End contract in order to appear in the Broadway production, and another British actor, Ernest Clark – who had taken over the role of John Cristow for the West End production of *The Hollow* when Hubert Gregg left the cast in order to appear in Disney's *Robin Hood* – flew out to play Mayhew.

Relations between Saunders and Miller got off to a bumpy start when doubts were raised over the original short story's copyright status in the USA, and when Miller discovered that Harold Ober had already sold some American television rights. Miller felt that this risked stealing the Broadway production's thunder and could also jeopardise the future sale of film rights. In the end it was confirmed that the television rights had only been sold for a number of one-off broadcasts, originally on both the BBC and NBC in 1949, and then again in America on CBS in 1950 and 1953, the last of these starring Edward G. Robinson. As these television adaptations were based on Christie's original short story they bore little resemblance to her own masterful dramatisation and, despite much heated correspondence on the subject, this all turned out to be something of a storm in a teacup.

It rang a bell with Edmund Cork, though, who remembered that when the 1953 television play was broadcast in America, Francis L. Sullivan had written to Christie to say that it would destroy any chance of a Broadway production. Christie's understandable concerns had been allayed by Ober's assurances that the broadcast would, in fact, create interest in the play. Now, believing that Sullivan was likely to be responsible for stirring up trouble with Miller as well, Cork wrote to Ober:

> You ask what is behind all this. I cannot tell you definitely, but I have seen in the press that Miller proposes to star Francis Sullivan in this play. Sullivan has always been a thorn in our flesh – he was very close to Agatha at one time, and has always imagined himself as the embodiment of Hercule Poirot. On a number of occasions over the years he has tried to make trouble over the way we have handled the Christie property. You will remember that it was his cabling Agatha that started the previous excitement when Edward G. Robinson starred in the J. Walter Thomson television show. Sullivan is rather an overpowering person, and if, when Miller was fixing up the arrangement with him, he made heavy weather about the TV exploitation of the subject – about which apparently Miller was unaware – I can just imagine Miller writing rather an

intense letter to Saunders, which started the whole
wretched business.[49]

All of this serves to highlight what an unknown quantity the
new medium of television was when it came to the licensing
of rights in the 1940s and 50s.

Sullivan was not the only Briton involved with Christie's stage
work in the UK to make contact with Miller. Douglas Clarke-
Smith, who played Myers the prosecuting counsel in the London
production, reminded him that he had another Christie connection: 'Did you know I produced [i.e. directed] Black Coffee for
Alec Rea at the St Martin's in 1931 with Sullivan as Poirot. I
have done four or five for Bronnie Albery since the war – they
were all successes. Could I direct Witness for the Prosecution
or something? If you do it in New York. Please. Yours ever,
Clarkie.'[50] Clarke-Smith, who had appeared alongside Sullivan
and Wallace Douglas in the 1937 broadcast of *The Wasp's Nest*,
and whose Oxford law degree made him well qualified for the
role of Myers, didn't get the job, and sadly was to be involved
in a serious domestic accident that would see Hubert Gregg
standing in for him at the Winter Garden in the autumn of 1954.

In the meantime, Robert Lewis had been appointed director
of the Broadway production. 'Gilbert Miller had sent me a list
of possible directors,' writes Saunders in *The Mousetrap Man*,
'and I suggested Robert Lewis, whose productions of *Brigadoon*
and *Teahouse of the August Moon* had been so brilliant. I
couldn't have made a better choice . . . Bobby Lewis had never
seen *Witness* in London and yet he directed it with exactly the
same feel and touch.'[51] In fact, the general consensus was that
Lewis's production was superior to Wallace Douglas's; hardly
surprising given that this was an exciting and credible directorial appointment in the same league as Irene Hentschel and
Peter Cotes. In the 1930s Lewis had been a founder-member
of New York's Group Theatre, which took their inspiration from
Constantin Stanislavski's pioneering work at the Moscow Art
Theatre. Stanislavski's techniques, which informed his successful
interpretations of Chekhov's plays, are examined in some detail

in *Theatre in Soviet Russia* by Andre van Gyseghem, the original director of *Black Coffee* at the Embassy Theatre before Clarke-Smith was put at the helm for its West End transfer. Stanislavski and New York's Group Theatre were to inspire Peter Cotes' London experiments in ensemble theatre, and Lewis meanwhile went on to co-found New York's legendary Actors Studio in 1947 before leaving to focus on his career as one of Broadway's most successful and respected directors.

Although this is probably the first time that the names Constantin Stanislavski and Agatha Christie have appeared in the same sentence, it is interesting to note the associations between some of her most successful stage work and advocates of the Group Theatre ethic like Lewis, Cotes and van Gyseghem. Cotes adopted the title *No Star Nonsense* for his 1949 book championing ensemble theatre; and it was Christie's aversion to 'star nonsense' from Laughton and Sullivan that led her to excise the character of Poirot from her stage work. When Hubert Gregg observes that Christie's plays were difficult to cast because each role only enjoys a brief moment in the limelight before fading into the background,[52] he is effectively identifying the fact that they are best delivered by an ensemble company. And when actress Mary Law remarks of Christie's dialogue that if actors 'can make it real, make it sincere, then it works 100 per cent, let's face it, but if they can't it is better to give it up',[53] she seems to be implying that it could be best suited to Stanislavskian 'method' actors.

I am not implying that Christie herself was in any way a conscious disciple of the Group Theatre ethic, or that she would even have been aware of Stanislavski and his work. She knew that her plays needed stars in them to sell tickets, and even considered Charles Laughton 'lucky' for her despite his comprehensive destruction of the role of Poirot. But it is interesting to note that her work shines when it is interpreted by those who have an appreciation of these methodologies; and it is perhaps ironic that *The Hollow*, with its Chekhovian resonances, was entrusted to the relatively lightweight Hubert Gregg. When Richard Attenborough recommended Peter Cotes as director for *The Mousetrap* he would have been well aware of Cotes' commitment to 'Group' work; now, on Broadway, a Christie play was again in the hands of an advocate of, and skilled practitioner in, ensemble theatre.

The pre-Broadway tour opened in New Haven on 18 November and it is clear that from the outset all was not well. Sullivan was slow to learn his part and erratic in its delivery; by the time the production reached its second touring date in Boston, he had lost his voice and was missing performances. In early December, with the Broadway opening a fortnight away, Miller's lieutenant George Banyai wrote to Saunders that there was 'so far no improvement' in Sullivan and that Robert Lewis wanted him replaced as soon as possible 'on a permanent basis'.[54] Matters were made worse by the fact that business on tour was poor, although Saunders was able to reassure Banyai that this had also been the case on the pre-West End tour.

Clearly it was not practical to replace Sullivan before the Broadway premiere, but he appears to have been no more reliable once the production had opened in New York. Lewis, who was by that time in Hollywood directing *Anything Goes* for Paramount, wrote to Banyai, 'As for Sullivan, I cannot tell you how shocked I am at the many letters and reports I receive about his sloppy performance. This is the first time this has ever happened to me in a production of mine and I frankly am at a loss how to act from this distance.'[55] Sullivan, an egotist both on and off stage, of course represented the antithesis to Lewis' cherished ensemble ethic. To make matters worse, Miller agreed to give Sullivan a week off from the Broadway run to undertake a television role. Lewis was apoplectic, writing to Saunders, in whom he appears to have found an unexpected ally, 'This is outrageous and I don't see why Agatha Christie permits such behaviour.'[56]

Witness for the Prosecution opened at Broadway's Henry Miller's Theatre on 16 December 1954 and the reception was every bit as good as it had been in London. Two days later, a clearly ecstatic Patricia Jessel wrote to Peter Saunders:

The first night reception was simply tremendous – as good as our London first night. My dressing room overflowed with flowers and cables before the show and with enthusiastic people after the show. Later, having sent a cable to George [her husband], I went over to join some people at Sardi's and Peter, it was New Haven all over again. The entire restaurant applauded!! I couldn't believe my ears! All sorts of people kept coming up to say nice things, and it was altogether wonderful. And Peter, don't think that I have forgotten where all this began because I haven't, and I shall always be grateful.

Father Miller [i.e. Gilbert Miller] now calls me Pat, he kisses me(!), and last night he brought in the proof of the new ad. for my approval. A large picture of me and a smaller one of Larry [Sullivan] – and lots of quotes from the reviews, most of which say lovely things about me. Heaven! I'm a very spoilt brat! I'm an ecstatically happy girl! . . . Don't look now but Jessel's a star! Get her!![57]

The hugely successful American radio entrepreneur Donald Flamm, a friend of Saunders – though he had distinguished himself by turning down investment in both *The Mousetrap* and *Witness for the Prosecution*, much to both his own and Saunders' amusement – cabled him in London at 2 a.m. with news of the show's reception and wrote the next morning to say:

Your holiday season should be very happy indeed! The audience last night was wildly enthusiastic. Cheers for Sullivan and Jessel and many curtain calls. When Jessel made her grand entrance at Sardis after the opening everyone in the restaurant applauded her – the kind of an ovation that is usually reserved only for our theatrical 'greats' when they do something quite outstanding. That should give you an idea . . . Aren't you going to come over and take some bows? After all you are the original producer and this is your once-in-a-lifetime opportunity to cash in on the avalanche of personal publicity that is yours for the asking. And in this business modesty does not pay off; on the contrary, publicity sells tickets at the box office![58]

On the face of it, Flamm was perhaps an unlikely ally, being a leading light of the American Anti-Defamation League which, in 1947, had taken Christie's American publishers Dodd, Mead & Co. to task for allegedly anti-semitic references in the novel of *The Hollow*.

Miller's own postbag from the great and the good of New York confirms the production's sensational reception, and the audience's response was echoed by the press. *The New York Times'* legendary drama critic Brooks Atkinson had led the derision of *Hidden Horizon*, but he devoted three columns to his plaudits for Christie's latest Broadway venture:

> In the murder mystery the British are the expert technicians. Frederick Knott's *Dial M for Murder* played the game according to the rules for 552 performances in this city. And now Agatha Christie's *Witness for the Prosecution* has skipped across the Atlantic to establish a career of its own. The rules of crime fiction are so exacting that they are known best to postgraduate students in the field. But *Dial M for Murder* and *Witness for the Prosecution* have one thing in common; they are frankly make-believe. You enjoy them all the more because you know that they are not real. In the last scene Miss Christie switches everything around so swiftly and decisively that the curtain falls on a sensational climax . . . good mystery plays are acted as if they were masterpieces of dramatic art. That is a traditional part of the game. In this respect *Witness for the Prosecution* is above reproach . . . Francis L. Sullivan . . . gives a grandiloquent performance with an undertone of humour. Imperiously realistic on the surface, he has his tongue in his cheek . . . by the breadth of his playing he represents the true spirit of the murder mystery. It's a game. In the twists of the plot and the expertness of the playing, *Witness for the Prosecution* is one of the best.[59]

Peter Saunders' new friend, Walter Kerr of the *Herald Tribune*, agreed:

Miss Christie is gloriously in her element. That element – the whodunit with a corpse, a chief suspect, and a thundering surprise at the thrill finish – isn't regarded as one of the higher reaches of literature at the moment and most purveyors of simple-minded theatrical excitement feel called upon to dress their humble puzzles in various more worthy guises . . . Miss Christie is unembarrassed by her materials. She loves them, without apology . . . the plotting is beautifully deceptive; the tug and pull as our sympathies switch from one suspect to another is infinitely adroit. Everything is ingeniously prepared for, everything is meticulously laid before our eyes, and – a miracle in this day of weary formulas – everything is astonishing at eleven o'clock. Because Miss Christie takes her limited craft seriously, because she is perfectly at home in all its devious corridors, because she is superbly equipped to engage in a battle of wits and win it, this guessing-game at the Henry Miller is a perfect sample of its kind. Director Robert Lewis has caught the head-on, do-it-straight spirit of his author and succeeded in staging a crowded, crackling, tight-reined performance that is superior to the long-running London original. He has brought Patricia Jessel over – after two years in the part – to give dignity and unfaltering tension to the role of a wife whose testimony will either save or destroy her accused husband. Just how good Miss Jessel is cannot be suggested without giving away half of the plot . . .[60]

Despite a couple of doubters, it appears that the highbrow Broadway critics lambasted by Saunders in his correspondence with Kerr were prepared on this occasion to let their hair down and engage with the piece on its own terms. 'The most delightful mystery-murder-melodrama in years. In *Witness for the Prosecution* Agatha Christie has given us something wonderful,' said the *New York Post*.[61] 'The new Agatha Christie thriller is a major Broadway hit. The solution is a humdinger,' said *Life*.[62]

'Expert Agatha Christie has fetched us a finely conducted English courtroom trial and then, when all is over, overturned it with not one shattering twist, but three,' said *Time*;[63] I count four, but they definitely stuck with the London ending. In a review headlined 'Christie Mystery 100% entertainment', the *World-Telegram and Sun* remarked that 'For sheer, unadulterated entertainment there is nothing around town to equal *Witness for the Prosecution*. Surely Agatha Christie is responsible for more mystery stories and plays than anyone else alive. This time she has surpassed even herself for ingenuity and excitement . . . It is grand, tingling fun.'[64] And the *Daily News* gifted the production's publicist, the legendary Richard Maney, the headline 'Murder Will Sell Out'.[65]

Neither Christie nor Saunders had been able to attend the Broadway premiere of *Witness for the Prosecution*, as they were busy preparing for their next West End production, *Spider's Web*, though Saunders had managed to get to New Haven for the opening of its pre-Broadway tour. There was still unfinished business with the Shuberts relating to their licence for *The Hollow* which Saunders hoped he could resolve on his visit to America, and he was keen to meet with Harold Ober's lawyers Howard Reinheimer and Irving Cohen to discuss this. Edmund Cork wrote a formal letter for Ober to use when presenting Saunders to third parties: 'This will introduce Peter Saunders who, as you know, is coming to New York in connection with the production of *Witness for the Prosecution*. Peter Saunders has become about the most successful independent theatre manager here, and is very important to us as he presents all the Christie plays, but it is more to the point that he is a very good friend, and I would appreciate anything you can do for him while he is in America.'[66]

In the covering note to Ober accompanying the letter of introduction, Cork reminds him that Saunders has had *The Mousetrap* running for two years and *Witness for the Prosecution* for almost a year. He comments that business on the *Spider's Web* tour is indicative that it will be the 'biggest success of the three' and that Saunders' production of William

Douglas Home's *The Manor at Northstead* is also playing to 'packed houses'. Delightfully, and veraciously, Cork adds that 'Peter is a man of great integrity but he is much less easy-going than most theatrical people, and I should think it quite possible that his relations with American managers will need a little lubrication.' Although Cork's word of warning was not without justification, Saunders appears to have charmed the Americans: 'I find Peter Saunders a very attractive man and he spoke very warmly of you,' wrote Ober to Cork.[67] There is a marvellous picture of Saunders taken on this visit, standing next to a large car outside the Shubert Theatre in New Haven and looking every inch the successful impresario. Although the Shuberts no longer owned the New Haven theatre that bore their name, it is ironic that Saunders, having switched allegiance to Miller, found himself standing under signage that advertised it.

Despite Francis L. Sullivan's excellent reviews, and his long and chatty 'letters home' to Saunders (in which he urged Saunders to cast him in the rumoured film of *Witness for the Prosecution*, and to look out for work for his actress niece),[68] the management seem to have been keen to dispense with their troublesome male star at the earliest opportunity. They were clearly intending to replace him as soon as his contract expired at the end of June 1955, and as early as February Saunders was writing to Banyai, 'The part of Sir Wilfred Robarts must be played by an unusual personality, and not just a good actor. I don't have to tell you, too, how important the girl is – although curiously enough Robarts is at least as important . . . If Mr Miller liked the idea, I would urge you to sign him [David Horne] up now, and I think you could get him more cheaply than Sullivan, especially if you could give his wife a non-speaking part at a nominal salary.'[69] However, events were about to secure Sullivan's position in the role.

In 1955 the Broadway production of *Witness for the Prosecution* scooped a number of prestigious awards. At the ninth annual Tony Awards in March, Francis L. Sullivan and Patricia Jessel were honoured as Best Featured Actor and Best

Featured Actress in a Play; this was an extraordinary achieve-ment for the two British performers, although it rather makes one wonder what the judges considered the *leading* male and female roles in the play to be. In April, Christie herself received the Edgar Allan Poe Award from the Mystery Writers Guild of America for *Witness for the Prosecution*, and the following month the play won the New York Drama Critics Circle Award for Best Foreign Play, keeping good company with the Best Play, Tennessee Williams' *Cat on a Hot Tin Roof*. All of this, of course, put a premium on the performances of Sullivan and Jessel, and in the end both of their contracts were extended until the end of the Broadway run, after which they headlined Miller's tour of the play to major US cities including Chicago and Los Angeles. Sullivan was even awarded a six-week holiday and a salary of $1,000 per week as part of his new deal.[70]

Witness for the Prosecution played for 645 performances on Broadway and, as in London, the production was a huge finan-cial success as well as a critical one. I have been unable to locate accounts (in fact, Saunders frequently criticised Miller for failing to supply detailed accounting), but it is noted in corre-spondence between the producers that at its height the Broadway production, which ran for almost two years, was averaging well over $4,000 profit per week ($1,000 of which went to Saunders), with Christie's royalties worth over $2,000 per week.[71]

In my view it can be no coincidence that Christie's two big Broadway successes were also the subjects of two of the most successful films of her work, René Clair's *And Then There Were None* (1945) and Billy Wilder's *Witness for the Prosecution* (1957). But if negotiations over film rights with the Shuberts had seemed tortuous, then these were to pale into insignificance when it came to dealing with Gilbert Miller on the subject; 'I have never known such hell!' Cork wrote to Ober in September 1955.[72] Not only did Miller initially maintain that the previous licensing of television rights to the short story in the USA might compromise the sale of film rights but, when the time came, Saunders and Cork proved unable to agree with him on a timetable for such a sale. The English producer and agent were

Captain Peter Saunders with the Intelligence Corps in Germany (1945).

Top left: Jeanne de Casalis.

Top right: Hubert Gregg directing Jessica Spencer in *The Hollow* (1951).

Bottom left: Peter Cotes and wife Joan Miller.

Bottom right: Richard Attenborough and Sheila Sim in the original cast of *The Mousetrap* (1952).

Top: The Duke and Duchess of Windsor attending *Witness for the Prosecution (1 December, 1953)*.

Bottom: The Broadway production of *Witness for the Prosecution* (1954).

Top left: Hugh 'Binkie' Beaumont.

Top right: Gilbert Miller.

Bottom: Peter Saunders in New Haven, USA (1954).

all for securing an immediate sale off the back of the Broadway reviews, but the more experienced Miller wanted to protect his Broadway revenues and in any case felt that the longer the show ran in New York the higher the price they would be able to command; and there were certainly plenty of bidders. Contractually, it was up to Saunders when to sell the film rights and for how much (Saunders would receive 30 per cent of the price and Miller 20 per cent); but it was discovered that the small print of the American Dramatists Guild Minimum Basic Agreement had given Miller himself the right to match any offer made by a third party. Suspicion thus grew in the English camp that Miller had a vested interest in keeping the price as low as possible and was doing his best to jeopardise a lucrative sale.

In using the Dramatists Guild Agreement as the basis for the deal with Miller for *Witness for the Prosecution*, Cork and Saunders had been unaware that it included certain 'Supplemental Provisions' which they appear not to have had a copy of. Miller's 'matching right' was part of these provisions and, according to Ober, would have been deleted as a matter of course had his office had sight of it. Ironically, therefore, it was Cork and Saunders' maladroit attempt to apply the Agreement that had created the problem. Ober's weary admonition of Cork in March 1955 was once more by way of closing the stable door: 'I hope that in future neither you nor Peter Saunders will sign a contract with an American manager or picture company without having it gone through by an American lawyer or agent, preferably by both.'[73]

In the end, much to Miller's chagrin, Ober was brought in to assist with brokering the sale of the film rights. Miller's lieutenant, George Banyai, complained to Saunders that Ober was 'slow, old-fashioned and thinks $100,000 is a lot of money'.[74] Saunders replied to Banyai, 'I do so regret that after my friendly association with the Gilbert Miller office this slight feeling of acrimony has crept in.'[75] Shortly afterwards Saunders wrote to Robert Lewis, the play's director, 'When I am told that Miller is the best of American managements to deal with, I wonder what the others are like';[76] this elicited the response,

'Please don't even repeat such nonsense that Miller is the best of the American managers. He has been for years among all intelligent people a laughing stock. I have told you of some good American managers and there are a few more. Probably the same percentage as in England or elsewhere.'[77]

The Hollywood press followed the convoluted negotiations for the film sale with interest, and substantial figures from $250,000 to $450,000 were talked about. Warner Brothers, United Artists, 20th Century Fox, Columbia and MGM were all at the table at some point, and the labyrinthine and sometimes acrimonious film negotiations fill several files on both sides of the Atlantic. At the end of 1955 Miller, with some partners, eventually paid $325,000 (reported in the UK as £116,000[78]) to exercise his matching right and outbid Louis B. Mayer, who had reached a widely reported deal with Ober for $300,000.[79] Miller immediately sold the rights on to American film producer Edward Small for $435,000.[80] The sale to Miller was thus not quite the unqualified triumph reported by Cork to his client and trumpeted by Saunders in the British press. In any event, the eventual 1957 film was produced by Arthur Hornblow Jr and Edward Small, and released by United Artists. The film's opening credits billed *Witness for the Prosecution* as 'Agatha Christie's international stage success' and its cast included Charles Laughton as Robarts, a singing Marlene Dietrich as Christine (Broadway audiences had sniggered at the name Romaine, believing it meant 'lettuce') and Tyrone Power as Vole (in his last role before his death in 1958 at the age of forty-four). It also featured popular Irish actress Una O'Connor repeating her Broadway success in the role of housekeeper Janet Mackenzie, and Laughton's wife, Elsa Lanchester, in a part written in especially for her. Francis L. Sullivan, who had become an American citizen after the Broadway opening, had died in New York the previous year, aged fifty-three. He had written to Saunders expressing his hope that he would be cast in the film, and the final irony of his career was that, having won a Tony award for his role in the play, he was posthumously and conclusively upstaged by Charles Laughton.

Agatha had taken the precaution of organising in advance of the film sale for its proceeds to be gifted to Rosalind as part of Edmund Cork's ongoing tax avoidance strategy (not tax 'evading', as stated in Laura Thompson's biography of Christie, I am happy to assure readers). Rosalind wrote to Cork, 'I am content to leave it to you to do your best with Gilbert Miller but hope you will fix something with him soon – 300,000 dollars will suit me.'[81] The letter is dated simply 'July 12th'. You would think that for a missive of such import it might have been appropriate to make a note of the year (1955). But like mother, like daughter.

It was not until *Witness for the Prosecution* was installed on Broadway that Cork felt it safe to experiment with American licensing for the relatively low-key *The Mousetrap*. There was some excitement when Jack Benny's agent asked to see a script at the end of 1954: 'The idea appears to be outrageous at first,' wrote Cork to Ober, 'but I am inclined to think this is just the sort of gimmick that is necessary to put this play over in America.'[82] Quite which role in *The Mousetrap* the sixty-year-old comedian was considering is unclear but, perhaps fortunately for all concerned, the idea went no further.

On 3 May 1955 Cork wrote to Rosalind:

The Mousetrap has passed its thousandth performance in London [which it had celebrated on 22 April] and as from yesterday the cast has been completely changed, with the exception of Patric Doonan [who had replaced Attenborough] and we are hoping that it will go on for some time at the Ambassadors, and that this will be followed by a long tour with the London company . . . Whether this is a play that will stand up to Broadway is very doubtful indeed. Half a dozen American managements have been interested, but finally decided that it was too 'small' a play for them. However, we are embarking on rather an interesting experiment, which will show how the Americans react to it. We have made arrangements for one of the best of the summer theatres –

the Arena Theatre in Washington DC – to put it on for a season of eight weeks. This will probably not bring in more than about a thousand dollars in cash, but it will give us a chance of judging how God's Own People like it. If it clicks, then on to Broadway in the autumn.[83]

Ober was less convinced that Washington was a potential stepping-stone to Broadway, advising Cork that 'it is my experience that it is difficult to tell from a summer production whether a play will be a Broadway success.' He had, however, heard good things about the 247-seat Arena Stage from his son and from F. Scott Fitzgerald's daughter, Frances, both of whom lived in Washington, and he spoke highly to Cork of Zelda Fichandler, 'who seems a very intelligent woman and whose small theatre in Washington is successful'.[84] Co-founded by Fichandler five years previously in a converted former burlesque and movie house, Arena Stage was one of America's first not-for-profit theatres and a pioneer of the regional theatre movement. Perhaps most interestingly, *The Mousetrap*, like all its productions, was to be performed in the round, which must have presented the set designer with some challenges.

And so it was that the American premiere of *The Mousetrap* took place in Washington DC on 17 May 1955, directed by Zelda Fichandler. Ober was right: the outcome in Washington was a happy one, but it did not propel the play to Broadway. The *Washington Post and Times Herald* reviewed it favourably: 'Arena, I suspect, has a major hit in this take-you-out-of-yourself evening.'[85] On 15 June, Cork wrote to Rosalind, 'The Mousetrap does well at Washington. The house is sold out every night and they would like to run it all summer. I don't think there is any reason why they should not. There doesn't seem to be any interest in a Broadway production so far, the general idea being that it would be rather an anti-climax to Witness for the Prosecution if it were done on Broadway. However, I don't think there is any doubt that it will do very well with amateurs, and bring in a lot of money for Mathew.'[86] Ironically, Arena Stage, which moved to larger premises after the run of *The Mousetrap*, would in future years become a major supplier of productions for Broadway.

Witness for the Prosecution closed on Broadway on 30 June 1956, but it was not until 5 November 1960 that *The Mousetrap* finally received its New York premiere at the Maidman Playhouse, 'off Broadway's finest theatre' according to a profile of its young producer, Robert Feldstein, in the *New York Journal-American* three weeks before it opened.[87] In the article, Feldstein claimed to have been in negotiation for the rights for a year and a half and that the production had broken all off-Broadway records for advance sales. He also confidently predicted a run of 'four years'. He was certainly an energetic promoter, feeding amusing stories to the press and providing audiences with forms on which they were encouraged to indicate who they thought the murderer was before the start of the second act.

The New York reviews were not raves, but neither were they as damning as those for *Hidden Horizon*. They praised the acting, direction and set and, whilst finding some flaws in the script, seemed generally happy to enter into the spirit of the piece despite it lacking the high drama of *Ten Little Indians* and *Witness for the Prosecution*. 'It is a paradox of the London theatre that, although Agatha Christie's *The Mousetrap* is not her best play it is her most successful,' observed the *New York Times*, adding that 'it is not exactly a blood-curdling experience. One murder does take place on the stage, and another impends through most of the evening. But it is the Christie skill and polish in throwing you off the scent that keeps the entertainment going' and concluding, '*The Mousetrap* will not exactly shake you up, but neither will it let you down.'[88] The *Morning Telegraph* was less supportive, describing the play as a 'mild little mystery charade' and remarking that 'Agatha Christie has written excellent mystery thrillers for the stage such as *Witness for the Prosecution* and *Ten Little Indians*. The latest detective story is not in the same class. It is not even up to grade C Christie, which is too low on the scale even for off-Broadway, where you have to be more thrilling, more stimulating than the Broadway fat cats to attract audiences.'[89]

On 10 November, Cork wrote to Christie, 'I enclose the New York Times review of The Mousetrap. The reception has not been quite as good as I hoped it might be, but the Ober office think it has a chance of a fair run. These off-Broadway productions, although they can be remunerative, are on a small scale and do not interfere with other rights. I see I wrote fully about the pros and cons on the 13th of July, and I am sorry to find now that you are rather against it.'[90] The production moved to the off-Broadway Greenwich Mews Theatre on 15 February and completed a total of 192 performances. *The Mousetrap* never played Broadway, and the best that can be said of its New York premiere is 'no harm done'.

It seems, however, that the 1960 production was not technically the play's New York premiere. A typewritten flyer archived in the New York Public Library for the Performing Arts advertises *The Mousetrap* for the 'First Time in New York!' for four performances from 5 to 7 December 1957 at 263 West 86th Street.[91] This is the address of the West End Theatre, a small community theatre on the second floor of the Methodist Church of St Paul and St Andrew. The production was directed by Franklyn Lenthall, a notable collector of theatrical artefacts who in the same year purchased the Boothbay Playhouse in Maine. Whatever the status of the Lenthall Players, they were presumably presenting the play under an amateur licence. But in doing so they made theatrical history.

Agatha herself never saw one of her plays performed on Broadway. She visited New York in 1956, after *Witness for the Prosecution* had closed, when accompanying Max to America to collect a gold medal that he had been awarded by the University of Pennsylvania. They also took the opportunity to go to Hollywood, where at least she was able to see *Witness for the Prosecution* being filmed. This was the first time Agatha had been to America since the Grand Tour with Archie in 1922 and she greatly enjoyed the experience. She was to go once more, ten years later, again accompanying Max who was giving a lecture tour, and on this occasion taking the opportunity to visit her American paternal grandfather's grave in New York's Greenwood cemetery.

SCENE FOUR

Hat-Trick

Amongst Gilbert Miller's papers from this period is a letter from John Gielgud dated 26 November 1953. It reads,

> Dear Gilbert,
>   Thank you so much for thinking of me on the first night at the Haymarket. The warmth of the audience and their enthusiastic reception was touching and thrilling, as you can imagine, and I have never been more aware of the kindness and love that has surrounded me at this time.
>   As ever, John[1]

Gielgud had just opened in in N.C. Hunter's *A Day by the Sea* at the Theatre Royal, Haymarket for Tennent Productions, playing alongside Ralph Richardson, Lewis Casson and Sybil Thorndike. This was his first West End appearance since his arrest and fine the previous month for importuning men 'for immoral purposes' in a public lavatory, and Miller had been amongst the numerous members of the theatrical community to send their good wishes at what was clearly a very difficult time for him.

As it turned out, though, *A Day by the Sea* was about to become the centre of media attention for a very different reason than the sexual proclivities of one of its stars. Growing resentment amongst theatre producers about the monopolistic tendencies of the Tennent empire had led Labour MP Woodrow

Wyatt to undertake a detailed investigation of its activities. Binkie Beaumont's skilful operation of an entertainments tax-exempt, non-profit distributing theatre production company (Tennent Productions Ltd) in tandem with his commercial company (H.M. Tennent Ltd) had enabled him to create a seemingly unassailable position of dominance in West End theatre. But now Wyatt was gathering evidence to support the tabling of a bill in Parliament. Specifically designed to put an end to Beaumont's exploitation of the exemption from the tax on ticket sales offered to non-profit distributing companies, the Theatrical Companies Bill was introduced by Wyatt as a Private Members' Bill under the 'ten minute rule' on Wednesday 10 March 1954, using the example of *A Day by the Sea* to demonstrate how Tennent Productions Ltd was saving around £500 in ticket sales tax a week, but was paying H.M. Tennent Ltd £40 per week to manage the production. Wyatt maintained that the commercial company's entire £10,000 profit for the year was accountable to its charging of management fees to the non-commercial company, and the bill itself was designed to prevent commercial and non-profit distributing companies from sharing directors and staff, as Tennents' did, and from working in tandem in this way. Wyatt concluded, 'What Mr Beaumont is very cleverly and skilfully doing is using the concession which was intended for another purpose to build himself up as the greatest theatrical impresario in London and operating what is nothing less than a capitalist monopoly.'[2]

By the early 1950s, the Tennent empire was indeed exhibiting all the characteristics of a monopoly, and paranoia and rumour had begun to spread amongst Beaumont's rivals. It was alleged not only that Beaumont was operating a blacklist but that performers were frightened to accept contracts with other managements (even, in some recorded instances, at higher wages) lest they were subsequently refused work by Tennents. Many actors appeared to be under permanent contract to 'the Firm' and several West End theatres, including the prestigious Theatre Royal Haymarket, were seemingly on permanent rental to him. It was the clever and perfectly legal way in which Beaumont had operated the companies in tandem that had enabled him to reach a position of dominance, and it was less the direct financial question of management fees that was the significant factor than the huge negotiating power which the additional company gave him, combined with the sheer quantity of work it enabled him to produce. It was as if while H.M. Tennent Ltd provided a decent living for all concerned, Tennent Productions Ltd simply soaked up all the remaining plays, theatres and actors and thus denied a living to other managements. Yet, because his rivals had quite simply failed to spot a business opportunity, the anti-Tennent arguments would always be hampered by the fact that they did smack somewhat of sour grapes.

According to Peter Saunders:

Two people went to see Woodrow Wyatt, MP for Birmingham Aston. One was a producer, the late Bill Linnit, the other a major international star whose name I am still pledged not to reveal. They started a train of thought in Wyatt's mind that led him to make long and exhaustive enquiries . . . He said he had had many representations from people of every sort and description in the theatrical industry – actors and actresses, producers, managers, etc – not only in London but up and down the country, all of whom (with very few exceptions) were strongly in favour of the bill. The exceptions, said Mr Wyatt, were employees or associates of one or other of the Tennent companies.[3]

There was a problem, though:

Wyatt said that almost invariably those who had made representations in favour of the bill had said, 'Please do not use my name, because if you do, and it becomes known that I have made representations to you about this matter, I shall be banned by the Tennent organisation either from acting or from carrying on my business in the theatrical profession.'

In the months between the bill's first reading on 10 March and its second on 24 June, Tennents mounted a media and parliamentary lobbying campaign of ruthless efficiency, oiled when necessary by free theatre tickets. This carefully orchestrated campaign is documented in the Tennent business papers, which were unaccountably 'missing' for two decades before being anonymously donated to the V&A's theatre collection in 2011.[4] Tennents' biggest coup was to enlist the services of another Labour MP, Sydney Silverman, to fight their cause. Silverman, who was to be a key player in the abolition of capital punishment, had opposed the bill's first reading, although he does not appear to have had a proper grasp of the issues at stake; and it is clear from Hansard's report of the 24 June debate that few Members of Parliament actually did. Hampered by the anonymity of his informants and by his parliamentary colleagues' seeming inability to understand the complexities of Beaumont's business model, Wyatt's bill was eventually 'talked out'.[5]

The Conservatives had returned to power under Churchill in 1951 and, as an overtly anti-capitalist measure tabled by a Labour MP, the Theatrical Companies Bill would doubtless not have stood much of a chance in any case, but despite its failure it is important not to underestimate the legacy of extreme bad feeling, betrayal and mistrust that Wyatt's evidence-gathering created within the theatrical community. Although the industry rapidly closed ranks to limit the damage, and the events surrounding the Theatrical Companies Bill are rarely referred to these days, it is clear that, in some quarters at least, the scars took a long time to heal. Typical of this is director Frith Banbury's claim that Wyatt, in questioning him, had referred to allegations by *Mousetrap* director Peter Cotes that Beaumont only employed homosexuals. Banbury, himself a homosexual who worked for Beaumont, claims to have put Wyatt right on this. His interview with Wyatt was reported by Banbury to Charles Duff, author of *The Lost Summer – The Heyday of West End Theatre*, who duly referred to it in his book.[6] According to Duff, Banbury later flatly denied telling him that Wyatt had mentioned Cotes by name. 'Nothing I have ever done in my life caused me as much anxiety as the short "West End 1950s" section of The Lost Summer,' Duff wrote to me, when I was carrying out research on Wyatt's bill several years ago.[7]

It is clear from Peter Saunders' autobiography that he was, in many respects, Beaumont's nemesis, and that it was his championing of populist theatre, as represented by Agatha Christie, that put him in a position of strength in this respect. In 1995, Lord Wyatt, whose political affinities had changed markedly in the intervening years, and who had himself dabbled in playwriting, refused to talk with me about his bill but suggested that 'the best person to enquire about my role in bringing the manipulation of the entertainment tax laws in the 1940s–50s to the public's attention is Peter Saunders, the impresario. You could tell him that I suggested you write to him. His address is . . .'[8] Saunders, though, also refused to discuss the matter, and simply referred me to his book.[9] Peter Cotes, who believed himself to have been blacklisted by Beaumont, wrote to me a few years later that 'the less I have to say about Mr Beaumont and what you term his creation of a theatrical monopoly through his manipulation of the Entertainment Tax laws, the better.'[10] He eventually agreed to answer a questionnaire, but died a few weeks later, before I could get it to him. As for the 'major international star' whose name Saunders pledged not to reveal, we will never know.

One major international star with whom Saunders was delighted to advertise his association in 1954 was Margaret Lockwood. RADA-trained Lockwood had become Britain's most popular and highly paid screen actress in the 1940s, appearing in a number of thrillers that included *Doctor Syn* (1937), *The Lady Vanishes* (1938), *Night Train to Munich* (1940), *The Man in Grey* (1943), *The Wicked Lady* (1945), *Bedelia* (1946), *Highly Dangerous* (1950) and *Trent's Last Case* (1952). On stage, Lockwood had starred in tours of *Pygmalion* and *Private Lives* but had not appeared in the West End (other than two Christmas seasons as Peter Pan) since working as a young graduate in the 1930s. In September 1953, aged thirty-seven and finding herself near the end of a film contract, Lockwood and her agent Herbert de Leon had decided that it was time for her to embark upon a change of direction and to launch herself as a West End star.

De Leon had masterminded Lockwood's career from the outset. Having started in the business as a professional singer, he was widely regarded as the biggest and most important of the 'one man' agencies. With a client list that included Greer Garson, Anna Neagle, Wilfrid Hyde White, Dora Bryan, Jack Hulbert, Cicely Courtneidge, Patricia Hayes and Jean Kent, de Leon was famous for his unorthodox methods; he never asked his clients to sign a contract with him and they were free to leave if and when they wanted to. He had seen Lockwood performing in her end-of-term RADA showcase in 1934 and, amazed that she didn't receive an award, offered to represent her on the spot. When he died forty-five years later he was still representing her and they still didn't have a contract.

In Margaret Lockwood's autobiography, which tells the story of her life up to the mid-1950s, she recalls that it was her agent who, aware of her 'passion for Agatha Christie', suggested asking Christie to write a play for her to star in. De Leon, a friend of Peter Saunders, talked to 'the skilful young theatrical manager who was already presenting two of Mrs Christie's plays in London, who accepted the idea enthusiastically . . . Mrs Christie travelled to London from her Devonshire home, and the four of us lunched together. I was charmed to meet my favourite authoress at last . . . She willingly entertained the idea of writing a play for me, and only six weeks later we had a message from her that she had already decided upon the plot and expected the whole work to be completed in two or three months.'[11] *Witness for the Prosecution* had not yet opened when the lunch at the Mirabelle took place, so Lockwood's choice of Christie pre-dated its phenomenal success and would have been based largely on the reputation of *The Mousetrap*. Coincidentally, the following August Lockwood and her daughter were to find themselves holidaying in the South of France in the same hotel as Richard Attenborough and Sheila Sim. Attenborough had just completed his extended run in *The Mousetrap* and Lockwood was about to start rehearsals for *Spider's Web*.

Christie remembers of her first meeting with Lockwood that she 'said at once that she didn't want to continue being sinister and melodramatic, that she had done a good many films lately in which she had been the "wicked lady". She wanted to play comedy. I think she was right, because she has an enormous flair for comedy, as well as being able to be dramatic. She is a very good actress, and has that perfect timing which enables her to give lines their true weight.'[12] This was the first time that Christie had consciously written a star role since she had created Canon Pennefather for Francis L. Sullivan, and I have no doubt that her willingness to do so on this occasion was motivated by the fact that it was for a woman, and one whose company she enjoyed and whose talent she admired. Lockwood and Christie were clearly kindred spirits; in an interview with *Reynolds News* in January 1954, Lockwood remarked that 'Agatha has the gift of doing what all women want to do, but only men have the chance. She achieves something. Men climb Everest, race fast cars, invent atom bombs, fight wars, become famous surgeons and man lifeboats. In her heart every woman, too, would like to do these things. But all we can do is dream. It is all we can do. It's a man's world. The only consolation I get is that Agatha kills off a few of you.'[13] The admiration was mutual and, astonishingly, Christie even agreed to appear with Lockwood in a series of highly staged publicity photographs, which feature Herbert de Leon as 'the corpse'.

The role she created for Lockwood, Clarissa, notably shares a name with Agatha's mother (Clarissa was also both Agatha's and Rosalind's middle name), although early notes for the play indicate that the character might originally have been called Laura. We get no description of Clarissa in Christie's stage directions (doubtless a diplomatic move on her part), although we know that, according to another character, her husband is 'years older' than her at 'about forty' and that she has a twelve-year-old stepdaughter. The dreamy but resourceful wife of a Foreign Office official, Clarissa is given to fantasising about a world of high drama and adventure: 'Supposing I were to come down one morning and find a dead body in the library, what should I do? Or supposing a woman were to be shown in here one day and told me that she and Henry had been secretly married in Constantinople, and that our marriage was bigamous, what should I say to her? Or supposing I had to choose between betraying my country and seeing Henry shot before my very eyes?'[14] It is as though *The Mousetrap*'s Mollie Ralston were dreaming of leading the life of *Chimneys*' Virginia Revel. Inevitably a body does turn up (before vanishing again), and we end up in a scenario that has many of the complexities and much of the lightness of touch of *Chimneys*, as well as similarly bubbling dialogue; there is even a subtext of international diplomacy and a reference to the fictional Balkan state of Herzoslovakia, last heard of in *Chimneys*.

The plot of *Spider's Web* deliberately includes a number of devices that would have been familiar to readers of Christie's stories, and involves an element of conscious self-parody of her work and of the detective thriller genre. The 'country house' setting is, once again a red herring; as in *The Mousetrap*, the house's inhabitants are by no means landed gentry, and in this case are renting the property, which comes complete with a priest's hole concealed behind a bookcase, allowing Clarissa the delightful curtain line 'Exit Clarissa mysteriously.' The whole thing rattles along at a fair old pace, greatly assisted by the fact that it is performed in real time over the course of one evening, leading Clarissa to conclude, 'How extraordinary it is; all my life nothing has really happened to me and tonight I've had the lot. Murder, police, drug addicts, invisible ink, secret writing, almost arrested for manslaughter and very nearly murdered. You know, in a way it's almost too much all in one evening.' A delightfully wry comment from Christie on the genre in which she wrote. Clarissa's husband, of course, doesn't believe her, and asks her to put the kettle on.

The Spider's Web was a title that Christie had wanted to use for the 1943 UK release of her novel *The Moving Finger*, originally published in America the previous year. Collins, however, had advised Edmund Cork that there had recently been another book of that title and that they were 'rather doubtful' about Christie's suggested alternative, 'The Tangled Web'.[15] In the end, Collins had stuck with the title used by Dodd, Mead & Co. for the book's American debut, but now Christie saw an opportunity to experiment with the 'Spider's Web' idea again; from the evidence of draft scripts, she was clearly torn between this and 'Clarissa Finds a Body' for the title of her new play.

Christie went diligently about her task, missing rehearsals for *Witness for the Prosecution* and making twenty pages of preparatory notes (in Notebook 12) for what was to be the first entirely original stage play of hers to be performed since *Black Coffee*, all of the others having been adaptations (although often quite radical ones) of either novels or short stories. *Spider's Web* was not technically a commission, but Christie entirely fulfilled her brief, creating a delightful star vehicle for Lockwood that would show off her talents to great effect in a comedy role and help her to dispel her cinematic 'wicked lady' image. Lockwood was thrilled: 'Before I'd finished reading the first act I knew the part of Clarissa Hailsham-Brown was "me". I loved it. It was light, saucy, endearing, packed with good lines and, above all, funny.'[16] Christie had written the role of Pippa, Clarissa's young stepdaughter, for Lockwood's thirteen-year-old daughter Julia (or 'Toots' as her mother called her), although in the end a filming contract, followed by a Christmas engagement to play Goldilocks at Brentford's Q Theatre, prevented her from taking part. The role of Sir Rowland Delahaye was created, at Lockwood's request, for another of de Leon's clients, Wilfrid Hyde White; but he turned it down and the part was taken by Felix Aylmer. Oxford-educated Aylmer had learned his craft with Barry Jackson's Birmingham Rep, and then as part of the regular ReandeaN company at the St Martin's Theatre, before going on to make notable appearances in Olivier's films of *Henry V* and *Hamlet* and, in 1950, becoming president of the actors' union, Equity. Saunders gave him second billing to Lockwood, who can be been seen smothering Aylmer to death in her signature role as the Wicked Lady. A first-rate cast also included the young Desmond Llewelyn (later to be James Bond's 'Q') in the role of Constable Jones, alongside Campbell Singer as Inspector Lord. Singer had the distinction of having played the role of Blore in the first full-length Christie play script to be televised, 1949's BBC broadcast of *Ten Little Niggers*.

Securing Lockwood as his star was a major coup for Saunders, and he made the most of it, booking an unusually long eleven-week pre-London tour which commenced on 27 September and opened, as usual, in Nottingham. As with the promotion of Attenborough and Sim for *The Mousetrap*, the poster design for *Spider's Web* consisted largely of a picture of Lockwood, and her name appeared on the publicity and programme in considerably larger type than Christie's; Saunders' oft-repeated mantra that he 'made Christie the star' only held good so long as there was nobody else to step into the shoes.

The production was directed by Wallace Douglas, who had made such a success of *Witness for the Prosecution* – just for once, Hubert Gregg does not claim that the job was offered to him first. Douglas's star was in the ascendant, and on 2 September 1954 *The Stage* reported, 'With the opening of *Dry Rot* at the Whitehall this week, Wallace Douglas has directed three plays now running in the West End, the others being *Witness for the Prosecution* at the Winter Garden and *The Manor at Northstead* at the Duchess. He is now working on *Spider's Web*, the play that is to bring Margaret Lockwood back to London.' It was indeed fortuitous that Douglas embarked on Christie's comedy immediately after opening John Chapman's *Dry Rot*, which was destined to become one of the longest-running and most successful of the farces presented by Brian Rix at the Whitehall Theatre during the 1950s and 60s. His experience at the helm of the Whitehall farce team must have proved invaluable to him in the staging of Christie's larky comedy, and with London evidently in the mood for farce the timing could not have been better. Saunders again teamed Douglas with designer Michael Weight, although *Spider's Web* presented fewer design challenges than their previous collaboration on *Witness for the Prosecution*.

Douglas and Christie clearly got on well although, like Gregg, she does not mention him in her autobiography. Unlike Gregg, Douglas was hugely respectful of the playwright with whose work he was entrusted. The draft script in the Agatha Christie archive opens with Clarissa's house guests, Sir Rowland Delahaye and Hugo Birch, discussing butterflies at great length. In some cases, the names of the butterflies have been left blank in the typescript and filled in later by hand, presumably following consultation with someone who was in a position to advise on the subject; possibly Christie's son-in-law Anthony Hicks, who she remarked in her autobiography 'could talk knowledgeably on butterflies'.[17]

Delightful though the conceit is of two eccentric fellows engaged in a passionate lepidopteral debate, Wallace Douglas believed that this would not be a dramatically effective opening to the play. Although Christie dug her heels in, she changed her mind after seeing the first performance in Nottingham, and she and Douglas worked in a room at their hotel to create the opening that we now know, involving Delahaye and Birch taking part in a blindfolded port tasting. 'That is what was so very sweet and generous of her,' remarked Douglas to unofficial Christie biographer Gwen Robyns. 'Once she was convinced that she was wrong she was never so discourteous as not to admit it.'[18] This new scenario may also have owed something to Hicks, of whom Christie observed affectionately, 'If he has a fault, it is that he discusses wine at too great length.'[19]

As is so often the case with the edits Christie made to her plays at the request of directors, the original version is far more interesting as a piece of writing than what we have been left with, although in strictly dramatic terms it would probably be difficult to argue with the decision to cut. Here, then, is the butterfly conversation – which, it should be noted, includes some wry observations on the male–female dynamic and the scientific and legal professions, all of which are absent from its replacement. It is a 'wet evening in March':

ROWLAND: What I say is, there's a lot of nonsense in these books. Why, I found a Heath Fritillary myself in my own herbaceous border.

HUGO: Nothing against that, but the Large Copper is entirely different. Lycaena Dispar has been extinct in this country since 1847. Consult any authority you like, they all say the same.

ROWLAND: Doesn't prevent them all being wrong.

HUGO: It's highly unlikely that they'd *all* be wrong.

ROWLAND: Most likely thing in the world! These scientific fellows are all the same, like a pack of sheep. All repeat what the other feller said. But here we've got a reliable witness. Clarissa's aunt definitely saw –

HUGO: Probably saw Polychloros – the Large Tortoiseshell.

ROWLAND: Not at all. Clarissa's aunt was a meticulous observer. You didn't know her.

HUGO: No – but what I say is, anyone can be mistaken.

ROWLAND: Not Clarissa's aunt! Why if Clarissa's aunt was alive now and came to me and said she'd seen a flying saucer – dash it all, I'd believe in flying saucers! . . .

HUGO: Now, look here, Rowly, let's go back a bit. Clarissa's aunt wasn't exactly what you'd call a professional ento-mologist –

ROWLAND: Of course she wasn't a professional entomologist. She was a country woman and what she didn't know about birds, butterflies, wild flowers –

HUGO: What I'm getting at is that she wasn't an *expert*.

ROWLAND: (snorting) Expert! Experts are the curse of this age. Give me an expert and I'll show you a fellow who's pretty certain to be wrong.

HUGO: That's a mere generalisation. But let's go back a bit. You admit the story is that Clarissa's aunt was out for a walk with her brother-in-law and her brother-in-law said 'My dear there is a Large Copper.' It's not really *her* word you have for it, it's *his*.

ROWLAND: I see no reason to disbelieve the story. Her husband's brother was Wainwright. You know, high court judge. Don't tell me that a high court judge would commit himself by saying 'There's a Large Copper' unless it was a Large Copper. You know how careful these legal wallahs are.

HUGO: What I'm getting at is that she didn't know of her own knowledge that it was a Large Copper, she just agreed with what he said because he was a man and sure to know best. Wish we had a little more of that delightful Victorian spirit nowadays.

ROWLAND: My point is that two people saw the Large Copper by the Harford River, and they can't both have been mistaken, and you're entirely wrong about Clarissa's aunt. She was a charming woman, but she had plenty of spirit.

HUGO: It's a well known fact that the Large Copper only breeds where the great water dock grows.

ROWLAND: Heaps of great water dock by the Harford River.

HUGO: How do you know, Rowly? You don't know a bee orchid from a stitchwort.

ROWLAND: Ah, but I was lunching at the club the other day. There was one of those botanical fellows there, just come back from Dartmoor. Had been looking for a lesser bogwort or something like that. I could swear he mentioned the great water dock. 'No rarity grows like a weed,' he said. Well, I mean, it *is* a weed of course.

ROWLAND: It's common in the Norfolk Broads but I don't believe it grows in the West of England. We'll look it up. (He rises and goes to door of library)

HUGO: You'll see. 'Found in marshy places and near streams.' That's what it will say. Clarissa's aunt knew all about wild flowers.[20]

The draft script also shows that the play originally consisted of three acts each of one scene, but that what were originally the first twenty-seven pages of a rather long Act Three were renumbered and converted into a second scene for Act Two. This change to the early draft, which clearly pre-dates rehearsals and the involvement of a director, gives a better balance to the piece and allows for an excellent curtain line at the new end of Act Two, which has been inserted on an additional page. John Curran identifies preparatory notes for the play which include Act Two action under the heading 'Act Three', and his surmise that the act structure must have been changed in this way is correct.[21] Three sections of additional dialogue (one in Act Two and two in Act Three) appear to have been added at a later stage and have been inserted, along with the new opening, into the copy held in the Lord Chamberlain's plays collection.[22]

One other change was made during the West End run of the play, according to correspondence in the Lord Chamberlain's files. In Act One, in a conversation about autographs, young Pippa says that she wishes she had 'Neville Duke's and Roger Bannister's. These historical ones are rather mouldy, I think.' In April 1956, in an acknowledgement of the marriage that month of Prince Rainier of Monaco to Grace Kelly, this was changed to 'I wish I had Grace Kelly's and Prince Rainier's'.[23] This change was evidently not passed on to Samuel French, who used the original line when they published the script in 1957.

Spider's Web opened in the West End at the Savoy Theatre, owned by the Savoy Hotel, on 14 December 1954. Once again, Saunders had been forced to find a home outside of 'the Group', many of whose theatres were contracted to Tennents. There was no orchestra on this occasion, but two pianists entertained the audience with a selection of Gershwin and Porter melodies, and the play featured the specially composed 'Spider's Web Theme Music'.[24] Saunders celebrated his trio of West End Christies by taking an advertisement for *The Mousetrap* and *Witness for the Prosecution* in the programme for *Spider's Web*. The first night audience's response was less emphatic than it had been for *Witness for the Prosecution*, although the play was undoubtedly a crowd-pleaser.

Kenneth Tynan had replaced Ivor Brown as the *Observer*'s theatre critic and, despite his later advocacy of British theatre's 'new wave', appears to have shared his predecessor's soft spot for Christie's idiosyncratic contributions to the West End stage. 'Those who grieve that our drama is a ritualistic art no longer should see Mrs Christie's *Spider's Web* and be consoled,' he wrote, 'for the detective play, in which a nameless avenger strikes down a chosen victim, is governed by conventions every bit as strict as those of Greek tragedy.'[25] He then goes on wittily to explain in some detail the parallels between ancient Greek drama and Christie's work, before lamenting that her characters were too well-drawn to serve the thriller genre and concluding, 'Audiences who emerged from *Witness for the Prosecution* murmuring "How clever she is" will probably emerge from *Spider's Web* murmuring "How clever I am!" Yet there are, I suppose, more unpleasant things to murmur.'

The *Times* review was less supportive, however: 'Miss Agatha Christie tries this time to combine a story of murder with a comedy of character. As Edgar Wallace showed more than once, the thing can be done. There is no reason why the special tension of the one should not support the special tension of the other. In this instance, however, the support is at best intermittent . . . the play as a whole is the least exciting and not the most amusing of the three Agatha Christies now running in London.'[26] A view which seems to have been shared by most of the critics.

The royal family continued to be enthusiastic in their support of Christie's work; on 1 March 1955 the Queen Mother saw a performance of *Spider's Web* and the following week the play was attended by the Queen, accompanied by the Duke of Edinburgh and Princess Margaret. According to Lockwood, 'More nerve-wracking than the first night was the night when the Queen came to see the play.'[27] Two months after attending *Spider's Web*, the Queen and the Duke of Edinburgh would be in Windsor watching *Witness for the Prosecution*. Lockwood's own career, like so many in our story, had previously benefited from the unexpected endorsement of Queen Elizabeth's grandmother,

Queen Mary, who at the age of seventy-eight had insisted on attending the premiere of her controversial film *The Wicked Lady*.

As with *The Mousetrap*, Cork and Saunders' strategy for *Spider's Web* deliberately excluded New York. Harold Ober reported that the agent of veteran Broadway leading lady Dorothy Stickney had expressed an interest in the play as a possible vehicle for their client, but at fifty-eight she would hardly have been suitable for the role of Clarissa. In January 1955, Cork wrote to Ober that 'This play was specially written for our film star Margaret Lockwood . . . I think Saunders expects about a four months' run, and there seems to be an idea that Lockwood would then make a film of it, which I suppose would rule out an American production.'[28] The Hughes Massie archive contains a two-page treatment for a film, apparently written by Christie herself; 'Commence with vast spider's web gradually dissolving into Clarissa studying a spiders's web in country house . . .'[29], but this was not pursued. A low-budget British colour film was eventually made by the American Danziger brothers, who were based at Elstree, and was released as a 'second feature' in UK cinemas in 1960. It appears not have been released in the USA, although it was shown on television there. Glynis Johns played Clarissa, alongside the much-loved husband and wife duo of Jack Hulbert as Sir Rowland Delahaye and Cicely Courtneidge as Mildred Peake (the eccentric gardener who had been played in the West End to great effect by Judith Furse).

In 1962 Hulbert and Courtneidge, both clients of Herbert de Leon, undertook a lengthy and successful stage tour of *Spider's Web* for Geoffrey Hastings (who had invested £125 in the West End run), under licence from Peter Saunders. On this occasion Courtneidge played the role of Clarissa. At the age of sixty-nine. The New York premiere of *Spider's Web* would eventually take place at the off-off-Broadway Lolly's Theatre Club in 1974, two years before Christie's death.

When Margaret Lockwood eventually left the cast after a run of fifteen months, the role of Clarissa was taken on by the popular thirty-five-year-old film and television actress Anne Crawford, Wallace Douglas's third wife. Tragically suffering from leukaemia,

Crawford died on 17 October 1956, and Saunders recalls that he 'watched with admiration the gallant but hopeless battle of her last weeks. Often in agony, she never missed a performance until the end.'[30] The understudy, Elizabeth Bird, took over for the last few weeks of the run, but Saunders had arranged for the production to play weeks at Golders Green and Streatham after it finished in the West End. According to Saunders, Bird was pregnant and unable to play these dates, although I suspect that it may have been more of a case of the management not wanting to risk fielding an understudy to headline two potentially lucrative touring dates. In any event it was here, according to Saunders, that 'Margaret Lockwood showed her professionalism and her generosity. She was having a much needed holiday in the South of France and, without telling me, her agent Herbert de Leon, phoned her and told her of my problems. Margaret immediately flew back from her holiday and played those two touring dates for me. I know of very few stars who would have done this.' I've not seen a record of Margaret Lockwood's deal, but Felix Aylmer and Ann Crawford were each earning £125 per week, and the lowest paid members of the company were on £20. In the week at Golders Green Hippodrome which Lockwood came to the rescue of, the production made a profit of £916 and Christie received a royalty of £348.[31]

Despite the lukewarm critical response, *Spider's Web* went on to enjoy the longest first run of any Christie play (after *The Mousetrap*, of course), clocking up an impressive 744 performances. Saunders found himself with yet another commercial hit on his hands, courtesy of Christie. The production's finances followed the usual pattern of a £5,000 capitalisation (with an actual production cost of £4,101), in which Saunders himself took the majority share; 72.5 per cent on this occasion, entitling him to 82.8 per cent of overall profit. After Saunders, Herbert de Leon was the biggest investor, backing his star to the tune of £1,000. The final profit on the enterprise was £63,388, calculated in 1963,[32] seven years after the end of the West End run, and including a share of subsidiary income from the modest film sale and the licensing of two post-West End tours and numerous repertory productions. Although actual dividends would have been paid over the previous eight years, that's well over a million pounds in today's money, of which de Leon would have received 12.5 per cent. Interestingly, Saunders' accounts show that amongst those entertained by him at *Spider's Web* was none other than Woodrow Wyatt, MP.

Under Saunders' diligent stewardship, Agatha Christie on stage had become big business. At the age of sixty-four, she had three big hits running in the West End and she remains, to this day, the only female playwright to have achieved this record.[33] She was also enjoying huge acclaim on Broadway. Only a dozen Agatha Christie novels were published in the 1950s, and some commentators believe this to indicate that her creative output was slowing down. On the contrary, her dedicated application to her day job had finally put her in a position where she was free to spend time on the work that she really enjoyed and found fulfilling. The journey from the Embassy Theatre in Swiss Cottage had not been an easy one for 'Mrs Pooper – cheap novelist', and success had been a long time coming, but when it suddenly arrived her position as the Queen of the West End was unassailable. Or so it appeared.

On the night that both Agatha Christie and Wallace Douglas scored their West End hat-tricks, Robert Morley and Wilfrid Hyde-White, both of whom had turned down Christie plays, were appearing at the Lyric in *Hippo Dancing*, and Terence Rattigan's *Separate Tables* was playing at the St James's Theatre. Elsewhere in the West End, theatregoers could see the musicals *Salad Days*, *The Boy Friend* and *The King and I*, or could enjoy an evening with Joyce Grenfell. Prince Littler's two-and-a-half-thousand-seat Stoll Theatre on Kingsway, meanwhile, was hosting the first of several West End Christmas seasons of Enid Blyton's *Noddy in Toyland*, performed largely by a cast of children drawn from the Italia Conti stage school and complete with wicked golliwogs. *Noddy in Toyland* was directed by Andre van Gyseghem, the original director of *Black Coffee* and the author of *Theatre in Soviet Russia*. It was produced by Bertie Meyer.

Blyton's agent George Greenfield notes in his amusing autobiography:

Early in 1954, she rang me and asked, 'George, do you think I could write a children's pantomime?'

I replied – and I meant it sincerely – 'If you put your mind to it, Enid, I reckon you could write almost anything.'

She sounded pleased and soon rang off. Two or three weeks later, she sent me the complete book and lyrics of the *Noddy in Toyland* pantomime. When it was staged at the huge Stoll theatre in Kingsway that Christmas, where every performance was fully sold out, neither the producer, B.A. Meyer nor the stage director, Andre van Gyseghem, had changed it to any great extent.

Bertie Meyer was in his seventies when I introduced him to Enid and Kenneth [her husband] as the potential producer. Tall, with luxuriant white hair, a Roman nose and a clipped moustache, he was a commanding and courteous figure. He had been involved in the West End theatre for over fifty years; soon after the turn of the century, Sir Henry Irving had been one of his leading actors.

After the meeting, when Bertie had left us, Kenneth Darrell Walters said in his bleating falsetto, 'He's far too old. He'll drop dead on us in the middle of a run – and then we'll be stuck.'

I told Kenneth that I had already discussed this delicate point with Bertie Meyer, who had a clean bill of health from his Harley Street doctor and who was quite prepared to undergo any further tests Kenneth might care to suggest . . . Enid said firmly that she liked and trusted Mr Meyer, and wanted to appoint him as the pantomime's producer. Still grumbling, Kenneth half-heartedly assented. In the event, Bertie Meyer produced *Noddy in Toyland* for the next five or six years until the demand did not warrant a West End production. Kenneth died in 1967 and Enid the following year. Bertie Meyer, then close on ninety, though naturally frail still had all his wits about him.[34]

Greenfield, who was clearly no fan of Blyton's husband, notes in passing that 'There is an interesting thesis to be researched and written on the husbands of successful women writers. The sensible ones, like Dr [sic] Mallowan, get on with their own life's work and maintain their self-respect by establishing a reputation in a separate field.'

Bertie Meyer was to play a key role in the development of the next 'Christie' work to appear in the West End, although he did not ultimately produce it: in 1956 an adaptation of her 1944 novel *Towards Zero* was finally staged in London, but it was not the play that Christie had written for the Shuberts and its origins are complicated.

In November 1947, shortly after the Shuberts' option on Christie's original script expired, a deal was done with L. Arthur Rose, best known for the book and lyrics of Noel Gay's 1937 musical *Me and My Girl*, giving him two years in which to dramatise the novel. A typescript of Rose's version of *Towards Zero* was discovered recently by an antiquarian bookseller, who kindly allowed me to read it, but it evidently did not pass muster with Christie herself.[35] In February 1950 she wrote to Cork from Iraq about what appears to have been yet another attempt at a stage adaptation:

It may be the natural apathy of the Near East, but I don't feel very enthusiastic about the proposed dramatisation of Towards Zero . . . I have become a bit bored with the perennial humorous policeman, but don't really care . . . the Whodunnit with everyone suspected in turn, and plenty of comic red herrings thrown in, really by now quite sickens me on the stage! And it's not the kind of story that Towards Zero is! . . . Don't twist the kind of book that hasn't the right atmosphere. You might just as well start with an entirely new story. There is a large class of my books which is not full of 'thrills' and 'humour', such as, for instance Towards Zero, Sparkling Cyanide, Five Little Pigs, Sad Cypress, the Hollow, etc. And you really can't turn a Class B story into a

Class A story – it doesn't lend itself to such treatment, and it doesn't seem fair to encourage Robert Brenon who is an intelligent and artistic young man to do so when I probably shan't like the result.

Frankly, as you know, I have never seen Towards Zero as good material for a play . . . its point is *not* suspicion on everybody – but suspicion and everything pointing towards the incrimination of *one* person – and rescue of that victim at the moment when she seems to be hopelessly doomed. But if fun and thrills are wanted, go to some other of my fifty offspring!

I think, really, it might be better to give the whole thing up. What do you think?[36]

It may have been at this point that Christie herself started making notes for a 'new version of Towards Zero', in which the action does not move to the familiar setting of Lady Tressilian's until Act Two.[37] Nothing was to come of the idea, but I do wonder whether it was the exchange with Cork that put her in mind to attempt her own version of *The Hollow*, without Hercule Poirot.

In March 1951 yet another writer, Gerald Verner, was granted the right 'To make a dramatic adaptation' of *Towards Zero* within six months, provided that a West End contract was entered into within eighteen months, and a West End production presented within two and a half years.[38] Income was to be divided 50/50 with Christie, which, significantly on this occasion, was the usual deal offered to third-party adaptors. A week later, Joseph Lucas at Hughes Massie wrote to Christie, 'We have not yet received the script of Gerald Verner's version of Towards Zero, but the one scene I have read of it looks most promising.'[39]

The man behind all these efforts to get a new script of *Towards Zero* written was Bertie Meyer, whose production of *Murder at the Vicarage* had closed twelve months earlier. In April 1951 he finally took out a one-year option to produce Verner's new adaptation,[40] and the following week Cork wrote to Christie by way of explanation:

I am afraid Bertie Meyer is going to do Towards Zero. He held us to the arrangement that you had told him that if he could get a good version made then he could – because of old associations – do the play. Gerald Verner's version was quite unobjectionable, in fact we think it is damn good, so this is all in train now, and the Howard and Wyndham people who, as you know, control most of the Number One dates, like the play, and are not only giving Bertie a selection of good dates in the autumn, but are taking a share in the show. The Howard and Wyndham participation is contingent on the parts of Neville [sic] and his two wives being played by suitable stars, which is useful reassurance from our point of view![41]

Christie responded, 'I must hand it to Bertie Meyer for sticking to it!! Am glad about the "stars" proviso!'[42]

On 6 June Cork wrote to Christie, 'I am sending you a copy of Gerald Verner's version of Towards Zero, which several people think is pretty good. I was talking to Bertie Meyer about it this morning, and he doesn't seem to have got very far with the casting.'[43] The following night, Peter Saunders' production of *The Hollow* opened at the Fortune.

In *The Mousetrap Man*, Saunders recalls that when he asked whether he would be treading on Meyer's toes in taking an option for *The Hollow* he was told by Cork that 'Bertie had another of her plays which he had never presented and she was not prepared to let him have another one until it was put on in town.'[44] Given that this conversation between Cork and Saunders had taken place in September 1950, when the new stage version of *Towards Zero* had not yet been written by Verner or optioned by Meyer, and given Christie's own reticence about the idea, I am not sure that this was entirely the case. Nonetheless the bizarre situation now arose where Bertie Meyer held an option for a new third-party Christie adaptation literally on the eve of the first West End production to be mounted by Peter Saunders, the producer who was to bring her own writing centre stage.

But the planned autumn 1951 tour of *Towards Zero* did not materialise. At the end of January 1952, with *The Hollow* successfully transferred to the Ambassadors and *Three Blind Mice* also under option to Saunders, *The Stage* printed an article headlined 'BERTIE MEYER'S JUBILEE – HALF A CENTURY IN MANAGEMENT'. It ran:

A man who has completed 40 or 50 years in any branch of work is usually considered to have earned his retirement. But B.A. Meyer, who this year sees his fiftieth year of active management, plans to celebrate his jubilee with three new projects. It is fitting that one of these should be a new adaptation from Agatha Christie, *Towards Zero*, for he was responsible, in 1928, for the first production of a Christie play, *Alibi*, which Gerald Du Maurier directed and in which Charles Laughton created the part of Inspector [sic] Poirot. He also brought a number of other Christie plays to the West End, including *Ten Little Niggers*, *Appointment with Death* and *Murder at the Vicarage*. One of Mr Meyer's colleagues in his new ventures will be Gerald Verner, who is adapting both the Christie play and a new Peter Cheyney play . . .

Mr Meyer believes that a manager must be guided by public taste to a large extent; attempting to guide taste oneself can often be a costly business. 'Looking back over the years,' he said, 'I think taste has changed very little. At the present time it is still very unsophisticated and the long runs are all light-hearted plays. At the same time I have always been a believer in clean plays; those dealing with sordid problems usually have a very limited appeal.[45]

Gerald Verner, the man who had finally created a script for *Towards Zero* that was deemed to be workable, was a prolific writer for the stage, television and radio, and was himself the author of more than a hundred books. He was said to have been able to write a thriller in a fortnight, and once wrote thirty-five books in five years. Verner had turned to writing in the 1920s after a career as an actor, a nightclub cabaret producer, a worker in Billingsgate fish market, a calendar designer and a pavement artist. It was while living as a down-and-out on the Embankment in London after the First World War that he wrote *The Embankment Murder* and was paid £70 for his manuscript; now the Duke of Windsor was a fan, and always had Verner's latest works sent to him.

Verner's biggest stage success was to be his other adaptation for Meyer, *Meet Mr Callaghan*, a dramatisation of crime writer Peter Cheyney's 1938 novel *The Urgent Hangman*. *Meet Mr Callaghan* opened at the Garrick Theatre in May 1952; directed by Derrick de Marney, who also alternated the title role with his brother Terence, it ran for almost a year. A sequel the following year, another Verner script based on Cheyney's 1939 novel *Dangerous Curves* and this time with Terence both directing and starring, followed it into the Garrick but was less successful.

Terence de Marney, who made a not insignificant contribution to Christie's own stage work as the original Lombard in *Ten Little Niggers* and the director of *Appointment with Death*, was to die in an accidental fall under a tube train in 1971 at the age of sixty-two. His *Times* obituary commented that he was an actor who had 'obviously relished the sinister, the indefinably frightening and the strange, but his range was not limited to them and he could provide romantic charm and sheer physical excitement . . . without plunging into extravagance he had the art of harnessing the audience's imagination to the service of any play in which he appeared.'[46]

An advertisement in *The Stage* in January 1952 from the leading tour booker of the day, Renee Stepham, seeks bookings for Peter Saunders' forthcoming production of *To Dorothy, a Son*, the play that Hubert Gregg would later turn down *The Mousetrap* for.[47] Both Saunders and Meyer used Stepham to book their tours, and the same advertisement also seeks pre-West End bookings for *Meet Mr Callaghan* ('One and only Peter Cheyney play' starring Terence de Marney) and for *Towards Zero* ('New Agatha Christie play' – no mention of Verner). So we know that Meyer at least made an attempt to get *Towards*

Zero on, although the advertisement advises that it was still 'not fully cast'.

This state of affairs was not without its problems, and threatened to compromise Saunders' ability to schedule first *The Mousetrap* and then *Witness for the Prosecution*. Bizarrely, though, Cork continued to renew Meyer's option on the Verner script, writing to Christie in March 1952:

> Bertie Meyer still thinks that he is going to do Towards Zero this Spring. His contract requires production by April 12th, which as I see it, makes it impossible for performance now, but Bertie has written me a long screed hoping that in view of his even longer association with the Christie plays, we will not close down on him. If you are agreeable, what I think we might do is to tell him he must produce either in the country or in London before the end of April, and that if the production is in the country, then he must bring it into the West End in the middle of July. This would give sufficient lapse of time not to interfere with The Mousetrap.[48]

Exactly a year later, Cork was to write, regarding *Witness for the Prosecution*, 'The rough idea for this is to have a Number One tour starting in August with the West End production in November, but this is to some extent dependent on Towards Zero. Bertie is still just on the point of completing his plans.'[49]

In April 1953 Christie wrote to Cork from Iraq, where she had been exchanging letters with Saunders on the development of the script for *Witness for the Prosecution*, 'P Saunders seems to think he can't do Witness for P when he thought because Bertie Meyer is putting on Towards 0. But is he really? I'm really fed up with Bertie – He's had *years* to get that play on – Peter does *put* my plays on.'[50] Cork responded with some interesting news:

> I believe you know that Bertie Meyer interested Peter Cotes in Towards Zero. He wanted to produce [i.e. direct] it, and Bertie in his incredible way said 'well that's marvellous; we

will keep in touch' – and nothing more was heard from him. Peter Cotes rang me up yesterday to say that if Bertie were out, his own production company would like to buy the play, as he feels if certain small things were done to it, he could make it into another Mousetrap. I could not give him any promise, as I think Peter Saunders ought to have first crack at it when Bertie fades away. Peter Saunders has said he would like to do it in order to avoid clashes, and probably when the time comes we can arrange to have the satisfactory business drive of the one Peter combined with the artistic assistance of the other.'[51]

It was not, in fact, Meyer who had suggested to Peter Cotes that he direct *Towards Zero*, but Christie herself; she had presented him with a copy of the script as his first night gift for *The Mousetrap*.[52] The playwright, if not the producer, was clearly an admirer of his work. Three months later, the Peter with the 'business drive' would write to the 'artistic' Peter dispensing with his services on *The Mousetrap*.

In August 1953 Meyer finally bowed out and Saunders took an option on Verner's script for *Towards Zero*.[53] A year later he arranged to extend his licence for six monthly periods until six months after the end of *The Mousetrap*, paying £100 for each such extension; it was clearly Saunders' intention to put *Towards Zero* into the Ambassadors Theatre when *The Mousetrap* closed.

Except it didn't. In April 1954, Cork wrote to Christie:

As you know, we have been putting off the production of Towards Zero so that it would not clash with your other plays. These postponements have not been entirely and altogether convenient to Gerald Verner, who is not directly interested in the other plays. He would be willing to dispose of his interest in the play for a cash sum, and I wonder if you would have any objection to . . . buying out Verner? Actually, Verner's rights under his original contract would expire next September if the play is not produced by that time, but I don't suppose you would mind giving an extension of his rights for say a year, as it was to suit us that the play has not been done.[54]

Verner thus assigned his rights to Christie, via an intermediary company, for £2,000, no doubt in the belief that at this stage a bird in the hand was worth two in the bush.[55] The same quirk in copyright law that was to see the rights of *The Mousetrap* revert to Rosalind in 2001 would mean that in 2005, twenty-five years after Verner's death, these assigned rights reverted to his son; but for now the position was clear-cut. Christie herself owned 'all rights of copyright' in Verner's work on *Towards Zero*.

With *The Mousetrap* showing no sign of vacating the Ambassadors, it was not until 4 September 1956 that Verner's adaptation of *Towards Zero* would eventually reach the West End, in a production presented by Peter Saunders at the St James's Theatre, following a four week tour which had again commenced at Nottingham. The St James's Theatre had been the home of Saunders' first West End production, *Fly Away Peter*, less than ten years previously, and although now managed by a company which counted Laurence Olivier and Vivien Leigh amongst its directors, it was actually a joint venture between the Group's ubiquitous Prince Littler and *Witness for the Prosecution*'s Broadway producer Gilbert Miller. Whatever the realities of the *Witness for the Prosecution* film sale, on paper it had ultimately been a success, and the Miller connection here cannot have been insignificant. Littler, too, had been known personally to support Saunders' efforts and, indeed, his wife held a small financial interest in *The Mousetrap*'s home at the Ambassadors. So while the St James's was by no means a first-rank 'Group' theatre, Saunders found that on this occasion the doors were open to him.

Saunders entrusted direction of the piece to Murray MacDonald, who had been responsible for the eventual West End production of *Love from a Stranger* in 1936. MacDonald had enjoyed a big West End hit in 1949 with James Bridie's *Daphne Laureola* starring Edith Evans, which transferred to Broadway less successfully the following year, and had also notably directed Dodie Smith's adaptation of her novel *I Capture the Castle* in 1954. Saunders again engaged Michael Weight as designer, although the standard 'drawing room' setting was considerably less of a challenge than *Witness for the Prosecution*, or even *Spider's Web* with its revolving bookcase. Film and television actor George Baker, later to become known to television viewers as Inspector Wexford in the Ruth Rendell mysteries, was paid £70 per week to play the leading role of the charismatic Nevile Strange, a man perhaps not unrelated to Gerald Strange in Christie's own script of *The Stranger*. The cast also featured Frederick Leister as Battle, Cyril Raymond as Royd and Gwen Cherrell as Audrey, Nevile Strange's first wife. This was a respectable but by no means stellar line-up, with salaries ranging between £45 and £60 per week, but the casting seems to have been insufficiently impressive for Howard & Wyndham to remain involved; or it may have been that they simply didn't want to switch allegiance from Meyer to Saunders. Unknown actress Mary Law was paid £23 per week to play Strange's second wife, Kay, having turned down the job of understudy. According to Law, in an interview with Gwen Robyns, Christie had been present at auditions and told her that she was delighted that she had been given the role. '"I am so glad," Christie said, "The first day I saw you I wanted you because you are absolutely as I imagined Kay would be so I was determined to have you."'[56]

Mary Law had recently finished her second run as Mollie in *The Mousetrap* (which she played in 1957–8 and 1975–6) when she was interviewed by Robyns, famously remarking of Christie's dialogue that it 'does not bear any resemblance to what one says in normal life'. She noted in particular that actors rehearsing *Towards Zero* 'all found her lines very difficult to say', but that Christie, quite rightly in Law's opinion, was resistant to changing them. Law identifies her as the playwright because, since Saunders had taken over the option from Meyer, the play had somehow become a 'co-adaptation' between Verner and Christie herself. Logic dictates that if

Christie had indeed been the co-writer of the script from the start then she would have received her usual 50 per cent of the writer's royalty as the author of the original book plus half of the adaptor's 50 per cent share. But this was not the case in Verner's original deal, in which he took the full adaptor's share of the royalty.

Saunders had by now presented four successful scripts from Christie's own pen, and Cork's standard response to the numerous enquiries from would-be adaptors of Christie's novels was that Christie wrote her own adaptations these days. And yet, following the closure of *Witness for the Prosecution*, the play that was to run alongside *The Mousetrap* and *Spider's Web* and take the number of Christie's works in the West End back up to three, was not actually written by her and had indeed been trailed by Bertie Meyer as an adaptation by Verner alone. Anticipating this problem, it appears that Saunders had succeeded in persuading Christie to undertake some work on the script so that he could legitimately put her stamp on it. This she undertook grudgingly. In a 1968 letter to a researcher she diplomatically states that she 'had a certain amount of collaboration with Gerald Verner in Towards Zero';[57] in a 1971 letter to Rosalind she was more blunt, writing that Saunders 'urged me into helping with Towards Zero' and that she 'never liked it'.[58]

There is no evidence that Christie made any significant changes to Verner's version, although in the absence of any working drafts or indeed any correspondence between the two writers, it is impossible to identify either Verner's original material or the exact extent of her contribution. Intriguingly, the scripts held in the Christie archive credit neither of the 'collaborators' and even the copy submitted to the Lord Chamberlain's office carries neither of their names, although it is filed under Christie's alone. There are some desultory scribbles from her on what appears to be, to all intents and purposes, a performance-ready typescript, and this already includes a sequence in the opening stage directions for which, from Notebook 17, we know she was responsible. Some undetailed jottings relating to her work on this version of the play can be found elsewhere in the notebooks, and at some point between the undated typescripts a few minor changes are made and the action is reordered from two acts of three scenes each to the three two-scene acts with which we are now familiar. Most notably, all available typescripts of the play contain a dramatic plot twist which does not feature in the book but for which there is a prototype in Christie's 1944 version.

Other than that, there are remarkably few parallels with her original adaptation. Instead of Christie's ambitious open air setting, the entire 'action of the play passes in the drawing room at Gull's Point, Lady Tressilian's house at Saltcreek, Cornwall'.[59] The specification of Cornwall is unique to this version of the play – the novel and Christie's script appear to be set in Salcombe, Devon. Superintendent Battle has been reinstated and Angus McWhirter, the failed suicide who features in the novel and makes a significant contribution to Christie's adaptation, is absent. Of Christie's 1944 thirteen-person dramatis personae only six are shared with Verner's eleven-person script, sadly not including an entertainingly dour Scottish housekeeper. Like *Ten Little Niggers* and *The Hollow* the drama is underscored with the time-honoured dramatic device of a storm, but the plot twists of the novel and its extraordinary premise are less successfully achieved on stage. Christie's instincts about its unsuitability for stage adaptation were ultimately to prove correct and it is little wonder that her heart wasn't in it.

In asking her to contribute to the script, it cannot have been lost on Saunders that Verner's rights in his work had been assigned to Christie, who consequently now received Verner's adaptation royalty as well as her own for the original source material. Saunders' promotion of the play took ruthless advantage of this, implying a much greater authorial input from Christie than I believe actually to have been the case. The classified advertisements for the production in *The Times* were worded simply 'George Baker in Towards Zero by Agatha Christie' and on the title page of the programme the play was billed as

TOWARDS ZERO
By Agatha Christie
Adapted from Agatha Christie's book by the authoress and
Gerald Verner[60]

The critics responded as if they were simply watching an unusually weak offering from the writer of *The Mousetrap*, *Witness for the Prosecution* and *Spider's Web*; and matters weren't helped when Milton Shulman gave away the identity of the killer in the *Evening Standard*. The *Times* critic, in a substantial review headlined 'Towards Zero by Agatha Christie' (with no mention of Gerald Verner), was relatively supportive, concluding that 'The piece, compactly full of all the ripest ingredients, remains a fair specimen . . . a not too strenuously diverting evening in which we do not smell a rat until too late.'[61] Kenneth Tynan in the *Observer*, however, did smell a rat:

> Agatha Christie's *Towards Zero* is a double parlour-game; before guessing the killer's name, we are invited to guess who is going to be killed. The writing is flat, and the setting one of those impregnable fortresses which pass in such plays for country houses. Among the accused are George Baker, stiff and shrill, and Mary Law, a dashing redhead. This tame affair taught me, if nothing else, why murder plays are so popular in London. All the characters must perforce be represented as harbouring dark and repressed criminal impulses, which gives them a likeness to everyday British life seldom approached by other dramatic conventions.[62]

Once again, this critical heavyweight was tickled by the genre, but he had noted correctly the inadequacy of the writing. Christie's own writing may be accused of many things, including being difficult for actors to deliver, but 'flat' it is never is. This is why I do not believe the play to be to any significant extent of her authorship. The strategy of marketing what I believe to have been essentially Verner's work in Christie's name had backfired, and the playwright whose last four West End plays had been hits was suddenly seen to be responsible for one that wasn't. The 1956 adaptation of *Towards Zero*, in my view, is a fake, and not a particularly good one at that. And as such, it should have no place in Christie's 'collected works' as a dramatist.

I don't believe that Christie herself was complicit in the subterfuge; no doubt she was cajoled by Saunders into putting her name to whatever contribution she made and probably didn't think twice about her billing. She dutifully attended rehearsals, but clearly felt uneasy about the outcome; significantly, she makes no mention at all of the play in her autobiography. Perhaps even more significantly, Saunders himself only gives it a few lines in his own book; we are told nothing at all about its origins or the process of its production other than that 'later that year I put on another Agatha Christie play, *Towards Zero*'[63] and that it got a 'medium' press and was not a success: 'We struggled along for six months but it was the most I could manage.' He does, however, give some space to the occasion on which the Queen visited unexpectedly and, to his horror, witnessed a half-full auditorium.

Towards Zero cost £3,456 to put on[64] (notably less than *Witness for the Prosecution* and *Spider's Web*) and, after 205 West End performances, went out on a national tour under licence to Geoffrey Hastings Ltd. Thereafter it thrived in repertory and amateur productions throughout the country courtesy of Samuel French's 1958 'acting edition' although, unusually, it had been published the previous year in America by the Dramatists Play Service.

On 9 July 1956, exactly a month before *Towards Zero* opened at Nottingham, the premiere of Christie's pre-war play *A Daughter's a Daughter* finally took place. Christie had reminded Edmund Cork about the piece at the end of 1950, and its production would have been of a great deal more interest to her than that of Verner's play. Cork had duly sent *A Daughter's a Daughter* to Peter Saunders, who at that point had optioned *The Hollow* but not yet produced it.

A Daughter's a Daughter is set in a London flat, where widowed thirty-nine-year-old Ann Prentice lives with her daughter, Sarah. Sarah objects to her mother's suitor, Richard Cauldfield, to whom she takes an instant, jealous dislike, not helped by his view that 'Girls take on a job just like men do nowadays'. Ann abandons her plans to remarry in order to pacify her daughter but, as her friend the 'celebrated' Dame Laura Whitstable remarks, 'The trouble with a sacrifice is that once it's made it's not over and done with.' The tables are then turned when Sarah has to choose between two suitors – the hapless and impecunious but devoted Jerry Lloyd and the dangerous, wealthy bounder Lawrence Steene – and Ann appears to encourage her daughter to marry the one who will make her least happy. Dame Laura is a wry and knowing observer as events unfold.

Saunders suggested some minor updates to make the vocabulary and references less specifically pre-war. Setting the end of the play, which covers a five-year timespan over its three acts, in 'the present' of 1950 neatly placed its opening scene at the end of the war, and Christie duly rewrote it in this context, with Sarah returning from service with the WAAF rather than a skiing holiday at the start of the play and Jerry introduced as a squadron leader. This serves the piece very well, adding a sense of post-war displacement to the characters' efforts to redefine themselves in a period of accelerated social change. Jerry's new status as a demobbed airman means that we also, thankfully, lose a sequence in which he reports that he has been fired from his job for having the girls at work 'in fits' of laughter by impersonating a 'frightful old Jewboy' who visits his employer. Although we are clearly not intended to empathise with Jerry's predicament, Christie herself needed no prompting from the Anti-Defamation League to appreciate that it was no longer acceptable even for her characters to adopt the casual anti-semitism that had been prevalent in her own Edwardian youth. Interestingly, Jerry's personality has improved in the process. In the early draft he is described as 'A dark, lazy-looking creature with charm and a slight air of ineffectiveness' but in the updated version he simply 'has a charm and is obviously in love with Sarah'.

The Agatha Christie archive holds a number of typescripts for *A Daughter's a Daughter*, the earliest of which appears to be the version incorporating the revisions requested by Basil Dean in 1939. This includes a number of handwritten notes, resulting in a revised typescript which sets the opening of the play firmly in 1945. As ever, the scripts themselves are not dated, but the final draft I believe to have been prepared in late 1950 or early 1951.

Much has been made of whether the play's scenario of a loving but mutually destructive mother–daughter relationship reflects elements of Christie's relationship with her own daughter, or indeed that of her friend Nan Kon with her daughter Judith. Certainly both Rosalind and Judith were of an age that could have informed the role of Sarah when the piece was originally written in the late 1930s. Of more interest than these resonances, though, is the play's portrayal of a young woman whose life-changing choices are ultimately dictated by a desire for excitement and danger, rather than dutiful stability, effectively making it the third in a trio which starts with *The Lie* and includes Christie's own version of *The Stranger*.

For Sarah, her excitement and danger come in the form of the dissolute Lawrence Steene, 'an attractive, rather dissipated-looking man of forty. He has a lazy voice and a vicious mouth – the kind of man most women find attractive and most men dislike.' In Act Two, the loyal housekeeper, Edith, cannot hide her obvious mistrust of Steene, leading him to question Sarah:

LAWRENCE: She hates me, doesn't she?

SARAH: She oughtn't to be so rude.

LAWRENCE: Oh, I don't mind. It gives me a kick – it's so in keeping. She's a period piece, of course. The faithful family servant – now almost extinct. Besides, quite a lot of people dislike me. I'd feel terribly upset if they didn't.

SARAH: I agree with you. I hate people whom everybody likes. They are usually too frightful.

LAWRENCE: Mothers won't let me talk to their daughters.

SARAH: Why? Do you seduce them?

LAWRENCE: Oh no, darling, nothing so crude. I'm supposed to have nameless orgies at my house.

SARAH: You do have rather peculiar parties, don't you?

LAWRENCE: (Smiling) I'm not conventional. There's so much to be done with life if you've only got the courage to experiment.

SARAH: That's what I think.

LAWRENCE: I don't like girls much – silly, fluffy crude little things. You're different, Sarah. You've got a mind – and a body, rather a nice body. (Pause) You don't bore me.

SARAH: Am I supposed to be grateful for that? Perhaps you bore me.

LAWRENCE: (Softly and with meaning) Do I?

SARAH: (A little breathless) No – you don't . . . You are a beast!

LAWRENCE: Yes, and you like me for it. I can give you a good deal, Sarah. It's not only that I can afford to wrap minks and fox furs around that adorable body, to hang jewels on your white skin. I can show you life, Sarah, I can teach you to feel. I can show you the depths and heights of human emotion. All life is experience.

SARAH: (Fascinated) Yes – I suppose that's true.

LAWRENCE: What do you know of life? Less than nothing. I can take you places, sordid horrible places, where you'll see life running fierce and dark, where you can feel – *feel* – till being alive is a dark ecstasy!

SARAH: (Pulling away from him) I think – I'm rather afraid of you.

LAWRENCE: I hope you are, you enjoy that feeling, don't you?[65]

Ann, who has cancelled her remarriage plans in order not to upset her daughter, has also started living life on the edge: 'She's got far more boyfriends than I have and she's never home until dawn,' Sarah tells Lawrence. The stage directions inform us that in Act Two 'Ann is quite metamorphosed. Her eyebrows are plucked, her hair is dressed in an exaggerated style and is touched up so that the colour is slightly brighter. She is restless and vivacious in manner and is dressed in the latest fashion.' 'I've become shockingly gay,' she remarks. 'After all, there's no need to be a frump just because one's middle-aged, is there?' The flat, too, has been 'redecorated in a modern style – plastic curtains and chromium chairs. There is a cocktail bar built in.'

Amongst the men Ann brings home is the flamboyant Basil, who is not unrelated to *The Mousetrap*'s Christopher Wren, and who talks enthusiastically about interior design and going to the ballet. 'It's no good, Mother, I don't like your pansy friend,' says Sarah. 'Oh but darling, he's very amusing. So marvellously spiteful about people,' comes the response. Ann's next gentleman caller (who we never actually meet) is Nigel. 'He's one of mother's specials – a he-man back from the Malay Straits,' says Sarah who, alone with her mother's friend Dame Laura, confides in her:

SARAH: Mother's in a flat spin from morning to night.

DAME LAURA: She's a good-looking woman.

SARAH: Oh, she's frightfully attractive. She's got lots of boyfriends. Some of them are a bit lousy, but I don't like to interfere. After all, the poor pet must enjoy herself before it's too late.

DAME LAURA: I suppose to you life ends at fifty.

SARAH: Well it must be awful when your face goes and your figure, and nobody wants to take you out any more. I hope I shall die at thirty-nine.

DAME LAURA: I remember you saying something like that a couple of years ago. But the age limit has gone up. It was twenty-nine then.

SARAH: It must be awful to be old.

DAME LAURA: No, it's very comfortable.

In an extraordinary scene of sustained discomfort in Act Two, Ann's former suitor Richard visits her with his new young wife,

Doris, who is described as 'pleasant, conventional and distinctly provincial'. The scene's opening stage directions read, 'Ann compares her own elegance favourably with Doris's provincial appearance. Doris, who has been a little jealous of this unknown Mrs Prentice, thinks "why, she's quite old." Richard thinks, looking at Ann: "she wouldn't really have done for me." He is quite besotted with his Doris.' The three of them engage in a brilliantly tortuous conversation about Richard and Doris's life in the country, where they have an Aga and keep dogs, find it difficult to engage servants ('They're talking about importing foreigners,' says Doris, 'Poles, I believe, are quite pleasant') and, worst of all, Richard has taken up golf. The talk turns to flowers, and Ann comments, 'I don't object to our labelling the garden varieties, but I do think the wild flowers might be allowed to grow in peace keeping their own secrets – or just being known by their local names – Ragged Robin – Traveller's Joy – Love-in-a-Mist – Love-Lies-Bleeding.' Ann is disconcerted to find that she is no longer attracted to Richard.

Sarah, having destroyed her own mother's hopes of happiness, discusses her own situation with Dame Laura:

SARAH: I'm getting awfully tired of doing nothing.

DAME LAURA: Not thinking of getting married?

SARAH: I'm not keen on getting married. It always seems to turn out so rottenly.

DAME LAURA: Not always.

SARAH: Most of my friends seem to have come croppers. Of course if you marry someone with pots of money, I suppose it's all right.

DAME LAURA: That's your view?

SARAH: Well it's really the only sensible one. Love's all right, but, after all, it's only based on sexual attraction and that never lasts . . . the only sensible thing is to marry someone really well off.

DAME LAURA: That mightn't last either.

SARAH: I suppose money does come and go a bit these days.

DAME LAURA: I didn't mean that. I meant that the pleasure of being rich is like sexual attraction. One gets used to it. It wears off like everything else.

Sarah eventually introduces Dame Laura to Lawrence, but her disapproval is as evident as Edith's:

DAME LAURA: I was broadcasting yesterday.
SARAH: Oh, that must be marvellous! What about?
DAME LAURA: The stability of marriage.
LAWRENCE: Surely it is the impermanence of marriage nowadays which constitutes its greatest charm?
SARAH: Lawrence has been married a good deal.
LAWRENCE: Only three times, Sarah.
DAME LAURA: Are you a mass poisoner, Mr Steene?
SARAH: Oh no, he sheds them in the divorce courts.

Not surprisingly, Sarah's decision to marry Lawrence turns out disastrously, and at the end of the play neither mother nor daughter has succeeded in finding happiness. This is all about as far removed from a country house whodunit as it is possible to get, and yet it is very much in keeping with Christie's preoccupations as a playwright and is a fine example of her abilities to explore serious subjects through the medium.

Basil Dean had hoped to cast Gertrude Lawrence as Ann in 1939, and in 1951 there was some excitement when Saunders thought he might be able to interest distinguished classical stage actress Fay Compton, who had played Ophelia opposite both John Gielgud and John Barrymore; but in the end Cork reported that Compton 'could not see herself in A Daughter's a Daughter, and as Peter Saunders does not want to do it unless he can get absolutely the right casting, this matter has not moved much'.[66] Cork's own suggestion, Martita Hunt, best known as Miss Havisham in David Lean's 1949 film of *Great Expectations*, was dismissed by Christie as 'not at all right'; a 'smart, sophisticated' actress, she thought, but not a sufficiently 'soft and sympathetic' one.[67]

After the Fay Compton setback, *A Daughter's a Daughter* appears to have gone on to the back burner again until it suddenly appeared, reworked as a novel, in 1952; this makes it, incidentally, the only Christie novel to be based on a play, rather than the other way round. In publishing it, however, Christie opted to issue it as a work by Mary Westmacott, the pen name which she had adopted for a series of non-crime novels that, in her own theatrical terminology, might be described as 'domestic dramas'. As Max Mallowan notes:

> Agatha's success as a writer of detective fiction had one disadvantage, in that her publisher discouraged her if she ever expressed a desire to work in some other literary medium. No other writer of detection has written in that form for so long . . . Nevertheless the time came when Agatha insisted on release and began writing under the name Mary Westmacott . . . As Mary Westmacott, Agatha was able to embark on many themes in which she was interested. Music, drama, the psychology of ambition, the problems of artists . . . But I think that in this form of writing the true release came in that it gave her freedom to range over characters in depth, freed from the constriction of the detective plot to which every personality had to be subordinated.[68]

The novelised *A Daughter's a Daughter* starts with the earlier scenario of Sarah on a skiing holiday, indicating that as a piece of writing it pre-dates the changes made to the play; although Gerry (in this case with a 'G') is not, even jokingly, anti-semitic. This was the fifth Westmacott title and the second to be published by Heinemann, Collins having lost the franchise when they opted out of publishing 1947's *The Rose and the Yew Tree*. In a piece written to mark her mother's centenary, Rosalind commented:

> The Mary Westmacott books have been described as romantic novels but I don't think it is really a fair assessment. They are not 'love stories' in the general sense of the term, and

they certainly have no happy endings. They are, I believe, about love in some of its most powerful and destructive forms. The possessive love of a mother for her child, or a child for its mother in both *Giant's Bread* (1930) and *Unfinished Portrait* (1944). The battle between the widowed mother and her grown-up daughter in *A Daughter's a Daughter*. A girl's obsession with her younger sister in *The Burden* and the closeness of love to hate – the Burden in this story being the weight of one person's love on someone else.[69]

In a *Sunday Times* interview in 1961, Agatha herself commented of the Westmacott novels that 'I enjoy thinking of a detective story, planning it, but when it comes to write it, it is like going to work every day, like having a job. Writing detective stories is your job, and it is a job, but writing the others feels pleasant.'[70] This is very similar to the way she compared her work on detective novels with the pleasure she derived from her playwriting, and biographer Laura Thompson, who devotes much of her book to exploring the thesis that the Westmacott novels provided a 'door that opened into her most private and precious imaginative garden', might have done well to pay equal attention to Christie's plays, rather than dismissing them as 'lightweight things on the whole'.

In the Westmacott books Agatha takes refuge in her alter ego to explore some of the more painful themes of her own life, particularly in the second book, 1934's *Unfinished Portrait*. Separating the work of 'Westmacott' from that written by 'Agatha Christie' ensured that, in so doing, the expectations of the latter's readers were not subverted. In her work as a dramatist, however, where her words were effectively spoken by her characters rather than herself, she felt no need for such distancing. Agatha Christie, playwright, was free to explore whatever themes, subtexts and dramatic constructions she wished, and the result was that the stage sometimes became a battlefield between her aspirations as a writer and the expectations of her audiences and producers.

Ironically, the one piece that could have conclusively defined Christie's work as a playwright on her own terms had now been published as a novel under the Westmacott name, so when it was finally performed there was no option but to promote the stage version as a Westmacott work as well. This had plainly never been Christie's intention, and even the revised early 1950s typescript states that *A Daughter's a Daughter* is a play 'by Agatha Christie'. Only when it was submitted to the Lord Chamberlain's office in 1956, four years after the novel-isation, did the play become credited to Westmacott.[71] The true identity of Westmacott had in fact been revealed in 1949, much to Christie's distress, by the *Sunday Times'* Atticus column which, appropriately enough, was written at that time by former secret agent Sir Robert Bruce Lockhart. Readers of the novel are therefore likely to have been well aware of its true author-ship, although Christie herself persisted with the pretence, issuing a sixth and final novel in the Westmacott name, *The Burden*, in 1956.

In May 1955, Edmund Cork wrote to Christie to confirm that her tickets had been reserved for the Queen's visit to *Witness for the Prosecution* at the Theatre Royal Windsor and with some updates about the proposed film of *Spider's Web* for Margaret Lockwood. He also mentions that 'The woman director who is so keen on A Daughter's a Daughter is Chloe Gibson. I don't know her work very well, but I understand she has come on wonderfully during the last year or so. Probably you know all about her, as she hails from Torquay.'[72] Gibson, who was nine years younger than Christie and was indeed a native of Torquay, had started her career acting in rep at Paignton and had the distinction of having 'discovered' Dirk Bogarde when making her West End directorial debut in 1947, with Michael Clayton-Hutton's play *Power Without Glory*. Gibson's work was highly regarded and she went on to become head of drama at Irish television station RTE, but we know from correspondence relating to finding a director for *The Hollow* that, according to Saunders, 'Miss Christie is not keen on Chloe Gibson.'[73] Quite why this was we may never know – it may even have related to childhood and family matters in Torquay – but for whatever reason Gibson, who would have been an interesting choice, was not entrusted with the project.

Having produced four consecutive Christie plays in the West End, and having firmly established her brand in the stage thriller market, Saunders was clearly at something of a loss as to what to do with *A Daughter's a Daughter*. Eventually, though, he concocted a scheme that would get the play off his desk and on to a stage with a minimum of fuss or, indeed, of financial outlay.

Amongst Saunders' smaller investors was Ralph Wotherspoon, a former satirist for *Punch* magazine who was now a director of Smith and Whiley Productions, which presented repertory seasons under the management of Geoffrey Hastings. Himself an investor with Saunders, Hastings had worked alongside him on his early theatrical projects, and was regularly licensed by him to produce post-West End tours of Christie plays. Smith and Whiley had engaged Hastings to run repertory seasons at the Theatre Royal Stratford East before the theatre was taken over by Joan Littlewoood's Theatre Workshop in 1953, and by 1956 he was managing successful seasons for them at Newquay and at the Theatre Royal, Bath. Now Saunders turned to Wotherspoon and Hastings' repertory company at Bath, the London Resident Company, to host the premiere of *A Daughter's a Daughter*. The production was scheduled to run for a week and would be cast from within the local repertory players. It was a low-maintenance operation, not in itself designed for West End transfer, but it would at least get the play on its feet.

The *Bath Chronicle* was well aware of the playwright's identity, and in July 1956 ran an article which read:

The London Resident Company are privileged to announce that they have been chosen to produce for the first time on any stage the new drama 'A Daughter's a Daughter' by Mary Westmacott. The author is, of course, more widely known

as Agatha Christie, the world famous novelist who also
specialises in stage thrillers. When writing novels other than
thrillers she uses the name Mary Westmacott. There is always
something exciting about the production for the first time
of a new play, particularly if its author is a popular figure,
and the London Resident Company are grateful for the opportunity of participating on such an occasion. Agatha Christie
and the London impresario Peter Saunders, who has exclusive rights on all Miss Christie's stage productions, will be
paying a visit to the Bath Theatre Royal one night during
the week to see this, her latest work.[74]

Strangely, for a local event of this importance ('First time
on any Stage' trumpeted the Theatre Royal's programme), the
Bath Chronicle appears not to have run a review of the play,
and this means that the review in *The Stage* newspaper, like
that of *Towards Zero* in the *Martha's Vineyard Gazette*, is the
only first-hand account that we have of the production. Unlike
the *Chronicle*'s journalist, *The Stage*'s critic was either ignorant
of, or chose not to reveal, the playwright's true identity. The
newspaper's review, which ran under the headline 'THE HATE
THAT GROWS IN WOMEN', oddly categorised the piece as a
'domestic comedy', perhaps as a result of local advertising,
and went on to say:

It has a nice workman-like plot and some unusual angles
and has much to commend it. It is scarcely a comedy, although
it contains much amusing dialogue. It portrays the hate that
can grow in women who have made a sacrifice and can
never forget the smell of its burning. A mother is about to
marry again. Her teenage daughter greatly resents this and
breaks off the marriage. From this time a happy home is
disrupted. The mother takes to the gay life and the daughter
marries a dissolute rich young man. Drink and drugs cloud
the mind of both, despite the efforts of a kindly elderly relative. Audrey Noble plays the part of the mother with effect,
and her duologues with her daughter are finely given. The

daughter is played brilliantly by Mary Manson, a clever and attractive young actress.[75]

The rest of the London Resident Company, led by their director Maurice Jones in the role of Ann's suitor, Richard Cauldfield, are also praised by the reviewer. Playing Sarah's hapless suitor Jerry was twenty-two-year-old Trevor Bannister, later to appear in the long-running television comedy *Are You Being Served?*

Doubtless to Saunders' relief, this was hardly the sort of response that was going to put pressure on him to put the play into the West End. And in any case, Christie herself was immediately distracted by rehearsals for *Towards Zero*. The truth was that Saunders wasn't really the man for this particular job, and he probably knew it. If Basil Dean had produced *A Daughter's a Daughter* back in 1939 with Gertrude Lawrence as Ann, it may well have been a sensation and sent Christie on an entirely different course as a playwright. Even if Saunders had produced the play when he himself first received it in the early 1950s, it might well have passed muster in a West End where Emlyn Williams explored middle-class flirtations with the seamier side of London life in 1951's *Accolade* and, the following year, Terence Rattigan's *The Deep Blue Sea* presented audiences with Peggy Ashcroft as Hester Collyer, a female protagonist who has suffered severe emotional damage as a result of the choices she has made in her pursuit of love. Both these productions were presented, of course, by Tennents, in whose hands *A Daughter's a Daughter* might well have been better positioned. For all they may have been accused of focusing their efforts on the work of gay men, Tennents produced a number of new plays by women writers, including Clemence Dane, Lesley Storm, Dodie Smith, Lillian Hellman and Daphne du Maurier; and two months before *A Daughter's a Daughter* opened in Bath, they had presented the London premiere of Enid Bagnold's *The Chalk Garden*, her first West End venture since Farndale had produced her debut play *Lottie Dundas* in 1943.

Although twenty years her junior, Rattigan, like Christie, had come into his own as a playwright in the post-war West End. We know from ticket orders held by Cork that Christie attended Rattigan's *Separate Tables* at the St James's Theatre in 1954, possibly in this case to support its designer Michael Weight, who was about to design *Spider's Web*; and there is every reason to believe that, as an avid theatregoer, she would have seen *The Deep Blue Sea* as well. When *A Daughter's a Daughter* finally received its West End premiere in 2009, almost thirty-four years after Christie's death, *Daily Telegraph* critic Charles Spencer wrote, 'Christie's clear-eyed, long-neglected account of the way the English middle-class can make their lives unutterably miserable can stand comparison with Rattigan at his best',[76] and Paul Taylor of the *Independent* agreed; 'I would have hazarded that A Daughter's A Daughter was a hitherto undiscovered collaboration between the J. B. Priestley of the socially aware "Time" plays, and the Terence Rattigan who understood the secrets of hearts female as well as male. In fact, it's by Agatha Christie, writing under the pseudonym of Mary Westmacott.'[77] The *Guardian*'s Lyn Gardner noted that 'Christie catches the uncertainty and desperation of a post-war Britain in rapid social change', while observing, 'It's a clever fake that looks and sounds like a Rattigan play, but it never feels like the real thing.'[78] In fact, of course, *A Daughter's a Daughter* pre-dates the majority of Rattigan's work, and the period of rapid social change which it addresses was originally a much earlier one. As a play, it is remarkably ahead of its time; the time, that is, when it was originally written. Developments in theatreland in 1956, however, had conspired to make it seem immediately out of date.

Two months before *A Daughter's a Daughter* opened at Bath, the newly established English Stage Company at the Royal Court, a beneficiary of a recent expansion in the Arts Council's funding remit, had presented their third production, John Osborne's *Look Back in Anger*. Osborne's play, which was set in a small, squalid Midlands flat and featured the truly shocking sight of a woman ironing on stage, introduced audiences to Jimmy Porter, the prototype 'angry young man'. It heralded a new wave of 'realist' playwriting and as such, if literary historians are to be believed, constituted a seminal moment in British theatre, arriving as it did less than a year after twenty-four-year-old director Peter Hall's London premiere of the distinctly non-realist *Waiting for Godot*. The *Observer*'s Kenneth Tynan was to lead the charge for *Look Back in Anger* (his predecessor, Ivor Brown, hated it) and, given this, Tynan's review of the notably substandard *Towards Zero* four months later was remarkably good-natured. As the normally unquotable Hubert Gregg puts it rather nicely, 'Coward had been clipped by Pinter, Beckett had rubbed out Rattigan. White ties and tails had surrendered to no ties and sweatshirts. Technique gave place to the grunt, the graceful gesture to the scratch. A witty line lost out to an interminable pause . . . One thing was certain amidst the shifting sands . . . nobody, but nobody was going to spring The Mousetrap.'[79]

The decades of delays in producing Christie's Rattiganesque *A Daughter's a Daughter* meant that it had, to all intents and purposes, missed the boat. With Jimmy Porter ranting and his wife Alison doing the ironing, Rattigan himself, like Coward after the war, suddenly found that he was yesterday's man; not helped, of course, by his advocacy, in the 1953 second volume of his *Collected Plays*, of playwriting that would find favour with audiences whom he characterised as 'Aunt Edna' – a 'nice, respectable, middle-class, middle-aged maiden lady'. Shaw had always challenged the 'well-made plays' of Rattigan, but now the 'angry young men' could have a field day promoting themselves as the antithesis to Aunt Edna.

Coward reinvented his career in Vegas and Rattigan re-invented his in film, but Christie herself was not caught in the crossfire between Aunt Edna and Jimmy Porter. With Saunders as her producer she was categorised as a provider of populist entertainment rather than the sort of art that people actually bothered arguing about. She was part of neither the culture (as represented by Tennents) nor the counter-culture (as represented by the Royal Court), and while this means that she has effectively been written out of theatre history, had she kept her head down and focused on writing detective thrillers for the stage she might well have remained above the fray. But Agatha Christie, playwright, didn't play by the rules.

Whilst the Royal Court benefited from the new era of public subsidy for theatre, Tennents cleverly continued to create their own subsidy by operating a tax-exempt company alongside their commercial one. Peter Saunders, in analysing the failure of Woodrow Wyatt's Theatrical Companies Bill, notes that 'The Tory Government of the day did not see fit to give way to a Socialist's plea on a matter like this. But the campaign for the Entertainment Tax's abolition was mounting. Deputations went to the House of Commons. Normally reticent producing managers opened their accounts to show how they were suffering, and how unfair it all was.'[80]

Amongst those raising their voices in protest was Frank G. Maddox, general manager of the Theatre Royal, Bath, who in 1956 wrote in the introduction to the programme for *A Daughter's a Daughter*, 'This will be a sad week and one of disappointment in the live theatre, for once again the Chancellor has refused the opportunity afforded him to put things right and abolish the Entertainment Tax. With a solemn promise that in the next budget he hopes that it will no longer be necessary for him to defend this imposition, and that he will look into the whole structure of the Entertainment Duty, he has again washed his hands of the theatre's present plight.'[81] He went on to note that eighty theatres had closed down in the UK in the previous two years, that London cabaret clubs were circumventing the tax by charging excessively for food and offering 'free' entertainment and that television was pulling stars away from live theatre.

The theatre industry was indeed facing new challenges; the coronation, three years previously, had given rise to a substantial increase in television ownership and 1955 had seen the launch of ITV. Saunders notes that

by drawing attention to the way in which the non-profit distributing companies were being used, Mr Wyatt convinced the government that the easiest way out would be to remove the entertainment tax completely. If there was no tax to pay, there would be no point in tax-exempt companies and everybody would be equal. In the Budget two years later, Mr Harold Macmillan, the Chancellor of the Exchequer, gave a firm promise that the entertainment tax would be removed the following year. Mr Peter Thorneycroft, in 1957, carried out that pledge. In doing so, he removed an enormous injustice from the industry at a cost of a little more than a million pounds a year.[82]

Macmillan himself had by this time stepped in as Prime Minister, following Anthony Eden's resignation in the aftermath of the Suez crisis, and Thorneycroft's 9 April budget led on various tax-cutting measures with the ending of entertainment tax effectively the headliner. The news was greeted by cheers in Parliament, and Cork wrote immediately to Christie explaining its significance: 'The important thing for us in the Budget is the cancellation of the Entertainment Tax. This will make all the difference to theatre managers, and according to my arithmetic should add about 20% to your royalty.'[83]

Saunders asks:

What, then, will be the final verdict of the theatre historian on the fantastic manipulations of Hugh Beaumont? Some will say that because he raised the state of British theatre to its greatest heights the ends justified the means. Others may say that by achieving almost the power of a dictator certain talents of authors, artistes, directors and producers were stillborn, and that the British theatre lost as much as or more than it gained. My own belief is that the enormous good Binkie did to the theatre has never disappeared, and indeed never will. But nevertheless I believe that his omnipotence was taken from him at the right moment. Had it continued much longer, all concerned with the industry would inevitably have suffered, because dictatorship or benevolent feudalism (whatever one might call it) is never in the end successful.[84]

Beaumont continued to produce until his death, aged sixty-three, in 1973. Amongst the various letters about his achievements published in the press at the time was one in *The Times* from Enid Bagnold, who wrote that 'He sat on his throne (and at one time it was a throne) disguised as a charming mouse. He was the romantic Mount Everest of my theatrical struggles – its steepest face . . . Playwrights, maybe, were not his closest friends. The "word" was dim to him. What he knew was whether the Whole would appeal . . .'[85] Saunders, whose book was published the year before Beaumont's death, magnanimously gives the man himself the last word on the subject, with his oft-quoted observation, 'If it was a dictatorship I agree it was a bad thing. But it wasn't. At least, I don't think it was.'

For Saunders, in 1957, the battle had finally been won. Binkie's business empire had proved unassailable but, by taking the lateral step of removing the tax itself, the government had also removed the advantage he gained by avoiding it. His biographer, Richard Huggett, notes that 'Nothing was ever quite the same again. Binkie looked on the abolition of the entertainment tax as Al Capone viewed the end of Prohibition. Their two empires did not collapse overnight but their days were numbered.'[86] It is perhaps the case, though, that Saunders had played Bugs Moran to Binkie's Al Capone, cleverly and determinedly constructing an alternative, and equally lucrative, operation based largely on a genre of populist theatre, typified by Christie, that did not fall within the decidedly highbrow agenda of 'the Firm'. With the ending of Binkie's tax advantage his nemesis, as represented by Saunders' rival empire, arguably lost something of its own *raison d'être*; and it may be that, imperceptibly, some of the fight went out of Saunders at that moment. For now, though, Saunders had another problem on his plate, courtesy of Christie herself.

On 30 December 1955 Saunders had taken out an option for a new Christie play called *No Fields of Amaranth*.[87] This, then, is clearly the piece that Christie herself had intended would follow the courtroom drama *Witness for the Prosecution* and the comedy *Spider's Web*, when she was at the height of her West End success; like the latter it was an entirely original piece, and not based on an existing source. Instead, 1956 saw a one-week repertory production of the updated *A Daughter's a Daughter* at Bath, presented in the name of Mary Westmacott, and a West End production of Gerald Verner's pedestrian adaptation of *Towards Zero*, to which she reluctantly lent her own name. Following four consecutive West End hits, Christie suddenly found herself in a position where her name was appearing on someone else's work, and her own work as a playwright was being presented under a pseudonym. It seems that those responsible for the management of 'brand Christie' were working somewhat to their own agenda.

Christie herself was awarded a CBE in the 1956 New Year's Honours, and it can be no coincidence that this followed a five-year period in which her profile as the West End's most successful female playwright had been firmly established. But, as was her habit, she then departed to Iraq until May, leaving Saunders and Cork to strategise the schedule for her theatrical work. *No Fields of Amaranth* mysteriously disappeared for over two years; like *A Daughter's a Daughter* it was clearly not a play that they felt would sit comfortably alongside the established Christie repertoire, and it may well be that the half-hearted 1956 production of *A Daughter's a Daughter* was by way of a consolation prize to Christie for allowing *Towards Zero* to jump the queue.

It is no surprise that Cork and Saunders were disconcerted by *No Fields of Amaranth*; a 'whodunit' it certainly wasn't. The play concerns the idealist Professor Karl Hendryk, whose subject appears to be moral philosophy. He is a political refugee from Eastern Europe, having lost his chair at the university in his homeland because he assisted 'the Schultzes', the family of an arrested colleague. Hendryk (called Henschel in early drafts, perhaps as an *homage* to Christie's similarly named favourite director) lives in a Bloomsbury flat with his self-pitying wheelchair-bound wife Anya, whom he cares for with the assistance of her cousin Lisa Koletsky, a trained physicist who has given up her career to play housekeeper to Anya and her husband. Lisa's relationship with Karl goes back a long way and their mutual devotion has grown into an unacknowledged love. This does not go unnoticed by Anya, however, who confides in the sagacious Dr Stoner her hope that when she dies Lisa and Karl will marry. Karl's students include a boy with an obviously Jewish name and a miner's son (neither of whom we meet), but tycoon Sir William Rollander persuades Karl also to take on his spoilt and objectionable twenty-three-year-old daughter, Helen, by offering in return the prospect of his paying for treatment for Anya.

Helen becomes infatuated with Karl and, seeing his crippled wife as an obstacle, gives her an overdose of medication, making it look like suicide. 'One feels so often that one would be better dead,' Anya has told Helen. Karl roundly rejects Helen's advances, and she then admits to him that she has killed his wife. Karl, astonishingly, does not report her to the police, believing that she is too naïve to understand the implications of her actions; significantly, in the context of 1958, he thereby spares her from the gallows. There is a very brief appearance by the methodical DI Ogden, a pointedly unshowy stage detective in the tradition of *The Hollow*'s tailor-made Inspector Colquhoun. Suspecting foul play and, based on evidence of a relationship between Lisa and Karl provided by their housekeeper, Ogden arrests Lisa. Only at this point does Karl tell the police that Helen is the culprit, but it is too late; Helen has been killed crossing the road, the implication being that she has committed suicide ('The lorry driver claims that Miss Rollander gave him no time to brake'), and Lisa remains the prime suspect.

There is an off-stage trial and the eventual verdict, awaited nervously by Karl, is that Lisa is innocent. Appalled that Karl's initial forgiveness of Helen could have sent her instead to the gallows, Lisa leaves him: 'you put ideas first, not people. Ideas of loyalty and friendship and pity. And because of that the people who are near suffer.' Karl is left alone in despair but in a final moment, reminiscent of the ending of *My Fair Lady*, Lisa returns to him 'because I am a fool'.

For those who believe that a playwright incorporating various elements of their life experiences into their work is in some way newsworthy, the play offers rich pickings. By 1955, when Saunders optioned it, Agatha Christie was extraordinarily famous, wealthy and successful, but there was no escaping the fact that she was a matronly woman in her sixties married to a renowned archaeologist fourteen years her junior. Max enjoyed close relationships with various female colleagues including, notably, his assistant, epigraphist Barbara Hastings Parker, whom he eventually married the year after Agatha's death.

The relatives-by-marriage of Agatha's sister who for some reason considered themselves qualified to offer author Jared Cade so much information about the famous 'disappearance' also have plenty to say about the exact nature of Max's friendships with Barbara Hastings. But to suggest that Agatha based the relationship between Karl, Lisa and Anya on that between Max, Barbara and herself, and that for her the play was, according to Cade, 'a brave, if unsuccessful, attempt to reconcile herself to Max's infidelity',[88] is to beg the question as to how, if this was indeed the case, she expected Max to react to such a public portrayal of their life together. In the novel *Unfinished Portrait*, sheltering behind Mary Westmacott, Agatha draws on painful incidents from her past in a semi-autobiographical manner, and I believe that she may once have hoped for a scene of reconciliation with Archie similar to the one she had portrayed in her unperformed play *The Lie*. But it is impossible to imagine such an intensely private person effectively laying bare any current domestic concerns she may have had in front of a West End audience and critics. All of this, in any case, is to ignore the real themes of the play and, by reducing them to the purely personal, to diminish Christie's ability to tackle universal issues that are central to the human experience and her wide frame of reference in so doing.

In *No Fields of Amaranth*, Christie was in fact exploring ideas that had been preoccupying her since her early playwriting experiments. The misguided idealist we have already seen (although audiences, of course, hadn't) in *Akhnaton*, but he is now portrayed as a European intellectual émigré of the sort Christie rubbed shoulders with at Lawn Road Flats; people like the antiquarian bookseller and Jewish socialist Berliner Louis Bondy, who we know she dined with at Lawn Road (a reference to a housekeeper called 'Mrs Bondy' had been cut from the script of *The Hollow*).[89] The fascistic Helen Rollander, with her belief that 'people who are sick and worn out and useless should be removed so as to leave room for the ones who matter', is a brutal post-war incarnation of the eugenicists Christie poked fun at in *Eugenia and Eugenics*. Other regular Christie themes are present too, as in the following exchange between Anya's doctor and one of Karl's students:

> DOCTOR: Love isn't glamour, desire, sex appeal – all the things you young people are so sure it is. That's nature's start of the whole business. It's the showy flower, if you like. But love's the root. Underground, out of sight, nothing much to look at, but it's where the life is.
>
> LESTER: I suppose so, yes. But passion doesn't last, sir, does it?
>
> DOCTOR: God give me strength. You young people know nothing about these things. You read in the papers of divorces, of love tangles with a sex angle to everything. Study the columns of deaths sometimes for a change. Plenty of records there of Emily this and John that dying in their seventy-fourth year, beloved wife of So-and-so, beloved husband of someone else. Unassuming records of lives spent together, sustained by the root I've just talked about which still puts out its leaves and its flowers. Not showy flowers, but still flowers.[90]

It would be easy enough to interpret this as a paean to the relationship between Agatha and Max, but we heard it first way back in *The Lie*, when Agatha was married to Archie, and Nell reminds us that 'It's the dull brown earth that endures, not the gay flowers that grow there.' Another familiar Christie leitmotif is explored when Karl and Lisa remember a concert in their homeland at which they heard a performance of the 'Liebestod' – the final aria in Wagner's 1859 opera *Tristan and Isolde*. Christie, who had once hoped to be an opera singer, chooses this particular work for a reason: its story, inspired by the ideas of philosopher Arthur Schopenhauer, is of a love so intense that it is destructive and unattainable.

This idea of unattainable desires is further reflected in the play's original title. Early on in the piece, Lisa quotes from the eccentric nineteenth-century Welsh poet and philosopher Walter Savage Landor's 'Imaginary Conversations', in this case the one between Aesop and Rhodope, when Aesop tells his legendarily beautiful lover, 'There are no fields of Amaranth on this side of the grave.' In an early draft, after the list of characters, Christie offers us the note, 'AMARANTH – another name for the plant called Love-lies-bleeding. An imaginary flower that never fades. From the Greek *amarantos* – never fading.' The note was reprinted in the play's programme, although by this time it would explain only the use of the quotation in the play, rather than its title. In mythology, amaranth represents immortality because of its reputedly never-fading flower, and Aesop here is effectively saying that nothing in this life lasts for ever. As we have seen, in *A Daughter's a Daughter*, written in the 1930s, Ann refers to the plant's real-life manifestation as 'love-lies-bleeding'; so, again, this is not something new to Christie's theatrical vocabulary and the play's title clearly carries a deep significance for her.

There are echoes of these themes in the background of much of Christie's stage work, and she is not presenting them in the foreground here simply in order publicly to exorcise concerns over her own marriage. There are even tantalising indications in one of the draft scripts (undated, of course) held at the Christie archive that at least some elements of the play originate from a much earlier period; the typography and layout on a small number of inserted pages is similar to that for work dating from over a decade previously. This would be consistent with the use of the name Henschel and with the Lawn Road inspiration for East European academic refugees living in a

London flat. It would also place it closer chronologically to both *Akhnaton* and *A Daughter's a Daughter*, both of which share themes with *No Fields of Amaranth*. Although Max had known Barbara Parker from at least the early 1940s, it would set the play's alleged portrayal of this relationship in an entirely different context, or even bring Stephen Glanville, who lived at Lawn Road for a while, into the frame. It was Glanville, after all, who had originally encouraged Barbara to study archaeology, and who tutored Agatha in matters Egyptian and wrote so passionately to her. As with *A Daughter's a Daughter* it would also, of course, mean that the original concept for *No Fields of Amaranth* pre-dated her attendance at Rattigan's plays in the 1950s, although it may well be that their stylistic resonance with some of her own earlier work was what encouraged her to revisit it.

As with much of Christie's playwriting, it is impossible to offer any definitive chronology or interpretation, and I am certainly not attempting to do so here; I am simply suggesting that we consider a number of options rather than leaping to conclusions. Whatever its origins, sources and inspirations, *No Fields of Amaranth* is a profound and deeply thoughtful play that examines ordinary people who are the victims of extreme circumstances arising from the practical application of conflicting moral philosophies. Even the murder, which takes place in full view of the audience and is thus no mystery, can be seen in this context. The tragedy is that Christie felt the necessity to introduce, however grudgingly, a detective of any sort into this scenario; but, given the difficulties she had experienced with *A Daughter's a Daughter*, she perhaps now regarded this as a necessity in order to get her work produced.

At the end of October 1957 Saunders, who clearly disliked the play's title, had what he must have regarded as a bit of good luck. In response to an interview given by Christie, a prolific author of romantic fiction called Hebe Keogh contacted him to say that she had written a book called *No Fields of Amaranth* and requested therefore that Christie retitle her play (and, by the way, when the change was announced, please could mention be made of her book?).[91] Although the book was out of print, Saunders seized the opportunity and wrote back, 'As good as the title is for a book it is a very bad one for a play . . . I am sure Agatha Christie will now agree to change it.'[92] Exactly when the play was renamed, and to what extent Christie was involved in the decision, is unclear; but we do know that at the end of November 1957 actors were being contracted for a play called simply 'Amaranth', and by the end of February 1958 they were being reviewed in a play called *Verdict*.

No Fields of Amaranth's title change, however, did not have a similarly happy outcome to that made to the title of *Three Blind Mice*. In fact it proved to be a hugely detrimental move, leading both audiences and critics to believe that they were about to experience a courtroom drama in the same vein as *Witness for the Prosecution*. Not since the Shuberts advertised *The Suspects* as a follow-up to *Ten Little Indians* had expectations for a Christie play been so comprehensively subverted. Just how little Christie's team understood about her more challenging work is apparent from a letter from Cork to Ober in April 1958. In fairness, he concedes that *No Fields of Amaranth* would have been a more suitable title for the play, but he goes on to say, 'Although I don't think it is a good play, I am inclined to think a very good film could be made out of it. The point is that one of the high spots of the play is a murder trial, and on stage it happens "off", while obviously in a film it could be written up so that Verdict could be the logical successor to Witness for the Prosecution.'[93] Such an idea would have been so far from Christie's aspirations for the piece that, in this instance, one has to question Cork's judgement.

And it wasn't only the title that was to be an issue. Christie often agonised over the opening and closing moments of her plays, and in the case of *Verdict* the final page was to be the subject of numerous rewrites. The burning issue was whether, in the closing moments of the piece, Lisa, having abandoned Karl and all that he stands for, should walk back in – and if she did so then what she should say. This was not dissimilar to the problems experienced by Shaw regarding the staging and filming of the final moments of *Pygmalion*, which were definitively resolved after his death, and in a manner contrary to his original intentions, by the creators of the musical *My Fair Lady*. The Agatha Christie archive contains a draft where Lisa does not return at all and Karl is left alone on the stage in despair, reading the Landor poem as his voice dies away and the book falls; another where Karl is left listening to Rachmaninov on the record player and Lisa returns and runs into his arms saying only his name; and further versions where Lisa returns and there is some brief dialogue, the eventual final line apparently being something of a last-minute addition. The version sent to the Lord Chamberlain's office, in which the final pages have been attached by adhesive tape in a manner that prevents us from seeing what is being replaced, sees Karl listening to the Rachmaninov and reads thus;

KARL: . . . Lisa – Lisa – How can I live without you?
(Door opens after a moment or two, Lisa comes in very softly, stands an instant, then comes softly down behind him, puts hands on his shoulders. He starts, thinks for a moment he is imagining, then turns, springs up)
Lisa? (afraid to believe) You have come back – why?
LISA: (between laughing and crying) Because I am a fool! (comes into his arms)
(Music comes up in triumphant passage)
CURTAIN[94]

Here is the same sequence as currently published:

KARL: Lisa – Lisa – how can I live without you? (He drops his head into his hands)
(The door up Centre opens slowly. Lisa enters up Centre, moves slowly to Right of Karl and puts her hand gently on his shoulder. He looks up at Lisa.)
Lisa? You've come back. Why?
LISA: (kneeling at Karl's side) Because I am a fool.

(Lisa rests her head on Karl's lap, he rests his head on hers
    and the music builds up as the Curtain falls)[95]

If ever an example were needed of how an 'acting edition'
impoverishes a writer's original stage directions through the
incorporation of stage manager's 'blocking' notes from
the prompt copy, then this is it. Historically, of course, it has
often been this version of the script that goes 'on the record'
and by which a playwright's work has been judged by future
academics. Christie's plays suffer particularly badly from this,
with much of what we now read having been aimed specifically at enabling amateurs to recreate, as far as possible, the
original staging.

Verdict also gives rise to a particularly fine example of another
of the problems that Christie's reputation as a dramatist is up
against in certain academic quarters. In the introduction to
British and Irish Women Dramatists Since 1958, edited by
Trevor R. Griffiths and Margaret Llewellyn-Jones (1993), we
read that 'some plays written by women may conform both
ideologically and formally to the established patriarchal norm,
for example Agatha Christie's 1950s Poirot-style plays, notwithstanding Miss Marple's appropriation of such apparently male
skills to solve mysteries in other plays.'[96]

I am not aware that Christie wrote any 'Poirot-style' plays
in the 1950s, and she certainly never wrote a play featuring
Miss Marple. Her one full-length Poirot play was produced in
1930, and even then his skills are notably not portrayed as
inherently 'male' (but that's another story). In the Poirotless
The Hollow, the female roles dominate the stage while the men
are by and large weak and ineffectual, in *The Mousetrap* Miss
Casewell hardly conforms to gender stereotypes, in *Witness for
the Prosecution* Romaine runs circles around the self-satisfied
male lawyers, in *Spider's Web* the resourceful female protagonist calls the shots as she sits at the centre of her web, and in
Verdict, which is in no sense 'Poirot-style', we see how a prin-
cipled but misguided male idealist wreaks unintentional havoc
on the lives of those around him like a modern-day Akhnaton.

Lib Taylor, in her chapter in the book, 'Early Stages', notes under the heading 'The West End, Collusion or Subversion' that 'Christie's plays reveal an underlying collusion with patriarchy' – citing 'The Verdict' [sic] as an example of this. Lisa, she says, 'denies her own future in favour of his [Karl's] and even after prison – in a sense her punishment for her transgression against the marriage vow – she continues this sacrifice despite an apparent awareness of male oppression . . .'[97] In this and other Christie plays, Taylor continues, 'redemption comes through the suffering of women whose only crime is their sexuality, whilst men remain irreproachable . . . the women collude by rejecting the possibility of challenging their oppressors, preferring the *status quo.*'

Anyone with a proper understanding of Christie's work for the stage, or even the basic plot of *Verdict*, will emphatically reject this thesis. Karl is not 'oppressing' anyone (except, argu- ably, himself); he is loyal to his wife, but he and Lisa are in love. He is trapped, like Akhnaton, by his own well-intentioned but ultimately destructive belief system, which is signposted in a minor way when he forgives a student for stealing a book. Far from being 'irreproachable', the extreme events of the play conclusively challenge his misguided philosophical outlook. Lisa makes her own choices, and her decision to return to Karl at the end of the play makes her the stronger partner, not the weaker one. As with all of Christie's work for the stage, *Verdict* is approached from the perspective of women being innately the stronger of the sexes and men the weaker: 'Men aren't realists like we are,' declares Helen to Anya. And I would respectfully suggest that if you are going to offer a critique of a play then you at least take the trouble to get its title right.

Taylor is, of course, restricted by the book's 1958 starting point to examining the relatively inglorious tail end of Christie's playwriting career. This date is chosen, according to its editors, because it is the year in which Shelagh Delaney's debut play *A Taste of Honey*, her first and last success, was premiered by Joan Littlewood's Theatre Workshop at the Theatre Royal Stratford East. The dramatis personae of nineteen-year-old

Delaney's brave and extraordinary, Salford-set working-class domestic drama includes an alcoholic single mother, a pregnant teenager, a black sailor and a homosexual art student. The play has achieved the same sort of iconic status as *Look Back in Anger* with some theatre historians and, we are told by the editors of *British and Irish Women Dramatists Since 1958*, 'seemed to offer a new way forward for women's theatre.' It is worth noting in the context of this claim that in 1931, the year of Agatha Christie's first West End production, twenty plays written or co-written by women enjoyed runs in the West End, and there were also numerous one-off 'try-out' performances of new plays by women writers in West End theatres. In the four years between 1956 and 1959 over fifty plays by women were presented in the West End, including work by Agatha Christie, Enid Bagnold, Lesley Storm, Lillian Hellman and Clemence Dane. And yet, at time of writing, the only play in the West End by a female playwright is *The Mousetrap*.

Perhaps unsurprisingly, given the challenges presented by the piece, casting *Verdict* proved problematic, and although the team that Saunders eventually assembled was certainly top-notch in terms of its ability to deliver the play, it did not offer any 'star name' insurance against poor reviews. There had been much excitement the previous year when it seemed that French film star Charles Boyer might accept the role of Karl; in 1952 he had received a Tony award for his Broadway appearance in Shaw's *Don Juan in Hell*, directed by Charles Laughton, and casting him in what would have been his first London stage appearance since 1924 would indeed have been something of a coup. In the end, though, Saunders reported that Boyer had felt 'he could not play the last act'[98] and the role eventually went to German-born film and stage actor Gerard Heinz: the same actor who, as Gerard Hinze, had played Dr Gerard in the West End production of *Appointment with Death*. Though a busy and well-regarded film and television actor who had notably appeared in the 1942 premiere of Terence Rattigan's *Flare Path*, Heinz was by no means a head-line star. One Tony award winner who did join the company was Patricia Jessel in the role of Lisa, her last Christie appearance having been as the toast of Broadway in *Witness for the Prosecution*; and playing Helen was former Windmill girl Moira Redmond. Recently returned from Australia and an unsuccessful marriage, Redmond had been Vivien Leigh's understudy in the 1957 West End season of Peter Brook's production of *Titus Andronicus* and, by all accounts, she made the most of the role of the young murderess in *Verdict*.

Taking the helm as director was RADA-trained Charles Hickman, who had been responsible for the popular *Sweet and Low* wartime revues that briefly made way for *Murder on the Nile* at the Ambassadors in 1946. Hickman was the director of Reandco's hugely successful premiere of Lesley Storm's *Black Chiffon* at the Westminster Theatre in 1949, and the following year he enjoyed a similar success with *His Excellency* by Dorothy and Campbell Christie at the Piccadilly. He had already worked with Saunders, staging his production of a new musical of *The Water Gipsies* which opened at the Winter Gardens six months after *Witness for the Prosecution* closed there.

The scheduling of *Verdict* early in the year was unusual, not least because it meant that Christie herself was in Iraq when the production rehearsed and opened on tour on 25 February 1958. It also meant that Nottingham's Theatre Royal was unable to play its usual role hosting the first performance, and the production opened instead in Wolverhampton, much to the chagrin of the local critic in Nottingham. A review in *The Stage* from Wolverhampton was promising, assessing the play on its own merits rather than its writer's reputation. Under the rather uninspiring headline, 'Mrs Christie Examines a Professor's Character', the critic's favourable response noted:

> Agatha Christie's new play, *Verdict*, which was presented at the Grand, Wolverhampton last week, shows a new point of departure for the author. The emphasis shifts from the creation of an atmosphere of suspicion to a psychologising of the characters involved. Moral problems, too, are drawn in. The bare pattern of the play is made quite shapely with

the same skill that appears in the author's more popular style of mystery play. When the murder of the professor's ailing wife is committed, no mystery surrounds it. Instead, we are invited to examine the character of the professor and the way his single-minded attachment to his ideals brings suffering to all those devoted to him.[99]

From early on, though, it was clear that the ending of *Verdict* was going to be problematic. In a courteous correspondence with the *Birmingham Post*'s critic, J.C. Trewin (later to contribute an entertaining chapter on Christie's theatre work to H.R.F. Keating's book, *Agatha Christie, First Lady of Crime*), Peter Saunders took issue with the poor review that he had given to the play:

Although naturally disappointed that you did not like my production of Verdict, may I say that at least it was a reasoned criticism, and as such, I feel I must answer it.

1. You say it is as artificial an anecdote as you have heard for some time. Do you really think it more so than Witness for the Prosecution which you liked?
2. You complain that the ultimate clue is all too predictable. But you have overlooked the fact that this is neither a thriller nor a whodunit. It is a *play*. You may indeed say – in fact you do say – that it is a bad play, but should you look for a surprise ending in something that was never intended to surprise?
3. The final minute to which you object is as much a bone of contention as the final twist in Witness for the Prosecution, when the majority of provincial critics urged Agatha to take it out. Already, with this ending we are having the same tug-of-war. I know that if I leave it in, it will be criticised as a phoney ending, and if I take it out the author will be accused of letting her play 'fade into nothingness'.

In your final paragraph you ask, I gather, for a return to the straightforward whodunit. It is in response to criticism that the characters are always the same, with butlers, maids and country vicars, that Mrs Christie has tried to be different. Her difficulty is, of course, that her name on the jar proclaims the kind of jam it is. Perhaps this time theatregoers will be disappointed.

Please do not take this letter in any way as an aggrieved producer who thinks he knows best. I am well alive to the kindness with which you have treated many of my plays in the past.[100]

Trewin replied, 'It was charming of you to write. I felt very guilty about Verdict, if I can put it in that way, because as a rule Agatha Christie gets me – and complaints seem almost disloyal. I look forward to seeing the play again. Here it may very well be that preparation, foreknowledge, helps . . . Mrs Christie sentimentalises the last curtain, I think falsely. Better, surely, to let the play remain ruthless (I've always wondered whether Rattigan was right to alter the original tragic end of Deep Blue Sea).'[101]

Saunders responded, 'I must confess that a lot of criticism has been aroused at the return of Lisa and it may be that this will still be changed, although I don't think so. As I know that you will not be influenced by anything I say in this personal letter, I admit freely that I am not looking forward to the London First Night. I am sure one or two of the critics will really have a lovely time – if you know what I mean.'[102]

As well as problems with the casting and the script, Saunders had once again experienced difficulties when seeking a West End theatre for a Christie play; but he eventually secured the Strand Theatre, yet another non-'Group' venue, where the play opened on 22 May 1958. Other West End attractions on offer that night included *Simply Heavenly*, an 'All-Negro musical' presented by Jack Hylton at the Adelphi; Lesley Storm's *Roar Like a Dove*, produced and directed by *Towards Zero*'s Murray MacDonald at the Phoenix and heralded by Kenneth Tynan as 'a resounding, self-evident hit'; Terence Rattigan's less well-received *Variation on a Theme* produced by Tennents at the Globe; and the London premiere of *My Fair Lady*, a rare Tennents venture into musical theatre, which had opened to huge acclaim the previous month at the Theatre Royal, Drury Lane and which, as the company's largest scale commercial venture to date, took full advantage of the abolition of the entertainment tax. Meanwhile, at the Ambassadors, *The Mousetrap* was advertising its 'Sixth Dazzling Year'.

With astonishing irony after all the debates about the ending, the young stage manager, Wendy Noel, who had worked on a number of previous Saunders productions including *Witness for the Prosecution* and *Towards Zero*, called the final curtain early on opening night and created the ending that J.C. Trewin had wanted, curtailing the performance before Anya's return and leaving Karl, bereft, on the stage. This did not go down well with the audience, and there were boos from the gallery. In a review in the *Daily Telegraph* headlined 'GALLERY BOOS CHRISTIE PLAY – A MELANCHOLY OCCASION', W.A. Darlington wrote:

> It seems that there is no grace in our gallery-goers – in those, at any rate, who booed when the curtain fell at the Strand last night on Agatha Christie's new play *Verdict*. If there is a writer in existence who has deserved gratitude from the many-headed, it is Mrs Christie. So when, for once, trying herself out in a new sort of play, she fails to bring it off, could not they let the melancholy occasion go by in silence? . . . There was no dextrous twist at the end, which solved everything and brought the lovers together. Instead there was a great scene of renunciation and parting, which rang false and fell flat.[103]

Booing from the gallery in West End theatres had become something of an issue in 1958, and one on which Saunders, of course, had strong opinions; its occurrence at the end of *Verdict* was by no means an isolated incident, but it was certainly a first for an Agatha Christie play. Under the headline 'AN

IMPROBABLE VERDICT: PLAY BY AGATHA CHRISTIE BOOED',
the *Times* critic wrote, 'Miss Agatha Christie has brought off
some mighty fine stage surprises in her time. Alas, all the
surprises in her latest play are surprises that people should
behave as she makes them behave . . . The lady companion is
obviously "on a spot" but after her acquittal she, who has all
the time impressed as a sensible and sympathetic woman,
surprises us by tearing the quixotry of her adored professor to
shreds and leaving him for ever . . . And the gallery booed, a
surprising thing to happen to an Agatha Christie, but all things
considered perhaps on this occasion not so surprising.'[104]

It is important to put the 'booing' incident in context,
however. A year later, man of the moment John Osborne's
short-lived West End musical *The World of Paul Slickey* was
also booed on its opening night, on this occasion from the stalls
rather than the gallery.

Even with *Verdict*'s correct ending restored, there was no
pleasing the press. *The Stage*'s London critic disagreed with
his provincial counterpart, although he clearly did not see the
ill-fated opening performance, noting that 'the professor and
Lisa at last come together in a musical aura of true love and
understanding which is unbelievably sloppy'. Under the headline 'REAL LIFE DEFEATS THE THRILLER QUEEN', the
review concluded that

> Agatha Christie, Queen of the thriller writers, apparently
> attempted in *Verdict*, at the Strand, to write a play about
> real life and living people. Having for the time abandoned
> her murder puzzles, cardboard characters and reliance on
> technical ingenuity and a gift for creating suspense, she had
> to face a variety of fresh problems, none of which is satis-
> factorily solved in *Verdict*. Mrs Christie in trying to create
> flesh and blood characters succeeds only in giving us
> dummies . . . Probably Charles Hickman should not be
> blamed too much for a thoroughly pedestrian production; a
> genius could not have saved the play.[105]

The 25 May 1958 edition of the *Observer* is interesting in a number of respects. Kenneth Tynan praises the Moscow Art Theatre, performing *Uncle Vanya* at Sadler's Wells, and gives a less than enthusiastic review to the premiere of Harold Pinter's *The Birthday Party* at the Lyric, Hammersmith. Laurence Kitchen is left to review *Verdict*, and comments that it is

> a dislocation of the Christie formula, trying to do an Ibsen on us and achieving lesser Pinero . . . beyond the patter of tiny clichés there are frustrating murmurs of a strong theme struggling to make itself heard. The murderess (Moira Redmond) remarks at one point 'I'm not a virgin, if that's what you've been worrying about'. Voraciously Beat Generation and neo-Fascist, she is brought to dramatic life without compromise, wielding a corrupt logic and the Sack line [the latest dress fashion]. Alarmed, it seems, by her own creation, Mrs Christie has this girl run over by a bus and takes refuge in the consoling babble of a shaggy old family doctor.

This is at least a considered response to the play, although it would have been interesting to see what Tynan himself made of it. Elsewhere in the newspaper there is a major article on the excavations at Nimrud, in which the reporter remarks that 'The good living, and a feeling of good sense not always found in such expeditions, was in large part due, I suspect, to the presiding influence of Mrs Mallowan, wife of the distinguished Director. I was allowed to make use of a small, almost secret, room that she has had added to the end of the house and where, during the opening phase of each season, she retreats to work and becomes once more Agatha Christie.'

Beresford Egan, theatre critic of the *Courier* magazine, seems to have been alone in identifying a strand of Christie's previous work in *Verdict*. He wrote to Saunders the week after the West End opening:

Once again, I find myself at variance with my fellow critics. While granting them a certain justification, I enjoyed Verdict. It was magnificently played, and, on that score alone, deserved a better fate. I am afraid Miss Christie got herself rather entangled with 'Mary Westmacott' – which is an interesting experiment, but obviously risky. The public, like mice, can only be attracted by the same trap. They are naturally wary of anything new. Agatha Christie and Whodunit are synonyms, and should never be separated. Nevertheless, I wouldn't have missed Verdict for the world. May fortune smile on your next production.[106]

Arguably, as with *A Daughter's a Daughter*, there may have been a case for selling *Verdict* as a Mary Westmacott play. Even though the cat was out of the bag as to Westmacott's true identity, it would neatly have circumvented the issue of audience expectation and might even have given Saunders the confidence to ignore Mrs Keogh. Although no writer at all is credited for *The Lie*, and it pre-dated Christie's adoption of her *nom de plume*, it was in effect the first 'Westmacott' play. *A Daughter's a Daughter* is the second. And *Verdict* is indeed arguably the third; even biographer Laura Thompson likes it. Or it may simply be the case that these are actually the only three 'Agatha Christie' plays, and that the rest of her repertoire as a playwright bears witness to a lifelong struggle against what audiences expected to see.

The damning reviews were reflected in poor ticket sales, and in the two weeks after the opening night the box office income fell below Saunders' weekly cost of running the production, a scenario which allowed the theatre to give him two weeks' notice to close; this they duly did, in a regretful and politely worded letter.[107] Saunders would doubtless have been grateful that he was thus relieved of the responsibility for closing the production, after a mere thirty-six performances. It is a great shame that Patricia Jessel's happy memories of the night she was cheered when she walked into Sardi's on Broadway would have been clouded by the memories of the night she was booed from the gallery in the West End. Jessel, who was to die in 1968 at the age of forty-seven, had by all accounts given the definitive interpretation of a Christie stage role in her performance as Romaine, and her own reviews for *Verdict* were also complimentary: 'establishes Patricia Jessel as a must for any Christie play', said the *Daily Mirror*.[108]

Charles Hickman would go on to direct a successful run of Jack Popplewell's *A Day in the Life of* . . . for Saunders at the Savoy in October 1958, with the unfortunate Wendy Noel, who had evidently been forgiven by both Hickman and Saunders, as stage manager. Typically, Christie's first thought on the night had been for the distress caused to the young stage manager who called the cue early, and she wrote to Noel the next day to assure her that the play would have received poor reviews in any case.[109] From what we know of the critical response to the correct ending, Christie wasn't wrong; but it is nonetheless something of a mystery how such an error came to be made, given that the production had been well run-in on tour prior to its West End opening. I can't help wondering whether Saunders, following the Trewin correspondence and in Christie's absence, had been experimenting with different endings on tour and that an alternative cue had therefore been marked in to the prompt copy, causing confusion on the opening night.

Verdict was the first Christie flop of the Saunders regime, and the first of her plays not to return a handsome profit to his investors. Two investors had each contributed the not inconsiderable sum of £1,000 to the production, with Saunders himself covering the remaining £3,000.[110] Herbert de Leon, who had invested in *Spider's Web*, notably was not among those financing the show on this occasion despite the fact that two of his clients, Patricia Jessel and Viola Keats (playing Anya), were performing in it. It is very clear that no one on the management side gave much for its chances from the outset. The production actually cost £4,791, making it the most expensive Christie play to date,[111] despite the fact that considerably less was spent on the set and on the advertising than for *Witness for the Prosecution*.

In 1966, when his licence expired, Saunders wrote to his investors to advise them that, once income from the pre-West End tour, numerous repertory productions and a post-West End tour by Geoffrey Hastings had been taken into account, 'All things considered, it seems we were lucky to only lose a total of £20 on a play which ran for four and a half weeks in the West End.'[112] It was indeed not a bad result under the circumstances, and is indicative of how buoyant the Christie brand remained in secondary markets. French's published their 'acting edition' at the end of 1958 and the amateur rights were released in 1959; and despite its West End fate, the play, with its cast of ten and single set, proved as popular with amateurs as it had with repertory companies. Saunders took up his option to participate in amateur rights,[113] as he always did, although investors were not entitled to a share in this income so it did not appear on the final statements.

As well as the investment details, the accounts files for *Verdict* contain two lovely examples of Saunders' legendary high principles in his financial dealings. Upmarket couturiers, Rahvis of Mayfair, had the audacity to demand payment prior to delivery for a costume that they had made. Outraged, Saunders took this as an affront to his reputation as a prompt payer and sent the company a solicitor's letter.[114] They immediately agreed to standard payment terms. By contrast, the boss of Morden Park Sound Studios requested no payment for his work because the production was not a success, eliciting the immediate response from Saunders, 'I understand you have made no charge for your own work and this is something that is not fair. It is extremely nice of you but the fact that the show was a failure isn't really your fault and had it been a success I would not have paid any extra, so will you please send me an amended account.'[115]

For Christie herself, the vagaries of theatre could scarcely have been more pointed or more poignant. The first night of *Verdict* (her shortest West End run) came just over a month after *The Mousetrap*'s attainment of the longest run in British theatre history had been celebrated with a party at the Savoy that was trumpeted by the *Daily Mail* as London's 'biggest-ever theatrical shindig'.[116] Christie was outwardly stoic in her acceptance of *Verdict*'s failure, but in her autobiography she makes it clear that it was a play:

> which, though not a success with the public, satisfied me completely. It was put on under the title of *Verdict* – a bad title. I had called it *No Fields of Amaranth*, taken from the words of Walter Landor's 'There are no flowers [sic] of amaranth on this side of the grave'. I still think it is the best play I have written, with the exception of *Witness for the Prosecution*. It failed, I think, because it was *not* a detective story or a thriller. It *was* a play that concerned murder, but its real background and point was that an idealist is always dangerous, a possible destroyer of those who love him – and [it] poses the question of how far you can sacrifice, not yourself, but those you love, to what you believe in, even though they do not.[117]

As Hubert Gregg observes, 'The clown wants to play Hamlet . . . The thriller writer wishes he or she doesn't have to thrill. Laudably, Agatha had her go in a play called *Verdict*. It didn't work. The public will take an unexpected guest but not an unexpected Christie. Its failure must have been a disappointment to Saunders who presented it. I don't think it can have been a surprise . . .'[118] Saunders himself tells the story of going to photograph the sign at the front of the theatre, only to discover that one of the lights had gone out, so that it now read 'Peter Saunders resents Verdict'.[119]

SCENE FIVE

The Late Plays

Verdict had opened at the Strand on 22 May 1958 and closed on 21 June 1958. 'After the disaster of *Verdict* I had begged Agatha Christie to write another play as quickly as she could,' writes Peter Saunders in *The Mousetrap Man*. 'I was afraid that if she didn't she might lose interest. Within a month she had produced *The Unexpected Guest*. Like driving a car immediately after an accident, I made certain this play would go on quickly.'[1]

He certainly did, and the result was a textbook operation in the production of a Christie hit. Hubert Gregg was tracked down on a beach in Portugal (Saunders' long-serving general manager Verity Hudson personally delivered the script, along with a copy of the *Spotlight* casting directory) and now-veteran Christie set designer Michael Weight was enlisted to work alongside him. Leading cast members were contracted at the beginning of July,[2] rehearsals commenced on 14 July (Saunders didn't technically option the play from Hughes Massie until 31 July),[3] and the production opened at the inappropriately large Bristol Hippodrome on 4 August. There wasn't even time to book the usual pre-West End tour; after a week at Bristol, *The Unexpected Guest* opened on 12 August at the Duchess Theatre, where it was to prove a critical and financial success and played for a total of 612 performances, according to Gregg breaking all box office records for the small, independently owned, thirty-year-old theatre.

The play, although imbued with trademark Christie quirkiness, was a whodunit set in a country house with French
windows and involved plenty of police procedurals. As a quick-
fix exercise in theatrical damage limitation it was ruthlessly
efficient. Christie's critical reputation as a purveyor of finely
crafted thrillers was restored: 'Verdict atoned for' she wrote
to Cork upon receiving copies of the largely favourable reviews.[4]
By the end of 1960, Saunders and his investors had shared in
profits of £38,000, including £32,000 from the West End run
and a share of income from over fifty repertory licences as
well as the usual post west-End tour presented by Geoffrey
Hastings.[5] And yet this was one of the few times that Christie
herself had been in the country but not attended a first rehearsal
for one of her plays; reportedly she sent a message that she
was unable to be there as she was making raspberry jam.[6]
And in her autobiography she notes simply that she wrote 'a
play called *The Unexpected Guest*'. To Gregg, who had in his
own estimation salvaged Christie's theatrical reputation, this
was an unforgivable slight.

Lest the speed and efficiency of the operation seem unfeasible, it should be noted that according to Saunders, Christie
'produced' *The Unexpected Guest* within a month of the opening
of *Verdict*, not that she necessarily actually wrote it within this
timeframe. There is, in fact, plenty of evidence that Christie
had been developing the idea for the play for at least eight
years, and every indication that it was in any case ready to
bring to the boil at about this moment. The agency-typed script
held in the Agatha Christie archive, although it contains a few
handwritten amendments, is to all intents and purposes a
performance text for the play as it is now known, the only
significant change being that its original three-act structure
was reduced to two in the course of the rehearsal process by
the simple expedient of combining the first two acts into one;
Hubert Gregg's rehearsal notes show him working out the
practicalities of this.[7]

The accelerated production process meant that there simply
wasn't time for the usual to-ing and fro-ing with director and

producer amendments, and it has to be said that the result is none the poorer for it. Agatha Christie was clearly more than capable of writing a full-length, ready-to-perform stage play without the necessity for third-party intervention. Gregg, of course, felt that she had by now taken on board the lessons learnt from experts like himself, and notes grudgingly that 'Much thought had been given to this Guest . . . much attention having been paid to the manipulation of that Hollow.'[8] In this case he takes personal credit only for the police sergeant's penchant for poetry – the sort of comic police 'stage business' that Christie is on record as disliking.

Unusually for a Christie play, it is to her notebooks, rather than draft scripts, that we must therefore turn for an insight into the origins and development of the piece. As we have seen, in her autobiography Christie remarks that, after writing *The Hollow*, her intention was 'to write a play that was not adapted from a book. I was going to write a play as a play.'[9] Although her next completed script turned out to be *The Mousetrap*, this comment makes perfect sense of the heading 'Play' in Notebook 34, followed by notes (unusually and clearly dated '1951') in which she outlines what is unmistakably an early version of the plot of *The Unexpected Guest*.[10] Notebook 53 and Notebook 47 also contain work on the piece, apparently dating from the early 1950s and mid-1950s respectively, and in the former case under the heading 'Play – The Unexpected Guest'.[11]

In certain elements of its structure and setting *The Unexpected Guest* is indeed a natural successor to *The Hollow*; in both plays a wife is found holding a gun over the body of her husband in the supposedly classic Christie dramatic setting of the country house. *The Unexpected Guest*, though, is a much darker piece, and the psychological interplay of the characters far more complex. Without the necessity to unweave Poirot from the story, Christie presents us with the efficient, sarcastic and no-nonsense Inspector Thomas; like *Verdict*'s Inspector Ogden he is a natural successor to *The Hollow*'s made-for-stage Inspector Colquhoun, and a man who is in any event guaranteed not to distract from the characters at the centre of the play's intense domestic drama.

It is clear from her notes that Christie does not regard the role of the inspector as in any way a central one; he is not named in the plot outlines and is not even included in some of the draft character lists. Similarly, the eventual identity of the killer is evidently not a priority, and various outcomes are experimented with; 'whodunit' does not appear to be of particular concern to Christie herself. Over the lengthy gestation of this story, the female protagonist starts life as Vera – a name presumably abandoned as it would have duplicated that of the leading female role in *Ten Little Niggers* – and eventually becomes Laura, the name that was rejected in favour of Clarissa for the heroine of *Spider's Web*. The character who eventually becomes Major Julian Farrar, her lover, is portrayed as an MP in the notes but is eventually demoted to a parliamentary candidate; if *Appointment with Death*'s Lady Westholme had been believed by the censor to resemble too closely Nancy Astor, then the prospect of portraying an MP involved in blackmail and an affair with a married woman was doubtless considered too much of a hostage to fortune in that respect. 'Excuse my ignorance, but what are you, Tory?' he is asked. 'I'm a Liberal,' replies Farrar. 'Oh, are they still at it?' comes the response.

By Notebook 28 the title of the play has changed temporarily to 'Fog', perhaps inspired by the dramatic potential of the killer smog that engulfed London in December 1952. The play is set in a house in South Wales near the Bristol Channel, a location which, although not geographically identical, may have been inspired by the house at Pwllywrach which Rosalind inherited from her first husband, Hubert Prichard, and where Christie had spent time with her daughter and grandson. The action of the play is punctuated by the 'melancholy boom' of the Bristol Channel foghorn and, significantly, it is the last thing we hear, even once the metaphorical fog besetting the characters appears to have cleared. In practical terms, it is the fog that causes the road accident that results in the titular 'unexpected guest' seeking refuge in the house where, on entering, he discovers Laura holding the gun over her wheelchair-bound husband's body. Inevitably, all is not as it appears, and the new arrival unearths a web of intrigue, deception and distrust in a sinister and dysfunctional household living in the shadow of the murder victim's bullying.

Like The Hollow, the house has a well-stocked gun cupboard, and it is clear from the start that this is going to be no vicarage tea party. The dramatis personae includes a terminally ill matriarch, a shifty male nurse and the mentally 'retarded' teenage boy, Jan; but arguably the dominant character in the play is dead from the outset, although we do spend the first scene in the company of his corpse. Amongst Richard Warwick's objectionable practices, we are told, was his penchant for shooting at animals, birds and the occasional passer-by through his open window: it was a habit he shared with Agatha's wayward brother, Monty, who had similarly spent time in Africa and who also required the services of a full-time nurse. According to Agatha's autobiography, Monty delighted in announcing that he had fired in the air around 'some silly old spinster going down the drive with her behind wobbling'.[12] In *The Unexpected Guest*, Laura reports a similar incident in which her husband boasted of having sent shots to the right and left of a woman 'going away down the drive', her 'fat backside . . . quivering like a jelly'.[13] In each case, the police were eventually called. Given the chronology of the writing of her autobiography (between 1950 and 1965) there is every chance that these similarly worded *homages* to her brother, who had died in 1929, were penned at around the same time. Monty himself, however, whilst both troubled and troublesome, was clearly not the model for the deeply unpleasant Richard Warwick, even if they did share an alarming inclination for using passers-by as target practice.

The Unexpected Guest is tense and well-constructed, and perhaps its greatest achievement is its extraordinary sixteen-page opening duologue between the intruder and the apparent murderess. In the wrong hands this unusual and risky piece of dramatic construction could compromise the play at the outset, but Christie skilfully sustains the tension and subtexts whilst interweaving exposition and back-story with intriguing stage business and a growing relationship between the two characters. As for the enigmatic 'guest', Michael Starkwedder is the ultimate embodiment of a recurring Christie character, be it Mortimer Cleveland whose car breaks down in the 1926 short story 'SOS' or the unexplained Mr Paravicini whose Rolls-Royce runs into a snowdrift in *The Mousetrap*. In this case, though, he has a much more significant narrative function and also provides the tantalising, but in this case unfulfilled, prospect of 'love from a stranger'. Here, as he departs into the fog at the end of the play, we see yet another example of how changes in the published edition can undermine the writer's original intention. What we now read is this:

> (As Laura stares at him, dazed, Starkwedder takes her hand and kisses the palm.)
> STARKWEDDER: (gruffly) Goodbye Laura.
> (Starkwedder goes quickly out of the window and disappears R into the mist. Laura runs out onto the terrace and calls after him)
> LAURA: Wait – wait. Come back.

Here is what Christie originally wrote; spot the difference!

> (As Laura stares at him, dazed, he tilts up her chin and kisses her lips quickly)
> STARKWEDDER: Goodbye, my darling.
> LAURA: Wait – wait. (she rushes after him to the window and calls out) Michael – come back.[14]

As for the unexpected guest's unusual name, when Gregg questioned Christie about its origins, she replied that the audience would assume that anyone calling himself Starkwedder must be genuine, as no one would invent such a name.[15] Gregg was suitably impressed by the ingenuity of her response, but would perhaps have been amused to know that in the early notes for the play the character is known simply as 'Trevor'.

Lib Taylor, whose feminist deconstruction of 'The Verdict' falls so short of the mark, also has it in for *The Unexpected Guest*, another play where apparently 'The women collude by rejecting the possibility of challenging their oppressors, preferring the status quo.'[16] This accusation is levelled at the writer of the line (spoken by Starkwedder), 'Men are really the sensitive sex. Women are tough. Men can't take murder in their stride. Women apparently can.' When Taylor maintains that 'the audience remain uncertain who the murderer was', it is apparent that her understanding of the text is minimal. Academics can sometimes forget that plays are written for performance rather than reading; and I have never seen a performance of *The Unexpected Guest* in which either a woman 'rejected the possibility of challenging her oppressor' or the audience wasn't entirely clear 'whodunit'. What we do see is an intriguing exploration of the idea of an avenging angel meting out justice to someone who appears to have escaped the law; in this case the victim of the self-appointed executioner has committed the same crime as the first victim of the avenger in *Ten Little Niggers* – killing a child through careless driving. Unusually, but not without precedent in Christie's work, the dispenser of this summary justice apparently walks free. Meanwhile, others attempt to take the blame in order to protect the innocent. None of the elements of this intriguing and complex moral maze were new to Christie's work, of course, but the characters and context of *The Unexpected Guest* imbue them with a highly effective immediacy.

As with the first set of notes for *The Unexpected Guest* there is, unusually, also a date on the last: 'Nov 1957'. *Towards Zero* had closed in March that year, and it may be that Christie had been toying with the idea of this as a somewhat superior successor; a conclusive demonstration that Agatha Christie, unaided, could do it better than Gerald Verner. In any event, the concept was clearly sufficiently developed by late May 1958 for a completed script to be on Saunders' desk within a month, and he forwarded it immediately to Hubert Gregg, who was in the midst of his seven-year stint as resident director of *The Mousetrap*. Six Christie pieces had been produced since Gregg had directed *The Hollow* for Saunders in 1951 but, despite his claims to have ensured *The Hollow*'s success through extensive rewrites of the text, none of them had been staged by Gregg. Now Saunders needed a safe pair of hands who would deliver a straightforward thriller, who was immediately available and who would not be phased by the timeframe.

Saunders was also no doubt responding to the fact that Gregg's most recent West End directorial offering, the American thriller *Speaking of Murder*, had just opened at the St Martin's, opposite *The Mousetrap*, advertising itself with a press quote that called it 'The Best Thriller in Town'. The skilfully plotted and entertaining play by prolific husband and wife mystery novelists Audrey and William Roos (known jointly to their readers as Kelley Roos), had been underfunded by its Canadian producers and only ran for 173 performances, but was nonetheless a highly regarded critical success. Now Gregg, back in the Saunders fold, began to cast *The Unexpected Guest*. 'Again, I couldn't get any major stars', notes Saunders. Agents were, perhaps, wary after the critical response to *Verdict*, although in this case the extremely short notice can't have made the casting process any easier.

In the end, a highly credible if not immediately commercial cast was led by forty-three-year-old Renee Asherson in the challenging role of Laura Warwick. Asherson was a well-regarded classical stage actress of the sort who would these days doubtless consider Christie's work as being beneath them. A graduate of Webber Douglas, where she had been a contemporary of Hubert Gregg's, she had worked with Barry Jackson's Birmingham Rep before going on to enjoy critical acclaim as a regular leading actress with the Old Vic company and memorably playing Princess Katherine to Laurence Olivier's Henry V in Olivier's film. She had also appeared regularly on stage and screen with her husband Robert Donat. Another respected Old Vic and West End player, thirty-nine-year-old Nigel Stock, took second billing as Starkwedder. His supporting roles in *Brighton Rock* (1947) and *The Dam Busters* (1955) did not qualify him as a 'name' in 1958 but he was later to become a popular television star, initially in the role of Doctor Watson in the long-running 1960s Sherlock Holmes series, opposite Douglas Wilmer and then Peter Cushing as Holmes. Veteran character actress Violet Farebrother, celebrating her seventieth birthday shortly after the play opened in London, completed the trio of 'above title' performers in the role of Mrs Warwick.

Despite the fact that the excellent cast Saunders had assembled was hardly stellar, he once again billed the performers far more prominently than the playwright on the production's publicity material,[17] in what was doubtless a case of post-*Verdict* bet-hedging. If you don't have 'major stars' then at least make it look like you have, particularly when the writer's last piece was a major flop. The line in the *Times* classified advertisements ran, 'RENEE ASHERSON, NIGEL STOCK, VIOLET FARE-BROTHER THE UNEXPECTED GUEST AGATHA CHRISTIE'S NEW WHODUNIT!' A lot of water had flowed under the bridge since Saunders, at Christie's insistence, had refrained from publicising *The Hollow* as a 'whodunit'.

The opening at Bristol Hippodrome was not without its problems. Clearly a last-minute booking, the huge theatre, which normally hosted musicals and which was in the habit of projecting advertisements on to its safety curtain during the interval, was entirely inappropriate for the presentation of a Christie play. Designer Michael Weight offered to make changes to the set in order to accommodate the vast expanses of the Hippodrome stage, but Gregg wisely opted to allow the actors to prepare for the West End run on a design configured in a way that would mirror the confined stage of the tiny Duchess, even though the result, he said, looked like a 'peep show'. There was also a practical issue with the fog idea. As Gregg was inevitably quick to point out, the play is set indoors, and it is difficult to achieve a fog effect on stage where it is seen through a window without it seeping onto the rest of the set; 'I should have said to myself "she thinks she's writing a book.

Forget it,"' he notes.[18] But, in fairness, he seems to have persevered, and a grateful Agatha sent him a first night telegram jokingly reminding him of their difference of opinion over the climactic thunderstorm in *The Hollow*: 'WOT NO THUNDER STOP ONLY MISERABLE MISSED STOP APOLOGIES NEXT PLAY WILL BE CALLED LIGHTNING STRIKES TWICE GOOD WISHES AND THANKS AGATHA'.[19] (For 'missed' read 'mist' – clearly a misunderstanding by the telegraphist!)

Western Daily Press reporter Peter Rodford managed to grab a rare first night interview with Christie in her seat at the front of the circle during the interval and, despite the considerable challenges presented by the space, she was evidently very pleased with how the performance was going. Responding to a question about how long it took her to write a play, Christie said, 'This one I did quite quickly, but then usually I spend some time thinking about them before writing. I have to make sure I have got all the ends tied up.'[20] This certainly seems a fair enough comment on the writing of *The Unexpected Guest*; she appears to have spent at least eight years thinking about it. Rodford then enquired whether Christie found crime plays or novels easier to write, eliciting the response, 'Crime plays. Keeping the plot in one setting is a help.' He went on to ask what she thought of third-party stage adaptations of her novels, and she replied tactfully, 'They are sometimes not stern enough. They try to leave too much in – too many clues.' I like the sound of Peter Rodford; he certainly knew which questions to ask this particular playwright in the very short time available to him.

A week later, *The Unexpected Guest* opened at the Duchess. Elsewhere in the West End that night, Rex Harrison, Julie Andrews and Stanley Holloway in *My Fair Lady* were continuing to compete successfully for the musical theatre audience with the long-running *The Boy Friend* and *Salad Days*; while, alongside their star-studded Drury Lane production, Tennents' repertoire included Peter Shaffer's West End debut *Five Finger Exercise*, directed by John Gielgud at the Comedy Theatre. The Prince's Theatre, by contrast, was hosting Michael V. Gazzo's

A Hatful of Rain, a hard-hitting play about drug dealing and addiction heralded by Saunders' friend Walter F. Kerr as 'an electrifying social study' and advertised as 'London's first Method Production'. At the New, Charles Laughton and Elsa Lanchester were appearing in Jane Arden's *The Party*, no doubt basking in the publicity generated by the release of the film of *Witness for the Prosecution* earlier in the year, while at the Winter Garden, previously the London home of Christie's greatest theatrical triumph, the Folies Bergeres had taken up residence with their 'all French revue'.

The heady days of *Witness for the Prosecution* at the Winter Garden were long gone, but with Christie at least on the face of it reclaiming what was regarded as familiar territory – the clown no longer aspiring to play Hamlet, to use Gregg's analogy – the theatre critics appear to have breathed a collective sigh of relief. It is as if Christie thrillers were perceived as inhabiting a territory of their own, no doubt offering some respite from the war zone of Aunt Edna versus Jimmy Porter, and she was consequently welcomed back to her pigeonhole with open arms, like an errant child returning home. 'Mrs Christie returns to her old form,' ran the headline in *The Stage*, above a review that started, 'Agatha Christie's latest play, *The Unexpected Guest*, which opened at the Duchess on Tuesday last, is an intriguing, deft and sharply characterised whodunnit which should go a long way towards restoring the author to public favour after the fiasco of *Verdict*.'[21] The *Telegraph* agreed: 'After the failure of her last play, *Verdict*, it was suggested in some quarters that Scotland Yard ought to be called in to discover who killed Agatha Christie. But *The Unexpected Guest*, turning up last night at the Duchess before even the reverberations of her last failure have died away, indicates that the corpse is still very much alive. Burial of her thriller reputation is certainly premature.'[22] The *Daily Mail* noted, 'In *Verdict* the motherly queen of whodunits tried for a change to substitute character for suspense but last night she beamed down from her box on the routine parade of thriller puppets playing the old guessing game.'[23] The *Star* added, 'After her recent failure – with *Verdict*

– to climb into a higher dramatic bracket, Agatha Christie has reverted to the old formula that has paid her so well in *The Mousetrap*.'[24] The *Manchester Guardian* damned with faint praise: '*The Unexpected Guest* is standard Agatha Christie. It has nothing as ingenious or exciting as the court scene and double twist of *Witness for the Prosecution* . . . I have known more tension and greater surprise from other of Mrs Christie's classics but this is quite a decent specimen of her craft.'[25]

Even a lukewarm review in *The Times* seemed reassured that as the play opened, 'we are already deep in the Christie country with its famous landmarks, the French windows, the lonely house, and the closed ring of suspects. But the author is vigilantly resourceful in suggesting throughout the first act that these surroundings are unfamiliar.'[26] By Act Two the play is running 'to formula, with repetitious police interviews, each one disclosing some fresh particle of evidence, none of which gives any clue to Miss Christie's closely guarded secret'. The review concludes, 'one's sympathy goes out to Mr Phillip Newman, as the dead man, for all the nightly vigils ahead.'

Laurence Hitchin in the *Observer*, deputising for Kenneth Tynan who was at the Edinburgh Festival, noted that 'The corpse in Agatha Christie's *Unexpected Guest* cools un-regarded in a wheel-chair while the widow and an intruder embark on complicated exposition. Provided you can accept such unreality and the abysmal humour, there is an ingenious display of suspects, as if lids were being taken off wells of depravity and hastily put back.'[27] This latter echoes Tynan's own comment on *Towards Zero*, when he noted that 'All the characters must perforce be represented as harbouring dark and repressed criminal impulses, which gives them a likeness to everyday British life seldom approached by other dramatic conventions.' Perhaps offering the glimpses of 'wells of depravity' in humanity, as represented in a more forthright manner by Laurence Steene in *A Daughter's a Daughter*, comes closer to the playwright's real concerns than playing a game of Cluedo with the audience.

If Christie herself continued to harbour aspirations to 'climb into a higher dramatic bracket', her producer evidently didn't.

Saunders' marketing strategy was relentless in driving home the message that *The Unexpected Guest* was indeed 'standard Agatha Christie' and would not disappoint whodunit fans in the way that *Verdict* had. The production's publicity leaflet deliberately ran with a selection of quotes from the press underlining the fact that the Thriller Queen was back on form:

'The impact is tremendous . . . when the murder seems solved, all the ends tied up and you are groping for your hat, Miss Christie pulls her almighty knock-out punch. From a dazed, horizontal position I admit her complete victory.' (*Evening News*)

'Agatha Christie is back with a bang . . . a really well-tangled whodunit.' (*The People*)

'It's Okay this time, Agatha!' (Herbert Kretzmer, *Daily Sketch*)

'Whodunnit? You won't guess.' (*Sunday Pictorial*)

'You will be kept guessing to the end.' (Harold Hobson, *Sunday Times*)

'This one is authentic Agatha.' (*News of the World*)

'Mrs Christie has us all groping in another little fog, mental this time, as we try to find out who did kill Richard Warwick.' (*Daily Telegraph*)

'Agatha hears the applause again.' (*Daily Mail*)

'I was completely baffled.' (*News Chronicle*)

'It kept the audience in a state of stunned uncertainty, guessing wrongly to the last.' (*Manchester Guardian*)

'Gasping at the final adroit twist sent me home grumbling "Fooled again".' (*The Star*)

'Agatha Christie is back with a success.' (*Daily Herald*)

'You will never guess who did the murder.' (*Sunday Empire News*)[28]

Amongst those joining in the guessing game was the Queen, who made her now traditional visit to the latest Christie play, accompanied by fellow Christie fans Lord and Lady Mountbatten.

On the night they visited in February 1959 further drama was added to proceedings when nineteen-year-old Christopher Sandford, playing Jan, was taken ill and replaced in at the interval by twenty-eight-year-old company manager and understudy Peter Fox.

With Christie apparently writing successful 'whodunits' to order again, the question now arose as to whether to attempt a large-scale production of *The Unexpected Guest* in America, or to hold back in order to protect the brand, as had been the case with *The Mousetrap* and *Spider's Web*. The play itself did not fall into the more melodramatic category of Christie's work that appeared to find favour on Broadway. *Ten Little Indians* and *Witness for the Prosecution* are both exceptional works of high drama; but the (at least on the face of it) 'by the book' English country house setting and police procedural format of *The Unexpected Guest* seemed in danger of predestining it to the same 'lost in translation' fate as had befallen *The Suspects*. And it has to be said that American producers were not exactly falling over themselves to sign up the new play, as they had been only five years earlier with Christie's extraordinary courtroom drama.

The careful strategy according to which the release of Christie's dramatic work in America was organised also suffered a sad setback when Harold Ober, her tireless American agent, died of a heart attack in New York in 1959 at the age of seventy-eight. Edmund Cork's ally and co-conspirator in the tactful management of Christie's hugely complex business affairs was indeed a sad loss. His witty and perceptive correspondence with Cork offers an invaluable insight into the challenges faced by those responsible for licensing Christie's intellectual property on both sides of the Atlantic, particularly in the context of the ascendancy of television as the dominant medium. The two men shared a healthy cynicism about the realities of staging theatrical productions and the people responsible for doing so, and whilst in hindsight some of their strategies may appear to have been naïve or ill-informed there can be no doubt about their absolute integrity in attempting to safeguard the long-term interests of their client. Ober himself had an excellent understanding of the extraordinary contractual complexities of American theatrical production and of how to deal with colourful personalities like the Shuberts and Gilbert Miller, and his advice on these matters, when Cork and Saunders chose to take it, was invariably accurate. Harold Ober's successor as president of the agency which he had founded in 1929 was the formidable Dorothy Olding, who had been with the company for twenty-one years. She already enjoyed a good working relationship with Cork and with Ober's distinguished clients, who as well as Christie included the notoriously reclusive J.D. Salinger and the crime novelist and theatre director Ngaio Marsh, who was also a client of Hughes Massie.

Saunders appears not to have exercised his own American option on *The Unexpected Guest*, although he was quick to secure his share of UK amateur income from this handy, single-set ten-hander, and the 'acting edition' was published within months by Samuel French.[29] In May 1965, an American licence was eventually issued by Dorothy Olding to Bruce Becker[30] who, with his wife Honey Waldman, had recently renovated the Broadway Theatre in Nyack, New York, and was about to reopen it as the Tappan Zee Playhouse. This enterprising couple were later to found the off-Broadway Bouwerie Lane Theatre, converted from the German Exchange Bank building; but for now *The Unexpected Guest* would be the first play of their opening season at Nyack from 5 to 10 July 1965, following a gala opening with Jack Benny (he who had expressed an interest in *The Mousetrap* a decade previously).

But this was only part of the strategy; *The Unexpected Guest* actually opened at the Town and Country Playhouse in Rochester, New York, on 29 June, and the week at Nyack was to be the second date on a ten-week tour that was evidently intended to prepare it for Broadway. And key to this was the casting of Hollywood legend Joan Fontaine in the role of Laura Warwick. Forty-eight-year-old Fontaine had won the 1942 Best Actress Oscar playing opposite Cary Grant in Hitchcock's *Suspicion*, and had also been nominated for the prize for Hitchcock's *Rebecca*, playing opposite Laurence Olivier, in 1941, and for Margaret Kennedy and Basil Dean's *The Constant Nymph* in 1944. On paper, at least, she was one of the biggest names to be cast in a Christie role. The *New York Times* announced, '*The Unexpected Guest*, a revised version of Agatha Christie's mystery play that ran in London in 1958, may be shown on Broadway with Joan Fontaine in the starring role. The presentation will be made by Bruce Becker, operator of the Tappan Zee Playhouse in Nyack, New York.'[31]

We know from press reports that the tour was a big success at the box office (it won a gold cup for breaking the attendance record at Westport Country Playhouse[32]) but for some reason the production never made it to Broadway. The answer as to why may lie in the *Palm Beach Post*'s review, headlined 'An Unexpected Mistake at Grove', which commented: 'Agatha Christie has written so many books and plays she's bound to make a mistake now and again. One of them, *The Unexpected Guest*, opened last night at the Coconut Grove Playhouse . . . more than 200 million Christie murder mysteries have been sold, so the 74-year-old writer doesn't really need this play to add to her reputation.'[33]

How much the critic's intense dislike of the play was down to yet another 'revised' American version of Christie's work we will never know, but he had no problem with Fontaine's performance, saying that she 'did a fine job, all things considered . . . That's the main redeeming feature of the play – looking at Miss Fontaine. I'm not sure just how old she is, but she's still a doll.' If this was indicative of the overall critical response, then there was clearly no basis on which to take the gamble of Broadway and, having cleaned up at the box office on the touring circuit, the producers took the no doubt wise decision to quit while they were ahead.

It must also be remembered that Fontaine, though not yet fifty, had all but quit her Hollywood career and was no stranger to lending her name to dinner theatre and out-of-town productions. Her only Broadway experience consisted of taking over from Deborah Kerr in the hit *Tea and Sympathy* in 1954 and she would later appear, again as a take-over, in the long-running

Top: Margaret Lockwood and company in *Spider's Web* (1954).

Bottom: Margaret Lockwood and Agatha Christie in a publicity photograph; the corpse is played by Lockwood's agent Herbert de Leon.

Top left: Patricia Jessel.

Top right: Verity Hudson.

Bottom left: The 1956 programme for *A Daughter's a Daughter*.

Bottom right: Agatha's daughter, Rosalind.

THEATRE ROYAL, BATH
Telephone 3700.   Box-Office Hours 10 a.m. to 9 p.m.
Lessee and General Manager — Frank G. Maddox.

MONDAY, JULY 2nd, 1956.

Smith & Whiley Productions Ltd.
present the
London Resident Company
in
"A DAUGHTER'S
A DAUGHTER"
By MARY WESTMACOTT
■ FIRST TIME ON ANY STAGE ■

Booking Office Open Daily 10 a.m. to 9 p.m.

PROGRAMME :: 6d.

L. F. SENNITT   Newsagent
8, TERRACE WALK   Tobacconist
BATH
                       Stationer
Also at :-
18, Northumberland Place - Bath

Top left:*Verdict* at the Strand Theatre (1958).

Top right: *The Unexpected Guest* at the Duchess Theatre (1958).

Bottom left: Renée Asherson.

Bottom right: The Playbill for the 1965 US production of *the Unexpected Guest* starring Joan Fontaine.

Top: Agatha Christie enjoying the company of Verity Hudson, Hubert Gregg, Robertson Hare, Margaret Lockwood, Pat Kirkwood, Peter Saunders and Marie Löhr to celebrate Verity Hudson's twenty-one years working for Peter Saunders (1969).

Bottom: Mathew Prichard, Max Mallowan, Agatha Christie and Peter Saunders at *The Mousetrap*'s 21st birthday party (1973).

Forty Carats. Such are the vagaries of show business that the Hollywood legend seems to have been good novelty billing for boosting dinner theatre and touring box office revenues, but perhaps simply not regarded as a sufficient stage heavyweight to sustain a Broadway opening in her own right. Or maybe she just preferred it that way, having left Hollywood for New York, she claimed, when they tried to cast her as Elvis Presley's mother.[34] As well as various TV appearances, Fontaine went on to tour regularly in *Dial M for Murder* and, in the summer of 1967, played Clarissa in a tour of Christie's *Spider's Web* (no doubt in a 'revised' version) seven years before its off-off-Broadway New York premiere.

Although it never played Broadway, *The Unexpected Guest*'s numerous international productions included a notable Parisian staging in 1968, adapted by French playwright Robert Thomas, whose *Trap for a Lonely Man* had enjoyed a successful run at the Savoy in 1963. Less happily, in 1999 *The Unexpected Guest* was the second of three original Christie plays to be 'novelised' by Charles Osborne; *Black Coffee* (1997) and *Spider's Web* (2000) were similarly adapted. I readily acknowledge that Osborne's 1982 book *The Life and Crimes of Agatha Christie* made a significant contribution to her readers' appreciation of Christie's work as a playwright, but to me the idea of turning her original stage plays into novels seems to be a curiously retrograde step. At least *Verdict* was spared.

On 8 January 1960, Saunders optioned Christie's latest play, *Go Back for Murder*;[35] and, with the next one in the bag, he closed *The Unexpected Guest* on 30 January. *Go Back for Murder* opened its short pre-West End tour in Edinburgh three weeks later. Saunders, who had perhaps been lulled into a false sense of security by *The Unexpected Guest*, and maybe by the fact that the title of the new piece contained the word 'murder', had booked the Duchess Theatre for a 23 March opening. The Duchess had provided a happy home for *The Unexpected Guest*, and had also hosted two other successes for Saunders; William Douglas Home's *The Manor at Northstead* and Ronald Millar's *The Bride and the Bachelor*. Now that the Christie stage thriller production line appeared to have overcome its brief malfunction, the Duchess had evidently been earmarked as a regular home for her work. But if Saunders had been expecting another detective yarn to keep the Queen of Crime's seemingly insatiable whodunit fans happy, he should perhaps have paid a little more attention to her chosen subject matter.

Go Back for Murder (the only play Christie ever wrote with the word 'murder' in the title) is based on her novel *Five Little Pigs*, originally serialised as *Murder in Retrospect* in the American magazine *Colliers Weekly* in 1941, and first published by Dodd, Mead & Co. in America the following year. Christie herself had not adapted a play from one of her novels since 1951's *The Hollow* had finally laid to rest the memories of her struggles in the 1940s with *Hidden Horizon*, *Towards Zero* and *Appointment with Death*. Having enjoyed in the interim four major successes with plays that did not use her novels as their source material, this seemed like an odd moment to return to a formula where her hands were tied by the logistics of the adaptation process. It also seems perverse that she should have specifically chosen one of five titles that she had highlighted to Cork in 1950 (when discussing the folly of adapting *Towards Zero*) as being unsuitable for adaptation as stage thrillers.[36] But that list, of course, had also included *The Hollow*, a challenge to which she had successfully risen. And, as *Ten Little Niggers* had amply demonstrated, if there was one thing that Agatha Christie, playwright, enjoyed it was a challenge.

Like other works of the period which Christie adapted for the stage (1937's *Death on The Nile*, 1944's *Towards Zero* and 1946's *The Hollow*), *Five Little Pigs* presents us with a man who finds himself under the same roof as both his new and old loves: a scenario which proves the catalyst for murder. In this case, the artist Amyas Crale is working on a portrait of his mistress Elsa, in the presence of his wife, Caroline. But who in the household put the poison in his beer? On stage, this question keeps the audience's eyes glued on the drink in question in the same way that they try to spot who is tampering with those ten notorious little figurines. But it is not the premise of the plot that fascinated Agatha so much as the unusual narrative structure by which the book delivers it. The action actually starts sixteen years after these events. Amyas and Caroline's daughter, Carla, is attempting to clear the name of her mother, who died in prison having been convicted of her father's murder. She enlists Poirot to interview five potential witnesses (the 'five little pigs' of the title), and he obtains both verbal and written accounts from them giving their own differing recollections of the circumstances leading up to the murder, and of the event itself. Simply by comparing these accounts, Poirot is eventually able to ascertain the truth of the matter.

At the centre of Christie's narrative premise is the critical legal conundrum of how far it is possible to ascertain the accuracy of personal testimony. Every individual's view of events is clouded by their own perception and prejudices and, in this case, also by the distance of time. Christie's contention here is that it is by identifying the very contradictions and inconsistencies in different individuals' recollections of events that the truth can be ascertained; and it is this that becomes Poirot's fascinating challenge. As a literary experiment this is ingenious; and it is deeply satisfying for the detective novel reader, who can work alongside Poirot to piece it all together by analysing the characters' various written and verbal communications. Like *Ten Little Niggers*, it is a masterpiece of narrative construction of the sort on which Christie's reputation as a novelist was based. As the basis for a piece of theatre, though, the problems it presents would appear to be well-nigh insurmountable; particularly if the first thing you do is to cut the character of Poirot. But I have no doubt that this is precisely why she took it on; and the solutions she provides are ingenious and, in terms of stagecraft at least, show Christie at the top of her game.

At the age of sixty-nine, Christie, buoyed up by her West End success, had set herself arguably the biggest challenge of her playwriting career. Like her fellow beneficiary of the People's Entertainment Society, J.B. Priestley, she had always been fascinated by the dramatic potential of the concept of time but, while 'murder in retrospect' had become a recurring theme in her novels, it was not something that she had ever achieved on stage. The unperformed *Someone at the Window* presents us with a substantial sequence in which we see a number of the same characters in flashback, and the 'alternative ending' to *Hidden Horizon* would have to some extent replicated the denouement of Priestley's 1932 play *Dangerous Corner*. Now, Christie was to produce a work which would push director, designer and actors to their limits but which, if successfully delivered, should have created an astonishing *coup de théâtre*.

In Act One of *Go Back for Murder*, Carla arrives from Canada, where she has been living, and enlists the help of solicitor Justin Fogg to organise one-to-one interviews, each in a different location, between herself and the five potential witnesses to her father's murder sixteen years previously. In Act Two, she persuades them to revisit the scene of the crime (the garden room and terrace of a now-deserted country house 'in the West of England' – complete with French windows, of course) and again recount their versions of events; but this time, as they do so, the action switches seamlessly in and out of the night of the crime, so that we see it acted out as the characters remember it. The actress playing Carla also plays her own mother, Caroline, and Christie gives intriguing notes in the 'acting edition' on how the other performers should subtly adjust their performances to indicate whether they are in the past or the present. Fogg acts as a sort of master of ceremonies, anchored in the present, and serves Poirot's function of spotting the vital clues as presented in the flashbacks, which we assume he himself is hearing simply as narrative from the five witnesses. The true killer is revealed but, once again, appears to escape justice, as there is no evidence of a sort that would hold up in a court. Carla has achieved her objective of seeing her mother exonerated to her own satisfaction, and the killer, we are told, has already been sentenced; the knowledge of their guilt, and of the miscarriage of justice inflicted on Caroline, has condemned them to 'life imprison-ment' inside themselves.

Christie has not only successfully dispensed with Poirot but, as in *Hidden Horizon*, has removed the role of the detective completely. She has also brilliantly made use of the highly theatrical device of re-enactment in a manner that suspends the audience's disbelief and engages them simultaneously in the present and the past. The 'present' of the play is 1959, and the 'past' is (wartime) 1943 which, in another interesting timewarp, is the 'present' of the novel's UK publication. We (and the actors) literally do 'go back' for murder. As a dramatic exercise it is daring but effective. At least, it should be. If it is properly directed. And designed. And acted.

Even Lib Taylor has to admire Christie's use of 'metatheat-rical devices', conceding that she is 'certainly here raising questions about linearity, and in representing multiplicity she foreshadows the preoccupations of feminist writers'.[37] Unfortunately, however, the solicitor apparently 'functions uncritically as male author, sustaining the narrative structure and "speaking for" characters, especially females, thereby denying plurality in favour of singularity and resolution. The deconstructive process reinforces rather than dislodges stereo-types, as the perceived villainess now coincides with the "true" murderess, and the mother is restored to her ideologically defined position. Moral justice prevails; the status quo remains undisturbed.' Well, now we know. To satisfy the feminists, the mother would have had to murder her husband; it is a shame that *The Hollow* pre-dates the time frame of Taylor's thesis.

What Taylor has spectacularly failed to appreciate, of course, is that by removing Poirot from the story altogether, Christie has placed Carla right at the centre of the action. Fogg, acting under her direction, has a certain stage management role in Act Two, but in Act One it is Carla rather than Poirot who interviews the suspects. Carla's single-minded determination to discover the truth is the driving force of the piece and, for good measure, she rids herself of a distinctly oppressive fiancé in the process. This gentleman, who goes by the name of Jeff, has some disturbing and distinctly outdated views on eugenics, which take us right back to Sydney Fairfield's dilemma in Clemence Dane's 1921 play *A Bill of Divorcement* and, indeed, to Christie's own early 'Eugenia' parody. Here, in conversation with Fogg, he reveals his dismay on discovering that his fiancée's mother was a convicted murderess:

> JEFF: There I was, all set to marry a nice girl, uncle and aunt some of the nicest people in Montreal, a well-bred girl, money of her own. Everything a man could want. And then – out of the blue – *this*. . . . I'll admit that, just at first, I thought of backing out – you know, kids – things like that?
>
> JUSTIN: You have strong views about heredity?
>
> JEFF: You can't do any cattle-breeding without realizing that certain strains repeat themselves. 'Still', I said to myself, 'it isn't the girl's fault. She's a fine girl. You can't let her down. You've just got to go through with it.'
>
> JUSTIN: Cattle breeding.
>
> JEFF: So I told her it made no difference at all.[38]

Later, in conversation with the brandy-swigging archaeologist Angela Warren, Carla expresses her doubts about Jeff:

> ANGELA: He minds about this?
>
> CARLA: He's very magnanimous.
>
> ANGELA: How bloody! I shouldn't marry him.
>
> CARLA: I'm not sure that I want to.
>
> ANGELA: Another man?
>
> CARLA: Must everything be a man?
>
> ANGELA: Usually seems to be. I prefer rock paintings.

Just so we are clear about Angela's sexual orientation, we are told that 'she is a tall woman of thirty, of distinguished appearance, well-dressed in a plain suit with a mannish hat.' As for Carla herself, in Christie's extensive theatrical pantheon of independent, determined female protagonists, she leads the field: single-mindedly pursuing her own agenda, irrespective of the men around her.

In terms of *Go Back for Murder*'s complex moral outcomes, it is worth noting, in passing, that the miscarriage of justice which put Caroline Crale behind bars instead of the real killer was not in this case compounded by the death penalty. We are told specifically that 'The jury made a strong recommendation to mercy. Her sentence was commuted to imprisonment.' The death sentence for murder was technically mandatory until the 1957 Homicide Act created various exceptions, and there is reference to this in 1958's *The Unexpected Guest*, when Starkwedder states that prison for Laura would be 'just as bad as being hanged by the neck, or is this the kind of crime you are hanged for? I can never remember.' But even in the early 1940s the jury's recommendation, provided the judge and the Home Secretary were of the same mind, could have resulted in a reprieve. Whilst the existence of the death penalty substantially raises the stakes in many a Christie drama, and specifically for the wrongfully accused women in *Towards Zero* and *Verdict*, 40 per cent of men and 90 per cent of women sentenced to the death penalty in the UK in the first half of the twentieth century were actually reprieved in this way.[39] Christie is thus not, as some have suggested, deliberately avoiding the issue of a misapplied death penalty, and thereby missing an opportunity to fuel the increasingly virulent opposition to it in the wake of the 1955 hanging of Ruth Ellis, but is simply realistically reflecting the most likely outcome. The play's narrative and psychological concerns are in any case not driven by the same agendas as *Come and Be Hanged!*, and if they were then the real killer could certainly not be allowed to walk free at the end. The death penalty for murder was finally suspended in 1965, when Labour MP Sydney Silverman, the man who had supported Binkie Beaumont in Parliament, introduced a Private Member's Bill of his own. It was abolished completely five years later.

As well as *The Unexpected Guest*'s restoration of her reputation as a playwright, the last years of the decade had brought with them the end of several significant chapters in Agatha's life. In 1958, following the death of Nancy Neele, she and Archie had exchanged some conciliatory correspondence; perhaps at last this had allowed her to achieve some closure on the distressing incidents of over thirty years before. In the same year, James Watts, Madge's widower, finally sold the cherished family home Abney Hall, the inspiration for many a Christie setting, most notably Chimneys. And in December 1959, just as Agatha was completing the script for *Go Back for Murder*, her close friend Nan Kon, James's sister, died.

There were changes, too, in Max's life, as he handed over the directorship of the Nimrud excavations in Iraq to a colleague. The British School of Archaeology was to continue its work at Nimrud after 1958's coup, which had overthrown the monarchy and established a republic in Iraq, but in early 1960 Agatha and Max chose to travel instead to India and Pakistan.

In January, Cork wrote to Agatha in Bombay, 'Peter seems to be very happy about the new play, plans for which have gone ahead along the lines discussed with you before you left, except that the actor who was to play the lawyer has got caught up with some film commitment and has had to be replaced with Robert Urquhart, who Peter seems to think will give quite as good a performance.'[40] Tantalisingly, I can find no clues as to who was originally to have played the role, but thirty-seven-year-old Scottish actor Urquhart, a respected stage and film performer, should have been a safe pair of hands. Hubert Gregg, now it seems automatically entrusted by Saunders with the direction of Christie plays, praises Urquhart's contribution to the production in his book, although I suspect he may have been Gregg's own suggestion as a replacement, having played the lead in his thriller *Speaking of Murder* ('the best thriller in town').

When *Go Back for Murder* started its short pre-West End tour at the King's Theatre Edinburgh on 22 February, *The Stage*'s regional critic seemed to appreciate it. Under the headline

'Ingenious new thriller by Agatha Christie' the review went on to call it 'an ingenious whodunit, making use of an unusual technique, calling for intricate staging and lighting. The characters, as one expects from Agatha Christie, are well differentiated, and we are kept guessing . . . we see the tragedy reconstructed, in memory, with Carla's lawyer as onlooker, ready to spot the vital clue.'[41]

On 23 March, when the play opened in London, the West End was offering its usual lively mix of thrillers, comedies, new plays, musicals and revues. At Drury Lane *My Fair Lady* had been recast and had finally seen off *Salad Days* and *The Boy Friend*, but was facing competition from *West Side Story* – 'a musical with full New York Cast' – and the transfer of the Theatre Royal Stratford East's *Fings Ain't Wot They Used T'Be*. Margaret Lockwood was appearing for Peter Saunders in the comedy *And Suddenly It's Spring* at the Duke of York's, and the Royal Court was presenting the transfer from Hampstead Theatre Club of the Harold Pinter double-bill *The Dumb Waiter* and *The Room*. *Go Back for Murder* had itself displaced Michael Gilbert's ingenious thriller *A Clean Kill*, directed by Alistair Sim and advertised as the 'Best Crime Play Since Dial M for Murder', which had taken up temporary residence at the Duchess (between Christies) en route to its final home at the Westminster Theatre.

By 1960 the problem of regular outbreaks of booing at West End first nights had ended as unaccountably as it had started; which, in the case of *Go Back for Murder*, was probably fortunate. Once again, Christie had comprehensively subverted expectations, but on this occasion Saunders' production itself seems to have fallen uncharacteristically short of the mark. Kenneth Tynan, who had previously expressed some appreciation, albeit ironically, of Christie's idiosyncratic work for the stage, was taking a sabbatical from the *Observer* to work at the *New Yorker*. His replacement's brief review said, '*Go Back for Murder* is another example of unexpected collapse, due to inept handling, of a very moderate idea . . . The whole matter is gone through at a snail's pace and in the teeth of every possible obstacle put in the way of the actors by Michael Weight's décor.'[42] In its 'theatre round-up', the *Observer* commented, 'Careless work; Agatha can do much better when she tries.'

The *Guardian* felt that

This is low octane Agatha Christie mousetrap cheese which only the very hungry will find palatable. It is roughly produced and contains some of the cheapest acting to have been seen on the London stage for many a day. As it may well run for seven years, it would honour the theatre if the producer [i.e. director] and players, with the honourable exception of Margot Boyd in a small part as a huffy governess, would try to establish a workable tempo and passably naturalistic style . . . it might be worse; is not devoid of ingenuity; but is, all the same, a sorry job for the author of *Witness for the Prosecution*.[43]

As had been the case with *Verdict*, *The Stage*'s London critic was sterner than his regional counterpart. Under the headline 'Mrs Christie! It's not as easy as it seems', the review ran:

Agatha Christie has hardly accomplished a neat, convincing piece of stagecraft in *Go Back For Murder*, which opened at the Duchess last week. In fact, it is an adaptation of one of her novels, and bears all the signs of a clumsy, inexpert, attempt to bring that totally different medium to life in a theatre. On paper the characters were conventional puppets given a superficial appearance of reality and manipulation with some plausibility purely in the service of puzzlement and plot. But it is not so simple as was evidently thought to write them down in a play-script and expect a group of living actors and actresses to make them compelling to an audience.[44]

Under the ominous headline 'Miss Christie varies the routine', *The Times* remarked:

Audiences show no obvious signs of growing tired of watching suspects in a case of murder rounded up and put through the hoop, one by one or in selected groups, by a dogged policeman. But Miss Agatha Christie evidently thinks it time they had a change. She tries to vary the routine without altering its fundamental pattern. *Go Back for Murder* at the Duchess puts the murder some sixteen years back in time and dispenses with the policeman . . . it must be said, however, that Miss Christie has often got more excitement from the routine police investigation than she manages to get from this variation on the routine. She requires in this instance a great many brief scenes which only with difficulty sustain the story's momentum; her dialogue is so strictly utilitarian that it hardly pretends to have the colour of life . . . Miss Ann Firbank is a vigorous heroine . . . the acting as a whole is as utilitarian as the dialogue.[45]

Of course, the very idea that 'Miss Christie' was daring to alter the 'routine' in any way and was unleashing another of her theatrical experiments on her unsuspecting public was enough to send the box office into rapid decline, and the production closed after an inglorious thirty-seven performances. History seems to have overlooked the fact that *Go Back for Murder* was actually a much bigger disaster than *Verdict*. It played one more performance (thirty-seven to *Verdict*'s thirty-six) but the multiple sets, in themselves costing over £2,000, had contributed to it being the most expensive Christie production staged to date, at £5,821. Although Peter Saunders waived some legitimate recharges from his own companies for props and set items, running accounts show substantial weekly losses in addition to the loss of the entire up-front expenditure.[46]

There was, of course, some additional income to help offset these losses; the pre-London tour had only been four weeks long but the usual licensed tour took place immediately after the West End run and, despite the staging difficulties, there was a level of repertory uptake. When the books closed and

Saunders wrote to investors with final accounts, it was to say, 'I am sorry your investment shows a loss, but I hope you will feel that, for a six set show to run for four and a half weeks in London and to lose just under £3,000 is quite a feat!'[47] *Verdict*, it will be remembered, had lost only £20 for the same length of run; but its costs had been lower and its repertory uptake higher.

The London premiere of *Go Back for Murder* had coincided with the press announcement that Christie herself had secured a million-pound deal with Metro-Goldwyn-Mayer for the screen rights to her work.[48] Hubert Gregg and Peter Saunders held the news responsible for a critical backlash; they both quote the *Daily Mail*'s new critic, Robert Muller, who remarked, 'I don't care how rich Miss Christie is. This stinks.'[49] Saunders and Gregg, though, must themselves take at least some of the responsibility for the production's failure. Saunders, happily, had married actress Ann Stewart the previous year, and in the autumn, as Christie finished her script, was focused on furnishing their impressive new home on exclusive Bishop's Avenue in Hampstead. Gregg, flushed with the success of both *The Hollow* and *The Unexpected Guest*, was confident in his belief that Christie and he seemed to be becoming a 'theatrical sure bet' – although not, it should be noted, as sure a bet as Christie and Wallace Douglas.

What neither Saunders nor Gregg appear to have appreciated is the complexity of the piece that Christie had presented them with. Michael Weight, as ever, came up with ingenious design solutions, not only for the first act's five different locations, but also for Act Two, with its stage split between the garden room and terrace. The fact was, however, that the theatre was far too small successfully to accommodate the concept of the production; according to Gregg, 'The wee Duchess Theatre was surprised out of its scene dock'.

With the exception of the honourable mentions for Margot Boyd and Ann Firbank, the performers mostly came in for as much criticism as the cramped design, and there seems to have been no attempt at all to cast the piece with star actors, even pretend ones. When the *Guardian*'s critic accused the performers of 'cheap' acting he wasn't far wrong. The payroll is notably lacking in star salaries,[50] although a number of the ten-strong cast enjoyed modest television and film profiles; in Lisa Daniely's case in the title role of the 1950s Lilli Marlene films. Cast as Amyas Crale's mistress Elsa, Daniely was represented by Herbert de Leon – who again, wisely, did not invest. Whereas *The Unexpected Guest*, despite its lack of major stars, at least appears to have benefited from a cast who were committed to doing justice to the play, the same, sadly, does not appear to have been the case with *Go Back for Murder*.

Arguably, the actors may simply have been the victims of the fact that Hubert Gregg himself was clearly well out of his comfort zone. He refers to *Go Back for Murder* as a 'problem piece' and appears to have been genuinely nonplussed by the whole thing. Even the lighting seems to have been beyond his capabilities on this occasion. *The Stage*'s Edinburgh critic had noted that the play called for 'intricate' lighting, and this was eventually provided when Saunders drafted in Michael Northen to undertake a redesign. So successful was the outcome that Northen, a leading pioneer in the field and the first person to be credited as a lighting designer in the UK, went on to light Saunders' productions on a regular basis, including a complete relight of *The Mousetrap* the following year. Gregg, who prided himself on his lighting abilities, does not mention Northen's involvement in his book, but in his own book Northen says that when he was invited to watch the production, 'I agreed, as tactfully as I could, that the lighting could certainly be improved.'[51]

Unusually for Gregg, he lays claim to the authorship of only three lines in the play, in this case some innocuous banter about the lack of heating in Fogg's office, and his overall verdict on the script is that 'It wasn't bad. It was different, very different, but it wasn't bad. I suppose it might have been better as a novel.'[52] He takes Christie to task for having adapted a book rather than coming up with a new idea, and goes on to state, with typical arrogance, that he didn't bother to read

Five Little Pigs. 'I had no intention of reading the book . . . I hadn't with *The Hollow*. With Christie I wore theatrical blinkers, it was the only way.' Perhaps in this case Gregg should have done so; he would then maybe have appreciated and properly understood the new idea that she had in fact come up with. As indeed might have Lib Taylor, had she read the novel.

One issue that Gregg does raise is the apparent lack of drama in the play's denouement. The real killer is identified by Fogg, and is singled out by him in front of a room full of people halfway through a long speech explaining how he has arrived at his conclusion. But the moment where the killer is identified can appear to be slightly ill-defined, relying on eye contact between accuser and accused at the point when the revelation is made. There is no violent reaction to the accusation. The accused listens impassively before remarking, 'He deserved to die,' adding, quite correctly, 'You're a clever man, Mr Fogg. But there isn't a damn thing you can do about it,' and then exiting. There is further dialogue amongst the characters left on stage but no final twist. Again, in the right hands this play should not require one; what has gone before should be sufficiently remarkable.

Gregg's papers, like the Christie archive and indeed the Christie notebooks, give us very few clues about the genesis of *Go Back for Murder*; and a fire at Peter Saunders' office in 1960 may account for the paucity of correspondence regarding this and other later Christie plays (although contractual and accounting material has been preserved). In Gregg's papers there is, however, one letter about the play from Christie, who wrote to him three weeks after the opening to commiserate over the reviews: 'Yes we've *all* copped it this time – even the music of Ravel did not escape. It's a bit disheartening, I must say – still plays are like racehorses, always either amazing or disappointing their stables.' She goes on to comment that Gregg's wife, the actress Pat Kirkwood, looked extremely glamorous and 'could have done a much better job of being "irresistible" than our Elsa [Lisa Daniely]', and that 'I still feel I can do better over that ending. The space is so cramped that one feels Justin is picking someone by means of the pin trick.'[53]

Christie goes on to point out in some detail that, as the accused had their back to the audience at the key moment, the audience saw no sign of a response to Fogg's accusation. 'You feel rather doubtful' whether Fogg actually meant that person or whether they even heard him. She concludes that it would of course be different if the performer playing the accused 'could *act* – but when they can't they can't and it wouldn't have made any difference to the critics anyway!!' Magnanimous as ever, it had nonetheless clearly not been lost on her that the production had been badly let down by the direction and some of the acting, as well as by attempting to squeeze the design into such a small space. It is interesting to note that, Christie had not been present for rehearsals of either *Verdict* or *Go Back for Murder*. It is all too easy to underestimate her own lively contribution to the rehearsal process.

Gregg quotes an unnamed critic in support of his thesis that Christie herself had botched the ending: 'Agatha Clarissa Christie seems to have lost her corkscrew . . . the one she used with such effect to give those typical twist endings to her most successful mystery plays. This latest . . . is short of this one ingredient. Miss Christie has produced some 60 such crime pieces in book or play form varying on this basic formula. Here one wonders whether or not the variation imposes too much on director Hubert Gregg and his assistants.'[54] The fact was that it clearly had; but in that case I would regard the fault as lying with the director rather than the playwright. Or, indeed, with the producer who appointed the director. J.B. Priestley's seminal 'time play', *Time and the Conways*, had received its West End premiere at the Duchess Theatre in 1937; it was directed by Irene Hentschel. One can't help but wonder how much better Christie's own 'time play' might have fared had it been entrusted to her favourite director.

The nationwide appetite for Christie's plays was undiminished by a second West End flop in three years, however; and, once again, the Hughes Massie sales ledgers bear witness to the enormous ongoing popularity of her work in regional theatres, with as many as half a dozen simultaneous repertory productions of a single title in the 1950s and 60s. In August 1961, *The Stage* reported on the Llandudno summer season:

> Now firmly established as one of the resort's major attractions is the season of Agatha Christie thrillers which Harold Fielding and Melville Gillam present at the Palladium. It is some five years since the Palladium was first put to this use and wet or fine the company plays before full houses. This season's plays, which are changed every Wednesday, are *Verdict*, *Go Back for Murder* and *Murder on the Nile*. The plays are proof that Mrs Christie reigns supreme as the queen of detective fiction and stage thrillers and the only regret felt by residents is that there are only three plays for them to view.[55]

The fact that legendary promoter Harold Fielding appears to have assembled a season consisting entirely of Christie's worst flops is neither here nor there. And in this case we are, of course, straying perilously close to the pier, if not actually onto the end of it. But my point is that, irrespective of the context, similarly well-attended productions of Christie's work would continue to take place up and down the country throughout the second half of the twentieth century. Irrespective of her West End fortunes, Agatha Christie was to remain, indisputably, the people's playwright.

Peter Saunders, meanwhile, was continuing to consolidate his own position in the West End. He already owned the lease on the Ambassadors, and in October 1961 he bought the freehold on the Duchess. The purchase was facilitated by a bank loan organised by Edmund Cork, and this was to be the foundation of a West End theatrical property empire, based on the leases of small playhouses bought from independent owners, that would later also include at various points the Vaudeville, the Duke of York's and the St Martin's. The following year, the Duchess would provide a home for Agatha's final West End offering, with Saunders now in the dual role of producer and landlord. But, ironically, owning the theatre was to prove no advantage when it came to scheduling the production's West End opening.

It seems that *Rule of Three*, an evening of three one-act plays, really was 'Saunders' Folly'. In his autobiography he notes, 'It will be remembered that one of my major successes had been *Witness for the Prosecution*, which I had persuaded Agatha Christie to write against her inclination. I had long since wanted to do a Christie evening of three one-act plays. My idea was that, as many people prefer her short stories to her full-length novels, the theatre-going public might like three plays for the price of one. Agatha was very unwilling to do this, but I am afraid I didn't refrain from reminding her how right I was about *Witness for the Prosecution* and, in due course, she produced *Rule of Three*, three one-acters.'[56]

The earliest reference to the project in Christie's papers is in Notebook 3, in a list headed 'General projects 1955' which also includes 'The Unexpected Guest'. The relevant note reads,

Three plays (Rule of Three?)
1. Accident?
2. Rajah's Emerald?
3. SOS?[57]

All three titles were published Christie short stories, 1929's 'Accident' having been the subject of Margery Vosper's one-act play, *Tea for Three*, in 1939. Perhaps Christie had considered including Vosper's piece in *Rule of Three*, but it seems more likely that she had simply forgotten that it existed, and that 'Accident' was eventually ruled out because it shares a poisoning theme with 'SOS' (1926). There are quite extensive notes that appear to develop the idea of turning 'SOS' into a play but, as it features the arrival at a remote house of a stranger whose car has broken down, it may be that she felt the premise was too similar to that of *The Unexpected Guest*, which she was also developing at the time. Of the three story titles originally listed by her, the only one that Christie continued to pursue as a potential adaptation was 'The Rajah's Emerald' (first published in *Red* magazine in 1926), which contains elements that were later to feature in the piece eventually known as *Afternoon at the Seaside*. By Notebook 24 the list of plays has been amended to 'The Patient', 'Seaside Holiday' and 'SOS', and is headed 'Rule of Three 3 1-act plays for PS', thus acknowledging Saunders' influence on the project.

Rule of Three (more often referred to in correspondence between Cork, Christie and Saunders as 'Triple Bill') ended up comprising three short plays: *The Rats*, *Afternoon at the Seaside* and *The Patient* (performed in that order). More helpfully than the notebooks, the Christie archive also contains loose-leaf first drafts for each of these plays. Apparently typed by Agatha herself, they are (inevitably) undated, and are covered in handwritten notes, amendments and corrections; giving a fascinating insight into Christie the playwright at work.

In the first play, the titular 'rats' in a trap are secret lovers Sandra and David, who are lured to a flat whose owners have gone away. There, bizarre and terrifying events unfold in an atmosphere of increasing tension and claustrophobia, as it becomes apparent that they are being framed for the murder of Sandra's husband, John, whose body they find in a chest where he appears to have hidden himself for the purpose of spying on their clandestine activities.

In Christie's original version, their gay acquaintance, Alec, who briefly joins the two lovers in the flat, actually murders the concealed John before their eyes. In the following extraordinary sequence Alec opens the chest in which Sandra's husband is hiding and kills him, without them (or probably most of the audience) noticing. But first, he is at pains to point out that the flat's balcony could provide an ideal setting for suicide:

ALEC: (goes out through door onto balcony) Perfect for suicide! Five flights and concrete at the bottom. (comes back in and shuts the door. Picks up knife from where David has put it down, holding it rather carefully towards the middle) Now let's see what else we can explore. Nothing very much is there, except the chest. That I believe is what they call a Kuwait Bride Chest. Oh listen, darling, do you think somebody could be hiding inside it? I must see. (opens lid, leans down inside. He holds the knife in his hand. There is a faint groaning noise masked by Alec's rather high-pitched voice) Delicious embroideries. Do you think the Torrances smuggled all these things through customs? (shuts down lid again) Well, I must say I'm disappointed.[58]

In the published version, the reference to suicide is recontexualised so as not to be so suggestive of the act, and Alec does not carry out the murder of John on stage, evidently having killed him at some point before Sandra and David's arrival at the deserted flat. In both versions he gets their fingerprints on the murder weapon, an ornamental knife, before departing, although only in the published script does he 'accidentally' drop the knife over the balcony. Sandra and David discover John's body and, realising that they are locked in the room and are being framed, they argue and their love quickly turns to hate.

By contrast, *Afternoon at the Seaside* is just what it says on the tin; a delightful observational comedy set in the English resort of 'Little-Slippyng-on-Sea', it pokes gentle fun at the British on holiday, and is framed in a wafer-thin plot about stolen jewellery.

One draft has an 'alternative' ending, resulting in the play being split into two scenes; Scene One is set in 'Late afternoon' and Scene Two, which is five hours later, 'Follows immediately. Moonlight. Beach deserted. Harlequinade atmosphere, Distant voice singing Me and My Girl.' The singing of 'Me and My Girl' is intentionally evocative of a bygone era, and I particularly like the fact that, after all her intervening theatrical adventures, Christie's mind turns once again to the childhood delights of a Harlequinade.

The third play, *The Patient*, is set in a private nursing home, where a paralysed woman is attempting to use a 'new electrical gadget' to assist with the identification of the person who pushed her off a balcony. The suspects are assembled and eventually the villain is entrapped. The play's conclusion involves the victim's assailant melodramatically stepping out from behind a curtain just as Inspector Cray identifies them by name as the culprit.

On the face of it, *Rule of Three* presents us with three unconnected plays, each in different styles and each with a crime element. But, as with much of Christie's stage work, there is a lot more to it than may at first appear. *The Rats* draws its storyline, of a murdered man concealed in a chest from which he had been spying on his unfaithful wife, from the 1932 Poirot short story 'The Mystery of the Baghdad Chest'. First published in the *Strand Magazine*, it was later reworked into the longer 'The Mystery of the Spanish Chest', published in *Women's Illustrated* in 1960. Christie would have been working on the expanded version, with its references to marital jealousy that draw parallels with *Othello*, at a time when the idea for *The Rats* was already well-developed. In the original version of the story, Hastings comments that the events it concerns would make a good plot for a play, and Poirot responds that it has already been done. Poirot could be referring to *Othello* or to the 1928 Patrick Hamilton play, *Rope*, in which party guests are served a buffet from the lid of a trunk containing a dead body. But I suspect that it may in fact be a reference to a short play called *Crime*, which featured in the first London Grand Guignol season at the Little Theatre. *Crime*, which premiered in November 1921, starred Sybil Thorndike and her brother Russell, and was written by her husband Lewis Casson.[59] In it, a woman is murdered with a breadknife by an unsavoury pair of characters and her body put in a trunk. Due to circumstances beyond their control, they are forced to remain in the room with their victim, and fall out between themselves. In their nervousness, they eventually give the game away to a third party and the trunk is opened, exposing her horribly mutilated corpse; in the ensuing fracas, one of the killers shoots the other.

The Times was not impressed by *Crime*, declaring that there was 'not a single thrill' in the piece and that the corpse was 'an obvious dummy', although the actors 'make the best of a bad job'.[60] But there was to be a real-life twist to the tale; Russell Thorndike, in his book about his sister's work, tells the story of a rehearsal at which Sybil became trapped inside the trunk, which did not have air holes, and fainted.[61] All of this – the killing with the knife, the conspirators falling out with each other, the question of air holes – finds resonances in *The Rats*. As Christie's *The Last Séance* demonstrates, she was well aware of the Grand Guignol concept, and we know that she attended a Grand Guignol performance when visiting France with Archie in 1924. *Black Coffee* had played at the Little Theatre in 1931; and it is more than likely that, if Christie had not actually seen *Crime* there ten years earlier, she at least read the reviews and heard the stories about it, and that it is therefore this that Poirot is referring to in 'The Mystery of the Baghdad Chest' when he observes that a play has already been made out of the scenario. By 1961, of course, Christie was a friend of Sybil Thorndike and would have heard all about it first hand. Whatever the origins of its storyline, *The Rats*, particularly in its original version featuring an onstage murder, is clearly an exercise in Grand Guignol and, as such, is Christie's second. A few of the critics picked up on this, and even the censor, in recommending it for licence, refers to it as 'Quite a good Guignol.'[62]

The Grand Guignol programmes had provided some light relief from the horrors by including short comedy plays of the sort that Christie herself had once written, and even Noël Coward had contributed such a piece to the original London Grand Guignol season. As a concept, *Rule of Three* is not dissimilar to Coward's own collections of short plays, *Tonight at 8.30*, with which he and Gertrude Lawrence enjoyed huge success in the 1930s; and it is also in Coward's work that we can find a direct inspiration for *Afternoon at the Seaside*.

Elements of the setting, and of the plot such as it is, had been borrowed by Christie from 'The Rajah's Emerald'; but in theatrical terms the play appears to have its origins in Coward's 1928 musical revue *This Year of Grace*, the show in which his enduringly popular song 'A Room with a View' first appeared. Produced by Agatha's friend, the impresario C.B. Cochran, it enjoyed successful runs at the London Pavilion and at the Selwyn Theatre (now the American Airlines Theatre) on Broadway.

The Act Two opener of *This Year of Grace* was a routine called 'The Lido Beach' (showing the English upper classes holidaying abroad), followed by 'The English Lido Beach' (showing the English working-class holiday at home). In the foreground of the first piece there is 'a row of cabanas with coloured, striped awnings' facing the audience, which are replaced in the second by a row of bathing machines. In Christie's piece, over thirty years later, 'Three bathing huts face the audience on a rostrum.' After we have observed the upper classes at play in 'The Lido Beach', the compere announces, 'Ladies and Gentlemen, it has been suggested in several newspapers of late that English seaside resorts hold out fewer attractions to visitors than Continental ones. Any true patriotic Englishman naturally resents this reflection on our national gaiety, and Mr Cochran perhaps more keenly than anyone – so he has determined to prove conclusively once and for all that no holiday resort in the world can equal in charm, gaiety and light-hearted carefree enjoyment an average watering-place on the shores of the English Channel.'[63]

What follows is, in spirit, very similar to *Afternoon at the Seaside*, although considerably shorter and obviously without the 'crime' element. Coward's piece, of course, also contains musical sequences, although for good measure Christie does specify a chorus of 'I Do Like to Be Beside the Seaside' ('rather out of tune') as the curtain goes up on hers.[64] There is no direct duplication of dialogue, and Christie puts her own unique stamp on the whole thing, yet *Afternoon at the Seaside* as a piece of theatre seems likely to have been inspired by an affectionate memory of the *mise en scène* and characters in Coward's 'The English Lido Beach', a fact which more than one reviewer of Christie's play would make reference to. She may well also have been remembering the title of another sketch in *This Year of Grace!*, a spoof of the dramatic style of J. M. Barrie, Frederick Lonsdale and Edgar Wallace called 'Rules of Three'.

Christie's own *Rule of Three*, with its direct references to Grand Guignol and pre-war revue, is I believe a very specific theatrical exercise; but one that it is possible her younger producer and his team did not fully appreciate. She herself was an enthusiastic and well-informed theatregoer, and we know that she attended the plays of Samuel Beckett alongside those of Terence Rattigan. She would have been fully aware of current theatrical trends, and if elements of *Rule of Three* appear to be old-fashioned then I have no doubt that Christie had very deliberately crafted them to be so. However, unless the staging and marketing of the piece could succeed in reflecting her intentions in this regard, she was running the risk of simply appearing to be behind the times.

Although hospital rooms were a favourite Guignol setting, and helpless patients a favourite Guignol premise, the plotting of *The Patient*, unlike the other two plays, appears to have no antecedents in Christie's own work. Her notebooks show that she was toying with a number of different endings for the play including 'Patient is really a policewoman – whole thing is rigged'; as it happens, the idea of a policewoman in disguise would eventually be used in *Afternoon at the Seaside*. Even more intriguingly, the first draft of *The Patient* concludes with the highly original concept that the curtain should come down just as the culprit is about to be revealed, so that the audience never discovers their identity. We hear instead a poem containing a wonderful sideswipe at the critics:

> Don't let whodunnit make you mad,
> Don't let it make the critics sad,
> Because they cannot give away,
> The murderer! If they *can* they *may*![65]

What isn't clear from the script is that this poem was intended to be heard on a recording of the playwright's own voice; 'We agreed to Agatha making this record' says Hubert Gregg, yet again at the helm as director: 'She seemed convinced it would work and we wanted her to get it out of her system.'[66]

An alternative to the poem, in which a voice simply asks the audience who they think did it, and the critics are spared, is inked in to the script. And following this is a page that reads,

A suggestion
If plays run satisfactorily, at some unadvertised date, the ending of the Patient will be different. Inspector Cray will have a few extra lines and the screen will be drawn aside, so that the audience sees who is hiding behind it! This could be done at odd intervals.

Work in progress on *The Patient* indicates that Christie may even have been toying with the idea that any of the five suspects could actually have been the culprit, and that this would have been the play's unique twist. In early drafts, there is no summation from Inspector Cray and the audience is left truly in the dark. When Christie adds her 'suggestion' for an occasional alternative ending in which the culprit is revealed, there is still no indication to the director as to who exactly this should be. When a summation was later added, enabling Cray to identify a particular suspect, it was so perfunctory as to appear to be an afterthought, and still required the culprit to incriminate themselves through their own actions. The two 'clues' upon which the identification hinges have been added on pages that have clearly been inserted into the script at a later stage.

Intriguingly, a South African Christie fan called James Chapman wrote to her at around the time the script was being completed to suggest a 'crazy idea for a play, which only you would be able to make use of at its best . . . Five different endings, in each of which one of the five suspects is the guilty party . . . Knowing your love of fooling your audiences, you may think it has possibilities.' But Chapman received a standard response from Hughes Massie and there is no indication that Christie herself ever saw the letter.[67]

Cork wrote to Christie in August 1961 enclosing a professionally typed 'good copy' of the *Rule of Three* script, but explaining that 'when it was "acted" it took precisely 81 minutes, which is rather too little to give the customers for their money. If you could see your way to adding 17 pages – say 7, 5 and 5 respectively, this would be perfect. I think you will agree when you see Peter that he is now going ahead with this project with terrific enthusiasm. With this he will probably overcome all difficulties.'[68] The plays had actually been 'acted' by Gregg to Saunders over dinner at Saunders' house in Bishop's Avenue, and the version of the script referred to would clearly have been too short for a full evening's entertainment. Christie dutifully added further material; in the case of *The Rats* by creating a scene with an additional character, the inquisitive Jennifer, so that a three-hander became a four-hander. Jennifer has come to feed the budgie belonging to the flat's owners, and is surprised to find Sandra there, but less so when Sandra's lover David also turns up. Jennifer puts two and two together and leaves the two of them together. David and Jennifer are then joined briefly by Alec.

Christie had previously kept the Lord Chamberlain's office happy by complying with the accepted codification of homosexual characters, including Christopher Wren (who wears an 'artistic' tie) in *The Mousetrap* and the 'pansy' Basil in *A Daughter's a Daughter*. But now, four years after the Wolfenden Report had recommended that 'homosexual behaviour between consenting adults in private be no longer a criminal offence', she attempted something more direct. Alec Hanbury is described as 'a young man of twenty-eight or nine, the pansy type, very elegant, amusing, inclined to be spiteful . . . dressed in the height of fashion, even wearing gloves'. When David remarks to Sandra that Alec clearly does not like her she responds, 'I don't think he likes any women very much.' Alec, of course, is a nasty piece of work, but then so are all the characters in *The Rats*; a heterosexual woman in the piece also proves to be a murderer. Christie's point is that crimes of passion are not a heterosexual preserve.

But it wasn't to be as simple as that. On 30 October 1961, Saunders wrote to the Lord Chamberlain's office to request approval for two amendments in the script for *The Rats*. The first was to change a line of Sandra's from 'You swine, you swine!' to 'You bastard! You filthy, rotten bastard!'; the censor has written 'OK' in blue ink next to this, and the word 'YES' is then written in red ink. The second was to change David's line describing Alec's love for Sandra's first husband from 'one of those unnatural, hysterical devotions I should guess' to 'Alex [sic] – obviously a homo – it was that kind of devotion I should guess.' Next to this, the censor has written in blue ink 'Why? I see no reason for underlining this character', and the word 'NO' is written in red ink.[69]

On 2 November, the Lord Chamberlain's office wrote to Saunders stating, 'The following dialogue is allowed: "You bastard! You filthy, rotten bastard." The following dialogue is not allowed: "Alex – obviously a homo – it was that kind of devotion I should guess."'[70] Under this, on the copy of the letter now held in the Lord Chamberlain's Plays archive, someone has handwritten (as if scribbled in rehearsals and sent straight back) 'Alex – obviously a queer' (next to which the censor has written 'NO') and 'Alex – obviously a bit feminine' (next to which the censor has written 'YES'). In a letter to Saunders dated 4 November, Assistant Comptroller E. Penn then states, 'I am desired by the Lord Chamberlain to inform you that the lines "Alex – obviously a bit feminine – it was that kind of devotion, I should guess," submitted by you on 3 November, have been passed for inclusion in the licensed manuscript of the above play.'[71] After all that, the published version we now know has replaced this hard-won line with 'You've only got to take one look at Alec to see what kind of devotion that was.'

The proposed use of the word 'homo' in this context is deliberately pejorative, and is intended to tell us as much about the prejudices of David, who speaks the line, as it does about Alec himself. The replacement line does not really serve this purpose, which is doubtless why it was itself eventually replaced. Six years later, in 1967, the Sexual Offences Act would finally decriminalise homosexual acts carried out in private between men; whatever *The Mousetrap*'s Miss Casewell or *Go Back for Murder*'s Angela Warren were getting up to in private had never been the concern of the law. The following year saw the abolition of theatre censorship in the UK. And the year after that, man landed on the moon.

Rule of Three opened to mixed reviews in Aberdeen on 6 November 1961 and toured to Glasgow, Oxford, Newcastle and Blackpool. The programme from Oxford presents us with the delightful prospect of the evening being punctuated by performances from the theatre's 'resident orchestra'.[72] Agatha and Max were visiting Kashmir and Iran throughout this period; Max, who had recently been made a fellow of All Souls College, Oxford, was involved with the Institute of Persian Studies in Tehran. Christie remained in communication by telegram while she was travelling, and a series of detailed letters sent by Saunders and Cork to her care of the British Embassy in Iran ('Persia' according to Saunders) awaited her arrival there. It is notable that, whereas in 1931 Agatha had hurried back from Nineveh in the hope of seeing the premiere of *Chimneys* at the little Embassy Theatre in Swiss Cottage, she was now prioritising her travels with Max, and seemed happy enough to leave Saunders and his team to their own devices. Following the failures of her brave theatrical experiments with *Verdict* and *Go Back for Murder*, the short-lived re-emergence of *A Daughter's a Daughter*, the faked collaboration on *Towards Zero* and the success of the relatively formulaic *The Unexpected Guest*, it is hardly surprising that, at the age of seventy-one, Agatha appears to have lost some of her appetite for the processes of theatrical production.

Saunders' report on the Aberdeen premiere, written three days later, reads:

Starting with the worst, I should say right away that I didn't like The Rats at all and I don't think that I ever shall. (Let

me interpose here and say that Edmund, I think, likes it the
best of the three.) Hubert worked all day on it yesterday, but
there are difficulties that I am not sure we can ever get over.
When you see Alec in his gloves taking the knife out of the
sheath and 'casually' handing it to the girl, about a quarter
of the audience got the implication. When he opened the
chest, I think 99 per cent realised what was going on. This
means that the play is just a slanging match, with an ending
that doesn't ring true. After all, why should the man commit
suicide for a murder he may not be charged with, and in any
case didn't commit? I spoke to Rosalind, and she had spoken
to Cecil Mallowan [Max's brother] who also disliked this play,
but thought it was bad acting. Yet he liked the acting in the
other two plays which, of course, included the same people.[73]

It is apparent from this that the play opened in the version,
approved by the Lord Chamberlain's office, that includes Alec's
murder of John as part of the action of the piece, and in which
David exits to the balcony at the end, inspired by Alec's carefully planted suggestion that jumping from it would be a good
way to end it all.

Saunders was much happier with the second play:

Afternoon at the Seaside is quite delightful in every way. It
is light, gay and amusing, but still has a twist at the end,
and I had nostalgic memories of Spider's Web, and wondered
what would have happened had you written it as a full-length
play . . . it was certainly the hit of the evening.

Patient . . . the ending was rather strange. We used the
prose rather than the poetry ending, and when your voice
said 'Who do *you* think is behind the curtain?' by some sixth
sense the audience seemed to realise immediately that it was
your voice, and there was such a hubbub that your next few
words weren't heard. For one moment I thought the idea
was going to be a terrific success, but when the audience
realised it was your voice telling them that they weren't going
to be given the *answer*, there was a wave of disappointment

that could be felt. No-one actually threw anything, but I asked the Manager of the theatre to enquire from various patrons he knew, and without exception they all said very uncomplimentary things about not being told who did it.

Saunders goes on to say that they had since been using a different ending where a recorded voice highlighted key clues before a curtain was drawn back to reveal the culprit. This, apparently, was a 'spectacular success'. Saunders' plan was to make sure Rosalind saw both versions in Oxford: 'What she doesn't know yet is that she is going to make the final decision. I haven't broken that to her yet. The ending is such a personal thing, that I feel it far better that in your absence she should decide rather than the combination of Edmund, Hubert and myself.' He goes on to note that, in the event that he fails to secure a West End theatre, 'the whole thing is self-solving' and Agatha will be able to make her own decision about the ending, based on recordings of each of them in performance, along with the audience's reaction.'

Cork sent Christie his own appraisal of *Rule of Three*'s opening:

The reception on the first night at Aberdeen was on balance both friendly and favourable. The Rats did not come over quite as well as we had hoped. It is pretty difficult to get over that claustrophobic sense of horror on a wide stage and in such a big theatre, but I think the production can be tightened up (and incidentally Hubert Gregg agrees with me while Peter does not) and that it will be all right when it comes to town. Afternoon at the Seaside was an absolute riot – I really had no idea it could please an audience so much. The Patient was played on the first night without the solution being given. Your record asking the audience what they thought the answer was came over well, but I fear it rather upset the audience . . . I'm afraid the general feeling was one of frustration, and actually one gaggle in the foyer used the word 'swindle', which I did not like at all. . . . by and large it looks as though the customers are there for easy entertainment, and are inclined to resent the riddle they cannot answer. I am very sorry to have to report in this way, but there it is.[74]

He also explained the plan to involve Rosalind in deciding which ending to use, and warned Agatha that 'Goodnight Mrs Puffin has caught on at the Duchess, so it seems unlikely that Peter will be able to chuck them out before Christmas – you will recall he had to take over the previous owner's contract with these people. Peter is exploring every avenue – not by any means limited to "Shaftesbury" – but I am afraid there is nothing definite to report at the moment.'

When Saunders took possession of the Duchess on 2 October 1961, he was obliged to honour the contract with the incumbent production, Arthur Lovegrove's hugely popular comedy, starring Irene Handl, which had transferred from the Strand Theatre only two weeks previously. As the landlord, he would have been unable to terminate the production's contract with the theatre unless its weekly income fell below its weekly costs.

On 5 December, Cork wrote to Christie, now in India:

I entirely agree with you that it would have been marvellous to get it into the West End for Christmas, but alas, the last hope – the Comedy [Theatre] – faded away yesterday. This is not personal to us, as there are five plays that have been doing excellent business in the country that are having to fold up as they cannot get into the West End. There was certainly part of the audience at Oxford that liked Triple Bill but unfortunately the business for the preceding and succeeding week [i.e. for other plays appearing at Oxford's New Theatre] amounted in each case to twice what we played to. Peter is coming to think that our best hope of getting a success at any other time than Christmas is to get a star in the bill, but this might involve more re-writing than you would want to undertake. Anyway, this problem is one that can wait until you get home again.[75]

Saunders wrote on the same day to confirm the postponement of the West End transfer: 'At least it gives us the time to reassess the position with your help rather than in your absence . . . we are now playing The Patient with the ending that you wrote, i.e. the Inspector disclosing who it was, and I think that this is probably the best thing, anyway until you come back.' Rosalind's role as arbitrator was not, in the end, required, and a version similar to the one that we now have, in which the inspector names the culprit as they step from behind a curtain, was used for the remainder of the first tour.

There appear to have been a number of attempts to create a new ending for *The Patient* during the course of the first tour, even including one put forward by the stage manager, for which a script still survives in the Gregg papers, in which the villain of the piece commits suicide. 'Can you imagine Agatha's face!' wrote Saunders to Gregg.[76] In Gregg's rehearsal script *The Patient* simply ends:

INSPECTOR: So now let's see if you're who I think you are.
(Lays hold of screen) . . .

The rest of the page is then torn out, with the words END TO FOLLOW written in blue ink.[77]

There has been some confusion over the timeframe of the original production of *Rule of Three*, because neither Saunders nor Gregg make it clear in their accounts that an entire year (and two tours) elapsed between its premiere in Aberdeen and its eventual West End opening. In respect of casting, Gregg says simply, 'There was some reshuffling before we reached London,' but the genesis of the production ultimately proved to be far more troublesome and time-consuming than either of them imply.

All things considered, it seems unlikely that Saunders would have pursued the idea of a West End run for *Rule of Three* at the end of 1961 with any great enthusiasm. He evidently felt that work needed to be done on the piece, and with Christie away travelling, there was little prospect of this being carried out. Lack of theatre availability is the classic excuse offered to playwrights by reluctant producers, followed closely by the need for star casting, and Saunders may well in any case have wanted to ensure that he could eventually host the piece at the Duchess once it had been rewritten and Mrs Puffin had flown. It is also apparent from his correspondence with Hubert Gregg that they were both less than happy with the cast they had assembled; of the thirteen who opened in Aberdeen only five would eventually be re-engaged for the West End the following year, although some of them, of course, may not have been available. The halcyon days of casting Richard Attenborough and Margaret Lockwood in Christie plays, although relatively recent, seemed long gone.

In August 1962, Gregg wrote a six-page letter to Saunders from his place in the Algarve which discussed various matters relating to the remounting of the production. The first thing it addressed was the vexed issue of Alec's murder of John in *The Rats*:

If Alec kills John before the action of the play begins there is no reason for the air holes. It is unlikely that John would lie in the chest alive while Alec drills the air holes. . . . Alec wouldn't have stabbed John outside the chest because of cluttering the place with blood, etc. If he stabbed him inside, as I say, why bore holes? Moreover, too, there's something chilling about the idea of a live man lying there listening. Alec may have managed the stabbing badly, or the fault may have been mine if you felt that the audience weren't held here. My own feeling was they were interested in the antics of Alec – in his movement about the room and, if some of the audience realise the truth (that he was stabbing a man) they were elated at their own cleverness. If you feel strongly enough by all means let John be dead before the curtain rises. But I think if we do this we are shying away from what I'm sure Agatha intends to be the high spot of the play, 'John was killed more or less in front of our eyes'. Remember that the stabbing is the only real 'introduction' of John to the audience. If we have just a box with a stiff in it does the description by David of what must have happened lose impact? Why don't we sort this out in, or just before, rehearsal? Perhaps with Agatha? Even see it performed as is once again before deciding?[78]

Hubert Gregg's papers contain a loose-leaf copy of a four-page additional scene, evidently intended to be a new opening for the play, in which we actually meet John, so that the three-hander that became a four-hander is now a five-hander. 'As the curtain rises, Alec is kneeling beside the chest drilling holes. He is in morning dress, but minus his coat, which is thrown over a nearby chair. John Grey, a pleasant, well built man is pacing restlessly.'[79] They are preparing the chest so that John can lie in it and eavesdrop on Sandra and her lover, and Alec is provoking John with tales of his wife's infidelity:

ALEC: A pity you're so old fashioned, John.
JOHN: What do you mean?
ALEC: The modern husband knows how to accept infidelity, I'm told. You're not like that.

Alec, who has been to a royal garden party, has gained entry to the flat using a key that he had cut for his friend 'Benjy' when they were using it together during the owners' absence. He clears up the sawdust, looks down at his dustpan and brush, and remarks, 'Quite the little housemaid, aren't I?' John eventually gets into the chest, but just as he does Alec suddenly 'draws the knife from behind his back and stabs John, out of sight of the audience. Apparently, he wipes the knife clean on the embroidery. Then he goes to replace the Kurdish knife in its sheath. He closes the lid of the chest, and begins to dust, carefully removing fingerprints.'

This scene was presumably written before rehearsals started for the second production, in order to deal with some of the issues raised in the correspondence between Saunders and Gregg. It provides a less unlikely scenario than Alec successfully killing John in the chest without the two other people in the room noticing, but still gives the audience the frisson of the eventual realisation that the murder was effectively carried out before their very eyes. The scene was never submitted to the Lord Chamberlain's office, so it can never have been tried out in performance, and no author is credited. There are no references to it in Christie's notes or draft material, so there is a possibility that it was actually written by Gregg. If that is the case then I have to take my hat off to him for an excellent fake.

Gregg's letter to Saunders goes on to discuss casting the new production of *Rule of Three* at some length, reviewing the previous actors' performances and suggesting who should be re-engaged and who replaced. The first tour had included a notable appearance by a poodle belonging to one of the actors, but it seems that the actor concerned must have been amongst those being considered for replacement: 'the dog would be a serious "miss"', says Gregg, 'I certainly think we should have one.' It is not clear whether they succeeded in finding a substitute canine.

Gregg also touches on the dilemma that Saunders was facing in his new role as theatre owner. It seems that *Goodnight Mrs Puffin* had been playing to poor box office figures during the summer of 1962, at last giving Saunders the opportunity to terminate its contract at the Duchess. But this would have been too early to assist with the West End scheduling of *Rule of Three*, and in any case a successful comedy could expect its business to pick up as Christmas approached. 'What a difficult decision you have re Puffin', wrote Gregg. 'Can you make them transfer if they climb above their break figure after falling below it? Indeed would you want to – not only from the kindness view but from the business angle? What you want is another theatre of your own. Simple.' Saunders wrote straight back to Gregg confirming that rehearsals for a new production of *Rule of Three* would commence on 29 October, with a tour starting on 19 November and the West End run opening in the week of 17 December.[80] He makes it clear that this is contingent on Christie herself being available for the first performance week; her absence had been felt the previous year, when the production got off to its false start.

Auditions were held for cast replacements, and amongst the candidates turned down for a role was Honor Blackman, much to Saunders and Gregg's subsequent embarrassment; her first episodes in *The Avengers* were broadcast in the autumn of 1962, as *Rule of Three* finally made its way into the West End, and two years later she was to play Pussy Galore in *Goldfinger*. Amongst those re-engaged from the first tour was Margot Boyd, who had notably achieved a good review in the role of Miss Williams in *Go Back for Murder*. Christie, it has to be said, had done her producer and director no favours on the casting front by concocting an evening of three short plays consisting of a four-hander Guignol, a nine-hander melodrama and a twelve-hander comedy, and it is clear form Gregg's notes, and Saunders' payroll, that the casting process was challenging on a number of levels.

The Stage subsequently announced that the new tour would open in Wolverhampton before playing Bath, Birmingham and the Nottingham Theatre Royal (no longer fulfilling its once traditional role as the opening venue), with the West End premiere set for Thursday 20 December.[81] *Goodnight Mrs Puffin*, which was having a 'successful run at the Duchess' after transferring from the Strand Theatre, would move to the Duke of York's Theatre. Saunders must have done exactly the deal that Gregg had suggested with the producers of *Goodnight Mrs Puffin*, allowing them to continue at the Duchess through the summer despite their poor box office figures on condition that they vacated the theatre in time to allow *Rule of Three* in before Christmas. At last, everything was set. The Christie theatre brand was, however, to suffer an unexpected setback before *Rule of Three* could finally make its London debut.

Taking advantage of the continued delays in presenting Christie's latest dramatic offering in the West End, the irrepressible Bertie Meyer had bypassed Cork and approached her directly at the end of June 1962 with a suggestion for a West End revival of *Ten Little Niggers*, eliciting the response: 'I think it would be fun to give Ten Little Niggers a new lease of life! I don't know what production difficulties there are or if it "dates" – anyway talk it over with Edmund Cork because he always arranges all these things and knows far more about all my affairs than I do.'[82] Despite the advanced state of Saunders' plans for *Rule of Three,* and presumably in his full knowledge, a licence was duly issued to Meyer; such was the eighty-five year-old impresario's status within the West End firmament that neither Cork nor Saunders were likely to have wanted to argue with the man who had produced Christie's first West End hit. On 21 August *The Times* carried a story under the headline 'Famous Thriller to be revived' announcing that *Ten Little Niggers*, having been presented in productions around the world, would open at St Martin's Theatre on 10 September. On the same day as this announcement, but without making reference to it, Saunders wrote to Gregg in Portugal to confirm arrangements for *Rule of Three.*

It was not the first time that Meyer's seemingly somewhat arbitrary agenda had conflicted with Saunders' well-laid plans; and it would be fair to say that to have the theatre opposite *The Mousetrap* opening a revival of *Ten Little Niggers* produced by a rival management, with Christie's latest West End offering due to open just over three months later, was not particularly helpful.

Although the American civil rights movement was reaching a crescendo, and Martin Luther King was to deliver his 'I have a dream' speech the following year, the idea of emblazoning the play's naïve 1943 title across the front of a theatre in post-*Empire Windrush* London, with the decolonisation of Africa in full swing, did not appear to raise any eyebrows. Or, if it did, then they were raised behind the scenes. Bertie Meyer, notably, seems to have been happy to retain the title despite knowing that complaints made about it to the Lord Chamberlain's office had come close to jeopardising the original production. In September 1962, *The Stage* reported, apparently without irony, that Langston Hughes' Gospel musical *Black Nativity* was transferring from the Criterion to the Phoenix on the same night that *Ten Little Niggers* was due to open at the St Martin's,[83] and *The Times* unashamedly headlined its review 'Back to Nigger Island'.[84] A letter subsequently appeared in the *Guardian* politely suggesting that it might be time to consider a title change for the play,[85] but it was not until a production in Birmingham in 1966 that protests outside the theatre were actually to achieve this. Since then it has been known as *And Then There Were None*, the title adopted for the American publication of the novel in 1940, although there were certainly still productions touring the UK under the original title in the 1970s, and the book itself was not renamed in the UK until the 1980s.[86]

The problem with the 1962 London presentation, however, was not so much the play's title as the universal critical condemnation with which the production itself was met, although the former may well have informed the latter by firmly positioning the piece as a product of a bygone theatrical era, and it is perhaps instructive to consider in this context Christie's own concern about whether the play 'dates'. The director of this unfortunate enterprise, which closed after twenty-six performances, was none other than Wallace Douglas. Perhaps his alignment with a rival management was by way of protest at being overlooked by Saunders for Christie's plays since *Spider's Web*, but in any event the result comprehensively put paid to his successful association with Christie's stage work.

By contrast, the critical response to the second tour of Christie's latest piece was initially encouraging. *The Stage*'s regional reviewer remarked:

Agatha Christie's trio of plays, *Rule of Three*, with some rewriting since they were tried out in the North and at Oxford last year, are now running for a week at the Grand Wolverhampton as the start of a pre-London tour. Miss Christie brings to the horror piece, The Rats, a highly ingenious plot, and to the whodunnit piece, The Patient, an electronic machine that enables an almost completely paralysed woman to answer questions. The author has to establish the basic situation so quickly that more than usual concentration is required to follow her. Miss a couple of words and one is done for: but Christie addicts are not likely to do this. In these plays it is often at her least typical that Miss Christie scores best.[87]

Of *An Afternoon at the Seaside*, he felt that its 'comedy is very much in the usual run but is served up most professionally and it is in this play that the director, Hubert Gregg, can make his stamp more obvious. The acting fulfils the requirements of the author.'

But Saunders was to have less luck with one of the leading national critics of the day. His files relating to *Rule of Three* include an entertaining exchange with Bernard Levin, who had recently moved from his job as theatre critic of the *Daily Express* to fulfil the same role at the *Daily Mail*.

In November 1962 Levin wrote to Saunders objecting to a leaflet advertising the forthcoming West End run of the production. Although the leaflet itself made it clear that all the glowing reviews quoted on it were from 'provincial' newspapers (in fact, from the previous year's tour), it included one from the *Mail*'s Northern edition calling the plays 'vintage Christie' and credited simply 'Daily Mail'.[88] Levin felt this implied that the review was his, and pointed out that the protocol whereby national critics did not attend 'out of town' performances should work both ways, and that producers should not quote reviews from national newspapers prior to a West End opening. Saunders responded that, in his opinion, he was entitled to quote a review from the Northern edition in this context, but that he would in future clarify that this was the case.

This, of course, did little to satisfy Levin, and Saunders eventually agreed to stop using the quote in question. For all Saunders' efforts to please him, Levin, who had mercilessly attacked the revival of *Ten Little Niggers* in verse, gave *Rule of Three*'s West End premiere at the Duchess a bad review as well. A few days later, Saunders wrote to fellow theatre-owner Leslie Macdonnell, managing director of Moss Empires, expressing his outrage that Levin had eaten sandwiches throughout *The Rats* and had been absent from his seat for much of the rest of the evening. Saunders told Macdonnell that there was no point in the theatre managements complaining to the *Mail* about their critic's behaviour, as 'the more fuss one makes of Levin the more likely they are to keep him on',[89] but asked if there was anything that could be done to ensure that Levin 'sees shows that he criticizes through from beginning to end, and that he doesn't behave like a peasant'. Despite all this, as Saunders makes clear in his book, he, along with most other producers at the time, actually had a sneaking admiration for Levin and the publicity he brought to theatre through his forthright critical style.

Levin was by no means the only national critic to dislike *Rule of Three*, and the now traditional critical drubbing of Agatha Christie's stage work was pretty well universal. Once again, *The Stage*'s London reviewer proved much harder to please than his regional counterpart:

> Not much need be said about *Rule of Three*. The first play is a Grand Guignol in which a couple of lovers are trapped in a Hampstead flat by a homosexual who has lured them there . . . Afternoon at the Seaside is the sort of thing one saw in West End revue years ago – fun at the expense of 'ordinary' people on holiday. But in revue we would have a sketch of five or seven minutes. . . . the Patient is the feeblest of the plays . . . the play creaks and pants through stuff that would be laughable if it were not so depressing. . . . Hubert Gregg has obviously put a lot of work into his direction. The players all work extremely hard. Alas, they are defeated.[90]

The *Guardian*'s Philip Hope-Wallace, who was no fan of Agatha Christie, commented that 'These Grand Guignol playlets may be feebly popular . . . but judged by the standards obtaining for the authoress of *Witness for the Prosecution* I fear I must call them cheap, coarse, obvious and forced.'[91] Under the headline 'LOOSE ENDS IN TRIPLE BILL – NAÏVE EVENING WITH AGATHA CHRISTIE', the *Times* critic wrote:

> As the talents of short story writer and novelist often do not go hand in hand, so the successful writer of one-act plays quite frequently fails with a full length play. And vice versa of course, as the new Agatha Christie programme demonstrates. Although the advertisements describe it as 'Agatha

Christie's latest play', it is in fact a bill of three plays, two dramatic and one comic sandwiched in between . . . In short, it is a harmless, naïve evening . . . it will probably appeal to amateurs and to the less demanding reps, but it is hardly, one would have thought, a probable addition to West End entertainments. Unfortunately, the actors do little to change one's opinion on this score . . .[92]

Kenneth Tynan, back from his sojourn in New York and now firmly established as an advocate of the theatrical 'new wave', finally seems to have run out of patience with Christie on stage. *Rule of Three*, he wrote in the *Observer*, is 'a trio of playlets devoted, like the rest of her work, to whetting one's appetite for retribution. . . . the writing is banal, the titillation unthrilling, and the implied view of life suggestive of Broadstairs in the Baldwin epoch.'[93] Next to his review, Tynan pays tribute to Charles Laughton, who had died a few days previously. Laughton, he said, was 'exorbitant, overweening and unskilled in the humility of teamwork, but a prodigious orator, a man of voluminous mind, and a master of showmanship, who bestowed on the science of scene-stealing a unique dimension of kleptomania. Even those he robbed will mourn him.'

The Broadstairs/Baldwin comment presumably refers specifically to *Afternoon at the Seaside*, and is hardly a criticism. Christie specifies that the 'time' setting of the play is simply 'a summer afternoon' and, although the 'daring bikini' worn by 'The Beauty' tells us that we are very much in the 1960s, the whole piece is a deliberately constructed stylistic exercise in nostalgia for an era that if it is not Baldwin's may be even earlier. The tragedy is that, to read Tynan and many of the other critics, one would get the impression that Christie was just an old lady of seventy-two whose portrayal of contemporary Britain was pitifully out of date. Gregg, in his book, treats us to several pages about his genius in taking his cue for the play from 'naughty seaside postcards', and his consequent directorial and textual embellishments of a scene where a lady gets changed from her swimming costume under a towel whilst attempting to preserve her modesty. In fairness, this routine (as delivered by Patricia Heneghan in the first tour and Betty McDowall in the West End) does appear to have brought the house down, but Gregg notes that whilst he himself may have seen the play as the theatrical equivalent of a naughty seaside postcard, 'I don't think Agatha had. She didn't complain at the result but she didn't thank me.'[94]

The postcards he refers to were presumably those of Donald McGill, whose hugely popular saucy cartoons, with their classic double entendres, enjoyed their heyday in the 1930s and 1940s. Extraordinarily, in 1954 at the age of seventy-nine, McGill had been tried and found guilty of publishing obscene images, and a number of his works had been banned. He died two months before *Afternoon at the Seaside* reached the West End. Whilst the play undoubtedly lends itself to this interpretation, it presents it in a context which, I suspect, was not intended and, in doing so, arguably coarsens it. Philip Hope-Wallace had found the playlet 'vulgar and patronising'. As directed by Gregg it may well have been, but Christie seems have found her own inspiration for the piece in a much older comic tradition than 1940s McGill. Her abandoned 'alternative ending', with its 'Harlequinade atmosphere', includes this delightful moment:

SOMERS: I don't look like a burglar, do I?
    (suddenly flings off coat and begins springing about, turning handsprings)
GEORGE: (alarmed) Stop it – stop it, you Clown! Have you gone mad?
SOMERS: I feel a bit mad. It's the moonlight. Relax, you old Pantaloon.
GEORGE: What do you think this is? A Pantomime? The silent young lovers. Me, Pantaloon. You playing the Clown. All we need now is a comic policeman.[95]

Needless to say, they get one.

The *Telegraph*'s critic appears to have been pretty much

alone in finding something to enjoy in *Rule of Three*, and the advertisements for the production subsequently quoted a line from his review, 'Three thrilling denouements for the price of one.' 'What a spiteful lot critics are,' concluded Christie in a letter to Cork,[96] pointing out that, contrary to the assertion in one review that she was 'quite out of touch with today's beach life' she was, in fact, 'an AUTHORITY', as a result of regular trips to Devon beaches with young relatives.

To make matters worse, in January 1963, in a round-up of the previous theatrical year, the *Financial Times* upset Saunders by claiming that *Rule of Three* had 'only just struggled into the New Year'.[97] Never one to countenance misreporting, Saunders took up the matter of this 'most damaging' article with the paper's editor, claiming that *Rule of Three* was in the best of health and stating that he hoped the journalist concerned would have the 'grace to blush' when the production celebrated its first anniversary.[98]

The *Financial Times* article in question actually offers a fascinating snapshot of London theatre at that time. Business in 1962, we are told, had suffered because 'Over the Cuba crisis, theatre-goers stayed at home listening to the news, while the economic gloom has been accurately reflected in the barometer of theatre attendances.' Nonetheless *My Fair Lady* and *Beyond the Fringe* had both returned a substantial profit. The Royal Shakespeare Company, which had been founded in 1961, was presenting *King Lear* at the Aldwych, and there were high hopes for the National Theatre, which was due to present its inaugural season at the Old Vic later in 1963. A list of theatrical hits that had opened in 1962 and were still running in January 1963 included *Signpost to Murder*, *Boeing-Boeing*, *Come Blow Your Horn*, *Blitz!*, *The Private Ear and the Public Eye* and Arnold Wesker's *Chips with Everything*, 'the only play to come out of the Kitchen Sink revolution' to have been a success that year. The corresponding list of the previous year's flops of course now included *Ten Little Niggers*, which was thereby humiliatingly demoted from its previous status as a West End hit.

Much of Saunders' own optimism hinged on the fact that he had clinched a deal with the BBC for a live television broadcast of *Afternoon at the Seaside* (or 'A day by the Seaside' as it was referred to on the licence) which was due to take place on 7 February. The BBC paid Christie £75 for the broadcast rights, of which Saunders was entitled to keep a third.[99] Saunders and Cork had high hopes that this exposure would revive the production's fortunes but, according to Saunders, although 'it seemed to televise beautifully' it 'had absolutely no effect on the box office whatsoever'.[100] Writing to Anthony Hicks on 12 February, Cork said that the broadcast 'made me laugh . . . but, alas, the box office has not responded.'[101]

Rule of Three closed on 9 March after a run of ninety-two performances over eleven and a half weeks, so the *Financial Times*' reporter, as it turned out, had no need to blush. I have not seen budgets or accounts, but the financial outcome cannot have been good. 'I felt dreadfully responsible over this one . . . I don't think I have ever fought so hard for a play,' says Saunders. And the production's failure, of course, meant that he was also facing the expensive prospect, as a theatre owner, of seeing the Duchess go 'dark'. *Rule of Three* eventually staggered on until a replacement could be found: a 'new revue' called *See You Inside*. It may have been some consolation to Saunders that, two weeks later, *Goodnight Mrs Puffin* closed at the Duke of York's.

The Times' summation that *Rule of Three* was likely to find a home with amateur and repertory companies proved remarkably prescient. Saunders had no hesitation in paying an advance of £200 to take up his 50 per cent share of Christie's income from amateur rights for the seven-year duration of his licence, and the three plays were rushed into print by Samuel French, published separately under their own titles. In May 1963 Hughes Massie took an advertisement in *The Stage* announcing that they were 'available for repertory', the author's royalty being 4 per cent for each play or 10 per cent if the three were presented together.[102] As it turned out, they did indeed end up as three plays for the price of one, although not in the way that the publicity had originally intended. As a business strategy for these particular works, it wasn't a bad one – but it was a sad West End finale for the playwright who, less than ten years before, had been the toast of London and Broadway.

It should not be forgotten, though, that none of the three plays was presented as Christie herself had originally envisaged. By the time the production reached the West End, the Grand Guignol 'before your very eyes' stabbing and the implied suicide, which she had seen as the centrepiece and the denouement of *The Rats*, had been cut completely; and her unique ending for *The Patient* had been replaced with something far more conventional, eventually scribbled by her on some small sheets of hotel notepaper at the start of the second tour in Wolverhampton. And *Afternoon at the Seaside*, which seems likely to have taken its cue from the revues of the 1920s, had been reinterpreted as a naughty postcard, complete with a line added by Gregg for a lady complaining that there was sand in her bra. As was so often the case, Christie's own theatrical imagination displayed a far more intriguing frame of reference than that of those responsible for delivering her work. Christie had written 'The Rule of Three Doth Puzzle Me . . . Old Rhyme' on the front page of her script, and the line also appeared on the title page of the play's programme. It certainly puzzled her producer, her director and the critics. I shall leave the last word on *Rule of Three* with Agatha herself; in a 1971 letter to Rosalind she says simply, 'I wrote the three short plays entirely to please Peter Saunders but I didn't enjoy them – and they were not really successful.'[103]

Rule of Three was the last occasion on which Peter Saunders premiered a play by Agatha Christie. There can be no doubt that she owed her theatrical success in the early 1950s very largely to Saunders' diligence, honesty and perspicacity; he was a tireless and resourceful ambassador for her plays, a charming, witty and skilful business ally and a loyal and valued friend. But, as an independent theatre producer launching his career in the early 1950s, he faced unprecedented challenges from within the industry, which he overcame to a large extent by characterising Christie's work in a manner that suited his own agenda. For a good deal of the time the playwright and her producer were creative fellow travellers, and when they were they created some of the West End's most legendary successes. But, on the occasions when they were not, the results could be disastrous. Against considerable odds, Saunders successfully maintained his position in a hugely competitive marketplace by defining himself as a purveyor of 'beer' rather than 'wine'. Agatha, however, continued to regard playwriting as an activity that allowed for creative experimentation and, right up to the end, she would continue to be full of surprises.

In 1964, when asked by the *Evening Standard* for his views on 'dirty' plays in the context of Joe Orton's *Entertaining Mr Sloane*, Saunders said, 'Filth and obscenity have become an unhappy trend in recent years, and if there is to be a place in theatre for this kind of thing, let the Lord Chamberlain issue F for Filth certificates. The public would at least be warned about what they are likely to see.'[104] Christie's other principal producer held similar views; in an article in *The Stage* two years later, celebrating Bertie Meyer's sixty years in show business, we hear that 'Mr Meyer prefers plays with a good story, well told, and free from kitchen sink associations' and that he was in favour of the censorship role of the Lord Chamberlain, with whom he had 'had the happiest of relationships for the past sixty years. His presence lends dignity to the theatre in Mr Meyer's estimation.'[105] Christie herself believed that theatre should be accessible to people of all ages, and had been delighted to discover that the British Ambassador to Iraq had taken his 'entire family, ranging in years from 79 to 11', to see *Spider's Web*.[106] In old age, her cherished ambition became to write another comedy for family audiences in the same vein as *Spider's Web*, partly as a deliberate counterpoint to what she saw as current trends.

Comedy had always been one of Christie's strong suits. *Ten Little Indians* had been advertised on Broadway as a 'comedy thriller' (which would doubtless have horrified Christie had she known at the time) and there had been much debate during the pre-West End tour of *The Mousetrap* about whether the play's comedy element was at risk of eclipsing its thrills. Her early one-act plays are mostly comedies, and the observational humour and witty dialogue that pervades all of her work are skilfully crafted; Saunders himself suggested that *An Afternoon at the Seaside* could have been expanded into a full-length play.[107]

Key to the success of *Spider's Web* had been the casting of Margaret Lockwood, who went on to work for Saunders on several more projects. 'She was a wonderful person to have in a company,' he writes. 'She was always punctual, never complained if she was kept hanging around, and rather disconcerted the cast because, having a photographic memory, she used to come to the first rehearsal knowing her lines.'[108] *Spider's Web* had been one of Christie's happiest theatrical experiences, and she envisaged that the new comedy on which she now spent much of her time would be another vehicle for Lockwood, along with her daughter Julia. In 1972 Julia was to become the third wife of Ernest Clark, who had played John Cristow in *The Hollow* and Mr Myers QC in *Witness for the Prosecution* on Broadway.

Amongst the many treatments for the new 'M and J play' is the following from Notebook 4a, with 'M' indicating Margaret Lockwood and 'J' indicating Julia. These brief, intriguing aides-memoires for a work in progress are typical of the gloriously jumbled and frequently indecipherable jottings that fill the 73 volumes of Christie's notebooks:

Spy Trial background Play
- M. good-natured landlady – ex actress
Spivy boy Ronnie – soft spot for him
J. comes through window – girl 'wanted' in bank robbery (at Worthing)
M. packs her off as Miss Jones – Rumanian student who is due to arrive –
Other lodgers – one borrows M.'s shopping bag –
'She's always doing it' – Another – man – has

done his own decorating etc.
Spy ring head waiter with M. as fall guy –
Ron is 'taken' with Miss I. (J)
End of 1st Act Revealing sentences between J. + R
'She fell for it like a lamb' Inference is J + R
are the bank robbery 'Wanteds' –
Act II
Appearing + disappearing papers – a
Murder? – +so on
M. taken off by police for questioning – her shopping
Bag. End of Act – Is it she who is crook?
Act III ends with unmasking of Murderer
Mrs. K(?) or Mr. Lewis (nice New Zealander?)
Or Finkelstein who has set up M. – in business –
really for his own ends –
Denouement – J + R are MI5 Security agents[109]

An outline for another of these 'Lockwood' plays, *Miss Perry*, appears in Notebook 53, and there are also a number of 'work in progress' scripts for it in the Christie archive; most interestingly one that appears to be a first draft typed by Christie herself, with numerous handwritten corrections, annotations and amendments. The dramatis personae in this draft has 'ML' written next to the role of Poppy and 'JL' next to that of Miss Perry. There is also a 'clean' typed version, incorporating the amendments. This copy has timings scribbled next to the scenes (23, 21 and 45 minutes) and has the letter 'M' next to male characters. The timings, and the clarification about casting, indicate that at some point a reading of the play probably took place. There are three plastic-bound copies of a retyped version, which looks as if it may have been created for such a reading, with a typist's telephone number which indicates that it dates from after 1966. In 2011, Dutch collector Ralf Stultiëns purchased a copy of *Miss Perry*, evidently from a stock of Christie's manuscripts that appear to have been 'recycled' by a former Hughes Massie employee. From what I have seen of pictures of this, it may be the first draft of the professionally typed version, containing Christie's corrections of the typist's work. In a television interview, Stultiëns either misstates (or is mistranslated as stating) that the play is 'about an elf who takes part in a bank robbery'.[110] This is not actually the case.

A twelve-hander, two-act play, *Miss Perry* is a full-length (but relatively short) piece which reads rather in the style of an episode of a television sitcom. It is set in the fictional village of Saddlebridge, where the residents are organising a pageant under the watchful eye of Poppy, 'a handsome woman with a vast fund of vitality'. They are using the front room of the Queen of Diamonds pub as their headquarters. A young woman, who introduces herself as Miss Perry, turns up and convinces the local residents that she is a fairy by performing a series of magic tricks, including turning someone into a tortoise and rustling up a live elephant: interesting challenges for a theatre designer. The play's title is taken from the word 'peri', a fairy-like creature of mythology referred to in the sub-title of Gilbert and Sullivan's 1882 *Iolanthe* ('The Peer and the Peri'), and of course nothing turns out to be quite as it seems. We eventually discover that 'Miss Perry' is actually an actress called Tania, and her 'magic tricks' are part of a plot to expose the criminal activities of a local bigwig and to put right a historic miscarriage of justice whereby the wrong man was imprisoned for a bank heist.

In the play, Christie enjoys a couple of sideswipes at recent trends in theatre. Here Martin Wylie, the young writer who has been brought in to prepare a script for the pageant, is upbraided by his father:

MR WYLIE: Nothing degrading about money, my boy. It's useful. I can use it. Your mother can use it – and I've no doubt in spite of your sentiments that you can use it. You can put on some of those new-fangled plays about a tramp and a drunk and a tart all meeting in a public lavatory . . .[111]

Martin later recruits Tania to appear in his next play, which is evidently no country house whodunit:

TANIA: He says I'm a very good actress. He's writing a play
and he thinks I'd be good enough to play the leading part
in it. It's a wonderful part – wonderful.

POPPY: Not a fairy queen, I presume!

TANIA: No indeed! It's a girl in a remand home. She's had
two abortions and has tried to be a prostitute. She falls
in love with this man, but it's no good. She goes back to
fulfilling her real nature. Back to the brothel.

POPPY: Well really – (laughs) – you children nowadays!

Another sign of the times is the distinctly Cold War, comically
'reds-under-the bed' police superintendent, here in conversation with the PC who is assisting him:

SUPERINTENDENT: Tania's a Russian name, and for all we
know she may be a prominent member of the Communist
party.

BARNSTABLE: I wouldn't think that's likely, sir. She seems
a very nice young lady.

SUPERINTENDENT: They catch 'em young, boy. So as to
indoctrinate them proper. And naturally she'd seem a nice
young lady. Because she's supposed to make converts, see?

And, when Miss Perry magics up a suitcase full of clothes, we
hear Christie's view on the latest fashion trends; 'everything a
young lady of today wants,' declares Miss Perry, naming the
items as she unpacks them 'as though it was a foreign language':

MISS PERRY: A skirt. A Blouse . . . a play suit? An evening
dress. A little black number. That's a funny name!
Stockings. Shoes. Panties. And – (frowns) – oh yes, a
brassiere . . . a . . .

MARTIN: (embarrassed) Stop.

WILLIAM: Gorblimey!

MISS PERRY: And something – very odd. (holds up jeans)

WILLIAM: Jeans.

MISS PERRY: Jeans? They are not pretty at all.

Once 'Miss Perry' becomes Tania we see her quite happily 'wearing jeans and a sloppy sweater'. Whatever Christie's personal wardrobe preferences, her female characters were, as ever, moving with the times.

On 22 March 1962, Christie lunched with Margaret Lockwood, an arrangement she apparently made without telling Peter Saunders. The previous day Cork had written to her, 'We had arranged to have a serious talk with Peter Saunders today, but he has apparently heard from Margaret Lockwood of tomorrow's lunch, and he has suggested that we put off our talk to see if anything transpires tomorrow that might alter the situation.'[112] Three weeks later, in a letter that starts with an update on Cork's efforts to track down a particular brand of American maple sugar that Agatha had requested, we find the following intriguing reference to *Miss Perry*: 'There have been no developments regarding the musical of Miss Perry, but there is nothing sinister in this as it is due to Mr Sekers being in Italy. He wrote me a civil note saying he would be in touch the moment he got back. I daresay you will hear from Peter that he is very excited about this project. I told him about it in general terms, as we and Sekers agreed that it would be treating him rather badly, if after the long and close association we did not give him a chance of coming in on it.'[113]

The 'Mr Sekers' referred to would have been 'Miki' (later Sir) Nicholas Sekers, a Jewish-Hungarian immigrant silk tycoon and one of the leading arts philanthropists of the day. A board member of Glyndebourne and the Royal Opera House, in 1959 he had opened the Rosehill Theatre on his Cumbrian estate, a few miles from Britain's first nuclear power station at Windscale. Peggy Ashcroft performed the opening ceremony, Emlyn Williams and John Gielgud were booked to give entertainments in the opening season, and *The Stage* had heralded the new theatre as 'The Glyndebourne of the North' and 'one of the most luxurious theatres of its size and type in Europe'.[114]

We hear nothing more either of the meeting with Lockwood or of Miki Sekers' interest in a musical of *Miss Perry*, but the proximity of these two letters from Cork offer the intriguing prospect of Agatha Christie involving herself in the development of a musical for Margaret Lockwood; although it has to be said that a whimsical comedy about a village pageant would hardly seem to be the stuff of musical theatre.

It is clear, though, that by the beginning of 1962, with the West End opening of *Rule of Three* delayed, Christie was taking steps to develop her own theatrical agenda, independently of Saunders. The following year there was to be some discussion about a third-party musical adaptation of Christie's 1955 Poirot novel, *Hickory Dickory Dock*. The rights for the book had been assigned to a trust set up to pay for the schooling of Max's nephews, Peter and John Mallowan, and Cork expressed some hope that the project might swell the trust's coffers.[115] But, again (and, perhaps, thankfully), nothing came of it.

Sekers may not have pursued his Agatha Christie project, but his firm was to provide the silk that formed part of the décor when Peter Saunders refurbished the Vaudeville Theatre, which he bought in 1969. Two years later, Saunders' latest acquisition would become the home of Ray Cooney and John Chapman's successful comedy, *Move Over Mrs Markham*, which Saunders co-produced with Cooney. Master farceur Cooney, who had performed with Brian Rix at the Whitehall, played Detective Sergeant Trotter in *The Mousetrap* in 1964, joining the company just as the production celebrated its 5,000th performance. Christie's own aspirations to pen a new stage comedy remained undiminished, and she saw and admired *Move Over Mrs Markham* on its pre-West End tour, although Max evidently did not share her enthusiasm for farce.

Oddly for someone who achieved Christie's huge commercial success, much of her life was dogged by financial uncertainty. Her father's premature death and her separation and divorce from Archie had made matters difficult in the early years and, like many successful writers of the day, she was involved in frequent disputes with the tax authorities in both the UK and the USA. Much of the correspondence between Edmund Cork, Harold Ober and Ober's lawyer Howard Reinheimer deals with these issues in considerable detail, and many of the problems they encountered regarding the taxation of income generated through the exploitation of intellectual property were unique to the period in which Christie was writing. This was particularly bad luck for Christie, but it also meant that, in terms of finding solutions to the numerous issues created by the punitive taxation policies of the era, her advisors frequently found themselves to a certain extent improvising. In retrospect, some of their advice and decisions may appear to have been slightly ill-judged: Cork, in particular, was clearly no expert in these matters, although he tried his very best to be so.

In later years, Christie was particularly fortunate to benefit from the direct involvement of her legally trained son-in-law, Anthony Hicks, in the conduct of her business affairs. Rosalind and he moved into a cottage on the Greenway estate in 1968, and the tactful and perceptive guidance that he provided to Cork and others on numerous occasions was invaluable. Despite the constant assistance of her professional advisors and her family, Agatha's seemingly endless battles with the tax authorities were distressing and time-consuming for her, and although she generally dealt with them with good humour they were the cause of considerable anxiety throughout her life.

The problems had started in the late 1930s, when, following a test case in the USA, the authorities there started to tax Christie's American earnings although she was non-resident and was already paying tax on them in the UK. A claim for back payments was made, and her American earnings (her most important source of income at the time) were frozen in the USA pending the outcome of lengthy legal wranglings.[116] Matters were eventually resolved following the 1945 double taxation treaty between Britain and the USA, which at least clarified matters for the future; a substantial settlement, however, still had to be negotiated regarding back payments, and arguments about this dragged on until 1954, further complicating the already labyrinthine business dealings with the Shuberts. Meanwhile, the post-war taxation regime in the UK had become notoriously punitive, with particularly high earners also facing substantial 'surtax' liabilities, as the public purse took on responsibility for funding the new Welfare State alongside a robust defence budget.[116]

The easiest way to avoid this was to become a tax exile but, unlike Noël Coward and Terence Rattigan, that was an option which Christie always refused to take. Instead, arrangements were made for her to become the salaried employee of a company (a solution also adopted by Enid Blyton). Agatha Christie Ltd was set up in 1955, and would own the copyrights on all work of hers produced thereafter; licences for plays written after this date were thus with the company rather than with Christie herself. The issue then became one of share ownerships and corporation tax on the profits from the exploitation of Christie's work, rather than of tax on her personal income.

At his death, Bernard Shaw's estate had been valued by the Inland Revenue based on the income generated by his most successful work multiplied by the number of his works, although in doing so they failed of course to include income from *My Fair Lady*, which was to premiere six years after his death. On a similar basis Cork estimated that Christie's death duties bill, based on *Witness for the Prosecution*, could have amounted to £20 million.[118] When the Christie Copyrights Trust was established in 1957, taking ownership of the rights in most of her work that pre-dated the founding of Agatha Christie Ltd, the issue of punitive death duties was avoided. A number of smaller trusts were also created to administer specific copyrights on behalf of certain individuals and organisations, and Christie was given the pleasure of seeing charities, friends and family members, including Max's two nephews, benefit from her work.[119]

Christie herself continued to receive problematic tax demands relating to the small number of copyrights that she personally retained, and was distressed to find that she was still being heavily taxed on her salary from Agatha Christie Ltd. But, throughout, she was always at pains to ensure that the numerous and complicated tax avoidance schemes diligently concocted by her advisors were both legal and ethical, and expressed her 'complete trust' in her team.[120] There were later to be issues for some of Agatha's beneficiaries regarding the reversion of assigned copyrights but, under the circumstances, the work put in by Cork, Ober, Reinheimer and Hicks made the best of a wearisome and very complicated scenario. 'How are all my tax affairs, companies and trusts?' Agatha wrote to Cork, 'Don't let them get you down! And don't tell me about them unless it's absolutely necessary!'[121] and in another letter, she noted that 'in tax, the dice are always loaded against one.'[122] Cork in turn lamented that the more successful an agent was in their client's lifetime, the worse were the problems created by their client's death. At Christie's death, the estate of the best-selling novelist, and best-selling female playwright, of all time was valued at £106,000.[123] Cork and his colleagues had certainly done their job.

To a certain extent, we perhaps owe the sudden blossoming of Agatha Christie, playwright, in the 1950s to the tax regime. At she notes in her autobiography, 'Seeing the point to which taxation has now risen, I was pleased to think it was no longer really worth-while for me to work so hard: one book a year would be ample. If I wrote two books a year, I should hardly earn more than by writing one, and only give myself a great deal of extra work. Certainly, there was no longer the old incentive. If there was something out of the ordinary that I really *wanted* to do, that would be different.'[124] What she really wanted to do, of course, was write plays, and given that she had nothing to lose by switching her focus as a writer to the stage, that is exactly what she did. 'Why not write a play instead of a book? Much more fun. One book a year would take care of finances, so I could now enjoy myself in an entirely different medium.'

Not surprisingly, Christie saw dramatic potential in her tax problems, and she was particularly tickled by the idea that, in order to avoid death duties on the assets she had gifted to various trusts, it was necessary for her to live for another five years. 'The doll will do her best to live another five years,' she wrote to Cork,[125] and in her autobiography she observed, 'As far as I could make out from what lawyers and tax people told me about death duties – very little of which I ever understood – my demise was going to be an unparalleled disaster for all my relations, and their only hope was to keep me alive as long as possible!'[126] Christie now set about combining the idea of a play about death duties with her other pet project of a comedy for Margaret and Julia Lockwood.

In Notebook 15, under the heading 'Oct 1958', Christie wrote:

Projects

A play – light-hearted (a Spider's Web type) Where? – girl's school?

Or Cheating Death Duties? Pretending a death? Or smuggling away a natural death – devoted fluffy secretary?

Then, in Notebook 39 under the heading 'M and J play', there are two outline plots for a 'death duties' play, one of which developed into a full-length script called *This Mortal Coil*, the second Christie play to take its title from a line in *Hamlet*. We hear nothing more of the 'girls' school' idea, but it is clear from the notebooks that *Miss Perry*, the 'Spy' play and *This Mortal Coil* were being developed in parallel as alternative comedy vehicles for the Lockwoods. Alongside these, Christie was also making notes for an altogether different play, unaccountably given the working title 'Mousetrap II', which centres on a party in Soho and a poisoning scenario that sounds not dissimilar to that in her 1937 short story and radio play *The Yellow Iris*.

'Mousetrap II' never got as far as a draft script, but the Agatha Christie archive contains a number of drafts for the 'death duties' play *This Mortal Coil*, along with extensive typed and handwritten notes. Christie's notoriously illegible writing became clearer as she grew older, and her struggle to get this play written and staged, despite resistance from her family, her agent and her regular producer, took up much time and fills several files. The earliest copy, with each act bound separately, appears to have been typed by Christie herself at around the same time that she typed the first draft of *Miss Perry*, and includes numerous handwritten corrections and amendments. The dramatis personae of eleven includes Sally (next to which name Christie has written 'ML') and Gina (next to which she has written 'JL'). Three alternative titles are suggested on the front page: *Fiddle De Dee*, *Sixpence Off* and *Fiddlers All*. The issues surrounding death duties are explained by the lawyer Truscott:

> TRUSCOTT: Your father is a very rich man. Death duties on his estate will, of course, be high, but his various trusts and dispositions will do much to mitigate that. He was wise enough to make them some time ago. He has taken fullest advantage of everything the law allows . . . Your deed of gift was the last of the various arrangements, and I believe I am correct in saying that the necessary five year period of survival expires tomorrow. It was quite an obsession with him. He regarded it as a kind of game. I shouldn't be surprised if he's saying to the doctor now: 'Only one day to go.' It would be like him.[127]

Although the details of the storyline were to undergo many revisions, the central premise of a man whose inheritance depends on his father living to a certain date remained the central plot point; the titular 'fiddlers', whose business schemes depend on the inheritance coming through, find their plans compromised when the father (inevitably) dies before the date in question. A sometimes farcical comedy about business and finance, with a strong undercurrent of criminal activity, it rejoices in characters with names like Bogusian (conveniently shortened to 'Bogus' in one of the typescripts) and Panhacker (three letters away from 'Panhandler'). It's not a bad idea for a comedy, and corporate tax avoidance scandals are never far from the headlines, but Christie was in her late sixties when she started working on the idea and in her eighties when it was finally performed, so if the comic dialogue lacks her usual sparkle it is perhaps not surprising.

This Mortal Coil may well have been on the agenda at Agatha's 1962 lunch with Lockwood, but seems, like *Miss Perry*, to have disappeared from the radar shortly thereafter. It was a letter from Hubert Gregg eight years later, congratulating Christie on her eightieth birthday, that was to get the ball rolling again. On 8 September 1970, a week before her birthday and in the midst of the media circus surrounding it, she replied to him from Greenway:

Dear Hubert,

How very nice to hear from you. Thanks for the birthday greetings – I am snowed under with demands from Journalists of periodicals with incredible names that I have never heard of – and from countries that I did not know existed!

How delightful therefore to hear from a real friend! [In the light of his book, I'm not sure he was, but we'll let it pass.]

I'm interested in what you say about plays – I got a letter only yesterday from a woman who had gone to see The Mousetrap (after waiting to for 9 years) and 'Oh the joy of seeing a play that was exciting and where nobody took their clothes off! I am recommending it to all my friends!'

I have got two plays laid aside which I quite like myself – one I started for Margaret Lockwood and her daughter to play in – and then they had a row, I think, and parted company – and so I laid it aside for the time being – there was a general feeling voiced by Peter that it would damage The Mousetrap if another play of mine saw the light of day.

I think now that that is not so. Every year I expect the Mousetrap to come off – and every year it stands up like a permanent monument – it's uncanny!

When I get back to Wallingford, if you'd like me to, I'll hunt up these two plays – they are both comedies – and more on the lines of Spider's Web – and I think there are some good acting parts in both of them.

'This Mortal Coil' has a first act in a business office and a second act in a Seaside Luxury Hotel – The other play takes place in a Pub. It's too short and wants another scene which I was going to write – but never did. I'll also think over my more recent books with a view to one that might be adaptable.

Perhaps we can meet in London or Wallingford when I get back and talk things over. [Agatha now divided her time between Greenway, her house in Wallingford and her London flat.]

We leave here about 20th September. It would be great fun to see you of course and have a nice theatrical talk –

Yours ever

Agatha Mallowan[128]

In 1968 the London opening of the hippy musical *Hair*, with its famous nude sequence at the end of Act One, had been delayed until the Theatres Act of that year – which finally abolished censorship – came into effect. Two years later, Kenneth Tynan's revue *Oh! Calcutta!*, another import from New York, also gained notoriety for featuring nudity. And now, at the end of 1970 and the beginning of 1971, Agatha busied herself with rewriting *This Mortal Coil*, renaming it *Fiddlers Five* in the process, and relishing the idea of creating a comedy in which no one took their clothes off in the newly censor-free West End. Work in progress for the revised version, again using as its basis a draft that appears to have been typed by Christie herself, has a label saying 'Fiddlers Five' stuck over the original title, and includes extensive interleaved amendments. A later version is professionally typed.

In April, once it was finished, she wrote to Gregg again. There had been a postal strike and problems with the telephone. 'Everything has been chaotic and I have also been trying to get a new book more or less finished,' she said. But the play-script was ready. 'I always liked it and have now rewritten it – if you'd care to have a look at it – Hughes Massie have a copy of the newest version. I didn't know whether it was tied up to Peter Saunders but I gather not – *I* think it is rather good!! But never go by what the author thinks – rather on the lines of Spider's Web – anyway, quite good fun – no nudity – which I think people are heartily sick of!'[129]

Saunders, as it happens, thought no more of *Fiddlers Five* than he had of *This Mortal Coil* and turned it down; as indeed did Gregg. Saunders later said, 'I would, of course, have put it on out of gratitude to her, but felt it would not do her reputation any good. When it was tried out later on I think everyone agreed that it was not vintage Christie.'[130] But the resourceful Cork, aware that, as ever, there would be no shortage of touring managements more than happy to take on a new Christie play, did a deal with veteran actor-manager James Grant Anderson, and on 6 May 1971 he was issued with a twelve-month touring licence for *Fiddlers Five*.[131] Whilst Grant Anderson himself was not a West End player, it seems that there was some hope that his production would garner interest in the project from those who were, and the deal included a clause whereby he would receive a one per cent royalty if a West End licence was issued within this period.

Although she was absent from some of Peter Saunders' own later productions of her work, Agatha made a point of being in attendance for the touring premiere of her new play at the King's Theatre Southsea on 7 June 1971, at which seventy-four-year-old Grant Anderson made a gracious and stirring curtain speech applauding her lifetime's contribution to theatre. The advertisements for the production read, 'J Grant Anderson has the great privilege to present the world premiere of Agatha Christie's FIDDLERS FIVE: AN OUTSTANDING EVENT IN THE THEATRE – DAME AGATHA'S FIRST NEW PLAY FOR YEARS.'[132]

The next day, the *Portsmouth Evening News* reported: 'The name of Dame Agatha Christie is one automatically associated with thrillers and mystery; comedy isn't reckoned to be her *forte*. But last night, with the world premiere of her *Fiddlers Five* at the King's Theatre Southsea, the Queen of suspense proved that she had a light hand with comedy.'[133] Two days later, the *Hampshire Telegraph*'s review noted that 'Miss

Christie introduces no detectives, no policemen, no interroga-
tions. Everything is in the lightest vein, verging at times on
farce.'[133] *The Stage*, under the headline 'A Different Agatha
Christie', announced that 'Agatha Christie's latest play . . . has
deserted the familiar path of the "whodunit" type of thriller
with those well-known guides Hercules Poirot [*sic*] and Miss
Marples [*sic*], in order to go a little off-beat into the realms of
black comedy . . . all the time the action is played for laughs
rather than chills, but once the story-line has been established
there is plenty of humour and sparkle to carry it along to the
usual surprise climax.'[135] Barry Howard, later to enjoy success
as a television comedy actor, scored a particular hit in the
dual role of an undertaker and a 'long-bearded Pakistani
doctor', both 'shrewdly conceived comic creations'. The mind
boggles.

Like the Beatles' George Harrison in his 1966 song 'Taxman',
Christie made the most of the opportunity to express her frustration with the tax regime through her work. Over forty years
earlier, her sister Madge had observed in *Oranges and Lemons*,
'Now we're taxing wealth. What harm does wealth do a
country? If there *is* a man capable of making money, for
Heaven's sake encourage him to make more!' *Fiddlers Five*
offers Agatha's own scathing verdict on the Inland Revenue,
and it pulls no punches:

BOGUSIAN: Fortunately on a bus, one does not have to pay.
    There is a special technique. I adopt it always.
FLETCHER: That's the way of business, Sally.
SALLY: Not all business. There are some kinds of business
    that aren't like that.
BOGUSIAN: And then what happens? The tax collector takes
    all. Why should I do business to please the Inland Revenue?
SALLY: Don't talk to me about Income Tax and the Inland
    Revenue! Barefaced robbers they are! Look what they did
    to Lil West. Just went out to work, casual like, to get a bit
    of extra pay for her washing machine. Took the best of it
    away from her. And why, I'd like to know? She worked

for it, didn't she? Why should they count it in with her husband? And poor old Ma Grant, they docked her Old Age Pension – said she did too much sewing at home. And then there was the poor old Smiths – on National Assistance and they cut that because –

FLETCHER: Ease up, Sally, ease up. We know all about that.

SALLY: Well, it makes me mad, it does! I'll give them Inland Revenue!

BOGUSIAN: You see, in business you do the business in a way that the tax collector, he cannot touch it. And when the business comes off nicely and you have the big money, why then you look round for some more business that will be like that again . . .

. . .

FLETCHER: Look here, Sally, if you don't want to be a criminal, say so.

SALLY: I'm all for crime. But it's got to be the right sort of crime.

FLETCHER: Aren't you particular? Quite the little lady. And what's the right kind of crime?

SALLY: Well, smuggling – something like that. Or doing down the income tax. I'd swindle them any day. Monstrous what they did to Lil and poor old Mrs Grant. Let's do down the income tax! I wouldn't have conscience at all about that!

BOGUSIAN: Ah, but it is highly specialised that. I tell you, I know.

FLETCHER: I bet you do, you old crook!

BOGUSIAN: Last year, they dare to question my return. I go there. I see this Mr Blood Sucker. I say to him, 'Listen,' I say, 'In this return I make, I cheat you very little – hardly at all. If I wish I could have cheated you much more. But no, I like to be honest.' 'So,' I say to him, 'You better to accept this. Otherwise I take it back and I fill you up another return, and in that I cheat you a great deal – but you will not be able to find out how. Because if I wish to cheat, I can cheat very good. So, you see, you better to accept this.'

SALLY: And what did he do?

BOGUSIAN: He accepted it. He knows me.[136]

Rosalind was horrified. The previous year her mother had been feted as a national treasure on her eightieth birthday, and in the 1971 New Year's Honours she had been made a Dame Commander of the British Empire, Max having been knighted three years previously. Much of Christie's literary career had been centred around the theme of criminals receiving their comeuppance, and yet suddenly she appeared to be endorsing criminal activity, apparently from a position of knowledge. Rosalind was even more horrified to hear that there had been a serious offer to present the play in the West End, particularly as the production itself appears to have been somewhat low rent. On 20 July Cork wrote to Grant Anderson in no uncertain terms, expressing his dismay at numerous aspects of the performances and staging,[137] and on the same day, Rosalind wrote to her mother:

As you know, there has been quite a good offer to put Fiddlers Five on in London in the winter. I think Cork is tempted partly as usual by the prospect of it earning some more money and partly because he thinks *you* would like to see it put on in London. I think he is doubtful about it though, as he doesn't like it himself. Whatever he may say about it, Mathew is not sure about it and didn't think it was very well done or well received in Bristol. I am sending you the press cuttings from Nottingham and Manchester not because I want to be unkind but because I know Mr Cork doesn't send you anything he thinks might upset you. Actually, I don't expect you would be nearly as upset about them as I am! I as you know haven't seen it but I didn't like it when I read it, and as I am always honest with you I may say I should be *most* upset to see it on in London. A lot of people would obviously go to see it because it was by you, whatever the reviews were like. Peter Saunders genuinely thought it wouldn't do in London. I expect you and Max will think it is very feeble of me but your fans do admire your work and indeed you yourself to a quite frightening degree. I don't think this play is worthy of *you*, and you are in this play letting people get away with crime and cheating the income tax and even in fun I don't think it is funny.[138]

This, of course, was a red rag to a bull, and elicited by way of response one of the most extraordinary letters Agatha ever wrote. In a handwritten missive ten pages long, she is clearly apoplectic about her daughter's interference, and takes the opportunity to itemise the many swings and roundabouts of her theatrical career in great detail. Much of this letter is quoted elsewhere in this book, in the context of the plays to which she refers, but here is a filleted version:

Dear Rosalind,

I'm sorry you are so upset about the awful prospect of Fiddlers Five possibly being done in London.

I've not urged it specially – I can't see why you are so opposed to it being a commercial success on tour . . . if anyone is prepared to put up big money to put it on with a good cast in London – it will be presumably because it has been commercially a success. It is, as always, a pure gamble on their part.

If they are really influenced by bad notices they presumably won't put it on!! I shan't mind – I have had the great pleasure of seeing it acted myself – I am delighted it has gone onto tour – Like Verdict it will probably go on tour again at intervals in the years to come!

Spider's Web, a pure farce if there ever was one – ran for 2 years at the Savoy and took £1800 at Richmond a week or so ago. I knew I'd get bad reviews [for *Fiddlers Five*] and I've had several rather surprising good ones – and 5 curtain calls at many theatres.

The Mousetrap – on tour originally – had only *one* criticism that could be used in adverts – all the others were somewhat unfavourable.

Verdict was not a success in London – but I am *very* glad

it came on – I've had to put up with several plays and films that I *hate* to have been associated with my name. I hated Murder At the Vicarage and a Miss Marple of twenty odd – and several other of the 'adapted' plays from my books. It was because I hated them so much that I determined to adapt the Hollow myself . . . you did your utmost to persuade me not to! . . . If you'd succeeded in making me stick to books – there would probably have been no Mousetrap – no Witness for the Prosecution – no Spider's Web.

I could have stopped any more adaptation of my books – but I should not have been a playwright and should have missed a lot of fun!

[She goes on to say how she had her arm twisted with *Rule of Three* and Gerald Verner's *Towards Zero*, to explain how Bertie Meyer had a hit with the original production of *Ten Little Niggers* when C.B. Cochrane had turned it down and that she was pleased she had persuaded Peter Saunders to put on *Verdict* . . .]

I have *not* in any way urged him to put on Fiddlers in London. He doesn't like it, is quite probably right and I shouldn't want him to do anything of the kind . . . All theatrical things are a pure gamble. If there's no London production I'll be quite glad for your sake!

But I wrote the play (some years ago now), have always liked it – and I shan't mind unduly if it is a flop – whatever I write in the play line would get nasty notices – chiefly because of The Mousetrap which is much resented by all the younger journalists.

I know you have my best interests at heart – as AP did when she implored me not to marry Max (apparently for religious reasons?) and even refused to come to the wedding. I'm thankful I didn't listen to her! Forty years of happiness I should have missed.

If one doesn't take a few risks in life one might as well be dead.

A lot of love to you,
Nima[139]

We seem to be entering *A Daughter's a Daughter* territory here, with Rosalind apparently advocating that her mother should abandon a course of action that will bring her happiness.

On 2 August Cork, ever the diplomat, stepped in to avert what appeared to be developing into a family crisis. He wrote to Agatha ostensibly agreeing with her that the play deserved a West End life. 'How many plays are there in London at the moment to which one could take the whole family?' he asked, knowing that this would be music to her ears. 'My attitude about this has always been that what you want goes.'[140] However, he continued, 'we must face the fact that we will get a hostile press – maybe any new play of yours would at this time . . . but people who have seen it have enjoyed it, and there is a lot of evidence that it is good entertainment. And this despite the fact that the production is far below West End standard. Star casting and first class directing would bring out all sorts of potentialities that have yet to be realised . . .'

Cork sent a copy of his letter to Rosalind, with a covering note saying, 'In fifty years of dealing with authors I have become very chary of stopping production of works against a writer's wishes. Occasionally it has to be done if faculties fail, but I do assure you it is a most dangerous thing to do!' As he did not insist that production of the piece should be stopped, we must assume that he at least did not believe that in Agatha's case faculties were failing.

Perhaps as a result of Cork's wonderfully artful letter, which expresses full support to Agatha whilst cleverly sowing the seeds of doubt, there appears to have been a compromise between her and her advisors. A plan was put in place to revise the script of *Fiddlers Five* and create a new production of it before the play was presented in the West End. The director was to be Allan Davis who, having opened the hit comedy *No Sex Please, We're British* a few months earlier, was very much the 'go to' comedy director of the day. Peter Saunders would later buy out John Gale's Volcano Productions, the company behind *No Sex Please . . .*, but it seems that Davis' introduction to *Fiddlers Five* may have come by another route; according to some sources it was young impresario Cameron Mackintosh who took Davis to see the production on its original tour.[141]

On 24 September 1971 producer James Verner was issued with a West End licence for *Fiddlers Five*.[142] Verner (no relation of *Towards Zero* adaptor Gerald) had directed a production of *Murder at the Vicarage* for Cameron Mackintosh in 1969, at a time when Mackintosh was also touring *Black Coffee* and *Love From a Stranger*, and had himself produced the London production of *Hair*, which Mackintosh assisted on, the previous year. Ironically, the comedy which Christie hoped would attract family audiences was thus now in the hands of the director of *No Sex Please, We're British* and the producer of *Hair*.

As soon as the licence had been issued to Verner, Christie wrote again to Hubert Gregg. After discussing her deteriorating health, she promised him, 'If I *am* considering writing another play I'll let you know – I've got a new book coming out next month – and a book a year is about enough to occupy me. I didn't think Fiddlers Five would have been your kind – but I thought you might as well have a look at it, as I was thinking of doing things to it if anyone fancied it!! The critics mostly dislike it – but it also seems to play to good houses and to be commercially successful. Parts of it are fun which is why I enjoyed writing it originally, but it is in no way a thriller.'[143]

Davis, who met with Christie before commencing work on the script, set about the task of revising it with great alacrity, and there was some lively correspondence between them at the start of 1972, in which she gave her comments on his amendments and interpolations. The five 'fiddlers' had now become three, partly through the amalgamation of the older and younger female roles originally intended for the Lockwoods: 'Sally now comes out a very good leading-lady's part . . . and I even wonder if Sally Blunt might not be developed for the play "you are going to write when you are 83!"' Davis explained, going on to say that he was hoping to interest Irene Handl in the role, and emphasising that 'Speed is now of the essence if we are to get the play off the ground this season . . . and if we could we'd like to be well established in the West

End when all your American fans arrive – so we need your OK to go ahead just as soon as you can give it, please.'[144]

Despite increasing ill health, Agatha relished the opportunity to reshape her play yet again, and made it clear that she was not prepared to relinquish the driving seat to Davis. In particular, she was keen to retain a scene where one of the conspirators sends a cheque to the Chancellor by way of 'conscience money' at the end of the play: 'I think Sally wanting to send conscience money to the Chancellor of the Exchequer shows herself as a very endearing and lovable character.'[145] This concept had appeared in one of the very first notes for the piece.

Fiddlers Three (not to be confused with the 1991 Eric Chappell comedy of the same title) opened at the Yvonne Arnaud Theatre, Guildford, on 1 August 1972, again in the presence of the now very fragile Agatha, who received a standing ovation when she entered the auditorium on the arm of the theatre's director. 'In all the creative arts there are exponents who transcend the rules . . .' reported the *Surrey Advertiser*. 'No one could disguise the play's basic weaknesses, but a playwright whose box office support outstrips that of Coward, Rattigan and Bolt, not to mention Shaw and Sheridan, can afford to make her own laws. And a mere journalist denigrates a cult goddess at his peril.'[146]

The play included the following exchange, as Henry explains to Sally that his father has bequeathed him £100,000 that he once won in a bet:

HENRY: Father drew up a deed making that money mine – on the day he reached seventy years of age . . . He gave it to me because he said it would teach me a sharp lesson.

SALLY: Teach you not to gamble, you mean?

HENRY: The other way round – teach me the advantages of gambling and of taking risks. He's always thought I'm a terrible sissy not to want to gamble.

SALLY: Your father must be an extraordinary man.

HENRY: Oh he is. I've always been a great disappointment

to him. I'm so – well, ordinary and cautious.[147]

As a crushing put-down aimed by the cult goddess at her own daughter, this could not have been more direct.

Irene Handl hadn't bitten, but popular Welsh comedienne Doris Hare took the role of Sally, which had originally been written ten years previously for Margaret Lockwood, and by all accounts made a good job of it. Although the Guildford production, and the short tour thereafter, had been intended as a stepping stone to the West End, nothing was to come of it. James Verner instead mounted yet another production for a twenty-week tour in 1973, with yet another director at the helm. Peggy Mount now took on the role of Sally, and the indomitable James Grant Anderson, having stepped aside at Guildford, again took on the relatively small role of solicitor Mr Truscott.

It seems that Verner was, perhaps, less of a player than he himself had made out. In his book *The Worst It Can Be Is a Disaster* (2009), Braham Murray, director of his 1975 production of *The Black Mikado*, is less than complimentary about Verner's business dealings.[148] I couldn't possibly comment; but consigning Christie's final play to the touring circuit evidently suited her advisors, so I can't imagine that any objections were raised. Had *Fiddlers Three* transferred to the West End, as intended, in September 1972, it would have been performed in a very different theatrical environment from that in which *Black Coffee* had opened in 1931. Alongside the Royal Shakespeare Company's repertoire at the Aldwych and the National Theatre's at the Old Vic, and an Arnold Wesker play at the Royal Court, the Palace Theatre was showing *Jesus Christ Superstar* and *Godspell* was playing at Wyndham's. Meanwhile, *No Sex Please, We're British* was at the Strand, *Hair* was in its fourth year at the Shaftesbury, *Oh! Calcutta* was in its third year at the Royalty, the Whitehall was home to 'London's controversial sex comedy' *Pyjama Tops* and the Duchess was hosting *The Dirtiest Show in Town* ('makes *Oh! Calcutta* seem like *Little Women*' said the *New York Times*). The title of *Ten Little Niggers* may have been changed in 1966, but in 1972 *The Black and White Minstrel Show* was playing at the Victoria Palace as the Dance Theatre of Jamaica arrived to perform at Sadler's Wells. You couldn't make it up.

Amidst this smorgasbord of theatrical delights, *The Mousetrap* was advertising its 'twentieth proud year' and Anthony Shaffer's *Sleuth* was in its 'third thrilling' year at the neighbouring St Martin's Theatre, where Peter Saunders had acquired the lease four years previously. West Street was now known as 'thriller alley', and in June Christie had attended *Sleuth* at Shaffer's invitation.

In November 1973 Christie, now aged eighty-three, was enthused by what she saw as an opportunity for *Miss Perry* to reach the stage. She had received an enquiry about a possible play from her friend Cicely Courtneidge, now aged eighty, to tour with her husband Jack Hulbert, and urged Cork to send them her unperformed comedy; evidently this was with a view to Courtneidge playing the role of Poppy, which had been written for a considerably younger Margaret Lockwood. 'It could be made very funny by Cicely going all out and people seem to love her doing it!!' she wrote to Cork. 'It's a funnier play than Fiddlers Three and I should really like to see it done.'[149] It wasn't; and the following month Hughes Massie took an advertisement in *The Stage* to say that Agatha Christie's 'high comedy' *Fiddlers Three* was 'now available for repertory', the main selling point evidently being that it only required 'two easy sets'.[150] By contrast, 1973 had also finally seen the publication of Christie's then unperformed historical drama *Akhnaton*, with its epic staging requirements. She had found it in a drawer the previous year and, encouraged by the success of the Tutankhamun exhibition which was attracting big crowds at the British Museum, carried out some final edits and sent it to Collins.

In early 1974 Saunders' lease on the Ambassadors came up for renewal and, unable to agree terms with the owners, he decided to move *The Mousetrap* across the alley to his own St Martin's Theatre (no longer the home of *Sleuth*); a manoeuvre that took place over the weekend of 23 March without a performance being missed. It has remained in its new home ever since: the longest running theatrical production of any kind, ever. Despite the protests of Rosalind, the very frail Agatha, who had suffered a heart attack the previous month, proudly co-hosted the play's annual birthday party in November. In December, she suffered a fall at her house, Winterbrook, in Wallingford, where she now spent her time.

When Agatha Christie died, aged eighty-five, at home with her beloved Max, on 12 January 1976, two West End theatres dimmed their lights: the St Martin's and the Savoy, where a successful touring revival of Moie Charles and Barbara Toy's *Murder at the Vicarage*, produced by Ray Cooney, had found a home. Barbara Mullen was reprising the role of Miss Marple, which she had first played in 1949. This time, she was old enough for the part.

Curtain Call

I can think of no better phrase to sum up Christie's legacy as a dramatist than that adopted by J.C. Trewin in his entertaining contribution to H.R.F. Keating's *Agatha Christie, First Lady of Crime* (1977). Hers was indeed 'A Midas gift to the theatre'. Theatrical empires, from Peter Saunders to Cameron Mackintosh, have been founded on her work, which has been seen and enjoyed in countless productions in numerous languages around the world. In 2001 the Agatha Christie Theatre Festival, comprising her complete dramatic works as then known, was staged over twelve weeks at the Palace Theatre, Westcliff-on-Sea. Five years later, the Agatha Christie Theatre Company was established; presented by Bill Kenwright and endorsed by her estate, it has since enjoyed great success touring her plays in the UK. In Hubert Gregg's words, 'She has defied changes of taste, sharpenings of critical view, the breaking of New Waves. She is a mighty anomaly. A square peg in a round world.'[1] In the extraordinarily small window of opportunity between entrusting her theatrical work to Peter Saunders in 1950 and the Royal Court revolution of 1956, she wrote, as a woman in her sixties, four hit plays: *The Hollow*, *The Mousetrap*, *Witness for the Prosecution* and *Spider's Web*. In doing so she created the longest-running piece of theatre of all time and became the only woman ever to have three plays running in the West End simultaneously. As Trewin puts it, Christie 'fortified the theatre of entertainment'.

Arguably the principal beneficiary of Christie's 'Midas gift' was Peter Saunders, who was quoted as saying that the true extent of his earnings from *The Mousetrap* was 'a secret between God and my accountant'.[2] Saunders remarks in his book, 'People have said to me, "You are lucky. Anyone could make money with the Agatha Christie plays." But was it luck? . . . I was the lowliest of all the producers at the time, and there is no question that if anybody else had "recognised this opportunity and taken advantage of it" *they* could have had the Christie plays . . . No. Luck has only a minimal part to play in the success of a producer.'[3] Saunders was knighted in 1982 (an honour never afforded to Binkie Beaumont) and retired to his Bishop's Avenue House, Monkswell, in 1994, happy in the company of his second wife, Katie Boyle. He died, aged ninety-one, in 2003. Edmund Cork had died in 1988 at the age of ninety-four, having represented Agatha Christie for sixty-five years. Bertie Meyer had died in 1967, aged ninety.

According to Saunders' *Daily Telegraph* obituary, 'Unsurprisingly, he lamented in 1955, "I don't want people to think that Mrs Christie's is the only egg I can sit on". Saunders was, in fact, a highly skilled producer of more than 100 plays, many of them in the West End and on Broadway. He was particularly associated with comedies and light thrillers, including *Alfie*, *Arsenic and Old Lace*, *No Sex Please We're British* and *Lloyd George Knew My Father*.'[4]

Former *Sunday Times* critic Harold Hobson, in *The Mousetrap*'s fortieth anniversary brochure, eulogises him thus:

No man without an extraordinary degree of fighting spirit and determination could have done what he did; that is overthrow the nearest thing to a monopoly we have ever come to in the theatrical profession. During and after the war the H.M. Tennent management dominated the London theatre. Tennent's did a great deal of admirable work in the theatre, and gained a great reputation for their polish and style. But the role they played came to restrict unduly the activities of other managements, and consequently the

range of theatre itself. Many managements chafed impo-
tently under the hardships inflicted on them by this
monopoly but only Peter Saunders studied the laws
governing the theatre so carefully that he was able to
establish in the realm of the drama an era of managerial
freedom . . . Much of the most influential opinion in the
theatre world of the last quarter of the century (and even
before) has been built on the assumption that somehow
there is something disgraceful in giving pleasure in the
theatre . . . Fortunately, Peter Saunders has never believed
this absurd fallacy any more than Shakespeare, Dr Johnson,
or the greatest of French dramatists did. Believing then,
as he does, in entertainment, he has demonstrated the
potency of this belief with rare power. Few others have
done it so unequivocally.[5]

That Saunders ran this article with pride in a publication of
his own indicates that he was happy to be known as the man
responsible for the 'overthrow' of Tennents; and the plays with
which he achieved this extraordinary David and Goliath feat
were, of course, Christie's.

After Christie's death, third-party adaptations of her novels
continued to arrive in the West End with depressing regularity,
confusing and sullying her own reputation as a playwright.
Saunders himself was responsible for commissioning and
producing two pedestrian adaptations from Leslie Darbon: *A
Murder is Announced* (1977), starring Dulcie Gray as Miss
Marple, and *Cards on the Table* (1981), both presented at his
own Vaudeville Theatre. The less said about these ventures the
better, and Saunders, of all people, should arguably have been
more respectful of Christie's dramatic legacy; although she had
agreed to the adaptation of *A Murder is Announced* before her
death and at least Poirot was cut from *Cards on the Table*, as
she no doubt would have wished. In 1993 Clive Exton's adaptation of *Murder is Easy* played for a few weeks at the Duke
of York's and in 2005 Kevin Elyot's unnecessary new adaptation
of the novel *And Then There Were None* played for a few

months at the Gielgud, giving the story, according to press announcements, a 'pulp fiction revamp' which was 'awash with blood'.[6] I saw it, and it was. Another unnecessary adaptation was Louise Page's new version of *Love From a Stranger*, premiered at the Mill at Sonning in 2010. Christie herself had a very low opinion of other people's dramatic tinkerings with her work but, with yet more stage adaptations in the pipeline, it seems that her own remarkable legacy as a dramatist is doomed to recede ever further towards a hidden horizon.

In 1992, British Telecom controversially ended a major sponsorship deal with the Royal Shakespeare Company in favour of supporting a sadly rather low-rent commercial tour of *Witness for the Prosecution*. *Guardian* theatre critic Michael Billington was outraged: 'Why in heaven's name switch their support from the greatest popular dramatist in history to arguably the worst popular dramatist of this century?' he demanded. 'Where BT once got brownie-points for backing Shakespeare tours, I see no kudos arising from its association with Mrs C.'[7] British Telecom, however, were more than happy to eschew 'kudos' in favour of reaching the widest possible audience demographic over a forty-week nationwide tour. Their spokesman said, 'It is important to note that traditionally sponsorship from major companies is directed towards opera, ballet and classical theatre. BT recognises that in serving the whole of the community which in turn are probably BT subscribers in every socio-economic group, we should address as large a segment of the population as possible.'[8] Like the People's Entertainment Society, BT had recognised Christie's status as the people's playwright. The irony was that Christie herself would have regarded Shakespeare as fulfilling that brief.

Billington's appraisal of Christie's work is based on his belief that 'She is a lousy dramatist precisely because her dialogue is a function of plot rather than an index of character. I can still hear, from the days when I worked in rep, the agonising groans that used to go up from actors when forced to animate the walking dead in yet another revival of *Peril at End House*.' I hope that this book has gone some way towards challenging that preconception, but in any event I would respectfully point out that, as a national newspaper's theatre critic, Mr Billington should be aware that *Peril at End House* is not in fact an Agatha Christie play.

Gwen Robyns asks, 'Will Agatha Christie's plays stand the test of time like those of Somerset Maugham or Noël Coward? They may date . . . but they do recall a visual nostalgia for a middle-class way of life that will never return to England. Of spacious, chintzy country houses, cultivated morning-room talk, impeccable servants, bowls of potpourri, croquet on the lawn, Earl Grey tea poured from Georgian silver, and wafer-thin brown bread cucumber sandwiches. Perhaps this is what many of us are longing for.'[9]

This misrepresentation of Christie as a playwright is by no means unique to Robyns, and seems to be some sort of confusion with the image portrayed in film and television adaptations of some of her novels or, indeed with plays adapted from her work by third parties. Of the fifteen of her own plays which were performed in her lifetime, few come anywhere close to the setting described above, and even those that do are notable for the absence of cucumber sandwiches, Earl Grey tea and croquet on the lawn.

And Then There Were None, *The Hollow*, *The Mousetrap*, *Witness for the Prosecution*, *Spider's Web* and *The Unexpected Guest* are six substantial, hugely successful plays which between them represent a notable contribution to the British dramatic repertoire. The less successful *Black Coffee*, *Murder on the Nile*, *Appointment with Death*, *Verdict*, *Go Back for Murder* and *Rule of Three* are a further six that continue to do very well off the back of the others. *A Daughter's a Daughter*, *Fiddlers Three*, *Akhnaton* (premiered on the fringe after Christie's death) and *Chimneys* remain barely performed and do not form part of the established Christie canon. The version of *Towards Zero* that she didn't write continues to be performed and included in anthologies, whilst the one that she did write has never been published, and has not been produced since its week at Martha's Vineyard Playhouse. *The Wasp's Nest* has never been given the stage presentation for which it was written, and a short play possibly intended for puppets has been published but not performed. A further five full-length plays and six one-act plays remain unpublished and, as far as we know, unperformed.

Christie's two masterpieces of dramatic construction, *Witness for the Prosecution* and *And Then There Were None*, are not detective stories and represent, in each case, the absolute pinnacle of their respective genres: often imitated but never bettered. Meanwhile, *The Lie*, *A Daughter's a Daughter* and *Verdict* give a tantalising glimpse of the playwright that Christie might have been had she not acceded to the seemingly unending demand for thrillers from her producers and audiences. As we have seen, much of her early work, like that of Clemence Dane, examines then much-debated issues such as divorce and eugenics; she even, in the mid-1920s, took on the subject of what was at that time regarded as incest. In *The Mousetrap*, the lady of the house struggled across the stage with a vacuum cleaner[10] four years before the sight of a woman doing the ironing caused a sensation at the Royal Court, and in 1961 the censor banned her from using the word 'homo' three years before Joe Orton's *Entertaining Mr Sloane*. In *The Last Séance* the stage was literally 'awash with blood' and in *Fiddlers Five*, to the horror of her family, the newly appointed Dame appeared to condone hoodwinking the taxman.

Christie colluded with neither the patriarchy nor the censor with respect to the content of her plays, which consistently and wittily subverted both. However, in order to get her work to the stage, and thus gain access to the theatrical world and companionship that she so cherished, she was frequently obliged to dance to other people's tunes. Or at least to appear to. Christie's theatrical fortunes were, of course, inextricably linked to those of Peter Saunders, but it is important to remember that, for her, playwriting was a source of creative fulfilment rather then necessary income, and that the 'Midas gift' of her theatrical imagination gave audiences an extraordinary range of work that often challenged and surprised them.

I will leave the last word with Agatha herself, as she describes the first night of *Witness for the Prosecution*:

I was happy, radiantly happy, and made even more so by the applause of the audience. I slipped away as usual after the curtain came down on *my* ending and out into Long Acre. In a few moments, while I was looking for a waiting car, I was surrounded by crowds of friendly people, quite ordinary members of the audience, who recognised me, patted me on the back and encouraged me – 'Best you've written, dearie!' 'First class-thumbs up, I'd say!' 'V-signs for this one!' and 'Loved every minute of it!' Autograph books were produced and I signed cheerfully and happily. My self-consciousness and nervousness, just for once, were not with me. Yes it was a memorable evening. I am proud of it still. And every now and then I dig into the memory chest, bring it out, take a look at it, and say 'That was the night, that was!'[11]

Endnotes

Abbreviations used in the Endnotes

The names of some of the people most frequently referred to in the Endnotes are abbreviated thus:

AC: Agatha Christie
Cork: Edmund Cork
HG: Hubert Gregg
MM: Max Mallowan
Ober: Harold Ober
PS: Peter Saunders

For a full list of archives consulted see Bibliography. Some of those most frequently referred to in the Endnotes are abbreviated thus:

ACA: Agatha Christie Archive; Christie Archive Trust
BDA: Basil Dean Archive; John Rylands Library, University of Manchester
HMA: Hughes Massie Archive of Agatha Christie's business papers; Exeter University Special Collections
HML: Hughes Massie's stage Licensing records; Agatha Christie Ltd.
HGP: Hubert Gregg's Papers; private collection
LCP: Lord Chamberlain's Plays collection; British Library
LCPC: Lord Chamberlain's Plays Correspondence; British Library
LOC: Library of Congress, Washington DC; Music Division, Gilbert Miller archive

PESA: People's Entertainment Society Archive; National Co-operative Archive, Manchester
PSP: Peter Saunders' business papers, Mousetrap Productions
SA: Shubert Archive, New York

For a full list of books and other publications consulted, see Bibliography. Where editions of works cited differ from the editions listed in the Bibliography, a publisher's name is given in the Endnotes. Where only a date is given, the edition cited is that listed in the Bibliography. Some of the publications most frequently referred to in the Endnotes are abbreviated thus:

ACATM: *Agatha Christie and All That Mousetrap* by Hubert Gregg (1980)
ACAuto: *An Autobiography* by Agatha Christie (HarperCollins, 2011)
MAC: *The Mystery of Agatha Christie* by Gwen Robyns (Penguin, 1979)
MMem: *Mallowan's Memoirs* by Max Mallowan (HarperCollins, 2010)
MOP: *The Mousetrap and Other Plays* (HarperCollins, 2011)
MTM: *The Mousetrap Man* by Peter Saunders (1972)
NYT: *New York Times*

Agatha Christie's Autobiography

Agatha Christie's autobiography (ACAuto) was transcribed by others from recordings which she dictated over more than ten years up to 1965, which may account for the occasional misspelling of names in the printed text. The transcribed material was extensively edited following Christie's death in 1976, prior to publication the following year. Recordings of some of her dictation for the last quarter of the book, as well as the full original transcripts, are held at the Agatha Christie Archive by the Christie Archive Trust (ACA), and a selection from these recordings was issued to accompany its most recent edition in hardcover (HarperCollins, 2011). I have highlighted a small number of discrepancies between the recordings and the text which I consider to be of particular relevance to the subject of this book.

Agatha Christie's Correspondence

Much of Christie's correspondence is penned in writing that is difficult to decipher, so gaps in the text cited here may indicate that some
of the content is illegible. Correspondence which benefits from the
use of a typewriter includes her wartime letters to Max on the subject
of Shakespeare (ACA), her letters to Saunders about *Witness for the
Prosecution* (PSP), and that with Cork about her financial affairs
(HMA). She rarely includes a full date, often opting simply to put the
day of the week, in which case I have listed the letter concerned as
'undated'. In these cases I hope that my attempts to ascertain approximate dates through referring to the letters to which she was
responding (where available), and by identifying particular family
events and theatrical projects which she mentions, have been by and
large successful. Where she provides more information (i.e. 'March
23rd') I have offered what I believe to be the correct year in order
to complete the date. The misdating of Christie's correspondence has
been a source of scholarly error in the past and, whilst my own
results may in some cases differ from previous attempts, I make no
claim that my efforts in this regard are in any way definitive.

Agatha Christie's Notebooks

Agatha Christie herself did not number her notebooks (held by the
Christie Archive Trust); this task was carried out in the 1990s. The
numbering of the notebooks does not reflect the chronology of their
content and, whilst there are obvious clusters of entries from similar
periods of time, her choice of which particular book to use for the
recording of her latest (mostly undated) thoughts appears to have been
entirely arbitrary. For a full explanation of these unique documents
see John Curran's *Agatha Christie's Secret Notebooks* (2009) pp.41–59.

Play Scripts

A variety of sources are referred to for Agatha Christie play scripts.
These include typescripts held at the Agatha Christie Archive by the
Christie Archive Trust (ACA), typescripts held at the Lord
Chamberlain's Plays collection at the British Library (LCP) and
current published editions. For most of the plays the published
version cited is the collection *The Mousetrap and Other Plays* (*MOP*,
HarperCollins, 2011). For published plays not included in this volume

(apart from *Akhnaton*), the most recent Samuel French acting edition is cited. Only in the case of extracts from published versions are Act, Scene and page references given. Where a number of quotations from the same script follow in succession, only the first is given a note reference.

The Lord Chamberlain's Plays Collection

Where the Lord Chamberlain's Plays collection (LCP) and Lord Chamberlain's Plays Correspondence files (LCPC) are cited, the relevant reference number within the collection is given (year followed by the number of the file in which stored). The collection may be viewed, by holders of a British Library Reader Pass, in the British Library Manuscripts Reading Room. At the time of writing, the digital cataloguing of the collection is an ongoing exercise, and although various publications and listings assist with the referencing of plays from certain periods, that in which we are most interested (1930–1968) remains principally catalogued by play title on a card index. For the period 1900–1968 there are also seventeen volumes of handwritten lists in chronological order of submission. For more information on the Lord Chamberlain's Plays collection and how it works, see: www.bl.uk/reshelp/pdfs/readerguide3.pdf

Family Tree

The extract from Agatha Christie's Family Tree at the front of the book has been prepared with the assistance of the Christie Archive Trust, and makes use of their latest research into the spelling of family names.

Historic Sterling and Dollar Values

There follows an approximate guide to historic sterling and dollar values, showing their "buying power" relative to 2016. There are a variety of methodologies for calculating inflation, but the sources referred to below (provided by the Bank of England and the US Bureau of Labor Statistics) are generally regarded as authoritative.

Date:	£1 was worth:	$1 was worth:
1930	£59.98	$14.37
1935	£65.26	$17.52

1940	£51.37	$17.14
1945	£39.61	$13.33
1950	£31.45	$9.96
1955	£24.08	$8.96
1960	£21.13	$8.11
1965	£17.77	$7.62
1970	£14.20	$6.19
1975	£7.70	$4.46

www.bankofengland.co.uk/education/pages/resources/inflationtools/
calculator/index1.aspx
www.bls.gov/data/inflation_calculator.htm

Dates

Dates are given in the form dd/mm/yy throughout.

Behind the Scenes

1. *ACAuto*: pp. 473-4.
2. *The Stage*: 7/6/1951.
3. BBC Radio interview with AC: 13/02/1955.
4. *Sunday Times*: 15/10/1961. Interview with AC by crime writer Julian Symons (1912-1994)
5. *ACAuto*: p.471.
6. BBC Radio interview with AC: 13/02/1955.
7. AC letter to *The Times*: 3/2/1973. Amongst other matters relating to Shakespeare, she applauds Dr A.L. Rowse's identification of Emilia Bassano as Shakespeare's 'Dark Lady' of the sonnets.
8. *ACAuto*: p.171.
9. Ibid.
10. AC letter to MM: 31/8/1942.
11. AC letter to MM: 23/8/1942.
12. A.L. Rowse, *Memories of Men and Women* (1980): p.89.
13. AC letter to MM: 14/1/1944.
14. *ACAuto*: pp.489-10.
15. *ACAuto*: p.514.
16. Ibid.
17. 'The Actress' was originally published as 'A Trap for the

Unwary' in *Novel Magazine* in May 1923. It is published in the AC short story collection *While the Light Lasts* (HarperCollins 1997), which benefits from interesting background notes by Tony Medawar.

18. Maggie B. Gale, *West End Women* (1996): p.59.
19. Maggie B. Gale, *Women, Theatre and Performance* (2001): pp.137–8.
20. *The Status of Women in British Theatre 1982–1983*, Conference of Women Theatre Directors and Administrators. The survey collected statistics relating to women directors, administrators and playwrights in national, repertory, fringe and community theatres in England, Wales and Northern Ireland. Scotland was not included although, as the survey's authors maintain, there is every reason to believe that the trends it demonstrates would have been repeated there. As we shall see, Christie enjoyed a particularly strong following in Scotland where, in her case, the results may well have been even better.
21. *The Stage*: 7/6/1951
22. See: John Earl, 'How West End Theatreland Happened' (*The Matcham Journal*, Edition 1, 2014).
23. Peter Haining, *Murder in Four Acts*: p.23.

ACT ONE: THE PEOPLE'S PLAYWRIGHT

Scene One: The Early Plays

1. *ACAuto*: p.107. Christie herself does not identify the theatre that the family attended, and I am grateful to Torquay local historian and tour guide John Risdon for assisting me in doing so.
2. *ACAuto*: p108.
3. *ACAuto*: p.55.
4. *ACAuto*: p.148.
5. *ACAuto*: pp.85.
6. *ACAuto*: p.148.
7. *ACAuto*: p.122.
8. *ACAuto*: p.158-9.
9. ACA: Photographs and programme of *The Blue Beard of Unhappiness* (undated). The archive also contains a programme for an entertainment at a charity bazaar at Torquay's Bath Saloons, dated 'Wednesday 10 April' (likely 1907, making Agatha sixteen), in which a 'Miss Miller' is listed as appearing

in 'A Play entitled *Let The Lady Go'*. A 'Mrs Watts', perhaps Agatha's sister Madge, is listed as directing another of the pieces being presented.

10. Miller Family Album of Confessions, Torquay Museum: page dated 'Nov 27/10'.

11. ACA: AC, *A Masque From Italy*: typescript (undated).

12. BBC Radio interview with AC: 13/02/1955.

13. ACA: AC, *The Conqueror* typescript (undated).

14. Eden Phillpotts, *From the Angle of 88* (1951): p.55.

15. ACA: Eden Phillpotts letter to AC: 6/2/1909.

16. See: Adelaide Ross (née Phillpotts), *Reverie* (1981) p.29. The nature of Eden Phillpotts' relationship with his daughter from the age of 'six or seven' is not the subject of this book, but is apparent both from her autobiography (cited here) and from his *Selected Letters* (ed. James Y. Dayananda, 1982).

17. ACA: AC, *Teddy Bear*: typescript (undated).

18. AC, *Death Comes as the End* (HarperCollins, 2001: p.303/first published in the USA by Dodd, Mead & Co., 1944/first published in the UK by Collins, 1945) '. . . as for men, let them breed and die early,' Kait goes on to remark.

19. ACA: AC, *Eugenia and Eugenics*: typescript (undated).

20. George Bernard Shaw, preface to *Getting Married: The Dramatic Works of George Bernard Shaw*, no.xvii (Constable, 1913): p.111.

21. *ACAuto*: p.221.

22. ACA: AC letter to Clara Miller: 9 May 1922. Also cited in *The Grand Tour* (ed. Mathew Prichard, 2012).

23. ACA: AC Notebook 43.

24. Noël Coward, *The Better Half* (1922), published in *London's Grand Guignol and the Theatre of Horror* by Richard J Hand and Michael Wilson (2007): p.255.

25. *The Times*: 8/9/1920.

26. ACA: AC, various unpublished short story typescripts .

27. ACA: AC, *The Last Séance*; one act play typescript (undated).

28. The short story version of AC's 'The Last Séance' can be read in the AC short story collection *The Hound of Death* (1933/ HarperCollins, 2003).

29. ACA: AC, *Ten Years*: typescript (undated).

30. ACA: AC, *Marmalade Moon*: typescript (undated).

31. See note 22 above.

32. Theatre Royal Windsor *Curtain Up* Magazine: September 1957

(Basil Dean Archive, John Rylands Library, University of Manchester).

33. Basil Dean, *Seven Ages* (1970): pp.129–30.

34. Ibid. p.143.

35. For a fuller discussion of the topic of the divorce laws as reflected in women's playwriting of the time, see Rebecca S. Cameron, *Irreconcilable Differences: Divorce and Women's Drama Before 1945* (*Modern Drama*, vol.44, no.4, 2001): p.476, to which I am indebted for this information.

36. *The Times*: 24/4/1978.

37. Basil Dean, *Seven Ages* (1970): p.143.

38. LCP (Ref: 1924/25): label on M.F. Watts, *The Claimant.*

39. ACA: various undated correspondence between Madge Watts and her husband James Watts: August–September, 1924. This correspondence is quoted at some length by biographer Laura Thompson in *Agatha Christie: an English Mystery* (2007), pp.46–48.

40. LCP (Ref: 1924/25): Lord Chamberlain's Office Reader's Report for *The Claimant* by M.F. Watts: 9/8/1924.

41. *The Times*: 4/9/1924.

42. *The Times*: 12/9/1924.

43. HMA: Letter from Cork to the Lord Chamberlain's Office: 8/12/1969 (The Lord Chamberlain's Office had relinquished its censorship role the previous year). Cork wrote: 'A play entitled The Claimant by M.F. Watts was produced by ReandeaN at the St Martin's Theatre in 1924. Our client, Lady Mallowan (Agatha Christie), who is the sister of the author, wishes to read the play, and the other beneficiaries of the author's will are happy that she should do so. In the circumstances we would be glad if two copies of the play could be made at our expense for the use of the owners of the copyright.' AC appears have been reminded of the play by an enquiry the previous month from a solicitor in Manchester, presumably in respect of her sister's estate. The resulting copy of *The Claimant*, complete with Reader's Report, remains at the ACA.

44. ACA: M.F. Watts, *Oranges and Lemons* typescript (undated).

45. *ACAuto*: p.127.

46. ACA: AC, *The Clutching Hand*, typescript, undated.

47. *ACAuto*: p.434.

48. Arthur B. Reeve, *The Exploits of Elaine: A Detective Novel* (Hodder and Stoughton, 1915): p.9.

49. ACA: AC Notebook 34.

50. *ACAuto*: p.319 (AC either misremembers the original title as 'Anna the Adventuress', or there is an error in transcribing her dictation).

51. *ACAuto*: p.335.

52. ACA: AC, *The Lie*: typescript (undated).

53. For a fuller discussion of The Deceased Wife's Sister's Marriage Act, see: Diane M. Chambers, 'Triangular Desire and the Sororal Bond: The Deceased Wife's Sister Bill' (*Mosaic – a journal for the interdisciplinary study of literature*, Volume 29 Number 1, 1996), to which I am indebted for this information.

54. The change in title may well have been prompted by the 1923-4 West End production of Henry Arthur Jones' *The Lie*, starring Syblil Thorndike.

Scene Two – Poirot Takes the Stage

1. HML: Licence summary card for dramatisation of *The Murder of Roger Ackroyd*, 2/4/1927.

2. *The Stage* of 21/12/1922 carries an entertaining article reporting on the company's first anniversary dinner, at which Lionel Bute's endeavours were saluted by his grateful actors.

3. ACA: programme for *Alibi* at the Prince of Wales' Theatre.

4. *Observer*: 4/3/1928.

5. *ACAuto*: p.434.

6. *Sunday Times*: 15/10/1961. Interview with AC by crime writer Julian Symons (1912-1994).

7. *MTM*: p.7.

8. *ACAuto*: p.433.

9. Ibid.

10. LCP: Typescript for *Alibi* by Michael Morton. LCP Ref: 1928/24.

11. According to *The Stage* of 9/9/2015, the opening performance of the tour at Swansea Grand, 'presented by Lionel Bute and BA Meyer' on 6/8/1928 'was well received by an appreciative crowd, as played by a capable company.' This was, in fact, one of two Bute/Meyer units to launch tours of *Alibi* on that date (*The Stage*, 12/7/1928) shortly before the London production's transfer to the Haymarket Theatre. Both tours ran concurrently with the West End production in the second half of 1928. On 7 September 1932 an adaptation of Morton's play entitled *Signor Bracoli*, by French playwright/director Jacques

Deval, opened at the Théâtre des Nouveautés in Paris. The script (published in *La Petite Illustration* magazine on 10/12/1932) reveals the titular Cesare Bracoli (as Poirot had here become) to be an 'attractive, exuberant, thirty year-old Neapolotan', and photographs of fifty-eight year-old Lucien Rozenberg in the role show him clearly giving Charles Laughton a run for his money. Morton's French Poirot thus became an Italian in the French version of the play, thereby preserving his credentials as a foreigner.

12. Observer: 20/3/1928.
13. *The Star*, interview with AC: 16/5/1928.
14. ACA: AC, *Chimneys* typescript with Marshalls Bureau date stamp '5 July 1928'.
15. Dr John Curran, 'Black Coffee; A Mystery within a Mystery' (*Crime and Detective Stories* magazine, no.67, 2014).
16. *ACAuto*: p.433-4.
17. HML: Licence summary card for *After Dinner/Black Coffee*, 18/11/1930. A typescript dated 1932 was included in the 2015 catalogue of Sanctuary Books in New York. Its first page clearly states, 'All communications to L.E. Berman, 32 Shaftesbury Avenue, W1.'
18. Basil Dean, *Seven Ages* (1970): pp.332–3.
19. *Daily Telegraph*: 11/12/1930.
20. ACA: AC letter to MM (undated, early November, 1930). There has previously been some confusion over the dating of this letter, and therefore the play to which it refers, not least as a result of the truly Christiesque occurence of the pages from one letter apparently having been folded inside those of another of a completely different date.
21. LCP: Typescript for *After Dinner/Black Coffee* (registered as '*Black Coffee*'): LCP Ref: 1930/52.
22. ACA: AC letter to MM: 26/11/1930.
23. ACA: AC letter to MM: 10/12/1930.
24. *ACAuto*: p.434.
25. *The Times*: 20/11/1956.
26. LCP: Typescript for *Alibi* by Michael Morton: LCP Ref: 1928/24.
27. See 21 above.
28. *The Times*: 9/12/1930.
29. ACA: AC letter to MM: undated (January 1931).
30. I am grateful to Peter Harrington Books for giving me access to a rare copy of Arthur Ashley's 1934 edition of *Black Coffee*,

from which this extract is quoted. It is effectively the text now used in the current Samuel French Acting Edition (1961).

31. *Observer*: 12/4/1931.
32. *The Times*: 11/5/1931.
33. HML: Licence summary card for *Chimneys*, 22/4/1931.
34. LCP: Typescript for *Chimneys* by AC, with licence date, annotations by actor and pencil notes on cast list. LCP Ref: 1931/40.
35. ACA: AC letter to MM (undated: without even a day of the week specified, but clearly from its context December 1931).
36. V&A: Embassy Theatre archive: Programme for Britannia of Billingsgate: 10/11/1931.
37. ACA: AC letter to MM: This is a continuation of the same letter, as in note 35 above, which effectively provides a diary of her journey.
38. V&A: Embassy Theatre archive: Programme for *Mary Broome*: 1/12/931.
39. ACA: AC letter to MM: 23/12/1931.
40. ACA: AC letter to MM: 31/12/1931.
41. *Observer*: 1/11/1931.
42. *The Times*: 26/1/1932.
43. LCPC: *Chimneys* correspondence file. Ref: 1931/10889. Reader's report by G.S. Street: 20/11/1931.
44. ACA: AC, *Chimneys*: typescript, undated.
45. AC, *The Secret of Chimneys* (Pan Books, 1956 edition) pp.72–73.
46. HML: Licence summary card for Broadway production of *Alibi*, 11/12/1931.
47. Booth Theatre Playbill for *The Fatal Alibi*: 9/2/1932 (Theatre Collection, Museum of the City of New York).
48. *New York Times*: 3/10/1932.
49. 'Tintypes': undated syndicated press cutting (Theatre Collection, Museum of the City of New York). From its context, this appears to have been written shortly after the Broadway opening of *The Fatal Alibi.*

Scene Three: Stranger and Stranger

1. HML: Licence summary card for *The Wasps' Nest*, 12/4/1932.
2. *The Times*: 8/6/1932. 'Gala matinee at Drury Lane'.
3. *Radio Times*: 13/6/1937.
4. HMA: Cork to Ober: 20/01/1949.

5. *ACAuto*: p.215.
6. *The Times*: 3/8/1937.
7. *MAC*: p.169.
8. Charles Osborne, *The Life and Crimes of Agatha Christie* (1982): p.95.
9. HML: Licence summary card for 'play and film' adaptation of *The Stranger/Philomel Cottage*, 1/2/1935.
10. HMA: AC to Michael Prichard (no relation): 30/3/1968.
11. ACA: AC, typescript for *The Stranger*, 10/3/1932.
12. Frank Vosper, *Love From a Stranger*, Samuel French Acting Edition (1937): Act III, Scene 2, p.75.
13. Emlyn Williams, *Emlyn* (Penguin, 1976): pp.417–418.
14. Basil Dean, *Seven Ages* (1970): p.332.
15. *The Stage*: 11/4/1935.
16. HML: Licence summary card for tour of *Love From a Stranger*: 11/2/1936. Refers to correspondence with 'HM Tennent' in which Tennent evidently succeeds in reducing the base royalty rate from 5% to 4% and eventually to 3%. It is interesting to note that presentation in New York increased Moss Empires and Howard & Wyndham's share of Christie and Vosper's film sale income from one third to 50%.
17. Emlyn Williams, *Emlyn* (Penguin, 1976): p.424.
18. *The Stage* of 2/5/1935 carries reviews of *Night Must Fall* in Edinburgh and *Love From a Stranger* in Glasgow. In the latter, credited as 'by Agatha Christie and Frank Vosper', the role of 'A Stranger' is listed as having been played by Gwenda Wren. The version of the script being reviewed here is LCP 1935/17.
19. *The Stage*: 6/2/1936. This version of the script was to become LCP 1936/21.
20. *Observer*: 5/4/1936.
21. *The Times*: 1/4/1936.
22. *Daily News* (New York): 30/9/1936.
23. Playbill for *Love From a Stranger*: 29/9/1936 (Theatre Collection, Museum of the City of New York).
24. *New York Times*: 30/9/1936.
25. *New York Evening Journal*: 30/9/1936.
26. *The Times*: 8/3/1937.
27. Records of The *Société des Auteurs et Compositeurs Dramatiques*, Paris. Registration for *L'Inconnu* by Agatha Christie, 23/02/1935.
28. ACA: AC, *Someone at the Window*: typescript (undated). A

further copy of the script appeared in the 2015 catalogue of Sanctuary Books in New York, and I am grateful to Daniel Weschler of Sanctuary Books for photographing opages from it for me, thereby enabling me to verify L.E. Berman's address on the typescript held at ACA. Like the ACA copies of the script, it is undated.

29. *ACAuto*: p.183.
30. Charles Osborne, *The Life and Crimes of Agatha Christie* (1982): p.101.
31. ACA: AC's unpublished handwritten draft Foreword for *Akhnaton*.
32. *MMem*: p.219–220.
33. *ACAuto*: p.335.
34. ACA: Letter from John Gielgud to AC: undated, sent from 31 Avenue Close, NW8.
35. Adelaide Ross (née Phillpotts), *Reverie* (1981): p.184.
36. Ibid.: p.89.
37. *The Times*: 29/9/1922.
38. Eden Phillpotts, *Selected Letters* (1982): Eden Phillpotts' letter to Adelaide Phillpotts: 21/11/1926.
39. Ibid. Eden Phillpotts' letter to Adelaide Phillpotts: 23/1/1927.
40. Adelaide Eden Phillpotts, *Akhnaton* (1926): pp.231–232.
41. AC, *Akhnaton* (1973): pp.152–153.
42. A.E. Grantham, *The Wisdom of Akhnaton* (1920): pp.xi–xvii.
43. *The Times* placed this advertisement on 16/3/1923, under the heading 'A Book About Tutankhamen's Father'; evidently making the most of the opportunity provided by the discovery of Akhnaton's son's tomb a few months earlier. On 12/12/ 1937 yet another play on the subject received a Sunday performance at the Fortune Theatre. Penned by Thomas Baden Morris (1905-1986), best-known as a prolific dramatist for the amateur market, the cast of *The Beautiful One* included Basil Langton as Akhnaton and Anthony Qualye as Thutmis.
44. LCP: Adelaide Eden Phillpotts and Jan Stewart, *The Wasps' Nest*, LCP Ref: 1935/24. Apart from the differently placed apostrophe, the title is identical to that of AC's play.
45. ACA: Two letters from Adelaide Ross to AC dated 1/3/66 and 16/3/66. I have not seen AC's side of the correspondence, but Adelaide's second letter is responding to news contained in AC's reply to her first, and they exchange invitations to visit each other.

46. BDA: Letter from Bernard Merivale (Hughes Massie) to Basil Dean: 13/3/1939. Bernard Merivale (1882–1939) was himself a playwright (including collaborations with Hughes Massie client Arnold Ridley) and screenwriter.
47. BDA: Letter from AC to Basil Dean: 5/4/1939.
48. BDA: Letter from Cork to Basil Dean: 26/5/1939.
49. BDA: Letter from M.F. Watts to Basil Dean: dated 'Tuesday', shown as having been received (Friday) 3 September, 1937. 'You probably won't remember me, but you produced my "The Claimant . . ."' she writes. She sends her congratulations on an unspecified production of Dean's that she has seen and goes on to invite him to lunch; although she expects that 'you are all too busy'.
50. ACA: M.F. Watts, *Oranges and Lemons*: typescript (undated).
51. BDA: Letter from Cork to Basil Dean: 20/6/1939.
52. BDA: Letter from AC to Basil Dean: 14/8/1939.
53. HMA: Letter from Cork to AC: 11/1/1942.
54. Agreement between AC and Arnold Ridley for stage adaptation of *Peril at End House*: 18/7/1938 (University of Bristol Theatre Collection).
55. HML: Licence summary card, 18/7/1938 re: 'Collaboration Agreement' between AC and Arnold Ridley for stage adaptation *Peril at End House*.
56. HML: Licence summary card 11/8/1938, re: 'Commission to adapt play from novel' between Eleven Twenty Three Ltd (Francis L. Sullivan) and Arnold Ridley/Agatha Christie.
57. *Peril at End House* programme, Vaudeville Theatre (University of Bristol Theatre Collection).
58. HMA: Letter from Cork to AC: 11/1/1940.
59. HMA: Letter from Cork to AC: 7/3/1940.
60. *Daily Telegraph*: 2/5/1940.
61. Charles Landstone, *Off-Stage* (1953): p.13.
62. HML: licence summary card of agreement between AC/Arnold Ridley and Samuel French Ltd for 'sole exclusive rights of representation by amateurs and right to publish play in book form' for *Peril at End House*.
63. *The Times*: 14/10/1981.

Scene Four: Broadway Bound

1. For an entertaining insight into the colourful residents of The

Lawn Road flats at this time see David Burke's *The Lawn Road Flats: Spies, Writers and Artists* (2014).

2. For the received wisdom on the history of the book's original title, and subsequent changes to it, see Dennis Sanders and Len Lovallo, *The Agatha Christie Companion* (1985) pp.178–84.

3. HMA: Letter from Cork to AC: 11/1/1940.

4. HMA: Letter from AC to Cork: 16/1/1940.

5. HMA: Letter from Cork to AC: 19/1/1940.

6. HMA: Letter from Cork to AC: 29/1/1940.

7. *ACAuto*: p.471. On the recording of AC's dictation for her autobiography she clearly distinguishes between 'detective stories' and 'thrillers'; commenting that, 'A thriller would be possible to adapt into a play, or more easily at any rate.'

8. *MTM*: p.8.

9. HMA: Letter from AC to Cork: 18/4//1940.

10. HMA: Letter from Cork to AC: 25/4/1940.

11. HMA: Letter from Cork to AC: 10/9/1940.

12. HMA Letter from AC to Cork: 22/10/1940.

13. HMA: Letter from AC to Cork: 17/9/1942.

14. HMA: Letter from Cork to AC: 21/9/1942.

15. HMA: Letter from Cork to AC: 29/9/1942.

16. BBC Radio interview with AC: 13/2/1955: 'Plays are better written quickly,' she says (as opposed to three months for a novel).

17. Barbara Toy, unpublished letter to unknown recipient: 11/10/1994. Cited in the *Dictionary of Literary Biography, Volume 204: British Travel Writers, 1940–1997*: p.288.

18. ACA: *Ten Little Niggers* illustrated nursery rhyme book, signed for AC by Bertie Meyer, Barbara Toy, Irene Hentschel and the original West End cast.

19. HMA: Letter from Cork to AC: 28/10/1942.

20. ACA: Letter from AC to MM: 5/11/1942.

21. HMA: Letter from Cork to AC: 20/11/1942.

22. HMA: Letter from Cork to AC: 24/12/1942.

23. A small private collection of Bertie Meyer's business papers relating to his presentation of AC's plays contains an annotated draft of the four-page licence agreement for *Ten Little Niggers* between Agatha Christie, Bertie Meyer and Farndale Pictures Ltd. A copy of the fully executed agreement is held in the Shubert Archive, New York.

24. ACA: Letter from AC to MM: 18/2/1943.

25. *The Times*: 16/11/1979.

26. *ACAuto*: p.472.
27. ACA: Letter from AC to MM: 23/6/1943.
28. ACA: Letter from AC to MM: 20/9/1963.
29. ACA: Letter from AC to MM: 1/10/1943.
30. ACA: Letter from AC to MM: 30/10/1943.
31. PESA: 'Rules of the People's Entertainment Society', printed by the Co-operative Press Ltd, Manchester, 1942.
32. PESA: Annual Report of The People's Entertainment Society, 1943.
33. PESA: PES Share Application form and accompanying information, 1944.
34. ACA: Letter from AC to MM: 17/11/1943.
35. ACA: Letter from Stephen Glanville to AC: 18/11/1943.
36. *The Times*: 18/11/1943.
37. *Observer*: 21/11/1943.
38. *ACAuto*: p.472.
39. AC, *Ten Little Niggers*, Samuel French Acting Edition, 1944: Act II; Scene I. p.46. (As *And Then There Were None* in *MOP*: p.47).
40. See Anselm Heinrich, 'Theatre in Britain During the Second World War', *New Theatre Quarterly*, 26:1 (2010), in which he argues that the change in both government policy and public responses to theatre caused by the Second World War directly resulted in what Laurence Olivier described as the 'rebirth of the theatre'. See also Charles Landstone, *Off-Stage: A Personal Record of the First Twelve Years of State Drama in Great Britain* (1953), and Basil Dean, *The Theatre at War* (1956). The latter includes an extraordinary photograph of Ivor Novello performing *Love From a Stranger* for ENSA on an open-air stage to the troops in Normandy.
41. ACA: programme for *Ten Little Niggers* at the St James's Theatre, 1943.
42. LCPC: *Ten Little Niggers* correspondence file. Ref: 1943/4955.
43. Quoted in Darrell M. Newton: *Paving the Empire Road; BBC Television and Black Britons* (2011): pp.23-4.
44. HML: Licence summary card for the US Production of *Ten Little Indians*: 26/6/44.
45. Chach/Fletcher/Swartz/Wang, *The Shuberts Present: 100 years of American Theater* (2001): p.6.
46. *The Times*: 28/12/1953.
47. Basil Dean, *Seven Ages* (1970): p.162.

48. SA: Memo from Adolph Kaufman to Lee Shubert: 2/6/1944.
49. SA: Memo from Adolph Kaufman to Lee Shubert: 4/3/1944.
50. The lengthy negotiations between the Shuberts and RKO fill several files at the Shubert Archive, and are summarised in a memo from Kaufman to Lee Shubert and others dated 27/3/44.
51. SA: Memo from C.P. Grenecker to Lee and J.J. Shubert: 'The new Jed Harris play, *The Fatal Alibi*, opened at the Booth Theatre last night and in the opinion of many it did not get over . . . the morning notices are not good.'
52. Hamlin Garland in *My Friendly Contemporaries: A Literary Log* (Macmillan, New York, 1932: p.493) notes that, according to Conrad, 'America would not buy a book about niggers, so my publishers changed the title to *Children of the Sea*. I accepted the change. I was in no situation to object.' The *Catalogue of the Ashley Library, Vol.1*, edited by T.J. Wise (limited edition private printing, London, 1922) contains a photograph of Joseph Conrad's undated handwritten flyleaf inscription to Wise on a copy of *The Children of the Sea: A Tale of the Forecastle* (Dodd, Mead and Company, 1897) in which Conrad notes that 'I consented to change of title under protest. The argument was that the American public would not but a book about a Nigger.' *The Nigger of the Narcissus* was, in fact, subsequently reissued in the USA under its original title. The intervening forty years had seen the significant cultural changes brought about by mass migration of the African American population from the rural South to the industrial North, but although the American edition of Christie's novel changed its setting from 'Nigger Island' to 'Indian Island', and the poem's protagonists accordingly from 'Nigger boys' to 'Injuns', the phrase 'Nigger in the woodpile' was retained; indicating, as Alison Light observes, 'some confusion about the issue' (Alison Light: *Forever England: Feminism, Literature and Conservatism between the Wars* (1991): p.243), and implying that the publisher's agenda was not necessarily motivated principally by a desire to avoid offence to African Americans, as some commentators have contended.
53. *NYT*: 19/12/1943.
54. Two months prior to completing their acquisition of the stage rights for *Ten Little Niggers*, the Shuberts applied to the United States Copyright Office to register a play called *Ten Little Indians* and a "melodrama" called *The Unknown Host*. On 5/5/1944,

both titles received copyright registration certificates valid for an initial twenty-eight years. In each case the owner of the copyright was listed as Select Theatres Corp., while the "author" was credited as Barre Dunbar, who was head of the Shuberts' script licensing department. The certificates, and correspondence relating to them, are held in the SA.

55. SA: interim statement of Operating Profit for *Ten Little Indians*: 9/12/1944.
56. Laura Thompson, *Agatha Christie; an English Mystery* (Headline Review, 2008): p.357.
57. *NYT*: 28/6/1944.
58. *New York Herald Tribune*: 28/6/1944.
59. *New York Post*: 28/6/1944.
60. *New York Journal – American*: 28/6/1944.
61. *New York World – Telegram*: 28/6/1944.
62. SA: Promotional leaflets for *Ten Little Indians*, 1944.
63. SA: Memo from Adolph Kaufman to Lee Shubert: 21/7/44.
64. SA: Playbill for *Ten Little Indians*, Broadhurst Theatre, 1944.
65. SA: Letter from Lee Shubert to the Actors' Equity Association: 16/3/1944.
66. SA: Playbill for *Ten Little Indians*, Broadhurst Theatre, 1944.
67. SA: Letter from the Actors' Equity Association to Lee Shubert: 17/3/1944.
68. HML: Overseas licence summary card for *Ten Little Niggers*: 13/11/44. Herbert Lom would go on to star in both the 1974 and 1989 films of the novel.
69. HML: Overseas licence summary card for *Ten Little Niggers*: 1/12/44.
70. *The Stage*: 27/9/1945.
71. ACA: Letter from AC to Rosalind Hicks: undated (July 1971).

Scene Five: Towards Zero

1. ACA: Letter from AC to MM: 30/10/1943.
2. HMA: Letter from Cork to AC: 4/9/1942.
3. HMA: Letter from AC to Cork: 17/9/1942.
4. HMA: Letter from AC to Michael Prichard: 30/3/1968.
5. HMA: Letter from Cork to AC: 18/10/1942.
6. HMA: Letter from AC to Cork: 27/10/1942.
7. ACA: Letter from AC to MM: 9/12/1942.
8. AC, *Murder on the Nile*: Samuel French Acting Edition (1948):

Act I, Scene I: p.20.

9. ACA: Letter from Cork to AC: 24/12/1942.

10. HML: Licence summary card for *Moon on the Nile*: 18/1/1943.

11. ACA: AC to Cork: 8/2/1943.

12. ACA: Letter from AC to MM: 14/2/1943.

13. AC, *Murder on the Nile*: Samuel French Acting Edition (1948): Act I, Scene I: p.25.

14. ACA: AC, *Moon on the Nile*: typescript (undated).

15. LCP: AC, *Hidden Horizon*: typescript (LCP Ref: 1934/35).

16. ACA: AC, *Hidden Horizon*, typescript (undated).

17. ACA: Letter from AC to MM: 9/1/1944.

18. ACA: Letter from AC to MM 14/1/1944.

19. *Dundee Evening Telegraph*: 15/1/1944.

20. *Dundee Evening Telegraph*: 18/1/1944.

21. HML: Licence summary card for *Appointment with Death*, 5/3/1944.

22. Co-production agreement for *Appointment with Death* between Bertie Meyer and Derrick de Marney, 15/11/1944 (private collection of Meyer/Christie contracts).

23. AC, *Appointment with Death*: Act I, Scene 1: *MOP*: p.97.

24. LCPC: *Appointment with Death* correspondence. Ref: 944/5971. Internal memo from H.G. Game: 27/12/1944.

25. SA: Commissioning Agreement between Select Operating Corp (Shuberts) and AC for an adaptation of *Towards Zero*: 9/8/1944.

26. HML: Licence summary card for *Towards Zero*, play commissioned by Select Operating Corp (Shuberts) from AC: 9/8/1944.

27. ACA: Letter from AC to MM: 3/1/1945.

28. ACA: Letter from AC to MM: 31/1/1945.

29. ACA: Programme for *Appointment with Death*, King's Theatre, Glasgow: 29/1/1945.

30. HMA: Letter from Cork to AC: 20/2/1945.

31. HMA: Letter from Bertie Meyer to AC: 22/2/1945.

32. HMA: Letter from Cork to AC: 19/3/1945.

33. *The Times*: 2/4/1945.

34. *Observer*: 8/4/1945.

35. *The Stage*: 5/4/1945.

36. HML: Licence summary card for assignment of Eleven Twenty Three Ltd's licence for *Hidden Horizon* to Reandco: 7/2/1945.

37. ACA: letter from AC to MM: 11/2/1945.

38. *The Stage*: 12/4/1945.

39. HMA: Letter from Cork to AC: 6/6/1945.

40. HMA: Letter from Cork to AC: 23/8/1945.
41. SA: US licence for *Hidden Horizon* between Reandco and Albert de Courville/Lee Shubert: 1/8/1945.
42. SA: Memo from Adolph Kaufman to Lee Shubert: 9/8/1944.
43. HMA: Letter from Cork to AC: 16/1/1945.
44. SA: Agreement between Select Operating Corp (Shuberts) Robert Harris: 5/6/1945.
45. SA: Memo from Adolph Kaufman to Lee Shubert: 30/6/1945.
46. HMA: Letter from Lee Shubert to AC: 18/10/1945.
47. SA: AC, *Towards Zero* typescript (undated: autumn 1944). Some fairly detailed notes for this script appear in AC's Notebook 32 at the ACA. In her forward to her autobiography, dated 2 April 1950, AC explores some similar ideas to those discussed by Audrey and Angus:

I have always thought life exciting and I still do.

Because one knows so little of it – only one's own tiny part – one is like an actor who has a few lines to say in Act I. He has a type-written script with his cues, and that is all he can know. He hasn't read the play. Why should he? His but to say 'The telephone is out of order, Madam' and then retire into obscurity.

But when the curtain goes up on the day of the performance, he will hear the play through, and he will be there to line up with the rest, and take his call.

To be part of something one doesn't understand is, I think, one of the most intriguing things about life.

I like living. I have sometimes been wildly despairing, acutely miserable, racked with sorrow, but through it all I know that just to *be* alive is a grand thing. (*ACAuto:* p.13)

48. *NYT:* 3/9/1945. *NYT* (3/3/1945) had announced 'Agatha Christie has dramatized another of her mysteries, *Towards Zero*, and the completed script is expected in the Shubert offices momentarily'; it had in fact been received by them at the end of the previous year.
49. *Martha's Vineyard Gazette*: 7 September, 1945 (*Martha's Vineyard Gazette* archive). A truly historic press cutting. The Martha's Vineyard Playhouse where *Towards Zero* was presented is not the theatre of the same name that exists today. Clarence Derwent's long out-of-print autobiography, *The*

Clarence Derwent Story (1953), notes simply that, 'Before leaving Martha's Vineyard I directed a new Agatha Christie mystery play, *Towards Zero*, but its title proved prophetic and it joined the long list of summer-theatre tryouts which never reach Broadway.' (p.216)

50. HMA: Ober to Cork: 28/11/1945.
51. HMA: Ober to Cork: 5/12/1945.
52. HML: Licence summary card for *Murder on the Nile*: 29 October 1945.
53. Ibid.
54. *The Times*: 20/3/1946.
55. *Daily Mail*: 20/3/46.
56. *Observer*: 24/3/1946.
57. *The Stage*: 21/3/1946.
58. *Daily Telegraph*: 20/3/46.
59. *The Times*: 22/6/1963

60. SA: Memo from J.J. Shubert to Lee Shubert: 4/7/1946.
61. HMA: Letter from Ober to Cork: 13/7/1945.
62. SA: Letter from Ober to Lee Shubert: 27/7/1945.
63. SA: *Hidden Horizon* US licence extension, between Ober (on behalf of Reandco) and Shubert/de Courville).
64. *NYT*: 30/8/1946.
65. SA: Press release for *Hidden Horizon*: 14/9/1946.
66. *NYT*: 19/9/1946.
67. SA: Playbill for *Hidden Horizon*: 19/9/1946.
68. *New York Post*: 20/9/1946.
69. *Herald Tribune*: 20/9/1946.
70. *NYT*: 20/9/1946.
71. *New Yorker*: 29/9/1946.
72. Final accounts for the Broadway production of *Hidden Horizon* (Katharine Cornell papers: Billy Rose Theatre Division, New York Public Library for the Performing Arts, Lincoln Centre, NY).
73. HMA: Memo from Cork to Ivan von Auw (on behalf of Ober): 3/10/1947.
74. *The Stage*: 22/4/1948.
75. ACA: most of these ideas appear in AC's Notebook 63A, around notes for the stage adaptation of *Death on the Nile*.
76. ACA: AC's Notebook 63.
77. HML: licence summary card for adaptation rights to *Murder*

at the Vicarage, with subsequent production licence (9/9/49) to Bertie Meyer.

78. BDA: Letter from AC to Basil Dean: 3/8/1939.
79. HMA: Letter from EC to AC: 24/12/1942.
80. HMA: Letter from AC to Cork: 22/6/1949.
81. HMA: Letter from Cork to AC: 2/3/1949.
82. Draft investment agreement for *Murder at the Vicarage* between Bertie Meyer and Howard & Wyndham Ltd: 6/9/1949. (Meyer/Christie contracts, private collection).
83. HMA: Letter from AC to Michael Prichard: 30/3/1968.
84. A Notice in the London Gazette of 30/1/1945 announces that 'Marion Gywnedd Beevor, Spinster, a natural born British subject at present residing at Flat 3, 73 St. James's Street, Westminster, SW1, intends after the expiration of twenty-one days from the date of publication of this notice to assume the name of Moie Charles.' The Notice of her death placed by her family in *The Times* (19/12/1957) confirms that she had been known by both names.
85. See Michael Thornton, *Daily Mail Online*: 28/3/2008: 'The Siren Who Disappeared: Uncovering the Mystery of Britain's First Sex Symbol' (re: Frances Day).
86. *The Times*, 30 June 1959.
87. *The Stage*: 20/10/1949.
88. PESA: Programme for *Murder at the Vicarage*, Royal Court Theatre, Liverpool: 5/12/1949.
89. *The Times*: 15/12/1949.
90. *Observer*: 18/12/1949.
91. PESA: PES Annual Report: 1950.
92. HMA: Letter from Cork to AC: March 1950.
93. Laura Thompson, *Agatha Christie: An English Mystery* (Headline Review, 2008): p.357.
94. *ACAuto*: pp.474-5. On the recording of AC's dictation for her autobiography she is at pains to point out that whilst a play may fail because of its cast, 'I don't mean that they acted it badly, but because very often they were just the wrong people to act that particular part.'
95. *ACAuto*: p.472.

ACT TWO: SAUNDERS SAVES THE DAY

Scene One: The Binkie Effect

1. Kitty Black, *Upper Circle* (1984): pp.154–5.
2. Director Tyrone Guthrie's oft-quoted assertion that Beaumont's 'iron fist was wrapped in fifteen pastel-shaded velvet gloves, but no-one who has known Binkie can for a moment fail to realise that there is an iron fist', first appeared in his autobiography, *A Life in the Theatre* (Hamish Hamilton, 1960: p.143).
3. Kitty Black, *Upper Circle* (1984): p.21.
4. *The Times*: 23/3/1973: The 'make or break' comment is from Tyrone Guthrie's *A Life in the Theatre* (see 2 above): p.142.
5. *MTM*: pp.68–70.
6. *MTM*: p.106.
7. HML: Licence summary card, *Murder at the Vicarage* post-West End tour: 16/2/1950.
8. *MTM*: p.107.
9. *ACAuto*: p.472-3.
10. ACA: Letter from AC to Rosalind Hicks (undated: July, 1971).
11. *ACAuto*: p.473.
12. *MMem*: p.217.
13. AC, *The Hollow*, Act I (*MOP*: p.204).
14. *Daily Telegraph*, Obituary of HG: 31/3/2004.
15. HG's third wife, Carmel Lytton, in editing his posthumously published autobiography, notes that 'the later Hubert was somehow mellower' (*Maybe It's Because . . . ?*, 2005: Foreword). Not having met him, I can only respond to his writings on the subject of his work with Christie.
16. *MTM*: p.108.
17. *MTM*: p.109.
18. HML: Licence summary cards: PS optioned the touring rights to *Black Coffee* on 24/8/1950, the West End rights to *The Hollow* on 7/9/1950 and the West End rights to *Black Coffee* on 7/12/1950.
19. *MTM*: p.111.
20. PSP: Letter from Mary Glasgow (Secretary General, Arts Council of Great Britain) to Peter Saunders: 9/12/1950.
21. David Pattie, *Modern British Playwriting: the 1950s* (2012): p.207.
22. *The Stage*, Obituary of Anthony Field: 21/4/2014.

23. *Bath Chronicle*: 3/5/1969. In an interview with Mackintosh, 'probably the youngest manager in the country' and at that time about to present a tour of *Black Coffee* at the Theatre Royal, Bath, he comments 'Agatha Christie is dependable, good box-office, and we aim to put one of her thrillers and a classic on tour every spring and autumn.'

24. *MTM*: p.111.

25. Richard Huggett, *Binkie Beaumont* (1989): p.329.

26. *The Times*: 20/8/1966.

27. *MMem*: p.216.

28. HMA: AC to Cork: 6/1/1951.

29. PPS: PS to Cork: 10/1/1951.

30. HMA: Letter from AC to Cork, sent from Iraq, dated 'Monday': 'Can you arrange for some flowers to be delivered to my actresses? . . . Oh dear, I hope it will be a success. I do think it is a good cast and well produced and I *want* it to be a success. The omens are good since it opens on St Agatha's day – a candle for St Agatha.'

31. HMA: Letter from Cork to AC: 8/2/1951.

32. HMA: Letter from Cork to AC: 22/8/1952.

33. HMA Letter from Cork to AC 8/2/1951.

34. HMA: Letter from AC to Cork 14/2/1951.

35. PSP: Letter from Rosalind Hicks to PS: 18/2/1951.

36. PSP: Letter from PS to Rosalind Hicks: 28/2/1951.

37. ACA: Letter from AC to Rosalind Hicks: 23/2/1951.

38. HMA: Letter from Cork to AC: 1/3/1951.

39. *MTM*: p.114.

40. HMA: Letter from Cork to AC: 20/4/1951.

41. *The Stage*: 7/6/1951.

42. *Evening Standard*: 8/6/1951.

43. *Evening News*: 8/6/951.

44. *Illustrated London News*: 23/6/1951.

45. *Observer*: 10/6/1951.

46. *News of the World*: 10/6/1951.

47. *Sunday Chronicle*: 10/6/1951.

48. PSP: Publicity leaflet for *The Hollow*, 1951.

49. HGP: rehearsal script of *The Hollow*, signed by PS.

50. *ACATM*: p.50.

51. HGP: HG's rehearsal script of *The Hollow*.

52. HG, *Maybe It's Because* (2005): p.255.

53. *The Stage*: 11/10/1951.

54. *MTM*: p.115.
55. *The Stage*: 11/10/1951.
56. PSP: Programme for *The Hollow*, Fortune Theatre, 1951.
57. PSP: PS to Beryl Baxter: 15/2/1951.
58. PSP: From a shop in Gerrard St, London to PS: 18/10/1951 (signature and name of shop unclear).
59. PSP: PS correspondence with H.J. Malden, manager of The Ambassadors, 9–12/2/1952.
60. PSP: Letter from PS to R B Salisbury re; investment terms in *The Hollow*: 13/1/1951.
61. PSP: Statement of weekly running accounts for *The Hollow*, Ambassadors Theatre, week ending 24/11/1951.
62. PSP: *The Hollow*, artists' contracts summary sheet.
63. PSP: Letter from PS to investors in *The Hollow*: 31/10/1951.
64. PSP: *The Hollow* final accounts statement (undated; probably September, 1958).
65. *MTM*: p.7.
66. SA: Licence for Select Theatres Corp to produce *The Hollow* in the USA: 20/6/51.
67. SA: Agreement between Select Theatres Corp and Sherman S Krellberg: 12/6/1952.
68. HMA: Letter from Ober to Cork: 2/8/1952.
69. HMA: Comments made by Howard Reinheimer in a telephone call to a member of Ober's staff: transcribed by the staff member and forwarded to Ober (1/8/1952). Forwarded by Ober to Cork (2/8/1952).
70. SA: Letter from PS to Lee Shubert: 19/3/1952.
71. SA: Letter from Cork to Lee Shubert: 17/6/1952.
72. SA: Letter from Cork to Lee Shubert.
73. SA: This exchange took place between 30/8/1952 and 2/9/1952.
74. SO: A series of telegrams and letters between Cork and Lee Shubert, relating to changing the title of *The Hollow* to *The Suspects*, culminates with this on 23/9/1952. A similar exchange had taken place the previous month relating to changing it to *The House Guest*, with Cork expressing his client's dislike of the suggestion whilst leaving the decision to Shubert.
75. Programme for *The Suspects*: Lester Sweyd Collection, Billy Rose Theatre Division of the New York Public Library for the Performing Arts, NY.
76. Unattributed press cutting: w/c 6/10/1952: Lester Sweyd

Collection (see 71 above).

77. *Boston Herald*: 19/10/1952.
78. *Boston Post*: 28/10/1952.
79. *NYT*: 31/10/1952.
80. For Jerome Robbins' role in giving evidence to the House Committee on Un-American activities, see Deborah Jowitt, *Jerome Robbins: His Life, His Theater, His Dance* (Simon & Schuster, USA, 2005) p.228–30.
81. HMA: Letter from Ober to Cork: 7/11/1952.
82. SA: Select Theatres Corp licence for *The Hollow*: 20/6/1951.
83. HML: licence summary card for *The Hollow* (9/7/1950) and SA: Agreement between PS and Lee & J.J. Shubert for American presentation of *The Hollow* (20/6/1951).
84. SA: Letter from PS to Lee Shubert: 14/1/1953.
85. SA: Letter from Lee Shubert to PS: 22/1/1953.
86. SA: Letter from John Shubert to Ober: 16/7/1954.
87. SA: Memo from Milton Weir (Shubert lawyer) to Lee Shubert: 17/12/1953: 'it is extremely doubtful in our opinion that you could earn the subsidiary rights by reviving the play.'

Scene Two: The Disappearing Director

1. HMA: Letter from AC to Cork: 18/8/51.
2. HMA: Letter from Cork to AC: 20/8/51.
3. Details of this delightful ditty were sent to the author by Eileen Cottis of the Society for Theatre Research on 8/3/2104. As an Assistant Examiner of Plays, Troubridge reported to Charles Heriot (the Senior Examiner of Plays), who in turn reported to Brigadier Sir Norman Wilmhurst Gwatkin (the Assistant Comptroller of the Lord Chamberlain's Office), who in turn reported to Sir Terence Nugent, the Comptroller of the Lord Chamberlain's Office. By all accounts, they were a lively bunch of characters.
4. *ACAuto*: p.475.
5. *ACAuto*: p.510-511.
6. Miller Family Album of Confessions, Torquay Museum: page dated 'Nov 27/10'.
7. ACA: AC, *Three Blind Mice* typescript (undated). The current published version replaces the 'one or two rather incongruous bits of Victorian furniture' with a single Victorian armchair amongst the 'shabby and old-fashioned' furniture.
8. 'Peter Saunders Presents *The Mousetrap Story*' (1992): p.5.

9. LCPC: *The Mousetrap* correspondence file. Ref: 1952/4570. Reader's Report for *The Mousetrap* by C.D. Heriot 17/9/1952.

10. ACA: AC, *Three Blind Mice* typescript (undated). On 20/4/1951 Cork wrote to AC: 'I am not at all sure that we can get away with a twelve minute scene in the London street dominated by Alf and Bill.'

11. LCPC: *The Mousetrap* correspondence file. Ref: 1952/4570. Reader's Report for *The Mousetrap* by C.D. Heriot: 17/9/1952. The copy given to AC was actually a certified duplicate of that submitted to the Lord Chamberlain's office, which retained the original, with the word 'cancelled' stamped over the opening pages featuring Bill and Alf.

12. HMA: Letter from Cork to AC: 30/8/1951.

13. As *The Mousetrap* was owned by Mathew Prichard's Trust, Hughes Massie's own licensing records do not include any significant information about the play. The underlying contracts form part of the current business affairs of the operation, but PSP includes a two-page typewritten summary of the production's labyrinthine contractual history, presumably drawn up in preparation for its sale on Saunders' retirement in 1994. Of the dozen transactions listed, the first is AC's assignment of the rights to her grandson, and the second is Saunders' acquisition of his original licence on 5/11/1951.

14. HMA: Letter from Cork to AC: 17/9/1952.

15. *ACAuto*: p.512.

16. *MMem*: p.218.

17. MTM: p.213.

18. *ACAuto*: p.530. In 2015, a year after Richard Attenborough's death, the Garrick Club in London, which he had joined in 1950, acquired his rehearsal script of *The Mousetrap* as a memento of their much-treasured member. Carrying the play's original title, this is one of the few extant copies of the script to include the subsequently deleted 'Bill and Alf' scene.

19. *Independent*: 12/11/1998.

20. Peter Cotes, *Thinking Aloud* (1993): p.118.

21. PSP: Letter from PS to John Boulting: 11/1/1952.

22. Letter from AC to Mrs Fink, 12/6/1972, included in the 1976 sales catalogue of Kenneth W Rendell Inc historical manuscripts dealer (South Natick, Massachusetts).

23. *MTM*: p.120.

24. *ACATM*: p.98.

25. In 1982, at the age of 76, John Fernald would eventually become the sixteenth resident director of *The Mousetrap*.
26. Peter Cotes, *Thinking Aloud* (1993): p.118.
27. PSP: Letter from PS to Peter Cotes: 30/8/1952.
28. Peter Cotes, *Thinking Aloud* (1993): p.117.
29. *Observer*: 30/10/1952.
30. *Sketch*: 17/12/1952.
31. *Punch*: 10/12/1952.
32. *The Times*: 26/11/1952.
33. *Variety*: 3/12/1952.
34. PSP: Letter from PS to Eric Glass, Peter Cotes' agent: 27/7/1953.
35. *ACATM*: p.156.
36. Peter Cotes, *Thinking Aloud* (1993): p.117.
37. Letter from PS to Birnberg & Co, solicitors: 1/8/1985: marked 'not sent'.
38. *ACAuto*: p.518. There are pictures of AC cutting splendidly decorated cakes at such events, but none of her cutting 'tapes.' I suggest this may be an error by those responsible for transcribing the recordings which she dictated for her autobiography.
39. PSP: Publicity leaflet for *The Mousetrap*, 1952.
40. Sent on 9/9/1957 from Bermuda to AC c/o The Ambassadors Theatre, Coward's telegram was discovered by Gloucestershire furniture restorer Clive Payne, while working on an old bureau purchased at auction at Greenway. Along with it was a receipt, dating from 1952 and addressed to Mrs Mallowan, for underwear and other items of clothing. (BBC News digital archive: 4/8/2011).
41. The Noël Coward Archive contains AC's reply to Coward, dated 'Sept 14';
    'Dear Noel (*sic*) Coward,
    How very charming of you to send me a cable of congratulation. It restored my morale which was seriously impaired by constantly being photographed in juxtaposition to young and beautiful stars – which made my aged face look even worse than it is!
    It's fine to have an unexpected success in one's (old) age – but as one fan wrote to me reproachfully: "I had no idea what an old lady you were. It makes me feel quite differently towards you – "
    I'll send you a cable when "Nude with Violin" does me down.

It's a glorious play – one of your best – I do admire real wit
– there's little enough of it about, goodness knows.

As you may gather I've always been one of your most fervent
admirers – from The Vortex (a most moving play) onwards –

Mes homages! And thank you –

Agatha Chrsitie

How wise you are to live in a decent climate!'

The sentiments expressed about being photographed with
actresses are similar to those in a passage from AC's autobiography (*ACAuto*: p.518); it was clearly something that preyed
on her mind.

Nude with Violin, which had opened almost a year previously at the Globe Theatre starring John Gielgud, had proved
a modest success; but would fail to give *The Mousetrap* a run
for its money, and closed the following February.

The Coward archive also contains a similar AC response to
a telegram which he evidently sent in January 1971 to congratulate her on the announcement of her damehood. 'I must say
that I'm very surprised to find myself a dame. Success of a
sausage machine perhaps' she observes in a letter dated
4/1/1971.

42. *ACATM*: p.112.

43. *MMem*: p.218. Mallowan cites the seating capacity of The
Ambassadors as having been 490 but, despite the fact that
Saunders increased its capacity by removing an aisle, this
seems highly unlikely given the very small dimensions of the
auditorium. The Ambassadors opened in 1913, and was
designed by architect W.G.R. Sprague, who three years later
would also be responsible for the St Martin's Theatre opposite.
The highest seating capacity for the Ambassadors that I can
find reference to during the run of *The Mousetrap* (other than
Mallowan's) is 453 (theatrestrust.org.uk).

44. *Sunday Times*: 15/10/1961. Interview with AC by crime writer
Julian Symons (1912-1994)

45. *ACAuto*: pp.511-12.

46. *MMem*: p.216.

47. Although it has never appeared at the National Theatre,
Christie's work has been played on the stage of the Shakespeare
Memorial Theatre (from 1961 the Royal Shakespeare Theatre),
Stratford-Upon-Avon. Three weeks before *The Mousetrap's*
London opening, while *The Mousetrap* itself was on its pre-

West End tour, Geoffrey Hastings' post-West End tour of *The Hollow* appeared at Stratford. (Leaflet for *The Hollow*, Shakespeare Memorial Theatre, 3 November 1952; private collection).

48. *The Stage*: 2/4/1955: 'Peter Saunders's Long-Term Deal'.
49. Peter Cotes, *Thinking Aloud* (1993): p.127.
50. PSP: Letter from PS to Jack Tinker: 30/8/1985.
51. PSP: Letter from PS to Peter Cotes' agent, Eric Glass: 6/4/1992.
52. PSP: Contract between PS and Peter Cotes 3/10/1952. Interestingly, the contract, of which there are various drafts, was not actually signed until three days before the production opened.
53. *MTM*: p.121.
54. PSP: Letter from PS to Peter Cotes: 30/8/1952.
55. PSP: Handwritten letter from Peter Cotes (on BBC notepaper) to PS: 1/9/1952.
56. *MTM*: p.9.

Scene Three: Saunders' Folly

1. *MTM*: p.139.
2. PS, *Scales of Justice*: Samuel French Acting Edition, 1988. The Samuel French edition states that the play was 'first presented' at the Redgrave Theatre Farnham on 17 June 1987, and gives full details of the production. Confusingly, it then says that it was 'originally produced at the Perth Theatre, Scotland, September 1978'. Perth Rep's Fiftieth Anniversary brochure (1985) states that the production was directed by Joan Knight.
3. *Daily Express*: w/c 6/2/1956: 'By Agatha Christie: special adaptation for *Daily Express* by Peter Saunders'.
4. See: James E Wise and Scott Baron, *International Stars at War* (2001): p.215 – Leo Genn. Genn would later appear as 'General Mandrake' in George Pollock's 1965 film of *Ten Little Indians*.
5. *Daily Telegraph*: 10/2/14.
6. ACA: AC, *Witness for the Prosecution* typescript (undated).
7. *ACATM*: pp.109–10.
8. *MTM*: p.140.
9. PSP: Contract between PS and Wallace Douglas (c/o Film Rights Ltd): 21/7/1953.
10. *ACAuto*: p.515.

11. *MTM*: p.140.
12. PSP: Letter from Peter Saunders to Roger Livesey: 15/3/1953.
13. *MTM*: p.140.
14. PSP: *Witness for the Prosecution* production file. Letters from AC to PS are originals (all typed, but with her signature), but the ones from PS to AC are carbon copies, so some of his sign-offs are missing. The ACA does not appear to hold the originals of the PS side of the correspondence.
15. AC, *Witness for the Prosecution*, Author's Note: *MOP*: p.370.
16. *MTM*: p.141.
17. Ibid.
18. PSP: Contract between PS and Winter Garden Theatre (London) Ltd: 29/9/1953.
19. PSP: Letter from PS to Roy J Bowles of the Musicians' Union 15/10/1953, and reply 21/10/1953.
20. PSP: Publicity leaflet for *Witness for the Prosecution*, Winter Garden Theatre, 1953.
21. *MTM*: p.73. Saunders' papers show that he subsequently sub-licensed the Australian rights to *Witness for the Prosecution* to Prince Littler's brother, Emile (he who had objected to the title of *Three Blind Mice*), and it occurs to me that this might have been by way of a 'thank you' for Prince's intervention. Of Howard & Wyndham's cancellation of the booking Saunders notes 'There was just nothing I could do. I could have sued them, of course, but what good would that have done me? They knew that although legally they had no right to do it, in this close-knit business I had to accept the position.'
22. *MTM*: p.143.
23. *MMem*: p.216.
24. PSP: Letter from PS to Malcolm MacDougall: 30/10/1953.
25. *Sunday Express*: 1/11/1953.
26. *Daily Telegraph*: 29/10/1953.
27. *Daily Express*: 29/10/1953.
28. *Daily Mail*: 29/10/1953.
29. *Daily Mirror*: 29/10/1953.
30. *Herald Tribune*: 14/8/1954.
31. PSP: Letter from PS to Walter F Kerr: 21/9/1954.
32. John Counsell, *Counsell's Opinion* (1963): p.200..
33. PSP: Letter from PS to Graham Muir (BBC TV): 13/10/1933.
34. PSP: Letter from PS to Ralph Wotherspoon: 12/8/1953.
35. PSP: Aurora Productions: *Witness for the Prosecution* Final

Statement of Profit (undated: February 1962).

36. *ACAuto*: pp.514–6.
37. *MTM*: p.7.
38. *MMem*: p.216.
39. HMA: Letter from Cork to Ober: 2/12/1953.
40. Basil Dean, *Seven Ages* (1970): p.163.
41. *The Times*: 3/1/1969.
42. *MTM*: p.148.
43. PSP: Letter from PS to S.J. Passmore (on behalf of Gilbert Miller): 10/11/1953.
44. HML: Licence summary card: 26/11/1953.
45. *Witness for the Prosecution* Playbill (Theatre Collection, Museum of the City of New York).
46. *Witness for the Prosecution* brochure (Theatre Collection, Museum of the City of New York): This glossy publication was packed with photographs and biographies of the performers and creative team, along with a page about the history of the Old Bailey. It appears to have been produced and marketed by Miller as an alternative to the (free) Playbill.
47. HML: Licence summary card: 27/11/1953.
48. LOC: Letter from Francis Sullivan to Gilbert Miller: 25/1/1954.
49. HMA: Letter from Cork to Ober: 29/4/1954.
50. LOC: Letter from D.A. Clarke-Smith to Gilbert Miller: undated.
51. *MTM*: p.149.
52. *ACATM*: p.52. To use HG's own, inimitable phraseology, 'every character is 'an inflated doll whose air gets let out as the play progresses.'
53. *MAC*: p.187. Law's analysis of Christie's dialogue, in which she also maintains that '. . . if you can act in an Agatha Christie play you can play in anything. It's rather like a lesson. I think that everyone at drama school should be made to do an Agatha Christie . . . it is a real test for everyone,' has been interpreted as criticism; particularly as it leads off with 'Christie's dialogue does not bear any resemblance to what one says in normal life . . .' However, the same could be said of the work of many highly successful playwrights; and Robyns is, I think, wrong to characterise these comments, presumably made in an interview with Law, as necessarily negative. My own experience of working with actors on Agatha Christie plays is that, as Law says, the dialogue 'works 100%' if the actors 'make it real'. Peter Cotes repeats Law's remarks verbatim, and without attri-

bution to Robyns, in *Thinking Aloud* (1993) at the start of his chapter on working with Christie (p.113).

54. LOC: Letter from George Banyai to Peter Saunders: 3/12/1954.
55. LOC: Letter from Robert Lewis to George Banyai: 5/2/1954.
56. PSP: Letter from Robert Lewis to PS: 29/3/1954.
57. PSP: Handwritten letter from Patricia Jessel to PS.
58. PSP: Letter from Donald Flamm to PS: 17/12/1954.
59. *NYT*: 17/12/1954.
60. *New York Herald Tribune*: 17/12/1954.
61. *New York Post*: 17/12/1954.
62. Cited in *Witness for the Prosecution* souvenir brochure (see 46 above).
63. Ibid.
64. *World-Telegram and Sun*: 17/12/1954.
65. *Sunday News*: 19/12/1954: Strictly speaking, John Chapman's article in the Sunday edition of the paper reviews *Witness for the Prosecution* in the context of an article about the wider subject of the public's fascination with murder generally. However, that didn't prevent Maney from making the most of the article's headline on advertising material for the production. Chapman's original review had run in the Friday (17/12/1954) edition under the less catchy headline 'Slick and Surprising Courtroom Play'.
66. HMA: Cork to Ober: 14/10/1954.
67. HMA: Ober to Cork: 18/11/1954.
68. PSP: Handwritten letters from Francis L Sullivan to PS: 8/6/1955 and subsequent (undated) letter in response to PS's reply.
69. PSP: Letter from PS to George Banyai: 4/2/1955.
70. LOC: Letter from Gilbert Miller to George Banyai confirming Sullivan's deal: 8/6/1955.
71. PSP: Figures cited in letter from George Banyai to PS.
72. PS: HMA: Letter from Cork to Ober: 8/9/1955.
73. HMA: Letter from Ober to Cork: 15/3/1955.
74. LOC: Letter from George Banyai to PS: circa February 1955.
75. LOC: Letter from PS to George Banyai: 7/3/1955.
76. PSP: Letter from PS to Robert Lewis: 21/3/1955.
77. PSP: Letter from Robert Lewis to PS: 29/3/1955.
78. The Stage: 26/1/1956. The sum of £116,000 was 'believed to be an all-time record for a British play'. By that time Miller had in fact already sold the film rights on for a healthy profit.

79. A *Hollywood Reporter* news item (23/6/1955), stating errone-
    ously that Louis B. Mayer was understood to have acquired
    the rights to the play for $300,000, triggered other articles to
    this effect in the media; including in *The Stage* (30/6/1955;
    retracted 7/7/1955) .
80. See: Scott Eyman, *Lion of Hollywood – The Life and Legend
    of Louis B. Mayer* (Simon and Shuster, USA, 2005): p.482.
81. HMA: Letter from Rosalind Hicks to Cork: 12/7/1955.
82. HMA: Letter from Cork to Ober: 4/1/1955.
83. HMA: Letter from Cork to Rosalind Hicks: 3/5/1955.
84. HMA: Letter from Ober to Cork: 25/4/1955.
85. *The Washington Post and Times Herald*: 19/4/1955.
86. HMA: Letter from Cork to Rosalind Hicks: 15/6/1955.
87. *New York Journal American*: 18/10/1960.
88. *NYT*: 7/11/1960.
89. *Morning Telegraph*: 8/11/1960.
90. HMA: Letter from Cork to AC: 10/11/1960.
91. Typewritten flyer advertising *The Mousetrap* in New York,
    1957: Billy Rose Theatre Division, New York Public Library for
    the Performing Arts. This collection also contains playbills for
    the Arena Stage (Washington D.C.) American premiere produc-
    tion and the 1960 off-Broadway production.

Scene Four: Hat-Trick

1. LOC: Letter from John Gielgud to Gilbert Miller: 30/11/1953.
2. *Hansard*: 10/3/ 1954.
3. *MTM*: p.74.
4. The Tennent business papers' un-trumpeted 2011 arrival at
   the Victoria and Albert Museum's Theatre and Performance
   Collection should be a cause for celebration amongst theatre
   historians; in a 1995 letter to me, the Head Librarian at the
   V&A's then Theatre Museum observed that 'it is a matter of
   immense frustration that these vital records have apparently
   disappeared without trace'. Amongst them is a file of correspondence relating to the Theatrical Companies Bill of 1954,
   showing Beaumont and his lieutenants monitoring and manip-
   ulating the situation in the minutest detail. Although little
   mention of the bill is made in theatreland these days, the
   extensive newspaper coverage of its progress at the time
   (included in the archive) bears witness to the importance of

these events and the extreme bad feeling within the industry that they generated.

5. *Hansard*: 24/6/1954.
6. Charles Duff, *The Lost Summer: The Heyday of the West End Theatre* (1995): p.104.
7. Letter from Charles Duff to the author: 28/9/1998.
8. Letter from Lord Wyatt to the author: 19/9/1995.
9. Letter from Sir Peter Saunders to the author: 18/9/1998.
10. Letter from Peter Cotes to the author: 17/9/1998 (Cotes died 10/11/1998).
11. Margaret Lockwood, *Lucky Star* (1955): p.179.
12. *ACAuto*: p.519.
13. *Reynolds News*: 17/1/1954.
14. AC, *Spider's Web*: Act I, Scene I (Samuel French Acting Edition: 1956): p.6.
15. HMA: Letter from Cork to AC: 4/12/1942.
16. Margaret Lockwood, *Lucky Star* (1955): p.179.
17. *ACAuto*: p.511.
18. *MAC*: p.216. Denied access to official archives, but writing at a time when many of the Christie story's colourful theatrical dramatis personae were still alive, Robyns diligently applied her journalistic skills to tracking down and interviewing a number of the key players. Her interview with Wallace Douglas about his work with Christie is a rare example of him going on the record on the subject.
19. *ACAuto*: p.511.
20. ACA: AC, *Spider's Web* typescript (undated).
21. John Curran, *Agatha Christie's Secret Notebooks* (2009): pp.181–2. Curran is here referring to twenty pages of notes for *Spider's Web* in 'Notebook 12'. As this book was going to press another Christie notebook, containing amongst other things some forty further pages of notes for the script, has come to light. It was originally donated by AC to a 1960 charity auction raising money for the 'Friends of the National Library'. Curran's scholarly analysis will follow in due course, but the fact that (as far as we know) AC made more preparatory notes for this play than for any other, confirms the seriousness with which she set about the task of writing a comedy thriller for Margaret Lockwood.
22. LCP: AC, *Spider's Web* typescript. LCP ref: 1954/47.
23. LCPC: *Spider's Web* correspondence file. Ref: 1954/6990. Letter

from PS to the Lord Chamberlain's Secretary: 4/4/1956. Reply from Assistant Comptroller N.W. Gwatkin (name rubber stamped in lieu of signature): 5/4/1956. The speed and efficiency with which such enquiries were dealt with is remarkable, as indeed was the speed and reliability of the postal service in those days.

24. PSP: *Spider's Web* programme, Savoy Theatre, 1954.
25. *Observer*: 19/12/1954.
26. *The Times*: 15/12/1954.
27. Margaret Lockwood, *Lucky Star* (1955): p.188.
28. HMA: Cork to Ober: 12/1/1955.
29. HMA: Film treatment for *Spider's Web*: Unattributed, and dated (unclearly and possibly by an archivist) either 1956 or 1958.
30. *MTM*: p.150.
31. PSP: *Spider's Web*: Running accounts for week ending 17/11/1956 at Golder's Green Hippodrome.
32. PSP: *Spider's Web* final accounts to investors: 10/12/1963.
33. Perhaps most significantly, AC was the only playwright of either sex to achieve this record in the 1950s, seen by so many historians as some sort of watershed in British theatre. From 14 December 1954 to 29 January 1955, *The Mousetrap*, *Witness for the Prosecution* and *Spider's Web* were all playing. Some would count this record as having been repeated when Gerald Verner's *Towards Zero* opened on 4 September 1956, playing alongside *The Mousetrap* and *Spider's Web* until the latter's closure on 3 November. To put this achievement in perspective, four of Somerset Maugham's plays ran simultaneously in the West End in 1908, four of Coward's in the 1920s and three of Rattigan's in the 1940s. Alan Ayckbourn boasted five in 1975, but this by virtue of three of the five being a trilogy playing in repertoire. Christie and Ayckbourn (counting *The Norman Conquests* as a single production) are thus the only two playwrights who can claim to have achieved three plays running simultaneously in the West End in the second half of the twentieth century.
34. George Greenfield, *A Smattering of Monsters* (1995): pp.118–119.
35. HML: Licence summary card for *Towards Zero* – L. Arthur Rose to adapt: 11/11/1947. Born in Aberdeen, L. Arthur Rose (1882-1958) was a prolific playwright, actor and director. The script itself was kindly made available to me by James Pickard

of James M. Pickard Fine and Rare Books in Leicester, U.K..
In Rose's version, the murder takes place before the action
of the play commences, running contrary to the concept
inherent in the title *Towards Zero* that it is the sequence of
events *leading up* to the 'zero hour' of murder which is
significant. Superintendent Battle is also unaccountably
renamed Detective Sergeant Brittle; Christie took great care
in naming her characters, and this again appears directly to
undermine her original intention. Rose's play, which has
twelve characters and a classic drawing room set (of which
a roughly-drawn plan is included in the typescript), reduces
Christie's complex psychological drama to a fairly basic game
of *Cluedo*, and it is not difficult to see why it was rejected by
her. It is, however, a significant chapter in the intriguing saga
of the stage adaptation of *Towards Zero*, and doubtless
contributed to Christie's own growing belief that in this case
she had written a novel which did not lend itself to stage
adaptation.

36. HMA: Letter from AC to Cork: 28/2/1950. The following year,
    the 'intelligent and artistic' Robert Brenon's co-adaptation (with
    Birmingham Rep director Barry Jackson) of Moliere's 1673
    comedy *Le Malade Imaginare*, re-titled as *The Gay Invalid*,
    would play for 68 performances in the West End, starring Peter
    Cushing. Kenneth Tynan, reviewing it in The Spectator on
    2/2/1951, described the production as 'feebly repetitive'.
37. ACA: AC's Notebook 63.
38. HML: Licence summary card for *Towards Zero* – Gerald Verner
    to adapt: 2/3/1951.
39. HMA: Letter from Joseph Lucas to AC: 6/3/1951.
40. HML: Licence summary card for *Towards Zero* – B.A. Meyer
    to produce: 12/4/1951.
41. HMA: Letter from Cork to AC: 20/4/1951.
42. HMA: Letter from AC to Cork: 28/4/1951.
43. HMA: Letter from Cork to AC: 6/6/1951.
44. *MTM*: p.108.
45. *The Stage*: 31/1/1952.
46. *The Times*: 26/5/1971.
47. *The Stage*: 24/1/52.
48. HMA: Letter from Cork to AC: 11/3/1952.
49. HMA: Letter from Cork to AC: 5/3/1953.
50. HMA: Letter from AC to Cork : 13/4/1953.

51. HMA: Letter from Cork to AC: 24/4/1953.
52. Peter Cotes, *Thinking Aloud* (1993), p119: '. . . Agatha sent me a memento of that first night. Bearing the inscription 'Many thanks for all your help, dear Peter', it was a leather-bound copy of her play *Towards Zero*. She was keen to get me interested in directing this play later on, and obviously felt after our successful association at rehearsals, I was the right director for the job.' This would have been Verner's adaptation of *Towards Zero* prior to Christie herself becoming involved as nominal co-writer. Or perhaps it was even a copy of her own version . . .
53. HML Licence Card for *Towards Zero* – PS to produce: 4/8/1953.
54. HMA: Letter from Cork to AC: 8/4/1954.
55. HML: Licence summary card for *Towards Zero* – Verner assignment to AC: 15/4/1954.
56. *MAC*: p.217. According to Robyns, 'Agatha Christie, who was keenly interested in music, was intrigued to know that the man in Mary Law's life was in fact the conductor Kenneth Alwyn, and she followed this romance with interest . . .'
57. HMA: Letter from AC to Michael Prichard: 30/3/1968.
58. ACA: Letter from AC to Rosalind Hicks (undated: July 1971).
59. 'AC and Gerald Verner', *Towards Zero* (*MOP*: p.461).
60. ACA: *Towards Zero* programme, St James's Theatre, 1956.
61. *The Times*: 5/9/1956.
62. *Observer*: 16/9/1956.
63. *MTM*: p.176. *Towards Zero* does not even warrant a mention in Saunders' book's index.
64. *Towards Zero* production account: dated August 1956.
65. ACA: AC, *A Daughter's a Daughter*, typescript (undated: c.1950).
66. HMA: Letter from Cork to AC: 20/4/1951.
67. HMA: Letter from AC to Cork: 28/4/1951.
68. *MMem*: p.209.
69. Rosalind Hicks, 'The Secret of Mary Westmacott' (*Agatha Christie Official Centenary Celebration* brochure: 1990).
70. *Sunday Times*: 15/10/1961. Interview with AC by crime writer Julian Symons (1912-1994).
71. LCP: AC, *A Daughter's a Daughter* typescript. LCP ref: 1956/35. At the Lord Chamberlain's Office *A Daughter's a Daughter* landed on the desk of Assistant Examiner of Plays Sir Thomas St Vincent Troubridge (see pp.302-3). As the former head of

the Hughes Massie Drama Department he was well qualified to point out the true identity of the playwright. 'Mary Westmacott is the *nom de plume* used by Agatha Christie for those of her books and plays that are not thrillers,' he wrote in his Reader's Report (dated 28 June 1956). 'This is a guarantee that the work will be void of offence, the construction deft and the dialogue good – but her thrillers are better.' Troubridge remarks that the play reminds him of 'early Noël Coward' and goes on to point out Sarah's use of the word 'pansy' when describing the character Basil (see p.432), 'I am not sure about the official attitude to the word 'pansy'. My instinct is that the word itself should be allowed, as very much part of the current speech, but that when a character is specifically fescribed as a 'pansy', the question of a warning as to the degree of effeminacy in playing should be considered. I do not think a warning is here necessary, as the character is a very subsidiary one, and the submitting management discreet.' In response, someone has scribbled in the margin, 'I really don't think we can cut this word and not appear ridiculous'. (LCPC: *A Daughter's a Daughter* correspondence file. Ref: 1956/9294).

72. HMA: Cork to AC: 12/3/1955.
73. PSP: Letter from PS to Joseph Lucas (Hughes Massie): 23/10/1950.
74. *Bath Chronicle*: 7/7/1956.
75. *The Stage*: 12/7/1956.
76. *Daily Telegraph*: 17/12/2009.
77. *Independent*: 17/12/2009.
78. *Guardian*: 4/1/2010.
79. *ACATM*: p.121.
80. *MTM*: p.77.
81. Programme for *A Daughter's a Daughter*, Theatre Royal, Bath (1956): Theatre Royal Bath archive.
82. *MTM*: p.78.
83. HMA: Letter from Cork to AC (10/4/1957).
84. *MTM*: p.78.
85. *The Times*: 29/3/1973. Letter from Enid Bagnold.
86. Richard Huggett, *Binkie Beaumont: Eminence Grise of the West End Theatre* (1989): p.457.
87. HML: licence summary card for *No Fields of Amaranth*: 30/12/1955. The original 12 month option, which cost £500 on account of royalties, was subsequently extended at 6 monthly

intervals for further payments of £100.

88. Jared Cade, *Agatha Christie and the Eleven Missing Days* (1998): p.240.

89. I am grateful to David Burke, author of *The Lawn Road Flats* (2014), for sharing with me a letter sent to him by a friend of Louis Bondy, who recalls that Bondy 'mentioned dining in the restaurant with Agatha Christie . . .' Christie very much enjoyed socialising in the flats' highly-regarded Isobar Restaurant, and the cosmopolitan company she kept there during the war would certainly have broadened her perspective on life.

90. AC, *Verdict*, Act II, Scene 1 (*MOP*: p.591).

91. PSP: Correspondence between Mrs Hebe Keogh and PS: October/November 1957. Keogh, who wrote under the name Hebe Elsna, published some 100 books between 1928 and 1982 Now all out of print, they boasted such titles as *The Love Match*, *The Wise Virgin*, *The Pursuit of Pleasure* and *My Lover the King*. Hebe Elsna's *No Fields of Amaranth* had been published by Christie's publisher, Collins, in 1943; at the time when Christie herself was living at the Lawn Road flats.

92. PSP: Letter from PS to Hebe Keogh: 31/10/1957.

93. HMA: Letter from Cork to Ober: 11/4/1958.

94. LCP: AC, *Verdict* typescript: LCP Ref: 1957/56. The Lord Chamberlain's Office Reader's Report (by G. Deamer, dated 14/12/1957) notes that *Verdict* is 'A good and unusual Agatha Christie, not a thriller... At first Lisa refuses to marry Karl saying he brings suffering wherever he goes through his ideals, but she relents finding him alone and in need of her. There are no fields of Amaranth this side of the grave, he laments, but Lisa takes a chance on it. Perhaps the poet was wrong'. (LCPC: *Verdict* correspondence file. Ref: 1957/568).

95. AC, *Verdict*, Act II, Scene 3 (*MOP*: p.622).

96. Trevor R. Griffiths and Margret Llewellyn-Jones, *British and Irish Women Dramatists since 1958: A Critical Handbook* (1993): p.7.

97. Ibid.: Lib Taylor, Chapter One, 'Early Stages': pp.12–13.

98. HMA: Letter from Cork to AC: 28/3/1957.

99. *The Stage*: 6/3/1958.

100. PSP: Letter from PS to J.C. Trewin: 5/3/1958.

101. PSP: Letter from J.C. Trewin to PS: 9/3/1958.

102. PSP: Letter from PS to J.C. Trewin: 11/3/1958.

103. *Daily Telegraph*: 23/5/1958.

104. *The Times*: 23/3/1958.
105. *The Stage*: 29/5/1958.
106. ACA: Letter from Beresford Egan to PS: 5/6/1958. Forwarded to AC by PS on 6/6/1958.
107. PSP: Letter from R.L. Wells, Send Manor Trust Ltd (Strand Theatre) to PS: 2/6/1958.
108. PSP: Publicity leaflet for *Verdict*, quoting *Daily Mirror* review. These leaflets normally quoted a few words from a large number of newspapers. In the case of *Verdict*, the *Daily Mirror* is the only one quoted, and at some length. Even this sounds as though it has been heavily edited, but Saunders presumably wanted to give his leading lady the boost afforded by its final line.
109. Mathew Prichard and I met Wendy Noel, quite by chance, in 2011, and she told us of his grandmother's thoughtfulness towards her.
110. PSP: *Verdict* statement of distribution of income to investors: 31/3/1960.
111. PSP: *Verdict* final statement of accounts for investors: 12/5/1966. The costume and furniture budgets are noticeably high, although this is offset by the 'sale of wardrobe and set', presumably to a Saunders-licensed touring production.
112. PSP: PS letter to *Verdict* investors accompanying accounts 12/5/1966: 'We have now lost our rights in this play,' he states, although interestingly the seven year licence period for participation in subsidiary rights (calculated from the first West End performance for a run of less than six months, or from the last performance for a run of more than six months) would have expired a year previously. Either there was an error, or Cork had allowed an extra year of subsidiary participation for the purposes of damage limitation.
113. HML: licence Summary card for *No Fields of Amaranth*. Under his original option, Saunders had the right to participate in amateur rights for a payment of £200 within 1 month of the West End opening, which a handwritten note shows that he made on 20/6/1958 (a day before the deadline). Samuel French Ltd were subsequently licensed to administer the amateur rights (HML licence summary card 7/7/1958), resulting in a deal whereby he would receive 30% of amateur income, Samuel French Ltd would receive 20% and Christie would receive 50%.
114. PSP: Letter from Hall Brydon solicitors to Rahvis of Mayfair

20/2/1958. It is little wonder that the costume budget for *Verdict* was unusually high if the ladies' dresses were being supplied by Rahvis. One of the reviews refers to the character of Helen Rollander (played by Moira Redmond) as being dressed in the latest fashions, and it may also be that Saunders was treating his Broadway star, Patricia Jessel, to some upmarket costuming.

115. PSP: Letter from PS to R.G. Jones, Morden Park Sound Studios: 8/8/1958.
116. *Daily Mail*: 14/4/1958: The party was held on Sunday 13/4/1954 to celebrate *The Mousetrap* playing its 2,239th performance the previous night – putting it ahead of Chu Chin Chow, which had achieved 2,238 performances between 1916 and 1921.
117. *ACAuto*: p.538.
118. *ACATM*: p.129.
119. *MTM*: p.181.

Scene Five: The Late Plays

1. *MTM*: p.181.
2. PSP: Cast contracts for *The Unexpected Guest*, 6/7/1958.
3. PSP: Licence Agreement for PS to present *The Unexpected Guest*, 31/7/1958.
4. HMA: Letter from AC to Cork: 14/8/58.
5. PSP: Interim Statement of Profit for *The Unexpected Guest*: 8/10/1960.
6. Actor Nigel Stock (who played Starkwedder in *The Unexpected Guest*) recounted this story when he spoke on the BBC's 85th birthday tribute to AC, *The Mysterious Dame Agatha*, broadcast on BBC Radio 4 on 17/9/1975.
7. HGP: Hubert Gregg's rehearsal script for *The Unexpected Guest*.
8. *ACATM*: p.122.
9. *ACAuto*: p.475.
10. ACA: AC's Notebook 34.
11. ACA: Notebooks 53 and 47. This dating is arrived at by placing the notes for the play in the context of surrounding material relating to works with known publication dates. Christie's use of particular notebooks was so arbitrary that this methodology is by no means fail-safe, although in this case it seems fairly certain.
12. *ACAuto*: pp.326–7.

13. AC, *The Unexpected Guest* (Samuel French Acting Edition, 1960): Act I, Scene 1: p.6.
14. The first extract is from AC, *The Unexpected Guest* (Samuel French Acting Edition, 1960): Act 2: p.69. The second is from LCP: AC, *The Unexpected Guest*. LCP Ref: 1958/30.
15. *ACATM*: p.127.
16. Lib Taylor, writing in *British and Irish Women Dramatists Since 1958* (1993: eds Trevor R. Griffiths and Margaret Llewellyn-Jones): p.12.
17. PSP: publicity leaflet for *The Unexpected Guest*.
18. *ACATM*: p.128.
19. *ACATM* p.129: photograph of telegram dated 4/8/1958.
20. *Western Daily Press*: 5/8/1958.
21. *The Stage*: 14/8/58.
22. Cited in *ACATM*: p.130.
23. Ibid.
24. Ibid.
25. *The Manchester Guardian*: 13/8/1958.
26. *The Times*: 13/8/1958.
27. *Observer*: 17/8/58.
28. PSP: publicity leaflet for *The Unexpected Guest*.
29. HML: Licence summary card for *The Unexpected Guest*: 9/12/1958.
30. HMA: Reported in a memo from 'J.R.' (Harold Ober Associates) to Cork: 20/3/1965.
31. *NYT*: 31/5/1965.
32. *NYT*: 11/8/1965.
33. *Palm Beach Post*: 20/8/1965.
34. *Guardian*, obituary of Joan Fontaine: 16/12/2013.
35. HML: licence summary card for *Go Back for Murder*: 8/1/1960.
36. HMA: Letter from AC to Cork: 28/2/1950.
37. Lib Taylor (see 16 above).
38. AC, *Go Back for Murder*: Act I, Scene 1 (*MOP*: p.638).
39. See: Lizzie Seal, 'Public Reactions to the Case of Mary Wilson, the Last Woman to be Sentenced to Death in England and Wales' (*Papers from the British Criminology Conference*, Vol.8, 2008).
40. HMA: Letter from Cork to AC: 15/1/1960.
41. *The Stage*: 3/3/60.
42. *Observer*: 27/3/60.
43. *The Guardian*: 24/3/1960.

44. *The Stage*: 31/3/60.

45. *The Times*: 24/3/1960.

46. PSP: *Go Back for Murder* 'Final Statement' and weekly 'summary of receipts and expenses' for the Duchess Theatre run (w/e 23/4/1960 the production showed a loss for the week of £636).

47. PSP: Letter from PS to investors in *Go Back for Murder*. Interestingly, these accounts closed on the same day as those for *Verdict*: 12/5/1966 (see Act Two/Scene 4/Note 108 above). But whereas PS and his investors seem to have enjoyed an extra year of residual participation in *Verdict*, the books appear to have closed a year short of the usual seven on *Go Back for Murder*. It may be that, given the higher subsidiary yields on *Verdict*, Cork had allowed PS to trade one for the other. Saunders, who as usual held the largest financial stake in *Go Back for Murder*, himself took a much bigger hit than any of the other investors; although it has to be said that the losses on a Christie failure were extremely modest compared to the vast profits made on the successes.

48. *The Stage* reported this a few weeks after the event, on 21/4/62, under the headline '£MGMillion For Christie'. As was often the case with Christie's film and TV deals, however, the reality of the situation diverged considerably from the press reports, and there is another book to be written about Christie's unhappy dealings with MGM.

49. *MTM*: p.185/ *ACATM*: p.139.

50. PSP: *Go Back for Murder* 'Contracts Chart': Apart from Robert Urquhart on £60 per week and Nigel Green (playing Amyas Crale) on £45 per week, cast salaries ranged from £20 per week to £40 per week (for the two leading ladies).

51. Michael Northen, *Northen Lights* (1997): p.184.

52. *ACATM*: p.136.

53. HGP: Letter from AC to HG: 3/4/1960. Pat Kirkwood was Gregg's second wife of three; he was her third husband of four.

54. *ACATM*: p.139.

55. *The Stage*: 3/8/1961.

56. *MTM*: p.195.

57. ACA: AC's Notebook 3.

58. ACA: AC, typescript for *The Rats* (undated).

59. LCP: Lewis Casson, *Crime*. LCP Ref: 1921/28.

60. *The Times*: 29/11/1921.

61. Russell Thorndike, *Sybil Thorndike* (1929): p.280.

62. LCPC: *The Rats* correspondence file. Ref: 1961/2024. C.D. Heriot's Reader's Report for *The Rats*: 27/9/1961.

63. Noël Coward, *This Year of Grace* (Noël Coward Collected Revue Sketches and Parodies, Methuen Drama, 1999): p.84.

64. ACA: AC, typescript for *Afternoon at the Seaside* (undated).

65. ACA: AC, typescript for *The Patient* (undated).

66. *ACATM*: p.151.

67. HMA: Letter from James Chapman to AC: 30/8/1961. The Hughes Massie archive contains several files full of letters from fans, some of them suggesting scenarios for stories and plays, and some asking Christie to comment on their own writing efforts. With the volume of correspondence increasing as she reached old age, it was clearly impractical for her to offer personal responses to all of them, although it is notable that she was particularly diligent in replying to letters from younger fans.

68. HMA: Letter from Cork to AC: 24/8/1961.

69. LCPC: *Rule of Three* correspondence file. Ref: 1961/2024. Letter from PS to the Lord Chamberlain's Office: 30/10/1961.

70. Ibid. Letter from E. Penn (Assistant Comptroller, Lord Chamberlain's Office) to PS: 2/11/1961. Penn's name is rubber-stamped onto the signature line (upside down).

71. Ibid. Letter from E. Penn (Lord Chamberlain's Office) to PS: 4/11/1961.

72. ACA: *Rule of Three* Programme, Oxford New Theatre, w/c 20/11/1961.

73. PSP: Letter from PS to AC: 9/11/1961.

74. HMA: Letter from Cork to AC: 11/11/1961.

75. HMA: Letter from Cork to AC: 5/12/1961.

76. HGP: Letter from PS to HG: 29/11/1961. Suicide was a theme frequently explored by AC, so it must be assumed that PS was anticipating her adverse reaction to the stage manager rewriting her script rather than the suggestion itself.

77. HGP: HG's rehearsal script for *Rule of Three* (undated).

78. PSP: Letter from HG to PS 19/8/1962.

79. HGP: Typescript for new opening scene of *The Rats* (undated: author unknown).

80. PSP: Letter from PS to Hubert Gregg: 19/8/1962.

81. *The Stage*: 25/10/62.

82. Letter from AC to Bertie Meyer: 29/6/1962. This letter appeared

in the sales catalogue of American autograph dealers Schulson Autographs (yours for $2,850). Efforts, kindly assisted by the Schulson emporium, to trace its provenance via the American auction house that sold it to them proved fruitless; I had been hoping that this rare letter from AC to Meyer might lead me to an archive of Bertie Meyer correspondence, but it didn't . . .

83. *The Stage*: 6/9/62 'Playgoers' Diary'.

84. *The Times*: 11/9/1962.

85. John Ringrose's letter to *The Guardian* (20/9/1962) concluded; 'Surely some change could be made in a title which can give great offence to a number of people who, God knows, have enough to bear already?' The *Guardian*'s review of *Ten Little Niggers* (11/9/1962) had pointed out that 'Its period flavour is well established by the title. Who, now, could set their play on Nigger Island and get away with it? But the events of the last twenty years had plainly passed by the first night audience . . .' It was probably just coincidence that the following day's edition carried an article entitled 'The Driven Wedge' in which distinguished Barbadian diplomat and journalist Oliver Jackman bemoaned the growth of racism in the UK over the previous decade and argued that the 'Immigration Act has exactly reflected the confusion and the negrophobia I have found in Britain in 1962.' The Commonwealth Immigrants Act, which had been passed five months previously, placed controls on immigration to the UK from the Commonwealth, and in this context the timing of the revival of Christie's play was particularly unfortunate.

86. The 1966 UK edition of the novel, published by Fontana, retained its original UK title and also referred to the previous year's film, which had taken its title from the Broadway production of the play. The result was the bizarre juxtaposition of both titles in large type on the front cover; '*Ten Little Niggers*: *Ten Little Indians* is the film based on this chilling novel.'

87. *The Stage*: 22/11/62.

88. PSP: *The Unexpected Guest* West End publicity leaflet, 1962.

89. PSP: Letter from PS to Leslie Macdonell, OBE: 1/1/1963.

90. *The Stage*: 27/12/62: 'Mrs Christie Does Not Do It Again' ran the headline over *The Stage*'s review of *Rule of Three*.

91. *Guardian*: 22/12/62.

92. *The Times*: 21/12/1962.

93. *Observer*: 23/12/1962

94. *ACATM*: p.147.

95. ACA: AC, typescript for *An Afternoon at the Seaside* (undated).
96. HMA: Letter from AC to Cork: 2/1/1963.
97. *Financial Times*: 11/1/1963.
98. PSP: Letters from PS to J.D. Higgins, *Financial Times* (headed 'not for publication'): 14/1/1963 and 17/1/1963: An appropriate apology was forthcoming. The article also maintained that the profits from *The Mousetrap* had enabled Saunders to buy two theatres, on which matter he was also at pains to set the record straight; pointing out that whilst he did indeed own the Duchess, the Ambassadors was on a lease.
99. HML: licence summary card for television broadcast of *A Day by the Seaside*: 25/1/1963.
100. *MTM*: p.195.
101. HMA: Letter from Cork to Anthony Hicks: 12/2/1963.
102. *The Stage*: 2/5/63.
103. ACA: Letter from AC to Rosalind Hicks (undated: July 1971).
104. Cited in *MTM*: p.205.
105. *The Stage*: 17/11/1966.
106. ACA: Letter from AC to Rosalind Hicks (undated). Writing from Baghdad, she tells Rosalind that she had met the "new" ambassador at an embassy dinner the previous night. This would have been Sir Michael Wright, who took up his post on 21 January 1955.
107. PSP: Letter from PS to AC: 9/11/1961.
108. *MTM*: p.150.
109. ACA: AC's notebook 4a.
110. The television interview with Stultiëns, originally produced by Radio Netherlands Worldwide (RNW), can be seen on YouTube.
111. ACA: AC, typescript for *Miss Perry* (undated).
112. HMA: Letter from Cork to AC: 21/3/1962.
113. HMA: Letter from Cork to AC: 14/4/1962.
114. *The Stage*: 10/9/1959.
115. HMA: Letter from PS to MM: 18/9/1963.
116. HMA: Extensive correspondence shows Christie's US tax liability for the 1930s–40s being revised, re-assessed and renegotiated for over a decade. According to a letter to Ober from his lawyer Howard Reinheimer (24/3/47; copied to Cork) AC was liable for tax arrears of $201,679 (including penalties and interest) for the years 1930–1941, for which Reinheimer was hoping to negotiate a settlement figure of $149,314, of which $30,000 would be outstanding. That would then leave the matter of the further

liability of $74,000 for the years 1942–1944 to be dealt with.

117. By 1966, Britain's highest earners were facing an income tax liability of just over 90% (George Harrison exaggerated slightly in his song *Taxman*) and Agatha, despite the best efforts of her advisors, found herself faced with a bill for £200,000 in personal income tax arrears.

118. HMA: Letter from Cork to AC: 21/8/1961. Cork goes on to explain that this had been his motivation for attempting to sort out AC's long-term tax affairs.

119. From 1954, the Hughes Massie archive contains separate yearly files relating to the conduct of the various Trusts operated on Christie's behalf, the affairs of which were all managed by Cork. 'I presume there is some sort of proviso that I get *some* money?!' AC wrote jokingly to Cork on 1/3/1956.

120. HMA: Letter from AC to Cork: 19/2/1956: 'I'd like to be clear in an entirely unlegal way what I feel about all this. First I presume it's ethical? So difficult to know nowadays.' Letter from AC to Cork: 1/3/1956: 'I am reposing complete trust in you and Anthony – but if I can't trust you after all these years, who can I trust?'

121. HMA: Letter from AC to Cork: 23/3/1957.

122. HMA: Letter from AC to Cork: 19/2/1956.

123. *Daily Telegraph*, 1/5/1976: 'Dame Agatha Christie's will, which it was thought would leave a huge fortune from her output of books, plays and films, came out yesterday with the sort of ending she would have hoped for – an estate of £106,683 to keep the tax man at bay.'

124. *ACAuto*: p.510.

125. HMA: AC to Cork: 19/2/1956.

126. *ACAuto*: p.528.

127. ACA: AC, *This Mortal Coil* typescript (undated).

128. HGP: Letter from AC to Hubert Gregg: 8/9/1970.

129. HGP: Letter from AC to Hubert Gregg: 8/4/1971.

130. Letter from PS to Charles Osborne, 24/11/1981, cited in Charles Osborne, *The Life and Crimes of Agatha Christie* (1982): p.224.

131. HML: licence summary card: *Fiddlers Five*: 6/3/1971.

132. ACA: Publicity leaflet for *Fiddlers Five* at the Theatre Royal, Nottingham: 21/6/1971.

133. *Portsmouth Evening News*: 8/6/1971.

134. *Hampshire Telegraph*: 10/6/1971.

135. *The Stage*: 17/6/71.

136. ACA: AC, *Fiddlers Five* typescript (undated).
137. HMA: Cork to James Grant Anderson: 20/7/1971.
138. ACA: Rosalind Hicks to AC: 20/7/1971.
139. ACA: AC to Rosalind Hicks (undated: July 1971). 'Nima' was the family nickname for Agatha, derived from her grandson Mathew's childhood mispronunciation of the word 'Grandma'. 'AP' here stands for 'Auntie Punkie', Rosalind's nickname for Agatha's sister Madge .
140. HMA: Cork to AC: 1/8/1971.
141. Charles Osborne, *The Life and Crimes of Agatha Christie* (1982): p.225 and Peter Haining, *Murder in Four Acts* (1990): p.37.
142. HML: licence summary card for *Fiddlers Five*, 24/9/1971.
143. HGP: Letter from AC to Gregg: 9/10/1971.
144. ACA: Letter from Allan Davis to AC: 26/1/1972.
145. ACA: Letter from AC to Allan Davis, 3/2/1972.
146. *Surrey Advertiser*: 4/8/1962, cited in Charles Osborne, *The Life and Crimes of Agatha Christie* (1982): pp.226–7.
147. ACA: AC, typescript for *Fiddlers Three* (undated).
148. See: Braham Murray, *The Worst It Can Be Is a Disaster* (2009). Murray was advised by his agent that James Verner had a 'dubious reputation . . . there had been rumours of embezzlement' (p.138), and Murray's experience of working with Verner did nothing to allay these suspicions.
149. HMA: Letter from AC to Cork: 5/11/1973.
150. *The Stage*: 6/12/73.

Curtain Call

1. *ACATM*: p.161.
2. *Daily Telegraph*, Peter Saunders obituary, 8/2/2003.
3. *MTM*: pp.245–6.
4. *Daily Telegraph*: 8/2/2003.
5. 'Peter Saunders Presents *The Mousetrap Story*' (1992): p.5.
6. *Evening Standard*: 13/5/2005.
7. *Guardian*, 25/3/1992. 'Michael Billington laments a sponsorship system that values the bad above the bard', we are told, under the headline 'Something rotten in the state.'
8. *Independent*, 12/3/1992.
9. Gwen Robyns, *The Mystery of Agatha Christie* (Penguin, 1979): p.219.
10. AC's original script specifies a 'carpet sweeper' although by

the time the play opened in Nottingham the programme was acknowledging Hoover's product-placement of their latest appliance ('electric cleaner by Hoover Ltd.'). The published script refers to a 'vacuum cleaner' in the stage directions and a 'carpet sweeper' in the dialogue.

11. *ACAuto*: p.516.

Bibliography

Publication dates listed below are for UK first editions unless otherwise indicated. Plays written by Agatha Christie that were performed in her lifetime are listed in the order in which they were premiered, with others in approximate order of writing. With the exception of those listed on pp.616–17, plays referred to in this book by writers other than Agatha Christie are not included here. Novels and short stories by Agatha Christie that are referred to but which were not adapted for the stage in her lifetime are also not listed. There are numerous websites and books offering 'definitive' lists of Christie's published work and, of these, Robert Barnard's *A Talent to Deceive* (Collins, 1980) includes a particularly helpful record of the UK and US publication histories of her novels and short stories in book form.

I am delighted that as a result of my research, Agatha Christie Ltd has started working with Samuel French Ltd to publish and make available for performance a number of the scripts listed below as unpublished and/or unperformed; although it should be noted that the texts of these plays have in some cases been edited in accordance with what Agatha Christie Ltd considers to be the requirements and sensibilities of today's theatre practitioners and audiences. In line with my research, the latest edition of the script for *Love from a Stranger* is credited as being jointly authored by Agatha Christie and Frank Vosper.

Abbreviations used in the Bibliography

ACA = The Agatha Christie Archive; Christie Archive Trust
LCP = Lord Chamberlain's Plays collection; British Library

The Plays of Agatha Christie

A Masque from Italy
 Original one-act stage play
 Typescript in ACA
 Unperformed
 First published: *The Road of Dreams*, Geoffrey Bles, 1924

The Conqueror
 Original one-act stage play
 Typescript in ACA
 Unperformed/unpublished

Teddy Bear
 Original one-act stage play
 Typescript in ACA
 Unperformed/unpublished

Eugenia and Eugenics
 Original one-act stage play
 Typescript in ACA
 Unperformed/unpublished

The Clutching Hand
 Full-length stage play
 Adapted from: *The Exploits of Elaine* (novel by Arthur B. Reeve:
   Hodder & Stoughton, 1915)
 Typescript in ACA
 Unperformed/unpublished

The Last Séance
 Original one-act stage play
 Typescript in ACA
 Unperformed
 Play unpublished. Short story in *The Hound of Death*, Odhams, 1933

Ten Years
 Original one-act stage play
 Typescript in ACA
 Unperformed/unpublished

Marmalade Moon
 Original one-act stage play
 Typescript in ACA
 Unperformed/unpublished

The Lie (aka *The Sister-in-Law*)
Original full-length stage play
Typescript in ACA
Unperformed/unpublished

Chimneys
Full-length stage play
Adapted from: *The Secret of Chimneys* (novel: John Lane, 1925)
Typescript in ACA. LCP Ref: 1931/40
First performed: 16 October 2003, Vertigo Theatre, Calgary
Unpublished

1930: *Black Coffee*
Original full-length stage play
No typescript in ACA. LCP Ref: 1930/52
First performed: 8 December 1930, Embassy Theatre, London
First published: Alfred Ashley, 1934

The Wasp's Nest
One-act stage play
Adapted from: 'The Wasp's Nest' (short story: originally published
    in the *Daily Mail*, 20 Nov 1928: included in *Double Sin*, Dodd,
    Mead & Co., USA, 1961/*Poirot's Early Cases*, Collins, 1974)
Typescript in ACA
Unperformed on stage (broadcast on BBC Television, 18 June
    1937)
Unpublished

The Stranger
Full-length stage play
Adapted from: 'Philomel Cottage' (short story: included in *The
    Listerdale Mystery*, Collins, 1934)
Typescript in ACA
Unperformed/unpublished

Someone at the Window
Full-length stage play
Adapted from: 'The Dead Harlequin' (short story: included in *The
    Mysterious Mr Quin*, Collins, 1930)
Typescript in ACA
Unperformed/unpublished

Akhnaton
Original full-length stage play

Typescript in ACA
First performed: Fountains Abbey Pub Theatre, London, January 1980
First published: Collins, 1973

1943: *Ten Little Niggers* (aka *Ten Little Indians/And Then There Were None)*
Full-length stage play
Adapted from: *Ten Little Niggers* (novel: Collins, 1939)
No typescript in ACA. LCP Ref: 1943/16
First performed: 20 September 1943, Wimbledon Theatre, London
First published: Samuel French, 1944

1944: *Hidden Horizon* (aka *Murder on the Nile)*
Full-length stage play
Adapted from: *Death on the Nile* (novel: Collins, 1937)
Typescript in ACA. LCP Ref: 1943/35
First performed: 17 January 1944, Dundee Repertory Theatre
First published: Samuel French, 1948

1945: *Appointment with Death*
Full-length stage play
Adapted from: *Appointment with Death* (novel: Collins, 1938)
No typescript in ACA. LCP Ref:1944/39
First performed: 29 January 1945, King's Theatre, Glasgow
First published: Samuel French, 1956

1945: *Towards Zero*
Full-length stage play
Adapted from: *Towards Zero* (novel: Collins, 1944)
Typescript in ACA, donated by the Shubert Organisation
First performed: Martha's Vineyard Playhouse, 4 September 1945
Unpublished

1951: *The Hollow* (aka *The Suspects)*
Full-length stage play
Adapted from: *The Hollow* (novel: Collins, 1946)
No typescript in ACA. LCP Ref: 1950/62
First performed: 5 February 1951, Cambridge Arts Theatre
First published: Samuel French, 1952

1952: *The Mousetrap*
Full-length stage play
Adapted from: *Three Blind Mice* (radio play: broadcast by the

BBC, 30 May 1947) and 'Three Blind Mice' (short story: included in *Three Blind Mice*, Dodd, Mead & Co., USA, 1950)
Typescript in ACA. LCP Ref: 1952/45
First performed: 6 October 1952, Theatre Royal, Nottingham
First published: Samuel French, 1954

1953: *Witness for the Prosecution*
Full-length stage play
Adapted from: 'The Witness for the Prosecution' (short story: included in *The Hound of Death*, Odhams, 1933)
Typescript in ACA. LCP Ref: 1953/46
First performed: 28 September 1953, Theatre Royal, Nottingham
First published: Samuel French, 1954

1954: *Spider's Web*
Original full-length stage play
Typescript in ACA. LCP Ref: 1954/47
First performed: 27 September 1954, Theatre Royal, Nottingham
First published: Samuel French, 1957

1956: *A Daughter's a Daughter* by Mary Westmacott
Original full-length stage play
Typescript in ACA. LCP Ref: 1956/35
First performed: 9 July 1956, Theatre Royal, Bath
Play unpublished. Published as a novel by Mary Westmacott: Heinemann, 1952

1958: *Verdict*
Original full-length stage play
Typescript in ACA. LCP Ref: 1957/56
First performed: 25 February 1958, Grand Theatre, Wolverhampton
First published: Samuel French, 1958

1958: *The Unexpected Guest*
Original full-length stage play
No typescript in ACA. LCP Ref: 1958/30
First performed: 4 August 1958, Hippodrome, Bristol
First published: Samuel French, 1958

1960: *Go Back for Murder*
Full-length stage play
Adapted from: *Five Little Pigs* (novel: Dodd, Mead & Co., USA, as *Murder In Restrospect*, 1942; Collins, 1943)

No typescript in ACA. LCP Ref: 1960/5
First performed: 22 February 1960, King's Theatre, Edinburgh
First published: Samuel French, 1960

1961: *Rule of Three (The Rats, Afternoon at the Seaside, The Patient)*
Three original one-act stage plays
Typescript in ACA. LCP Ref: 1961/49
First performed: 6 November 1961, His Majesty's Theatre, Aberdeen
First published (individually): Samuel French, 1963

Miss Perry
Original full-length stage play
Typescript in ACA
Unperformed/unpublished

1971: *Fiddlers Five (aka Fiddlers Three)*
Original full-length stage play
Typescript in ACA
First performed: 7 June 1971, King's Theatre, Southsea
Unpublished

Plays adapted from Agatha Christie's work in her lifetime by other writers

*Alibi (*aka *The Fatal Alibi)*
Adapted by Michael Morton from *The Murder of Roger Ackroyd*
    (novel: Collins, 1926)
First published: Samuel French, 1929

Love from a Stranger
Adapted by Frank Vosper from *The Stranger* (original stage play:
    unpublished/ACA)
Published: Collins, 1936/Samuel French, 1937

Tea for Three
Adapted by Margery Vosper from 'Accident' (short story: included
    in *The Listerdale Mystery*, Collins, 1934)
First published: *Theatrecraft Plays Book Two*, Nelson & Sons, 1939

Peril at End House
Adapted by Arnold Ridley from *Peril at End House* (novel: Collins,
    1932)
First published: Samuel French, 1945

Towards Zero
  Adapted by L. Arthur Rose from *Towards Zero* (novel: Collins, 1944)
  Typescript in private collection
  Unperformed/unpublished

Murder at the Vicarage
  Adapted by Moie Charles and Barbara Toy from *The Murder at the Vicarage* (novel: Collins, 1930)
  First published: Samuel French, 1950

Towards Zero
  Adapted by Gerald Verner (with nominal assistance from Agatha Christie) from *Towards Zero* (novel: Collins, 1944)
  Published: Dramatists Play Service, USA, 1957/Samuel French 1958

Other plays of interest

Casson, Lewis (adapted from Level, Maurice), *Crime* (unpublished: LCP 1921/28)
Coward, Noël, *This Year of Grace* (Chappell, 1928)
Coward, Noël, *The Better Half* (1922 – published in Hand, Richard J. and Wilson, Michael, *London's Grand Guignol and the Theatre of Horror*, 2007)
Dane, Clemence, *A Bill of Divorcement* (Heinemann, 1921)
Delaney, Shelagh, *A Taste of Honey* (Methuen, 1959)
Grantham, A. E., *The Wisdom of Akhnaton* (The Bodley Head, 1920)
Osborne, John, *Look Back in Anger* (Faber and Faber, 1957)
Phillpotts, Adelaide Eden, *Akhnaton: A Play* (Thornton Butterworth, 1926)
Priestley, J. B., *Dangerous Corner* (Samuel French, 1933)
Priestley, J. B., *Time and The Conways* (Heinemann, 1937)
Rattigan, Terence, *The Deep Blue Sea* (Hamish Hamilton, 1952)
Saunders, Peter, *Scales of Justice* (Chappell Plays, 1988)
Shaw, George Bernard, *Getting Married, A Disquisitory Play* (Constable, 1908)
Shaw, George Bernard, *Misalliance* (Constable, 1914)
Watts, M. F., *The Claimant* (unpublished: ACA. LCP Ref: 1924/25)
Watts, M. F., *Oranges and Lemons* (unpublished: ACA, date unknown)

Books about Agatha Christie and her work

Aldridge, Mark, *Agatha Christie on Screen* (Palgrave MacMillan, 2016)

Barnard, Robert, *A Talent to Deceive* (Collins, 1980)

Bloom, Harold (ed.), *Modern Critical Views: Agatha Christie* (Chelsea House, USA, 2002)

Cade, Jared, *Agatha Christie and the Eleven Missing Days* (Peter Owen, 1998)

Christie, Agatha, *An Autobiography* (Collins, 1977)

Curran, John, *Agatha Christie's Secret Notebooks* (HarperCollins, 2009)

Curran, John, *Agatha Christie's Murder in the Making* (HarperCollins, 2011)

Curran, John, *Agatha Christie's Complete Secret Notebooks* (HarperCollins, 2016)

Gill, Gillian, *Agatha Christie: The Woman and her Mysteries* (Robson, 1999)

Haining, Peter, *Agatha Christie: Murder in Four Acts* (Virgin Books, 1990)

Holgate, Mike, *Stranger Than Fiction: Agatha Christie's True Crime Inspirations* (History Press, 2010)

Keating, H.R.F., *Agatha Christie: First Lady of Crime* (Weidenfeld and Nicolson, 1977)

Light, Alison, *Forever England: Femininity, Literature and Conservatism Between the Wars* (Routledge, 1991)

Mackaskill, Hilary, *Agatha Christie at Home* (Frances Lincoln, 2009)

Makinen, Merja, *Agatha Christie: Investigating Femininity* (Palgrave Macmillan, 2006)

Morgan, Janet, *Agatha Christie: A Biography* (Collins, 1984)

Osborne, Charles, *The Life and Crimes of Agatha Christie* (Collins, 1982)

Prichard, Mathew (ed.), *Agatha Christie: The Grand Tour* (HarperCollins, 2012)

Ramsey, G.C., *Agatha Christie: Mistress of Mystery* (Dodd, Mead & Co., USA, 1967/Collins, 1968)

Robyns, Gwen, *The Mystery of Agatha Christie* (Doubleday, USA, 1978)

Rowland, Susan, *From Agatha Christie to Ruth Rendell: British Women Writers in Detective and Crime Fiction* (Palgrave, 2001)

Sanders, Dennis and Lovallo, Len, *The Agatha Christie Companion* (Delacorte Press, USA, 1984/W.H. Allen, 1985)

Thompson, Laura, *Agatha Christie: An English Mystery* (Headline Review, 2007)

Trumpler, Charlotte (ed.), *Agatha Christie and Archaeology* (British Museum Press, 2001)

Underwood, Lynn (ed.), *Agatha Christie: Official Centenary Celebration* (Belgrave Publishing, 1990)

Autobiographies and memoirs

Attenborough, Richard and Hawkins, Diana, *Entirely Up to You, Darling* (Hutchinson, 2008)

Black, Kitty, *Upper Circle: A Theatrical Chronicle* (Methuen, 1984)

Brown, Curtis, *Contacts* (Cassell, 1935)

Cotes, Peter, *No Star Nonsense: A Challenging Declaration of Faith in the Essentials of Tomorrow's Theatre* (Rockliff, 1949)

Cotes, Peter, *Thinking Aloud: Fragments of Autobiography* (Peter Owen, 1993)

Counsell, John, *Counsell's Opinion* (Barrie and Rockliff, 1963)

Dean, Basil, *The Theatre at War* (Harrap, 1956)

Dean, Basil, *Seven Ages: an Autobiography 1888–1927* (Hutchinson, 1970)

Dean, Basil, *Mind's Eye: an Autobiography 1927–1972* (Hutchinson 1973)

Derwent, Clarence, *The Clarence Derwent Story* (Henry Schuman, 1953)

Greenfield, George, *A Smattering of Monsters: a Kind of Memoir* (Little, Brown, 1995)

Gregg, Hubert, *Agatha Christie and all that Mousetrap* (William Kimber, 1980)

Gregg, Hubert, *Maybe it's Because . . .?* (IndePenPress, 2005)

Guthrie, Tyrone *A Life in the Theatre* (Hamish Hamilton, 1960)

Harris, Jed, *A Dance on the High Wire: a Unique Memoir of the Theatre* (Crown, USA, 1979)

Landstone, Charles, *Off-Stage: a Personal Record of the First Twelve Years of State Sponsored Drama in Great Britain* (Elek Books, 1953)

Landstone, Charles, *I Gate-Crashed* (Stainer and Bell, 1975)

Lockwood, Margaret, *Lucky Star* (Odhams, 1955)

Mallowan, Max, *Mallowan's Memoirs* (William Collins, 1977)

Murray, Braham, *The Worst it can be is a Disaster* (Methuen Drama, 2007)

Northen, Michael, *Northen Lights* (Summersdale, 1977)

Phillpotts, Eden, *From the Angle of 88* (Hutchinson, 1951)

Phillpotts, Eden, *Eden Phillpotts (1862–1960) Selected Letters*, ed. Dayananda, James Y. (University Press of America, USA, 1982)

Ross (née Phillpotts), Adelaide, *Reverie* (Robert Hale, 1981)

Rowse, A.L., *Memories of Men and Women* (Eyre Methuen, 1980)

Saunders, Peter, *The Mousetrap Man* (Collins, 1972)

Toy, Barbara, *A Fool on Wheels: Tangier to Baghdad by Land Rover* (John Murray, 1955)

Williams, Emlyn, *Emlyn* (Bodley Head, 1973)

Wolfit, Donald, *First Interval* (Odhams, 1954)

Books about theatre and theatre people

Aldgate, Anthony and Crighton Robertson, James, *Censorship in Theatre and Cinema* (Edinburgh University Press, 2005)

Aston, Elaine and Reinelt, Janelle (eds), *The Cambridge Companion to Modern British Women Playwrights* (Cambridge University Press, 2000)

Barker, Clive and Gale, Maggie B. (eds), *British Theatre Between the Wars: 1918–1939* (Cambridge University Press, 2000)

Billington, Michael, *State of the Nation: British Theatre Since 1945* (Faber and Faber, 2007)

Callow, Simon, *Charles Laughton: A Difficult Actor* (Methuen, 1987)

Cochrane, Clare, *Twentieth Century British Theatre: Industry, Art and Empire* (Cambridge University Press, 2011)

De Jongh, Nicholas, *Politics, Prudery and Perversions: The Censoring of the English Stage 1901–1968* (Methuen, 2000)

Du Maurier, Daphne, *Gerald: A Portrait* (Victor Gollancz, 1934)

Duff, Charles, *The Lost Summer: The Heyday of the West End Theatre* (Nick Hern, 1995)

Federation of Theatre Unions, *Theatre Ownership in Britain* (Federation of Theatre Unions, 1953)

Findlater, Richard, *The Unholy Trade* (Victor Gollancz, 1952)

Gale, Maggie B., *West End Women: Women and the London Stage, 1918–1962* (Routledge, 1996)

Gale, Maggie B. and Gardner, Viv (eds), *Women, Theatre and Performance: New Histories, New Historiographies* (Manchester University Press, 2000)

Gottfried, Martin, *Jed Harris: The Curse of Genius* (Little, Brown, USA, 1984)

Griffiths, Trevor R. and Llewellyn-Jones, Margaret (eds), *British and Irish Women Dramatists Since 1958: A Critical Handbook* (Open University Press, 1993)

Hand, Richard J. and Wilson, Michael, *London's Grand Guignol and the Theatre of Horror* (University of Exeter Press, 2007)

Harding, James, *Gerald du Maurier: The Last Actor-Manager* (Hodder and Stoughton, 1989)

Harris, Andrew B., *Broadway Theatre* (Routledge, 1994)

Harwood, Ronald, *Sir Donald Wolfit CBE: His Life and Work in the Unfashionable Theatre* (Secker and Warburg, 1971)

Higham, Charles, *Charles Laughton: An Intimate Biography* (W.H. Allen, 1976)

Hirsch, Foster, *The Boys from Syracuse: The Shuberts' Theatrical Empire* (Cooper Square Press, USA, 2000)

Hoare, Philip, *Noël Coward: A Biography* (Sinclair-Stevenson, 1995)

Holroyd, Michael, *Bernard Shaw* (Chatto and Windus, 1997)

Huggett, Richard, *Binkie Beaumont: Eminence Grise of the West End Theatre, 1933–1973* (Hodder and Stoughton, 1989)

Hume, Elizabeth, *A Laboratory of Theatre: The History of the Embassy* (Central School of Speech and Drama, 2002)

Kabatchnik, Amnon, *Blood on the Stage: Milestone Plays of Crime, Mystery and Detection 1925–1950* (Scarecrow Press, USA, 2010)

Kabatchnik, Amnon, *Blood on the Stage: Milestone Plays of Crime, Mystery and Detection 1950–1975* (Scarecrow Press, USA, 2011)

Kabatchnik, Amnon, *Blood on the Stage: Milestone Plays of Crime, Mystery and Detection 1975–2000* (Scarecrow Press, USA, 2012)

Lachman, Marvin, *The Villainous Stage: Crime Plays on Broadway and in the West End* (McFarland, USA, 2014)

Lane, Margaret, *Edgar Wallace: The Biography of a Phenomenon* (Heinemann, 1938)

Mander, Raymond and Mitchenson, Joe, *The Theatres of London*, revised and enlarged edition (New English Library, 1975)

Marshall, Norman, *The Other Theatre* (John Lehmann, 1947)

Nicholson, Steve *The Censorship of British Drama 1900–1968, Volume One: 1900–1932* (University of Exeter Press, 2003), *Volume Two: 1933–1952* (University of Exeter Press, 2005), *Volume Three: The Fifties* (University of Exeter Press, 2011)

Parker, John (original ed.), *Who's Who in the Theatre* (Pitman, 1912, 1914, 1916, 1922, 1925, 1930, 1933, 1936, 1939, 1947, 1952, 1957, 1961, 1967, 1972)

Pattie, David, *Modern British Playwriting, the 1950s: Voices, Documents, New Interpretations* (Methuen, 2012)

Pick, John, *The West End: Mismanagement and Snobbery* (John Offord, 1983)

Pick, John, *Vile Jelly: The Birth, Life and Lingering Death of the*

Arts Council of Great Britain (Brynmill Press, 1991)

Rebellato, Dan, *1956 And All That: The Making of Modern British Drama* (Routledge, 1999)

Sanderson, Michael, *From Irving to Olivier: A Social History of the Acting Profession in England 1880–1983* (Palgrave Macmillan, 1984)

Saunders, Peter, *The Mousetrap Story* (St Martin's Theatre, 1992)

Shafer, Elizabeth, *Ms-Directing Shakespeare: Women Direct Shakespeare* (The Women's Press, 1998)

Shellard, Dominic, *British Theatre Since the War* (Yale University Press, UK and USA, 1999)

Shellard, Dominic (ed.), *British Theatre in the 1950s* (Sheffield Academic Press, 2000)

Shellard, Dominic and Nicholson, Steve with Hadley, Miriam, *The Lord Chamberlain Regrets: British Stage Censorship and Readers' Reports from 1824–1968* (British Library, 2004)

Shepherd, Simon, *The Cambridge Introduction to Modern British Theatre* (Cambridge University Press, 2009)

Shubert Archive (Maryann Chach, Reagan Fletcher, Mark E. Swartz, Syvia Wang), *The Shuberts Present: 100 Years of American Theater* (Harry N. Abrams, USA, 2001)

Sinfield, Alan, *Out on Stage; Lesbian and Gay Theatre in the Twentieth Century* (Yale University Press, 1999)

Thorndike, Russell, *Sybil Thorndike* (Thornton Butterworth, 1929)

Van Gyseghem, Andre, *Theatre in Soviet Russia* (Faber and Faber, 1943)

Wearing, J.P., *American and British Theatrical Biography: A Directory* (Scarecrow Press, USA, 1979)

Wearing, J.P., *The London Stage, 1920–29: A Calendar of Plays and Players* (Scarecrow Press, USA, 1984)

Wearing, J.P., *The London Stage, 1930–1939: A Calendar of Plays and Players* (Scarecrow Press, USA, 1990)

Wearing, J.P., *The London Stage, 1940–1949: A Calendar of Plays and Players* (Scarecrow Press, US, 1991)

Wearing, J.P., *The London Stage, 1950–1959: A Calendar of Plays and Players* (Scarecrow Press, US, 1993)

Wilmeth, Don B and Bigsby, Christopher (Eds) *The Cambridge History of American Theatre Volume II: 1870–1945* (Cambridge University Press, 1999)

Wilmeth, Don B and Bigsby, Christopher (Eds) *The Cambridge History of American Theatre Volume III: Post-World War II to the 1990s* (Cambridge University Press, 2000)

Other books of interest

Burke, David, *The Lawn Road Flats: Spies, Writers and Artists* (Boydell Press, 2014)

Canjels, Rudmer, *Distributing Silent Film Serials: Local Practices, Changing Forms, Cultural Transformation* (Routledge, 2011)

Clarke, Peter, *Hope and Glory: Britain 1900–1990* (Allen Lane/ Penguin Press, 1996)

Dahlquist, Marina (ed.), *Exporting Perilous Pauline: Pearl White and the Serial Film Craze* (University of Illinois Press, USA, 2013)

Gardiner, Juliet, *The Thirties: An Intimate History* (HarperPress, 2010)

Hennessy, Peter, *Never Again: Britain 1945–51* (Jonathan Cape, 1992)

Humble, Nicola, *The Feminine Middlebrow Novel, 1920s–1950s: Class, Domesticity and Bohemianism* (Oxford University Press, 2001)

Knight, Stephen, *Form and Ideology in Crime Fiction* (Macmillan, 1980)

Kynaston, David, *Austerity Britain: 1945–51* (Bloomsbury, 2007)

Kynaston, David, *Family Britain: 1951–57* (Bloomsbury, 2009)

Kynaston, David, *Modernity Britain: 1957–59* (Bloomsbury, 2013)

Maltin, Leonard (ed.), *Leonard Maltin's Classic Movie Guide* (Plume/ Penguin, 2005)

Melman, Billie, *Women and the Popular Imagination in the 1920s: Flappers and Nymphs* (Macmillan, 1988)

Morgan, Kenneth O., *Britain Since 1945: the People's Peace* (Oxford University Press, 1990/2001)

Newton, Darrell M., *Paving the Empire Road; BBC Television and Black Britons* (Manchester University Press, 2011)

Pugh, Martin, *We Danced All Night: A Social History of Britain Between the Wars* (Bodley Head, 2008)

Sandbrook, Dominic, *Never Had It So Good: A History of Britain from Suez to the Beatles* (Little, Brown, 2005)

Steadman, Raymond William, *The Serials: Suspense and Drama by Installment* (University of Oklahoma Press, US, 1971)

Weigall, Arthur, *The Life and Times of Akhnaton, Pharoah of Egypt* (Thornton Butterworth 1910/revised edition 1922)

Other publications of interest

Allen, M.D., 'Barbara Toy', *Dictionary of Literary Biography*, Vol 204: *British Travel Writers 1940–1997* (Gale, USA, 1999)

Cameron, Rebecca S., 'Irreconcilable Differences: Divorce and Women's Drama before 1945' (*Modern Drama*, vol. 44, no. 4, 2001)

Chambers, Diane M, 'Triangular Desire and the Sororal Bond: The "Deceased Wife's Sister Bill"' (*Mosaic: A Journal for the Interdisciplinary Study of Literature*, vol. 29, no. 1, 1996)

Conference of Women Theatre Directors and Administrators, *The Status of Women in British Theatre 1982–1983* (Survey, 1983)

Curran, John, 'Black Coffee: A Mystery within a Mystery' (*Crime and Detective Stories*, no. 67, 2014)

Dalby, Richard, 'Spotlight on Agatha Christie', (*Book and Magazine Collector*, no. 174, 1998)

Dove, Richard, 'Gerhard Hinze' or Gerard Heinz? A Life in Two Acts' (*Yearbook of the Research Centre for German and Austrian Exile Studies* vol 14, 2013)'

Earl, John, 'How West End Theatreland Happened' (*The Matcham Journal*, edition 1, 2014)

Harmston, Joe (Artistic Director of the Agatha Christie Theatre Company), Programme notes for the ACTC's productions of *The Hollow* (2006), *The Unexpected Guest* (2007), *And Then There Were None* (2008/2015), *Spider's Web* (2009), *Witness for the Prosecution* (2010), *Verdict* (2011), *Murder on The Nile* (2012), *Go Back For Murder* (2013), *Black Coffee* (2014) (John Good)

Heinrich, Anselm, 'Theatre in Britain During the Second World War' (*New Theatre Quarterly*, vol. 26, no. 1, 2010)

Seal, Lizzie, 'Public Reactions to the Case of Mary Wilson, The Last Woman to be Sentenced to Death in England and Wales' (papers from the *British Criminology Conference*, vol 8, 2008)

Torremans, Professor Paul and Castrillon, Professor Carmen Otero Garcia, 'Reversionary Copyright: A Ghost of the Past or a Current Trap to Assignments of Copyright?' (*Intellectual Property Quarterly*, no. 2, 2012)

Wandor, Michelene, 'The Impact of Feminism on the Theatre' (*The Feminist Review*, no.18, 1984)

Websites

Doollee database of modern plays in English (doollee.com)

The Internet Broadway database (ibdb.com)

The Internet Movie database (imdb.com)

The Oxford Dictionary of National Biography (oxforddnb.com)

The Theatres Trust (theatrestrust.org.uk)

Archives visited by the author in the UK:

The Christie Archive Trust. Includes Agatha Christie's extensive correspondence with Max Mallowan and Rosalind Hicks; typescripts of the plays of Agatha Christie and M. F. Watts; Agatha Christie's notebooks and her unpublished works and draft scripts.

The Peter Saunders business papers; Mousetrap Productions. Extensive documentation of the production of all of Agatha Christie's major plays from 1951, including correspondence between Saunders and Christie.

The Hughes Massie Archive of Agatha Christie's business papers; Exeter University Special Collections. Extensive documentation of Christie's business affairs, including Edmund Cork's correspondence with Agatha Christie and Harold Ober.

The Hughes Massie stage licensing records; Agatha Christie Ltd. Details of all performance licences issued for Agatha Christie's plays by Hughes Massie Ltd, summarised on typed index cards created on the issue date of each licence.

The Theatre and Performance Collections, Victoria and Albert Museum. Includes the H. M. Tennent correspondence relating to the 1954 Theatrical Companies Bill, the Embassy Theatre archive, *The Mousetrap* programme and press archive, and the original prompt copy of *The Mousetrap*.

The Hubert Gregg Agatha Christie papers. Small, privately-held collection of Gregg's annotated director's scripts of Agatha Christie's plays and some of his correspondence with her.

The Basil Dean Archive; John Rylands Library, University of Manchester. Includes a small amount of Agatha Christie and M.F. Watts correspondence.

The Lord Chamberlain's Plays collection; British Library. Includes typescripts of every Christie play that received its UK premiere prior to 1968, as well as *Chimneys*, which didn't.

The Lord Chamberlain's Plays correspondence files; British Library. Includes Readers' Reports and correspondence between the Lord Chamberlain's Office and Christie's producers regarding her plays.

The People's Entertainment Society Archive; National Co-operative Archive, Manchester. Includes records of the P.E.S.'s productions of Agatha Christie plays.

The Noël Coward Archive Trust. Includes a small amount of Agatha Christie correspondence.

The Garrick Club Library. Includes Richard Attenborough's annoted rehearsal script for *The Mousetrap*.

The Royal Central School of Speech and drama archives. Includes various records of the Embassy Theatre.

Archives visited by the author in the USA:

The Shubert Archive, New York. Extensive documentation of the Shuberts' presentation of Christie's plays, including the only extant copies of Christie's own adaptation of *Towards Zero*.

The Gilbert Miller Collection; Music Division, Library of Congress, Washington DC. Includes correspondence relating to the New York production of *Witness for the Prosecution*.

The Billy Rose Theatre Division; New York Public Library for the Performing Arts. Includes materials relating to various US productions of Christie's plays.

The Theatre Collection; Museum of the City of New York. Includes materials relating to Gilbert Miller and to the New York production of *Witness for the Prosecution*.

Other archives contributing material

Companies House archive
Martha's Vineyard Gazette archive, USA
Bertie Meyer's Agatha Christie contracts (small private collection)
University of Bristol Theatre Collection
Scottish Theatre Archive; Glasgow University Special Collections
Theatre Royal, Bath archive

Digital archives

The BBC archive (bbc.co.uk/archive)
The *Guardian* and *Observer* archive (Cambridge University Library ejournals)
The Hansard archive (hansard-archive.parliament.uk)
The *London Gazette* archive (thegazette.co.uk)
The *New York Times* archive (Cambridge University Library ejournals)
The Stage archive (archive.thestage.co.uk)
The Times archive (Cambridge University Library ejournals)

Index of Agatha Christie Works

General Index

Mousetrap Theatre Projects

Mousetrap Theatre Projects is a theatre education charity founded with seed money from Agatha Christie's *The Mousetrap*, dedicated to bringing the magic of theatre into the lives of young people. Believing passionately in the power of theatre to transform young lives, Mousetrap Theatre Projects aims to engage young people through theatre and drama, using it creatively to educate, challenge and inspire them, focusing on those who experience disadvantage – whether economic, social or through a learning or sensory disability.

To learn more about our programmes or to support us, visit our website: **www.mousetrap.org.uk**